1994-95 Official Guide and Record Book
The New York Rangers Hockey Club
is a part of the Madison Square Garden Corporation.

RANGERS 1994-95 MEDIA GUIDE
Table of Contents

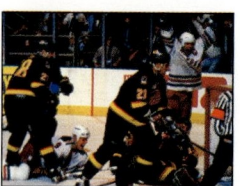

The Players
16-91

1993-94 In Review
94-142

Stanley Cup Playoffs
146-168

Page

FRONT OFFICE
Rangers Directory 4
Rangers 1994-95 Schedule 5
Smith, Neil 6-7
Campbell, Colin 8-9
Pleau, Larry 10
Assistant Coaches 11
Scouting Staff 12
Training Staff 13

THE PLAYERS
Player Biographies 16-77
In The System 78-84
Team Broadcasters 85
1994 Entry Draft Selections 86-89
Rangers Roster 90-91

1993-94 ... IN REVIEW
Final Standings 94
League Leaders 95-96
Final Rangers Scoring 97
Regular Season Highlights 98-99
Scoring Breakdown 100
Special Teams Scoring Breakdown 101
Individual Scoring vs. Each Division 102
Quarter-By-Quarter Scoring 103
Miscellaneous Statistics 104-105
Hat Tricks and Shorthanded Goals 106
Manpower Games Lost To Injury 107
Transactions/Off-Season Activity 108-109
Game-By-Game Results (Home and Away) 110-113
Game-By-Game Power Play Totals 114
Game-By-Game Penalty Killing Totals 115
Game-By-Game Home Attendance 116
Scoring of Rangers Draft Choices 117
Rangers vs. Each NHL Club 118-142

1994 STANLEY CUP PLAYOFFS
Final Scoring/Scoring Leaders 146-147
Special Teams Scoring Breakdown 148
Scoring Breakdown 149
Miscellaneous Statistics 150-151
Eastern Conference Quarterfinals 152-155
Eastern Conference Semifinals 156-159
Eastern Conference Finals 160-163
Stanley Cup Finals 164-167
Series-by-Series Recap 168

BINGHAMTON RANGERS
Coaching Staff 170
Club Directory/1994-95 Schedule 171
Final AHL Standings and Scoring 172
Rangers Alumni Association 173

BARRY WATKINS	JOHN ROSASCO	ROB KOCH
Managing Editor	Editor	Associate Editor

Editorial Assistants: Ann Marie Gilmartin, Dana Florio, Adam Sigler, Keith Soutar, Karin Strelec
Photography: Bruce Bennett Studios, pages 144-145 Jeffrey Markowitz
Production: Paul Gornstein, Michael Braun
Printed by Fleetwood Litho - Ken Marino, Joe Morris and Mike Sykora, Production Coordinators

(Rangers received National Hockey League franchise on May 15, 1926)
(All Contents Copyrighted)

Page

CAREER RECORDS
Players Career Records vs. Each NHL Team..........................176-179
Goaltenders vs. Each NHL Team..180
Lifetime Shutouts..181
Lifetime Hat Tricks..182
All-Star Game Appearances..183
Players Career Goal Breakdown/Scoring Streaks 184-187
Milestones Within Reach..188
How The Rangers Were Built..189

IN THE PAST
All-Time Record vs. Each NHL Team...192
Current Streaks vs. Each Team 193
Recent Record vs.Each Team..194
Last Shutout vs.Each Team 195
All-Time Won/Loss Record (Home and Away)..........................196-197
Year-By-Year Scoring Leaders...198
Rangers All-Time Scoring List...199
Career Leaders..200
Single Season Leaders 201
Longest All-Time Goal, Assist and Point Streaks...........................202
Longest Goal Scoring Streaks Year-By-Year...................................203
Longest Assist Streaks Year-By-Year..204
Longest Point Scoring Streaks Year-By-Year 205
Last Overtime Win/Loss vs. Each Team 206
Overtime History..207-209
All-Time Rangers Shutouts...210
10 Goal Games and 0-0 Ties 211
Rangers In NHL All-Star Game 212-213
Rangers NHL All-Stars (Post Season) 214
All-Time Longest Team Streaks..215
Longest Team Streaks Year-By-Year 216-217
Longest Team Streaks Year-By-Year, Home Games 218-219
Longest Team Streaks Year-By-Year, Road Games 220-221
All-Time Penalty Shots 222
The Last Time..223
Team Records..224-226
Player Records...227-228
Rookie/Defensemen/Goalie Records 229
Playoffs — Team Records..230
Playoffs — Player Records...231
Playoff Overtime Games 232
Playoff Record Year-By-Year..233
Rangers Playoff Records..234-235
Rangers Stanley Cup Champions...236-237
Rangers Management..238
Captains and Coaching Records..239
Brief History of Rangers 240-241
Power Play and Penalty Killing...242
Final Player Scoring, Year-By-Year, Since 1926 243-261
Final Goalie Records, Year-By-Year, Since 1926....................262-264
Game-By-Game Results, Year-By-Year, Since 1926 265-294
Steven McDonald "Extra Effort" Award...295
Lars-Erik Sjoberg Award..296
Rangers Award Winners...297-299
Milestone Winners and Hall of Famers..300
All-Time Draft Selections..301-304
All-Time Player Register...305-316

Binghamton Rangers
170-172

Career Records
176-189

In The Past
192-316

NEW YORK RANGERS DIRECTORY

Madison Square Garden
4 Penn Plaza, New York, New York 10001

Executive Management
President and General Manager ....Neil Smith
Executive Vice President and General Counsel ....Kenneth W. Munoz
Vice President and Controller ....Charles Groneman
Alternate Governors ....Neil Smith, Kenneth W. Munoz

Hockey Club Personnel
Assistant General Manager\Player Development ....Larry Pleau
Head Coach ....Colin Campbell
Assistant Coaches ....Mike Murphy, Dick Todd
Development Coach ....Al Hill
Assistant Development Coach ....Mike Busniuk
Goaltending Analyst ....Sam St. Laurent
Scouting Staff ....Darwin Bennett, Tony Feltrin, Herb Hammond,
Martin Madden, Christer Rockstrom
Director of Business Administration ....John Gentile
Director of Hockey Administration ....Kevin McDonald
Director of Team Operations ....Matthew Loughran
Scouting Manager ....Bill Short
Executive Administrative Assistant ....Barbara Dand
Senior Secretary...Nicole Wetzold

Medical\Training Staff
Team Physician and Orthopedic Surgeon ....Dr. Barton Nisonson
Assistant Team Physician..Dr. Anthony Maddalo
Medical Consultants ....Drs. Howard Chester, Frank Gardner, Ronald Weissman
Team Dentists ....Dr. Irwin Miller and Dr. Don Saloman
Sports Physiologist ....Howie Wenger
Medical Trainer ....Jim Ramsay
Equipment Manager..Mike Folga
Equipment Trainer ....Joe Murphy
Massage Therapist ....Bruce Lifrieri
Lockerroom Assistant ....Benny Petrizzi
Video Assistant ....Jerry Dineen
Staff Assistant ....Brad Kolodny

COMMUNICATIONS DEPARTMENT
Director of Communications...Barry Watkins
Assistant Director of Communications..John Rosasco
Communications Assistant ....Rob Koch
Administrative Assistant..Ann Marie Gilmartin

MARKETING DEPARTMENT
Director of Marketing ....Kevin Kennedy
Manager of Community Relations ....Rod Gilbert
Promotions Manager ....Caroline Calabrese
Manager of Marketing Operations ....Jim Pfeifer
Manager of Event Presentation..Jeanie Baumgartner

ADDITIONAL INFORMATION
Executive Offices..Madison Square Garden
Home Ice ....Madison Sqare Garden
Seating Capacity 18,200
Largest Crowd 18,200
Press Facilities...33rd Street
Television Facilities ....31st Street
Radio Facilities ....33rd Street
Rink Dimensions..200 feet x 85 feet
Ends and Sides of Rink..Plexiglass (8 feet)
Club Colors ....Blue, Red White
Uniforms..Home- Base color white, trimmed with blue and red
Road- Base color blue, trimmed with red and white
Practice Facility ....Rye, New York

1994-95 RANGERS SCHEDULE

OCTOBER

Sun	Mon	Tue	Wed	Thu	Fri	Sat
						1 NJ
2	3 PIT	4	5	6 PHI	7	8 FLA
9	10	11 T.B.	12	13 ST. L	14	15 HFD
16	17	18 QUE	19	20 LA	21	22 MTL
23 S.J.	24	25	26	27	28 CGY	29
30 VAN	31					

NOVEMBER

Sun	Mon	Tue	Wed	Thu	Fri	Sat
		1 LA	2 ANA	3	4	5 S.J.
6	7	8	9 HFD	10	11 NYI	12
13 WSH	14	15	16	17 PHI	18	19 OTT
20	21	22	23 PIT	24	25 WPG	26
27 FLA	28	29 HFD	30 BUF			

DECEMBER

Sun	Mon	Tue	Wed	Thu	Fri	Sat
				1	2 ANA	3
4 EDM	5	6 PIT	7	8 NYI	9	10
11	12	13 NYI	14 VAN	15	16	17 EDM
18 CGY	19	20	21	22 BOS	23 MTL	24
25	26	27 OTT	28 WSH	29	30	31 T.B.

JANUARY

Sun	Mon	Tue	Wed	Thu	Fri	Sat
1 FLA	2	3 ST. L	4	5 NYI	6	7 T.B.
8	9 FLA	10	11 PIT	12	13	14 WSH
15 NJ	16	17 DET	18	19	20	21 ALL STAR GAME
22	23 QUE	24	25 BOS	26	27 T.B.	28 QUE
29	30 NYI	31				

FEBRUARY

Sun	Mon	Tue	Wed	Thu	Fri	Sat
			1	2 CHI	3	4 OTT
5	6 WPG	7 BOS	8	9 PHI	10	11 T.B.
12	13	14	15 BUF	16 MTL	17	18 TOR
19	20 TOR ■	21	22	23	24 HFD	25
26 BUF	27	28 FLA				

MARCH

Sun	Mon	Tue	Wed	Thu	Fri	Sat
			1	2	3 PHI	4 NYI
5	6 NJ	7	8 BUF	9	10	11 MTL
12 PHI	13	14	15 NJ	16	17	18 WSH
19	20	21 DAL	22	23 CGY	24	25
26	27	28 DET	29	30 QUE	31	

APRIL

Sun	Mon	Tue	Wed	Thu	Fri	Sat
						1 BOS
2 CHI	3	4	5 WSH	6	7 OTT	8
9 NJ	10	11	12	13	14	15

Rangers home starting time is 7:30 PM, except: 10/13, 10/23, 10/27, 10/30, 11/4, 7:00 PM; 1/15, 8:00 PM; (■) 2/20 1:30 PM.

Season Subscription (212) 465-6073
Group Sales (212) 465-6080

 TICKETMASTER
(212) 307-7171 (609) 520-8383
(201) 507-8900 (914) 454-3388
(516) 888-9000 (203) 624-0033

■ HOME   ■ AWAY   ▨ NEUTRAL SITE

NEIL SMITH

PRESIDENT and GENERAL MANAGER

Born: January 9, 1954
Toronto, Ontario

Through the first five years of his tenure at the helm of the Rangers, Neil Smith has become one of the most successful men to ever run the club in the 68 year history of the franchise.

Last season, Neil's diligence and persistence to build the Rangers into a Stanley Cup Championship club came to fruition on June 14 when the team captured the fourth Stanley Cup in franchise history, defeating Vancouver four games to three. The championship was the culmination of a record setting season in which New York set a club record with 52 wins and 112 points. The Rangers captured their second Presidents' Trophy in the last three years and became the first team since the Presidents' Trophy was established to win it, along with the Conference Championship and Stanley Cup in the same year. Following the season Neil was awarded with The Hockey News Executive of the Year Award.

In his first three seasons as general manager after joining the Rangers on July 17, 1989 New York finished in first place twice and second place once, marking the best three consecutive finishes in club history. The Rangers also captured the Presidents' Trophy as the NHL's Regular Season Champions in 1991-92.

Neil's outstanding accomplishments with the Rangers were recognized following the '91-92 season with two tremendous honors.

First, he was named the NHL Executive of the Year by The Sporting News, as voted by NHL general managers and governors, becoming the first Rangers executive to ever capture the award.

Then on June 19, 1992, he was promoted to the position of president and general manager, becoming the ninth president in Rangers history and the first president to also hold the title of general manager.

Neil has built the Rangers through his extraordinary ability to recognize talent and by making bold moves when necessary.

Following the 1994 Stanley Cup Championship season, Neil has continued to improve the club, acquiring Petr Nedved from St. Louis, Glen Featherstone from Boston and Mark Osborne from Toronto. On August 9 he promoted Colin Campbell, whom Neil brought to the organization from Detroit in August of 1990, to head coach.

Through the NHL Entry Draft, Neil has added players like Sergei Nemchinov, Alexei Kovalev and Sergei Zubov to the Rangers roster, while loading the organization's depth chart with top prospects at every position: goaltenders Corey Hirsch, Jamie Ram and Dan Cloutier; defensemen Mattias Norstrom, Eric Cairns, Lee Sorochan, Adam Smith, Maxim Galanov; and forwards Peter and Chris Ferraro, Niklas Sundstrom, Dimitri Starostenko, Rudolf Vercik, Jeff Nielsen and Sergei Olympijev.

In addition, when given an opportunity to improve the club through trades or signing free agents, Neil has acted quickly to add even more talent to the Rangers lineup.

In his first four seasons as general manager, he made deals to acquire Mark Messier, Jeff Beukeboom, Eddie Olczyk, Kevin Lowe, Glenn Healy, Jay Wells and Joey Kocur and signed Adam Graves and Greg Gilbert as free agents. Last season he upgraded the team's talent level by obtaining Steve Larmer and Nick Kypreos in November, while making trades to acquire Glenn Anderson, Craig MacTavish, Brian Noonan and Stephane Matteau at the trade deadline.

A native of Toronto, Ontario, Smith played junior hockey at Brockville, Ontario, before entering Western Michigan University, where he became an All-America defenseman as a freshman and team captain in his second year. In September of 1991, Neil was inducted into the school's Hall of Fame, the first hockey player ever given the honor.

After being selected by the New York Islanders in the NHL Amateur draft and playing two seasons in the International Hockey League, Neil joined the Islanders scouting department during the '80-81 season.

Following two seasons in that capacity, he joined the Detroit Red Wings in 1982 as director of professional scouting and soon after became director of their entire farm system.

Smith was then named director of scouting, and general manager/governor of the Adirondack Red Wings of the AHL, where he won two Calder Cup championships.

Neil, who is a board member of the National Child Abuse Prevention Center, lives with his wife, Katia, in New York City. He enjoys racquetball and lists "Stripes" and "Animal House" as his favorite movies.

COLIN CAMPBELL

HEAD COACH

**Born: January 28, 1953
London, Ontario**

After serving in various capacities in the Rangers organization over the last four years, including assistant coach, associate coach and half of a 1992-93 season as head coach of the Rangers American Hockey League affiliate at Binghamton, Colin Campbell was introduced as the Rangers new head coach on August 9.

Campbell, 41, began his coaching career in 1985-86 with the Detroit Red Wings, following his retirement as a player after the 1984-85 season. He worked a total of five seasons as a Red Wings assistant coach, including one season under coach Harry Neale and four seasons under coach Jacques Demers.

The native of London, Ontario, joined the Rangers organization in August of 1990 as an assistant coach to Roger Neilson. He served in that role until January 4, 1993, when he became head coach of the Binghamton Rangers, New York's American Hockey League affiliate. He guided Binghamton to a record of 29-8-5, helping them set AHL records for wins (57) and points (124) in a single season.

On June 21, 1993, Campbell was promoted to associate coach of New York, under head coach Mike Keenan, helping the Rangers set team records for wins (52) and points in a season (112), while capturing the Presidents' Trophy and the Stanley Cup.

Before joining the coaching ranks, Campbell played 12 seasons of professional hockey as a defensive defenseman. After being drafted by the Pittsburgh Penguins as their third choice, 27th overall, in the second round of the 1973 Amateur Draft, he opted to join the Vancouver Blazers of the World Hockey Association where he was coached by former Rangers Phil Watson and Andy Bathgate.

Following one season in the WHA, he went on to play 11 seasons in the National Hockey League beginning with the Penguins in 1973-74. After two seasons with Pittsburgh he was dealt to the Colorado Rockies and played there for one year before being dealt back to Pittsburgh.

After two more years in Pittsburgh, he was claimed in the 1979 Expansion Draft by the Edmonton Oilers where he was teammates with Mark Messier and Kevin Lowe. Following his only season in Edmonton he was claimed by the Vancouver Canucks in the NHL Waiver draft where he played for two seasons. In 1981-82 he helped the Canucks to the Stanley Cup Finals under coach Roger Neilson, playing in 16 of 17 post-season matches.

Colin signed as a free agent with Detroit in July of 1982 and played for three seasons with the Red Wings before becoming an assistant coach with the club. He played in a total of 636 NHL contests, collecting 25 goals and 103 assists for 128 points along with 1,292 penalty minutes.

"Collie", who is a licensed pilot, owns and operates the Colin Campbell Hockey School in Tillsonburg, Ontario for three weeks each summer. He and his wife Heather reside in Rye, New York with their three children; daughters, Lauren and Courtney and son Gregory.

LARRY PLEAU
ASSISTANT GENERAL MANAGER/ PLAYER DEVELOPMENT

Larry Pleau, who joined the Rangers organization in August of 1989, enters his sixth season as the club's assistant general manager/player development.

Pleau assists Neil Smith, the team's president and general manager, with the development of all amateur players in the organization, while he also oversees the day-to-day operation of the Rangers scouting department. In addition, he is involved in player transactions and the selection of players at the NHL Entry Draft. Larry also served as the assistant general manager for the 1991 United States Canada Cup Team.

He travels extensively throughout the year to Europe, Canada and across the United States to prepare for the draft and check on the development of Rangers prospects playing in high school, college, junior hockey or in Europe.

Pleau, 45, played three seasons with the Montreal Canadiens (1969-70 - 1971-72) in the National Hockey League, before being the first player signed by the Hartford Whalers of the World Hockey Association. He was a center/left wing for the Whalers from 1972 until his retirement in 1979. He played in a total of 468 regular-season games for Hartford, accumulating 157 goals and 215 assists for 372 points. In 66 playoff contests, he registered 29 goals and 22 assists for 51 points.

During his time with the Whalers, Larry scored 25 goals or more on four occasions and was selected to play in the WHA All-Star Game three times (1973, 1974 and 1975).

Pleau also played for the 1968 United States Olympic Team, the 1969 U.S. National Team and for Team USA in the 1976 Canada Cup Tournament.

A native of Lynn, Massachusetts, Larry became an assistant coach with the Whalers in 1979. He remained in that position until Feb. 20, 1981, when he took the reins as head coach.

The following season he added to his responsibilities as head coach and became the club's director of hockey operations. During his tenure the Whalers drafted many current NHL players including; Kevin Dineen, Ulf Samuelsson, Ray Ferraro and Sylvain Cote.

After two seasons in that position and a year as assistant general manager under Emile Francis, Pleau became director of hockey operations and head coach of the Binghamton Whalers of the American Hockey League in 1984-85.

In his first season at Binghamton, he led the team to a first-place finish with a record of 52-20-8 and in his third season (1986-87) he guided the club to a mark of 47-26-7, as he was named the AHL's Coach of the Year.

Larry remained in Binghamton for three and a half seasons before returning to Hartford as head coach for the remainder of the 1987-88 campaign and all of the 1988-89 season.

Larry and his wife, Wendy, recently moved to Seabrook, New Hampshire, where they reside with their son, Steve, and daughter, Shannon. Steve recently completed his sophomore year at the University of New Hampshire, where he played on the school's hockey team.

ASSISTANT COACHES

Mike Murphy

Entering his first year as an assistant coach with the Rangers, following a three year stint as assistant coach with the Toronto Maple Leafs. Murphy was named to the post on August 24.

Murphy, 43, began his coaching career as an assistant coach with the Los Angles Kings on January 30, 1984. Murphy served briefly as a a special assistant to the general manager after his retirement as a player with the Kings in October of 1983 before joining the coaching staff.

The native of Toronto, Ontario worked as an assistant to head coach Pat Quinn for three seasons until January 10, 1987 when he took over as the club's head coach. Murphy signed on as an assistant coach with Vancouver on March 3, 1988 following his career with Los Angeles. He was named head coach of the Canucks International Hockey League affiliate in Milwaukee for the 1990-91 season and guided the Admirals for one season before joining the Maple Leafs coaching staff.

Murphy was originally drafted by the Rangers in the second round, 25th overall, in the 1970 NHL Amateur Draft. He was named the CHL Rookie-of-the-Year with the Ranger minor league affiliate in Omaha in 1970-71. He was dealt to St. Louis in 1971-72 and then dealt back to New York in March of 1973. After appearing in 31 games with New York, tallying six goals and five assists, Murphy was then traded to Los Angeles on November 30, 1973 where he played for 10 and a half seasons, including six as the team captain. The right-winger tallied 238 goals and 318 assists for 556 points in 831 career matches.

Mike and his wife Evon reside in Aurora, Ontario with their four children; Sean, Ryan, Breeann and Patrick.

Dick Todd

Dick Todd begins his second season as an assistant coach with the Rangers. Todd joined the Rangers on July 7, 1993 following a 21 year career with the Peterborough Petes, including the last 12 as head coach.

The native of Peterborough, Ontario posted a career record of 477-239-53 along with a .655 winning percentage. Under Todd's guidance, Peterborough has won four Leyden Division Championships, two OHL Playoff Championship and advanced to two Memorial Cup Finals. In his 12 seasons behind the bench, the Petes have finished lower than third only one time.

In his last two seasons, the Petes', led by the number two pick in the 1993 Entry Draft, Chris Pronger, compiled a record of 87-33-12 for a .705 winning percentage.

Todd, 48, led Team Canada to a gold medal at the 1991 World Junior Tournament in Saskatoon and in 1990, he was the assistant coach for Team Canada when they earned a silver medal at the World Junior Championships in Helsinki, Finland. In 1987-88 he was selected by his peers as the OHL Coach of the Year.

Over the past two decades, Todd has held many different positions with the Petes, including trainer, head coach, and general manager. He began his coaching career halfway through the 1981-82 season, replacing Dave Dryden. He remained as head coach through '92-93 season when he led Peterborough to a 46-15-5 record, finishing with the best record in the OHL and winning the OHL Playoff Championship.

In his 12 years behind the bench for the Petes, Todd has coached numerous players who have since gone on to the NHL including; Steve Yzerman, Kay Whitmore, Kris King, Jody Hull, Tie Domi, Mike Ricci, Terry Carkner, Randy Burridge, Bob Errey, Ron Tugnutt, Luke Richardson.

Dick currently resides in Rye with his wife, Mary and his daughter, Terri-Anne.

SCOUTING STAFF

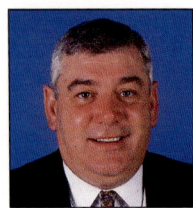

Darwin Bennett
Entering his second year with the Rangers ... Scouts players in the Ontario Hockey League and Western Hockey League ... Joined the scouting staff on August 4, 1993 after spending the previous eight seasons as a scout with the Quebec Nordiques ... Promoted to the position of assistant to the chief scout in 1989 ... Joined the Nordiques scouting staff in 1986, following four seasons scouting for the Prince Albert Raiders of the Western Hockey League ... Worked for 13 years in the Saskatchewan government, including six years as the director of personnel prior to joining the Nordiques in 1986 ... Single.

Tony Feltrin
Entering his ninth year as a scout with New York after retiring as a player in September of 1986 ... Primarily scouts players in the Western Hockey League, while also evaluating talent in the Ontario Hockey League and Quebec Major Junior Hockey League ... Played parts of four seasons in the National Hockey League, including 10 games with New York during the 1985-86 season ... Suffered a severe eye injury on Dec. 31, 1985, while playing with New Haven of the American Hockey League ... Married: wife, Kelly; children, Kurt and Carli.

Herb Hammond
Begins his sixth season with the Rangers ... Is responsible for scouting U.S. colleges and high schools ... Worked at Brown University from 1982-89 ... Was school's head coach from 1982 to 1988 and served as assistant athletic director in 1988-89 ... Coached prep schools in Albany and North Yarmouth beginning in 1958 ... Moved to the college coaching ranks in 1968 and guided Plattsburgh and Oswego State Colleges before going to Brown ... Earned his Bachelor's degree in history and physical education and his Master's degree in counseling from Springfield College ... Married: wife, Patricia; daughters, Leslie and Heather.

Martin Madden
Is now in his fourth season with New York ... Joined the Rangers scouting staff in 1990 as a part time scout in the Quebec area ... Served as General Manager of Quebec Nordiques from 1988 to February of 1990 ... Worked as the chief scout of Quebec from 1981 to 1988 ... Coached the Quebec Ramparts from 1978 to 1980 ... Worked with Central Scouting from 1975-78 ... Was a scout for the Philadelphia Flyers from 1969 to 1975 ... Married: wife, Nicole; children, Martin Jr. and Karen.

Christer Rockstrom
Beginning his sixth year as the Rangers European scout ... Covered Sweden and part of Europe for the Detroit Red Wings from 1984 to 1989 ... Is one of the most highly regarded evaluators of European talent in the NHL ... Has tremendous knowledge of players at all levels and in different areas including Sweden, Finland, Russia and Czechoslovakia ... Makes his home in Stockholm, Sweden... Single.

TRAINING STAFF

Mike Folga — Equipment Manager
Beginning his second season with the Rangers ... Served as one of the trainers for the 1994 NHL All-Star Game at MSG ... Joined the Rangers after working as head trainer for the Indianapolis Ice (IHL) in '92-93 ... Served as the head trainer for the St. Louis Blues from '87-88 through '90-91 ... Graduated from Mercyhurst College with a Bachelor of Science in Sports Medicine ... Played minor league baseball in the St. Louis Cardinals organization in '80 and '81 ... Head baseball coach at Behrend College following his baseball career ... Resides in Rye, New York ...son, Dakota.

Bruce Lifrieri — Massage Therapist
Bruce "The Masseuse" enters his second season as a full time member of the Rangers training staff ... Worked with the club on a part-time basis from 1986-87 to 1992-93 ... Worked the 1994 NHL All-Star Game at MSG ... Attended Westchester Community College and Pace University ... Attended the Dr. Victor Scherer Academy of Physiotherapy ... Is a lifelong resident of Westchester county ... Single.

Joe Murphy — Equipment Trainer
Senior member of the Rangers training staff is entering his 17th year with the club ... Served as one of the trainers for the 1994 NHL All-Star Game at MSG ... "Murph" was member of the training staff for the U.S. Team in the 1987 Canada Cup Tournament ... Was playing in a Westchester County men's hockey league when then Ranger trainer Nick Garen asked him to help out ... Born and raised in New York ... Married: wife, Joan; daughters, Peggy and Patti; son, Joe, who is the father of the Murphy's granddaughter, Jaqueline Nicole.

Benny Petrizzi — Lockerroom Assistant
Starting his 13th season working at the Rangers training facility in Rye, New York ... Began his career at Rye Playland in 1934 as a parking lot attendant ... Was born in Italy, he currently resides in Harrison ... Has been married to his wife Fannie for 44 years ... One son, Robert, and two grandchildren, Sara and Torrey.

Jim Ramsay — Medical Trainer
Begins his first season with the Rangers after spending the last five seasons with the Winnipeg Jets ... Was selected to be part of the training staff for the Western Conference team at the 1994 NHL All-Star Game held at MSG on Jan. 22 ... Began his career with the Jets in 1989 after working two years in a private sports medicine practice in Winnipeg ... Graduated with honors from the University of Manitoba ... Played junior hockey in Manitoba and was teammates with Toronto Maple Leafs center Mike Ridley ... Was engaged last summer to Anita Rhodes ... Son, Mason.

Howie Wenger — Sports Physiologist
Begins his second year with the Rangers ... Joined the staff last year after serving as a consultant with the Los Angeles Kings from 1986 to 1993 ... Has also worked as a consultant with Edmonton ('78-'80), and Vancouver ('81-83) and the 1991 Canadian Team in the Canada Cup Tournament ... Received his Ph.D. in Exercise Physiology from the University of Alberta ... Currently teaches exercise physiology courses at the University of Victoria ... Married; wife, Jan; sons, Matthew and Dave; daughter, Sonja.

THE PLAYERS

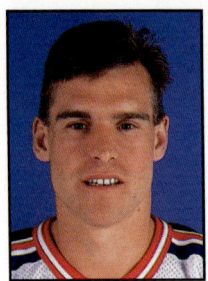

JEFF BEUKEBOOM

23

DEFENSE
6-5 • 230 • Shoots Right
Born: March 28, 1965 • Ajax, Ontario
Off-Season Home: Dunsford, Ontario

1993-94: Set a career-high, tallying eight goals ... Notched his first power play goal since Jan. 18, 1988 at Montreal, while with Edmonton, on Jan. 3 vs. Florida ... Notched his first career two-goal game, including his 100th career point on Nov. 13 vs. San Jose ... Tied for fifth on the club with a plus 18 rating ... Rangers were 12-2-1 when he registered a point and 5-1-0 when he scored a goal.

1994 PLAYOFFS: Tallied six assists in 21 matches, notching five of the six on the road ... Tallied a pair of assists, including one on Glenn Anderson's game-winning goal, and a plus four rating in Game Three of the Finals on June 4 at Vancouver ... Placed second on the team and second in the NHL with a plus 17 rating.

NHL CAREER: 1985-86: Began the season in Edmonton after a solid training camp, but was sent to Nova Scotia (AHL) on Oct. 15 before seeing any action ... Recalled on Feb. 10, but did not play and was returned the following day ... Made his NHL debut in a playoff game against Vancouver on Apr. 10. **1986-87:** Started the campaign with the Oilers and appeared in his initial regular-season contest on Oct. 17 vs. Detroit and notched his first NHL point with an assist on a goal by Jari Kurri ... Sent to Nova Scotia on Nov. 3 and played in 14 games ... Recalled on Dec. 3 and remained with Edmonton for the rest of the season... First NHL goal was a game-winning, power play tally in 7-3 win at Vancouver on Dec. 30. **1987-88:** Produced career highs in assists (20), points (25) and penalty minutes (201) in his first full season in NHL ... Registered the longest point scoring streak of his career, four games, from Jan. 11-Jan. 18 ... Accumulated a career high three assists in Buffalo on Nov. 29. **1988-89:** Suspended for 10 games in the beginning of the season for leaving the bench in a pre-season contest ... Sent to Cape Breton for conditioning on Nov. 17, returning on Nov. 30 ... Missed 11 games with knee injury suffered in Chicago on Jan. 16. **1989-90:** Appeared in only 46 games, collecting 13 points. **1990-91:** Plus six rating ranked fourth among club defensemen and 150 PIM placed fourth on the team ... Was unsuccessful on the first penalty shot of his career in the season opener on Oct. 6, when he was stopped by Winnipeg's Richard Tabaracci. **1991-92:** Obtained from Edmonton on Nov. 12 in exchange for David Shaw as future considerations from the Mark Messier trade ... Played in his 300th NHL game on Dec. 21 at Pittsburgh ... Compiled a plus 19 rating in 56 games with New York ... Missed four games due to suspension and one game to injury ... Tallied his first goal as a Ranger on Jan. 6 vs. Winnipeg. **1992-93:** Appeared in 82 games in his first full season with New York ... Placed third on the team and first among backliners with a plus nine rating ... Tied a career high for points and assists in game, with three vs. Tampa Bay on Dec. 9.

AHL CAREER: Played a total of 99 American Hockey League games in three different stints ... Spent almost the entire '85-86 season with Nova Scotia, where the leading scorer of the club was former Rangers center Mike Rogers ... Played 14 games with Nova Scotia in '86-87 and eight games in a conditioning stint with Cape Breton in '88-89.

JUNIOR CAREER: Played three seasons with the Sault Ste. Marie Greyhounds of the Ontario Hockey League from 1982 to 1985 ... Named as the OHL's best defenseman by the league's coaches in 1984-85 ... Named an OHL first-team All-Star and earned a spot on the Emms Division All-Star team in 1985.

INTERNATIONAL COMPETITION: Was a member of Canadian team that won the World Junior tournament in Finland in 1985.

BACKGROUND: Was a member of three Stanley Cup teams with Oilers... Selected by Edmonton in the first round of the 1983 Entry Draft, he is the only non-goaltender ever selected in the first round who did not score a goal in year prior to draft... His brother, John, played with the Adirondack Red Wings (AHL) and Kalamazoo Wings (IHL) in 1986-87 ... Wore uniform number six with Edmonton ... Is a nephew of former NHL'er Ed Kea ... Enjoys fishing and golfing in the off-season ... Married: wife, Sherri; daughter, Tyson and son, Brock.

CAREER TRANSACTIONS: *June 8, 1983* — Edmonton's first round choice (19th overall) in the 1983 NHL Entry Draft. *Nov. 12, 1991* — Traded by Edmonton to New York in exchange for David Shaw as the future considerations in the Mark Messier trade made on Oct. 4.

JEFF BEUKEBOOM #23

CAREER HIGHLIGHTS

MOST GOALS, GAME: 2, Nov. 14, 1993 vs. S.J., **MOST ASSISTS, GAME:** 3 (twice) last- Dec. 9, 1992 vs. T.B., **MOST POINTS, GAME:** 3 (twice) last- Dec. 9, 1992 vs. T.B., **MOST PIM, GAME:** 26, Oct. 8, 1991 vs. L.A., **MOST SHOTS, GAME:** 5 (3 times) last- Jan. 3, 1994 vs. Fla., **MOST SHOTS, SEASON:** 76, 1987-88, **HIGHEST +/-, SEASON:** 27, 1987-88, **FIRST NHL GAME:** Oct. 17, 1986 vs. Det., **FIRST NHL GOAL:** Dec. 30, 1986 at Van. (Brodeur)

AMATEUR AND PROFESSIONAL RECORD

Season	Club	Lea	Regular Season					Playoffs				
			GP	G	A	PTS	PIM	GP	G	A	PTS	PIM
1981-82	Newmarket	OPJHL	49	5	30	35	218	—	—	—	—	—
1982-83	Sault Ste. Marie	OHL	70	0	25	25	143	16	1	4	5	46
1983-84	Sault Ste. Marie	OHL	61	6	30	36	178	16	1	7	8	43
1984-85	Sault Ste. Marie	OHL	37	4	20	24	85	16	4	6	10	47
1985-86	Edmonton	NHL	—	—	—	—	—	1	0	0	0	4
1985-86	Nova Scotia	AHL	77	9	20	29	175	—	—	—	—	—
1986-87	Edmonton	NHL	44	3	8	11	124	—	—	—	—	—
1986-87	Nova Scotia	AHL	14	1	7	8	35	—	—	—	—	—
1987-88	Edmonton	NHL	73	5	20	25	201	7	0	0	0	16
1988-89	Edmonton	NHL	36	0	5	5	94	1	0	0	0	2
1988-89	Cape Breton	AHL	8	0	4	4	36	—	—	—	—	—
1989-90	Edmonton	NHL	46	1	12	13	86	2	0	0	0	0
1990-91	Edmonton	NHL	67	3	7	10	150	18	1	3	4	28
1991-92	Edmonton	NHL	18	0	5	5	78	—	—	—	—	—
1991-92	Rangers	NHL	56	1	10	11	122	13	2	3	5	47
1992-93	Rangers	NHL	82	2	17	19	153	—	—	—	—	—
1993-94	Rangers	NHL	68	8	8	16	170	22	0	6	6	50
NHL Totals			490	23	92	115	1178	64	3	12	15	147
Rangers Totals			206	11	35	46	445	35	2	9	11	97

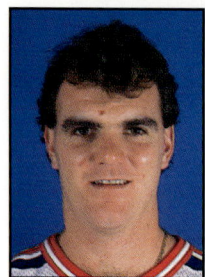

GLEN FEATHERSTONE

6

DEFENSE
6-4 • 212 • Shoots Left
Born: July 8, 1968 • Toronto, Ontario
Off-Season Home: Beacon Hill, Massachusetts

1993-94: Appeared in 58 games with Boston, collecting one goal and eight assists ... Placed second on the team with 152 penalty minutes ... Missed 17 games with shoulder and knee injuries ... Skated in his 200th NHL game on November 7 at Buffalo ... Two of his nine assists came on game winning goals.

NHL CAREER: 1988-89: Began the season with Peoria and was called up by St. Louis in January ... Made his NHL debut on January 4 vs. Detroit ... Registered his first NHL point on March 20 vs. the Rangers ... Appeared in 18 games with the Blues and tallied two assists and 22 penalty minutes ... Registered 25 penalty minutes in six playoff matches. **1989-90:** Began the season with Peoria but was recalled by Blues on October 26 ... Notched assists in three of his first four matches ... Was sent to Peoria on December 26 and was recalled on January 17 ... Placed third on the club with 145 penalty minutes ... Appeared in all 12 playoff matches, recording two assists, including one on Sergio Momesso's overtime, game winning goal in Game Three of the Norris Division Semi-Finals vs. Detroit. **1990-91:** Established career-highs in all categories, appearing in 68 games in his first full season in the NHL ... Collected five goals and 15 assists for 20 points ... Ranked second among Blues defensemen with a plus 19 rating and placed third on the team with 204 penalty minutes ... Recorded his first NHL goal, the game winner vs. Montreal, on October 27 ... Registered three multiple-point games and notched a three game point scoring streak from December 20 to 26 ... Skated in his 100th NHL game on December 2 at Chicago ... Missed 10 games due to injury. **1991-92:** Signed with Boston as a free agent on July 25 ... Skated in his first game with the club on October 3 vs. the Rangers ... Notched his first goal with the Bruins on October 24 vs. St. Louis ... Appeared in six more games before developing back problems ... Had surgery to remove a herniated disc on November 15 and missed the remainder of the season. **1992-93:** Equaled his career high of five goals despite playing in only 34 games due to thigh and knee injuries ... Began the season with Providence on a conditioning stint and notched three goals and four assists along with 60 penalty minutes in eight games before returning to Boston on November 27 ... Skated in 16 games before suffering a groin injury ... Returned to the lineup on January 19 and appeared in 18 games before suffering knee and thigh injuries which forced him to miss the remainder of the season.

IHL CAREER: Made his professional debut with Peoria in 1988-89, appearing in 37 matches before being called up by St. Louis ... Collected five goals and 19 assists for 24 points along with 97 penalty minutes ... Began the 1989-90 season with the Rivermen but was recalled by the Blues on October 26 ... Returned to Peoria on December 26 for a brief stint and rejoined the Blues on January 17.

JUNIOR CAREER: Played three seasons with the Windsor Spitfires in the Ontario Hockey League ... Was teammates in each of the three seasons with Adam Graves ... Had his most productive season in 1987-88 when he tallied seven goals and 27 assists for 34 points along with 201 penalty minutes while helping the Spitfires to the OHL championship, before losing in the finals of the Memorial Cup ... Notched six goals and nine assists for 15 points along with 47 penalty minutes in 12 playoff matches.

BACKGROUND: Is good friends with Adam Graves and was in Graves wedding party this past July ... Nickname is "Feather" ... Enjoys fishing and golfing in the off-season ... Lists "Stripes" as his favorite movie ... Married: wife, Kelly.

CAREER TRANSACTIONS: *June 21, 1986* — St. Louis' fourth choice (fourth round, 73rd overall) in the 1986 NHL Entry Draft. *July 25, 1991* — Signed by Boston as a free agent. *August 19, 1994* — Traded by Boston to Rangers for Daniel Lacroix.

GLEN FEATHERSTONE #6

CAREER HIGHLIGHTS

MOST GOALS, GAME: 1, (12 times) last- Nov. 7, 1993 at Buf., **MOST ASSISTS, GAME:** 2, (twice) last- Dec. 20, 1989 at Chi., **MOST POINTS, GAME:** 2, (3 times) last- Jan. 17, 1990 vs. Mtl., **MOST PIM, GAME:** 20, Mar. 17 1990 vs. Det., **MOST SHOTS, GAME:** 5, Nov. 18, 1990 at Wpg., **MOST SHOTS, SEASON:** 59, 1990-91, **HIGHEST +/-, SEASON:** 19, 1990-91, **FIRST NHL GAME:** Jan. 4, 1989 vs. Det., **FIRST NHL GOAL:** Oct. 27, 1990 vs. Mtl. (Roy)

AMATEUR AND PROFESSIONAL RECORD

Season	Club	Lea	Regular Season					Playoffs				
			GP	G	A	PTS	PIM	GP	G	A	PTS	PIM
1985-86	Windsor	OHL	49	0	6	6	135	14	1	1	2	23
1986-87	Windsor	OHL	47	6	11	17	154	14	2	6	8	19
1987-88	Windsor	OHL	53	7	27	34	201	12	6	9	15	47
1988-89	St. Louis	NHL	18	0	2	2	22	6	0	0	0	0
1988-89	Peoria	IHL	37	5	19	24	97	—	—	—	—	—
1989-90	St. Louis	NHL	58	0	12	12	145	12	0	2	2	47
1989-90	Peoria	IHL	15	1	4	5	43	6	0	2	2	8
1990-91	St. Louis	NHL	68	5	15	20	204	9	0	0	0	31
1991-92	Boston	NHL	7	1	0	1	20	—	—	—	—	—
1992-93	Boston	NHL	34	5	5	10	102	—	—	—	—	—
1992-93	Providence	AHL	8	3	4	7	60	—	—	—	—	—
1993-94	Boston	NHL	58	1	8	9	152	1	0	2	2	103
NHL Totals			243	12	42	54	645	28	0	4	4	181

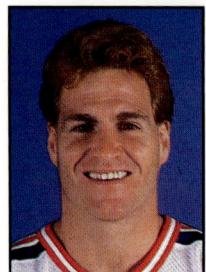

GREG GILBERT

LEFT WING
6-1 • 195 • Shoots Left
Born: Jan. 22, 1962 • Mississauga, Ontario
Off-Season Home: Hinsdale, Illinois

 # 17

1993-94: Veteran left wing skated in his first match with the Rangers on Oct. 5 vs. Boston ... Appeared in his 700th NHL match two nights later vs. Tampa Bay ... Tallied his first point with the club on Oct. 15 at Buffalo ... Initial Rangers goal came on Nov. 27 at Long Island ... Rangers were 11-3-1 when he collected a point ... Seven of his 11 assists were tallied at MSG.

1994 PLAYOFFS: Tallied his only goal of the post-season on May 1 in Game One of the Conference Semifinals vs. Washington ... Tallied an assist in Game Four of the Finals at Vancouver on June 7 ... Register his first point of the post-season in Game Four of the Conference Quarterfinals at Long Island on April 24.

NHL CAREER: 1981-82: Called up by the Islanders from the Toronto Marlboros (OHL) on Dec. 15 and registered his first NHL goal that night vs. Quebec ... Returned to Toronto after the game and was recalled during the playoffs after an injury to Bob Nystrom ... Registered a goal and an assist in four games vs. Pittsburgh. **1982-83:** Earned Henry Saranceno Award as Isles top rookie in training camp ... Began the season in Indianapolis (CHL) and was called up on November 30 ... Collected eight goals and 11 assists in 45 games. **1983-84:** Posted career-highs in all offensive categories in his first full season ... Played on line with Mike Bossy and Bryan Trottier from December through the end of the season ... 31 goals and plus 51 rating ranked fourth on club ... Placed third in NHL with a 26.3 shooting percentage ... Recorded his first NHL hat trick Feb. 25 vs. New Jersey ... Appeared in all 21 playoff games, scoring five goals and seven assists ... Recorded the game-winning goal in game two of the Stanley Cup finals vs. Edmonton. **1984-85:** Shattered left knee ended his season on Feb. 27 at Calgary. **1985-86:** Returned to the NHL on Nov. 17, following reconstructive knee surgery and a two-game conditioning stint with Springfield (AHL) ... Played in 60 of the team's final 64 games ... Notched game-winner in OT vs. Rangers on Nov. 24 at MSG. **1986-87:** Missed 21 games due to injury, including 10 with a fractured jaw and seven with a bruised shoulder ... Appeared in 10 of 14 playoff matches, collecting two goals and two assists along with a team-leading 28.6 shooting percentage ... Notched game-winner in game five of division semi-final match vs. Washington. **1987-88:** Potted a natural hat trick, including his 200th NHL point on Feb. 16 vs. Calgary ... Notched eight multiple-point games along with a plus 14 rating. **1988-89:** Acquired from the Islanders by Chicago on Mar. 7 ... Sidelined for nine games with a broken foot suffered in his Hawk's debut ... Skated in 15 of the team's 16 playoff matches, collecting a goal and five assists. **1989-90:** Collected 12 goals and 25 points in his first full season with Chicago ... Led the team with a plus 27 rating ... Notched three assists on Dec. 22 at Toronto along with his 100th NHL goal ... Tallied five goals and eight assists along with a team-leading plus 10 rating in 19 playoff matches. **1990-91:** Skated in his 500th NHL match on Oct. 4 vs. the Rangers. **1991-92:** Recorded his 300th career point with a goal at Montreal on Nov. 9 ... Skated in his 600th NHL contest on Dec. 14 at Philadelphia ... Played in 10 of 18 playoff matches notching a goal and three assists. **1992-93:** Skated in 77 games, marking the second highest total of his career and his most since playing in a career-high 79 in 1983-84 ... Posted a plus five rating ... Recorded his 200th NHL assist on Feb. 7 vs. Detroit.

JUNIOR CAREER: Played for three seasons with the Toronto Marlboros of the OHL ... Recorded 41 goals and 67 assists for 108 points in his final season ... Earned honors as the OHL's top defensive forward in 1980-81 and was named to the league's Third All-Star Team.

BACKGROUND: Member of two Stanley Cup Championship teams with the Islanders in 1982 and '83 ... Participated in the New York Skates program, he appeared at the South Street Seaport on July 30 ... Enjoys golfing during the off-season ... Lists Dire Straits as his favorite musical group ... Does considerable charitable work, including many hospital visits during the season ... Married: wife, Tammy; sons Dillon and Brenden; daughter, Lauren.

CAREER TRANSACTIONS: *June 11, 1980* — Islanders' fifth choice (80th overall) in the 1980 Entry Draft. *March 7, 1989* — Traded to Chicago by the Islanders for Chicago's fifth round choice in the 1989 Entry Draft. *July 29, 1993* — Signed by New York as a free agent.

GREG GILBERT #17

CAREER HIGHLIGHTS
MOST GOALS, GAME: 3, (twice) last- Feb. 16, 1988 vs. Cgy., **MOST ASSISTS, GAME:** 3, (twice) last- Dec. 23, 1989 at Tor., **MOST POINTS, GAME:** 4, Apr. 5, 1986 vs. N.J., **MOST PIM, GAME:** 17, Mar. 30, 1983 at Wsh., **MOST SHOTS, GAME:** 6, Nov. 11, 1990 at NYI, **MOST SHOTS, SEASON:** 118, 1983-84, **HIGHEST +/-, SEASON:** 51, 1983-84, **FIRST NHL GAME:** Dec. 15, 1981 vs. Que., **FIRST NHL GOAL:** Dec. 15, 1981 vs. Que. (Malarchuk)

AMATEUR AND PROFESSIONAL RECORD

Season	Club	Lea	Regular Season					Playoffs				
			GP	G	A	PTS	PIM	GP	G	A	PTS	PIM
1979-80	Toronto	OHA	68	10	11	21	35	—	—	—	—	—
1980-81	Toronto	OHA	64	30	37	67	73	5	2	6	8	16
1981-82	NY Islanders	NHL	1	1	0	1	0	4	1	1	2	2
1981-82	Toronto	OHL	65	41	67	108	119	10	4	12	16	23
1982-83	NY Islanders	NHL	45	8	11	19	30	10	1	0	1	14
1982-83	Indianapolis	CHL	24	11	16	27	23	—	—	—	—	—
1983-84	NY Islanders	NHL	79	31	35	66	59	21	5	7	12	39
1984-85	NY Islanders	NHL	58	13	25	38	36	—	—	—	—	—
1985-86	NY Islanders	NHL	60	9	19	28	82	2	0	0	0	9
1985-86	Springfield	AHL	2	0	0	0	2	—	—	—	—	—
1986-87	NY Islanders	NHL	51	6	7	13	26	10	2	2	4	6
1987-88	NY Islanders	NHL	76	17	28	45	46	4	0	0	0	6
1988-89	NY Islanders	NHL	55	8	13	21	45	—	—	—	—	—
1988-89	Chicago	NHL	4	0	0	0	0	15	1	5	6	20
1989-90	Chicago	NHL	70	12	25	37	54	19	5	8	13	34
1990-91	Chicago	NHL	72	10	15	25	58	5	0	1	1	2
1991-92	Chicago	NHL	50	7	5	12	35	10	1	3	4	16
1992-93	Chicago	NHL	77	13	19	32	57	3	0	0	0	0
1993-94	Rangers	NHL	76	4	11	15	29	23	1	3	4	8
NHL Totals			774	139	213	352	557	126	17	30	47	156
Rangers Totals			76	4	11	15	29	23	1	3	4	8

ADAM GRAVES

LEFT WING

9

6-0 • 205 • Shoots Left
Born: April 12, 1968 • Toronto, Ontario
Off-Season Home: Tecumseh, Ontario

1993-94: Named an NHL Second-Team All-Star following the season ... Established a team record for goals in a single season, notching 52, breaking Vic Hadfield's 22 year-old club record of 50 ... Tallied goals 50 and 51 only 2:54 apart at Edmonton on March 23 ... The 52 goals ranked fifth in the NHL and set a career high for goals in a season, surpassing his previous high of 36 set in 1992-93 ... Received the King Clancy Memorial Trophy following the season, becoming the first Rangers player to be so honored ... The award is given to the player who best exemplifies leadership qualities on and off the ice and has made a noteworthy humanitarian contribution to his community ... Also captured three of the team's five post-season awards, winning his third consecutive Steven McDonald Extra Effort award given to the player "who goes above and beyond the call of duty" as voted by the fans, along with his third straight Rangers MVP award as voted by the media and the Rangers Fan Club's Frank Boucher Trophy awarded to the team's most popular player on and off the ice ... Has played in 299 consecutive games, the second longest streak in the league, trailing only Trevor Linden of Vancouver ... Has played in 248 consecutive games with the Rangers the longest active streak on the club ... Was one of only two players to appear in all 84 contests ... Tied John Ogrodnick (1989-90) and Pierre Larouche (1983-84) for the fifth highest single season power play goal total after potting his 20th on March 16 vs. Hartford ... Tied for third on the team in scoring with 79 points ... The Rangers were 33-5-2 when he tallied a goal and 40-8-3 when he recorded a point ... Registered a plus or even rating in 67 of the 84 matches and placed second on the team with a plus 27 rating ... Tied for first on the club with 24 multiple point games ... Recorded his fourth career hat trick (third with New York) on February 2 vs. the Islanders ... Made his first NHL All-Star Appearance on January 22 at MSG, collecting a pair of assists ... Led all players in the game with eight shots on goal.

1994 PLAYOFFS: Placed third on the team and fifth in the NHL with 10 goals ... Notched the third highest single post-season goal total in club history, trailing Mark Messier (12) and Brian Leetch (11) set in 1994 ... Ranked fifth on the team in scoring with 17 points and also ranked fifth with a plus 12 rating ... Notched a goal and added an assist on Mark Messier's Cup-winning goal in Game Seven of the Finals vs. Vancouver on June 14 ... Led the team with four goals vs. Washington in the Conference Semifinals ... Placed second on the team with three power play goals.

NHL CAREER: 1987-88: Began the season with the Detroit Red Wings ... Made his NHL debut in the Wings' second game, October 9 in Edmonton ... Collected his initial NHL point on October 23 vs. Pittsburgh with an assist on a goal by Shawn Burr ... Returned to the OHL on November 18. **1988-89:** Began the season with Detroit and remained there until being sent to Adirondack on February 24 ... Returned to Detroit for the final two regular-season games and five playoff matches ... Sent back to Adirondack after Detroit's playoffs ... Potted his first NHL goal on October 15 ... Notched his first two-goal game on November 9 at Minnesota. **1989-90:** Dealt to Edmonton on November 2 ... Played in first game for Oilers and collected an assist on November 3 ... Recorded first career hat trick on December 17 at Chicago ... Accumulated five goals and six assists in 22 playoff games, helping Edmonton win the Stanley Cup ... Played with Joe Murphy and Martin Gelinas to form "The Kid Line" during the playoffs ... Scored a goal in four consecutive playoff contests from May 10-May 18. **1990-91:** Ranked fifth on the club with 127 PIM and sixth with 126 shots on goal ... 18 of his 25 points were notched in second half of season ... Appeared in all of team's 18 playoff outings and tied for the team lead with a plus eight rating. **1991-92:** Signed by the Rangers as a free agent in September ... Won the Steven McDonald Award and the Players' Player Award ... Scored 26 goals, surpassing his career total of 23 in his first 217 games ... Set career highs with 33 assists and 59 points ... Notched 26 goals

and 32 assists for 58 points in last 65 games, after collecting only one assist in first 15 outings ... Placed fourth on the team with 228 shots and recorded at least one shot in 79 of his 80 contests ... Was one of three Rangers to appear in all 80 contests. **1992-93:** Won the team's Most Valuable Player award as voted by the media and for the second consecutive year and captured the player's player award as voted by the players ... Winner of the Steven McDonald "Extra Effort" award for the second consecutive season ... Tallied a career-high four assists on March 19 vs. San Jose ... Registered 36 goals, placing second on the team and led the club with six game-winning goals, while also assisting on two game-winners ... Notched a career-high five points (three goals, two assists) at Pittsburgh on November 25 ... Was one of only two Rangers to play in all 84 contests.

AHL CAREER: Made his AHL debut in the 1987 playoffs ... Appeared in 14 regular season games for Adirondack in '88-89 and registered 10 goals and 11 assists ... Returned to Adirondack for the playoffs that season and helped them win the Calder Cup with 11 goals and seven assists in 14 outings.

JUNIOR CAREER: Played two and a half seasons with Windsor of the OHL, totalling 100 goals and 124 assists for 224 points in 165 matches ... Recorded 45 goals and 55 assists for 100 points in '86-87 ... Was Windsor's leading scorer in the playoffs all three seasons ... Captained the Spitfires to the OHL championship in 1988, before losing in the finals of the Memorial Cup ... That season, he led the OHL in playoff scoring with 14 goals and 18 assists for 32 points in 12 games.

INTERNATIONAL COMPETITION: Was a member of the Gold Medal winning, Canadian Junior team at the World Junior Championships in 1988 ... Captain of Team Canada at the 1993 World Championships in Munich, Germany, collecting three goals and three assists in eight games.

BACKGROUND: Married the former Violet Ravija this past July ... Serves as an active celebrity chairman for Family Dynamics, a New York CIty child abuse agency and for the Greater New York City Ice Hockey League ... "Gravy" makes several appearances with each organization during the season ... Won the Crumb Bum award in 1992-93 for work with New York youngsters ... Also captured the Good Guy award for cooperation with media presented by the New York chapter of the Professional Hockey Writers' Association ... Runs a hockey school each summer in Windsor ... Wore uniform number 11 in his Rangers debut, but switched to number nine for the second game, following the arrival of Mark Messier ... Wore uniform number 12 with Red Wings and Oilers ... His father, Henry, retired from the Ontario police department in May, 1993 after 20 years on the force ... Played organized soccer for 12 years as a youngster ... Favorite team is the Toronto Blue Jays ... Enjoys the music of U2 and Bruce Springsteen.

CAREER TRANSACTIONS: *June 21, 1986* — Detroit's second round choice (22nd overall) in the 1986 Entry Draft. *November 2, 1989* — Traded by Detroit to Edmonton along with Petr Klima, Joe Murphy and Jeff Sharples in exchange for Jimmy Carson, Kevin McClelland and a 1991 fifth round draft choice. *September 3, 1991* — Signed by New York as a group one free agent (compensation was Troy Mallette).

GRAVES CAPTURES THE KING CLANCY TROPHY

Last season Adam Graves on-ice contributions to the Rangers were quite clear, as he set a team record for goals in a single season and helped the Rangers to the Stanley Cup Championship. His off-ice contributions, however, usually don't get quite as much attention. At least that was true until June 16 in Toronto, when he was named the winner of the 1993-94 King Clancy Memorial Trophy, which is awarded annually to the "player who best exemplifies leadership qualities on and off the ice and has made a noteworthy humanitarian contribution to his community." Graves, who serves as chairman of Family Dynamics and the Greater New York City Ice Hockey League, became the first Rangers player to capture the award.

From top left, Adam at the annual Ice Hockey In Harlem clinic; with children from Family Dynamics; at GNYCIHL clinic; with his wife Violet and his parents Henry and Lynda at award dinner.

ADAM GRAVES #9

CAREER HIGHLIGHTS

MOST GOALS, GAME: 3, (four times) last-Feb. 2, 1994 vs. NYI, **MOST ASSISTS, GAME:** 4, Mar. 19, 1993 vs. S.J., **MOST POINTS, GAME:** 5, Nov. 25, 1992 at Pit., **MOST PIM, GAME:** 22, Oct. 6, 1990 vs. Wpg., **MOST SHOTS, GAME:** 9, Jan. 27, 1994 at L.A., **MOST SHOTS, SEASON:** 291, 1993-94, **HIGHEST +/-, SEASON:** 27, 1993-94, **FIRST NHL GAME:** Oct. 9, 1987 at Edm., **FIRST NHL GOAL:** Oct. 15, 1988 vs. Tor. (Bester)

AMATEUR AND PROFESSIONAL RECORD

			Regular Season					Playoffs				
Season	Club	Lea	GP	G	A	PTS	PIM	GP	G	A	PTS	PIM
1985-86	Windsor	OHL	62	27	37	64	35	16	5	11	16	10
1986-87	Windsor	OHL	66	45	55	100	70	14	9	8	17	32
1986-87	Adirondack	AHL	—	—	—	—	—	5	0	1	1	0
1987-88	Detroit	NHL	9	0	1	1	8	—	—	—	—	—
1987-88	Windsor	OHL	37	28	32	60	107	12	14	18	32	16
1988-89	Detroit	NHL	56	7	5	12	60	5	0	0	0	4
1988-89	Adirondack	AHL	14	10	11	21	28	14	11	7	18	17
1989-90	Detroit	NHL	13	0	1	1	13	—	—	—	—	—
1989-90	Edmonton	NHL	63	9	12	21	123	22	5	6	11	17
1990-91	Edmonton	NHL	76	7	18	25	127	18	2	4	6	22
1991-92	Rangers	NHL	80	26	33	59	139	10	5	3	8	22
1992-93	Rangers	NHL	84	36	29	65	148	—	—	—	—	—
1993-94	Rangers	NHL	84	52	27	79	127	23	10	7	17	24
NHL Totals			465	137	126	263	745	78	22	20	42	89
Rangers Totals			248	114	89	203	414	33	15	10	25	46

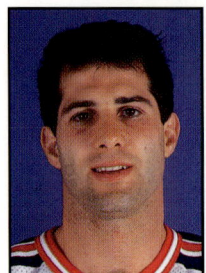

MIKE HARTMAN

LEFT WING — 18

6-0 • 195 • Shoots Left
Born: February 7, 1967 • Detroit, Michigan
Off-Season Home: Detroit, Michigan

1993-94: Collected his first point with New York, registering an assist on Oct. 24 vs. Los Angeles ... Notched his first goal with the Rangers on March 14 at Florida ... Posted a plus or even rating in 29 of his 35 outings.

NHL CAREER: 1986-87: Made his NHL and professional debut with Buffalo on October 15 vs. Montreal ... Scored his first NHL goal on October 17, in his second NHL game vs. Pittsburgh against Roberto Romamo ... Played in 17 games before being returned to North Bay (OHL)... **1987-88:** Registered 90 penalty minutes in 18 games ... 90 penalty minutes was the eighth-highest total by a Sabres rookie ... **1988-89:** Became a regular in his first full season with the Sabres ... Placed fourth among team forwards with a plus eight rating ... Set a club record with 316 penalty minutes, and was the first player in Sabres history to post over 300 penalty minutes in a season ... Notched two assists on March 28 vs. Hartford in his first multiple-point game ... **1989-90:** Set career-highs with goals (11), assists (10) and points (21) ... Missed 20 games due to an ankle injury ... **1990-91:** Played in his 200th NHL game on January 14 ... Finished his career with the Sabres in fifth place on the club's all-time PIM list with 890. **1991-92:** Traded to Winnipeg by Buffalo on October 11 ... Played in career-high 75 games ... Went over the 1,000 career PIM mark while leading the Jets with 264. **1992-93:** Acquired from Tampa Bay on March 22 in exchange for Randy Gilhen ... Made his debut with New York on April 12 at Philadelphia and skated in the final three games of the season ... Led Lightning with 154 penalty minutes ... Was even or plus in 45 of his 58 games with Tampa Bay and in each of his three games with New York ... Collected four goals and four assists ... Played in 39 of his last 41 games with Lightning after missing previous four games due to injury ... Missed eight games due to injury ... Skated in his 350th NHL game on February 27 at Pittsburgh.

AHL CAREER: Played in 57 games for Rochester, tallying 13 goals and 14 assists in 1987-88, his only season in the minor leagues ... Led the team with 283 penalty minutes ... Was voted the team's Most Improved Player following the season.

JUNIOR CAREER: Began his career with the Belleville Bulls (OHL) recording 13 goals and 12 assists along with 119 penalty minutes ... Was traded to North Bay four games into the 1985-86 season ... Posted his best goal total that season with 21 ... Teammates with Darren Turcotte at North Bay through the 1986-87 season ... Posted his highest point total in '86-87 with 39 in 32 games.

BACKGROUND: Hobbies include boating, golfing and softball ... Plans to pursue a degree in business following his career ... Lists Bobby Orr as his childhood idol ... Teammates with Eddie Olczyk at Winnipeg and Jay Wells at Buffalo ... While growing up in Detroit, he was a big fan of the Red Wings ... His father, John, is the team photographer for the Red Wings ... Married: wife, Lauren; daughter, Gabrielle.

CAREER TRANSACTIONS: *June, 1986* — Buffalo's eighth choice (131st overall) in the 1986 NHL Entry Draft. *October 11, 1991* — Traded to Winnipeg by Buffalo with Darrin Shannon and Dean Kennedy in exchange for Dave McLlwain, Gord Donnely, Winnipeg's fifth round choice (Yuri Khmylev) in 1992 Entry Draft and future considerations. *June 18, 1992* — Selected by Tampa Bay from Winnipeg in the 1992 Expansion Draft. *March 22, 1993* — Traded by Tampa Bay to Rangers in exchange for Randy Gilhen.

CAREER HIGHLIGHTS

MOST GOALS, GAME: 2, (twice) last- Nov. 5, 1989 vs. L.A., **MOST ASSISTS, GAME:** 3, Mar. 27, 1990 at Det., **MOST POINTS, GAME:** 3, (twice) last- Mar. 27, 1990 at Det., **MOST PIM, GAME:** 21, Dec. 21, 1991 vs. Cgy., **MOST SHOTS, GAME:** 7, Nov. 19, 1988 at Tor., **MOST SHOTS, SEASON:** 97, 1989-90, **HIGHEST +/-, SEASON:** 9, 1988-89, **FIRST NHL GAME:** Oct. 15, 1986 vs. Mtl., **FIRST NHL GOAL:** Oct. 17, 1986 vs. Pit. (Romano)

MIKE HARTMAN #18

AMATEUR AND PROFESSIONAL RECORD

Season	Club	Lea	Regular Season					Playoffs				
			GP	G	A	PTS	PIM	GP	G	A	PTS	PIM
1984-85	Belleville	OHL	49	13	12	25	119	—	—	—	—	—
1985-86	Belleville	OHL	4	2	1	3	5	—	—	—	—	—
1985-86	North Bay	OHL	53	19	16	35	205	10	2	4	6	34
1986-87	Buffalo	NHL	17	3	3	6	69	—	—	—	—	—
1986-87	North Bay	OHL	32	15	24	39	144	19	7	8	15	88
1987-88	Buffalo	NHL	18	3	1	4	90	6	0	0	0	35
1987-88	Rochester	AHL	57	13	14	27	283	4	1	0	1	22
1988-89	Buffalo	NHL	70	8	9	17	316	5	0	0	0	34
1989-90	Buffalo	NHL	60	11	10	21	211	6	0	0	0	18
1990-91	Buffalo	NHL	60	9	3	12	204	2	0	0	0	17
1991-92	Winnipeg	NHL	75	4	4	8	264	2	0	0	0	2
1992-93	Tampa Bay	NHL	58	4	4	8	154	—	—	—	—	—
1992-93	Rangers	NHL	3	0	0	0	6	—	—	—	—	—
1993-94	Rangers	NHL	35	1	1	2	70	—	—	—	—	—
NHL Totals			396	43	35	78	1384	21	0	0	0	106
Rangers Totals			38	1	1	2	76	—	—	—	—	—

GLENN HEALY

30

GOALTENDER
5-10 • 185 • Catches Left
Born: August 23, 1962 • Pickering, Ontario
Off-Season Home: Pickering, Ontario

1993-94: Made his Rangers debut on Oct. 7, posting a 5-4 victory vs. Tampa Bay ... Registered his sixth career shutout, stopping 20 shots at Washington on Dec. 23 ... Turned aside 28 shots and notched his second shutout of the season (seventh career) on Feb. 3 at Boston ... Allowed two or fewer goals in seven of his 17 starts and allowed three or fewer in 11 of the 17 ... 14 of his last 15 starts came on the road.

1994 PLAYOFFS: Appeared in two playoff matches, both in relief ... Made his first post-season appearance with New York on May 7 in Game Four of the Conference Semifinals at Washington ... Did not allow a goal and did not figure in the decision ... Relieved Mike Richter in the first period on May 21 in Game Four of the Conference Finals at New Jersey ... Allowed one goal and did not figure in the decision.

NHL CAREER: 1985-86: Called up by Los Angeles on Nov. 21 during a suspension to Bob Janecyk ... Made his NHL debut six days later, relieving Darren Eliot on Nov. 27 vs. Hartford ... Returned to New Haven on Dec. 2. **1987-88:** Started his first NHL contest on Oct. 25 vs. Boston, suffering a 3-2 defeat ... Earned his first NHL victory on Oct. 28, defeating the Rangers, 4-3 at MSG ... Notched his initial NHL shutout on Feb. 28 at Vancouver ... Co-winner of Kings Rookie of the Year award ... Started four of five playoff games. **1988-89:** Appeared in 48 games and led L.A. in games (48),and wins (25) ... Played in 45 of the first 61 games, going 25-16-2 ... Recorded a four-game winning streak from Nov. 5 and Nov. 15. **1989-90:** Notched second career shutout on Jan. 16, defeating Vancouver, 3-0 ... Earned second shutout of the season on Feb. 4, defeating Buffalo, 1-0 at the Aud ... Started four of Isles five playoff matches. **1990-91:** Goaltender of record in 18 of the Islanders 25 victories and in nine of the team's 10 ties, playing in a career-high 53 games. **1991-92:** Recorded Isles only shutout of the season, blanking N.J., 7-0 in the season finale ... Posted a career-high, five-game winning streak Feb. 2, to Feb. 20 ... Missed 28 games due to injury, including 13 games in March after severing his finger during practice. **1992-93:** Led the Islanders to the Wales Conference Finals with outstanding playoff performance ... Finished fourth in the NHL for the post-season with nine wins and a 3.19 goals against average, while starting all 18 playoff matches ... Stopped 42 shots in 4-3 victory, in game seven of the division finals at Pittsburgh ... Led Islanders with 22 victories during the regular season, 3.30 GAA was the best mark of his career ... Notched his fifth career shutout and only Islanders shutout of the season Mar.16 at San Jose, 6-0 ... Earned his 100th NHL victory Mar. 27 vs. San Jose ... Began the season with a five game unbeaten streak, (4-0-1) Oct. 10 to Oct. 23.

COLLEGE CAREER: Played four seasons at Western Michigan University ... Improved his win totals and GAA each season, posting a 21-14-2 record with a 3.26 average in his senior season ... Earned honors as an All-American in his final season.

AHL CAREER: Appeared in 43 games for New Haven in 1985-86, his first professional season ... Posted a record of 21-15-4 with a 3.98 GAA ... Named as the team's MVP ... Established himself as the Nighthawks top netminder in '86-87, notching 21 wins for the second consecutive season ... Went 4-6 in 10 shootout contests, second most in AHL ... ... Named Nighthawks MVP for the second consecutive season.

BACKGROUND: Has done extensive work with handicapped children for the National Center for Disability Services and has sold autographed pictures to benefit the Leukemia Society ... Has also worked with the Apple Institute, a drug rehabilitation center on Long Island ... Majored in business at Western Michigan University, the same school Rangers President and General Manager Neil Smith attended... Very active in the community ... 1991 recipient of the Long Island chapter of the PHWA's Good Guy award ... Married: wife, Susie.

CAREER TRANSACTIONS: *June 13, 1985* — Signed as a free agent by Los Angeles. *August 16, 1989* — signed as a free agent with the New York Islanders. *June 24, 1993* — Claimed by Anaheim in phase one of the NHL Expansion Draft. *June 25, 1993* — Claimed by Tampa Bay in phase two of the NHL Expansion Draft. *June 25, 1993* — Traded to the Rangers by Tampa Bay in exchange for a return of Tampa Bay's third round draft choice in the 1993 NHL Entry Draft.

CAREER HIGHLIGHTS

LONGEST WIN STREAK: 5, Feb. 2 - Feb 20, 1992, **LONGEST UNBEATEN STREAK:** 5, (twice) last— Feb. 2 - Feb 20, 1992, **MOST SHOTS FACED, GAME:** 51, Jan. 16, 1990 vs. Van., **FIRST NHL GAME:** Nov. 27, 1985 vs. Hfd., **FIRST NHL SHUTOUT:** Feb. 28, 1988 vs. Van. (2-0)

GLENN HEALY #30

AMATEUR AND PROFESSIONAL RECORD

Season	Club	Lea	GP	W	L	T	MINS	GA	SO	AVG	GP	W	L	MINS	GA	SO	AVG
1981-82	W. Michigan	CCHA	27	7	19	1	1569	116	0	4.44	—	—	—	—	—	—	—
1982-83	W. Michigan	CCHA	30	8	19	2	1732	116	0	4.01	—	—	—	—	—	—	—
1983-84	W. Michigan	CCHA	38	19	16	3	2241	146	0	3.90	—	—	—	—	—	—	—
1984-85	W. Michigan	CCHA	37	21	14	2	2171	118	0	3.26	—	—	—	—	—	—	—
1985-86	Los Angeles	NHL	1	0	0	0	51	6	0	7.06	—	—	—	—	—	—	—
1985-86	New Haven	AHL	43	21	15	4	2410	160	0	3.98	2	0	2	49	11	0	5.55
1986-87	New Haven	AHL	47	21	15	0	2828	173	1	3.67	7	3	4	427	19	0	2.67
1987-88	Los Angeles	NHL	34	12	18	1	1869	135	1	4.33	4	1	3	240	20	0	5.00
1988-89	Los Angeles	NHL	48	25	19	2	2699	192	0	4.27	3	0	1	97	6	0	3.71
1989-90	NY Islanders	NHL	39	12	19	6	2197	128	2	3.50	4	1	2	166	9	0	3.25
1990-91	NY Islanders	NHL	53	18	24	9	2999	166	0	3.32	—	—	—	—	—	—	—
1991-92	NY Islanders	NHL	37	14	16	4	1960	124	1	3.80	—	—	—	—	—	—	—
1992-93	NY Islanders	NHL	47	22	20	2	2655	146	3	3.30	18	9	8	1109	59	0	3.19
1993-94	Rangers	NHL	29	10	12	2	1368	69	2	3.03	2	0	0	68	1	0	0.88
NHL Totals			288	113	128	26	15798	966	7	3.67	31	11	14	1680	95	0	3.39
Rangers Totals			29	10	12	2	1368	69	2	3.03	2	0	0	68	1	0	0.88

COREY HIRSCH

31

GOALTENDER
5-10 • 160 • Catches Left
Born: July 1, 1972 • Medicine Hat, Alberta
Off-Season Home: Calgary, Alberta

1993-94: Spent the majority of the season as the number one goaltender with Team Canada, where he posted a record of 19-15-2 with a 2.91 GAA in 37 pre-Olympic contests ... Led the Canadian Olympic Team to a silver medal in the 1994 Winter Olympics in Lillehammer, Norway ... Posted a 5-2-1 record with a 2.35 goals against average in eight Olympic contests ... One the two losses came in the sudden death shootout in the gold medal game vs. Sweden ... Joined the Binghamton Rangers (AHL) following the Olympics and posted a 5-4-1 record and a 3.87 GAA in 10 games ... Was recalled by the Rangers on April 11 following the completion of Binghamton's season and remained with the club through the Stanley Cup playoffs.

NHL CAREER: 1992-93: Called up from Binghamton of the American Hockey League on December 6 and served as the backup goaltender for four games before being returned to Binghamton on December 12 ... Recalled from Binghamton on January 16 and made his NHL debut on January 19 at Detroit, stopping 32 shots in a 2-2 tie with the Red Wings ... Earned his first NHL victory, 8-3, on January 23 at Los Angeles turning aside 32 of 35 shots ... Returned to Binghamton on January 25 and was recalled on April 6 appearing in two games for New York.

AHL CAREER: 1992-93: Made his professional debut with Binghamton on October 10, 1992 vs. Utica and earned his first victory, 6-4 ... Began the season with a 15-game unbeaten streak, going 13-0-2 from October 10 through December 4 ... Posted his first professional shutout on November 21 at Hershey ... Led the AHL in wins (35) and goals against average (2.79) ... Set a Binghamton franchise record for wins and fell two short of Darren Puppa's AHL record of 37 ... Captured the Baz Bastien Trophy as the AHL's top goaltender as voted by AHL coaches along with the Dudley "Red" Garrett Memorial Trophy given to the AHL's top rookie performer ... Shared the Harry "Hap" Holmes Award with Boris Rousson awarded to the team with the lowest GAA ... Named to the AHL All-Star first team ... Finished third in the voting for the Les Cunningham Plaque awarded to the AHL's most valuable player.

JUNIOR CAREER: Played four seasons with Kamloops of the Ontario Hockey League ... Emerged as the Blazers top netminder in his second season with the club posting a record of 48-13-0 along with a 3.45 GAA in 63 games ... Registered a record of 14-3 along with a 3.45 GAA in 17 playoff matches ... Named to the WHL (West) All-Star second team ... Notched a record of 26-7-1 along with a 3.05 GAA in 38 games in 1990-91 ... Led Kamloops to a league-best 51-17-4 record in 1991-92, posting a record of 35-10-2 with a 2.72 GAA ... Led the WHL in GAA (2.72) and shutouts (five) ... Won 22 of his final 24 regular season matches ... Guided the Blazers to their first-ever Memorial Cup Championship emblematic of the best 43 major junior teams in Canada ... Posted a record of 11-5 with a 2.20 GAA in the playoffs and was named the Hap Emms Memorial Trophy winner awarded to the outstanding goaltender at the Memorial Cup Championships ... Placed first in the league in games (16), wins (11), shutouts (two), and GAA (2.20) ... Earned honors as a First-Team WHL All-Star and First-Team All-Star of the three Canadian Junior Leagues combined ... One of three finalists for the Canadian Junior Player of the Year ... Captured the Cooper/Goaltender of the Year Award as the top goalie of the 43 Canadian major junior teams along with The Hockey News/Cooper Junior Player of the Year Award as voted by a committee of scouts, coaches and media members... Recipient of the Del Wilson Trophy as the WHL's top netminder.

BACKGROUND: Nickname "Hershey" ... Finished his junior career as the WHL's all-time leader in shutouts with 13 ... Goals against average of 2.72 in his last season at Kamloops was the best mark in the WHL in the previous 20 years, surpassed only by former Rangers goaltender and current MSG broadcaster, John Davidson who posted a 2.37 GAA for the Calgary Centennials in 1971-72 ... Teammates with Petr Nedved on Team Canada last season ... Lists U2 and the Police as his favorite musical groups ... Enjoys golfing in the off-season ... Favorite non-hockey sports teams are the Portland Trail Blazers and the California Angels ... Single.

CAREER TRANSACTIONS: *June 22, 1991* — Rangers' eighth round choice (169th overall) in the 1991 NHL Entry Draft.

CAREER HIGHLIGHTS
LONGEST WIN STREAK: 1, Jan. 23 at L.A., **LONGEST UNBEATEN STREAK:** 2, Jan. 19 - Jan. 23, 1993, **MOST SHOTS FACED, GAME:** 35, Jan. 23, 1993 at L.A., **FIRST NHL GAME:** Jan. 19, 1993 at Det., **FIRST NHL SHUTOUT:** None

COREY HIRSCH #31

AMATEUR AND PROFESSIONAL RECORD

			Regular Season								Playoffs					
Season	Club	Lea	GP	W	L	T	MINS	GA	SO	AVG	GP	W	L	MINS	GA	SO	AVG
1988-89	Kamloops	WHL	32	11	12	2	1516	106	2	4.20	5	3	2	245	19	0	4.65
1989-90	Kamloops	WHL	63	48	13	0	3608	230	3	3.82	17	14	3	1043	60	0	3.45
1990-91	Kamloops	WHL	38	26	7	1	1970	100	3	3.05	11	5	6	623	42	0	4.04
1991-92	Kamloops	WHL	48	35	10	2	2732	124	5	2.72	16	11	5	954	35	2	2.20
1992-93	Rangers	NHL	4	1	2	1	224	14	0	3.75	—	—	—	—	—	—	—
1992-93	Binghamton	AHL	46	35	4	5	2692	125	1	2.79	14	7	7	831	46	0	3.32
1993-94	Binghamton	AHL	10	5	4	1	294	18	0	3.67	—	—	—	—	—	—	—
1993-94	Canadian National		37	19	15	2	2168	105	0	2.80	—	—	—	—	—	—	—
1993-94	Canadian Olympic		8	5	2	1	485	19	0	2.35	—	—	—	—	—	—	—
NHL and Rangers Totals			4	1	2	1	224	14	0	3.75	—	—	—	—	—	—	—

MIKE HUDSON

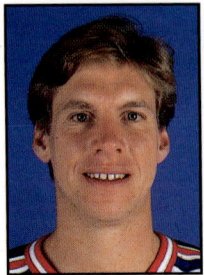

CENTER

15

6-1 • 205 • Shoots Left
Born: February 6, 1967 • Guelph, Ontario
Off-Season Home: Rockwood, Ontario

1993-94: Claimed from Edmonton in the NHL waiver draft on October 3 ... Appeared in 48 games, collecting four goals and seven assists ... Collected his initial point with the team, registering an assist, while making his Rangers debut on October 7 vs. Tampa Bay ... Notched his 100th career point with an assist on November 27 at Long Island ... Recorded his first goal with New York on December 15 vs. Hartford ... Missed 16 games due to a fractured left hand suffered on October 9 at Pittsburgh and missed 10 games due to suspension.

NHL CAREER: 1988-89: Made his NHL debut on October 6 vs. the Rangers and registered his first NHL point with an assist ... Registered a career-high 16 assists ... Potted his first NHL goal, a shorthanded tally, on October 12 vs. Winnipeg ... Collected a goal and two assists in 10 playoff outings. **1989-90:** Recorded nine goals and 12 assists in 49 games ... Missed 12 games due to a lacerated hand. **1990-91:** Potted six of his seven goals and 12 of his 16 points at home ... Notched a career-high three points with a goal and an assist on March 31 vs. Detroit ... Skated in his 100th NHL contest on October 25 vs. Washington. **1991-92:** Posted career-highs in games (76), goals (14), points (29) and penalty minutes (92) ... Registered seven goals and 12 assists for 19 points at home and seven goals and three assists for 10 points on the road ... Collected two game-winning goals, including an overtime, game-winner on January 27 at Calgary ... Skated in 16 of Hawk's 18 playoff contests, tallying three goals and five assists ... Posted a four-game scoring streak with two goals and four assists vs. St. Louis. **1992-93:** Collected a goal and seven assists in 41 games with Edmonton and Chicago ... Obtained by Edmonton from Chicago in exchange for Craig Muni on March 22 ... Missed 13 games from January 7 to January 29 due to a hand injury ... Registered a plus or even rating in 24 of his 36 games with the Blackhawks and in 27 of his 41 games overall ... Skated in his 250th NHL match on January 30 at Los Angeles.

IHL CAREER: 1987-88: Made his professional debut with Saginaw ... Registered 18 goals and 30 assists for 48 points in 75 games. **1989-90:** Collected 15 goals in 17 assists for 32 points in 30 games, splitting the season between Saginaw and Chicago.

JUNIOR CAREER: Began his junior career with Hamilton of the Ontario Hockey League in 1984-85 ... Collected 10 goals and 12 assists ... Traded to Sudbury by Hamilton seven games into the 1985-86 season ... Registered 35 goals and 42 assists for 77 points in 59 games with Sudbury ... Tallied 40 goals and 57 assists for 97 points in 63 games in 1986-87 to complete his junior career.

BACKGROUND: Spent some time vacationing in Australia during the summer ... Nickname "Huddy" ... Enjoys windsurfing and playing tennis in the off-season ... Teammates with Greg Gilbert and Steve Larmer in Chicago ... Lists Casablanca as his favorite movie ... Single.

CAREER TRANSACTIONS: *June 21, 1986* — Blackhawks' sixth choice, (140th overall) in the 1986 NHL Entry Draft. *March 22, 1993* — Traded to Edmonton by Chicago for Craig Muni. *October 3, 1993* — Claimed by the Rangers from Edmonton in the NHL waiver draft.

CAREER HIGHLIGHTS

MOST GOALS, GAME: 2, Mar. 23, 1991 at Pit., **MOST ASSISTS, GAME:** 2, (8 times) last- Oct. 13, 1991 vs. S.J., **MOST POINTS, GAME:** 3, (3 times) last- Oct. 13, 1991 vs. S.J., **MOST PIM, GAME:** 22, Oct. 16, 1990 at Stl., **MOST SHOTS, GAME:** 6, Nov. 5, 1989 vs. Wpg., **MOST SHOTS, SEASON:** 97, 1991-92, **HIGHEST +/-, SEASON:** 5, 1990-91, **FIRST NHL GAME:** Oct. 6, 1988 vs. NYR., **FIRST NHL GOAL:** Oct 12, 1988 vs. Wpg. (Reddick)

MIKE HUDSON #15

AMATEUR AND PROFESSIONAL RECORD

Season	Club	Lea	Regular Season					Playoffs				
			GP	G	A	PTS	PIM	GP	G	A	PTS	PIM
1984-85	Hamilton	OHL	50	10	12	22	13	—	—	—	—	—
1985-86	Hamilton	OHL	7	3	2	5	4	—	—	—	—	—
1985-86	Sudbury	OHL	59	35	42	77	20	4	2	5	7	7
1986-87	Sudbury	OHL	63	40	57	97	18	—	—	—	—	—
1987-88	Saginaw	IHL	75	18	30	48	44	10	2	3	5	20
1988-89	Chicago	NHL	41	7	16	23	20	10	1	2	3	18
1988-89	Saginaw	IHL	30	15	17	32	10	—	—	—	—	—
1989-90	Chicago	NHL	49	9	12	21	56	4	0	0	0	2
1990-91	Chicago	NHL	55	7	9	16	62	6	0	2	2	8
1990-91	Indianapolis	IHL	3	1	2	3	0	—	—	—	—	—
1991-92	Chicago	NHL	76	14	15	29	92	16	3	5	8	26
1992-93	Chicago	NHL	36	1	6	7	44	—	—	—	—	—
1992-93	Edmonton	NHL	5	0	1	1	2	—	—	—	—	—
1993-94	Rangers	NHL	48	4	7	11	47	—	—	—	—	—
NHL Totals			310	42	66	108	323	36	4	9	13	54
Rangers Totals			48	4	7	11	47	0	0	0	0	0

ALEXANDER KARPOVTSEV

DEFENSE
6-1 • 200 • Shoots Right
Born: April 7, 1970 • Moscow, Russia
Off-Season Home: Moscow, Russia

25

1993-94: Appeared in 67 games, tallying three goals and 15 assists for 18 points in his first season in the National Hockey League ... Acquired from Quebec on September 9 in exchange for Mike Hurlbut ... Made his NHL debut on October 9 at Pittsburgh ... Collected his first NHL goal, potting the game winner on the power play, on October 13 vs. Quebec ... Registered a plus or even rating in 51 of his 67 matches and finished the season with a plus 12 rating ... Notched 10 of his 15 assists on the road ... Saw time on the power play and penalty killing units and registered four power play assists and one shorthanded assist ... Collected a pair of assists on April 8 vs. Toronto, notching his first multiple-point game ... Missed 11 games due to injury.

1994 PLAYOFFS: Appeared in 17 of the 23 playoff matches, tallying four assists ... Made his initial NHL playoff appearance on April 17 in Game One of the Conference Quarterfinals vs. the Islanders ... Recorded his first point of the post-season with an assist on Stephane Matteau's goal on April 18 in Game Two vs. the Islanders ... Three of his four assists were collected during the Conference Semifinals vs. Washington ... Four assists tied for fourth among NHL rookies.

RUSSIAN CAREER: Played four seasons with Dynamo Moscow in the Russian Elite League ... Had his best offensive production in his last year with the club (1992-93), notching three goals and 11 assists for 14 points in 40 games while serving as the team captain ... Led the entire Russian Elite League with 100 penalty minutes in '92-93 ... Skated in eight games for the Russian team at the 1993 World Championships in Munich, Germany, collecting one assist ... Collected three goals and two assists in 28 matches in 1991-92 helping lead the club to a 25-2-3 record and the regular season and playoff championship ... Teammates included Alexei Kovalev, Alexei Zhamnov (Wpg.), Alexander Semak (N.J.), Igor Koralev (St. L.), Yan Kaminsky (NYI), Dimitri Filimonov (Ott.), Dimitri Yushkevich (Phi.), Alexei Yashin (Ott.), Darius Kasparaitis (NYI) and Andre Lomakin (Phi).

BACKGROUND: Nickname is "Pottsy" ... His hobbies include playing tennis, fishing, and playing pool ... Lists tennis star Andrei Medvedev as his favorite athlete ... His brother Andrei played briefly with Moncton in the AHL ... Enjoys listening to Aerosmith ... Married, wife Janna; daughter Dasha.

CAREER TRANSACTIONS: *June 16, 1990* — Quebec's seventh round choice (158th) overall in the 1990 NHL Entry Draft. *September 9, 1993* — Traded to the Rangers by Quebec for Mike Hurlbut.

ALEXANDER KARPOVTSEV #25

CAREER HIGHLIGHTS

MOST GOALS, GAME: 1 (3 times) last- Apr. 12, 1994 vs. Buf., **MOST ASSISTS, GAME:** 2, Apr. 8, 1994 vs. Tor., **MOST POINTS, GAME:** 3, Apr. 8, 1994 vs. Tor., **MOST PIM, GAME:** 4, (8 times) last- Mar. 23, 1994 at Edm., **MOST SHOTS, GAME:** 8, Oct. 19, 1993 vs. Ana., **MOST SHOTS, SEASON:** 78, 1993-94, **HIGHEST +/-, SEASON:** 12, 1993-94, **FIRST NHL GAME:** Oct. 9, 1993 at Pit., **FIRST NHL GOAL:** Oct. 13, 1993 vs. Que. (Fiset)

AMATEUR AND PROFESSIONAL RECORD

			Regular Season					Playoffs				
Season	Club	Lea	GP	G	A	PTS	PIM	GP	G	A	PTS	PIM
1989-90	Dynamo Moscow	USSR	35	1	1	2	27	—	—	—	—	—
1990-91	Dynamo Moscow	USSR	40	0	5	5	15	—	—	—	—	—
1991-92	Dynamo Moscow	CIS	28	3	2	5	22	—	—	—	—	—
1992-93	Dynamo Moscow	CIS	40	3	11	14	100	—	—	—	—	—
1993-94	Rangers	NHL	67	3	15	18	58	17	0	4	4	12
NHL and Rangers Totals			67	3	15	18	58	17	0	4	4	12

JOE KOCUR

26

RIGHT WING
6-0 • 205 • Shoots Right
Born: December 21, 1964 • Calgary, Alberta
Off-Season Home: Highland, Michigan

1993-94: Appeared in 71 games, tying the second highest mark of his career and his most since joining the Rangers in 1991 ... Placed fourth on the team with 129 penalty minutes.

1994 PLAYOFFS: Appeared in 20 of the 23 matches, including six of the seven matches in the Finals ... Missed three matches due to injury ... Tallied an assist in Game One of the Conference Semifinals on May 1 vs. Washington ... Tallied his only goal of the playoffs in Game Two of the Conference Semifinals vs. Washington.

NHL CAREER: 1984-85: Spent bulk of campaign with Adirondack (AHL) before being called up by Red Wings on Feb. 18 ... Made his NHL debut two nights later in a 3-2 victory over St. Louis ... Collected his initial fighting major in his second outing ... Tallied his first NHL goal on Mar. 9 vs. New Jersey (Glenn Resch) with assists from Gerard Gallant and Brad Park. **1985-86:** First nine games of season were spent with Adirondack before call-up on Oct. 29 ... After going scoreless in first 26 outings with Detroit, notched two goals and one assist in 6-5 triumph against Toronto on Jan. 5 while playing on a line with Steve Yzerman and Petr Klima ... Had another three-point performance on Feb. 14 against the Rangers, two goals and one assist ... Led the NHL and set a Detroit club record with 377 penalty minutes while appearing in 59 games ... Set a Red wings club record for PIM in a single game with 42 on Nov. 2 against St. Louis. **1986-87:** Played entire season with Red Wings leading club in PIM for second straight year with 276 ... Potted a pair of goals at Toronto on Jan. 31 ... Two goals and three assists in 16 playoff appearances, along with 71 penalty minutes, still a Wings record. **1987-88:** Was second on team in PIM with 263 ... Missed total of 16 games with four different injuries ... Missed final six straight outings with a separated right shoulder. **1988-89:** Potted nine goals for the third time in four seasons while also adding nine assists ... Second on Red Wings with 213 PIM ... Missed total of 17 games due to injuries and illness. **1989-90:** Ranked eighth on Red Wings in scoring with career high 36 points, 16 goals and 20 assists ... Tied for second on team with five game-winning goals, including his first career overtime score on Mar. 17 in 4-3 victory at St. Louis ... Best offensive stretch was a three-game span from Jan. 27-Feb. 2 when he notched four goals and three assists ... Team leader with 268 PIM. **1990-91:** Obtained from Detroit at the trading deadline along with Per Djoos for Kevin Miller, Dennis Vial and Jim Cummins ... Made his Rangers debut in Quebec on Mar. 7 playing in his 400th NHL contest ... Appeared in only five games with New York after trade due to an injury and a pair of suspensions ... Ranked fifth in NHL with 289 PIM ... Final goal as a Red Wing came on a penalty shot on Nov. 29 in Chicago. **1991-92:** Collected seven goals in his first full season in New York ... Missed 28 games due to injury, including 13 straight from Jan. 30 to Feb. 25, due to a shoulder injury suffered on Jan. 28 against San Jose ... Notched his first goal as a Ranger on Nov. 11 vs. Penguins ... Scored two goals at Detroit on Dec. 6 ... ... Recorded eight of his 11 points on the road ... Played in 12 of New York's 13 playoff matches and ranked second on the team with 38 penalty minutes. **1992-93:** Became the 19th player in NHL history to surpass the 2,000 mark in career penalty minutes on Apr. 4 at Washington ... Played in his 500th NHL match on Feb. 10 vs. Pittsburgh ... Collected two goals and one assist on the power play ... Six of his eight points were scored on the road.

AHL CAREER: Made his AHL debut in the 1984 playoffs, appearing in five contests ... Split the next season (1984-85) between Adirondack and Detroit, notching 12 goals in 47 AHL games ... Played first nine games with Adirondack in 1985-86 before being called up to Detroit.

JUNIOR CAREER: Joined the Saskatoon Blades of the WHL from the Yorkton Terriers of the Saskatchewan Junior Hockey League and notched 23 goals and 40 points in his rookie season ... The next season he doubled his point production with 40 goals and 41 assists for 81 points ... Ranked second on the team with 40 goals and 81 points and fourth with 41 ... Led team in penalty minutes each season.

BACKGROUND: Born in Calgary but moved to Kelvington, Saskatchewan at very early age ... Is a distant cousin of Quebec's Wendel Clark and his first cousin, Kory Kocur was Detroit's first pick in '88 Entry Draft ... Wore uniform number 26 during his entire career with Red Wings ... Is a scratch golfer and lists Pebble Beach as his favorite place to visit ... Also enjoys fishing during the off-season ... A big country music fan, his favorite singer is Garth Brooks and his favorite group is Alabama ... Is a fan of college football with his favorite being the Michigan Wolverines ... Has a golden retriever named "Molson" ... Married: wife, Kristen; daughter Kendall.

CAREER TRANSACTIONS: *June 8, 1983* — Detroit's sixth choice (fifth round, 91st overall) in the 1983 Entry Draft. *Mar. 5, 1991* — Traded by Detroit along with Per Djoos to Rangers for Kevin Miller, Dennis Vial and Jim Cummins.

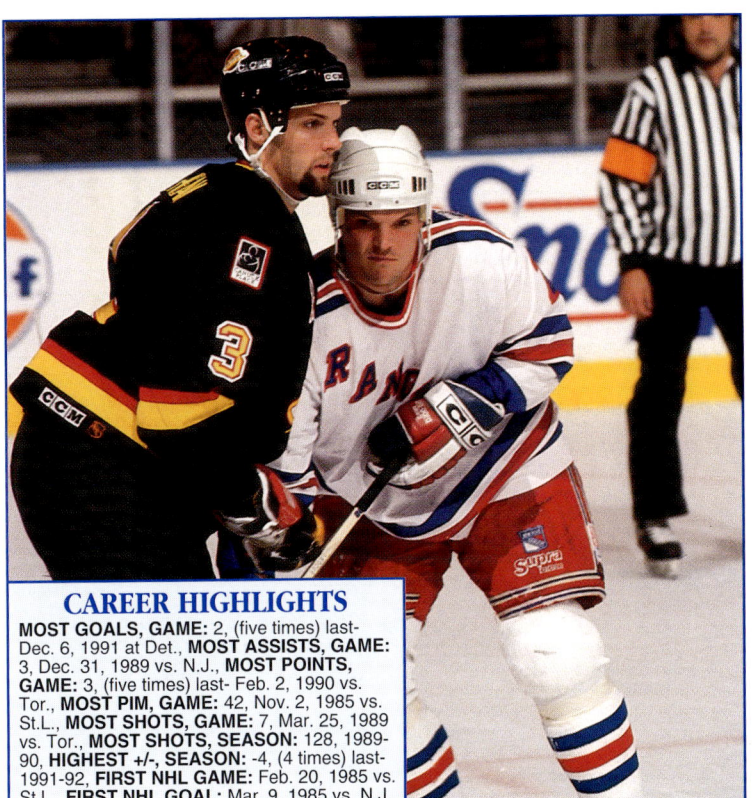

JOE KOCUR #26

CAREER HIGHLIGHTS

MOST GOALS, GAME: 2, (five times) last- Dec. 6, 1991 at Det., **MOST ASSISTS, GAME:** 3, Dec. 31, 1989 vs. N.J., **MOST POINTS, GAME:** 3, (five times) last- Feb. 2, 1990 vs. Tor., **MOST PIM, GAME:** 42, Nov. 2, 1985 vs. St.L., **MOST SHOTS, GAME:** 7, Mar. 25, 1989 vs. Tor., **MOST SHOTS, SEASON:** 128, 1989-90, **HIGHEST +/-, SEASON:** -4, (4 times) last- 1991-92, **FIRST NHL GAME:** Feb. 20, 1985 vs. St.L., **FIRST NHL GOAL:** Mar. 9, 1985 vs. N.J.

AMATEUR AND PROFESSIONAL RECORD

Season	Club	Lea	Regular Season					Playoffs				
			GP	G	A	PTS	PIM	GP	G	A	PTS	PIM
1982-83	Saskatoon	WHL	62	23	17	40	289	6	2	3	5	25
1983-84	Saskatoon	WHL	69	40	41	81	258	—	—	—	—	—
1983-84	Adirondack	AHL	—	—	—	—	—	5	0	0	0	20
1984-85	Detroit	NHL	17	1	0	1	64	3	1	0	1	5
1984-85	Adirondack	AHL	47	12	7	19	171	—	—	—	—	—
1985-86	Detroit	NHL	59	9	6	15	377	—	—	—	—	—
1985-86	Adirondack	AHL	9	6	2	8	34	—	—	—	—	—
1986-87	Detroit	NHL	77	9	9	18	276	16	2	3	5	71
1987-88	Detroit	NHL	64	7	7	14	263	10	0	1	1	13
1988-89	Detroit	NHL	60	9	9	18	213	3	0	1	1	6
1989-90	Detroit	NHL	71	16	20	36	268	—	—	—	—	—
1990-91	Detroit	NHL	52	5	4	9	253	—	—	—	—	—
1990-91	Rangers	NHL	5	0	0	0	36	6	0	2	2	21
1991-92	Rangers	NHL	51	7	4	11	121	12	1	1	2	38
1992-93	Rangers	NHL	65	3	6	9	131	—	—	—	—	—
1993-94	Rangers	NHL	71	2	1	3	129	20	1	1	2	17
NHL Totals			592	68	66	134	2131	70	5	9	14	171
Rangers Totals			192	12	11	23	417	38	2	4	6	76

ALEXEI KOVALEV

RIGHT WING
6-0 • 200 • Shoots Left
Born: February 24, 1973 • Togliatti, Russia
Off-Season Home: Mamaroneck, New York

1993-94: Established career highs in games played and all offensive categories in his first full season in the NHL ... Began the season at his natural position of right wing but was shifted to center in March ... Responded by tallying 13 goals and six assists for 19 points in his last 20 games ... Registered an 11-game point scoring streak from Mar. 16 to Apr. 8, collecting 10 goals and five assists over the span and tying Mark Messier for the longest point scoring streak on the team ... Also registered a career-high four-game goal scoring streak from Mar. 27 to Apr. 2 ... Potted 16 goals in his last 36 games after notching seven in his first 40 matches ... Ranked second on the team with 27 assists and 43 points at even strength ... Registered a plus or even rating in 55 of his last 66 matches, recording a plus 26 rating over the span.

1994 PLAYOFFS: Placed third on the team in scoring with nine goals and 12 assists for 21 points in 23 matches ... Tied with Mark Messier for second on the club in scoring during the Finals, collecting two goals and five assists ... Set a club record, notching his fifth power play goal of the post-season, in Game Six of the Finals ... Notched a point in each of the last five games of the Finals ... Recorded a goal and tallied a pair of assists on Messier's game-tying and game-winning goals on in Game Six of the Conference Finals ... Notched a point in each of the first seven playoff matches (four goals, seven assists) ... Registered a goal in each of the four Conference Quarterfinal matches vs. the Islanders, tying Pavel Bure for the longest goal scoring streak during the playoffs.

NHL CAREER: 1992-93: Made his NHL debut at MSG vs. Hartford on Oct. 12 and tallied his first NHL goal against Sean Burke ... Registered his first NHL assist in his first career multiple point outing vs. Washington on Oct. 21 ... Began the season with New York, tallying two goals and four assists in 14 games before being assigned to Binghamton on Nov. 23 ... Was recalled on Dec. 6 and collected 10 goals and eight assists in his next 20 contests ... Recorded his first career hat trick on Dec. 27 vs. Boston, including the game-winner with 36 seconds remaining ... Tallied a goal and three assists for a career-high four points vs. Montreal on Dec. 13.

RUSSIAN CAREER: Began his hockey career in Togliatti, on Volga-River, at the age of seven ... In 1988 was invited to Dynamo Moscow ... Played two seasons for Dynamo's junior team ... Made his debut in senior team at the end of the 1989-90 season, at the age of 17 ... Wore uniform No. 30 with Dynamo ... In last two seasons he received two gold medals for winning national championships. 1991-92: Became a regular with Dynamo Moscow after appearing in two pre-season contests with Rangers ... Played in 26 games and collected 16 goals and eight assists for 24 points ... Won national title with the team for the second straight year.

INTERNATIONAL CAREER: Made his debut with the national team on Aug. 14, 1991, in an exhibition game against Sweden ... Was in training camp of the national team before Canada Cup, but did not make the team ... Won title with the team at the World Junior Championships ... Collected five goals and five assists for 10 points in seven games ... Was the top scorer on the team and fifth overall in the league... Was named to the tournament's All-Star team ... Was a key member of the Russian team that won the gold medal at the 1992 Olympic Games ... Played at the World Championships in Czechoslovakia, appearing in six games, collecting one assist... Played two years at European Junior Championships ... Played at World Junior Championships, Olympics and World Championships in 1991-92... Wore uniform number 14 on the National Team.

BACKGROUND: The first Soviet player ever taken in the first round of the NHL Entry Draft ... Lists Wayne Gretzky as his hockey hero ... Enjoys soccer and water skiing ... Favorite actor is Saveli Kramarov ("Moscow on Hudson"), the former Soviet comedy actor ... Always keeps a troll with him for good luck ... Likes to read ... After attending Rangers' training camp in 1991, started to study English ... Single.

CAREER TRANSACTIONS: *June 9, 1991* — Rangers' first round choice (15th overall) in 1991 Entry Draft.

CAREER HIGHLIGHTS

MOST GOALS, GAME: 3, Dec. 27, 1992 vs. Bos., **MOST ASSISTS, GAME:** 3, (twice) last-Dec. 26, 1993 vs. N.J., **MOST POINTS, GAME:** 4, (twice) last-Dec. 26, 1993 vs. N.J., **MOST PIM, GAME:** 21, Jan. 6, 1992 at Ott., **MOST SHOTS, GAME:** 8, (twice) last- Mar. 19,1993 vs. S.J., **MOST SHOTS, SEASON:** 184, 1993-94, **HIGHEST +/-, SEASON:** 18, 1993-94, **FIRST NHL GAME:** Oct. 12, 1992 vs. Hfd., **FIRST NHL GOAL:** Oct. 12, 1992 vs. Hfd. (Burke)

ALEXEI KOVALEV #27

AMATEUR AND PROFESSIONAL RECORD

			Regular Season					Playoffs				
Season	Club	Lea	GP	G	A	PTS	PIM	GP	G	A	PTS	PIM
1989-90	Dynamo Moscow	Sov. Elite	1	0	0	0	0	—	—	—	—	—
1990-91	Dynamo Moscow	Sov. Elite	18	1	2	3	4	—	—	—	—	—
1991-92	Unified Olympic Team		8	1	2	3	—	—	—	—	—	—
1991-92	Dynamo Moscow	Sov. Elite	33	16	9	25	20	—	—	—	—	—
1992-93	Rangers	NHL	65	20	18	38	79	—	—	—	—	—
1992-93	Binghamton	AHL	13	13	11	24	35	9	3	5	8	14
1993-94	Rangers	NHL	76	23	33	56	154	23	9	12	21	18
NHL and Rangers Totals			141	43	51	94	233	23	9	12	21	18

NICK KYPREOS

19

LEFT WING
6-0 • 205 • Shoots Left
Born: June 6, 1966 • Toronto, Ontario
Off-Season Home: Willowdale, Ontario

1993-94: Acquired from Hartford along with Steve Larmer, Barry Richter and a draft choice on Nov. 2 ... Played in 10 games with the Whalers prior to the trade ... Collected three goals and five assists in 46 games with New York ... Notched his first point with the Rangers on Dec. 13 vs. Buffalo, assisting on Sergei Nemchinov's game winning goal ... Tallied his first goal as a Ranger on Jan. 10 vs. Tampa Bay.

1994 Playoffs: Appeared in three playoff matches, including Game Seven of the Stanley Cup Finals vs. Vancouver on June 14 ... Skated in Games Three and Four of the Conference Quarterfinals at Long Island.

NHL CAREER: 1989-90: Claimed by Washington from Philadelphia in the Waiver Draft, following an impressive training camp with the Flyers ... Made his National Hockey League debut on October 6 vs. Philadelphia ... Tallied his first NHL goal on November 29 at Detroit ... Two of his five goals were game-winners ... Posted a three-game scoring streak from December 5 to December 9, collecting two goals and two assists over the span ... Registered a plus two rating and 82 penalty minutes in 31 games ... Sent to Baltimore on March 8 after undergoing minor knee surgery ... Skated in his first NHL playoff game vs. the Rangers on April 21 at Madison Square Garden. **1990-91:** Played in 79 games after not dressing for the opener ... Collected three game-winning goals ... Registered his only multiple-point game of the season at Edmonton on March 10 ... Placed third on the club with 196 penalty minutes ... Tied a career-high with a three-game scoring streak from January 1 to January 5. **1991-92:** Recorded 206 penalty minutes, placing second on the team while playing in his first season with Hartford ... Notched his first career two-goal game on January 1 vs. the Islanders. **1992-93:** Posted career-highs with 17 goals, 10 assists, 27 points and a team-leading 325 penalty minutes ... Ranked fourth in the league in penalty minutes ... Recorded two goals vs. the Islanders on February 28 ... Three of his 17 goals were game-winners ... Whalers were 13-7-3 when he recorded a point and 10-40-2 when he didn't ... Missed the final seven games of the season with an abdominal muscle strain.

AHL CAREER: Joined the Hershey Bears following his final season with North Bay and appeared in 10 games in 1986-87 ... Recorded 24 goals and 20 assists for 44 points along with 101 penalty minutes in his first full professional season with Hershey in 1987-88 ... Skated in 12 playoff matches as Hershey captured the 1988 Calder Cup ... Missed the first 52 games of the 1989-90 season and was limited to 28 games due to pre-season knee injury ... Recorded two goals and three assists on March 16, 1990 vs. New Haven while playing with Baltimore.

JUNIOR CAREER: Played four seasons with the North Bay Centennials of the Ontario Hockey League ... Led the club in with 62 goals and 97 points and was named a first team OHL All-Star in 1985-86 ... The following year he placed second on the team in scoring in with 90 points despite playing in only 46 games ... Earned honors as a second team OHL All-Star ... Recorded 11 goals and five assists in 24 games as North Bay went to the finals of the OHL playoffs before losing in to the Oshawa Generals.

BACKGROUND: Majored in marketing at Candore College ... Enjoys playing soccer and baseball ... Received the Shawmut Bank Favorite Whaler Award as voted by the fans and also captured the Whalers Heavy Hitter Award in 1992-93 ... Following the team's Cup victory, he went with teammates Brian Leetch and Mark Messier to throw out the first pitch at Yankee Stadium, appeared in MTV's This Week in Rock with Glenn Healy and went with Brian Noonan to MTV's Summer Beach House in the Hampton's ... Does considerable charitable work and appearances ... Single.

CAREER TRANSACTIONS: *September 30, 1984* — Signed as a free agent by Philadelphia. *October 2, 1989* —Claimed by Washington in NHL Waiver Draft. *June 15, 1992* —Traded to Hartford by Washington for Mark Hunter and future considerations (Yvon Corriveau). *November 2, 1993* —Traded by Hartford to Rangers along with Steve Larmer, Barry Richter and a 1994 draft choice (Yuri Litvinov).

CAREER HIGHLIGHTS

MOST GOALS, GAME: 2, (3 times) last- Feb. 28, 1993 vs. NYI, **MOST ASSISTS, GAME:** 2, (twice) last- Feb. 20, 1993 vs. Edm., **MOST POINTS, GAME:** 2, (5 times) last- Feb. 20, 1993 vs. Edm., **MOST PIM, GAME:** 42, Dec. 11, 1992 at Buf., **MOST SHOTS, GAME:** 4, (twice) last- Dec. 12, 1992 vs. Buf., **MOST SHOTS, SEASON:** 81, 1992-93, **HIGHEST +/-, SEASON:** 2, 1989-90, **FIRST NHL GAME:** Oct. 6, 1989 vs. Phi., **FIRST NHL GOAL:** Nov. 29, 1989 vs. Det. (St. Laurent)

NICK KYPREOS #19

AMATEUR AND PROFESSIONAL RECORD

			Regular Season					Playoffs				
Season	Club	Lea	GP	G	A	PTS	PIM	GP	G	A	PTS	PIM
1983-84	North Bay	OHL	51	12	11	23	36	4	3	2	5	9
1984-85	North Bay	OHL	64	41	36	77	71	8	2	2	4	15
1985-86	North Bay	OHL	64	62	35	97	112	—	—	—	—	—
1986-87	Hershey	AHL	10	0	1	1	4	—	—	—	—	—
1986-87	North Bay	OHL	46	49	41	90	54	24	11	5	16	78
1987-88	Hershey	AHL	71	24	20	44	101	12	0	2	2	17
1988-89	Hershey	AHL	28	12	15	27	19	12	4	5	9	11
1989-90	Washington	NHL	31	5	4	9	82	7	1	0	1	15
1989-90	Baltimore	AHL	14	6	5	11	6	7	4	1	5	17
1990-91	Washington	NHL	79	9	9	18	196	9	0	1	1	38
1991-92	Washington	NHL	65	4	6	10	206	—	—	—	—	—
1992-93	Hartford	NHL	75	17	10	27	325	—	—	—	—	—
1993-94	Hartford	NHL	10	0	0	0	37	—	—	—	—	—
1993-94	Rangers	NHL	46	3	5	8	102	3	0	0	0	2
NHL Totals			306	38	34	72	948	19	1	1	2	55
Rangers Totals			46	3	5	8	102	3	0	0	0	2

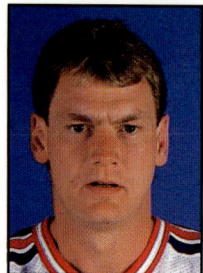

STEVE LARMER

RIGHT WING

28

5-11 • 195 • Shoots Left
Born: June 16, 1961 • Peterborough, Ontario
Off-Season Home: Peterborough, Ontario

1993-94: Acquired from Hartford on Nov. 2 after being dealt to the Whalers from Chicago earlier in the day ... Made his Rangers debut and tallied the game winning goal on Nov. 3 vs. Vancouver ... Tallied three assists three days later at Quebec and recorded three goals and three assists in his first three matches ... Skated in his 900th NHL contest on Nov. 23 vs. Montreal ... Missed three games due to a broken finger suffered on Jan. 5 vs. Calgary ... Returned two weeks ahead of schedule on Jan. 16 at Chicago and scored on a penalty shot and added an assist in his first appearance as a visiting player at Chicago Stadium ... Rangers were 44-17-7 with him in the lineup, 31-6-6 when he tallied a point and 15-3-1 when he scored a goal ... Led the club with seven game winning tallies and also assisted on seven game winners.

1994 PLAYOFFS: Placed sixth on the team in scoring with nine goals and seven assists for 16 points in 23 matches ... Tallied four of his nine goals in the Finals ... Notched a power play goal and added an assist in his first playoff appearance with New York on Apr. 17 ... Collected a point in five of the first six playoff matches.

NHL CAREER: **1980-81:** Made his NHL debut on Jan. 17 at Hartford, after being called up from Niagara Falls (OHL). **1981-82:** Appeared in three games after being called up from New Brunswick (AHL). **1982-83:** Won the Calder Trophy as the NHL's top rookie, scoring 43 goals and 47 assists for 91 points ... Set a Hawks record for goals by a right wing, playing with Denis Savard and Al Secord ... Collected his first NHL goal on Oct. 6 vs. Toronto ... Placed first among NHL rookies in goals and scoring, setting club records in both categories and tied for the lead in assists, tying the team record ... Led the Hawks with a plus 44 rating and was tops on the team with nine GWG's ... Ranked second among rookies in playoff scoring with five goals and seven assists for 12 points in 11 games. **1983-84:** Placed second on the club with 35 goals and 75 points and led Hawks with 13 PPG's. **1984-85:** Led the team with 46 goals ... Six GWG's tied for first on the club ... Collected nine goals and 13 assists for 22 points in 15 playoff outings. **1985-86:** Collected his first shg while regularly killing penalties for the first time in his career. **1986-87:** Led the team and set a new Hawks record for assists by a right wing with 56 ... Placed second on the club in scoring with 84 points ... Led the team with 10 PPG's and placed second with four game-winners ... Collected four assists on Nov. 1 at Minnesota. **1987-88:** Placed second on the team in scoring with 89 points ... Set a Hawks record with seven SHG's ... Placed first on the team with 21 PPG's ... Recorded his 500th career point with a goal on Mar. 30 vs. the Rangers. **1988-89:** Placed first on the team with 43 goals, 87 points and 19 PPG's ... Tallied a goal in six consecutive playoff games, establishing a new club record. **1989-90:** Led Hawks in scoring for the second consecutive season while collecting a career-high 59 assists ... Posted a nine-game assist streak from Dec. 6 to Dec. 23 ... Appeared in his first NHL All Star Game on Jan. 21 ... Tied for the team lead in playoff scoring with seven goals and 15 assists for 22 points in 20 games. **1990-91:** Notched over 100 points for the first time in his career, registering 44 goals and 57 assists for 101 points ... Broke Jim Pappin's club record for points in a season by a right wing ... Placed fifth in the league and first on the team with a plus 37 rating ... Made his second career All-Star appearance on Jan. 19 at Chicago Stadium. **1991-92:** Became the fourth player in Hawks history to reach the 100 point plateau in playoff scoring ... Tied Stan Mikita's club playoff record for most points in a game with five assists. **1992-93:** Did not miss a game for the 11th consecutive season, extending his consecutive games streak to 884 ... Led the team with a plus 23 rating ... Collected six points with two goals and four assists on Nov. 27 at Edmonton ... Collected his 900th career point on Jan. 10 vs. Los Angeles.

AHL CAREER: Spent one season with New Brunswick in 1981-82 and was named to the AHL's Second All-Star Team.

JUNIOR CAREER: Began his junior career with Peterborough in 1977-78 ... Earned honors by being named to the OHA's Second All-Star Team in 1980-81.

BACKGROUND: Lists the Rolling Stones as his favorite musical group ... Recipient of the 1990-91 Hockey News/Inside Hockey "Man of the Year" ... Played for Team Canada in the 1991 Canada Cup where he tallied the series-clinching goal vs. Team USA ... Played in 884 consecutive games, the third longest streak in NHL history ... Married, wife Rose; daughter, Bailey Rose.

CAREER TRANSACTIONS: *June 11, 1980* — Chicago's sixth choice (120th overall) in the 1980 NHL Entry Draft. *November 2, 1993* — Traded to Hartford from Chicago with Bryan Marchment for Patrick Poulin and Eric Weinrich. *November 2, 1993* — Traded by Hartford with Nick Kypreos, Barry Richter and a 1994 sixth round draft choice (Yuri Litvinov) for James Patrick and Darren Turcotte.

STEVE LARMER #28

CAREER HIGHLIGHTS

MOST GOALS, GAME: 3, (9 times) last- Dec. 23, 1992 at Ott., **MOST ASSISTS, GAME:** 4, (twice) last- Nov. 27, 1992 at Edm., **MOST POINTS, GAME:** 6, Nov. 27, 1992 at Edm., **MOST PIM, GAME:** 27, Mar. 17, 1991 vs. Stl., **MOST SHOTS, GAME:** 11, Feb. 22, 1989 vs. Min., **MOST SHOTS, SEASON:** 269, 1988-89, **HIGHEST +/-, SEASON:** 44, 1982-83, **FIRST NHL GAME:** Jan. 17, 1981 at Hfd., **FIRST NHL GOAL:** Oct. 6, 1982 at Chi. (Larocque)

AMATEUR AND PROFESSIONAL RECORD

			Regular Season					Playoffs				
Season	Club	Lea	GP	G	A	PTS	PIM	GP	G	A	PTS	PIM
1977-78	Peterborough	OHA	62	24	17	41	51	18	5	7	12	27
1978-79	Niagara Falls	OHA	66	37	47	84	108	—	—	—	—	—
1979-80	Niagara Falls	OHA	67	45	69	114	71	10	5	9	14	15
1980-81	Chicago	NHL	4	0	1	1	0	—	—	—	—	—
1980-81	Niagara Falls	OHA	61	55	78	133	73	12	13	8	21	24
1981-82	Chicago	NHL	3	0	0	0	0	—	—	—	—	—
1981-82	New Brunswick	AHL	74	38	44	82	46	15	6	6	12	0
1982-83	Chicago	NHL	80	43	47	90	28	11	5	7	12	8
1983-84	Chicago	NHL	80	35	40	75	34	5	2	2	4	7
1984-85	Chicago	NHL	80	46	40	86	16	15	9	13	22	14
1985-86	Chicago	NHL	80	31	45	76	47	3	0	3	3	4
1986-87	Chicago	NHL	80	28	56	84	22	4	0	0	0	2
1987-88	Chicago	NHL	80	41	48	89	42	5	1	6	7	0
1988-89	Chicago	NHL	80	43	44	87	54	16	8	9	17	22
1989-90	Chicago	NHL	80	31	59	90	40	20	7	15	22	2
1990-91	Chicago	NHL	80	44	57	101	79	6	5	1	6	4
1991-92	Chicago	NHL	80	29	45	74	65	18	8	7	15	6
1992-93	Chicago	NHL	84	35	35	70	48	4	0	3	3	0
1993-94	Rangers	NHL	68	21	39	60	41	23	9	7	16	14
NHL Totals			959	427	556	983	516	130	54	73	127	83
Rangers Totals			68	21	39	60	41	23	9	7	16	14

BRIAN LEETCH

2

DEFENSE
5-11 • 190 • Shoots Left
Born: March 3, 1968 • Corpus Christi, Texas
Off-Season Home: New York, New York

1993-94: Named an NHL Second-Team All-Star following the season ... Tied for third on the team in scoring and placed fourth among NHL defensemen with 79 points ... Tied his career high with 23 goals, equalling the mark he set in 1988-89 as a rookie ... The mark is tied for the third highest single season goal total by a defenseman in club history ... Led the team and notched a career-high 323 shots on goal ... Ranked second in the NHL with 53 power play points, finished fourth with 26 power play assists and was on the ice for 87 of the Rangers 96 power play goals ... Rangers were 36-9-6 when he tallied a point ... Tallied a pair of goals, including the 100th of his career on March 25 at Vancouver, becoming the third defenseman in club history to reach the plateau, joining Ron Greschner and James Patrick ... Tallied a pair of assists, including the 300th of his career on November 6 at Quebec ... Skated in his 400th NHL match on January 27 at Los Angeles ... Tied a career high with four assists vs. Washington on March 9 at Halifax ... Collected his 400th NHL point with an assist on December 4 at Toronto ... Registered a 10-game point scoring streak (four goals, 10 assists) from November 14 to December 5 ... Was voted as a starter and appeared in his fourth All-Star Game on January 22 at MSG.

1994 PLAYOFFS: Led the NHL in scoring with 11 goals and 23 assists for 34 points in 23 matches and was awarded the Conn Smythe Trophy as the most valuable player in the post-season, becoming the first American-born player to ever capture the award ... 34 points is the second highest total by a defenseman in playoff history, trailing only Paul Coffey's 37 in 1985 ... Is the first Ranger to lead the league in scoring since Pentti Lund in 1949-50 ... Led the team with five goals and six assists in the Finals and opened the scoring in Game Seven on June 14 ... Moved into second place on the Rangers all-time playoff scoring list with 58 points ... Set team playoff records for goals by a defenseman (11), points (34), assists (23), game-winning goals (four), and tied the club mark for power play goals with four ... Led the NHL with a plus 19 rating ... Was on the ice for 61 of the team's 81 goals, including 19 of the 22 power play tallies ... Collected a point in each of the first nine playoff matches and tallied a point in 19 of the 23 games overall.

NHL CAREER: 1987-88: Made his NHL debut on February 29 after competing with the U.S. Olympic Team at the games in Calgary ... Initial point was an assist in his first game ... Notched his first NHL goal and collected two assists on March 24 vs. Edmonton. **1988-89:** Won the Calder Trophy as the League's Rookie of the Year, becoming the first Ranger to win the award since Steve Vickers in '72-73 ... Led all league freshman in points (71), assists (48) and shots (268) ... Fifth among NHL defensemen with the 71 points ... 23 goals set an NHL record for most goals by a rookie defenseman, breaking the mark set by Barry Beck (22 in '77-78) ... Broke Ranger rookie defenseman records for most goals, assists and points in a season, all held by Reijo Ruotsalainen ... 13 shots on January 4 against Washington set a Ranger record for a defenseman ... Five points and four assists on February 17 vs. Toronto matched the team mark for a rookie in a single contest ... **1989-90:** Played in team's first 71 contests before suffering a fractured left ankle at Toronto on March 14 ... Led Rangers defensemen in assists (45) and shots (222) and was second among club backliners in goals (11) and points (56) ... Represented the Rangers in the All-Star Game. **1990-91:** Established team records for most assists in a season, 72, breaking Mike Rogers' mark of 65 set in '81-82 and for most points in a season by a defenseman with 88, breaking Brad Park's mark of 82 set in '73-74 ... Only Ranger to play in all 80 contests ... Appeared in second consecutive All-Star Game ... Named team MVP by members of the media. **1991-92:** Winner of the Norris Trophy as the NHL's best defenseman, becoming the first Ranger to capture the award since Harry Howell in '66-67 ... Named an NHL First-Team All-Star ... Broke his own club records for assists in a single season (80) and points by a defenseman in a single season (102) ... Became only the fifth defenseman in league history to collect 100

points in a season with 102 ... Recorded the longest point scoring streak in team history, notching a point in 17 straight contests from November 23 to December 31 ... The streak was the third longest for a defenseman in league history ... Also collected the longest assist streak in team history, 15 consecutive games, from November 29 to December 31, becoming only the fourth player in NHL history to tally a 15-game assist streak ... Established team record for most PPG's by a defenseman with 10 ... Led all NHL defensemen with 102 points, while placing ninth in the NHL ... 80 assists ranked third in the NHL ... Played in all 80 games for the second straight season ... Appeared in his third consecutive All-Star Game. **1992-93:** Missed 48 games due to injury, including 34 with a neck injury from December 17 to March 9 ... Suffered a fractured right ankle on March 19 and missed the final 13 games of the season ... Rangers were 20-13-3 when he was in the lineup and 14-26-8 when he was injured ... Opened the season with a seven-game point scoring streak, (two goals, eight assists) ... Tied a team-high for the season with 11 shots vs. Edmonton on March 17 ... Voted by fans as a starter for the Wales Conference in the NHL All-Star game, but missed the game due to injury ... Was tops among all team blueliners with 36 points despite playing in only 36 games.

INTERNATIONAL CAREER: Served as captain of the 1988 U.S. Olympic Team ... Participated for Team USA in the 1991 Canada Cup tournament ... Competed in the 1989 World Championships in Stockholm, Sweden, and was voted as the best player on Team USA ... Played with the 1987 National Team and the 1985, 1986, and 1987 National Junior Teams ... Named to the first All-Star Team at the 1987 World Junior Championship.

COLLEGE CAREER: Played one season (1986-87) for Boston College before leaving to play in the Olympics, and won the Hockey East Player of the Year and Rookie of the Year awards ... Led B.C. to the Hockey East Championship, while being tabbed an All-America and named to the All-Hockey East team ... Was a finalist for the Hobey Baker Memorial Award, symbolic of college hockey's best player, becoming the first freshman to ever be nominated for the award.

HIGH SCHOOL CAREER: Collected M.V.P. honors two consecutive seasons at Avon Old Farms ... All-New England Prep School selection and New England Prep School's Player of the Year in 1985-86.

BACKGROUND: Named the winner of the 1993-94 "Good Guy" award for cooperation with the media ... Does extensive work for the Leukemia Society and is the Celebrity Chairman for the Ice Hockey in Harlem program ... Also became involved with the Ronald McDonald House last season, as well as the Children's Health Fund ... "Leetchie" was a pitcher in high school with a fastball that was clocked at 90 miles an hour ... He, along with Mark Messier and Nick Kypreos, took batting practice with the Yankees this summer while bringing the Stanley Cup to Yankee Stadium ... Appeared along with Messier and Mike Richter on The Late Show with David Letterman following the team's Cup-victory, as well as The Today Show, Late Night with Conan O'Brien and The Howard Stern Show... Idol growing up was Ray Bourque ... His father, Jack, also played hockey for Boston College ... Enjoys fishing, tennis and golf ... Single.

CAREER TRANSACTIONS: *June 21, 1986* — Rangers' first round choice (ninth overall) in the 1986 Entry Draft.

RANGERS RECORDS OWNED OR SHARED BY BRIAN LEETCH

REGULAR SEASON RECORDS

INDIVIDUAL RECORDS
Most Assists, One Season: 88, 1991-92
Longest Consecutive Point Scoring Streak: 17, November 23 thru December 31, 1991 (five goals and 24 assists)

INDIVIDUAL ROOKIE RECORDS
Most Assists, One Season: 48, 1988-89
Most Goals by a Defenseman, One Season: 23, 1988-89
Most Assists by a Defenseman, One Season: 48, 1988-89
Most Points by a Defenseman, One Season: 71, 1988-89
Most Assists, One Game: 4 (tied with three others) - February 17, 1989 against Toronto at Madison Square Garden.
Most Points, One Game: 5, (tied with two others) - February 17, 1989 against Toronto at Madison Square Garden.
Most Shots, One Season: 268, 1988-89

INDIVIDUAL DEFENSEMAN RECORDS
Most Assists, One Season: 88, 1991-92
Most Points, One Season: 102, 1991-92
Most Points, One Game: 5, February 17, 1989 against Toronto at Madison Square Garden.
Most Power Play Goals, One Season: 17, 1993-94
Most Shorthanded Goals, One Season 3, 1988-89
Most Shots, One Season: 328, 1993-94
Most Shots, One Game: 13, January 4, 1989 against Washington at Madison Square Garden.
Longest Consecutive Assist Scoring Streak: 15, November 29 thru December 31, 1991 (23 assists during the streak).
Longest Consecutive Point Scoring Streak: 17, November 23 thru December 31, 1991 (five goals and 24 assists over the span).

PLAYOFF RECORDS

INDIVIDUAL PLAYER RECORDS
Most Assists, One Year: 23, 1993-94
Most Points, One Year: 34, 1993-94
Most Assists, One Period: 3, (tied with two others) - May 9, 1994 vs. Washington at Madison Square Garden during the first period.
Most Goals by a Defenseman, One Year: 11, 1993-94
Most Assists by a Defenseman, One Year: 23, 1993-94
Most Points by a Defenseman, One Year: 34, 1993-94
Most Points by a Defenseman, One Game: 4, twice (tied with two others) - May 9, 1994 vs. Washington at Madison Square Garden (one goal and three assists); June 7, 1994 vs. Vancouver at Vancouver (one goal and three assists).
Most Game-Winning Goals, One Year: 4, (tied) 1993-94

CAREER PLAYER RECORDS
Most Assists: 39 (four playoffs)
Most Points by a Defenseman: 58 (four playoffs)

BRIAN LEETCH #2

CAREER HIGHLIGHTS

MOST GOALS, GAME: 2, (11 times) last-Mar. 25, 1994 at Van., **MOST ASSISTS, GAME:** 4, (3 times) last- Mar. 11, 1992 vs. Chi., **MOST POINTS, GAME:** 5, Feb. 17, 1989 vs. Tor., **MOST PIM, GAME:** 15, Oct. 22, 1993 at T.B., **MOST SHOTS, GAME:** 13, Jan. 4, 1989 vs. Wsh., **MOST SHOTS, SEASON:** 328, 1993-94, **HIGHEST +/-, SEASON:** 28, 1993-94, **FIRST NHL GAME:** Feb. 29, 1988 vs. St.L., **FIRST NHL GOAL:** Mar. 24, 1988 vs. Edm. (Fuhr)

AMATEUR AND PROFESSIONAL RECORD

			Regular Season					Playoffs			
Season	Club	Lea	GP	G	A	PTS	PIM	GP	G	A	PTS	PIM
1984-85	Avon Old Farms	H.S.	26	30	46	76	15	—	—	—	—	—
1985-86	Avon Old Farms	H.S.	28	40	44	84	18	—	—	—	—	—
1986-87	Boston College	H.E.	37	9	38	47	10	—	—	—	—	—
1987-88	U.S. National Team		60	13	61	74	38	—	—	—	—	—
1987-88	U.S. Olympic Team		6	1	5	6	4	—	—	—	—	—
1987-88	Rangers	NHL	17	2	12	14	0	—	—	—	—	—
1988-89	Rangers	NHL	68	23	48	71	50	4	3	2	5	2
1989-90	Rangers	NHL	72	11	45	56	26	—	—	—	—	—
1990-91	Rangers	NHL	80	16	72	88	42	6	1	3	4	0
1991-92	Rangers	NHL	80	22	80	102	26	13	4	11	15	4
1992-93	Rangers	NHL	36	6	30	36	26	—	—	—	—	—
1993-94	Rangers	NHL	84	23	56	79	67	23	11	23	34	6
NHL and Rangers Totals			437	103	343	446	237	46	19	39	58	12

KEVIN LOWE

#4

DEFENSE
6-2 • 190 • Shoots Left
Born: April 15, 1959 • Lachute, Quebec
Off-Season Home: Tappen, British Columbia

1993-94: Skated in 71 games in his first full season with New York ... Tallied a pair of assists, including his 400th NHL point, on Jan. 25 at San Jose ... Collected four of his 14 assists on game winning goals ... Four of his five goals and 13 of his 19 points were registered on the road ... Rangers were 15-2-0 when he collected a point.

1994 PLAYOFFS: Appeared in 22 of the 23 playoff matches, collecting a goal on Apr. 18 in Game Two of the Conference Quarterfinals vs. the Islanders ... Moved past Denis Potvin into second place on the NHL's all-time games played list among defensemen on May 31 in Game One of the Finals and now ranks fourth overall with 193.

NHL CAREER: 1979-80: Went directly to the Oilers, without playing a minor league game, after being selected by Edmonton as their first choice (20th overall) in the 1979 draft ... Scored the first NHL goal in the history of the club in his initial NHL game on Oct. 10 in Chicago ... **1980-81:** Played in 79 games which was tied for third on the club ... Scored a career high 10 goals ... **1981-82:** One of five Oilers to play in all 80 contests ... Of his nine goals, two were game-winners ... **1982-83:** One of seven Oilers to play in all 80 matches ... Collected a career high five assists and six points on Feb. 19 at Pittsburgh ... **1983-84:** Played in all 80 outings for the third consecutive season ... Recorded a career high 42 assists and 46 points ... Appeared in his first NHL All-Star Game ... **1984-85:** Appeared in 80 games for the fourth straight season and played in his second All-Star Game ... **1985-86:** Consecutive game streak came to an end at 420 straight outings when he suffered a finger injury and missed six games ... The 420 games are still an Oilers record ... Played in his third All-Star Game ... **1986-87:** Named as an alternate captain on Mar. 6 after Lee Fogolin was traded ... Accumulated a seven-game point-scoring streak from Jan. 28 to Feb. 8 ... Plus 41 rating placed fourth on the team. **1987-88:** Missed 10 games with a wrist injury ... Played in his fourth NHL All-Star Game ... Scored overtime goal at Winnipeg on Feb. 3. **1988-89:** Plus 26 rating was second on the club and his 25 points were second among team defensemen ... Played in his fifth All-Star Game ... **1989-90:** Ranked second among Oilers defensemen with 33 points and placed fourth on the team with a plus 18 rating ... Played in his sixth All-Star Game ... **1990-91:** Missed seven games with an ankle injury. **1991-92:** Named team captain before the start of the season, replacing Mark Messier, who was traded to New York. **1992-93:** Obtained from Edmonton on Dec. 11 ... Made his Rangers debut on Dec. 15 vs. Calgary ... Recorded his first goal with New York on Dec. 23 vs. New Jersey ... Collected his 300th NHL assist on Jan. 9 at Philadelphia ... Tallied an assist in the NHL All-Star game on Feb. 6 while making his seventh All-Star appearance ... Skated in his 1,000th NHL game on Mar. 11 in 4-1 victory at Chicago.

INTERNATIONAL CAREER: Played for Team Canada in the 1982 World Championships and the 1984 Canada Cup.

JUNIOR CAREER: Played three seasons of junior hockey with the Quebec Remparts of the Quebec Major Junior Hockey League, serving as team captain in his final year ... Named a QMJHL Second-Team All-Star in '78-79.

BACKGROUND: Won the King Clancy Memorial Trophy for his leadership qualities on and off the ice and for his humanitarian contribution to the community and the BUD Light/NHL Man Of The Year award as a positive role model in the local community through his conduct on and off the ice in 1990 ... Completed his 13-year career with Edmonton as their all-time leader in games played in the regular season (966) and the playoffs (170) ... His total of 1,164 minutes in penalties are the second most in Oilers history ... Wore uniform number four during his career in Edmonton ... Member of five Stanley Cup Championship teams in Edmonton ... His brother, Ken, is the Oilers athletic trainer ... Married Olympic skier Karen Percy on June 16, 1990 ... Daughter, Devyn; son, Keegan.

CAREER TRANSACTIONS: August 19, 1979 — Edmonton's first choice (21st overall) in the 1979 Entry Draft. December 11, 1992 — Traded to Rangers by Edmonton in exchange for Roman Oksyuta and a third round draft choice in 1993.

KEVIN LOWE # 4

CAREER HIGHLIGHTS

MOST GOALS, GAME: 1, (81 times) last-Jan. 18, 1994 vs. Stl., **MOST ASSISTS, GAME:** 5, Feb. 19, 1983 at Pit., **MOST POINTS, GAME:** 6, Feb. 19, 1983 at Pit., **MOST PIM, GAME:** 22, Oct. 8, 1992 at L.A., **MOST SHOTS, GAME:** 7, Feb. 8, 1981 vs. Cgy., **MOST SHOTS, SEASON:** 115, 1980-81, **HIGHEST +/-, SEASON:** 46, 1981-82, **FIRST NHL GAME:** Oct. 10, 1979 at Chi., **FIRST NHL GOAL:** Oct. 10, 1979 at Chi. (Esposito)

AMATEUR AND PROFESSIONAL RECORD

Season	Club	Lea	Regular Season					Playoffs				
			GP	G	A	PTS	PIM	GP	G	A	PTS	PIM
1977-78	Quebec	QJHL	64	13	52	65	86	4	1	2	3	6
1978-79	Quebec	QJHL	68	26	60	86	120	6	1	7	8	36
1979-80	Edmonton	NHL	64	2	19	21	70	3	0	1	1	0
1980-81	Edmonton	NHL	79	10	24	34	94	9	0	2	2	11
1981-82	Edmonton	NHL	80	9	31	40	63	5	0	3	3	0
1982-83	Edmonton	NHL	80	6	34	40	43	16	1	8	9	10
1983-84	Edmonton	NHL	80	4	42	46	59	19	3	7	10	16
1984-85	Edmonton	NHL	80	4	22	26	104	16	0	5	5	8
1985-86	Edmonton	NHL	74	2	16	18	90	10	1	3	4	15
1986-87	Edmonton	NHL	77	8	29	37	94	21	2	4	6	22
1987-88	Edmonton	NHL	70	9	15	24	89	19	0	2	2	26
1988-89	Edmonton	NHL	76	7	18	25	98	7	1	2	3	4
1989-90	Edmonton	NHL	78	7	26	33	140	20	0	2	2	10
1990-91	Edmonton	NHL	73	3	13	16	113	14	1	1	2	14
1991-92	Edmonton	NHL	55	2	8	10	107	11	0	3	3	16
1992-93	Rangers	NHL	49	3	12	15	58	—	—	—	—	—
1993-94	Rangers	NHL	71	5	14	19	70	22	1	0	1	20
NHL Totals			1086	81	323	404	1292	192	10	43	53	172
Rangers Totals			120	8	26	34	128	22	1	0	1	20

STEPHANE MATTEAU

32

LEFT WING
6-3 • 210 • Shoots Left
Born: Sept. 2, 1969 • Rouyn-Noranda, Quebec
Off-Season Home: Rouyn-Noranda, Quebec

1993-94: Acquired from Chicago along with Brian Noonan on March 21 ... Collected four goals and three assists along with a plus six rating in 12 games with New York ... Established career highs with 19 goals and 38 points ... Recorded the game tying goal with 14 seconds remaining on March 22 at Calgary while making his Rangers debut ... Rangers were 8-2-2 with him in the lineup and 4-1-1- when he scored a goal ... Tallied 15 goals and 26 assists for 31 points, along with a plus 10 rating in 65 games with Chicago ... Notched a career-high three points on March 18 vs. the Rangers at Madison Square Garden.

1994 PLAYOFFS: Tallied six goals and three assists while appearing in all 23 matches ... Potted the game-winning and series clinching goal at 4:24 of the second overtime period in Game Seven of the Conference Finals vs. New Jersey ... Tallied the game-winning goal at 6:13 of the second overtime period on May 19 in Game Three at New Jersey and is one of only four players, including Mel Hill, Maurice Richard and Petr Klima to tally two double-overtime goals.

NHL CAREER: 1990-91: Placed second on the Flames among rookies in goals (15), assists (19) and points (34) ... Led club rookies and tied for first in the NHL among rookies with a plus 17 rating ... Made his NHL debut on October 4 vs. Vancouver ... Registered his first NHL goal on October 8 at Winnipeg ... Tallied one shorthanded goal and assisted on four shorthanded scores ... Was plus or even in 60 of his 78 matches ... Recorded a five-game point-scoring streak from February 15 to February 23, collecting three goals and two assists over the span. **1991-92:** Began the season with Calgary, appearing in four games before being dealt to Chicago in exchange for Trent Yawney on December 6 ... Missed 43 games due to a bruised thigh ... Made his Blackhawks debut on January 23 vs. Quebec ... Tallied his first point with the Blackhawks on January 27 at Calgary ... Potted his first goal with Chicago on March 10 vs. San Jose ... Placed fifth on the team with four playoff goals and ranked seventh with 10 points in 18 playoff matches. **1992-93:** Equaled his career-high of 15 goals, set in his rookie season with Calgary ... Recorded a pair of power play goals and two game-winning goals along with plus six rating ... Registered nine of his 15 goals at home.

IHL CAREER: Joined Salt Lake for the 1989 playoffs, following the completion of his junior career ... Registered four assists in nine playoff outings ... Notched 23 goals and 35 assists for 58 points along with 130 penalty minutes in 81 games with Salt Lake in his first professional season ... Ranked fifth on the club in goals and points ... Tallied six goals and three assists along with 38 penalty minutes in 10 playoff matches.

JUNIOR CAREER: Played four seasons with the Hull Olympiques (QMJHL) ... Appeared in his first season with Hull in 1985-86, collecting six goals and eight assists in 60 matches ... Recorded 27 goals and 48 assists for 75 points along with 113 penalty minutes in 69 games in 1986-87 ... Collected five goals and 14 assists for 19 points in 18 playoff matches in 1988, leading Hull to the Memorial Cup Tournament ... Tied for the team lead in scoring in 1988-89 with 44 goals and 45 assists for 89 points in 59 matches ... Also notched 202 penalty minutes ... Registered eight goals and six assists for 14 points in nine playoff matches to finish his junior career with 16 goals and 27 assists in 44 playoff matches.

BACKGROUND: Teammates with Greg Gilbert, Mike Hudson and Brian Noonan in Chicago ... Returns to Rouyn-Noranda in the off-season ... Skated on a line with Chicago's Jeremy Roenick and Vancouver's Martin Gelinas while with Hull ... Boyhood friends with the Islanders Pierre Turgeon, the two played hockey and organized baseball together, including the 1982 Little League World Sreies ... Married: wife Natalie; son, Stephane Jr.

CAREER TRANSACTIONS: *June 13, 1987* — Calgary's 2nd choice (25th overall) in the 1987 NHL Entry Draft. *December 6, 1991* —Traded to Chicago from Calgary in exchange for Trent Yawney. *March 21, 1994* — Traded to the Rangers from Chicago with Brian Noonan in exchange for Tony Amonte and Matt Oates.

STEPHANE MATTEAU #32

CAREER HIGHLIGHTS

MOST GOALS, GAME: 2 (twice) last- Oct. 10, 1993 vs. Wpg., **MOST ASSISTS, GAME:** 3, Mar. 18, 1994 at NYR., **MOST POINTS, GAME:** 3, Mar. 18, 1994 at NYR., **MOST PIM, GAME:** 19, Mar. 19, 1992 vs. Min., **MOST SHOTS, GAME:** 6, (twice) last- Nov. 29, 1993 at Van., **MOST SHOTS, SEASON:** 135, 1993-94, **HIGHEST +/-, SEASON:** 17, (1990-91), **FIRST NHL GAME:** Oct. 4, 1990 vs. Van., **FIRST NHL GOAL:** Oct. 8, 1990 at Wpg. (Beauregard)

AMATEUR AND PROFESSIONAL RECORD

Season	Club	Lea	Regular Season					Playoffs				
			GP	G	A	PTS	PIM	GP	G	A	PTS	PIM
1985-86	Hull	QMJHL	60	6	8	14	19	4	0	0	0	0
1986-87	Hull	QMJHL	69	27	49	75	113	8	3	7	10	8
1987-88	Hull	QMJHL	57	17	40	57	179	18	5	14	19	94
1988-89	Hull	QMJHL	59	44	45	89	202	9	8	6	14	30
1988-89	Salt Lake	IHL	—	—	—	—	—	9	0	4	4	13
1989-90	Salt Lake	IHL	81	23	35	58	130	10	6	3	9	38
1990-91	Calgary	NHL	78	15	19	34	93	5	0	1	1	0
1991-92	Calgary	NHL	4	1	0	1	19	—	—	—	—	—
1991-92	Chicago	NHL	20	5	8	13	45	18	4	6	10	24
1992-93	Chicago	NHL	79	15	18	33	98	3	0	1	1	2
1993-94	Chicago	NHL	65	15	16	31	55	—	—	—	—	—
1993-94	Rangers	NHL	12	4	3	7	2	23	6	3	9	20
NHL Totals			258	55	64	119	312	49	10	11	21	46
Rangers Totals			12	4	3	7	2	23	6	3	9	20

JOBY MESSIER

DEFENSE

6-1 • 200 • Shoots Right
Born: March 2, 1970 • Regina, Saskatchewan
Off-Season Home: Lansing, Michigan

29

1993-94: Began the season with New York, appearing in three of the first four matches of the season, before being assigned to Binghamton on October 21 ... Recorded two assists, including his first NHL point in the season opener on October 5 vs. Boston ... Notched six goals and 14 assists for 20 points along with 58 penalty minutes and a plus 10 rating in 42 games with Binghamton ... Five of his six goals were tallied on the power play ... Was recalled on April 11 and appeared in his fourth match of the season on April 12 vs. Buffalo.

NHL CAREER 1992-93: Was called up to New York on January 31 and made NHL debut at Long Island one night later in a 3-3 tie with the Islanders ... Was returned to Binghamton on February 4 ... Was recalled on March 24 and played in nine of New York's final 10 games ... Registered an even or plus rating in seven of his nine contests and in eight of his 11 overall.

AHL CAREER: 1992-93: Played in first professional season after four years at Michigan State University ... Tallied five goals and 11 assists for 16 points along with 63 penalty minutes in 60 games for Binghamton ... Led the entire American Hockey League with a plus 59 rating ... Scored his first professional goal on November 7 in Binghamton's 7-3 victory at Fredericton ... Registered four, two-point games at Binghamton, including two assists on December 19 in 11-3 victory over Providence and two assists in 8-7 triumph over Hershey on March 20.

COLLEGE CAREER: Four-year letterman at Michigan State ... Played for Ron Mason, the NCAA's all-time winningest coach ... Served as captain in his senior season ... Named as a first team West All-America, which also included Winnipeg Jets forward, Dallas Drake ... Selected to the Central Collegiate Hockey Association first All-Star team ... Named CCHA's best defensive defenseman for the 1991-92 campaign, while notching a career high 13 goals and 16 assists along with 85 penalty minutes ... Named as the team's Most Valuable Player while helping lead the Spartans to a berth in the NCAA semifinals after upsetting Maine, 3-2, in quarterfinals ... Named as the club's best defensive player for three consecutive seasons, from 1989-90 to 1991-92.

BACKGROUND: Teammates and roommates with Rangers 1990 first round draft selection Michael Stewart at Michigan State ... MSU coach Ron Mason called Messier, "The best defenseman I've ever had inside our blueline" ... Attended Athol Murray College of Notre Dame (prep school) in Wilcox, Saskatchewan, where he was teammates with current NHL'ers Curtis Joseph (St. Louis), and Rod Brind'Amour (Philadelphia) ... High school was also attended by former Ranger James Patrick ... Scored nine goals and 27 assists for 36 points in 53 games during his senior year, 1987-88 ... Is second cousins of Rangers' captain Mark Messier ... His father, Denny, and Mark's father, Doug, are first cousins ... His brother, Mitch, also an All-American at Michigan State, plays with the Milwaukee Admirals of the IHL ... Majored in psychology at MSU ... Single.

CAREER TRANSACTIONS: *June 17, 1989* — Rangers' seventh choice, sixth round (118th overall) in the 1989 Entry Draft.

CAREER HIGHLIGHTS
MOST GOALS, GAME: None, **MOST ASSISTS, GAME:** 2, Oct. 5, 1993 vs. Bos., **MOST POINTS, GAME:** 2, Oct. 5, 1993 vs. Bos., **MOST PIM, GAME:** 2 (three times) last- Apr. 5 vs. Hfd., **MOST SHOTS, GAME:** 3, (three times) last-Oct. 11, 1993 vs. Wsh., **MOST SHOTS, SEASON:** 11, 1992-93, **HIGHEST +/-, SEASON:** E, 1992-93, **FIRST NHL GAME:** Feb. 1, 1993 at NYI, **FIRST NHL GOAL:** None

AMATEUR AND PROFESSIONAL RECORD

			Regular Season					Playoffs				
Season	Club	Lea	GP	G	A	PTS	PIM	GP	G	A	PTS	PIM
1988-89	Michigan St.	CCHA	46	2	10	12	70	—	—	—	—	—
1989-90	Michigan St.	CCHA	42	1	11	12	58	—	—	—	—	—
1990-91	Michigan St.	CCHA	39	5	11	16	71	—	—	—	—	—
1991-92	Michigan St.	CCHA	41	13	16	29	85	—	—	—	—	—
1992-93	Rangers	NHL	11	0	0	0	6	—	—	—	—	—
1992-93	Binghamton	AHL	60	5	16	21	63	14	1	1	2	6
1993-94	Rangers	NHL	4	0	2	2	0	—	—	—	—	—
1993-94	Binghamton	AHL	42	6	14	20	58	—	—	—	—	—
NHL and Rangers Totals			15	0	2	2	6	—	—	—	—	—

JOBY MESSIER #29

MARK MESSIER

11

CENTER
6-1 • 205 • Shoots Left
Born: January 18, 1961 • Edmonton, Alberta
Off-Season Home: Hilton Head, S. Carolina

1993-94: Placed second on the team in scoring with 81 points ... Tied for first on the club with 24 multiple point games and ranked third with a plus 25 rating ... Notched his 800th assist on Dec. 4 at Toronto ... Moved past Alex Delvecchio into 10th place on the NHL's all-time scoring list with two points on Jan. 31 vs. Pittsburgh ... Tallied a pair of assists on Mar. 2 vs. Quebec, moving past Delvecchio into 10th place on the NHL's all-time assist list ... Registered an 11-game point scoring streak from Jan. 14 to Feb. 9 ... Assisted on all four of Adam Graves' shorthanded goals and tied for first in the NHL with seven shorthanded assists ... Assisted on 23 of Graves' 52 goals overall ... Notched four assists for the seventh time in his career on Feb. 2 vs. the Islanders ... Made his 12th NHL all-star appearance on Jan. 22 at MSG, tallying a goal and two assists, while serving as captain of the Eastern Conference.

1994 PLAYOFFS: Placed second on the team and third in the NHL with 30 points in 23 matches ... Netted the Stanley Cup clinching goal at 13:29 of the second period on June 14 in Game Seven ... Tied for second on the team with seven points in the Finals ... Nothched his fourth career playoff hat trick (first as a Ranger), including the game-tying and winning goals on May 25 in Game Six of the Conference Finals at New Jersey ... Set a club record for goals in one playoff year with 12 ... Tallied a point in each of the first 13 matches and in 21 of the 23 post-season matches ... Tied for first in the NHL with four game-winning goals and ranked third in the league with a plus 14 rating ... Registered a goal on Apr. 18 in Game Two of the Conference Quarterfinals vs. the Islanders, moving past Glenn Anderson into third place on the NHL's all-time playoff goal scoring list.

NHL CAREER: 1979-80: Played in his first NHL game, at 18 years old, on Oct. 10 vs. Chicago and registered his initial score on Oct. 13 against Detroit (Rogie Vachon) ... Sent to Houston of the Central Hockey League from Oct. 30 to Nov. 8,... Brief, four-game, stint with the Houston Apollos are the only games he has played in the minors.
1980-81: Nearly doubled his point production, improving his totals from 33 points to 63 ... Of the 63 points, 35 were scored in his final 24 games of season ... Collected first NHL three-point effort (all assists) on Jan. 28 vs. Montreal and notched his first four-point outing (two goals, two assists) on Mar. 3 vs. the Islanders ... Potted his first hat trick on Mar. 16 vs. Pittsburgh ... Helped Edmonton to a stunning three-game sweep of the Canadiens in the first round of the playoffs after Montreal had 29 more points than Edmonton during the regular season.. **1981-82:** Only 21 years old, he blossomed into one of the NHL's premier players, scoring 50 goals and being tabbed as the NHL's First-Team All-Star left wing. **1982-83:** Scored over 100 points for the first time in his career, collecting 48 goals and 58 assists for 106 points, placing seventh in the league and second on Edmonton, behind Wayne Gretzky ... Tabbed as the NHL's First-Team All-Start left wing ... Registered his first NHL four-goal game on Dec. 18 vs. Montreal ... Helped Oilers to their first-ever Stanley Cup Finals, despite playing with a sore shoulder ... Led team in playoffs with 15 goals in 15 games, including a four-goal outing vs. Calgary on Apr. 14. **1983-84:** Scored over 100 points for the second consecutive season, collecting 37 goals and 64 assists for 101 points, and was named as the NHL's Second-Team All-Star left wing ... Began playing regularly at center ice on Feb. 15 ... Led the Oilers in PIM with 165 ... Posted a career high six assists vs. Minnesota on Jan. 4 ... Led Edmonton to a record of 57-18-5 for 119 points and on to the first Stanley Cup in team history ... Captured the Conn Smythe Trophy as the playoff's most valuable player, tallying eight goals and 18 assists for 26 points.
1984-85: Limited to only 55 games due to a left knee injury suffered on Nov. 4 vs. Winnipeg that caused him to miss 15 contests and sat out a 10 game suspension for an altercation with Calgary's Jamie Macoun ... After posting 23 goals and 31 assists for 54 points in 55 regular-season outings, he collected 12 goals and 13 assists for 25 points in 18 playoff matches, helping Edmonton to their second consecutive Stanley Cup. **1985-86:** For the second season in a row his playing time was limited due to injury, as he suffered a left foot injury on Dec. 3 and missed 17 contests ... Recorded 10 two-point efforts, 12 three-point performances and two four-point outings. **1986-87:** Went over the 100-point plateau for the third time, tying for third in the NHL's scoring race with 107 points (37 goals, 70 assists) ... 70 assists ranked third in league and placed second on the club ... Member of the NHL team at Rendez-Vous '87 and was named the number one star of the first game ... Ranked second in NHL in playoff scoring with 28 points, including at least one point in 15 of 21 games ... Helped Oilers win their third Stanley Cup. **1987-88:** Notched over 100 points for the second consecutive year and for the fourth time in his career ... Ranked second on Edmonton and fifth in the NHL with

74 assists and 111 points and placed fifth on club with 37 goals ... Registered 20 two-point efforts, seven three-point outings, five four-point games and one five-point performance on Feb. 23 vs. St. Louis ... Led the team with seven game-winning goals ... Outstanding playoff performance included a 14-game point scoring streak along with four, four-point efforts ... 23 playoff assists and 34 playoff points were second in NHL along with his 11 goals, helping Edmonton to their fourth Stanley Cup in five seasons. **1988-89:** Named captain of the Oilers before the start of the season after Wayne Gretzky was traded to L.A. ... Led the club and placed seventh in the league with 61 assists, 94 points was third on team and 33 goals was fourth on Edmonton ... Suspended for six games after his stick hit Vancouver's Rich Sutter in the mouth ... Played for Team Canada in the World Championships after Edmonton was eliminated in the playoffs ... One goal and 11 assists for 12 points led Oilers in playoff scoring. **1989-90:** Established career highs with 84 assists and 129 points and was tabbed the NHL's Most Valuable Player ... Was also named winner of the Lester B. Pearson Award by the Players Association as the NHL's Outstanding Player, a First-Team NHL All-Star, winner of The Sporting News and Hockey News Player of the Year Awards ... Assist and point totals placed second in NHL, while he led the Oilers in each category, as well as in goals (45) and shots (211) ... Registered at least one point in all but 15 contests and on only one occasion failed to register a point in back-to-back games ... Collected 23 two-point outings, 13 three-point matches, four four-point affairs and one five-point performance (one goal, four assists) on Jan. 25 vs. L.A. ... Appeared in a career high 79 games, resting for the final regular-season contest ... Tied for NHL lead in playoff scoring with 31 points and led NHL with 22 playoff assists ... Also recorded an 11-game point scoring streak in playoffs, leading the Oilers to their fifth Stanley Cup Championship. **1990-91:** Limited to a career low 53 games due to two different injuries ... Injured his left knee on Oct. 16 vs. St. Louis and missed 19 games and fractured his left thumb on Feb. 18, sitting out the next eight outings ... Still scored over a point-per-game, notching 12 goals and 52 assists for 64 points in 53 tilts ... 52 assists led the Oilers and 64 points placed third on the squad ... With him in the lineup Edmonton was 29-20-4 and without him Oilers were 8-17-2. **1991-92:** Swept all of the MVP post season awards, including the Hart Trophy as the NHL's Most Valuable Player, becoming the first Ranger to win the award since Andy Bathgate in '58-59 ... Captured the Pearson Award as the league's top player as voted by all NHL players, The Sporting News Player of the Year Award and The Hockey News Player of the Year Award, while also earning a first-team All-Star berth ... Acquired from the Edmonton Oilers on Oct. 4 ... Made Rangers debut the following night at the Montreal Forum and was named team captain before the home opener on Oct. 7 ... Led team in scoring with 107 points, falling two points shy of tying Jean Ratelle's franchise record for most points in a single season ... Set team record for most assists by a center in a season (72), breaking Mike Rogers' mark of 65 set in '81-82 ... Joined Ratelle, Rogers, Vic Hadfield and Brian Leetch as the only players in club history to record 100 points in a season ... Tied for fifth in NHL with his 107 points and 72 assists ... Ranked third in the NHL with 65 even-strength points and placed second with nine shorthanded points ... Led club with three hat tricks, including a four-goal game vs. Devils on Mar. 22 ... Registered a career high 15-game point scoring streak from Feb. 5 to Mar. 7 ... Placed third on the club in playoff scoring with 14 points, despite missing two games due to a back injury. **1992-93:** Skated in his 1,000th NHL game at New Jersey on Apr. 7 ... With 66 assists he notched the fourth highest single-season assist total in Rangers history ... Posted a career-high 10 shots on Jan. 13 vs. Washington ... Tied his career-high with six-point effort at Pittsburgh on Nov. 25 ... First on the team with 66 assists and 91 points ... Led the team with 30 power play points ... Was named to the All-Star team for the 11th consecutive season, but missed the game due to injury.

WHA CAREER: Signed as a 17-year old by the Indianapolis Racers after only one year of junior hockey to replace Wayne Gretzky, who was sold to the Edmonton Oilers ... After five games with the Racers, he joined the Cincinnati Stingers, where he was teammates with Paul Stewart, a current NHL referee.

INTERNATIONAL COMPETITION: Helped Team Canada to three Canada Cup championships in 1984, 1987 and 1991 ... Also played for Team Canada in the 1989 World Championships at Stockholm, Sweden ... Was a member of the NHL team at Rendez-Vous '87.

BACKGROUND: During the season, he often organizes off-ice events that the entire team attends ... Raised over $100,000 for the Tomorrows Children's Fund last season after establishing the Mark Messier Point Club ... His father Doug, who played in the minor leagues for nine years, along with his brother Paul, who played in Europe for eight years and sister Mary Kay, operate Messier Management International. ... Owns the Tampa Bay Tritons of the Rollerhockey International League ... Appeared with teammate Brian Leetch in December of 1991 on the "Late Night with David Letterman" show in a skit that had the pair trying to break a camera with slapshots ... Also appeared with Leetch and Richter with the Stanley Cup on the Late Show with David Letterman following the Stanley Cup playoffs ... Also, appeared on The Howard Stern Show and threw out the first pitch at Yankee Stadium following Cup victory ... Became first player in league history to serve as captain for two different Stanley Cup-winning teams... Enjoys golfing, fishing and water skiing ... 14 playoff shorthanded goals are an NHL record ... Single.

CAREER TRANSACTIONS: *June 19, 1979* — Edmonton's second choice (third round, 48th overall) in the 1979 Entry Draft. *October 4, 1991* — Traded by Edmonton to New York along with future considerations in exchange for Bernie Nicholls, Steven Rice and Louie DeBrusk.

SCORING STREAKS AND MULTIPLE POINT GAMES

CAREER POINT SCORING STREAKS
(SIX GAMES OR MORE)

(Goals, Assists and Points during streak listed on right)

15	Feb. 5, 1992	- Mar. 7, 1992	(7-17-24)
14	Oct. 31, 1987	- Nov. 29, 1987	(11-16-27)
14	Jan. 11, 1983	- Feb. 14, 1983	(9-17-26)
12	Dec. 11, 1982	- Jan. 7, 1983	(13-18-31)
12	Feb. 19, 1989	- Mar. 5, 1989	(8-15-23)
11	Oct. 5, 1991	- Oct. 26, 1991	(5-11-16)
11	Mar. 1, 1985	- Mar. 26, 1985	(9- 6-15)
10	Oct. 22, 1983	- Nov. 12, 1982	(5- 8-13)
10	Dec. 12, 1986	- Jan. 3, 1987	(4-15-19)
9	Feb. 7, 1990	- Feb. 25, 1990	(4-14-18)
9	Nov. 25, 1989	- Dec. 16, 1989	(4-11-15)
9	Mar. 4, 1984	- Mar. 21, 1984	(9- 8-17)
9	Nov. 8, 1982	- Nov. 24, 1982	(7- 4-11)
9	Oct. 12, 1992	- Oct. 29, 1992	(6-10-16)
8	Nov. 3, 1985	- Nov. 17, 1985	(4- 8- 12)
8	Oct. 19, 1986	- Nov. 2, 1986	(5-11-16)
8	Oct. 22, 1989	- Nov. 4, 1989	(5- 9-14)
8	Nov. 19, 1992	- Dec. 4, 1992	(5-11-16)
8	Feb. 12, 1993	- Feb. 27, 1993	(2-11-13)
7	Oct. 31, 1991	- Nov. 13, 1991	(0- 8- 8)
6	Mar. 3, 1990	- Mar. 10, 1990	(7- 6-13)
6	Jan. 16, 1990	- Jan. 30, 1990	(8-11-20)
6	Oct. 5, 1989	- Oct. 18, 1989	(6- 6-12)
6	Mar. 12, 1988	- Mar. 24, 1988	(2- 9-11)
6	Dec. 16, 1987	- Dec. 28, 1987	(4- 5- 9)
6	Oct. 9, 1987	- Oct. 21, 1987	(6- 6-12)
6	Mar. 14, 1986	- Mar. 28, 1986	(7- 6-13)
6	Feb. 9, 1986	- Feb. 22, 1986	(1-10-11)
6	Jan. 24, 1986	- Feb. 1, 1986	(6- 8-14)
6	Nov. 11, 1981	- Nov. 19, 1981	(3- 4- 7)
6	Feb. 18, 1981	- Feb. 27, 1981	(3- 6- 9)
6	Nov. 26, 1980	- Dec. 10, 1980	(4- 4- 8)

GOAL SCORING STREAKS
(MINIMUM OF FOUR)

6	Mar. 14, 1986	- Mar. 28, 1986	(seven)
5	Jan. 15, 1983	- Jan. 23, 1983	(seven)
4	Feb. 7, 1992	- Feb. 14, 1992	(four)
4	Oct. 5, 1990	- Oct. 13, 1990	(four)
4	Mar. 4, 1987	- Mar. 11, 1987	(five)
4	Jan. 24, 1986	- Jan. 31, 1986	(five)
4	Mar. 9, 1985	- Mar. 17, 1985	(five)
4	Mar. 16, 1983	- Mar. 23, 1983	(five)
4	Nov. 16, 1982	- Nov. 24, 1982	(four)
4	Oct. 21, 1981	- Oct. 27, 1981	(four)
4	Oct. 9, 1981	- Oct. 16, 1981	(four)

ASSIST STREAKS
(MINIMUM OF FIVE)

8	Feb. 12, 1992	- Feb. 27, 1992	(11)
8	Feb. 11, 1990	- Feb. 25, 1990	(14)
7	Nov. 21, 1992	- Dec. 4, 1992	(11)
7	Oct. 31, 1991	- Nov. 13, 1991	(eight)
7	Nov. 3, 1985	- Nov. 16, 1985	(eight)
7	Jan. 22, 1983	- Feb. 4, 1983	(10)
6	Feb. 9, 1992	- Feb. 20, 1992	(eight)
6	Oct. 5, 1991	- Oct. 14, 1991	(eight)
6	Jan. 16, 1990	- Jan. 30, 1990	(11)
6	Mar. 12, 1988	- Mar. 24, 1988	(nine)
6	Dec. 10, 1986	- Dec. 20, 1986	(11)
5	Oct. 12, 1992	- Oct. 21, 1992	(seven)
5	Jan. 14, 1992	- Jan. 28, 1992	(seven)
5	Nov. 23, 1991	- Dec. 6, 1991	(six)
5	Nov. 25, 1989	- Dec. 3, 1989	(seven)
5	Feb. 11, 1988	- Feb. 19, 1988	(10)
5	Oct. 31, 1987	- Nov. 7, 1987	(seven)
5	Dec. 14, 1983	- Dec. 23, 1983	(seven)
5	Nov. 21, 1983	- Nov. 30, 1983	(seven)
5	Mar. 21, 1981	- Mar. 29, 1981	(eight)

ALL-TIME MULTIPLE-POINT GAMES

Two Goal Games	68	(last—Feb. 24, 1993 at Vancouver)
Three Goal Games	12	(last—Dec. 13, 1991 at Washington)
Four Goal Games	4	(last—Mar. 22, 1992 vs. New Jersey)
Two Assist Games	143	(last—Apr. 10, 1993 at Pittsburgh)
Three Assist Games	42	(last—Mar. 24, 1993 vs. Philadelphia)
Four Assist Games	6	(last—Nov. 25, 1992 at Pittsburgh)
Five Assist Games	None	
Six Assist Games	1	(Jan. 4, 1984 vs. Minnesota)
Two Point Games	217	(last—Mar. 10, 1993 at Pittsburgh)
Three Point Games	104	(last—Mar. 24, 1993 vs. Philadelphia)
Four Point Games	28	(last—Jan. 13, 1993 vs. Washington)
Five Point Games	2	(last—Jan. 25, 1990 vs. L.A.)
Six Point Games	2	(last—Nov. 25, 1992 at Pittsburgh)

CAREER HIGHLIGHTS

MOST GOALS, GAME: 4, (four times) last- Mar. 22, 1992 vs. N.J., **MOST ASSISTS, GAME:** 6, Jan. 4, 1984 vs. Min., **MOST POINTS, GAME:** 6, (twice) last- Nov. 25, 1992 at Pit., **MOST PIM, GAME:** 30, Jan. 19, 1980 vs. Pit., **MOST SHOTS, GAME:** 10, Jan. 13, 1993 vs. Wsh., **MOST SHOTS, SEASON:** 237, 1982-83, **HIGHEST +/-, SEASON:** 40, 1983-84, **FIRST NHL GAME:** Oct. 10, 1979 vs. Chi., **FIRST NHL GOAL:** Oct. 13, 1979 vs. Det. (Vachon)

AMATEUR AND PROFESSIONAL RECORD

			Regular Season					Playoffs			
Season	Club	Lea	GP	G	A	PTS	PIM	GP	G	A	PTS	PIM
1977-78	Portland	WHL	—	—	—	—	—	7	4	1	5	2
1978-79	Indianapolis	WHA	5	0	0	0	0	—	—	—	—	—
1978-79	Cincinnati	WHA	47	1	10	11	58	—	—	—	—	—
1979-80	Houston	CHL	4	0	3	3	4	—	—	—	—	—
1979-80	Edmonton	NHL	75	12	21	33	120	3	1	2	3	2
1980-81	Edmonton	NHL	72	23	40	63	102	9	2	5	7	13
1981-82	Edmonton	NHL	78	50	38	88	119	5	1	2	3	8
1982-83	Edmonton	NHL	77	48	58	106	72	15	15	6	21	14
1983-84	Edmonton	NHL	73	37	64	101	165	19	8	18	26	19
1984-85	Edmonton	NHL	55	23	31	54	57	18	12	13	25	12
1985-86	Edmonton	NHL	63	35	49	84	68	10	4	6	10	18
1986-87	Edmonton	NHL	77	37	70	107	73	21	12	16	28	16
1987-88	Edmonton	NHL	77	37	74	111	103	19	11	23	34	29
1988-89	Edmonton	NHL	72	33	61	94	130	7	1	11	12	8
1989-90	Edmonton	NHL	79	45	84	129	79	22	9	22	31	20
1990-91	Edmonton	NHL	53	12	52	64	34	18	4	11	15	16
1991-92	Rangers	NHL	79	35	72	107	76	11	7	7	14	6
1992-93	Rangers	NHL	75	25	66	91	72	—	—	—	—	—
1993-94	Rangers	NHL	76	26	58	84	76	23	12	18	30	33
NHL Totals			1081	478	838	1316	1346	200	99	160	259	214
Rangers Totals			230	86	196	282	224	34	19	25	44	39

MARK MESSIER #11

PETR NEDVED

CENTER
6-3 • 195 • Shoots Left
Born: Dec. 9, 1971 • Liberec, Czechoslovakia
Off-Season Home: Vancouver, British Columbia

10

1993-94: Tallied five goals and one assist for six points in eight games for Team Canada at the 1994 Winter Olympics in Lillehammer ... Tied for first on the team with five goals and placed second with eight points ... Recorded 19 goals and 12 assists for 31 points in 17 pre-Olympic matches ... Signed as a free agent by St. Louis on March 6 and collected six goals and 14 assists for 20 points in 19 games ... Tallied points in 15 of 19 matches with the Blues ... Notched one assist while appearing in four playoff matches.

NHL CAREER: 1990-91: Appeared in 61 games, tallying 10 goals and six assists for 16 points in his first NHL season ... Seven of his 10 goals were collected on the road and nine of the 10 came in his last 34 games after the Canucks traded Brian Bradley and he received more ice time ... Registered his first NHL goal on Oct. 27 at Hartford. **1991-92:** Placed 11th in team scoring with 15 goals and 22 assists for 37 points, appearing in 77 games ... Scored 10 goals in final 32 games ... Skated in his 100th NHL game on Jan. 7 vs. San Jose. **1992-93:** Placed sixth on the Canucks in scoring with 38 goals and 33 assists for 71 points, establishing career highs in all offensive categories ... Ranked second on the club with 38 goals and 35 even strength goals ... One of only four players to appear in all 84 matches ... Led the Canucks with a plus 20 ... Placed second in the NHL with a 25.5% shooting percentage ... Recorded a franchise record 15 game point scoring streak from Nov. 19 to Dec. 27, scoring 15 goals and nine assists fro 24 points ... Tallied two goals and three assists in 12 playoff matches.

JUNIOR CAREER: Played one season, 1989-90, in the Western Hockey League with the Seattle Thunderbirds and received the Jim Piggott Memorial Trophy as the WHL's top rookie and the Toshiba Cup, awarded to the Canadian Hockey League's top rookie performer ... Tallied 65 goals and 80 assists for 145 points in 71 games, establishing a WHL rookie record for points, while tying the league's rookie mark for assists ... Notched five points, collecting four goals and an assist on March 4 vs. Spokane ... Registered four goals and nine assists for 13 points in 11 playoff matches ... His rights were acquired by Seattle from Moose Jaw after he defected.

CZECHOSLOVAKIAN CAREER: Played midget hockey for Litvinov in 1988-89, registering 32 goals and 19 assists for 51 points in 20 games ... Was the leading scorer at the Mac's midget tournament in Calgary in December of 1988 with 17 goals and nine assists for 26 points in nine games for Chemical Works Litvinov ... Defected to Canada on January 2, 1989 while his teammates were traveling home from the tournament.

BACKGROUND: Lists Wayne Gretzky as his childhood idol ... Wore uniform number 19 with Vancouver and number 93 with St. Louis ... Teammates with Corey Hirsch on Team Canada ... Had two years of electro-technical training in Czechoslovakia ... Enjoys playing tennis and swimming in the off-season ... His parents Jaroslav, who is a civil engineer, and Sonja were in Vancouver to see him selected second overall by the Canucks in the 1990 NHL Entry Draft ... Is the second highest Czechoslovakian player ever drafted, second only to Roman Hamrlik who was taken first overall by Tampa Bay in 1992 ... Single.

CAREER TRANSACTIONS: *June 16, 1990* — Vancouver's first round choice, (second overall), in the 1990 NHL Entry Draft. *March 6, 1994* — Signed as a free agent by St. Louis. *July 24, 1994* — Traded by St. Louis to the Rangers for Doug Lidster and Esa Tikkanen.

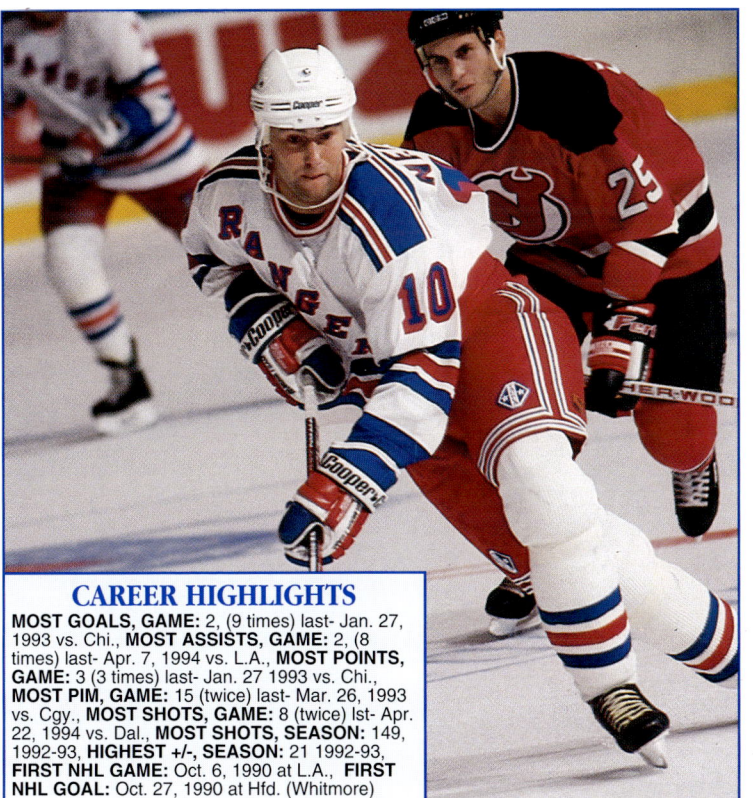

CAREER HIGHLIGHTS

MOST GOALS, GAME: 2, (9 times) last- Jan. 27, 1993 vs. Chi., **MOST ASSISTS, GAME:** 2, (8 times) last- Apr. 7, 1994 vs. L.A., **MOST POINTS, GAME:** 3 (3 times) last- Jan. 27 1993 vs. Chi., **MOST PIM, GAME:** 15 (twice) last- Mar. 26, 1993 vs. Cgy., **MOST SHOTS, GAME:** 8 (twice) lst- Apr. 22, 1994 vs. Dal., **MOST SHOTS, SEASON:** 149, 1992-93, **HIGHEST +/-, SEASON:** 21 1992-93, **FIRST NHL GAME:** Oct. 6, 1990 at L.A., **FIRST NHL GOAL:** Oct. 27, 1990 at Hfd. (Whitmore)

PETR NEDVED #10

AMATEUR AND PROFESSIONAL RECORD

			Regular Season					Playoffs				
Season	Club	Lea	GP	G	A	PTS	PIM	GP	G	A	PTS	PIM
1988-89	Litvinov	Czech.Jrs	20	32	19	51	12	—	—	—	—	—
1989-90	Seattle	WHL	71	65	80	145	80	11	4	9	13	2
1990-91	Vancouver	NHL	61	10	6	16	20	6	0	1	1	0
1991-92	Vancouver	NHL	77	15	22	37	36	10	1	4	5	16
1992-93	Vancouver	NHL	84	38	33	71	96	12	2	3	5	2
1993-94	Canadian Olympic Team		8	5	1	6	6	—	—	—	—	—
1993-94	Canadian National Team		17	19	12	31	16	—	—	—	—	—
1993-94	St. Louis	NHL	19	6	14	20	8	4	0	1	1	4
NHL Totals			241	69	75	144	160	32	3	9	12	22

SERGEI NEMCHINOV

13

CENTER
6-0 • 200 • Shoots Left
Born: January 14, 1964 • Moscow, Russia
Off-Season Home: Rye, New York

1993-94: Reached the 20-goal plateau for the third consecutive season, notching 22 along with 27 assists for 49 points in 76 matches ... Placed second on the team with six game-winning goals and also assisted on six game-winners ... Ranked second on the club with 18 even strength goals and was tied for third with 39 points at even strength ... Skated in his 200th NHL game on Jan. 25 at San Jose ... Rangers were 16-1-0 when he scored a goal and 26-8-1 when he scored a point ... Registered 10 multiple-point games, including four three point efforts and six two point games.

1994 PLAYOFFS: Collected two goals and five assists while appearing in all 23 matches ... Registered his first goal on May 15 in Game One of the Conference Finals vs. New Jersey and collected his second goal in Game Two ... Collected assists in three consecutive games from April 24 to May 5 ... Assisted on Glenn Anderson's game-winning goal on June 4 in Game Three of the Finals at Vancouver.

NHL CAREER: 1991-92: Became the first Russian-born player to play for the Rangers in franchise history ... Recorded 30 goals, ranking fourth in the NHL among first-year players and tied for fourth on the club ... Placed third on the team with five game-winning goals ... 24.2 shooting percentage ranked fifth in the league ... Recorded a six game goal scoring streak from Dec. 2 to Dec. 14, which was tied for the third longest in the NHL ... First NHL goal was overtime score at Montreal on Oct. 5 ... 28 of his 30 goals and 50 of his 58 points were collected at even-strength... Registered 15 goals and 10 assists at home and 15 goals and 18 assists on the road. **1992-93:** Tallied his 100th NHL point with a goal vs. Islanders on Feb. 12 ... Notched his first career NHL hat trick on Jan. 29 at Buffalo ... Led the team with a plus 15 rating ... Posted a career-high, six-game point scoring streak from Dec. 2 to Dec. 13 ... Team was 13-4-1 when he scored a goal and 23-12-6 when he tallied a point ... Collected 50 of his 54 points at even strength ... Placed third on the team with 50 points at even strength ... Missed the last three games of the season due to injury ... Collected 27 points at MSG and 27 points on the road.

SOVIET CAREER: Began with the Soviet Wings in 1981-82 at the age of 17 ... Played with the Wings for one season, before joining the Central Red Army team for three years ... Rejoined the Wings for the beginning of the '85-86 season and played there until joining Rangers ... In seven years with the Soviet Wings he totalled 91 goals and 86 assists for 177 points in 279 games and in three seasons with Central Red Army, he accumulated eight goals and nine assists in 62 matches ... Won the Soviet Elite League championship each year with Central Red Army ... ... Wore uniform number eight with Wings and 14 for Central Red Army ... In 1990-91 he led the Soviet Wings in scoring, reaching career highs in goals (21), assists (24) and points (45) ... 45 points ranked fifth in the league ... Named captain of the Wings for the second straight season ... Added to the Central Red Army team to compete against seven NHL clubs in Super Series '91 ... As part of Super Series, he played against the Rangers at MSG on Dec. 31, recording two assists.

INTERNATIONAL CAREER: Made his debut for the Soviet National team on Apr. 9, 1984 in a game against Finland during Sweden Cup tournament ... Before that he participated in the '81-82 European Junior Championships and the World Junior Championships in '82-83 and '83-84 ... Totalled nine goals and nine assists for 18 points in 14 World Junior Championship contests ... Appeared in five games during Canada Cup '87 and played one game for Soviet team in Rendez-Vous '87 against the NHL All-Stars ... Won gold medal at the World Championships in '89 and '90 and a bronze medal in '91 ... Won gold medal at '89 and '91 European Championships and silver medal in '90 ... Scored two goals and one assist in five games at '90 Goodwill Games, helping Soviet Union to gold medal ... In his final season he appeared in each of the National Team's 34 outings ... Teammates on National Team included Sergei Fedorov (Detroit), Alexander Mogilny (Buffalo) and Dimitri Khristich (Washington).

BACKGROUND: Is the first Rangers player to wear uniform number 13 since Bob Brooke was traded in 1986 ... Is one of only two 12th round draft choices to play for the Rangers along with Rudy Poeschek ... Favorite sports teams are the New York Knicks and the New York Yankees ... Was a teammate and roommate with goaltender Vladislav Tretiak while with Central Army ... Enjoys listening to the Beatles, reading history books and playing soccer and volleyball ... Married: wife, Yelena; daughters, Natasha and Elizabeth.

CAREER TRANSACTIONS: *June 16, 1990* — Rangers' 13th choice (12th round, 244th overall) in 1990 Entry Draft.

SERGEI NEMCHINOV #13

CAREER HIGHLIGHTS

MOST GOALS, GAME: 3, Jan. 29, 1993 at Buf., **MOST ASSISTS, GAME:** 3, (twice) last- Mar. 2, 1992 at N.J., **MOST POINTS, GAME:** 4, Mar. 2, 1992 at N.J., **MOST PIM, GAME:** 10, Oct. 12, 1992 vs. Hfd., **MOST SHOTS, GAME:** 7, Jan. 29, 1993 at Buf., **MOST SHOTS, SEASON:** 144, (twice) last- 1993-94, **HIGHEST +/-, SEASON:** 19, 1991-92, **FIRST NHL GAME:** Oct. 3, 1991 at Bos., **FIRST NHL GOAL:** Oct. 5, 1992 at Mtl. (Roy)

AMATEUR AND PROFESSIONAL RECORD

Season	Club	Lea	Regular Season					Playoffs				
			GP	G	A	PTS	PIM	GP	G	A	PTS	PIM
1981-82	Soviet Wings	Sov. Elite	15	1	0	1	0	—	—	—	—	—
1982-83	CSKA Moscow	Sov. Elite	11	0	0	0	2	—	—	—	—	—
1983-84	CSKA Moscow	Sov. Elite	20	6	5	11	4	—	—	—	—	—
1984-85	CSKA Moscow	Sov. Elite	31	2	4	6	4	—	—	—	—	—
1985-86	Soviet Wings	Sov. Elite	39	7	12	19	28	—	—	—	—	—
1986-87	Soviet Wings	Sov. Elite	40	13	9	22	24	—	—	—	—	—
1987-88	Soviet Wings	Sov. Elite	48	17	11	28	26	—	—	—	—	—
1988-89	Soviet Wings	Sov. Elite	43	15	14	29	28	—	—	—	—	—
1989-90	Soviet Wings	Sov. Elite	48	17	16	33	34	—	—	—	—	—
1990-91	Soviet Wings	Sov. Elite	46	21	24	45	30	—	—	—	—	—
1991-92	Rangers	NHL	73	30	28	58	15	13	1	4	5	8
1992-93	Rangers	NHL	81	23	31	54	34	—	—	—	—	—
1993-94	Rangers	NHL	76	22	27	49	36	23	2	5	7	6
NHL and Rangers Totals			230	75	86	161	85	36	3	9	12	14

BRIAN NOONAN

16

RIGHT WING
6-1 • 200 • Shoots Right
Born: May 29, 1965 • Boston, Massachusetts
Off-Season Home: Elmhurst, Illinois

1993-94: Acquired from Chicago along with Stephane Matteau on March 21 ... Collected four goals and two assists along with a plus six rating in 12 games with New York ... Made his Rangers debut on March 22 at Calgary ... Collected his first goal as a Ranger, netting the game-winner, on March 23 at Edmonton ... Rangers were 8-2-2 with him in the lineup, 3-0-0 when he scored a goal and 5-0-0 when he notched a point ... Three of his four goals with New York were game winners ... Established career highs with 23 assists and 41 points ... Tallied 14 goals and 21 assists for 35 points in 64 games with Chicago ... Ranked fourth on Chicago in scoring, second on the club with eight power play goals and tied for third with three game-winners at the time of the trade ... Notched five, two-goal games with Chicago.

1994 PLAYOFFS: Appeared in 22 of the 23 games, missing one game due to injury ... Notched four goals and seven assists for 11 points ... Three of his four goals were tallied in the Conference Semifinals vs. Washington ... Tallied an assist on Mark Messier's Stanley Cup clinching goal at 13:29 of the second period on June 14 in Game Seven.

NHL CAREER: 1987-88: Made his NHL debut on October 8 vs. Toronto, tallying his first NHL goal and adding an assist ... Placed eighth on the team in scoring with 10 goals and 20 assists for 30 points ...Tallied three of his 10 goals on the power play and notched two game-winners ... Played both right wing and center. **1988-89:** Began the season at Saginaw (IHL) and was recalled on November 2 ... Collected four goals and 12 assists in 45 games with the Blackhawks. **1989-90:** Appeared in eight games with Chicago, collecting two assists ... **1990-91:** Appeared in seven games with the Blackhawks, notching four assists ... Notched a career-high three assists in October 6 at St. Louis. **1991-92:** Notched career-highs with 19 goals and 31 points while appearing in a career-high 65 games ... Recorded four power play goals and reg- istered a plus nine rating ... Notched his first career hat trick vs. Los Angeles on December 5 ... Set a Blackhawks record for most consecutive goals scored by a single player, notching seven consecutive with a hat trick on December 27 and a career best four goal effort on December 29 vs. Detroit

... Became the first Blackhawks player to net back-to-back hat tricks since Stan Mikita on December 4 and December 5, 1965 ... Skated in his 200th NHL game on March 31 at Detroit ... Placed fourth on the club in playoff scoring, appearing in all 18 matches, collecting six goals and nine assists for 15 points ... Notched a pair of goals in Game Four of the Campbell Conference Finals vs. Edmonton ... **1992-93:** Collected 16 goals and 14 assists in 65 games ... Notched 12 of his 16 goals on the road and tallied five power play goals ... Tied for fifth on the club with three game-winning goals ... Recorded his 100th NHL point on January 23 at Hartford ... Led the team with three goals in four playoff matches, registering a hat trick in the first game of the Division Semi-Finals.

AHL/IHL CAREER: Notched 39 goals and 39 assists for 78 points with Saginaw (IHL) in 1985-86 ... Captured the Ken McKenzie Trophy as the league's top rookie performer ... Collected 25 goals and 26 assists for 51 points with Nova Scotia (AHL) in 1986-87 ... Notched 18 goals and 13 assists for 31 points in 19 game with Saginaw (IHL) ... Was named to the IHL All-Star second team in 1989-90 after recording 40 goals and 36 assists for 76 points in 56 games at Indianapolis ... Led the team with six goals and four assists for 10 points in seven play- off matches ... Selected to the IHL's All-Star first team in 1990-91 after registering 38 goals and 53 assists with Indianapolis.

JUNIOR CAREER: Played one season at New Westminster (WHL) collecting 50 goals and 66 assists for 116 points in 72 matches in the 1984-85 season.

BACKGROUND: Appeared with the Stanley Cup and teammate Nick Kypreos at MTV's Summer Beachouse in the Hampton's in July ... Teammates with Greg Gilbert, Mike Hudson and Stephane Matteau in Chicago ... Split the off-season between Chicago and the South Boston area ... Enjoys playing basketball and softball during the summer ... Single.

CAREER TRANSACTIONS: *June 8, 1983* — Chicago's 10th choice (179th overall) in the 1983 NHL Entry Draft. *March 21, 1994* — Traded to the Rangers from Chicago with Stephane Matteau in exchange for Tony Amonte and Matt Oates.

CAREER HIGHLIGHTS

MOST GOALS, GAME: 4, Dec. 29, 1991 vs. Det., **MOST ASSISTS, GAME:** 3, Oct. 6, 1990 at Stl., **MOST POINTS, GAME:** 4, Dec. 29, 1991 vs. Det., **MOST PIM, GAME:** 17, Oct. 10, 1991 vs. Van., **MOST SHOTS, GAME:** 8, Dec. 29, 1991 vs. Det., **MOST SHOTS, SEASON:** 160, 1993-94, **HIGHEST +/-, SEASON:** 9, 1991-92, **FIRST NHL GAME:** Oct. 8, 1987 vs. Tor., **FIRST NHL GOAL:** Oct. 8, 1987 vs. Tor.

BRIAN NOONAN #16

AMATEUR AND PROFESSIONAL RECORD

Season	Club	Lea	Regular Season GP	G	A	PTS	PIM	Playoffs GP	G	A	PTS	PIM
1984-85	N. Westminster	WHL	72	50	66	116	76	11	8	7	15	4
1985-86	Nova Scotia	AHL	2	0	0	0	0	—	—	—	—	—
1985-86	Saginaw	IHL	76	39	39	78	69	11	6	3	9	6
1986-87	Nova Scotia	AHL	70	25	26	51	30	5	3	1	4	4
1987-88	Chicago	NHL	77	10	20	30	44	3	0	0	0	4
1988-89	Chicago	NHL	45	4	12	16	28	1	0	0	0	4
1988-89	Saginaw	IHL	19	18	13	31	36	1	0	0	0	0
1989-90	Chicago	NHL	8	0	2	2	6	—	—	—	—	—
1989-90	Indianapolis	IHL	56	40	36	76	85	14	6	9	15	20
1990-91	Chicago	NHL	7	0	4	4	2	—	—	—	—	—
1990-91	Indianapolis	IHL	59	38	53	91	67	7	6	4	10	18
1991-92	Chicago	NHL	65	19	12	31	81	18	6	9	15	30
1992-93	Chicago	NHL	63	16	14	30	82	4	3	0	3	4
1993-94	Chicago	NHL	64	14	21	35	57	—	—	—	—	—
1993-94	Rangers	NHL	12	4	2	6	12	22	4	7	11	17
NHL Totals			341	67	87	154	312	48	13	16	29	59
Rangers Totals			12	4	2	6	12	22	4	7	11	17

MATTIAS NORSTROM

5

DEFENSE
6-1 • 205 lbs. • Shoots Left
Born: January 2, 1972 • Stockhom, Sweden
Off-Season Home: Stockholm, Sweden

1993-94: Began the season with New York after an impressive training camp in which he was awarded the Lars-Erik Sjoberg Trophy given to the team's best rookie performer in training camp ... Did not dress for the first two contests and was assigned to Binghamton of the American Hockey League on October 8 ... Appeared in his first AHL match on October 8, recording an assist in the club's 7-4 opening night victory vs. Hamilton ... Was recalled by New York on October 9 ... Made his National Hockey League debut in a 5-2 victory vs. Washington on October 11 ... Skated in one more match on October 13 vs. Quebec before returning to Binghamton on October 21 ... Appeared in 55 games with Binghamton, collecting one goal and nine assists along with 70 penalty minutes ... Notched his only multiple point effort on November 24, tallying a pair of assists in a 6-3 win at Providence ... Missed four games in mid-January due to the flu ... Collected his first professional goal on March 9 in Binghamton's 5-3 victory at Cornwall ... Binghamton posted a 7-2-0 record when he tallied a point ... Was recalled on March 11 and skated in four straight matches with New York from March 12 to March 18 ... Registered his first NHL point with an assist on Steve Larmer's game winning goal on March 16 vs. Hartford ... Collected his only other point on April 8 vs. Toronto, registering an assist ... Appeared in seven of New York's final 16 matches ... Remained with the club through the Stanley Cup playoffs but did not make a post season appearance.

SWEDISH CAREER: Played for two season (1991-92 and 1992-93) with AIK in the Swedish Elite League ... Placed third on the club in scoring among defensemen in 1991-92, tallying four goals and four assists for eight points in 39 games in his first season with the club ... Teammates included former NHL all-star defenseman and his childhood idol Borje Salming and Calgary Flames forward Mikael Nylander ... Notched one assist in 22 matches in his second season with the club.

BACKGROUND: Began the season wearing number 14 and switched to uniform number 5 after Craig MacTavish was acquired at the trade deadline ... Is an extremely well conditioned athlete, paying strict attention to training and eating habits ... Is a strong stay-at-home defenseman who can clear the front of the net with his strength ... Is an above average skater with a powerful stride and great lower body strength ... Rangers European scout Christer Rockstrom said of Norstrom, "As far as personality, drive and dedication goes, he along with Detroit's Nicklas Lidstrom are the best defensemen I've ever drafted" ... Had an impressive training camp with the Rangers in 1992 before returning to Sweden ... Single.

CAREER TRANSACTIONS: *June 20, 1992* — Rangers' second round choice (48th overall) in the 1992 NHL Entry Draft.

MATTIAS NORSTROM #5

CAREER HIGHLIGHTS

MOST GOALS, GAME: None, **MOST ASSISTS, GAME:** 1, (twice) last- Apr. 8, 1994 vs. Tor., **MOST POINTS, GAME:** 1 (twice) last- Apr. 8, 1994 vs. Tor., **MOST PIM, GAME:** 4, Mar. 27, 1994 at Wpg., **MOST SHOTS, GAME:** 1, (3 times) last Mar. 18, 1994 vs. Chi., **MOST SHOTS, SEASON:** 3, 1993-94, **HIGHEST +/-, SEASON:** E, 1993-94, **FIRST NHL GAME:** Oct. 11, 1993 vs. Wsh., **FIRST NHL GOAL:** None

AMATEUR AND PROFESSIONAL RECORD

			Regular Season					Playoffs				
Season	Club	Lea	GP	G	A	PTS	PIM	GP	G	A	PTS	PIM
1991-92	AIK	Swe.	39	4	4	8	28	—	—	—	—	—
1992-93	AIK	Swe.	22	0	1	1	16	—	—	—	—	—
1993-94	Rangers	NHL	9	0	2	2	6	—	—	—	—	—
1993-94	Binghamton	AHL	55	1	9	10	70	—	—	—	—	—
NHL and Rangers Totals			9	0	2	2	6	—	—	—	—	—

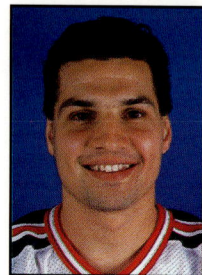

EDDIE OLCZYK

LEFT WING — 12

6-1 • 205 • Shoots Left
Born: August 16, 1966 • Chicago, Illinois
Off-Season Home: Barrington, Illinois

1993-94: Was awarded the prestigious Players' Player Award given to the best "team player" as voted by the players ... Missed 23 games due to a thumb injury suffered on Jan. 28 at Anaheim ... Each of his goals and three of his five assists were tallied at MSG ... Rangers were 7-0-0 when he registered a point and 3-0-0 when he scored a goal ... Notched the game-winning goal on Nov. 23 vs. Montreal ... Skated in his 700th NHL contest on Dec. 13 vs. Buffalo.

1994 PLAYOFFS: Made his only post-season appearance in Game Six of the Conference Finals at New Jersey.

NHL CAREER: 1984-85: Selected by Chicago as their first choice in the 1984 draft and went directly to the Blackhawks as an 18-year old ... Played in his first NHL game on Oct. 11 vs. Detroit and scored his initial goal ... Recorded his first NHL assist in his second game, Oct. 13 vs. the Islanders ... Spent most of the year on the "Clydesdales" line, playing with Troy Murray and Curt Fraser ... Ranked 10th among rookies with 50 points ... Led all rookies with six goals in the post-season and was second with 11 points. **1985-86:** Placed third on the team with 50 assists and 79 points and ranked sixth with 29 goals ... Recorded, eight PPG's, one SHG, one game-winner, and seven was against the Red Wings. **1986-87:** Played in 79 games for the second straight season ... Ranked fifth on the Hawks with 35 assists, sixth with 51 points and tied for seventh with 16 goals. **1987-88:** Traded to Toronto on Sept. 3 ... Led Maple Leafs with a career-high 42 goals and 75 points ... Led the team with 243 shots and placed third with 33 assists ... Scored one goal and five assists vs. Winnipeg on Nov. 4 ... One of only two Leafs to play in all 80 games. **1988-89:** Led Toronto in scoring for the second consecutive season with a career high 90 points ... 38 goals and 52 assists led the team ... Played in all 80 games for the second straight season, one of four Leafs to play all 80 ... Also led Leafs with 249 shots ... Recorded his first NHL hat trick on Mar. 25 vs. Detroit. **1989-90:** Tied Leafs record with 18-game point scoring streak that was halted on Jan. 10 (11 goals, 17 assists) ... Scored second career hat trick on Jan. 27 vs. Canadiens ... Played in 79 contests, missing one game with a knee injury. **1990-91:** Dealt to Winnipeg on Nov. 10 ... Scored 30 goals for the fourth consecutive season. **1991-92:** Led the Jets with 32 goals, seven game-winning goals and 245 shots on goal, despite missing 16 games due to elbow and ankle injuries ... Ranked second on the club with 65 points and 12 PPG's and placed fourth with 33 assists ... Plus 11 rating led team forwards. **1992-93:** Scored his 20th goal of the season on Apr. 2 vs. the Islanders, giving him 20 or more goals in six consecutive seasons and eight times in his first nine years in the NHL ... Registered 21 points in the last 27 games ... Collected 13 goals and 16 assists for 29 points along with a plus nine rating in 46 games with New York after being acquired on Dec. 28 from Winnipeg ... Recorded an assist on Feb. 20 at San Jose to become the 10th U.S. born player to reach the 600-point plateau ... Notched his first points as a Ranger with a goal and an assist vs. Ottawa on Jan. 6.

INTERNATIONAL CAREER: Played for the U.S. Olympic Team at the 1984 Games and was the youngest player on the team ... Accumulated 59 points in 56 games in pre-Olympic contests, then collected nine points in six Olympic Games ... Member of the U.S. teams in the '84, '87 and '91 Canada Cup tournaments ... Also appeared in the '87, '89 and '90 World Championships and served as captain of Team USA at the '93 World Championships.

BACKGROUND: Has never played in the minor leagues ... Very involved with numerous charitable organizations throughout his career ... Wore uniform number 16 with Chicago, Toronto and Winnipeg ... Chicago traded goaltender Pat Jablonski and their number one pick in '84 draft to acquire third overall selection and select him in Entry Draft ... Teammates with Mike Richter and Brian Leetch with Team USA in the '91 Canada Cup ... Loves horseracing, he owns two thouroughbred racehorses and he even brought the Stanley Cup to Belmont Park for a charity event... Has listed MSG as his favorite arena to play in ... Married: wife, Diana; two sons, Eddie and Tommy.

CAREER TRANSACTIONS: *June 9, 1984* — Drafted by Chicago as their first round choice (third overall) in the 1984 Entry Draft. *Sept. 3, 1987* — Traded to Toronto from Chicago with Al Secord for Rick Vaive, Steve Thomas and Bob McGill. *Nov. 10, 1990* — Traded by Toronto to Winnipeg with Mark Osborne for Dave Ellett and Paul Fenton. *Dec. 28, 1992* — Traded by Winnipeg to New York for Kris King and Tie Domi.

CAREER HIGHLIGHTS

MOST GOALS, GAME: 3, (3 times) last- Mar. 24, 1993 vs. Phi., **MOST ASSISTS, GAME:** 5, Nov. 4, 1987 vs. Wpg., **MOST POINTS, GAME:** 6, (twice) last- Dec. 21, 1992 vs. Cgy., **MOST PIM, GAME:** 27, Jan. 11, 1987 vs. Det., **MOST SHOTS, GAME:** 8, (six times) last- Dec. 10, 1991 vs. S.J, **MOST SHOTS, SEASON:** 249, 1988-89, **HIGHEST +/-, SEASON:** 11, (twice) last- 1991-92, **FIRST NHL GAME:** Oct. 11, 1984 vs. Det., **FIRST NHL GOAL:** Oct. 11, 1984 vs. Det. (Stefan)

EDDIE OLCZYK #12

AMATEUR AND PROFESSIONAL RECORD

			Regular Season					Playoffs				
Season	Club	Lea	GP	G	A	PTS	PIM	GP	G	A	PTS	PIM
1983-84	U.S. National Team		56	19	40	59	36	—	—	—	—	—
1883-84	U.S. Olympic Team		6	2	6	8	0	—	—	—	—	—
1984-85	Chicago	NHL	70	20	30	50	67	15	6	5	11	11
1985-86	Chicago	NHL	79	29	50	79	47	3	0	0	0	0
1986-87	Chicago	NHL	79	16	35	51	119	4	1	1	2	4
1987-88	Toronto	NHL	80	42	33	75	55	6	5	4	9	2
1988-89	Toronto	NHL	80	38	52	90	75	—	—	—	—	—
1989-90	Toronto	NHL	79	32	56	88	78	5	1	2	3	14
1990-91	Toronto	NHL	18	4	10	14	13	—	—	—	—	—
1990-91	Winnipeg	NHL	61	26	31	57	69	—	—	—	—	—
1991-92	Winnipeg	NHL	64	32	33	65	67	6	2	1	3	4
1992-93	Winnipeg	NHL	25	8	12	20	26	—	—	—	—	—
1992-93	Rangers	NHL	46	13	16	29	26	—	—	—	—	—
1993-94	Rangers	NHL	37	3	5	8	28	1	0	0	0	0
NHL Totals			718	263	363	626	670	40	15	13	28	35
Rangers Totals			83	16	21	37	54	1	0	0	0	0

MARK OSBORNE

20

LEFT WING
6-2 • 200 • Shoots Left
Born: August 13, 1961 • Toronto, Ontario
Off-Season Home: Toronto, Ontario

1993-94: Skated in 73 games with Toronto, collecting nine goals and 15 assists for 24 points and registered a plus two rating ... Placed third on the team with 145 penalty minutes ... Registered a plus or even rating in 60 of his 73 matches ... Two of his nine assists came on game winning goals ... Collected four goals and two assists along with a plus one rating in 18 playoff matches ... Led the club with two shorthanded goals and 52 penalty minutes in the post-season.

NHL CAREER: 1981-82: Went directly to the Red Wings following his junior career ... Led the team in scoring in his first season with the club, collecting 26 goals and 41 assists for 67 points, appearing in all 80 games ... Placed second with 26 goals and led the team in assists ... Scored his first NHL goal on Oct. 6, in the season opener vs. the Rangers at MSG, scoring the game-winner in a 5-2 Wings victory ... Was named the Red Wings Player of the Year following the season ... Joined Adirondack for the playoffs and helped the team to the AHL championship. **1982-83:** Played in all 80 games for the second consecutive season. **1983-84:** Collected 23 goals and 28 assists for 51 points in his first season with the Rangers after being acquired in a six player trade in June ... Ranked second on the team with five game winning goals, including two in overtime ... Missed four games due to the flu after playing in 193 consecutive contests. **1984-85:** Missed 57 games with a hip flexor injury suffered in the off-season and aggravated in training camp ... Played in 23 of the final 24 games after making his first appearance of the season on Feb. 17. **1985-86:** Appeared in the first 55 games of the season before suffering an ankle injury that forced him to miss 17 of 18 contests from Feb. 14 to Mar. 23 ... Recorded four assists vs. Detroit on Dec. 23 ... Skated in 15 of 16 playoff matches, tallying two goals and three assists, including the series winning goal in the first round vs. Philadelphia. **1986-87:** Tallied 17 goals and 15 assists for 32 points in 58 games with New York before being dealt to Toronto on Mar. 5 ... Tallied five goals and 10 assists in 16 matches with the club. **1987-88:** Tallied 23 goals and 37 assists for 60 points along with a career high 102 penalty minutes in 79 games in his first full year with the Maple Leafs ... Was named the Leaf's Masterton Trophy nominee by the local media and was named the Leaf's inaugural nominee for the King Clancy Memorial Trophy. **1988-89:** Skated in his 500th NHL match on Dec. 10 vs. Detroit ... Notched a career high 112 penalty minutes ... Was the Leaf's nominee for the King Clancy Award for the second consecutive year. **1989-90:** Notched a career high 50 assists and 73 points, while his 23 goals was tied for the second highest mark of his career ... Placed fifth on the team in scoring and ranked third in assists ... Led the club in game winning goals with six ... Tallied four assists on Jan. 8 vs. Washington ... **1990-91:** Appeared in 18 games with Toronto, tallying three goals and three assists, before being dealt to Winnipeg along with Eddie Olczyk on Nov. 10 ... Collected eight goals and eight assists in 37 games with the Jets. **1991-92:** Appeared in 43 games with Winnipeg before being re-acquired by Toronto from Winnipeg on Mar. 10 in exchange for Lucien Deblois ... Tallied three goals and one assist in 11 matches with the Leafs, with two of his three goals coming while shorthanded ... Skated in his 700th NHL game on Dec. 10 vs. San Jose. **1992-93:** Appeared in 76 games with Toronto, tallying 12 goals and 14 assists for 26 points ... Skated in his 800th NHL game on Mar. 10 vs. Hartford ... Scored his 200th NHL goal on Feb. 14 vs. Minnesota and recorded his 500th career point on Feb. 20 vs. Boston ... Missed seven games with a sprained knee.

JUNIOR CAREER: Played three seasons with Niagara Falls in the Ontario Hockey Association from 1978 to 1981 ... Teammates with Steve Larmer in each of the three seasons ... Notched 39 goals and 41 assists for 80 points in 54 games in his finals season with the club.

BACKGROUND: Teammates with Eddie Olczyk in Winnipeg and Toronto and Mike Hartman in Winnipeg ... Lists Bobby Orr as his childhood idol ... Enjoys golfing and fishing in the off season ... "Ozzie" does considerable charitable work and has twice been nominated for the King Clancy Award ... Is an avid Toronto Blue Jays fan ... Is married to actress Madolyn Smith ... Daughter, Abigail.

CAREER TRANSACTIONS: *June 11, 1980* — Detroit's second choice, (third round, 46th overall) in the 1980 NHL Entry Draft. *June 13, 1983* — Traded to the Rangers by Detroit along with Willie Huber and Mike Blaisdell for Ron Duguay, Ed Mio and Ed Johnstone. *Mar. 5, 1987* — Traded by the Rangers to Toronto for Jeff Jackson and a third round draft choice (Rob Zamuner) in 1989. *Nov. 10, 1990* — Traded to Winnipeg by Toronto with Eddie Olczyk for Dave Ellett and Paul Fenton. *Mar. 10, 1992* — Traded to Toronto by Winnipeg for Lucien DeBlois. *Sept. 6, 1994* — Signed by the Rangers as an unrestricted free agent.

CAREER HIGHLIGHTS

MOST GOALS, GAME: 3, Dec. 1, 1981 vs. St.L., **MOST ASSISTS, GAME:** 5, Feb. 7, 1982 vs. St.L., **MOST POINTS, GAME:** 5, Feb. 7, 1982 vs. St.L., **MOST PIM, GAME:** 17, Mar. 4, 1987 vs. NYI., **MOST SHOTS, GAME:** 6 (6 times) last- Jan. 3, 1990 vs. Que., **MOST SHOTS, SEASON:** 181, 1991-92, **HIGHEST +/-, SEASON:** 5, 1985-86, **FIRST NHL GAME:** Oct. 6, 1981 vs. NYR., **FIRST NHL GOAL:** Oct. 6, 1981 vs. NYR. (Weeks).

MARK OSBORNE #20

AMATEUR AND PROFESSIONAL RECORD

			Regular Season					Playoffs				
Season	Club	Lea	GP	G	A	PTS	PIM	GP	G	A	PTS	PIM
1979-80	Niagra Falls	OHA	52	10	33	43	104	10	2	1	3	23
1980-81	Niagra Falls	OHA	54	39	41	80	140	12	11	10	21	20
1980-81	Adirondack	AHL	—	—	—	—	—	13	2	3	5	2
1981-82	Detroit	NHL	80	26	41	67	61	—	—	—	—	—
1982-83	Detroit	NHL	80	19	24	43	83	—	—	—	—	—
1983-84	Rangers	NHL	73	23	28	51	88	5	0	1	1	7
1984-85	Rangers	NHL	23	4	4	8	33	3	0	0	0	4
1985-86	Rangers	NHL	62	16	24	40	80	15	2	3	5	26
1986-87	Rangers	NHL	58	17	15	32	101	—	—	—	—	—
1986-87	Toronto	NHL	16	5	10	15	12	9	1	3	4	6
1987-88	Toronto	NHL	79	23	37	60	102	6	1	3	4	16
1988-89	Toronto	NHL	75	16	30	46	112	—	—	—	—	—
1989-90	Toronto	NHL	78	23	50	73	91	5	2	3	5	12
1990-91	Toronto	NHL	18	3	3	6	4	—	—	—	—	—
1990-91	Winnipeg	NHL	37	8	8	16	59	—	—	—	—	—
1991-92	Winnipeg	NHL	43	4	12	16	65	—	—	—	—	—
1991-92	Toronto	NHL	11	3	1	4	8	—	—	—	—	—
1992-93	Toronto	NHL	76	12	14	26	89	19	1	1	2	16
1993-94	Toronto	NHL	73	9	15	24	145	18	4	2	6	52
NHL Totals			882	211	316	527	1133	80	11	16	27	139
Rangers Totals			216	60	71	131	302	23	2	4	6	37

MIKE RICHTER

35

GOALTENDER
5-11 • 185 • Catches Left
Born: Sept. 22, 1966 • Abington, Pennsylvania
Off-Season Home: New York, New York

1993-94: Appeared in a career high 68 matches and established a franchise record for wins in a single season with 42 ... Became the first Rangers goaltender to lead the NHL in wins since Ed Giacomin led the league with 37 in 1968-69 ... Set a career high and tied for fourth in the league with five shutouts ... Placed fifth in the NHL with a career best 2.57 GAA ... Notched his fifth shutout of the season on Apr. 1 vs. Dallas, his 38th victory, setting a club record for wins in a season ... After opening the season with a 0-4-0 mark, he went 42-8-6 with a 2.46 GAA and .913 save percentage in his final 64 outings ... Posted a franchise record 20-game unbeaten streak, going 17-0-3 from Oct. 24 to Dec. 19, surpassing Dave Kerr's club record of 19 (14-0-5) set in 1939-40 ... Started in a career-high 15 consecutive games from Oct. 19 to Nov. 23 ... Was named the NHL Player of the Month for November after posting a record of 9-0-1 with a 2.37 GAA and .917 save percentage in 12 games ... Appeared in his 200th NHL match on Mar. 4 vs. the Islanders ... Recorded his 100th NHL career win on Feb. 28 vs. Philadelphia ... Moved past Gilles Villemure into sixth place on the Rangers all-time win list on Feb. 18 vs. Ottawa ... Posted a career high eight game winning streak from Mar. 23 to Apr. 12, surpassing his previous high of seven set from Oct. 30 to Nov. 13, 1993 ... Finished the season with a nine game unbeaten streak from Mar. 23 to Apr. 14 and was named NHL Player of the Week for the week ending April 3 ... Was named as the MVP in the NHL All-Star Game on Jan. 22 at MSG, stopping 19 of 21 shots in the second period while making his second All-Star appearance ... Was the first goaltender to win the award since Grant Fuhr in 1986 and became the third Ranger to earn the award.

1994 PLAYOFFS: Started all 23 playoff matches and led the NHL with 16 wins, placed third with a 2.07 GAA and ranked fourth with a .921 save percentage ... Stopped 31 shots in Game Seven double overtime victory in the Conference Finals vs. New Jersey on May 27, setting a club record for wins in one playoff year, with 12 ... Notched his fourth shutout of the playoffs on May 17 in Game Two vs. New Jersey, tying the team and NHL record for shutouts in a single post season ... Stopped Pavel Bure's penalty shot attempt in the second period of Game Four of the Finals on June 7 at Vancouver ... Turned aside 28 shots in Game Seven Stanley Cup clinching victory ... Won his first seven matches, including consecutive 6-0 shutouts in the first two games of the Conference Quarterfinals vs. the Islanders on Apr. 17 and 18 at MSG ... Became the second Rangers player to post back to back shutouts in the playoffs, joining Dave Kerr who blanked the Bruins, 1-0 and 1-0 on Mar. 26 and Mar. 28, 1940.

NHL CAREER: 1988-89: Although he won the Lars-Erik Sjoberg Award as the best rookie of training camp, he spent most of the season with Denver (IHL) ... Served as New York's back up goalie on two occasions and made his NHL debut as starting goalie in game four of first round playoff series vs. Pittsburgh. **1989-90:** Made his NHL regular-season debut on Oct. 19, defeating the Whalers 7-3 at MSG ... Called up from Flint (IHL) on Dec. 31 to face the Soviet Wings and remained with the team for the rest of the season ... Posted a record of 7-4-2 with a 3.76 GAA in 13 games with Flint ... Lost a 4-3 decision in St. Louis on Jan. 6, then went unbeaten in his next seven games (5-0-2) and was named the NHL's Rookie of the Month for January ... Four of his five losses were by one goal and he allowed more than three goals in only six of his 22 starts ... Stopped two penalty shots during the regular-season and one in the playoffs. **1990-91:** Set an NHL record by alternating starts with John Vanbiesbrouck for the first 76 games of the season ... Started the final four regular season games and all six playoff matches ... Named as a finalist for the Vezina Trophy as the NHL's top goaltender ... .903 save percentage ranked third in the NHL and was the second best in club history ... Recorded a career-high eight-game unbeaten streak (5-0-3) from Jan. 25 to Mar. 4, including a 59 save performance in 3-3 tie at Vancouver on Jan. 31 that set a team record for saves in a game ... Won several team awards after the season, including the Players' Player Award. **1991-92:** Won over

20 games for the second consecutive season, despite missing 12 games from Feb. 1 to Feb. 25 due to injury ... Tied for fifth in the league with .901 save percentage and three shutouts ... Recorded his initial regular season shutout on Nov. 23 at St. Louis, while also posting shutouts vs. Boston on Dec. 8 and against New Jersey on Dec. 23 ... Posted a five game winning streak from Oct. 16 to Nov. 2 ... Played in first career All-Star Game in Philadelphia on Jan. 18 and allowed two goals on 15 shots while playing the third period ... Won the goaltending part of the Skills Competition the night before the All-Star Game ... Notched four of the Rangers' six playoff victories. **1992-93:** Turned aside 29 shots while posting his fourth career shutout at Edmonton on Feb. 27 ... With an assist vs. Ottawa on Jan. 6, he tied the Rangers all-time record for most assists in a season, matching John Vanbiesbrouck's mark of five tallied in '84-85 and again in '87-88 ... Allowed three of fewer goals in 12 of his last 16 decisions ... Completed a five-game conditioning stint at Binghamton on Jan. 23, where he posted a 4-0-1 record with a 1.18 GAA and a .964 save percentage ... Began the season by winning four of his first five starts.

IHL CAREER: Made his professional debut with the Colorado Rangers on Mar. 1, 1988 just a few days after playing with the U.S. Olympic Team ... Posted a 3-1 victory at Kalamazoo in his initial start and went on to record a 13-3-0 mark during the month to help Colorado win the West Division title ... 2.94 GAA and .905 save percentage during March earned him selection as IHL Player of the Month ... 5-3 record during playoffs, accounting for five of Colorado's six post season victories ... Spent the entire '88-89 campaign with Denver, leading all IHL goalies in games played (57) and ranking second in minutes (3,031).

COLLEGE CAREER: Played for two seasons at University of Wisconsin, going 14-9-0 in his freshman campaign in '85-86 and 19-16-1 in '86-87 ... Selected as WCHA Freshman of the Year in 1985-86 ... All-Western Collegiate Hockey Association All-Academic selection in 1986-87 ... Among his teammates while playing for the Badgers were Tony Granato (Los Angeles) and Paul Ranheim (Hartford).

INTERNATIONAL CAREER: Member of the 1986 and 1987 U.S. National Teams and 1987 Select Team ... Shared the 1988 60-game pre-Olympic schedule with Chris Terreri (N.J.), each accumulating a record of 17-7-3 ... Appeared in four matches during the Olympics in Calgary for the U.S. team ... Starting goalie for Team USA in 1991 Canada Cup ... Played in four games with Team USA at the 1993 World Championships in Munich, Germany.

BACKGROUND: Took classes at Columbia University for the second consecutive summer ... Appeared with Brian Leetch and Mark Messier on the Late Show with David Letterman, following the team's Stanley Cup victory ... Also appeared on the Howard Stern Show and the Today Show ... Does extensive work with charitable organizations including serving as honorary hockey chairman of the Children's Health Fund ... Won the 1990-91 "Good Guy" Award for cooperation with the press ... Visited The White House in 1991 to help kick off "The Great American Workout" ... His favorite sports team is the Philadelphia Phillies ... Avid reader ... Single.

CAREER TRANSACTIONS: June 15, 1985 — Rangers' second round draft choice (28th overall) in the 1985 Entry Draft.

RICHTER'S RECORD SETTING SEASON

42 WINS

Date	Opponent	Score	Saves
Oct. 24	Los Angeles	3-2	23
Oct. 30	@ Hartford	4-1	21
Oct. 31	New Jersey*	4-1	23
Nov. 3	Vancouver	6-3	33
Nov. 6	@ Quebec	4-2	19
Nov. 8	Tampa Bay	6-3	28
Nov. 10	Winnipeg	2-1	26
Nov. 13	@ Washington	2-0	21
Nov. 19	@ Tampa Bay	5-3	28
Nov. 23	Montreal	5-4	27
Nov. 28	Washington	3-1	33
Nov. 30	@ New Jersey	3-1	26
Dec. 4	@ Toronto	4-3	14
Dec. 5	New Jersey	2-1	26
Dec. 13	Buffalo	2-0	28
Dec. 15	Hartford	5-2	22
Dec. 19	Ottawa	6-3	22
Dec. 29	@ St. Louis	4-3	40
Jan. 3	Florida	3-2	25
Jan. 14	Philadelphia	5-2	22
Jan. 16	@ Chicago	5-1	32
Jan. 18	St. Louis	4-1	25
Jan. 25	@ San Jose	8-3	27
Jan. 27	@ Los Angeles	5-4(OT)	19
Jan. 31	Pittsburgh	5-3	22
Feb. 12	@ Ottawa	4-3(OT)	13
Feb. 14	@ Quebec	4-2	24
Feb. 18	Ottawa	3-0	24
Feb. 21	Pittsburgh	4-3(OT)	24
Feb. 24	@ New Jersey	3-1	35
Feb. 28	Philadelphia	4-1	26
Mar. 2	Quebec	5-2	32
Mar. 5	@ Islanders	5-4	14
Mar. 16	Hartford	4-0	27
Mar. 23	@ Edmonton	5-3	29
Mar. 25	@ Vancouver	5-2	30
Mar. 29	@ Philadelphia	4-3	27
Apr. 1	Dallas	3-0	28
Apr. 2	@ New Jersey	4-2	24
Apr. 4	Florida	3-2	29
Apr. 8	Toronto	5-3	34
Apr. 12	Buffalo	3-2	24

*Neutral site game in Halifax.

16 PLAYOFF WINS

Date	Opponent	Score	Saves
Apr. 17	Islanders	6-0	21
Apr. 18	Islanders	6-0	29
Apr. 21	@ Islanders	5-1	21
Apr. 24	@ Islanders	4-2	16
May 1	Washington	6-3	27
May 3	Washington	5-3	22
May 5	@ Washington	3-0	21
May 9	Washington	4-3	28
May 17	New Jersey	4-0	16
May 19	@ New Jersey	3-2(2-OT)	29
May 25	@ New Jersey	4-2	28
May 27	New Jersey	3-2(2-OT)	31
June 2	Vancouver	3-1	28
June 4	@ Vancouver	5-1	24
June 7	@ Vancouver	4-2	28
June 14	Vancouver	3-2	28

20 GAME UNBEATEN STREAK

Date	Opponent	Decision	Score	Saves
Oct. 24	Los Angeles	W	3-2	23
Oct. 28	Montreal	T	3-3	23
Oct. 30	@ Hartford	W	4-1	21
Oct. 31	New Jersey*	W	4-1	23
Nov. 3	Vancouver	W	6-3	33
Nov. 6	@ Quebec	W	4-2	19
Nov. 8	Tampa Bay	W	6-3	28
Nov. 10	Winnipeg	W	2-1	26
Nov. 13	@ Washington	W	2-0	21
Nov. 14	San Jose	T	3-3	18
Nov. 19	@ Tampa Bay	W	5-3	28
Nov. 23	Montreal	W	5-4	27
Nov. 28	Washington	W	3-1	33
Nov. 30	@ New Jersey	W	3-1	26
Dec. 4	@ Toronto	W	4-3	14
Dec. 5	New Jersey	W	2-1	26
Dec. 8	Edmonton	T	1-1	37
Dec. 13	Buffalo	W	2-0	28
Dec. 15	Hartford	W	5-2	22
Dec. 19	Ottawa	W	6-3	22

MIKE RICHTER #35

CAREER HIGHLIGHTS
LONGEST WIN STREAK: 8, Mar. 23, 1994-Apr. 12, 1994, **LONGEST UNBEATEN STREAK:** 20, (17-0-3) Oct. 24, 1993-Dec. 19, 1994, **LONGEST SHUTOUT STREAK:** 113:50, Nov. 19, 1991-Nov. 27, 1991, **MOST SHOTS FACED, GAME:** 62, Jan. 31, 1991 at Van., **FIRST NHL GAME:** Oct. 19, 1989 vs. Hfd. (7-3), **FIRST NHL SHUTOUT:** Nov. 23, 1991 at St.L. (3-0)

AMATEUR AND PROFESSIONAL RECORD

			Regular Season								Playoffs					
Season	Club	Lea	GP	W	L	T	MINS	GA	SO	AVG	GP	W	L	MINS	GA	SO	AVG
1985-86	Wisconsin	WCHA	25	14	9	0	1394	92	1	3.96	—	—	—	—	—	—	—
1986-87	Wisconsin	WCHA	36	19	16	1	2136	126	0	3.54	—	—	—	—	—	—	—
1987-88	U.S. National Team		29	17	7	2	1559	86	0	3.31	—	—	—	—	—	—	—
1987-88	U.S. Olympic Team		4	2	2	0	230	15	0	3.91	—	—	—	—	—	—	—
1987-88	Colorado	IHL	22	16	5	0	1298	68	1	3.14	10	5	3	536	35	0	3.92
1988-89	Rangers	NHL	—	—	—	—	—	—	—	—	1	0	1	58	4	0	4.14
1988-89	Denver	IHL	57	23	26	0	3031	217	1	4.30	4	0	4	210	21	0	6.00
1989-90	Rangers	NHL	23	12	5	5	1320	66	0	3.00	6	3	2	330	19	0	3.45
1989-90	Flint	IHL	13	7	4	2	782	49	0	3.76	—	—	—	—	—	—	—
1990-91	Rangers	NHL	45	21	13	7	2596	135	0	3.12	6	2	4	313	14	1	2.68
1991-92	Rangers	NHL	41	23	12	2	2298	119	3	3.11	7	4	2	412	24	1	3.50
1992-93	Rangers	NHL	38	13	19	3	2105	134	1	3.82	—	—	—	—	—	—	—
1992-93	Binghamton	AHL	5	4	0	1	305	6	0	1.18	—	—	—	—	—	—	—
1993-94	Rangers	NHL	68	42	12	6	3710	159	5	2.57	23	16	7	1417	49	4	2.07
NHL and Rangers Totals			215	111	61	23	12029	613	9	3.06	43	25	16	2530	110	6	2.61

JAY WELLS

24

DEFENSE
6-1 • 210 • Shoots Left
Born: May 18, 1959 • Paris, Ontario
Off-Season Home: East Amherst, New York

1993-94: Tied a career high, appearing in 79 games in his 15th NHL season ... Registered a plus or even rating in 65 of his 79 matches ... Skated in his 900th NHL game on Nov. 19 at Tampa Bay ... Rangers were 7-1-1 when he tallied a point ... Notched his 200th career assist on Oct. 16 at Philadelphia.

1994 PLAYOFFS: Appeared in all 23 playoff matches and played in his first Stanley Cup Finals.

NHL CAREER: 1979-80: Began the season with Los Angeles, but was sent to Binghamton (AHL) for a brief period ... Rejoined the Kings in late December and was a regular on defense for the Kings for the second half of season ... Led Los Angeles in PIM with 113 and was named the team's top rookie performer. **1980-81:** Scored initial NHL goal on Nov. 19 vs. Winnipeg ... Missed seven games with a charley horse ... Led the team with 155 PIM. **1981-82:** Led the team with 145 PIM, despite missing 18 games with a broken hand ... Accumulated 41 minutes in penalties, while appearing in all 10 playoff encounters. **1982-83:** Voted by his teammates as the Kings Outstanding Defenseman ... Led the team with 167 PIM ... Missed 11 games with a knee injury. **1983-84:** Was named as the Kings Outstanding Defenseman for the second consecutive season ... Led the club with 141 PIM ... Missed 11 games with an ankle injury. **1984-85:** Led all Kings defensemen with a plus five rating ... Led Los Angeles in PIM for the sixth straight season with 185 ... Missed three games with sore ribs. **1985-86:** Set career highs in goals (11), assists (31), points (42) and penalty minutes (226) ... The 42 points led club backliners ... Nine of his 11 goals were scored on the road ... Notched first two-goal game of his career on Nov. 2 at Hartford and collected three assists in a game on two occasions ... Only game missed was due to a suspension ... 226 penalty minutes was second on the club to Tiger Williams' 320. **1986-87:** Led Kings defensemen with 29 assists ... Six of his seven goals were scored on power play ... Missed two contests with an eye injury. **1987-88:** Ranked second among club defensemen with 23 assists and placed third on the club with 159 PIM ... Missed 18 games with a groin injury. **1988-89:** Traded to Philadelphia before the start of the season ... Ranked third on Flyers with 184 PIM. **1989-90:** Traded from Flyers to Sabres on Mar. 5 ... Missed four weeks with a fractured ankle ... Recorded an assist in his first game with Buffalo on Mar. 8. **1990-91:** Missed 20 games due to injury in his first full season in Buffalo. **1991-92:** Acquired by the Rangers from the Buffalo Sabres on Mar. 9 ... Played in 41 games for Buffalo, collecting two goals and nine assists along with 157 PIM ... Scoreless with a plus two rating in 11 contests with New York... Accumulated an even or plus rating in 10 of his 11 outings with New York... Recorded his 2,000th career penalty minute on Mar. 3 at Quebec... Appeared in all of the Rangers 13 playoff games. **1992-93:** Veteran NHL defenseman collected a goal and nine assists in his first full season in New York ... Collected his first goal as a Ranger on Dec. 19 at Hartford ... Missed 31 games due to knee injury suffered Jan. 27 vs. Winnipeg ... Recorded his first point as a Ranger with an assist on Paul Broten's goal Oct. 10 at New Jersey.

JUNIOR CAREER: Played two seasons with Kingston of the OHA... Selected to play in the OHA All-Star game in '78-79 and was named a post-season first team All-Star.

BACKGROUND: Wore number 24 with Buffalo and Los Angeles and number seven with Flyers ... 604 career games with Kings is the most of any defenseman in team history and 1,446 penalty minutes is second on the club's all-time list... Grew up on his parents' 320 acre farm... Married: wife, Colleen; daughters, Stephanie and Alexa.

CAREER TRANSACTIONS: *June 19, 1979* — Kings' first round draft choice (16th overall) in the 1979 NHL Entry Draft. *Sept. 29, 1988* — Traded by Los Angeles to Philadelphia for Doug Crossman. *March 5, 1990* — Traded by Philadelphia to Buffalo along with a 1991 second round draft choice in exchange for Kevin Maguire and a 1990 second round draft choice. *March 9, 1992* — Traded by Buffalo to New York in exchange for Randy Moller.

JAY WELLS #24

CAREER HIGHLIGHTS

MOST GOALS, GAME: 2, Nov. 2, 1985 at Hfd., **MOST ASSISTS, GAME:** 3, (twice) last- Mar. 17, 1986 at Tor., **MOST POINTS, GAME:** 3, (four times) last- Jan. 7, 1991 at Phi., **MOST PIM, GAME:** 36, Nov. 26, 1986 vs. Van., **MOST SHOTS, GAME:** 6, (twice) last-Oct. 24, 1993 vs. L.A., **MOST SHOTS, SEASON:** 115, 1986-87, **HIGHEST +/-, SEASON:** 11, 1982-83, **FIRST NHL GAME:** Oct. 13, 1979 vs. St.L., **FIRST NHL GOAL:** Nov. 19, 1980 vs. Wpg. (Hamel)

AMATEUR AND PROFESSIONAL RECORD

			Regular Season					Playoffs				
Season	Club	Lea	GP	G	A	PTS	PIM	GP	G	A	PTS	PIM
1976-77	Kingston	OHA	59	4	7	11	90	—	—	—	—	—
1977-78	Kingston	OHA	68	9	13	22	195	5	1	2	3	6
1978-79	Kingston	OHA	48	6	21	27	100	11	2	7	9	29
1979-80	Binghamton	AHL	28	0	6	6	48	—	—	—	—	—
1979-80	Los Angeles	NHL	43	0	0	0	113	4	0	0	0	11
1980-81	Los Angeles	NHL	72	5	13	18	155	4	0	0	0	27
1981-82	Los Angeles	NHL	60	1	8	9	145	10	1	3	4	41
1982-83	Los Angeles	NHL	69	3	12	15	167	—	—	—	—	—
1983-84	Los Angeles	NHL	69	3	18	21	141	—	—	—	—	—
1984-85	Los Angeles	NHL	77	2	9	11	185	3	0	1	1	0
1985-86	Los Angeles	NHL	79	11	31	42	226	—	—	—	—	—
1986-87	Los Angeles	NHL	77	7	29	36	155	5	1	2	3	10
1987-88	Los Angeles	NHL	58	2	23	25	159	5	1	2	3	21
1988-89	Philadelphia	NHL	67	2	19	21	184	18	0	2	2	51
1989-90	Philadelphia	NHL	59	3	16	19	129	—	—	—	—	—
1989-90	Buffalo	NHL	1	0	1	1	0	6	0	0	0	12
1990-91	Buffalo	NHL	43	1	2	3	86	1	0	1	1	0
1991-92	Buffalo	NHL	41	2	9	11	157	—	—	—	—	—
1991-92	Rangers	NHL	11	0	0	0	24	13	0	2	2	10
1992-93	Rangers	NHL	53	1	9	10	107	—	—	—	—	—
1993-94	Rangers	NHL	79	2	7	9	110	23	0	0	0	20
NHL Totals			958	45	206	251	2243	92	3	13	16	203
Rangers Totals			143	3	16	19	241	36	0	2	2	30

SERGEI ZUBOV

DEFENSE
21

6-1 • 200 • Shoots Right
Born: July 22, 1970 • Moscow, Russia
Off-Season Home: Mamaroneck, New York

1993-94: Led the team and placed second in the NHL in scoring among defensemen with 12 goals and 77 assists for 89 points in his first full season in the NHL ... Became the first defenseman to lead a team that finished first overall in the NHL in scoring ... Led the team, ranked first among NHL defensemen and placed fourth in the NHL with 77 assists ... Is one of only two defensemen in Rangers history along with Brain Leetch to tally 70 or more assists in a single season ... 77 assists is the second highest single season mark in team history, trailing only Brian Leetch's 80 in '91-92 ... Notched a career high eight game scoring streak from Mar. 4 to Mar. 16 ... Collected 40 power play assists, ranking first on the club and third in the NHL ... Registered one game-winning goal and assisted on 20 game-winners, placing first on the club ... Was fourth on the team with a plus 20 rating ... Collected a point in 55 of his 78 matches and tied for first on the club with 24 multiple point games ... Tallied four assists on Jan. 25 at San Jose, setting career highs for assists and points in a game ... Registered a career best 11 shots on goal on Jan. 5 vs. Calgary.

1994 PLAYOFFS: Placed fourth on the team and second among defensemen with five goals and 14 assists for 19 points in 22 matches ... Tallied a pair of assists in Game Seven of the Finals vs. Vancouver on June 14 ... Missed Game Three of the Finals due to injury ... Registered a goal and two assists on Apr. 17 in Game One of the Conference Quarterfinals vs. the Islanders while making his first playoff appearance.

NHL CAREER: 1992-93: Called up from Binghamton (AHL) on Dec. 6 and made his NHL debut vs. Toronto that night ... Played in three games (all Rangers wins) and returned to Binghamton on Dec. 12 ... Tallied seven goals and 28 assists for 35 points in 29 AHL contests ... Led the AHL with a plus 29 rating and was on a 13 game point scoring streak at the time of his recall on Dec. 27 ... Notched his initial NHL point with an assist on Dec. 27 vs. Boston ... Tallied his first NHL goal at Buffalo on December 31 ... Registered his only two-goal effort on Jan. 6 vs. Ottawa and finished first among team defensemen with eight goals ... Tallied 17 points in his last 26 games ... Collected three goals and nine assists on the power play.

RUSSIAN CAREER: Played four seasons for CSKA Moscow ... Helped lead the team to its 13th consecutive championship in '88-89 and to second place finishes in '89-90 and '91-92 ... Teammates with Pavel Bure (Van.), Sergei Fedorov (Det.), Vladimir Konstantinov (Det.), Valeri Kamensky (Que.), Alexei Kasatonov (Bos.), Andre Kovalenko (Que.), Vladimir Malakhov (NYI) and Igor Kravchuk (Edm.).

INTERNATIONAL CAREER: Competed for the Soviet Union team and won a silver medal at the '88 European Junior Championships ... Member of the '89 and '90 Soviet Union World Junior Championship teams, capturing the Gold Medal in '89 and silver in '90 ... Was named a second-team All-Star in '90 ... Teamed with New York Islanders defenseman, Vladimir Malakhov, on the backline for the 1992 Gold Medal-winning C.I.S team at the 1992 Olympics ... The duo was not on the ice for an even strength goal against ... Teammates with Alexei Kovalev as well as Darius Kasparaitis (NYI), Kravchuk, Kovalenko and Davydov.

BACKGROUND: Was the third Russian-born player to be drafted by the Rangers, following Roman Oksyuta in 1989 and Sergei Kapustin in 1982 ... Nickname "Zubie" ... Favorite music group is Guns 'N' Roses and his favorite off-season activity is fishing ... Enjoys watching basketball, his favorite team is the Chicago Bulls ... Lists his favorite all-time movie as "The Godfather" ... Married; wife, Irina; new baby boy, Pavel, was born in August.

CAREER TRANSACTIONS: *June 16, 1990* — Rangers' sixth choice (fifth round, 85th overall) in 1990 Entry Draft.

SERGEI ZUBOV #21

CAREER HIGHLIGHTS
MOST GOALS, GAMES: 2, Jan. 6, 1993 vs. Ott., **MOST ASSISTS, GAME:** 4, Jan. 25, 1994 at S.J., **MOST POINTS, GAME:** 4, Jan. 25, 1994 at S.J., **MOST PIM, GAME:** 2, (twice) last- Feb. 8, 1993 vs. N.J., **MOST SHOTS, GAME:** 11, Jan. 5, 1994 vs. Cgy., **MOST SHOTS, SEASON:** 222, 1993-94, **HIGHEST +/-, SEASON:** 20, 1993-94, **FIRST NHL GAME:** Dec. 6, 1992 vs. Tor., **FIRST NHL GOAL:** Dec. 31, 1992 at Buf. (Hasek)

AMATEUR AND PROFESSIONAL RECORD

Season	Club	Lea	Regular Season GP	G	A	PTS	PIM	Playoffs GP	G	A	PTS	PIM
1988-89	CSKA	USSR	29	1	4	5	10	—	—	—	—	—
1989-90	CSKA	USSR	48	6	2	8	16	—	—	—	—	—
1990-91	CSKA	USSR	41	6	5	11	12	—	—	—	—	—
1991-92	Unified Olympic Team		8	0	1	1	0	—	—	—	—	—
1991-92	CSKA	CIS	44	4	7	11	24	—	—	—	—	—
1992-93	Rangers	NHL	49	8	23	31	4	—	—	—	—	—
1992-93	Binghamton	AHL	30	7	29	36	14	11	5	5	10	2
1993-94	Rangers	NHL	78	12	77	89	39	22	5	14	19	0
1993-94	Binghamton	AHL	2	1	2	3	0	—	—	—	—	—
NHL and Rangers Totals			127	20	100	120	43	22	5	14	19	0

IN THE SYSTEM

SYLVAIN BLOUIN
DEFENSE
6'2"   225 lbs.   Shoots Left
Born: May 21, 1974, Montreal, Quebec
Obtained in Entry Draft, June 28, 1994; fifth choice, number 104 overall.

				Regular Season				Playoffs			
Season	Club	League	GP	G	A	PTS	PIM	GP	G	A	PTS	PIM
1991-92	Laval	QMJHL	28	0	0	0	23	9	0	0	0	35
1992-93	Laval	QMJHL	68	0	10	10	373	13	1	0	1	66
1993-94	Laval	QMJHL	62	18	23	41	492	21	4	13	17	177

ERIC CAIRNS
DEFENSE
6'5"   230 lbs.   Shoots Left
Born: June 27, 1974, Oakville, Ontario
Obtained in Entry Draft, June 20, 1992; third choice, number 72 overall.

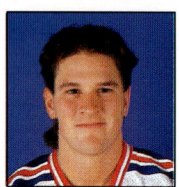

				Regular Season				Playoffs			
Season	Club	League	GP	G	A	PTS	PIM	GP	G	A	PTS	PIM
1991-92	Detroit	OHL	64	1	11	12	232	7	0	0	0	31
1992-93	Detroit	OHL	64	3	13	16	194	15	0	3	3	24
1993-94	Detroit	OHL	59	7	35	42	204	—	—	—	—	—

CRAIG DUNCANSON
LEFT WING
6'0"   200 lbs.   Shoots Left
Born: March 17, 1967, Sudbury, Ontario
Signed as a free agent on September 4, 1992.
Originally drafted by Los Angeles as their first choice, ninth overall, in the 1985 NHL Entry Draft.

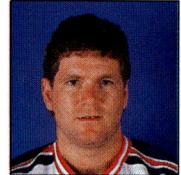

				Regular Season				Playoffs			
Season	Club	Lea.	GP	G	A	PTS	PIM	GP	G	A	PTS	PIM
1983-84	Sudbury	OHL	62	38	38	76	176	—	—	—	—	—
1984-85	Sudbury	OHL	53	35	28	63	129	—	—	—	—	—
1985-86	Los Angeles	NHL	2	0	1	1	0	—	—	—	—	—
1985-86	Sudbury	OHL	21	12	17	29	55	—	—	—	—	—
1985-86	Cornwall	OHL	40	31	50	81	135	6	4	7	11	2
1985-86	New Haven	AHL	—	—	—	—	—	2	0	0	0	5
1986-87	Los Angeles	NHL	2	0	0	0	24	—	—	—	—	—
1986-87	Cornwall	OHL	52	22	45	67	88	5	4	3	7	20
1987-88	Los Angeles	NHL	9	0	0	0	12	—	—	—	—	—
1987-88	New Haven	AHL	57	15	25	40	170	—	—	—	—	—
1988-89	Los Angeles	NHL	5	0	0	0	0	—	—	—	—	—
1988-89	New Haven	AHL	69	25	39	64	200	17	4	8	12	60
1989-90	Los Angeles	NHL	10	3	2	5	9	—	—	—	—	—
1989-90	New Haven	AHL	51	17	30	47	152	—	—	—	—	—
1990-91	Winnipeg	NHL	7	2	0	2	16	—	—	—	—	—
1990-91	Moncton	AHL	58	16	34	50	107	9	3	11	14	31
1991-92	Moncton	AHL	19	12	9	21	6	11	6	4	10	10
1991-92	Baltimore	AHL	46	20	26	46	98	—	—	—	—	—
1992-93	Rangers	NHL	3	0	1	1	0	—	—	—	—	—
1992-93	Binghamton	AHL	69	35	59	94	126	14	7	5	12	9
1993-94	Binghamton	AHL	70	25	44	69	83	—	—	—	—	—
NHL Totals			38	5	4	9	61	—	—	—	—	—
Rangers Totals			3	0	1	1	0	—	—	—	—	—

IN THE SYSTEM

PETER FIORENTINO
DEFENSE
6'1"   200 lbs.   Shoots Right
Born: December 22, 1968, Niagara Falls, Ontario
Obtained in Entry Draft, June 11, 1988; eleventh round choice, number 215 overall.

Season	Club	Lea.	GP	G	A	PTS	PIM	GP	G	A	PTS	PIM
1984-85	Niagara Falls	Jr.B	38	7	10	17	149	—	—	—	—	—
1985-86	Sault Ste. Marie	OHL	58	1	6	7	87	—	—	—	—	—
1986-87	Sault Ste. Marie	OHL	64	1	12	13	187	4	2	1	3	5
1987-88	Sault Ste. Marie	OHL	65	5	27	32	252	6	2	2	4	21
1988-89	Sault Ste. Marie	OHL	55	5	24	29	220	—	—	—	—	—
1988-89	Denver	IHL	10	0	0	0	39	4	0	0	0	24
1989-90	Flint	IHL	64	2	7	9	302	—	—	—	—	—
1990-91	Binghamton	AHL	55	2	11	13	361	1	0	0	0	0
1991-92	Rangers	NHL	1	0	0	0	0	—	—	—	—	—
1991-92	Binghamton	AHL	70	2	11	13	340	5	0	1	1	24
1992-93	Binghamton	AHL	64	9	5	14	286	13	0	3	3	22
1993-94	Binghamton	AHL	68	7	15	22	220	—	—	—	—	—
NHL & Rangers Totals			1	0	0	0	0	—	—	—	—	—

KEN GERNANDER
CENTER
5'10"   180 lbs.   Shoots Left
Born: June 30, 1969, Coleraine, Minnesota
Signed as a free agent on September 9, 1994.
Originally drafted by Winnipeg as their fourth choice, 96th overall, in the 1987 NHL Entry Draft.

Season	Club	Lea.	GP	G	A	PTS	PIM	GP	G	A	PTS	PIM
1987-88	U. Minnesota	WCHA	44	14	14	28	14	—	—	—	—	—
1988-89	U. Minnesota	WCHA	44	9	11	20	2	—	—	—	—	—
1989-90	U. Minnesota	WCHA	44	32	17	49	24	—	—	—	—	—
1990-91	U. Minnesota	WCHA	44	23	20	43	24	—	—	—	—	—
1991-92	Fort Wayne	IHL	13	7	6	13	2	—	—	—	—	—
1991-92	Moncton	AHL	43	8	18	26	98	1	1	2	2	
1992-93	Moncton	AHL	71	18	29	47	20	5	1	4	5	0
1993-94	Moncton	AHL	71	22	35	57	12	19	6	1	7	0

JON HILLEBRANDT
GOALTENDER
5'10"   185 lbs.   Catches Left
Born: December 18, 1971, Cottage Grove, Wisconsin
Obtained in 1990 Entry Draft, June, 16 1990; 10th round choice, number 202 overall.

Season	Club	Lea.	GP	W	L	T	AVG	GP	W	L	AVG
1990-91	Madison	USHL	28	10	14	3	4.08	—	—	—	—
1991-92	Univ. of Illinois-Chicago	CCHA	31	7	19	—	4.14	—	—	—	—
1992-93	Univ. of Illinois-Chicago	CCHA	33	8	22	2	4.51	5	2	3	4.80
1993-94	Binghamton	AHL	8	0	0	0	0	—	—	—	—
1993-94	U.S. National Team		2	1	1	0	3.9	—	—	—	—

IN THE SYSTEM

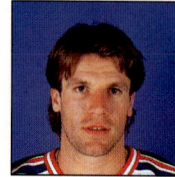

JIM HILLER
RIGHT WING
6'0"   200 lbs.   Shoots Right
Born: May 15, 1969, Port Alberni, Britsish Columbia
Claimed off waivers from the Detroit Red Wings on October 12, 1993
Originally drafted by the Los Angeles Kings as their 10th round pick, 207th overall, in the 1989 NHL Entry Draft.

Season	Club	Lea.	Regular Season					Playoffs				
			GP	G	A	PTS	PIM	GP	G	A	PTS	PIM
1989-90	N. Michigan	WCHA	39	23	33	56	52	—	—	—	—	—
1990-91	N. Michigan	WCHA	43	22	41	68	59	—	—	—	—	—
1991-92	N. Michigan	WCHA	39	28	52	80	115	—	—	—	—	—
1992-93	Los Angeles	NHL	40	6	6	12	90	—	—	—	—	—
1992-93	Phoenix	IHL	3	0	2	2	2	—	—	—	—	—
1992-93	Detroit	NHL	21	2	6	8	19	2	0	0	0	4
1993-94	Rangers	NHL	2	0	0	0	7	—	—	—	—	—
1993-94	Binghamton	AHL	67	27	34	61	61	—	—	—	—	—
NHL Totals			63	8	12	20	116	2	0	0	0	4
Rangers Totals			2	0	0	0	7	0	0	0	0	0

ROB KENNY
LEFT WING
6'1"   200 lbs.   Shoots Left
Born: October 19, 1968, Bronx, New York
Signed as a free agent on August 24, 1992.

Season	Club	Lea.	Regular Season					Playoffs				
			GP	G	A	PTS	PIM	GP	G	A	PTS	PIM
1989-90	Northeastern Univ.	H.E.	32	2	7	9	29	—	—	—	—	—
1990-91	Northeastern Univ.	H.E.	29	6	11	17	40	—	—	—	—	—
1991-92	Northeastern Univ.	H.E.	34	19	14	33	44	—	—	—	—	—
1992-93	Binghamton	AHL	66	12	11	23	56	8	2	4	6	8
1993-94	Binghamton	AHL	63	27	14	41	90	—	—	—	—	—

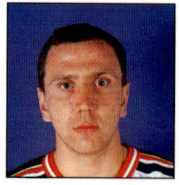

ANDREI KUDINOV
CENTER
6'0"   195 lbs.   Shoots Left
Born: June 28, 1970, Chelyabinsk, CIS
Obtained in Entry Draft, June 26, 1993; 10th round choice, number 242 overall.

Season	Club	Lea.	Regular Season					Playoffs				
			GP	G	A	PTS	PIM	GP	G	A	PTS	PIM
1990-91	Chelyabinsk	Sov. El.	24	2	3	5	20	—	—	—	—	—
1991-92	Chelyabinsk	CIS	36	9	7	16	40	—	—	—	—	—
1992-93	Chelyabinsk	CIS	41	13	23	36	50	8	0	1	1	6
1993-94	Binghamton	AHL	25	3	3	6	6	—	—	—	—	—

IN THE SYSTEM

DARREN LANGDON
LEFT WING
6'1"   205 lbs.   Shoots Left
Born: January 8, 1971, Deer Lake, Newfoundland
Signed as a free agent on August 16, 1993

			Regular Season					Playoffs			
Season	Club	Lea.	GP	G	A	PTS	PIM	GP	G	A	PTS	PIM
1991-92	Summerside	MJHL	44	34	49	83	441	—	—	—	—	—
1992-93	Binghamton	AHL	18	3	4	7	115	8	0	1	1	14
1992-93	Dayton	ECHL	54	23	22	45	429	3	0	1	1	40
1993-94	Binghamton	AHL	54	2	7	9	327	—	—	—	—	—

SCOTT MALONE
DEFENSE
6'1"   195 lbs.   Shoots Left
Born: January 16, 1971, South Boston, Massachusetts
Obtained from the Toronto Maple Leafs along with Glenn Anderson and a 1994 fourth round draft pick (Alexander Korobolin) for Mike Gartner on March 21, 1994. Originally drafted by Toronto as their 10th pick, 220th overall, in the 1990 NHL Entry Draft.

			Regular Season					Playoffs			
Season	Club	Lea.	GP	G	A	PTS	PIM	GP	G	A	PTS	PIM
1991-92	N. Hampshire	H.E.	27	0	4	4	52	—	—	—	—	—
1992-93	N. Hampshire	H.E.	36	5	6	11	96	—	—	—	—	—
1993-94	N. Hampshire	H.E.	40	14	6	20	162	—	—	—	—	—

SHAWN McCOSH
CENTER
6'0"   190 lbs.   Shoots Right
Born: June 5, 1969, Oshawa, Ontario
Signed as a free agent on August, 17, 1993
Originally drafted by Detroit as their fifth selection, 95th overall, in the 1989 NHL Entry Draft.

			Regular Season					Playoffs			
Season	Club	Lea.	GP	G	A	PTS	PIM	GP	G	A	PTS	PIM
1986-87	Hamilton	OHL	50	11	17	28	49	6	1	0	1	2
1987-88	Hamilton	OHL	64	17	36	53	96	14	6	8	14	14
1988-89	Niagara Falls	OHL	56	41	62	103	75	14	4	13	17	23
1989-90	Niagara Falls	OHL	9	6	10	16	24	—	—	—	—	—
1989-90	Hamilton	OHL	39	24	28	52	65	—	—	—	—	—
1990-91	New Haven	AHL	66	16	21	37	104	—	—	—	—	—
1991-92	Los Angeles	NHL	4	0	0	0	4	—	—	—	—	—
1991-92	Phoenix	IHL	71	21	32	53	118	—	—	—	—	—
1991-92	New Haven	AHL	—	—	—	—	—	5	0	1	1	—
1992-93	New Haven	AHL	46	22	32	54	54	—	—	—	—	—
1992-93	Phoenix	IHL	22	9	8	17	36	—	—	—	—	—
1993-94	Binghamton	AHL	75	31	44	75	68	—	—	—	—	—
NHL Totals			4	0	0	0	4	—	—	—	—	—

IN THE SYSTEM

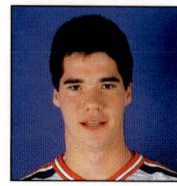

MIKE McLAUGHLIN
LEFT WING
6'1"   205 lbs.   Shoots Left
Born: March 29, 1970, Longmeadow, Massachusetts
Signed as a free agent on August 17, 1993
Originally drafted by Buffalo as their seventh selection, 118th overall, in the 1988 NHL Entry Draft

Season	Club	Lea.	GP	G	A	PTS	PIM	GP	G	A	PTS	PIM
1988-89	Univ. of Vermont	ECAC	32	5	6	11	12	—	—	—	—	—
1989-90	Univ. of Vermont	ECAC	29	11	12	23	37	—	—	—	—	—
1990-91	Univ. of Vermont	ECAC	32	12	14	26	34	—	—	—	—	—
1991-92	Univ. of Vermont	ECAC	30	9	9	18	34	—	—	—	—	—
1992-93	Rochester	AHL	71	19	35	54	27	16	4	2	6	8
1993-94	Binghamton	AHL	56	11	13	24	33	—	—	—	—	—

JEFF NIELSEN
RIGHT WING
6'0"   200 lbs.   Shoots Right
Born: September 20, 1971, Grand Rapids, Minnesota
Obtained in Entry Draft, June 16, 1990; fourth round choice, number 69 overall.

Season	Club	Lea.	GP	G	A	PTS	PIM	GP	G	A	PTS	PIM
1987-88	Grand Rapids HS	Minn. HS	21	9	11	20	14	—	—	—	—	—
1988-89	Grand Rapids HS	Minn. HS	25	13	17	30	26	—	—	—	—	—
1989-90	Grand Rapids HS	Minn. HS	28	32	25	57		—	—	—	—	—
1990-91	U. Minnesota	WCHA	45	11	14	25	50	—	—	—	—	—
1991-92	U. Minnesota	WCHA	44	15	16	30	74	—	—	—	—	—
1992-93	U. Minnesota	WCHA	42	21	20	41	80	—	—	—	—	—
1993-94	U. Minnesota	WCHA	41	20	16	45	94	—	—	—	—	—

JAMIE RAM
GOALTENDER
5'11"   175 lbs.   Catches Left
Born: January 18, 1971, Scarborough, Ontario
Obtained in Entry Draft, June 22, 1991, 10th round choice, number 213 overall.

Season	Club	Lea.	GP	G	A	PTS	PIM	GP	G	A	PTS	PIM
1990-91	Michigan Tech.	WCHA	14	5	9	0	4.14	—	—	—	—	—
1991-92	Michigan Tech.	WCHA	23	9	9	1	4.35	—	—	—	—	—
1992-93	Michigan Tech.	WCHA	36	16	14	5	3.32	—	—	—	—	—
1993-94	Michigan Tech.	WCHA	39	12	20	5	3.20	—	—	—	—	—

IN THE SYSTEM

SHAWN REID
DEFENSE
6'0"   200 lbs.   Shoots Left
Born: September 21, 1970, Toronto, Ontario
Signed as a free agent on July 6, 1994

				Regular Season				Playoffs				
Season	Club	Lea.	GP	G	A	PTS	PIM	GP	G	A	PTS	PIM
1990-91	Colorado	WCHA	38	10	8	18	36	—	—	—	—	—
1991-92	Colorado	WCHA	41	12	22	34	64	—	—	—	—	—
1992-93	Colorado	WCHA	32	3	11	14	54	—	—	—	—	—
1993-94	Colorado	WCHA	39	7	20	27	28	—	—	—	—	—

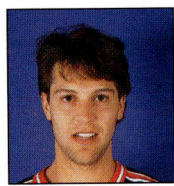

BARRY RICHTER
DEFENSE
6'2"   195 lbs.   Shoots Left
Born: September 11, 1970, Madison, Wisconsin
Obtained from the Hartford Whalers along with Nick Kypreos, Steve Larmer and a 1994 sixth round draft pick (Yuri Litvinov) for James Patrick and Darren Turcotte. Originally drafted by Hartford as their second round pick, 32nd overall, in the 1988 NHL Entry Draft.

				Regular Season				Playoffs				
Season	Club	Lea.	GP	G	A	PTS	PIM	GP	G	A	PTS	PIM
1989-90	Wisconsin	WCHA	42	13	23	36	36	—	—	—	—	—
1990-91	Wisconsin	WCHA	43	15	20	35	42	—	—	—	—	—
1991-92	Wisconsin	WCHA	39	10	25	35	62	—	—	—	—	—
1992-93	Wisconsin	WCHA	42	14	32	46	74	—	—	—	—	—
1993-94	Binghamton	AHL	21	0	9	9	12	—	—	—	—	—
1993-94	U.S. Olympic Team		8	0	3	3	4	—	—	—	—	—
1993-94	U.S. National Team		56	7	16	23	50	—	—	—	—	—

JEAN-YVES ROY
RIGHT WING
5'10"   180 lbs.   Shoots Left
Born: February 17, 1969, Rosemere, Quebec
Signed as a free agent on July 20, 1992.

				Regular Season				Playoffs				
Season	Club	Lea.	GP	G	A	PTS	PIM	GP	G	A	PTS	PIM
1989-90	Univ. of Maine	H.E.	46	39	26	65	52	—	—	—	—	—
1990-91	Univ. of Maine	H.E.	43	37	45	82	62	—	—	—	—	—
1991-92	Univ. of Maine	H.E.	35	32	24	56	62	—	—	—	—	—
1992-93	Binghamton	AHL	49	13	15	28	21	14	5	2	7	4
1992-93	Canadian National Team		23	9	6	15	35	—	—	—	—	—
1993-94	Binghamton	AHL	65	41	24	65	33	—	—	—	—	—
1993-94	Canadian Olympic Team		8	1	0	1	0	—	—	—	—	—
1993-94	Canadian National Team		6	3	2	5	2	—	—	—	—	—

ANDY SILVERMAN
DEFENSE
6'3"   205 lbs.   Shoots Left
Born: August 23, 1972, Beverly, Massachusetts
Obtained in Entry Draft, June 16, 1990; 11th round choice, number 181 overall.

				Regular Season				Playoffs				
Season	Club	Lea.	GP	G	A	PTS	PIM	GP	G	A	PTS	PIM
1991-92	Univ. of Maine	H.E.	30	2	9	11	18	—	—	—	—	—
1992-93	Univ. of Maine	H.E.	37	1	7	8	56	—	—	—	—	—
1993-94	Univ. of Maine	H.E.	35	0	3	3	80	—	—	—	—	—

IN THE SYSTEM

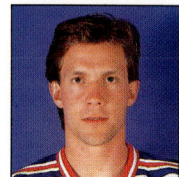

DAVE SMITH
CENTER
6'1"   180 lbs.   Shoots Left
Born: November 21, 1968, Arthur, Ontario
Signed as a free agent on September 9, 1994.

				Regular Season				Playoffs			
Season	Club	Lea.	GP	G	A	PTS	PIM	GP	G	A	PTS	PIM
1988-89	Ohio State	CCHA	21	5	7	12	26	—	—	—	—	—
1989-90	Ohio State	CCHA	35	19	16	35	76	—	—	—	—	—
1990-91	Ohio State	CCHA	34	11	19	30	115	—	—	—	—	—
1991-92	Ohio State	CCHA	36	22	41	63	181	—	—	—	—	—
1992-93	Fort Wayne	IHL	25	7	6	13	77	10	4	5	9	46
1993-94	Fort Wayne	IHL	65	22	22	44	196	18	2	6	8	68

DIMITRI STAROSTENKO
RIGHT WING
6'0"   195 lbs.   Shoots Left
Born: March 18, 1973, Minsk, Russia
Obtained in Entry Draft, June 20, 1992, fifth round choice, number 120 overall.

				Regular Season				Playoffs			
Season	Club	Lea.	GP	G	A	PTS	PIM	GP	G	A	PTS	PIM
1990-91	CSKA	USSR	20	2	1	3	—	—	—	—	—	—
1991-92	CSKA	CIS	32	3	1	4	12	—	—	—	—	—
1992-93	CSKA	CIS	42	15	12	27	22	—	—	—	—	—
1993-94	Binghamton	AHL	41	12	9	21	10	—	—	—	—	—

MICHAEL STEWART
DEFENSE
6'2"   208 lbs.   Shoots Left
Born: May 30, 1972, Calgary, Alberta
Obtained in Entry Draft, June 16, 1990; first round choice, number 13 overall.

				Regular Season				Playoffs			
Season	Club	Lea.	GP	G	A	PTS	PIM	GP	G	A	PTS	PIM
1989-90	Michigan State	CCHA	40	2	6	8	39	—	—	—	—	—
1990-91	Michigan State	CCHA	37	3	12	15	58	—	—	—	—	—
1991-92	Michigan State	CCHA	8	1	3	4	6	—	—	—	—	—
1992-93	Binghamton	AHL	68	2	10	12	71	1	0	0	0	0
1993-94	Binghamton	AHL	79	8	42	50	75	—	—	—	—	—

DARCY WERENKA
DEFENSE
6'1"   205 lbs.   Shoots Right
Born: May 13, 1973, Edmonton, Alberta
Obtained in Entry Draft, June 22 1991, second round, number 37 overall.

				Regular Season				Playoffs			
Season	Club	Lea.	GP	G	A	PTS	PIM	GP	G	A	PTS	PIM
1990-91	Lethbridge	WHL	72	13	37	50	39	16	1	7	8	4
1991-92	Lethbridge	WHL	69	17	58	75	56	5	2	1	3	0
1992-93	Binghamton	AHL	3	0	1	1	2	3	0	0	0	0
1992-93	Brandon	WHL	55	8	42	50	31	3	0	0	0	2
1993-94	Binghamton	AHL	53	5	22	27	10	—	—	—	—	—

MSG NETWORK BROADCAST TEAM

Marv Albert

John Davidson

Sal Messina

Howie Rose

Sam Rosen

Al Trautwig

Away from the ice and up in the broadcast booth, the Rangers have another star-studded lineup. Whether on radio or on television, at home or on the road, the Rangers are well-covered in the talent department by: Marv Albert, John Davidson, Sal Messina, Howie Rose, Sam Rosen and Al Trautwig.

Follow the Rangers-and their off-ice lineup-all season long on Madison Square Garden Network and MSG Radio, including WFAN-Radio (660-AM) and WEVD (1050). Consult your local radio and television listings for games being carried, game times, and station information.

NEW YORK RANGERS 1994

Name-Round/Overall-Position/Shoots-Ht.-Wt.-Birthdate-Birthplace

DAN CLOUTIER
1/26   G/L   6-1   182   4/22/76   Mont-Laurier, Quebec

Posted a 28-14-6 record with a 3.56 goals against average in 55 games with the Sault Ste. Marie Greyhounds of the Ontario Hockey League ... His 28 wins were tied for second in the league, while his 3.56 GAA placed seventh ... Appeared in 14 playoff matches, notching a 10-4 record along with a 3.75 GAA ... Was ranked third among goaltenders by Central Scouting ... Became the first goaltender ever to be drafted by the Rangers in the first round ... Is a "stand-up" goaltender who positions himself well and has a quick glove hand according to Central Scouting reports ... Played in 12 games with Sault Ste. Marie last season in his first year in the OHL helping the Greyhounds to the Memorial Cup ... Was the Greyhounds first choice, 15th overall in the 1992 OHL draft ... Lists Patrick Roy and Mario Lemieux as his idols ... Dan's older brother, Sylvain, was chosen by Detroit, 70th overall in 1990 ... Was coached for the last two years by former NHL defenseman Ted Nolan who played three seasons with Detroit and Pittsburgh ... Placed second an OHL coaches poll as the league's most improved player in 1993-94 ... Teammate at Sault Ste. Marie with Rangers 1993 fifth round draft choice Gary Roach. ... Enjoys playing baseball in the off-season.

RUDOLF VERCIK
2/52   LW/L   6-1   191   3/19/76   Bratislava, Slovakia

Improved steadily as the season progressed, skating in 17 games for Slovan Bratislava in the Slovakian Elite League ... Played for both the under 18 and under 20 junior national teams and also appeared in two games for the Slovak Republic senior national team ... Is a skilled forward with good hands and exceptional skating ability ... Outstanding skating speed and agility allows him to beat defenders to the outside ... Is considered by scouts to be the best skater among all European players selected in this year's draft ... Should play for the Slovak National Team next season, according to the team's coach, Julius Supler ... Lists Washington Capitals forward Peter Bondra as his favorite NHL player ... Was teammates last season at Bratislava with former NHL forward, Anton Stastny ... Peter Stastny also appeared in four games with the club in 1993-94 ... Was also teammates and linemates with the Rangers 10th round draft selection, Radoslav Kropac ... Has an excellent work ethic and is well respected by his older teammates.

Neil Smith and Larry Pleau welcome Dan Cloutier, the Rangers first round selection in the 1994 Entry Draft.

ENTRY DRAFT SELECTIONS

Name-Round/Overall-Position/Shoots-Ht.-Wt.-Birthdate-Birthplace

ADAM SMITH
3/78　　　　D/L　　　6-0　　190　　4/24/76　　　　Digby, Nova Scotia

Has played the last two seasons with the Tacoma Rockets of the Western Hockey League ... A "defensive" defenseman, Smith tallied four goals and 19 assists for 23 points in 66 games with Tacoma ... Is a good skater with agility, balance and lateral movement ... Was a member of Canada's Under 18 team ... Finishes his checks and uses his strength well along the boards and in the corners ... Is an above average passer who moves the puck effectively out of his own end ... Earned honors as the Scholastic Player of the Year in the British Columbia Junior Hockey League in 1992 as a member of the Kelowna Spartans in Junior A Tier 2 ... Lists Ray Bourque his favorite NHL player ... Teammates with the Rangers 11th round selection, Jamie Butt ... Works extremely hard in the off-season with weight training and aerobic exercise.

ALEXANDER KOROBOLIN
4/100　　　　D/L　　　6-2　　189　　3/12/76　　　　Chelyabinsk, Russia

Began last season with Tractor Chelyabinsk in the Russian Elite League and finished with Mechel ... A physical defenseman who plays a North American style game ... Continually improved his skating throughout the year ... Skates with a long, powerful stride ... Plays a sound positional game and uses his partner well ... Reads plays well and has the ability to make a good breakout pass ... Was teammates at Chelyabinsk with the Rangers 1993 11th round draft selection, Maxim Smelnitski.

SYLVAIN BLOUIN
4/104　　　　D/L　　　6-2　　216　　5/21/74　　　　Montreal, Quebec

Strong, physical defenseman led the Quebec Major Junior Hockey League with 492 penalty minutes playing for the Laval Titans ... Collected 18 goals and 22 assists for 40 points in 62 matches ... Led the QMJHL with 177 penalty minutes in four playoff matches ... Played in all game situations, including power play and penalty killing ... Played as a forward in front of the net on the power play ... Placed second in the league with 373 penalty minutes in 1992-93, while notching 10 assists in 68 matches.

MARTIN ETHIER
5/130　　　　D/R　　　6-1　　180　　9/3/76　　　　Ste. Eustache, Quebec

Tallied four goals and 19 assists for 23 points along with 53 penalty minutes with the Beauport Harfangs in the Quebec Major Junior Hockey League ... Is an above average skater with good lateral movement ... Has a long reach which he uses effectively ... Has excellent work habits at home and on the road and during practice according to Beauport coach Joseph Canale ... Has a hard, accurate shot from the point ... Nickname is E.T. ... Enjoys playing tennis, golf and baseball during the off-season ... Admires Ray Bourque and former Washington Capitals defenseman Rod Langway ... Trains at Olympic speedskater Gaetan Boucher's school in the summer.

YURI LITVINOV
6/135　　　　C/L　　　5-10　165　　4/11/76　　　　Donetsk, Russia

Tallied five goals and six assists in 42 games with Krylja Sovetov in his first season in the Russian Elite League ... Plays on the same team as Rangers center Sergei Nemchinov played for ... Is a two-way type center with above average skating and stickhandling ability ... Stickhandles well in traffic and moves the puck quickly at the right time ... Combines finesse and physical game very well according to Central Scouting reports ... Played on the first two lines and on the power play unit ... Missed the European Junior tournament due to a hand injury ... Is good friends with Oleg Tverdovsky who was selected in the first round, second overall by Anaheim ... Grew up in Ukraine and left for Moscow at age 14 to improve his hockey skills ... Played for Russia at the 1993 Pacific Cup and finished 10th overall in scoring with two goals and four assists.

NEW YORK RANGERS 1994

Name-Round/Overall-Position/Shoots-Ht.-Wt.-Birthdate-Birthplace

DAVID BROSSEAU
6/156   C/R   6-1   190   1/16/76   Montreal, Quebec

Collected 27 goals and 26 assists for 53 points in 65 matches with the Shawinigan Cataractes in the Quebec Major Junior Hockey League ... Placed seventh on the club in scoring ... Notched 10 power play goals and three game-winners ... Is a good strong skater with balance ... Is good at reading plays and getting into position to score ... Has good size and strength and is hard to knock off the puck ... Is a tenacious forechecker who uses his stick effectively ... Enjoys tennis and golf during the off-season ... Lists Mario Lemieux as his idol and likes to emulate Kirk Muller's style of play ... Tallied five goals and four assists in 56 games with Shawinigan in 1992-93.

ALEXEI LAZARENKO
7/182   L/RW/L   5-11   176   1/3/76   Moscow, Russia

Played with the CSKA Moscow Russian Penguins second team last season and has an excellent chance to make the first team this season ... Is a very aggressive forward who played both left and right wing last season and can play all three forward positions ... Has good hands, displaying both scoring and passing skills ... Drives to the net well ... Has very explosive one-on-one moves ... Is a feisty player who can play the physical game.

CRAIG ANDERSON
8/208   D/L   6-1   171   1/6/76   Minneapolis, Minnesota

Offensive defenseman tallied 24 goals and 18 assists for 42 points in 24 games with Park Center High School in Minnesota ... Is a smooth skater with speed and acceleration and good all around mobility ... Possesses a hard accurate shot with a quick release ... Handles the puck well and can beat opponents one-on-one ... Plays with poise and confidence, using his size and strength to his advantage ... Also captained soccer and golf teams in high school and made the all-conference team in soccer ... Will attend the University of Wisconsin this fall.

VITALI YEREMEYEV
9/209   G/L   5-10   167   9/23/75   Ust-Kamenogorsk, Kazakstan

Appeared in 19 games for Torpedo Ust-Kamenogorsk, playing 1015 minutes, allowing 38 goals for a 2.24 goals against average ... Grew up in Ust-Kamenogorsk, a small town in Kazakstan, 300 kilometers from the Chinese border ... Is a "butterfly" style goaltender with quick reflexes ... Signed with the Russian Penguins following last season and will compete for one of the top two goalie positions on the club.

ERIC BOULTON
9/234   LW/L   6-0   201   8/17/76   Halifax, Nova Scotia

Registered four goals and three assists in 45 games in his first season with the Oshawa Generals of the Ontario Hockey League ... Placed second on the club with 149 penalty minutes ... Teammates at Oshawa with the Rangers 1993 ninth round draft selection Ken Shepard.

ENTRY DRAFT SELECTIONS

Name-Round/Overall-Position/Shoots-Ht.-Wt.-Birthdate-Birthplace

RADOSLAV KROPAC
10/260   RW/L   6-0   187   4/5/75   Bratislava, Slovakia

Tallied seven goals and six assists in 33 matches with Slovan Bratislava ... Played right wing on a line with the Rangers 1994 second round draft choice Rudolf Vercik ... Is a grinding type forward with good forechecking and defensive skills ... Played last season on the team's top penalty killing unit ... Is an above average skater and keeps himself in excellent physical condition ... Teammates at Slovan Bratislava with former NHL forward Anton Stastny ... Peter Stastny also appeared in four games with the club last season.

JAMIE BUTT
11/267   LW/L   5-11   180   4/4/76   Richmond, British Columbia

Collected eight goals and 13 assists for 21 points in 64 games with the Tacoma Rockets of the Western Hockey League ... Placed third on the club with 214 penalty minutes ... Is good defensive, forechecking forward ... Is willing to play the physical game and works hard along the boards and in the corners ... Teammates at Tacoma with the Rangers third round selection in 1994 Adam Smith ... Appeared in 21 games for Tacoma in 1992-93.

KIM JOHNSSON
11/286   D\L   6-1   175   3/16/76   Malmo, Sweden

Played last season for the Swedish Junior National Team and Malmo in the Swedish Elite League ... Is versatile defenseman who can play an offensive or defensive style ... Is extremely well conditioned and is known for his extensive training habits ... Is a good passer with the ability to play the point on the power play ... Was the 286th selection in the Entry Draft, the latest selection in Rangers history.

Neil Smith and Christer Rockstrom greet Rudolf Vercik, the Rangers second round selection in the 1994 Entry Draft.

NEW YORK RANGERS

Player	Height	Weight	Shoots	Place of Birth
Forwards:				
Duncanson, Craig	6-0	200	L	Sudbury, Ontario
Gernander, Ken	5-10	180	L	Coleraine, Minnesota
Graves, Adam	6-0	205	L	Toronto, Ontario
Gilbert, Greg	6-1	195	L	Mississauga, Ontario
Hartman, Mike	6-0	195	L	Detroit, Michigan
Hiller, Jim	6-0	200	R	Port Alberni, B.C.
Hudson, Mike	6-1	205	L	Guelph, Ontario
Kenny, Rob	6-1	200	L	Bronx, New York
Kocur, Joe	6-0	205	R	Calgary, Alberta
Kovalev, Alexei	6-0	205	L	Moscow, Russia
Kudinov, Andrei	6-0	195	L	Chelyabinsk, CIS
Kypreos, Nick	6-0	205	L	Toronto, Ontario
Langdon, Darren	6-1	205	L	Deer Lake, Newfoundland
Larmer, Steve	5-11	195	L	Peterborough, Ontario
Matteau, Stephane	6-3	210	L	Rouyn Noranda, Quebec
McCosh, Shawn	6-0	190	R	Oshawa, Ontario
McLaughlin, Mike	6-1	205	L	Springfield, Massachusetts
Messier, Mark	6-1	205	L	Edmonton, Alberta
Nedved, Petr	6-3	195	L	Liberec, Czechoslovakia
Nielsen, Jeff	6-0	200	R	Grand Rapids, Minnesota
Nemchinov, Sergei	6-0	200	L	Moscow, Russia
Noonan, Brian	6-1	200	R	Boston, Massachusetts
Olczyk, Eddie	6-1	205	L	Chicago, Illinois
Osborne, Mark	6-2	200	L	Toronto, Ontario
Roy, Jean-Yves	5-10	180	L	Rosemere, Quebec
Smith, Dave	6-1	180	L	Arthur, Ontario
Starostenko, Dimitri	6-0	195	L	Minsk, Russia
Defensemen:				
Beukeboom, Jeff	6-5	230	R	Ajax, Ontario
Cairns, Eric	6-5	225	L	Oakville, Ontario
Featherstone, Glen	6-4	212	L	Toronto, Ontario
Fiorentino, Peter	6-1	200	R	Niagara Falls, Ontario
Karpovtsev, Alexander	6-1	200	R	Moscow, Russia
Leetch, Brian	5-11	190	L	Corpus Christi, Texas
Lowe, Kevin	6-2	190	L	Lachute, Quebec
Malone, Scott	6-0	195	L	South Boston, Massachusetts
Messier, Joby	6-0	200	R	Regina, Saskatchewan
Norstrom, Mattias	6-1	205	L	Mora, Sweden
Reid, Shawn	6-0	200	L	Toronto, Ontario
Richter, Barry	6-2	195	L	Madison, Wisconsin
Silverman, Andy	6-3	205	L	Beverly, Massachusetts
Stewart, Micheal	6-2	208	L	Calgary, Alberta
Wells, Jay	6-1	210	L	Paris, Ontario
Werenka, Darcy	6-1	205	R	Edmonton, Alberta
Zubov, Sergei	6-1	200	R	Moscow, Russia
Goaltenders			**Catches**	
Healy, Glenn	5-10	185	L	Pickering, Ontario
Hillebrandt, Jon	5-10	185	L	Cottage Grove, Wisconsin
Hirsch, Corey	5-10	160	L	Medicine Hat, Alberta
Ram, Jamie	5-11	175	L	Scarborough, Ontario
Richter, Mike	5-11	185	L	Abington, Pennsylvania

1994-95 ROSTER

		1993-94 Regular Season Statistics				
Birthdate	**1993-94 Team**	**GP**	**G**	**A**	**PTS**	**PIM**
3/17/67	Binghamton (AHL)	70	25	44	69	83
6/30/69	Moncton (AHL)	71	22	25	47	12
4/12/68	N.Y. Rangers	84	52	27	89	127
1/22/62	N.Y. Rangers	76	4	11	15	29
2/7/67	N.Y. Rangers	35	1	1	2	70
5/15/69	N.Y. Rangers	2	0	0	0	7
	Binghamton (AHL)	67	27	34	61	61
2/6/67	N.Y. Rangers	48	4	7	11	47
10/19/68	Binghamton (AHL)	63	27	14	41	90
12/21/64	N.Y. Rangers	71	2	1	3	129
2/24/73	N.Y. Rangers	76	23	33	56	154
6/28/70	Binghamton (AHL)	25	3	3	6	6
6/4/66	N.Y. Rangers	46	3	5	8	102
	Hartford	10	0	0	0	37
1/8/71	Binghamton (AHL)	54	2	7	9	327
6/16/61	N.Y. Rangers	68	21	39	60	41
9/2/69	N.Y. Rangers	12	4	3	7	2
	Chicago	65	15	16	31	55
6/5/69	Binghamton (AHL)	75	31	44	75	68
3/29/70	Binghamton (AHL)	56	11	13	24	33
1/18/61	N.Y. Rangers	76	26	58	84	76
12/9/71	St. Louis	19	6	14	20	8
	Canadian Olympic Team	8	5	1	6	6
	Canadian National Team	17	19	12	31	16
9/20/71	Minnesota (WCHA)	41	29	16	45	94
1/14/64	N.Y. Rangers	76	22	27	49	36
5/29/65	N.Y. Rangers	12	4	2	6	12
	Chicago	64	14	21	35	57
8/16/66	N.Y. Rangers	37	3	5	8	28
8/13/61	Toronto	73	9	15	24	145
2/17/69	Binghamton (AHL)	65	41	24	65	33
	Canadian Olympic Team	8	1	0	1	0
	Canadian National Team	6	3	2	5	2
11/21/68	Fort Wayne (IHL)	65	22	22	44	196
3/18/73	Binghamton (AHL)	41	12	9	21	10
3/28/65	N.Y. Rangers	68	8	8	16	170
6/27/74	Detroit (OHL)	59	7	35	42	204
7/8/68	Boston	58	1	8	9	152
12/22/68	Binghamton (AHL)	68	7	15	22	220
4/7/70	N.Y. Rangers	67	3	15	18	58
3/3/68	N.Y. Rangers	84	23	56	79	67
4/15/59	N.Y. Rangers	71	5	14	19	70
1/16/71	New Hampshire (HE)	40	14	6	20	162
3/2/70	N.Y. Rangers	4	0	2	2	0
	Binghamton (AHL)	42	6	14	20	58
1/2/72	N.Y. Rangers	9	0	2	2	6
	Binghamton (AHL)	55	1	9	10	70
9/21/70	Colorado (WCHA)	39	7	20	27	28
9/11/70	Binghamton (AHL)	21	0	9	9	12
	U.S. Olympic Team	8	0	3	3	4
	U.S. National Team	56	7	16	23	50
8/23/72	Maine (HE)	35	0	3	3	80
5/30/72	Binghamton (AHL)	79	8	42	50	75
5/18/59	N.Y. Rangers	79	2	7	9	110
5/13/73	Binghamton (AHL)	53	5	22	27	10
7/22/70	N.Y. Rangers	78	12	77	89	39
		GP	**W**	**L**	**T**	**AVG**
8/23/62	N.Y. Rangers	29	10	12	2	3.03
12/18/71	Binghamton (AHL)	7	1	3	0	3.67
	U.S. National Team	2	1	1	0	3.92
7/1/72	Binghamton (AHL)	10	5	4	1	3.73
	U.S. Olympic Team	8	5	2	1	2.35
	U.S. National Team	37	19	15	2	2.80
1/18/71	Michigan Tech. (WCHA)	39	12	20	5	3.20
9/22/66	N.Y. Rangers	68	42	12	6	2.57

SEASON IN REVIEW

NATIONAL HOCKEY LEAGUE FINAL STANDINGS

EASTERN CONFERENCE

Northeast Division

	GP	W	L	T	GF	GA	PTS	PCTG
PITTSBURGH	84	44	27	13	299	285	101	.601
BOSTON	84	42	29	13	289	252	97	.577
MONTREAL	84	41	29	14	283	248	96	.571
BUFFALO	84	43	32	9	282	218	95	.565
QUEBEC	84	34	42	8	277	292	76	.452
HARTFORD	84	27	48	9	227	288	63	.375
OTTAWA	84	14	61	9	201	397	37	.220

Atlantic Division

	GP	W	L	T	GF	GA	PTS	PCTG
NY RANGERS	**84**	**52**	**24**	**8**	**299**	**231**	**112**	**.667**
NEW JERSEY	84	47	25	12	306	220	106	.631
WASHINGTON	84	39	35	10	277	263	88	.524
NY ISLANDERS	84	36	36	12	282	264	84	.500
FLORIDA	84	33	34	17	233	233	83	.494
PHILADELPHIA	84	35	39	10	294	314	80	.476
TAMPA BAY	84	30	43	11	224	251	71	.423

WESTERN CONFERENCE

Central Division

	GP	W	L	T	GF	GA	PTS	PCTG
DETROIT	84	46	30	8	356	275	100	.595
TORONTO	84	43	29	12	280	243	98	.583
DALLAS	84	42	29	13	286	265	97	.577
ST LOUIS	84	40	33	11	270	283	91	.542
CHICAGO	84	39	36	9	254	240	87	.518
WINNIPEG	84	24	51	9	245	344	57	.339

Pacific Division

	GP	W	L	T	GF	GA	PTS	PCTG
CALGARY	84	42	29	13	302	256	97	.577
VANCOUVER	84	41	40	3	279	276	85	.506
SAN JOSE	84	33	35	16	252	265	82	.488
ANAHEIM	84	33	46	5	229	251	71	.423
LOS ANGELES	84	27	45	12	294	322	66	.393
EDMONTON	84	25	45	14	261	305	64	.381

TEAM STANDINGS BY CONFERENCE

EASTERN CONFERENCE

	GP	W	L	T	GF	GA	PTS	PCTG
NY RANGERS	**84**	**52**	**24**	**8**	**299**	**231**	**112**	**.667**
NEW JERSEY	84	47	25	12	306	220	106	.631
PITTSBURGH	84	44	27	13	299	285	101	.601
BOSTON	84	42	29	13	289	252	97	.577
MONTREAL	84	41	29	14	283	248	96	.571
BUFFALO	84	43	32	9	282	218	95	.565
WASHINGTON	84	39	35	10	277	263	88	.524
NY ISLANDERS	84	36	36	12	282	264	84	.500
FLORIDA	84	33	34	17	233	233	83	.494
PHILADELPHIA	84	35	39	10	294	314	80	.476
QUEBEC	84	34	42	8	277	292	76	.452
TAMPA BAY	84	30	43	11	224	251	71	423
HARTFORD	84	27	48	9	227	288	63	.375
OTTAWA	84	14	61	9	201	397	37	.220

WESTERN CONFERENCE

	GP	W	L	T	GF	GA	PTS	PCTG
DETROIT	84	46	30	8	356	275	100	.595
TORONTO	84	43	29	12	280	243	98	.583
CALGARY	84	42	29	13	302	256	97	.577
DALLAS	84	42	29	13	286	265	97	.577
ST LOUIS	84	40	33	11	270	283	91	.542
CHICAGO	84	39	36	9	254	240	87	.518
VANCOUVER	84	41	40	3	279	276	85	.506
SAN JOSE	84	33	35	16	252	265	82	.488
ANAHEIM	84	33	46	5	229	251	71	.423
LOS ANGELES	84	27	45	12	294	322	66	.393
EDMONTON	84	25	45	14	261	305	64	.381
WINNIPEG	84	24	51	9	245	344	57	.339

LEAGUE LEADERS

INDIVIDUAL SCORING LEADERS
FOR ART ROSS TROPHY

PLAYER	TEAM	GP	G	A	PTS
Wayne Gretzky	Los Angeles	81	38	92	130
Sergei Fedorov	Detroit	82	56	64	120
Adam Oates	Boston	77	32	80	112
Doug Gilmour	Toronto	83	27	84	111
Pavel Bure	Vancouver	76	60	47	107
Jeremy Roenick	Chicago	84	46	61	107
Mark Recchi	Philadelphia	84	40	67	107
Brendan Shanahan	St. Louis	81	52	50	102
Jaromir Jagr	Pittsburgh	80	32	67	99
Dave Andreychuk	Toronto	83	53	45	98
Brett Hull	St. Louis	81	57	40	97
Eric Lindros	Philadelphia	65	44	53	97
Rod Brind'Amour	Philadelphia	84	35	62	97
Pierre Turgeon	NY Islanders	69	38	56	94
Ray Sheppard	Detroit	82	52	41	93
Mike Modano	Dallas	76	50	43	93
Robert Reichel	Calgary	84	40	53	93
Ron Francis	Pittsburgh	82	27	66	93
Joe Sakic	Quebec	84	28	64	92
Vincent Damphousse	Montreal	84	40	51	91
Ray Bourque	Boston	72	20	71	91
Sergei Zubov	**NY Rangers**	**78**	**12**	**77**	**89**
Kevin Stevens	Pittsburgh	83	41	47	88
Luc Robitaille	Los Angeles	83	44	42	86
Dale Hawerchuk	Buffalo	81	35	51	86

Sergei Zubov placed 22nd among the scoring leaders with 89 points.

Adam Graves tied for fifth in goal scoring with 52 goals.

GOAL SCORING

NAME	TEAM	GP	G
Pavel Bure	Vancouver	76	60
Brett Hull	St. Louis	81	57
Sergei Fedorov	Detroit	82	56
Dave Andreychuk	Toronto	83	53
Brendan Shanahan	St. Louis	81	52
Ray Sheppard	Detroit	82	52
Adam Graves	**NY Rangers**	**84**	**52**
Cam Neely	Boston	49	50
Mike Modano	Dallas	76	50
Wendel Clark	Toronto	64	46
Jeremy Roenick	Chicago	84	46
Eric Lindros	Philadelphia	65	44
Luc Robitaille	Los Angeles	83	44
Steve Thomas	NY Islanders	78	42

ASSISTS

NAME	TEAM	GP	A
Wayne Gretzky	Los Angeles	81	92
Doug Gilmour	Toronto	83	84
Adam Oates	Boston	77	80
Sergei Zubov	**NY Rangers**	**78**	**77**
Ray Bourque	Boston	72	71
Craig Janney	St. Louis	69	68
Jaromir Jagr	Pittsburgh	80	67
Mark Recchi	Philadelphia	84	67
Joe Juneau	Bos-Wsh	74	66
Ron Francis	Pittsburgh	82	66
Sergei Fedorov	Detroit	82	64
Joe Sakic	Quebec	84	64
Paul Coffey	Detroit	80	63
Rod Brind'Amour	Philadelphia	84	62

Wayne Gretzky led the NHL with 92 assists.

LEAGUE LEADERS

DEFENSEMEN SCORING LEADERS

PLAYER	TEAM	GP	G	A	PTS
Ray Bourque	Boston	72	20	71	91
Sergei Zubov	**NY Rangers**	**78**	**12**	**77**	**89**
Al MacInnis	Calgary	75	28	54	82
Brian Leetch	**NY Rangers**	**84**	**23**	**56**	**79**
Scott Stevens	New Jersey	83	18	60	78
Paul Coffey	Detroit	80	14	63	77
Larry Murphy	Pittsburgh	84	17	56	73
Garry Galley	Philadelphia	81	10	60	70
Rob Blake	Los Angeles	84	20	48	68
Jeff Brown	St.L-Van	74	14	52	66

ROOKIE SCORING LEADERS

PLAYER	TEAM	GP	G	A	PTS
Mikael Renberg	Philadelphia	83	38	44	82
Alexei Yahin	Ottawa	83	30	49	79
Jason Arnott	Edmonton	78	33	35	68
Derek Plante	Buffalo	77	21	35	56
Bryan Smolinski	Boston	83	31	20	51
Alexandre Daigle	Ottawa	84	20	31	51
Jesse Belanger	Florida	70	17	33	50
Chris Gratton	Tampa Bay	84	13	29	42
Iain Fraser	Quebec	60	17	20	37
Boris Mironov	Wpg-Edm	79	7	24	31

Brian Leetch placed fourth among defensemen in scoring with 79 points.

GOALTENDING LEADERS

GOALS AGAINST AVERAGE

GOALTENDER	TEAM	GPI	MINS	GA	AVG
Dominik Hasek	Buffalo	58	3358	109	1.95
Martin Brodeur	New Jersey	47	2625	105	2.40
Patrick Roy	Montreal	68	3867	161	2.50
John Vanbiesbrouck	Florida	57	3440	145	2.53
Mike Richter	**NY Rangers**	**68**	**3710**	**159**	**2.57**

WINS

GOALTENDER	TEAM	GPI	MINS	W	L	T
Mike Richter	**NY Rangers**	**68**	**3710**	**42**	**12**	**6**
Ed Belfour	Chicago	70	3998	37	24	6
Curtis Joseph	St. Louis	71	4127	36	23	11
Patrick Roy	Montreal	68	3867	35	17	11
Felix Potvin	Toronto	66	3883	34	22	9

Mike Richter led the NHL with 42 wins.

SAVE PERCENTAGE

GOALTENDER	TEAM	GPI	MINS	GA	SA	SPCTG	W	L	T
Dominik Hasek	Buffalo	58	3358	109	1552	.930	30	20	6
John Vanbiesbrouck	Florida	57	3440	145	1912	.924	21	25	11
Patrick Roy	Montreal	68	3867	161	1956	.918	35	17	11
Martin Brodeur	New Jersey	47	2625	105	1238	.915	27	11	8
Mark Fitzpatrick	Florida	28	1603	73	844	.913	12	8	6

SHUTOUTS

GOALTENDER	TEAM	GPI	MINS	SO	W	L	T
Dominik Hasek	Buffalo	58	3358	7	30	20	6
Patrick Roy	Montreal	68	3867	7	35	17	11
Ed Belfour	Chicago	70	3998	7	37	24	6
Ron Hextall	NY Islanders	65	3581	5	27	26	6
Mike Richter	**NY Rangers**	**68**	**3710**	**5**	**42**	**12**	**6**

FINAL SCORING

POS	NO.	PLAYER		GP	G	A	PTS	+/-	PIM	PP	SH	GW	GT	S	PCTG
D	21	Sergei Zubov		78	12	77	89	20	39	9	0	1	0	222	5.4
C	11	Mark Messier		76	26	58	84	25	76	6	2	5	0	216	12.0
LW	9	Adam Graves		84	52	27	79	27	127	20	4	4	1	291	17.9
D	2	Brian Leetch		84	23	56	79	28	67	17	1	4	0	328	7.0
RW	28	Steve Larmer		68	21	39	60	14	41	6	4	7	0	146	14.4
C	27	Alexei Kovalev		76	23	33	56	18	154	7	0	3	0	184	12.5
LW	10	Esa Tikkanen		83	22	32	54	5	114	5	3	4	0	257	8.6
C	13	Sergei Nemchinov		76	22	27	49	13	36	4	0	6	0	144	15.3
RW	36	Glenn Anderson	TOR	73	17	18	35	6-	50	5	0	3	0	127	13.4
			NYR	12	4	2	6	1	12	2	0	0	0	22	18.2
			TOTAL	85	21	20	41	5-	62	7	0	3	0	149	14.1
RW	16	Brian Noonan	CHI	64	14	21	35	2	57	8	0	3	1	134	10.4
			NYR	12	4	2	6	5	12	2	0	3	0	26	15.4
			TOTAL	76	18	23	41	7	69	10	0	6	1	160	11.3
LW	32	Stephane Matteau	CHI	65	15	16	31	10	55	2	0	2	0	113	13.3
			NYR	12	4	3	7	5	2	1	0	0	1	22	18.2
			TOTAL	77	19	19	38	15	57	3	0	2	1	135	14.1
C	14	Craig MacTavish	EDM	66	16	10	26	20-	80	0	0	1	0	97	16.5
			NYR	12	4	3	7	6	11	1	0	1	1	25	16.0
			TOTAL	78	20	13	33	14-	91	1	0	2	1	122	16.4
D	4	Kevin Lowe		71	5	14	19	4	70	0	0	1	0	50	10.0
D	25	*Alexander Karpovtsev		67	3	15	18	12	58	1	0	1	0	78	3.8
D	23	Jeff Beukeboom		68	8	8	16	18	170	1	0	0	0	58	13.8
LW	17	Greg Gilbert		76	4	11	15	3-	29	1	0	0	1	64	6.3
C	15	Mike Hudson		48	4	7	11	5-	47	0	0	1	0	48	8.3
D	24	Jay Wells		79	2	7	9	4	110	0	0	0	0	64	3.1
C	12	Eddie Olczyk		37	3	5	8	1-	28	0	0	1	0	40	7.5
LW	19	Nick Kypreos	HFD	10	0	0	0	8-	37	0	0	0	0	5	.0
			NYR	46	3	5	8	8-	102	0	0	1	0	29	10.3
			TOTAL	56	3	5	8	16-	139	0	0	1	0	34	8.8
RW	26	Joe Kocur		71	2	1	3	9-	129	0	0	0	0	43	4.7
LW	18	Mike Hartman		35	1	1	2	5-	70	0	0	0	0	19	5.3
D	8	*Joby Messier		4	0	2	2	1-	0	0	0	0	0	7	.0
G	30	Glenn Healy		29	0	2	2	0	2	0	0	0	0	0	.0
D	6	Doug Lidster		34	0	2	2	12-	33	0	0	0	0	25	.0
D	5	*Mattias Norstrom		9	0	1	1	0	6	0	0	0	0	3	.0
RW	16	Jim Hiller		2	0	0	0	1	7	0	0	0	0	0	.0
LW	32	*Dan Lacroix		4	0	0	0	0	0	0	0	0	0	0	.0
G	35	Mike Richter		68	0	0	0	0	2	0	0	0	0	0	.0

GOALTENDING RECORDS

NO.	GOALTENDER	GPI	MINS	AVG	W	L	T	EN	SO	GA	SA	SPCTG	G	A	PIM
35	Mike Richter	68	3710	2.57	42	12	6	1	5	159	1758	.910	0	0	2
30	Glenn Healy	29	1368	3.03	10	12	2	2	2	69	567	.878	0	2	2
	NYR TOTALS	84	5089	2.72	52	24	8	3	7	231	2328	.901			

*Indicates Rookie

1993-94 REGULAR SEASON HIGHLIGHTS

Set a franchise record for wins in a season with 52, surpassing the 50 posted in 1991-92.

Establisthed a club record for points in a season with 112, surpassing the 1970-71 and 1971-72 point totals of 109.

Captured the Presidents' Trophy for the second time in the last three years, and have won the division title for the third time in the last five years.

Established a new team record for road victories in one season with 24, surpassing the previous record of 22 in 1991-92. Tied the 1991-92 record of 50 points on the road.

Tied for the second-highest home win total with 28, equalling the 1991-92 team. Nothced the second highest home point total with 62, the highest home point total since 1970-71 when the club record of 67 was achieved.

Improved on last season's point total of 79 by a club record of 33 points. The biggest previous jump had been 25 points in 1966-67 when the team posted 72 after posting 47 in 1965-66.

Improved on last season's win total of 34 by a club record of 18. The biggest previous jump had been 15, from 17 in 1954-55 to 32 in 1955-56.

Set a club record with nine 20-goal scorers, eclipsing the previous mark of eight established in 1972-73 and equalled in 1973-74, 1974-75 and 1983-84.

Posted a 14-game unbeaten streak, going 12-0-2 from October 24 to November 24, tying the fourth longest unbeaten streak in team history and longest since the 1972-73 season.

Notched the third longest road winning streak in team history, winning six consecutive road matches from October 30 to November 24.

Jeff Beukeboom, Stephane Matteau and Steve Larmer.

1993-94 REGULAR SEASON HIGHLIGHTS

Led the NHL with 24 road victories and a .595 winning percentage on the road.

Posted a 16-game home unbeaten streak, going 13-0-3 from October 24 to January 5, recording the fifth longest home unbeaten streak in team history and longest since 1971-72.

Recorded the league's best home record at 28-8-6 along with a .738 winning percentage.

Tied the club mark for best monthly record with an 11-1-1 record in November.

Set a club record for shorthanded goals in a season with 20, surpassing the previous mark of 14, set three times previously, most recently in 1991-92.

Have allowed 231 goals, the fewest the club has given up since allowing 208 in 1972-73.

Posted a 21-8-3 record and a .703 winning percentage vs. their own division, ranking first in the league and ranked second with a 31-16-5 record and .644 winning percentage outside the division.

Had the league's best inter-conference record at 39-16-5 along with a .692 winning percentage.

Ranked first in the NHL on the power play and is ranked third in penalty killing. Tied for the league lead the league with 96 power play goals and ranked first in the NHL with five shorthanded goals allowed (the fewest the club has given up since allowing four in 1985-86). Ranks third with 20 shorthanded goals and were plus 44 on special teams, ranking second in the NHL.

Notched the third-highest single-season power play goal total in team history, seven goals shy of the second-highest mark of 103 set in 1989-90. The club record of 111 was established in 1987-88.

Tallied six power play goals on October 13 vs. Quebec, setting a club record for power play tallies in a game, eclipsing the previous mark of five reached on February 24, 1980 vs. the Islanders and equalled on February 28, 1983 vs. Pittsburgh.

Recorded back-to-back 50-plus shot performances on January 3 vs. Florida (54) and on January 5 vs. Calgary (53), marking the first time New York had accomplished the feat since March 23, 1971 (50 vs. Buffalo) and March 27, 1971 (52 vs. Boston).

Were not outshot in the first 19 games of the season, the longest such streak since the 1972-73 club went 26 consecutive games without being outshot from January 28 to March 25.

Had four representatives in the NHL All-Star Game (Mark Messier, Brian Leetch, Adam Graves and Mike Richter) for the first time since 1972-73 (Ed Giacomin, Brad Park, Jean Ratelle and Gilles Villemure).

Tied the NHL and club record for fastest goal from the start of overtime on February 21 vs. Pittsburgh when Tony Amonte scored at :08 to give the Rangers a 4-3 victory. The win was New York's first overtime win vs. Pittsburgh since March 14, 1987.

Swept season series from New Jersey for the first time since the franchise moved from Denver in 1982. Also swept four-game season series from Toronto, Ottawa and Quebec and two game series from St. Louis, Los Angeles and Toronto.

Defeated the Islanders, 5-4, on March 5 at Long Island, marking the team's first victory at the Nassau Coliseum since October 28, 1989.

SCORING BREAKDOWN

Player	GP	Home G	Home A	Home PTS	GP	Road G	Road A	Road PTS	GP	Total G	Total A	Total PTS	Game Winning G	Game Winning A	Game Winning PTS	Game Tying G	Game Tying A	Game Tying PTS
Anderson (TOR)	35	9	7	16	38	8	11	19	73	17	18	35	3	0	3	0	0	0
Anderson (NYR)	5	2	1	3	7	2	1	3	12	4	2	6	0	1	1	0	0	0
Beukeboom	33	6	5	11	35	2	3	5	68	8	8	16	0	1	1	0	0	0
Gilbert	38	1	7	8	38	3	4	7	76	4	11	15	0	3	3	1	0	1
Graves	42	26	16	42	42	26	11	37	84	52	27	79	4	7	11	1	0	1
Hartman	18	0	1	1	17	1	0	1	35	1	1	2	0	0	0	0	0	0
Healy	9	0	1	1	20	0	1	1	29	0	2	2	0	1	1	0	0	0
Hiller	1	0	0	0	1	0	0	0	2	0	0	0	0	0	0	0	0	0
Hudson	22	3	4	7	26	1	3	4	48	4	7	11	1	0	1	0	1	1
Karpovtsev	28	3	5	8	39	0	10	10	67	3	15	18	1	0	1	0	0	0
Kocur	38	1	1	2	33	1	0	1	71	2	1	3	0	0	0	0	0	0
Kovalev	38	14	17	31	38	9	16	25	76	23	33	56	3	5	8	0	0	0
Kypreos (HFD)	4	0	0	0	6	0	0	0	10	0	0	0	0	0	0	0	0	0
Kypreos (NYR)	22	1	3	4	24	2	2	4	46	3	5	8	1	1	2	0	0	0
Lacroix	3	0	0	0	1	0	0	0	4	0	0	0	0	0	0	0	0	0
Larmer	32	9	16	25	36	12	23	35	68	21	39	60	7	7	14	0	1	1
Leetch	42	9	26	35	42	14	30	44	84	23	56	79	4	6	10	0	0	0
Lidster	21	0	1	1	13	0	1	1	34	0	2	2	0	0	0	0	0	0
Lowe	32	1	5	6	39	4	9	13	71	5	14	19	1	4	5	0	0	0
MacTavish (EDM)	32	10	9	19	34	6	1	7	66	16	10	26	1	0	1	0	0	0
MacTavish (NYR)	5	2	2	4	7	2	0	2	12	4	2	6	1	0	1	1	0	1
Matteau (CHI)	30	8	4	12	33	7	12	19	63	15	16	31	2	0	2	0	0	0
Matteau (NYR)	5	0	1	1	7	4	2	6	12	4	3	7	0	2	2	1	0	1
J. Messier	4	0	2	2	0	0	0	0	4	0	2	2	0	0	0	0	0	0
M. Messier	38	12	34	46	38	14	24	38	76	26	58	84	4	7	11	0	0	0
Nemchinov	39	13	17	30	37	9	10	19	76	22	27	49	6	6	12	0	1	1
Noonan (CHI)	30	6	8	14	34	8	13	21	64	14	21	35	3	0	3	1	0	1
Noonan (NYR)	5	1	2	3	7	3	0	3	12	4	2	6	3	0	3	0	0	0
Norstrom	6	0	2	2	3	0	0	0	9	0	2	2	0	1	1	0	0	0
Olczyk	21	3	3	6	16	0	2	2	37	3	5	8	1	0	1	0	0	0
Richter	39	0	0	0	29	0	0	0	68	0	0	0	0	0	0	0	0	0
Tikkanen	41	11	14	25	42	11	18	29	83	22	32	54	4	2	6	0	2	2
Wells	42	2	4	6	37	0	3	3	79	2	7	9	0	0	0	0	0	0
Zubov	39	5	33	38	39	7	44	51	78	12	77	89	1	20	21	0	1	1

GOALTENDING BREAKDOWN

HOME

	GP	W	L	T	GA	EN	MINS	AVG	SH	SHOTS	SAVES	PERCENTAGE
Healy	9	4	2	0	21	0	391	3.22	0	169	148	.876
Richter	39	24	6	6	90	0	2156	2.50	4	1045	955	.914

ROAD

	GP	W	L	T	GA	EN	MINS	AVG	SH	SHOTS	SAVES	PERCENTAGE
Healy	20	6	10	2	48	2	976	2.95	2	398	350	.879
Richter	29	18	6	0	69	1	1556	2.66	1	713	644	.903

Steve Larmer led the team with seven game winning goals.

Mark Messier collected a team high 46 points at home.

SPECIAL TEAMS SCORING BREAKDOWN

	Power Play			Shorthanded			Even Strength			Total		
	G	A	PTS	G	A	PTS	G	A	PTS	G	A	PTS
Anderson (TOR)	5	6	11	0	0	0	12	12	24	17	18	35
Anderson (NYR)	2	1	3	0	0	0	2	1	3	4	2	6
Beukeboom	1	0	1	0	0	0	7	8	15	8	8	16
Gilbert	1	0	1	0	0	0	3	11	14	4	11	15
Graves	20	8	28	4	1	5	28	18	46	52	27	79
Hartman	0	0	0	0	0	0	1	1	2	1	1	2
Healy	0	0	0	0	1	1	0	1	1	0	2	2
Hudson	0	0	0	0	0	0	4	7	11	4	7	11
Karpovtsev	1	4	5	0	1	1	2	10	12	3	15	18
Kocur	0	0	0	0	0	0	2	1	3	2	1	3
Kovalev	7	6	13	0	0	0	16	27	43	23	33	56
Kypreos (HFD)	0	0	0	0	0	0	0	0	0	0	0	0
Kypreos (NYR)	0	0	0	0	0	0	3	5	8	3	5	8
Lacroix	0	0	0	0	0	0	0	0	0	0	0	0
Larmer	6	15	21	4	2	6	11	22	33	21	39	60
Leetch	17	36	53	1	2	3	5	18	23	23	56	79
Lidster	0	0	0	0	0	0	0	2	2	0	2	2
Lowe	0	2	2	0	3	3	5	9	14	5	14	19
MacTavish (EDM)	0	2	2	0	0	0	16	8	24	16	10	26
MacTavish (NYR)	1	0	1	0	0	0	3	2	5	4	2	6
Matteau (CHI)	2	1	3	0	3	0	13	12	25	15	16	31
Matteau (NYR)	1	0	1	0	0	0	3	3	6	4	3	7
J. Messier	0	0	0	0	0	0	0	2	2	0	2	2
M. Messier	7	30	37	2	7	9	17	21	38	26	58	84
Nemchinov	4	3	7	0	3	3	18	21	39	22	27	49
Noonan (CHI)	8	9	17	0	0	0	6	12	18	14	21	35
Noonan (NYR)	2	0	2	0	0	0	2	2	4	4	2	6
Norstrom	0	0	0	0	0	0	0	2	2	0	2	2
Olczyk	0	0	0	0	0	0	3	5	8	3	5	8
Richter	0	0	0	0	0	0	0	0	0	0	0	0
Tikkanen	5	16	21	3	1	4	14	15	29	22	32	54
Wells	0	0	0	0	0	0	2	7	9	2	7	9
Zubov	9	40	49	0	1	1	3	36	39	12	77	89

Rangers Total Power Play Statistics

HOME				AWAY				TOTAL			
PPGF	ADV	PCTG	RANK	PPGF	ADV	PCTG	RANK	PPGF	ADV	PCTG	RANK
47	210	22.4	7th	49	207	23.7	2nd	96	417	23.0	

Rangers Total Penalty Killing Statistics

HOME				AWAY				TOTAL			
PPGA	TSH	PCTG	RANK	PPGA	TSH	PCTG	RANK	PPGA	TSH	PCTG	RANK
26	202	87.1	1st	41	233	82.4	9th	67	435	84.6	3rd

INDIVIUAL SCORING VS. EACH DIVISION

Player	ATLANTIC GP	G	A	PTS	NORTHEAST GP	G	A	PTS	PACIFIC GP	G	A	PTS	CENTRAL GP	G	A	PTS	TOTALS GP	G	A	PTS
Anderson (TOR)	14	1	1	2	13	5	1	6	26	5	11	16	20	6	5	11	73	17	18	35
Anderson (NYR)	5	0	0	0	1	0	0	0	3	2	1	3	3	2	1	3	12	4	2	6
Beukeboom	27	3	2	5	20	3	4	7	12	0	1	1	9	2	1	3	68	8	8	16
Gilbert	30	2	4	6	25	1	3	4	10	1	1	2	11	0	3	3	76	4	11	15
Graves	32	19	10	29	28	22	11	33	12	7	2	9	12	4	4	8	84	52	27	79
Hartman	13	1	0	1	13	0	0	0	5	0	0	0	4	0	1	1	35	1	1	2
Healy	12	0	1	1	10	0	1	1	4	0	0	0	3	0	0	0	29	0	2	2
Hudson	18	2	3	5	18	2	2	4	7	0	1	1	5	0	1	1	48	4	7	11
Karpovtsev	24	0	6	6	23	2	5	7	10	1	2	3	10	0	2	2	67	3	15	18
Kocur	27	2	0	2	22	0	0	0	10	0	0	0	12	0	1	1	71	2	1	3
Kovalev	30	9	14	23	25	5	9	14	10	6	2	8	11	3	8	11	76	23	33	56
Kypreos (HFD)	1	0	0	0	6	0	0	0	3	0	0	0	0	0	0	0	10	0	0	0
Kypreos (NYR)	15	2	2	4	14	1	2	3	9	0	0	0	8	0	1	1	46	3	5	8
Lacroix	1	0	0	0	3	0	0	0	0	0	0	0	0	0	0	0	4	0	0	0
Larmer	25	8	11	19	21	7	15	22	12	2	8	10	10	4	5	9	68	21	39	60
Leetch	32	11	16	27	28	3	24	27	12	4	5	9	12	5	11	16	84	23	56	79
Lidster	12	0	1	1	15	0	1	1	2	0	0	0	5	0	0	0	34	0	2	2
Lowe	28	1	9	10	22	1	2	3	10	3	0	3	11	0	3	3	71	5	14	19
MacTavish (EDM)	12	2	1	3	12	4	0	4	22	6	7	13	20	4	2	6	66	16	10	26
MacTavish (NYR)	5	3	0	3	1	0	1	1	3	1	1	2	3	0	0	0	12	4	2	6
Matteau (CHI)	13	3	6	9	10	1	3	4	20	4	4	8	22	7	3	10	65	15	16	31
Matteau (NYR)	5	2	3	5	1	0	0	0	3	0	0	0	3	2	0	2	12	4	3	7
J. Messier	2	0	0	0	2	0	2	2	0	0	0	0	0	0	0	0	4	0	2	2
M. Messier	29	7	20	27	27	13	22	35	10	1	7	8	10	5	9	14	76	26	58	84
Nemchinov	31	11	12	23	27	6	12	18	9	1	2	3	9	4	1	5	76	22	27	49
Noonan (CHI)	11	3	1	4	11	0	4	4	20	5	9	14	22	6	7	13	64	14	21	35
Noonan (NYR)	5	0	1	1	1	1	0	1	3	0	1	1	3	3	0	3	12	4	2	6
Norstrom	4	0	0	0	2	0	1	1	3	0	1	1	0	0	0	0	9	0	2	2
Olczyk	18	1	2	3	18	2	2	4	6	0	1	1	5	0	0	0	37	3	5	8
Richter	25	0	0	0	20	0	0	0	11	0	0	0	12	0	0	0	68	0	0	0
Tikkanen	32	8	10	18	28	7	12	19	11	4	3	7	12	3	7	10	83	22	32	54
Wells	30	1	3	4	26	1	2	3	11	0	1	1	12	0	1	1	79	2	7	9
Zubov	30	3	30	33	25	7	25	32	12	1	12	13	11	1	10	11	78	12	77	89

GOALTENDING BREAKDOWN

		GP	W	L	T	GA	EN	MINS	AVG	SH	SHOTS	SAVES	PERCENTAGE
						ATLANTIC							
Healy	HOME	5	3	1	0	13	0	247	3.16	0	95	82	.863
Healy	ROAD	7	3	3	0	18	0	318	3.40	1	123	105	.854
Healy	TOTAL	12	6	4	0	31	0	565	3.29	1	218	187	.858
Richter	HOME	14	8	1	3	27	0	728	2.23	0	364	337	.926
Richter	ROAD	12	7	3	0	27	0	640	2.53	1	292	265	.908
Richter	TOTAL	26	15	4	3	54	0	1368	2.37	1	656	602	.918
						NORTHEAST							
Healy	HOME	2	1	1	0	5	0	86	3.49	0	43	38	.884
Healy	ROAD	8	3	4	1	21	1	485	2.60	1	196	175	.893
Healy	TOTAL	10	4	5	1	26	1	571	2.73	1	239	213	.891
Richter	HOME	13	10	1	1	31	0	757	2.46	3	347	316	.911
Richter	ROAD	6	4	2	0	14	1	362	2.32	0	148	134	.905
Richter	TOTAL	19	14	3	1	45	1	1119	2.41	3	495	450	.909
						CENTRAL							
Healy	HOME	1	0	0	0	2	0	20	6.00	0	15	13	.867
Healy	ROAD	3	0	2	0	6	1	114	3.16	0	43	37	.860
Healy	TOTAL	4	0	2	0	8	1	134	3.58	0	58	50	.862
Richter	HOME	6	4	2	0	16	0	340	2.82	1	169	153	.905
Richter	ROAD	5	3	1	0	12	0	245	2.94	0	125	113	.904
Richter	TOTAL	11	7	3	0	28	0	585	2.87	1	294	266	.905
						PACIFIC							
Healy	HOME	1	0	0	0	1	0	38	1.58	0	16	15	.938
Healy	ROAD	2	0	1	1	3	0	59	3.05	0	36	33	.917
Healy	TOTAL	3	0	1	1	4	0	97	2.47	0	52	48	.923
Richter	HOME	6	2	2	2	16	0	331	2.90	0	165	149	.903
Richter	ROAD	6	4	0	0	16	0	309	3.11	0	148	132	.892
Richter	TOTAL	12	6	2	2	32	0	640	3.00	0	313	281	.898
						TOTALS							
Healy		29	10	12	2	69	2	1367	3.03	2	567	498	.878
Richter		68	42	12	6	159	1	3712	2.57	5	1758	1599	.910

QUARTER-BY-QUARTER SCORING

	First Quarter				Second Quarter				Third Quarter				Fourth Quarter				Totals			
	GP	W	L	T	GP	W	L	T	GP	W	L	T	GP	W	L	T	GP	W	L	T
Anderson	21	2	5	7	21	6	7	13	21	5	3	8	22	8	5	13	85	21	20	41
Beukeboom	7	2	0	2	21	2	5	7	19	1	1	2	21	3	2	5	68	8	8	16
Gilbert	21	0	3	3	21	1	2	3	13	1	2	3	21	2	4	6	76	4	11	15
Graves	21	15	6	21	21	11	4	15	21	18	9	27	21	8	8	16	84	52	27	79
Hartman	17	0	1	1	8	0	0	0	3	0	0	0	7	1	0	1	35	1	1	2
Healy	6	0	2	2	9	0	0	0	6	0	0	0	8	0	0	0	29	0	2	2
Hudson	4	0	1	1	20	1	3	3	18	2	1	3	6	1	2	3	48	4	7	11
Karpovtsev	12	1	3	4	18	0	4	4	19	1	3	4	18	1	5	6	67	3	15	18
Kocur	21	0	1	1	20	2	0	2	13	0	0	0	17	0	0	0	71	2	1	3
Kovalev	20	4	11	15	16	3	8	11	19	3	8	11	21	13	6	19	76	23	33	56
Kypreos	14	0	0	0	4	1	1	2	21	1	2	3	17	1	2	3	56	3	5	8
Lacroix	1	0	0	0	0	0	0	0	3	0	0	0	0	0	0	0	4	0	0	0
Larmer	8	3	6	9	19	5	10	15	20	8	11	19	21	5	12	17	68	21	39	60
Leetch	21	7	17	24	21	5	13	18	21	3	15	18	21	8	11	19	84	23	56	79
Lidster	20	0	2	2	3	0	0	0	6	0	0	0	5	0	0	0	34	0	2	2
Lowe	18	1	6	7	20	2	2	4	20	2	5	7	13	0	1	1	71	5	14	19
MacTavish	20	5	1	6	15	5	3	8	21	4	5	9	22	6	3	9	78	20	12	32
Matteau	21	7	6	13	14	4	2	6	20	2	4	6	22	6	7	13	77	19	19	38
J. Messier	3	0	2	2	0	0	0	0	0	0	0	0	1	0	0	0	4	0	2	2
M. Messier	21	7	15	22	15	5	11	16	21	12	21	33	19	2	11	13	76	26	58	84
Nemchinov	21	7	6	13	21	6	10	16	21	6	6	12	13	3	5	8	76	22	27	49
Noonan	18	5	4	9	19	4	5	9	20	4	9	13	19	5	5	10	76	18	23	41
Norstrom	2	0	0	0	0	0	0	0	0	0	0	0	7	0	2	2	9	0	2	2
Olczyk	10	0	0	0	21	3	4	7	5	0	1	1	1	0	0	0	37	3	5	8
Richter	17	0	0	0	16	0	0	0	19	0	0	0	16	0	0	0	68	0	0	0
Tikkanen	21	12	12	24	21	6	7	13	20	3	7	10	21	1	6	7	83	22	32	54
Wells	21	0	2	2	21	0	2	2	21	2	1	3	16	0	2	2	79	2	7	9
Zubov	15	1	16	17	21	5	16	21	21	3	25	28	21	3	20	23	78	12	77	89

GOALTENDING BREAKDOWN

	First Quarter				Second Quarter				Third Quarter				Fourth Quarter				Totals			
	GP	W	L	T	GP	W	L	T	GP	W	L	T	GP	W	L	T	GP	W	L	T
Glenn Healy	6	5	1	0	9	3	5	0	6	1	3	0	8	1	3	2	29	10	12	2
Mike Richter	17	9	4	2	16	10	2	1	19	13	3	1	16	10	3	2	68	42	12	6

	GA	SH	SV	SV%	GA	SH	SV	SV%	GA	SH	SV	SV%	GA	SH	SV	SV%	GA	SH	SV	SV%
Glenn Healy	15	115	100	.870	19	194	175	.902	11	123	112	.911	24	136	112	.824	69	568	499	.878
Mike Richter	40	438	398	.909	35	378	343	.907	42	489	447	.914	42	453	411	.907	159	1758	1599	.910

Alexei Kovalev tallied a team leading 13 goals in the fourth quarter of the season.

Adam Graves collected 18 goals during the third quarter of the season.

MISCELLANEOUS

WIN/LOSS BREAKDOWN

DIVISION	HOME	ROAD	TOTALS
Atlantic	11-2-3	10-6-0	21-8-3
Northeast	11-2-1	7-6-1	18-8-2
Central	4-2-0	3-3-0	7-5-0
Pacific	2-2-2	4-1-1	6-3-3
TOTALS	**28-8-6**	**24-16-2**	**52-24-8**

GOALS BY PERIODS

	1st	2nd	3rd	OT	TOTALS
Rangers	100	110	86	3	299
Opponents	78	81	71	1	231

SHOTS BY PERIOD

	1st	2nd	3rd	OT	TOTALS
Rangers	936	1000	902	33	2871
Opponents	784	804	717	23	2328

TEAM STATISTICS

Most Goals, Game– 8, (twice) last– (January 25, 1994 @ San Jose)
Most Goals Allowed, Game– 7, (March 18, 1994 vs. Chicago)
Most Goals, Period– 5, (twice) last– (April 8, 1994 vs. Toronto, 2nd period)
Most Goals Allowed, Period– 4, (3 times) last– (March 9, 1994 at Washington, 2nd period)
Largest Margin of Victory– 6, (November 24, 1993 @ Ottawa)
Largest Margin of Defeat– 4, (twice) last–(March 18, 1994 vs. Chicago)
Most Shots, Game– 54, (January 3, 1994 vs. Florida)
Most Shots Allowed, Game– 40, (December 29, 1993 @ St. Louis)
Most Shots, Period– 24, (January 5, 1994 vs. Calgary, 1st period)
Most Shots Allowed, Period– 18, (twice) last– (November 3, 1993 vs. Vancouver, 3rd period)
Least Shots, Game– 16, (March 25, 1994 @ Vancouver)
Least Shots Allowed, Game– 15, (November 24, 1993 at Ottawa)
Least Shots, Period– 2, (twice) last– (March 25, 1994 @ Vancouver, 3rd period)
Least Shots Allowed, Period– 3, (5 times) last– (March 5, at NY Islanders, 3rd period)
Most Power Play Goals, Game– 6, (October 13, 1993 vs. Quebec)
Most Power Play Goals Allowed, Game– 4, (December 17, 1993 Detroit)
Most Shorthanded Goals, Game– 2, (4 times) last– (March 25, 1994 @ Vancouver)
Most Shorthanded Goals Allowed, Game– 1, (3 times) last– (March 18, 1994 vs. Chicago)
Longest Winning Streak– 7, (October 30 to November 13)
Longest Losing Streak– 3, (twice) last– (January 5 to January 10)
Longest Unbeaten Streak– 14, October 24 to November 24 (12–0–2)
Longest Winless Streak– 3, (3 times) last– March 10 to March 14 (0–2–1)

INDIVIDUAL STATISTICS

Most Goals, Game– 3, (twice) – Graves, (February 2, 1994 vs. NY Islanders), Gartner (January 31, 1994 vs. Pittsburgh)
Most Assists, Game– 4, (3 times) – Messier (February 2, 1994 vs. NY Islanders), Zubov (January 25, 1994 at San Jose), Leetch (October 11, 1993 vs. Washington)
Most Points, Game– 4, (5 times) – Gartner (March 9, 1994 at Washington), Messier (February 2, 1994 vs. NY Islanders), Zubov (January 25, 1994 at San Jose), Leetch (October 13, 1993 vs. Quebec), Leetch (October 11, 1993 vs. Washington)
Most Shots, Game– 11, Zubov (January 5, 1994 vs. Calgary)
Most Shots, Period– 7, Leetch (March 22, 1994 at Calgary, 2nd period)
Most Penalty Minutes, Game– 17, (3 times) - Beukeboom (January 28, 1994 at Anaheim), Kovalev (October 11, 1993 vs. Washington), Wells (October 5, 1993 vs. Boston)
Longest Point Scoring Streak– 11, (twice) – Kovalev (March 16 to April 8), Messier (January 14 to February 9)
Longest Goal Scoring Streak– 4, (6 times) – Kovalev (March 27 to April 4), Messier (January 25 to January 31), (October 7 to October 13), Graves (November 16 to November 24), (November 3 to November 10), (October 11 to October 16)
Longest Assist Streak– 5, (3 times) - Zubov (January 14 to January 27), (October 22 to October 31), Leetch (November 14 to November 24)

STATISTICS

MONTHLY RECORD

	GP	W	L	T	GF	GA	PTS
October	13	7	5	1	46	38	15
November	13	11	1	1	54	30	23
December	12	8	3	1	40	29	17
January	11	7	4	0	42	30	14
February	13	7	5	1	39	35	15
March	14	7	4	3	51	45	18
April	7	5	1	1	24	17	11

QUARTER BY QUARTER

	W	L	T	PTS
1st quarter of season	14	5	2	30
2nd quarter of season	13	7	1	27
3rd quarter of season	14	6	1	29
4th quarter of season	11	6	4	26

RANGERS RECORD

	WON	LOST	TIED
When Scoring First	38	13	4
When Allowing First Goal	14	11	4
When Leading After First Period	29	6	2
When Trailing After First Period	9	11	2
When Tied After First Period	14	6	4
When Leading After Second Period	40	0	4
When Trailing After Second Period	4	18	3
When Tied After Second Period	8	5	1
In Overtime	3	1	8
When Outshooting Opponents	39	16	6
When Outshot by Opponents	13	6	2
When Shots Are Even	0	1	0
In Second Game of back-to back games	10	3	2
On Sundays	7	2	1
On Mondays	9	4	0
On Tuesdays	7	2	1
On Wednesdays	10	4	2
On Thursdays	5	0	3
On Fridays	8	4	1
On Saturdays	6	7	0
In One Goal Games	16	9	–
In Two Goal Games	15	6	–
In Three Goal Games	16	7	–
In Four Goal Games	2	1	–
In Five Goal Games	2	0	–
In Six Or More Goal Games	1	0	–

When Rangers Score

	WON	LOST	TIED
0 Goals	–	0	0
1 Goal	1	7	1
2 Goals	4	8	2
3 Goals	10	5	3
4 Goals	14	4	2
5 Goals	15	0	0
6 Goals	5	0	0
7 Goals	1	0	0
8 Goals	2	0	0
9 or More Goals	0	0	0

When Opposition Scores

	WON	LOST	TIED
0 Goals	7	–	0
1 Goal	11	0	1
2 Goals	14	1	2
3 Goals	14	6	3
4 Goals	5	9	2
5 Goals	1	2	0
6 Goals	0	5	0
7 Goals	0	1	0
8 Goals	0	0	0
9 or More Goals	0	0	0

HAT TRICKS AND SHORTHANDED GOALS

Hat Tricks

BY RANGERS (2)
Adam Graves vs. Islanders on Feb. 2. All against Ron Hextall.
Mike Gartner vs. Pittsburgh on Jan. 31. All against Ken Wregget.

AGAINST RANGERS (2)
Steve Thomas, Islanders, at Long Island on Nov. 27. Two scored against Richter and one scored against Healy.
Terry Yake, Anaheim, at Madison Square Garden on Oct. 19. All scored against Richter.

Shorthanded Goals

Rangers (20)

Gartner	5	(Phi., Pit., Buf., Wsh., NJ,)
Graves	4	(TB twice, Buf., Wpg.)
Larmer	4	(TB, Ott., Que., Van.)
Tikkanen	3	(Que, TB, Tor.)
Messier	2	(Wsh., Que.)
Andersson	1	(Que.)
Leetch	1	(Van.)

Opponents (5)

Drake	1	(Wpg.)
Gratton	1	(TB)
Hogue	1	(NYI)
Ricci	1	(Que.)
Roenick	1	(Chi.)

Penalty Shots

BY RANGERS
Alexei Kovalev (10/5/93 vs. Boston - unsuccessful against Jon Casey)
Steve Larmer (1/16/94 at Chicago - successful against Ed Belfour)
Tony Amonte (1/27/94 at Los Angeles - unsuccesful against Kelly Hrudey)

AGAINST RANGERS
NONE

Empty Net Goals

BY RANGERS (6)
Adam Graves vs. Buffalo on Dec. 13 at Madison Square Garden. Against the record of Dominik Hasek.
Eddie Olczyk vs. Hartford on Dec. 15 at Madison Square Garden. Against the record of Sean Burke.
Mike Hudson vs. Hartford on Dec. 15 at Madison Square Garden. Against the record of Sean Burke.
Jeff Beukeboom vs. Quebec on Mar. 2 at Madison Square Garden. Against the record of Stephane Fiset.
Sergei Nemchinov vs. Washington on Mar. 9 at Halifax, Nova Scotia. Against the record of Olaf Kolzig.
Alexei Kovalev vs. Dallas on Apr. 1 at Madison Square Garden. Against the record of Andy Moog.

AGAINST RANGERS (3)
Ray Sheppard of Detroit on Dec. 17 at Detroit. Against the record of Glenn Healy.
Yuri Khmylev of Buffalo on Dec. 31 at Buffalo. Against the record of Glenn Healy.
Pat Verbeek of Hartford on Feb. 19 at Hartford. Against the record of Mike Richter.

MANPOWER GAMES LOST TO INJURY OR ILLNESS

PLAYER	DATE OF INJURY	TYPE OF INJURY	DATES MISSED	GAMES MISSED
Beukeboom	2/9	bruised chest	2/12-2/14	2
Gilbert	1/14	bruised shoulder	1/16-1/18	2
	1/27	sprained knee	1/28-2/9	6
Hartman	11/10	charley horse	11/13-11/14	2
Hudson	10/9	fractured left hand	10/11-11/14	16
Karpovtsev	10/9	bruised buttocks	10/11	1
	11/3	bruised hip	11/6-11/16	6
		bruised hip	11/23	1
	2/28	facial injury	3/2-3/4	2
Kocur	1/28	bruised hand	1/31-2/3	3
		bruised hand	2/12-2/19	4
	4/4	back spasms	4/8 - 4/10	2
Kypreos		root canal surgery	4/4	1
Larmer	1/5	broken hand	1/8-1/14	3
Lowe	10/9	bruised foot	10/11-10/13	2
	10/15	bruised thigh	10/19	1
	12/31	flu	12/31	1
		back	3/2	1
		back	3/12	1
		back	3/16 - 3/18	2
	4/2	sprained wrist	4/4 - 4/14	5
Messier	12/22	sprained wrist	12/23-1/5	6
	3/16	bruised thigh	3/18 - 3/22	2
Olczyk	1/28	broken thumb	1/13-3/18	23
Tikkanen	1/14	bruised knee	1/18	1
Wells	3/25	sprained wrist	3/27	1

TOTAL MANPOWER GAMES LOST TO INJURY OR ILLNESS   **99**
(Includes all traded players)

TRANSACTIONS

October 3	Mike Hudson is claimed from Edmonton in the NHL waiver draft. Paul Broten is claimed by Dallas and John McIntyre is claimed by Vancouver.
October 7	Daniel Lacroix is assigned to Binghamton.
October 8	Mattias Norstrom and Sergei Zubov are assigned to Binghamton.
October 9	Mattias Norstrom and Sergei Zubov are recalled from Binghamotn.
October 10	Daniel Lacroix is recalled from Binghamton.
October 12	Jim Hiller is claimed off waivers from the Detroit Red Wings. Daniel Lacroix is assigned to Binghamton.
October 21	Joby Messier and Mattias Norstrom are assigned to Binghamton.
November 2	Rangers acquire Steve Larmer, Nick Kypreos, Barry Richter and a 1994 draft pick (Yuri Litvinov) from Hartford in exchange for James Patrick and Darren Turcotte.
November 5	Jim Hiller is assigned to Binghamton for two weeks of conditioning.
January 29	Daniel Lacroix is recalled from Binghamton.
February 4	Daniel Lacroix is returned to Binghamton.
March 11	Mattias Norstrom is recalled from Binghamton.
March 8	Corey Hirsch joins the club after his participation for Team Canada at the 1994 Winter Olympics.
March 16	Corey Hirsch is assigned to Binghamton.
March 21	Rangers acquire Stephane Matteau and Brian Noonan from Chicago in exchage for Tony Amonte and the rights to Matt Oates.
March 21	Ranger acquire Glenn Anderson, the rights to Scott Malone and a 1994 fourth round draft choice (Alexander Korobolin) from Toronto in exchange for Mike Gartner.
March 21	Rangers acquired Craig MacTavish from Edmonton in exchange for Todd Marchant.
March 21	Rangers trade Peter Andersson to Florida in exchange for a ninth round 1994 draft choice (Vitali Yeremeyev).
March 21	Rangers trade Phil Bourque to Ottawa for future considerations.
April 11	Rangers recall Corey Hirsch, Joby Messier and Barry Richter from Binghamton.

1994 OFF-SEASON ACTIVITY

July 6.........................Rangers sign free agent Shawn Reid.
July 15........................Mike Keenan resigns as Rangers head coach.
July 24........................Rangers trade Esa Tikkanen and Doug Lidster to St. Louis in exchange for Petr Nedved.
August 9....................Rangers name Colin Campbell head coach.
August 19..................Rangers trade Daniel Lacroix to Boston in exchange for Glen Featherstone.
August 24..................Rangers name Mike Murphy assistant coach.
August 25..................Rangers sign Scott Malone and Andy Silverman to professional contracts.
September 6.............Rangers sign free agent Mark Osborne.
September 7.............Rangers agree to terms with Eddie Olczyk and Jay Wells.
September 9.............Rangers sign free agents Ken Gernander and Dave Smith.
September 9.............Rangers sign Jeff Nielsen to a professional contract.

Colin Campbell and Neil Smith at the press conference introducing Campbell as the team's new head coach.

Rangers Birthdays in 1994-95

DECEMBER
 9- Petr Nedved (23)
21- Joe Kocur (30)

JANUARY
 2- Mattias Norstrom (23)
 9- Neil Smith (41)
14- Sergei Nemchinov (31)
18- Mark Messier (34)
22- Greg Gilbert (33)
28- Colin Campbell (42)

FEBRUARY
 6- Mike Hudson (28)
 7- Mike Hartman (28)
25- Alexei Kovalev (22)

MARCH
 2- Joby Messier (25)
 3- Brian Leetch (27)
28- Jeff Beukeboom (30)

APRIL
 7- Alexander Karpovtsev (25)
12- Adam Graves (27)
15- Kevin Lowe (36)

MAY
18- Jay Wells (36)
29- Brian Noonan (30)

JUNE
 4- Nick Kypreos (29)
16- Steve Larmer (34)

JULY
 1- Corey Hirsch (23)
 8- Glen Featherstone (27)
22- Sergei Zubov (25)

AUGUST
13- Mark Osborne (34)
16- Eddie Olczyk (29)
23- Glenn Healy (33)

SEPTEMBER
 2- Stephane Matteau (26)
22- Mike Richter (29)

(Number in parenthesis indicates age he will become)

GAME-BY-GAME RESULTS

Game No.	Date	Opponent	Score	Result	Ranger Goalie(s)	Winning/Tying Goal	Team Record	Position in Standings	SF	SA	(Total) GF	GA
1	Oct. 5	Bos	3-4	L	35	Neely	0 - 1 - 0	—	32	31	3	4
2	Oct. 7	T.B.	5-4	W	30	Leetch-1	1 - 1 - 0	3	38	19	8	8
3	Oct. 9	@ Pitt	2-3	L	35	Straka	1 - 2 - 0	4	33	33	10	11
4	Oct. 11	Wsh.	5-2	W	30	Tikkanen-1	2 - 2 - 0	3	48	19	15	13
5	Oct. 13	Que.	6-4	W	35/30(W)	Karpovtsev-1	3 - 2 - 0	2T	35	29	21	17
6	Oct. 15	@ Buf.	5-2	W	30	Gartner-1	4 - 2 - 0	1T	27	17	26	19
7	Oct. 16	@ Phi.	3-4	L	30	Brind'Amour	4 - 3 - 0	3	25	24	29	23
8	Oct. 19	Ana.	2-4	L	35	Yake	4 - 4 - 0	3	42	37	31	27
9	Oct. 22	@ T.B.	1-4	L	35	Cole	4 - 5 - 0	3	34	29	32	31
10	Oct. 24	L.A.	3-2	W	35	Tikkanen-2	5 - 5 - 0	3	41	25	35	33
11	Oct. 28	Mon.	3-3	T	35	Graves (T)-1	5 - 5 - 1	3	42	26	38	36
12	Oct. 30	@ Hfd.	4-1	W	35	Nemchinov-1	6 - 5 - 1	3	25	22	42	37
13	Oct. 31	vs. N.J.	4-1	W	35	Nemchinov-2	7 - 5 - 1	3	37	24	46	38
14	Nov. 3	Van.	6-3	W	35	Larmer-1	8 - 5 - 1	2	41	36	52	41
15	Nov. 6	@ Que.	4-2	W	35	Messier-1	9 - 5 - 1	3	31	21	56	43
16	Nov. 8	T.B.	6-3	W	35	Messier-2	10 - 5 - 1	2	38	31	62	46
17	Nov. 10	Win.	2-1	W	35	Amonte-1	11 - 5 - 1	2	42	27	64	47
18	Nov. 13	@ Wsh.	2-0	W	35	Nemchinov-3	12 - 5 - 1	1	24	21	66	47
19	Nov. 14	S.J.	3-3	T	35	Larionov (T)	12 - 5 - 2	1	35	21	69	50
20	Nov. 16	@ Fla.	4-2	W	35/30(W)	Amonte-2	13 - 5 - 2	1	27	30	73	52
21	Nov. 19	@ T.B.	5-3	W	35	Tikkanen-3	14 - 5 - 2	1	38	31	78	55
22	Nov. 23	Mon.	5-4	W	35	Olczyk-1	15 - 5 - 2	1	41	31	83	59
23	Nov. 24	@ Ott.	7-1	W	30	Larmer-2	16 - 5 - 2	1	37	15	90	60
24	Nov. 27	@ NYI	4-6	L	35/30(L)	Thomas	16 - 6 - 2	1	41	31	94	66
25	Nov. 28	Wsh.	3-1	W	35	Larmer-3	17 - 6 - 2	1	39	34	97	67
26	Nov. 30	@ N.J.	3-1	W	35	Leetch-1	18 - 6 - 2	1	26	27	100	68
27	Dec. 4	@ Tor.	4-3	W	35	Gartner-2	19 - 6 - 2	1	43	17	104	71
28	Dec. 5	N.J.	2-1	W	35	Gartner-3	20 - 6 - 2	1	35	27	106	72
29	Dec. 8	Edm.	1-1	T	35	Beers (T)	20 - 6 - 3	1	46	38	107	73
30	Dec. 13	Buf.	2-0	W	35	Nemchinov-4	21 - 6 - 3	1	35	28	109	73
31	Dec. 15	Hfd.	5-2	W	35	Messier-3	22 - 6 - 3	1	41	24	114	75
32	Dec. 17	@ Det.	4-6	L	35/30 (L)	Konstantinov	22 - 7 - 3	1	41	32	118	81
33	Dec. 19	Ott.	6-3	W	35	Amonte-3	23 - 7 - 3	1	37	25	124	84
34	Dec. 22	@ Fla.	2-3	L	35	Mellanby	23 - 8 - 3	1	35	20	126	87
35	Dec. 23	@ Wsh.	1-0	W	30	Graves-1	24 - 8 - 3	1	24	20	127	87
36	Dec. 26	N.J.	8-3	W	30	Nemchinov-5	25 - 8 - 3	1	32	26	135	90
37	Dec. 29	@ Stl.	4-3	W	35	Tikkanen-4	26 - 8 - 3	1	29	40	139	93
38	Dec. 31	@ Buf.	1-4	L	30	May	26 - 9 - 3	1	40	28	140	97
39	Jan. 3	Fla.	3-2	W	35	Graves-2	27 - 9 - 3	1	54	27	143	99
40	Jan. 5	Cgy.	1-4	L	35(L)/30	Nieuwendyk	27 - 10 - 3	1	53	24	144	103
41	Jan. 8	@ Mon.	2-3	L	30	LeClair	27 - 11 - 3	1	36	26	146	106
42	Jan. 10	T.B.	2-5	L	35/30(L)	Bergevin	27 -12 - 3	1	29	33	148	111

* At Halifax, N.S.

GAME-BY-GAME RESULTS

Game No.	Date	Opponent	Score	Result	Ranger Goalie(s)	Winning/ Tying Goal	Team Record	Position in Standings	SF	SA	(Total) GF	GA
43	Jan. 14	Phi.	5-2	W	35	Leetch-2	28-12-3	1	32	24	153	113
44	Jan. 16	@ Chi.	5-1	W	35	Lowe-1	29-12-3	1	32	33	158	114
45	Jan. 18	Stl.	4-1	W	35	Nemchinov-6	30-12-3	1	38	26	162	115
46	Jan. 25	@ S.J.	8-3	W	35	Larmer-4	31-12-3	1	21	30	170	118
47	Jan. 27	@ L.A.	5-4(OT)	W	35	Messier-4	32-12-3	1	48	23	175	122
48	Jan. 28	@ Ana.	2-3	L	30(L)/35	Dollas	32-13-3	1	30	36	177	125
49	Jan. 31	Pit.	5-3	W	35	Messier-5	33-13-3	1	23	25	182	128
50	Feb. 2	NYI	4-4	T	35	Ferraro (T)	33-13-4	1	31	37	186	132
51	Feb. 3	@ Bos.	3-0	W	30	Larmer-5	34-13-4	1	26	28	189	132
52	Feb. 7	Wsh.	1-4	L	35(L)/30	Pivonka	34-14-4	1	28	38	190	136
53	Feb. 9	@ Mon.	3-4(OT)	L	30	Desjardins	34-15-4	1	37	30	193	140
54	Feb. 12	@ Ott.	4-3(OT)	W	35	Gartner-4	35-15-4	1	37	16	197	143
55	Feb. 14	@ Que.	4-2	W	35	Kypreos-1	36-15-4	1	33	26	201	145
56	Feb. 18	Ott.	3-0	W	35	Graves-3	37-15-4	1	30	24	204	145
57	Feb. 19	@ Hfd.	2-4	L	35	Cassels	37-16-4	1	31	17	206	149
58	Feb. 21	Pit.	4-3(OT)	W	35	Amonte-4	38-16-4	1	45	27	210	152
59	Feb. 23	Bos.	3-6	L	35/30(L)	Stumpel	38-17-4	1	26	33	213	158
60	Feb. 24	@ N.J.	3-1	W	35	Graves-4	39-17-4	1	35	36	216	159
61	Feb. 26	@Dal.	1-3	L	35(L)/30	Hatcher	39-18-4	1	36	29	217	162
62	Feb. 28	Phi.	4-1	W	35	Kovalev-1	40-18-4	1	43	27	221	163
63	Mar. 2	Que.	5-2	W	35	Andersson-1	41-18-4	1	37	34	226	165
64	Mar. 4	NYI	3-3	T	35	King (T)	41-18-5	1	35	33	229	168
65	Mar. 5	@ NYI	5-4	W	35	Zubov-1	42-18-5	1	35	20	234	172
66	Mar. 7	Det.	3-6	L	35(L)/30	Sheppard	42-19-5	1	30	33	237	178
67	Mar. 9	vs. Wsh.	7-5	W	30	Hudson-1	43-19-5	1	22	25	244	183
68	Mar. 10	@ Bos.	2-2	T	30	Gilbert (T)-1	43-19-6	1	25	35	246	185
69	Mar. 12	@ Pit.	2-6	L	30	Lemieux	43-20-6	1	34	18	248	191
70	Mar. 14	@ Fla.	1-2	L	35	Hull	43-21-6	1	28	23	249	193
71	Mar. 16	Hfd.	4-0	W	35	Larmer-6	44-21-6	1	39	27	253	193
72	Mar. 18	Chi.	3-7	L	35	Cunneyworth	44-22-6	1	32	33	256	200
73	Mar. 22	@ Cal.	4-4	T	35/30/35	Matteau (T)-1	44-22-7	1	33	31	260	204
74	Mar. 23	@ Edm.	5-3	W	35	Noonan-4	45-22-7	1	20	32	265	207
75	Mar. 25	@ Van.	5-2	W	35	Noonan-5	46-22-7	1	16	32	270	209
76	Mar. 27	@ Win.	1-3	L	30	Drake	46-23-7	1T	34	18	271	212
77	Mar. 29	@ Phi.	4-3	W	35	Kovalev-2	47-23-7	1T	19	30	275	215
78	Apr. 1	Dal.	3-0	W	35	Leetch-4	48-23-7	1	29	28	278	215
79	Apr. 2	@ N.J.	4-2	W	35	Kovalev-3	49-23-7	1	23	26	282	217
80	Apr. 4	Fla.	3-2	W	35	Larmer-7	50-23-7	1	40	31	285	219
81	Apr. 8	Tor.	5-3	W	35	MacTavish-2	51-23-7	1	41	37	290	222
82	Apr. 10	@ NYI	4-5	L	30	Malakhov	51-24-7	1	27	22	294	227
83	Apr. 12	Buf.	3-2	W	35	Noonan-6	52-24-7	1	40	26	297	229
84	Apr. 14	Phi.	2-2	T	35	MacTavish (T)-1	52-24-8	1	54	29	299	231

* At Halifax, N.S.

HOME GAME-BY-GAME RESULTS

Game No.	Date	Opponent	Score	Result	Ranger Goalie(s)	Winning/ Tying Goal	Team Record	Position in Standings	SF	SA	GF (Total)	GA
1	Oct. 5	Bos	3-4	L	35	Neely	0 - 1 - 0	0	32	31	3	4
2	Oct. 7	T.B.	5-4	W	30	Leetch-1	1 - 1 - 0	3	38	19	8	8
3	Oct. 11	Wsh.	5-2	W	30	Tikkanen-1	2 - 1 - 0	3	48	19	13	10
4	Oct. 13	Que.	6-4	W	35/30(W)	Karpovtsev-1	3 - 1 - 0	2T	35	29	19	14
5	Oct. 19	Ana.	2-4	L	35	Yake	3 - 2 - 0	3	42	37	21	18
6	Oct. 24	L.A.	3-2	W	35	Tikkanen-2	4 - 2 - 0	3	41	25	24	20
7	Oct. 28	Mon.	3-3	T	35	Graves (T)-1	4 - 2 - 1	3	42	26	27	23
8	Oct. 31	N.J*	4-1	W	35	Nemchinov-2	5 - 2 - 1	3	37	24	31	24
9	Nov. 3	Van.	6-3	W	35	Larmer-1	6 - 2 - 1	2	41	36	37	27
10	Nov. 8	T.B.	6-3	W	35	Messier-2	7 - 2 - 1	2	38	31	43	30
11	Nov. 10	Win.	2-1	W	35	Amonte-1	8 - 2 - 1	2	42	27	45	31
12	Nov. 14	S.J.	3-3	T	35	Larionov (T)	8 - 2 - 2	1	35	21	48	34
13	Nov. 23	Mon.	5-4	W	35	Olczyk-1	9 - 2 - 2	1	41	31	53	38
14	Nov. 28	Wsh.	3-1	W	35	Larmer-3	10 - 2 - 2	1	39	34	56	39
15	Dec. 5	N.J.	2-1	W	35	Gartner-3	11 - 2 - 2	1	35	27	58	40
16	Dec. 8	Edm.	1-1	T	35	Beers (T)	11 - 2 - 3	1	46	38	59	41
17	Dec. 13	Buf.	2-0	W	35	Nemchinov-4	12 - 2 - 3	1	35	28	61	41
18	Dec. 15	Hfd.	5-2	W	35	Messier-3	13 - 2 - 3	1	41	24	66	43
19	Dec, 19	Ott.	6-3	W	35	Amonte-3	14 - 2 - 3	1	37	25	72	46
20	Dec. 26	N.J.	8-3	W	30	Nemchinov-5	15 - 2 - 3	1	32	26	80	49
21	Jan. 3	Fla.	3-2	W	35	Graves-2	16 - 2 - 3	1	54	27	83	51
22	Jan. 5	Cgy.	1-4	L	35(L)/30	Nieuwendyk	16 - 3 - 3	1	53	24	84	55
23	Jan. 10	T.B.	2-5	L	35/30(L)	Bergevin	16 - 4 - 3	1	29	33	86	60
24	Jan. 14	Phi.	5-2	W	35	Leetch-2	17 - 4 - 3	1	32	24	91	62
25	Jan. 18	Stl.	4-1	W	35	Nemchinov-6	18 - 4 - 3	1	38	26	95	63
26	Jan. 31	Pit.	5-3	W	35	Messier-5	19 - 4 - 3	1	23	25	100	66
27	Feb. 2	NYI	4-4	T	35	Ferraro (T)	19 - 4 - 4	1	31	37	104	70
28	Feb. 7	Wsh.	1-4	L	35(L)/30	Pivonka	19 - 5 - 4	1	28	38	105	74
29	Feb. 18	Ott.	3-0	W	35	Graves-3	20 - 5 - 4	1	30	24	108	74
30	Feb. 21	Pit.	4-3(OT)	W	35	Amonte-4	21 - 5 - 4	1	45	27	112	77
31	Feb. 23	Bos.	3-6	L	35/30(L)	Stumpel	21 - 6 - 4	1	26	33	115	83
32	Feb. 28	Phi.	4-1	W	35	Kovalev-1	22 - 6 - 4	1	43	27	119	84
33	Mar. 2	Que.	5-2	W	35	Andersson-1	23 - 6 - 4	1	37	34	124	86
34	Mar. 4	NYI	3-3	T	35	King (T)	23 - 6 - 5	1	35	33	127	89
35	Mar. 7	Det.	3-6	L	35(L)/30	Sheppard	23 - 7 - 5	1	30	33	130	95
36	Mar. 16	Hfd.	4-0	W	35	Larmer-6	24 - 7 - 5	1	39	27	134	95
37	Mar. 18	Chi.	3-7	L	35	Cunneyworth	24 - 8 - 5	1	32	33	137	102
38	Apr. 1	Dal.	3-0	W	35	Leetch-4	25 - 8 - 5	1	29	28	140	102
39	Apr. 4	Fla.	3-2	W	35	Larmer-7	26 - 8 - 5	1	40	31	143	104
40	Apr. 8	Tor.	5-3	W	35	MacTavish-2	27 - 8 - 5	1	41	37	148	107
41	Apr. 12	Buf.	3-2	W	35	Noonan-6	28 - 8 - 5	1	40	26	151	109
42	Apr. 14	Phi.	2-2	T	35	MacTavish (T)-1	28 - 8 - 6	1	54	29	153	111

* Indicates in Halifax

ROAD GAME-BY-GAME RESULTS

Game No.	Date	Opponent	Score	Result	Ranger Goalie(s)	Winning/ Tying Goal	Team Record	Position in Standings	SF	SA	(Total) GF	GA
1	Oct. 9	@ Pitt	2-3	L	35	Straka	0 - 1 - 0	4	33	33	2	3
2	Oct. 15	@ Buf.	5-2	W	30	Gartner-1	1 - 1 - 0	1T	27	17	7	5
3	Oct. 16	@ Phi.	3-4	L	30	Brind'Amour	1 - 2 - 0	3	25	24	10	9
4	Oct. 22	@ T.B.	1-4	L	35	Cole	1 - 3 - 0	3	34	29	11	13
5	Oct. 30	@ Hfd.	4-1	W	35	Nemchinov-1	2 - 3 - 0	3	25	22	15	14
6	Nov. 6	@ Que.	4-2	W	35	Messier-1	3 - 3 - 0	3	31	21	19	16
7	Nov. 13	@ Wsh.	2-0	W	35	Nemchinov-3	4 - 3 - 0	1	24	21	21	16
8	Nov. 16	@ Fla.	4-2	W	35/30(W)	Amonte-2	5 - 3 - 0	1	27	30	25	18
9	Nov. 19	@ T.B.	5-3	W	35	Tikkanen-3	6 - 3 - 0	1	38	31	30	21
10	Nov. 24	@ Ott.	7-1	W	30	Larmer-2	7 - 3 - 0	1	37	15	37	22
11	Nov. 27	@ NYI	4-6	L	35/30(L)	Thomas	7 - 4 - 0	1	41	31	41	28
12	Nov. 30	@ N.J.	3-1	W	35	Leetch-1	8 - 4 - 0	1	26	27	44	29
13	Dec. 4	@ Tor.	4-3	W	35	Gartner-2	9 - 4 - 0	1	43	17	48	32
14	Dec. 17	@ Det.	4-6	L	35/30 (L)	Konstantinov	9 - 5 - 0	1	41	32	52	38
15	Dec. 22	@ Fla.	2-3	L	35	Mellanby	9 - 6 - 0	1	35	20	54	41
16	Dec. 23	@ Wsh.	1-0	W	30	Graves-1	10 - 6 - 0	1	24	20	55	41
17	Dec. 29	@ Stl.	4-3	W	35	Tikkanen-4	11 - 6 - 0	1	29	40	59	44
18	Dec. 31	@ Buf.	1-4	L	30	May	11 - 7 - 0	1	40	28	60	48
19	Jan. 8	@ Mon.	2-3	L	30	LeClair	11 - 8 - 0	1	36	26	62	51
20	Jan. 16	@ Chi.	5-1	W	35	Lowe-1	12 - 8 - 0	1	32	33	67	52
21	Jan. 25	@ S.J.	8-3	W	35	Larmer-4	13 - 8 - 0	1	21	30	75	55
22	Jan. 27	@ L.A.	5-4(OT)	W	35	Messier-4	14 - 8 - 0	1	48	23	80	59
23	Jan. 28	@ Ana.	2-3	L	30(L)/35	Dollas	14 - 9 - 0	1	30	36	82	62
24	Feb. 3	@ Bos.	3-0	W	30	Larmer-5	15 - 9 - 0	1	26	28	85	62
25	Feb. 9	@ Mon.	3-4(OT)	L	30	Desjardins	15 -10 - 0	1	37	30	88	66
26	Feb. 12	@ Ott.	4-3(OT)	W	35	Gartner-4	16 -10 - 0	1	37	16	92	69
27	Feb. 14	@ Que.	4-2	W	35	Kypreos-1	17 -10 - 0	1	33	26	96	71
28	Feb. 19	@ Hfd.	2-4	L	35	Cassels	17 -11 - 0	1	31	17	98	75
29	Feb. 24	@ N.J.	3-1	W	35	Graves-4	18 -11 - 0	1	35	36	101	76
30	Feb. 26	@ Dal.	1-3	L	35(L)/30	Hatcher	18 -12 - 0	1	36	29	102	79
31	Mar. 5	@ NYI	5-4	W	35	Zubov-1	19 -12 - 0	1	35	20	107	83
32	Mar. 9	@ Wsh.*	7-5	W	30	Hudson-1	20 -12 - 0	1	22	25	114	88
33	Mar. 10	@ Bos.	2-2	T	30	Gilbert (T)-1	20 - 12 - 1	1	25	35	116	90
34	Mar. 12	@ Pit.	2-6	L	30	Lemieux	20 - 13 - 1	1	34	18	118	96
35	Mar. 14	@ Fla.	1-2	L	35	Hull	20 - 14 - 1	1	28	23	119	98
36	Mar. 22	@ Cal.	4-4	T	35/30/35	Matteau (T)-1	20 - 14 - 2	1	33	31	123	102
37	Mar. 23	@ Edm.	5-3	W	35	Noonan-4	21 -14 - 2	1	20	32	128	105
38	Mar. 25	@ Van.	5-2	W	35	Noonan-5	22 -14 - 2	1	16	32	133	107
39	Mar. 27	@ Win.	1-3	L	30	Drake	22 -15 - 2	1T	34	18	134	110
40	Mar. 29	@ Phi.	4-3	W	35	Kovalev-2	23 -15 - 2	1T	19	30	138	113
41	Apr. 2	@ N.J.	4-2	W	35	Kovalev-3	24 -15 - 2	1	23	26	142	115
42	Apr. 10	@ NYI	4-5	L	30	Malakhov	24 -16 - 2	1	27	22	146	120

* Indicates in Halifax

GAME-BY-GAME POWER PLAY TOTALS

					Season Totals			
GM	Date	Opponent	PPGF	ADV	PPGF	ADV	PP%	SGA
1	10-5-93	Boston	1	5	1	5	20.0	0
2	10-7-93	Tampa Bay	1	1	2	6	33.3	0
3	10-9-93	@ Pittsburgh	0	3	3	9	22.2	0
4	10-10-93	Washington	4	7	6	16	37.5	0
5	10-13-93	Quebec	6	7	12	23	52.2	0
6	10-15-93	@ Buffalo	0	6	12	29	41.4	0
7	10-16-93	@ Philadelphia	1	4	13	33	39.4	0
8	10-19-93	Anaheim	1	6	14	39	35.9	0
9	10-22-93	@ Tampa Bay	1	6	15	45	33.3	1
10	10-24-93	Los Angeles	1	3	16	48	33.3	0
11	10-28-93	Montreal	1	6	17	54	31.5	0
12	10-30-93	@ Hartford	3	7	20	61	32.8	0
13	10-31-93	New Jersey*	2	7	22	68	32.4	0
14	11-3-93	Vancouver	1	7	23	75	30.7	0
15	11-6-93	@ Quebec	2	6	25	81	30.9	0
16	11-8-93	Tampa Bay	1	4	26	85	30.6	0
17	11-10-93	Winnipeg	0	7	26	92	28.3	0
18	11-13-93	@ Washington	0	4	26	96	27.1	0
19	11-14-93	San Jose	1	4	27	100	27.0	0
20	11-16-93	@ Florida	1	3	28	103	27.2	0
21	11-19-93	@ Tampa Bay	1	3	29	106	27.4	0
22	11-23-93	Montreal	1	6	30	112	26.8	0
23	11-24-93	@ Ottawa	3	6	33	118	28.0	0
24	11-27-93	@ Islanders	2	6	35	124	28.2	1
25	11-28-93	Washington	2	4	37	128	28.9	0
26	11-30-93	@ New Jersey	1	5	38	133	28.6	0
27	12-4-93	@ Toronto	1	6	39	139	28.1	0
28	12-5-93	New Jersey	0	6	39	145	26.9	0
29	12-8-93	Edmonton	0	5	39	150	26.0	0
30	12-13-93	Buffalo	0	3	39	153	25.5	0
31	12-15-93	Hartford	1	4	40	157	25.5	0
32	12-17-93	@ Detroit	2	7	42	164	25.6	0
33	12-19-93	Ottawa	1	4	43	168	25.6	0
34	12-22-93	@ Florida	0	3	43	171	25.1	0
35	12-23-93	@ Washington	0	3	43	174	24.7	0
36	12-26-93	New Jersey	2	4	45	178	25.3	0
37	12-29-93	@ St. Louis	2	4	47	182	25.8	0
38	12-31-93	@ Buffalo	0	5	47	187	25.1	0
39	1-3-94	Florida	2	4	49	191	25.4	0
40	1-5-94	Calgary	0	10	49	201	24.4	0
41	1-8-94	@ Montreal	1	5	50	207	24.2	0
42	1-10-94	Tampa Bay	1	4	51	211	24.2	0
43	1-14-94	Philadelphia	1	4	52	215	24.2	0
44	1-16-94	@ Chicago	0	3	52	218	23.9	0
45	1-18-94	St. Louis	0	3	52	221	23.5	0
46	1-25-94	@ San Jose	3	6	55	227	24.2	0
47	1-27-94	@ Los Angeles	0	4	55	231	23.8	0
48	1-28-94	@ Anaheim	0	5	55	236	23.3	0
49	1-31-94	Pittsburgh	3	6	58	242	24.0	0
50	2-2-94	Islanders	1	5	59	247	23.9	0
51	2-3-94	@ Boston	1	2	60	249	24.1	0
52	2-7-94	Washington	0	4	60	253	23.7	0
53	2-9-94	@ Montreal	2	5	62	258	24.0	0
54	2-12-94	@ Ottawa	1	4	63	264	23.9	1
55	2-14-94	@ Quebec	2	1	64	268	23.9	0
56	2-18-94	Ottawa	1	4	66	279	23.7	0
57	2-19-94	@ Hartford	1	5	67	283	23.7	0
58	2-21-94	Pittsburgh	1	7	68	288	23.6	0
59	2-23-94	Boston	2	5	69	295	23.4	0
60	2-24-94	@ New Jersey	2	5	71	300	23.7	0
61	2-26-94	@ Dallas	1	6	73	305	23.9	0
62	2-28-94	Philadelphia	2	5	74	311	23.8	0
63	3-2-94	Quebec	1	6	76	316	24.1	0
64	3-4-94	Islanders	1	7	77	323	23.8	0
65	3-5-94	@ Islanders	1	7	78	330	23.6	0
66	3-7-94	Detroit	1	5	79	335	23.6	0
67	3-9-94	Washington*	1	4	80	339	23.6	0
68	3-10-94	@ Boston	1	4	81	343	23.6	0
69	3-12-94	@ Pittsburgh	2	7	83	350	23.7	0
70	3-14-94	@ Florida	0	5	83	355	23.4	0
71	3-16-94	Hartford	1	8	84	363	23.1	0
72	3-18-94	Chicago	0	5	84	368	22.8	1
73	3-22-94	@ Calgary	2	4	86	372	23.1	0
74	3-23-94	@ Edmonton	1	3	87	375	23.2	0
75	3-25-94	@ Vancouver	3	8	90	383	23.5	0
76	3-27-94	@ Winnipeg	1	7	91	390	23.3	1
77	3-29-94	@ Philadelphia	2	4	93	394	23.6	0
78	4-1-94	Dallas	1	5	94	398	23.6	0
79	4-2-94	@ New Jersey	1	2	95	400	23.8	0
80	4-4-94	Florida	0	5	95	402	23.6	0
81	4-8-94	Toronto	1	5	96	407	23.6	0
82	4-10-94	@ Islanders	0	3	96	410	23.4	0
83	4-12-94	Buffalo	0	3	96	413	23.2	0
84	4-14-94	Philadelphia	0	4	96	417	23.0	0
SEASON TOTALS					**96**	**417**	**23.0**	**5**

* indicates neutral site game in Halifax.

GAME-BY-GAME PENALTY KILLING TOTALS

GM	Date	Opponent	PPGA	TSH	Season Totals PPGA	TSH	PK%	SGF
1	10-5-93	Boston	1	3	1	3	66.7	0
2	10-7-93	Tampa Bay	1	4	2	7	71.4	1
3	10-9-93	@ Pittsburgh	1	5	3	12	75.0	1
4	10-10-93	Washington	1	6	4	18	77.8	0
5	10-13-93	Quebec	0	8	4	26	84.6	0
6	10-15-93	@ Buffalo	0	8	4	34	88.2	2
7	10-16-93	@ Philadelphia	1	3	5	37	86.5	0
8	10-19-93	Anaheim	2	8	7	45	84.4	0
9	10-22-93	@ Tampa Bay	1	5	8	50	84.0	0
10	10-24-93	Los Angeles	0	4	8	54	85.2	0
11	10-28-93	Montreal	1	6	9	60	85.0	0
12	10-30-93	@ Hartford	1	10	10	70	85.7	0
13	10-31-93	New Jersey*	0	7	10	76	86.8	0
14	11-3-93	Vancouver	1	5	11	81	86.4	0
15	11-6-93	@ Quebec	0	5	11	86	87.2	1
16	11-8-93	Tampa Bay	0	5	11	91	97.9	2
17	11-10-93	Winnipeg	0	8	11	99	87.9	1
18	11-13-93	@ Washington	0	5	11	104	89.4	1
19	11-14-93	San Jose	1	5	12	109	89.0	0
20	11-16-93	@ Florida	1	5	13	114	88.6	0
21	11-19-93	@ Tampa Bay	0	5	13	119	89.1	1
22	11-23-93	Montreal	1	5	14	124	88.7	0
23	11-24-93	@ Ottawa	1	6	15	130	88.5	1
24	11-27-93	@ Islanders	2	3	17	133	87.2	0
25	11-28-93	Washington	0	2	17	135	87.4	0
26	11-30-93	@ New Jersey	0	5	17	140	87.9	0
27	12-4-93	@ Toronto	1	8	18	148	87.8	1
28	12-5-93	New Jersey	1	7	19	155	87.7	1
29	12-8-93	Edmonton	0	3	19	158	88.0	0
30	12-13-93	Buffalo	0	2	19	160	88.1	0
31	12-15-93	Hartford	1	3	20	163	87.7	0
32	12-17-93	@ Detroit	4	6	24	169	85.8	0
33	12-19-93	Ottawa	0	4	24	173	86.1	0
34	12-22-93	@ Florida	2	3	26	176	85.2	0
35	12-23-93	@ Washington	0	5	26	181	85.6	0
36	12-26-93	New Jersey	0	3	26	184	85.9	0
37	12-29-93	@ St. Louis	0	7	26	191	86.4	0
38	12-31-93	@ Buffalo	1	3	27	194	86.1	0
39	1-3-94	Florida	1	3	28	197	85.8	0
40	1-5-94	Calgary	2	7	30	204	85.3	0
41	1-8-94	@ Montreal	0	3	30	207	85.5	0
42	1-10-94	Tampa Bay	2	2	32	209	84.7	0
43	1-14-94	Philadelphia	0	5	32	214	85.0	1
44	1-16-94	@ Chicago	0	6	32	220	85.5	0
45	1-18-94	St. Louis	0	6	32	226	85.8	0
46	1-25-94	@ San Jose	2	6	34	232	85.3	0
47	1-27-94	@ Los Angeles	1	5	35	237	85.2	0
48	1-28-94	@ Anaheim	1	3	36	240	85.0	0
49	1-31-94	Pittsburgh	2	9	38	249	84.7	0
50	2-2-94	Islanders	1	6	39	255	84.7	0
51	2-3-94	@ Boston	0	5	39	260	85.0	0
52	2-7-94	Washington	0	5	39	265	85.3	0
53	2-9-94	@ Montreal	3	7	42	272	84.6	0
54	2-12-94	@ Ottawa	0	4	42	277	84.8	1
55	2-14-94	@ Quebec	1	12	43	281	85.1	0
56	2-18-94	Ottawa	0	7	43	293	85.3	2
57	2-19-94	@ Hartford	1	6	44	300	85.7	0
58	2-21-94	Pittsburgh	1	5	45	306	85.6	1
59	2-23-94	Boston	1	3	46	311	85.5	0
60	2-24-94	@ New Jersey	0	4	46	314	85.4	0
61	2-26-94	@ Dallas	1	8	47	318	85.5	0
62	2-28-94	Philadelphia	0	4	47	326	85.6	0
63	3-2-94	Quebec	0	5	47	330	85.8	0
64	3-4-94	Islanders	0	3	47	333	85.9	0
65	3-5-94	@ Islanders	2	8	49	341	85.6	0
66	3-7-94	Detroit	1	5	50	346	85.5	0
67	3-9-94	Washington*	2	4	52	350	85.1	0
68	3-10-94	@ Boston	1	3	53	353	85.0	0
69	3-12-94	@ Pittsburgh	2	6	55	359	84.7	0
70	3-14-94	@ Florida	1	7	56	366	84.7	0
71	3-16-94	Hartford	0	6	56	372	84.9	0
72	3-18-94	Chicago	1	6	57	378	84.9	0
73	3-22-94	@ Calgary	0	4	57	382	85.1	0
74	3-23-94	@ Edmonton	2	8	59	390	84.9	0
75	3-25-94	@ Vancouver	0	7	59	397	85.1	0
76	3-27-94	@ Winnipeg	2	8	61	405	84.9	0
77	3-29-94	@ Philadelphia	1	5	62	410	84.9	0
78	4-1-94	Dallas	0	5	62	415	85.1	2
79	4-2-94	@ New Jersey	0	3	62	418	85.2	0
80	4-4-94	Florida	2	5	64	423	84.9	0
81	4-8-94	Toronto	2	4	64	427	85.0	0
82	4-10-94	@ Islanders	2	4	66	431	84.7	0
83	4-12-94	Buffalo	1	2	67	433	84.5	0
84	4-14-94	Philadelphia	0	2	67	435	84.6	0
SEASON TOTALS					**67**	**435**	**84.6**	**20**

* indicates neutral site game in Halifax.

GAME-BY-GAME HOME ATTENDANCE

NO.	DATE	DAY	VS.	ATTENDANCE	SEASON	SELLOUT	AVG
1	**Oct. 5**	**Tues.**	**Boston**	**18,200**	**18,200**	1	**18,200**
2	Oct. 7	Thurs.	Tampa Bay	16,596	34,796		17,398
3	Oct. 11	Mon.	Washington	16,834	51,630		17,210
4	Oct. 13	Wed.	Quebec	16,451	68,081		17,020
5	Oct. 19	Tues.	Anaheim	17,643	85,724		17,145
6	**Oct. 24**	**Sun.**	**Los Angeles**	**18,200**	**103,924**	2	**17,321**
7	Oct. 28	Thurs.	Montreal	17,811	121,735		17,391
8	Nov. 3	Wed.	Vancouver	18,001	139,736		17,467
9	Nov. 8	Mon.	Tampa Bay	16,618	156,354		17,373
10	**Nov. 10**	**Wed.**	**Winnipeg**	**18,200**	**174,554**	3	**17,455**
11	**Nov. 14**	**Sun.**	**San Jose**	**18,200**	**192,754**	4	**17,523**
12	**Nov. 23**	**Tue.**	**Montreal**	**18,200**	**210,954**	5	**17,580**
13	Nov. 28	Sun.	Washington	17,941	228,895		17,607
14	**Dec. 5**	**Sun.**	**New Jersey**	**18,200**	**247,095**	6	**17,650**
15	**Dec. 7**	**Wed.**	**Edmonton**	**18,200**	**265,295**	7	**17,686**
16	**Dec. 13**	**Mon.**	**Buffalo**	**18,200**	**283,495**	8	**17,718**
17	Dec. 15	Wed.	Hartford	17,967	301,462		17,733
18	**Dec. 19**	**Sun.**	**Ottawa**	**18,200**	**319,662**	9	**17,759**
19	**Dec. 26**	**Sun.**	**New Jersey**	**18,200**	**337,862**	10	**17,782**
20	**Jan. 3**	**Mon.**	**Florida**	**18,200**	**356,062**	11	**17,803**
21	**Jan. 5**	**Wed.**	**Calgary**	**18,200**	**374,262**	12	**17,822**
22	Jan. 10	Mon.	Tampa Bay	17,993	392,255		17,830
23	**Jan. 14**	**Fri.**	**Philadelphia**	**18,200**	**410,455**	13	**17,846**
24	**Jan. 18**	**Tue.**	**St. Louis**	**18,200**	**428,655**	14	**17,861**
25	**Jan. 31**	**Mon.**	**Pittsburgh**	**18,200**	**446,855**	15	**17,874**
26	**Feb. 2**	**Wed.**	**NY Islanders**	**18,200**	**465,055**	16	**17,887**
27	**Feb. 7**	**Mon.**	**Washington**	**18,200**	**483,255**	17	**17,898**
28	**Feb. 18**	**Fri.**	**Ottawa**	**18,200**	**501,455**	18	**17,909**
29	**Feb. 21**	**Mon.**	**Pittsburgh***	**18,200**	**519,655**	19	**17,919**
30	**Feb. 23**	**Wed.**	**Boston**	**18,200**	**537,855**	20	**17,929**
31	**Feb. 28**	**Mon.**	**Philadelphia**	**18,200**	**556,055**	21	**17,937**
32	**Mar. 2**	**Wed.**	**Quebec**	**18,200**	**574,255**	22	**17,945**
33	**Mar. 4**	**Fri.**	**NY Islanders**	**18,200**	**592,455**	23	**17,953**
34	**Mar. 7**	**Mon.**	**Detroit**	**18,200**	**610,655**	24	**17,960**
35	**Mar. 16**	**Wed.**	**Hartford**	**18,200**	**628,855**	25	**17,967**
36	**Mar. 18**	**Fri.**	**Chicago**	**18,200**	**647,055**	26	**17,974**
37	**Apr. 1**	**Fri.**	**Dallas**	**18,200**	**665,255**	27	**17,980**
38	**Apr. 4**	**Mon.**	**Florida**	**18,200**	**683,455**	28	**17,986**
39	**Apr. 8**	**Fri**	**Toronto**	**18,200**	**701,655**	29	**17,991**
40	**Apr. 12**	**Tue.**	**Buffalo**	**18,200**	**719,855**	30	**17,996**
41	**Apr. 14**	**Thu.**	**Philadelphia**	**18,200**	**738,055**	31	**18,001**

* Afternoon game

SCORING OF RANGERS DRAFT CHOICES

UNITED STATES COLLEGES

POS	NAME	BORN	HT-WT	RD/YR	SCHOOL	GP	G	A	PTS	PIM
D	Dan Brierley	1/23/74	6-2-185	9/92	Yale University	27	3	7	10	60
D	Eddy Campbell	11/26/73	6-2-212	8/93	University of Lowell	40	8	16	24	114
D	Davide Dal Grande	7/8/74	6-5-195	6/92	Notre Dame	32	2	4	6	20
D	Mickey Elick	3/17/74	6-1-180	8/92	University of Wisconsin	42	7	12	19	54
RW	Todd Hedlund	8/20/71	6-1-177	8/90	University of Wisconsin	—	—	—	—	—
C	Brett Lievers	6/18/71	6-0-170	11/90	St. Cloud State	32	16	16	32	2
D	Brian Lonsinger	7/21/72	6-3-193	7/90	Harvard University	33	1	5	6	14
RW	Corey Machanic	9/26/72	6-3-197	5/91	University of Vermont	29	2	6	8	24
D	Scott Malone	1/16/71	6-1-195	10/90	Univ. of New Hampshire	40	14	6	20	162
RW	Jeff Nielsen	9/20/71	6-0-170	4/90	University of Minnesota	41	29	16	45	94
C	John Rushin	9/12/72	6-5-207	7/91	Notre Dame	36	3	6	9	60
D	Andy Silverman	8/23/72	6-3-210	9/90	University of Maine	35	0	3	3	80
RW	Wayne Strachan	12/12/72	5-10-185	Sp/93	Lake Superior State	45	24	23	47	74
D	Jason Weinrich	2/13/72	6-2-189	6/90	University of Maine	18	3	4	7	30
LW	Rick Willis	1/09/72	6-0-185	4/90	University of Michigan	40	8	5	13	83
C	Brian Wiseman	7/13/71	5-7-180	12/91	University of Michigan	40	19	50	69	44

						GP	W	L	T	GAA
G	Jamie Ram	1/18/71	5-11-164	10/91	Michigan Tech.	39	12	20	5	3.20

U.S. OLYMPIC TEAM

POS	NAME	BORN	HT-WT	RD/YR	TEAM	GP	G	A	PTS	PIM
RW	Chris Ferraro	1/24/73	5-10-175	4/92	TEAM USA	48	8	34	42	58
C	Peter Ferraro	1/24/73	5-10-175	1/92	TEAM USA	68	36	34	70	93
D	Barry Richter	9/11/70	6-2-185	2/88	TEAM USA	64	7	19	26	54

						GP	W	L	T	GAA
G	Jon Hillebrandt	7/01/72	5-10-160	8/91	TEAM USA	2	1	1	0	3.9

CANADIAN OLYMPIC TEAM

POS	NAME	BORN	HT-WT	RD/YR	TEAM	GP	G	A	PTS	PIM
RW	Jean-Yves Roy	2/17/69	5-10-180	F/A	TEAM CANADA	14	4	2	6	2

						GP	W	L	T	GAA
G	Corey Hirsch	7/01/72	5-10-160	8/91	TEAM CANADA	45	24	17	3	2.80

ONTARIO HOCKEY LEAGUE/WESTERN HOCKEY LEAGUE

POS	NAME	BORN	HT-WT	RD/YR	SCHOOL	GP	G	A	PTS	PIM
D	Eric Cairns	6/27/74	6-5-217	3/92	Detroit (OHL)	59	7	35	42	204
C	Sergei Olympijev	1/12/75	6-3-190	4/93	Kitchener (OHL)	41	9	10	19	28
					Ottawa (OHL)	20	3	5	8	4
D	Gary Roach	2/04/75	6-2-190	5/93	Sault St. Marie (OHL)	45	5	35	40	28
D	Lee Sorochan	9/09/75	6-1-210	2/93	Lethbridge (WHL)	46	5	27	32	123

						GP	W	L	T	GAA
G	Ken Shepard	1/20/74	5-10-192	9/93	Oshawa (OHL)	45	20	15	5	3.95
G	Dave Trofimenkoff	1/20/75	6-1-190	6/93	Lethbridge (WHL)	42	18	18	1	4.66

EUROPEANS

POS	NAME	BORN	HT-WT	RD/YR	TEAM	GP	G	A	PTS	PIM
C	Vitali Chinakov	1/15/72	5-11-183	11/91	Molot Perm(CIS)	39	14	9	23	12
C	Heinz Ehlers	2/21/68	5-11-176	9b/84	Biel (Switzerland)	23	5	16	21	14
D	Maxim Galanov	3/13/74	6-1-175	3/93	Lada Togliatti (CIS)	7	1	0	1	4
D	Pavel Komarov	2/28/74	6-1-180	11a/93	Torpedo Nizhny (CIS)	18	1	0	1	20
RW	Sergei Kondrashkin	4/02/75	6-0-192	7a/93	Cherepovets (CIS)	41	7	2	9	26
C	Lubos Rob	8/05/70	5-11-183	5/90	Motor (Czech)	33	14	20	34	0
C	Maxim Smelnitski	3/24/74	6-3-207	11b/93	Chelybinsk (CIS)	23	4	0	4	4
C	Niklas Sundstrom	6/06/75	6-0-185	1/93	MoDo (Sweden)	37	7	12	19	28
RW	Vladimir Vorobiev	11/03/72	6-0-183	10/92	Moscow Dynamo (CIS)	36	9	14	23	10

MIGHTY DUCKS vs. RANGERS, 1993-94

	Overall Record:	0-2-0		at New York 0-1-0		at Anaheim 0-1-0	
	GP	W	L	T	GF	GA	PTS
Mighty Ducks	2	2	0	0	7	4	4
Rangers	2	0	2	0	4	7	0

Oct. 19 — Rangers 2, Mighty Ducks 4 at New York (Hebert & Richter)
Jan. 28 — Rangers 2, Mighty Ducks 3 at Anaheim (Hebert & Healy/Richter)

SCORING

Ducks	GP	G	A	PTS	PIM	S	+\-	Rangers	GP	G	A	PTS	PIM	S	+\-
Yake	2	3	3	6	6	9	2	Messier	2	2	0	2	0	7	2
Corkum	2	1	1	2	2	7	-1	Leetch	2	1	1	2	0	10	-1
Semenov	2	0	2	2	0	5	1	Kovalev	2	0	2	2	6	3	2
Dollas	2	1	0	1	2	5	-1	Amonte	2	1	0	1	2	7	1
Loney	2	1	0	1	5	2	1	Turcotte	1	0	1	1	2	1	E
Sweeney	2	1	0	1	0	6	E	Graves	2	0	1	1	2	5	1
Carnback	2	0	1	1	2	4	-1	Andersson	1	0	0	0	0	2	E
Hill	2	0	1	1	6	3	2	Beukeboom	1	0	0	0	17	1	E
Houlder	2	0	1	1	0	5	E	Gilbert	1	0	0	0	0	0	-1
Ladouceur	2	0	1	1	0	2	-1	Hartman	1	0	0	0	0	0	E
Sacco	2	0	1	1	0	7	2	Hudson	1	0	0	0	2	0	-2
Douris	1	0	0	0	0	1	-1	Kypreos	1	0	0	0	5	0	-1
Ferner	1	0	0	0	0	3	1	Larmer	1	0	0	0	0	2	E
Kasatonov	1	0	0	0	0	1	E	Lidster	1	0	0	0	0	1	E
King	1	0	0	0	2	5	E	Lowe	1	0	0	0	0	1	E
McSween	1	0	0	0	0	1	1	Patrick	1	0	0	0	2	1	E
Williams	1	0	0	0	0	1	E	Zubov	1	0	0	0	0	3	1
Ewen	2	0	0	0	9	0	E	Gartner	2	0	0	0	4	6	-1
Grimson	2	0	0	0	11	1	E	Karpovtsev	2	0	0	0	0	10	-2
Valk	2	0	0	0	0	3	-1	Kocur	2	0	0	0	7	1	-2
Van Allen	2	0	0	0	00	2	1	Nemchinov	2	0	0	0	2	1	-2
								Olczyk	2	0	0	0	0	1	E
								Tikkanen	2	0	0	0	4	9	E
								Wells	2	0	0	0	2	0	E

GOALTENDING

	GP	MINS	GA	EN	AVG	W	L	T
Hebert	2	120	4	0	2.00	2	0	0

	GP	MINS	GA	EN	AVG	W	L	T
Healy	1	59	3	0	3.05	0	1	0
Richter	2	59	4	0	4.07	0	1	0

Mighty Ducks Power Play: 3-11 (27.3%)
Power Play Goals: Yake, Loney, Sweeney
Shorthanded Goals: None
Game-Winning Goals: Yake, Dollas
Game-Tying Goals: None
Goals by Period: 1st 2nd 3rd OT Total
Mighty Ducks   3   2   2   0   7
Rangers   0   3   1   0   4
Last Win at MSG: 10/19/93 (4-2)
Last Win at Ana: 1/28/94 (3-2)

Rangers Power Play: 1-11 (9.1%)
Power Play Goals: Leetch
Shorthanded Goals: None
Game Winning Goals: None
Game Tying Goals: None
Shots by Period: 1st 2nd 3rd OT Total
Mighty Ducks   24 31 18   0   73
Rangers   18 27 27   0   72
Last Win at MSG: None
Last Win at Ana: None

Last Ranger trade with Anaheim: None.

BRUINS vs. RANGERS, 1993-94

	Overall Record: 1-2-1				at New York 0-2-0	at Boston 1-0-1		
	GP	W	L	T		GF	GA	PTS
Bruins	4	2	1	1		12	11	5
Rangers	4	1	2	1		11	12	3

Oct. 5	Rangers 3, Bruins 4 at New York (Casey & Richter)
Feb. 3	Rangers 3, Bruins 0 at Boston (Riendeau & Healy)
Feb. 23	Rangers 3, Bruins 6 at New York (Casey & Healy/Richter)
Mar. 10	Rangers 2, Bruins 2 at Boston (Casey & Healy)

SCORING

Bruins	GP	G	A	PTS	PIM	S	+/-	Rangers	GP	G	A	PTS	PIM	S	+/-
Juneau	4	2	3	5	0	6	E	Messier	4	2	3	5	4	9	-2
Oates	4	1	4	5	4	6	2	Leetch	4	0	5	5	4	15	4
Wesley	4	1	3	4	2	14	E	Larmer	3	1	3	4	0	5	E
Bourque	4	0	4	4	2	17	3	Graves	4	2	1	3	4	10	1
Murray	3	1	2	3	6	9	1	Zubov	3	1	2	3	0	9	-1
Kvartalnov	2	2	0	2	0	4	1	Kovalev	4	2	0	2	4	9	-1
Neely	4	1	1	2	0	8	1	Tikkanen	4	1	1	2	0	8	-2
Stumpel	4	1	1	2	0	3	2	J. Messier	1	0	2	2	0	2	1
Hughes	3	0	2	2	4	6	E	Nemchinov	4	0	2	2	2	3	E
Marois	1	1	0	1	2	1	E	Gilbert	3	1	0	1	2	1	-1
Reid	4	1	0	1	0	10	2	Gartner	4	1	0	1	2	14	-1
Smolinski	4	1	0	1	0	8	E	Hudson	2	0	1	1	0	2	E
Shaw	2	0	1	1	2	5	3	Andersson	1	0	0	0	0	2	E
Leach	1	0	0	0	0	2	E	Patrick	1	0	0	0	0	1	-1
McKim	2	0	0	0	0	1	E	Turcotte	1	0	0	0	0	2	-1
Stewart	2	0	0	0	0	1	E	Hartman	2	0	0	0	0	0	-1
Featherstone	3	0	0	0	9	1	-3	Lacroix	2	0	0	0	0	0	E
Heinze	3	0	0	0	0	6	-1	Lidster	2	0	0	0	0	1	-1
Huscroft	3	0	0	0	4	1	E	Beukeboom	3	0	0	0	4	1	-1
Stanton	3	0	0	0	0	3	2	Karpovtsev	3	0	0	0	2	0	-1
Donato	4	0	0	0	2	5	E	Kocur	3	0	0	0	2	4	-1
Roberts	4	0	0	0	2	3	-1	Kypreos	3	0	0	0	4	2	-1
Sweeney	4	0	0	0	4	7	2	Wells	3	0	0	0	17	1	-2
								Amonte	4	0	0	0	0	4	E
								Lowe	4	0	0	0	0	4	-4

GOALTENDING

	GP	MINS	GA	EN	AVG	W	L	T		GP	MINS	GA	EN	AVG	W	L	T
Casey	3	185	8	0	2.59	2	0	1	Richter	2	87	7	0	4.83	0	0	0
Riendeau	1	60	3	0	3.00	0	1	0	Healy	3	157	5	0	1.91	0	0	0

Bruins Power Play: 3-14 (21.4%)
Power Play Goals: Marois, Wesley, Kvartalnov
Shorthanded Goals: None
Game-Winning Goals: Neely, Stumpel
Game-Tying Goals: None
Goals by Period: 1st 2nd 3rd OT Total
Bruins   3   5   4   0   12
Rangers   3   3   5   0   11
Last Win at MSG: 2/23/94 (6-4)
Last Win at Bos: 10/3/91 (5-3)

Rangers Power Play: 5-16 (31.3%)
Power Play Goals: Kovalev (2), Messier, Leetch, Graves
Shorthanded Goals: None
Game Winning Goals: Larmer
Game Tying Goals: Gilbert
Shots by Period: 1st 2nd 3rd OT Total
Bruins   38 52 35   2   127
Rangers   35 38 36   0   109
Last Win at MSG: 12/27/92 (6-5)
Last Win at Bos: 2/3/94 (3-0)

Last Ranger trade with Boston: August 19, 1994, Bruins traded Glen Featherstone to Rangers for Daniel Lacroix.

SABRES vs. RANGERS, 1993-94

Overall Record: 3-1-0 at New York 2-0-0 at Buffalo 1-1-0

	GP	W	L	T	GF	GA	PTS
Sabres	4	1	3	0	8	11	2
Rangers	4	3	1	0	11	8	6

Oct. 15	Rangers 5, Sabres 2 at Buffalo (Fuhr/Hasek & Healy)
Dec. 13	Rangers 2, Sabres 0 at New York (Hasek & Richter)
Dec. 31	Rangers 1, Sabres 4 at Buffalo (Hasek & Healy)
Apr. 12	Rangers 3, Sabres 2 at New York (Hasek & Richter)

SCORING

Sabres	GP	G	A	PTS	PIM	S	+\-
Audette	4	2	2	4	4	10	E
Plante	4	1	2	3	0	4	1
Hawerchuk	4	2	0	2	0	11	-4
May	4	1	1	2	10	6	-2
LaFontaine	1	1	0	1	0	5	-3
Khmylev	2	1	0	1	2	4	1
Carney	1	0	1	1	0	1	1
Dawe	1	0	1	1	2	2	-1
Petrenko	1	0	1	1	0	1	-1
Sweeney	2	0	1	1	4	1	-1
Mogilny	3	0	1	1	0	14	-2
Bodger	4	0	1	1	2	3	-3
Moller	4	0	1	1	12	8	E
Sutton	4	0	1	1	0	3	-2
Boucher	1	0	0	0	0	3	-1
Simon	1	0	0	0	0	0	-1
Simpson	1	0	0	0	0	2	-3
Tsygurov	1	0	0	0	2	0	E
Barnaby	2	0	0	0	6	0	-1
Thomas	2	0	0	0	0	1	-1
Muni	3	0	0	0	4	0	2
Presley	3	0	0	0	2	4	-2
Svoboda	3	0	0	0	0	2	-2
Hannan	4	0	0	0	2	3	2
Ray	4	0	0	0	14	4	E
Smehlik	4	0	0	0	0	3	-4
Wood	4	0	0	0	0	3	-2

Rangers	GP	G	A	PTS	PIM	S	+\-
Graves	4	3	1	4	6	13	1
Gartner	3	2	2	4	0	16	5
Nemchinov	4	2	2	4	2	7	5
Karpovtsev	4	1	1	2	0	6	3
Tikkanen	4	1	1	2	6	12	1
Beukeboom	3	0	2	2	7	3	1
Larmer	3	0	2	2	2	7	-1
Zubov	3	0	2	2	0	8	2
Noonan	1	1	0	1	0	3	1
Turcotte	1	1	0	1	2	4	E
Bourque	1	0	1	1	2	1	1
Kypreos	1	0	1	1	0	0	1
MacTavish	1	0	1	1	0	4	1
Patrick	1	0	1	1	0	1	1
Healy	2	0	1	1	0	0	E
Amonte	3	0	1	1	0	4	-1
Messier	3	0	1	1	0	5	1
Gilbert	4	0	1	1	0	3	1
Leetch	4	0	1	1	0	18	1
Anderson	1	0	0	0	2	2	-1
Andersson	1	0	0	0	0	1	-1
Lidster	1	0	0	0	4	1	E
Matteau	1	0	0	0	0	2	E
J. Messier	1	0	0	0	0	1	E
Hartman	2	0	0	0	10	1	-1
Hudson	2	0	0	0	0	3	E
Lowe	2	0	0	0	0	2	E
Olczyk	2	0	0	0	0	1	E
Kovalev	3	0	0	0	0	6	E
Kocur	4	0	0	0	11	4	-1
Wells	4	0	0	0	16	3	3

GOALTENDING

	GP	MINS	GA	EN	AVG	W	L	T
Hasek	4	223	6	1	1.61	1	2	0
Fuhr	1	16	4	0	15.00	0	1	0

	GP	MINS	GA	EN	VG	W	L	T
Richter	2	120	2	0	1.00	2	0	0
Healy	2	120	5	0	2.50	1	1	0

Sabres Power Play: 2-15 (13.3%)
Power Play Goals: Audette (2)
Shorthanded Goals: None
Game-Winning Goals: May

Game-Tying Goals: None
Goals by Period:

	1st	2nd	3rd	OT	Total
Sabres	3	1	4	0	8
Rangers	5	1	5	0	11

Last Win at MSG: 3/8/89 (2-0)
Last Win at Buf: 12/31/93 (4-1)

Rangers Power Play: 0-16 (0.0%)
Power Play Goals: None
Shorthanded Goals: Gartner, Graves
Game Winning Goals: Gartner, Nemchinov, Noonan

Game Tying Goals: None
Shots by Period:

	1st	2nd	3rd	OT	Total
Sabres	39	28	32	0	99
Rangers	40	53	49	0	142

Last Win at MSG: 4/12/94 (3-2)
Last Win at Buf: 10/15/93 (5-2)

Last Ranger trade with Buffalo: March 9, 1992, Sabres traded Jay Wells to Rangers in exchange for Randy Moller.

FLAMES vs. RANGERS, 1993-94

	Overall Record: 0-1-1		at New York 0-1-0		at Calgary 0-0-1	
	GP	W	L	T	GF	GA	PTS
Flames	2	1	0	1	8	5	3
Rangers	2	0	1	1	5	8	1

Jan. 5 — Rangers 1, Flames 4 at New York (Trefilov & Healy/Richter)
Mar. 22 — Rangers 4, Flames 4 at Calgary (Vernon & Healy/Richter)

SCORING

Flames	GP	G	A	PTS	PIM	S	+\-	Rangers	GP	G	A	PTS	PIM	S	+\-
Reichel	2	2	3	5	2	6	3	Leetch	2	1	2	3	2	15	2
Walz	2	0	3	3	0	4	4	Anderson	1	2	0	2	0	4	1
Zalapski	1	2	0	2	0	5	2	Kovalev	2	0	2	2	0	4	E
MacInnis	1	1	1	2	2	6	E	Tikkanen	2	0	2	2	6	6	2
Nieuwendyk	1	1	1	2	0	6	E	Amonte	1	1	0	1	0	4	1
Fleury	2	1	1	2	4	6	E	Matteau	1	1	0	1	0	2	2
Roberts	1	1	0	1	2	3	-1	Larmer	2	0	1	1	0	5	-3
Kisio	1	1	0	1	2	0	1	Zubov	2	0	1	1	0	15	-1
Patrick	1	0	1	1	0	4	2	Gartner	1	0	0	0	0	4	-1
Schlegel	1	0	1	1	0	1	1	Hartman	1	0	0	0	0	7	-1
Stern	1	0	1	1	0	0	1	Hudson	1	0	0	0	0	2	E
Keczmer	2	0	1	1	6	1	1	Karpovtsev	1	0	0	0	0	0	-1
Petit	2	0	1	1	6	4	E	Kypreos	1	0	0	0	2	0	-2
Yawney	2	0	1	1	4	1	2	Lidster	1	0	0	0	0	0	-2
Dahlquist	1	0	0	0	0	0	-1	MacTavish	1	0	0	0	0	0	-2
Esau	1	0	0	0	7	0	E	Nemchinov	1	0	0	0	2	2	-1
Musil	1	0	0	0	2	0	-1	Noonan	1	0	0	0	0	1	E
Nylander	1	0	0	0	0	1	-1	Beukeboom	2	0	0	0	2	4	1
Paslawski	1	0	0	0	0	0	E	Gilbert	2	0	0	0	0	1	E
Ranheim	1	0	0	0	0	0	E	Graves	2	0	0	0	4	13	E
Struch	1	0	0	0	0	0	E	Kocur	2	0	0	0	2	1	E
Sullivan	1	0	0	0	0	2	E	Lowe	2	0	0	0	4	0	-3
Titov	1	0	0	0	0	2	-1	Olczyk	2	0	0	0	0	1	-2
Trefilov	1	0	0	0	2	0	E	Wells	2	0	0	0	2	0	-2
Wortman	1	0	0	0	0	0	E								
Kruse	2	0	0	0	0	2	1								
McCarthy	2	0	0	0	0	1	E								
Otto	2	0	0	0	2	1	-1								

GOALTENDING

	GP	MINS	GA	EN	AVG	W	L	T		GP	MINS	GA	EN	AVG	W	L	T
Trefilov	1	60	1	0	1.00	1	0	0	Healy	2	38	1	0	1.58	0	0	1
Vernon	1	60	4	0	3.69	0	0	1	Richter	2	86	7	0	4.88	0	1	0

Flames Power Play: 2-11 (18.2%)
Power Play Goals: Fleury, Roberts
Shorthanded Goals: None
Game-Winning Goals: Nieuwendyk
Game-Tying Goals: None

Goals by Period:	1st	2nd	3rd	OT	Total
Flames	3	3	2	0	8
Rangers	2	2	1	0	5

Last Win at MSG: 1/5/94 (4-1)
Last Win at Cgy: 12/15/92 (3-0)

Rangers Power Play: 2-14 (14.3%)
Power Play Goals: Anderson (2)
Shorthanded Goals: None
Game Winning Goals: None
Game Tying Goals: Matteau

Shots by Period:	1st	2nd	3rd	OT	Total
Flames	18	21	14	2	55
Rangers	32	31	21	2	86

Last Win at MSG: 1/16/92 (6-4)
Last Win at Cgy: 1/14/87 (8-5)

Last Ranger trade with Calgary: November 7, 1987, Flames traded Don Mercier to Rangers for Jim Leavins.

BLACKHAWKS vs. RANGERS, 1993-94

Overall Record: 1-1-1   at New York 0-1-0   at Chicago 1-0-0

	GP	W	L	T	GF	GA	PTS
Blackhawks	2	1	1	0	8	8	2
Rangers	2	1	1	0	8	8	2

Jan. 16   Rangers 5, Blackhawks 1 at Chicago (Belfour & Richter)
Mar. 18   Rangers 3, Blackhawks 7 at New York (Belfour & Richter)

SCORING

Blackhawks	GP	G	A	PTS	PIM	S	+\-
Roenick	2	2	2	4	2	8	-1
Carney	2	1	2	3	0	3	3
Matteau	2	0	3	3	0	5	1
Murphy	2	2	0	2	0	6	-2
Chelios	2	1	1	2	4	7	-1
B. Sutter	2	0	2	2	4	4	1
Cunneyworth	1	1	0	1	0	3	1
Graham	1	1	0	1	0	3	E
Dubinsky	1	0	1	1	0	0	1
Shantz	1	0	1	1	2	1	1
Droppa	1	0	0	0	4	1	1
Goulet	1	0	0	0	0	3	E
Horacek	1	0	0	0	0	0	E
Kimble	1	0	0	0	5	0	1
Kucera	1	0	0	0	0	1	E
Lemieux	1	0	0	0	0	2	-1
Russell	1	0	0	0	0	0	E
Smith	1	0	0	0	0	2	E
Suter	1	0	0	0	0	2	E
Weinrich	1	0	0	0	0	1	-3
Wilkinson	1	0	0	0	0	1	E
Noonan	2	0	0	0	0	1	1
Poulin	2	0	0	0	0	4	-1
Ruuttu	2	0	0	0	2	2	-2
Smyth	2	0	0	0	7	0	E
R. Sutter	2	0	0	0	0	6	E

Rangers	GP	G	A	PTS	PIM	S	+\-
Graves	2	3	0	3	0	9	1
Kovalev	2	1	2	3	5	4	1
Amonte	2	1	1	2	2	4	-1
Larmer	2	1	1	2	2	7	1
Gartner	2	0	2	2	2	6	1
Lowe	1	1	0	1	0	1	1
Messier	1	1	0	1	2	3	E
Gilbert	1	0	1	1	0	2	1
Olczyk	1	0	1	1	0	0	1
Leetch	2	0	1	1	0	7	1
Zubov	2	0	1	1	0	4	4
Bourque	1	0	0	0	2	1	-1
Hartman	1	0	0	0	7	1	-1
Hudson	1	0	0	0	2	0	E
Karpovtsev	1	0	0	0	0	1	E
Lidster	1	0	0	0	0	1	-1
Marchant	1	0	0	0	0	1	-1
Nemchinov	1	0	0	0	0	1	1
Norstrom	1	0	0	0	0	1	E
Beukeboom	2	0	0	0	2	0	-2
Kocur	2	0	0	0	6	3	-1
Kypreos	2	0	0	0	9	1	-2
Wells	2	0	0	0	0	2	-3

GOALTENDING

	GP	MINS	GA	EN	AVG	W	L	T
Belfour	2	120	8	0	4.00	1	1	0
Richter	2	120	8	0	4.00	1	1	0

Blackhawks Power Play: 1-12 (8.3%)
Power Play Goals: Murphy
Shorthanded Goals: Roenick
Game-Winning Goals: Cunneyworth
Game-Tying Goals: None
Goals by Period: 1st   2nd   3rd   OT   Total
Blackhawks   2   3   3   0   8
Rangers   3   2   3   0   8
Last Win at MSG: 3/18/94 (7-3)
Last Win at Chi: 3/10/91 (5-2)

Rangers Power Play: 0-8 (0.0%)
Power Play Goals: None
Shorthanded Goals: None
Game Winning Goals: Lowe
Game Tying Goals: None
Shots by Period: 1st   2nd   3rd   OT   Total
Blackhawks   17   23   26   0   66
Rangers   20   21   23   0   64
Last Win at MSG: 3/11/93 (4-1)
Last Win at Chi: 1/16/94 (5-1)

Last Ranger trade with Chicago: March 21, 1994, Blackhawks traded Brian Noonan and Stephane Matteau to the Rangers for Tony Amonte and Matt Oates.

STARS VS. RANGERS, 1993-94

	Overall Record: 1-1-0		at New York 1-0-0		at Dallas 0-1-0		
	GP	W	L	T	GF	GA	PTS
Stars	2	1	1	0	3	4	2
Rangers	2	1	1	0	4	3	2

Feb. 26   Rangers 1, Stars 3 at Dallas (Moog & Healy/Richter)
Apr. 1   Rangers 3, Stars 0 at New York (Moog & Richter)

SCORING

Stars	GP	G	A	PTS	PIM	S	+\-	Rangers	GP	G	A	PTS	PIM	S	+\-
Gagner	2	1	1	2	5	8	1	Leetch	2	2	1	3	0	11	E
P. Broten	2	1	0	1	0	4	1	Messier	2	0	2	2	2	5	E
Hatcher	2	1	0	1	0	9	E	Zubov	2	0	2	2	0	7	-2
Cavallini	1	0	1	1	2	1	E	Anderson	1	1	0	1	0	3	1
N. Broten	2	0	1	1	0	0	E	Kovalev	2	1	0	1	7	5	E
Courtnall	2	0	1	1	0	6	-2	Graves	2	0	1	1	4	7	1
Dahlen	1	0	0	0	0	2	E	Larmer	2	0	1	1	2	5	1
Klatt	1	0	0	0	2	2	E	Wells	2	0	1	1	0	2	1
Lalor	1	0	0	0	0	2	-1	Amonte	1	0	0	0	0	1	E
May	1	0	0	0	2	1	E	Gartner	1	0	0	0	0	4	-1
McKenzie	1	0	0	0	0	0	1	Hartman	1	0	0	0	5	0	E
Churla	2	0	0	0	7	0	-1	Hudson	1	0	0	0	0	0	E
Craig	2	0	0	0	0	3	E	Kocur	1	0	0	0	2	2	E
Donnelly	2	0	0	0	4	0	E	MacTavish	1	0	0	0	0	1	E
Evason	2	0	0	0	0	1	-1	Matteau	1	0	0	0	0	0	1
Gilchrist	2	0	0	0	0	2	E	Nemchinov	1	0	0	0	4	0	E
Ledyard	2	0	0	0	2	1	2	Noonan	1	0	0	0	0	1	E
Ludwig	2	0	0	0	6	3	1	Beukeboom	2	0	0	0	2	3	1
Matvichuk	2	0	0	0	4	2	-1	Gilbert	2	0	0	0	4	1	-1
McPhee	2	0	0	0	0	2	-1	Karpovtsev	2	0	0	0	0	0	1
Modano	2	0	0	0	0	8	-1	Kypreos	2	0	0	0	2	2	E
Moog	2	0	0	0	2	0	E	Lowe	2	0	0	0	2	3	E
								Tikkanen	2	0	0	0	4	2	-2

GOALTENDING

	GP	MINS	GA	EN	AVG	W	L	T
Moog	2	119	3	1	1.51	1	1	0

	GP	MINS	GA	EN	AVG	W	L	T
Healy	1	1	0	0	0.00	0	0	0
Richter	2	119	3	0	1.51	1	1	0

Stars Power Play: 1-13 (7.7%)
Power Play Goals: Gagner
Shorthanded Goals: None
Game-Winning Goals: Hatcher
Game-Tying Goals: None
Goals by Period: 1st 2nd 3rd OT Total
Stars   1   1   1   0   3
Rangers   1   1   2   0   4
Last Win at MSG: 11/30/92 (4-2)
Last Win at Dal: 2/26/94 (3-1)

Rangers Power Play: 2-10 (20.0%)
Power Play Goals: Leetch (2)
Shorthanded Goals: None
Game Winning Goals: Leetch
Game Tying Goals: None
Shots by Period: 1st 2nd 3rd OT Total
Stars   23   19   15   0   57
Rangers   18   21   26   0   65
Last Win at MSG: 4/1/94 (3-0)
Last Win at Dal: 2/1/92 (2-1)

Last Ranger trade with Dallas: March 9, 1992, Stars traded Mario Thyer and a 1993 third round draft choice to Rangers for Mark Janssens.

RED WINGS vs. RANGERS, 1993-94

Overall Record: 0-2-0 at New York 0-1-0 at Detroit 0-1-0

	GP	W	L	T	GF	GA	PTS
Red Wings	2	2	0	0	12	7	4
Rangers	2	0	2	0	7	12	0

Dec. 17   Rangers 4, Red Wings 6 at Detroit (Cheveldae/Osgood & Healy/Richter)
Mar. 7   Rangers 3, Red Wings 6 at New York (Cheveldae & Healy/Richter)

SCORING

Red Wings	GP	G	A	PTS	PIM	S	+\-
Fedorov	2	2	5	7	0	9	2
Sheppard	2	2	1	3	2	6	1
Coffey	2	1	2	3	0	4	E
Konstantinov	2	1	2	3	8	3	4
Kozlov	2	1	1	2	0	4	-1
Primeau	2	1	1	2	7	4	E
Lidstrom	2	0	2	2	0	5	-1
Burr	1	1	0	1	0	2	1
Drake	1	1	0	1	0	2	1
Draper	1	1	0	1	0	1	1
Chiasson	2	1	0	1	8	6	3
Johnson	1	0	1	1	0	0	E
Sillinger	1	0	1	1	0	0	-1
Ciccarelli	2	0	1	1	2	4	-1
Kennedy	2	0	1	1	0	4	4
McCarty	2	0	1	1	5	2	E
Probert	2	0	1	1	7	4	2
Aivazoff	1	0	0	0	0	0	-1
Halkidis	1	0	0	0	4	1	-1
Howe	1	0	0	0	0	2	1
Lapointe	1	0	0	0	0	0	E
Yzerman	1	0	0	0	0	2	1
Carkner	2	0	0	0	0	0	E

Rangers	GP	G	A	PTS	PIM	S	+\-
Zubov	2	1	3	4	4	2	-1
Leetch	2	2	1	3	2	0	-1
Gartner	2	1	1	2	1	5	1
Gilbert	2	1	0	1	0	6	-1
Kovalev	2	1	0	1	4	5	-1
Lowe	2	1	0	1	4	2	-1
Amonte	2	0	1	1	0	7	-1
Hudson	2	0	1	1	4	3	E
Messier	2	0	1	1	0	5	-3
Nemchinov	2	0	1	1	2	5	E
Tikkanen	2	0	1	1	0	7	-1
Kypreos	1	0	0	0	0	1	E
Olczyk	1	0	0	0	2	2	E
Beukeboom	2	0	0	0	2	1	-2
Graves	2	0	0	0	5	5	-1
Karpovtsev	2	0	0	0	0	3	-2
Kocur	2	0	0	0	12	2	E
Larmer	2	0	0	0	0	0	-1
Wells	2	0	0	0	2	3	-1

GOALTENDING

	GP	MINS	GA	EN	AVG	W	L	T
Osgood	1	17	0	0	0.00	0	0	0
Cheveldae	2	103	7	0	4.08	2	0	0

	GP	MINS	GA	EN	AVG	W	L	T
Healy	2	74	5	1	4.05	0	1	0
Richter	2	46	6	0	7.83	0	1	0

Red Wings Power Play: 5-11 (45.5%)
Power Play Goals: Sheppard, Coffey, Konstantinov, Kozlov, Primeau
Shorthanded Goals: None
Game-Winning Goals: Sheppard, Konstantinov
Game-Tying Goals: None

Goals by Period:	1st	2nd	3rd	OT	Total
Red Wings	6	3	3	0	12
Rangers	4	2	1	0	7

Last Win at MSG: 3/7/94 (6-3)
Last Win at Det: 12/17/93 (6-4)

Rangers Power Play: 3-12 (25.0%)
Power Play Goals: Leetch (2), Gartner
Shorthanded Goals: None
Game Winning Goals: None
Game Tying Goals: None

Shots by Period:	1st	2nd	3rd	OT	Total
Red Wings	22	16	27	0	65
Rangers	25	24	22	0	71

Last Win at MSG: 12/2/92 (5-3)
Last Win at Det: 3/20/92 (4-2)

Last Ranger trade with Detroit: December 26, 1991, Detroit traded an undisclosed draft pick for Greg Millen.

OILERS vs. RANGERS, 1993-94

	Overall Record: 1-0-1		at New York 0-0-1		at Edmonton 1-0-0		
	GP	W	L	T	GF	GA	PTS
Oilers	2	0	1	1	4	6	1
Rangers	2	1	0	1	6	4	3

Dec. 8 — Rangers 1, Oilers 1 at New York (Ranford & Richter)
Mar. 23 — Rangers 5, Oilers 3 at Edmonton (Ranford/Brathwaite & Richter)

SCORING

Oilers	GP	G	A	PTS	PIM	S	+\-
Arnott	2	2	1	3	6	5	1
McAmmond	1	1	2	3	2	3	-1
Beers	2	1	1	2	0	5	E
Mironov	1	0	2	2	0	2	-1
Byakin	1	0	1	1	2	0	1
DeBrusk	1	0	0	0	0	1	E
Grieve	1	0	0	0	0	1	E
MacTavish	1	0	0	0	0	1	E
Manson	1	0	0	0	0	1	E
Marchant	1	0	0	0	0	2	-1
Olausson	1	0	0	0	0	1	E
Rice	1	0	0	0	2	3	E
Stapleton	1	0	0	0	0	0	-1
White	1	0	0	0	0	1	E
Bennett	2	0	0	0	0	3	-2
Buchberger	2	0	0	0	9	1	-2
Ciger	2	0	0	0	2	6	2
Corson	2	0	0	0	0	4	E
Kravchuk	2	0	0	0	0	5	-2
Maltby	2	0	0	0	2	7	-2
Pearson	2	0	0	0	4	11	-2
Ranford	2	0	0	0	2	0	E
Richardson	2	0	0	0	2	3	-2
Thornton	2	0	0	0	0	1	-1
Weight	2	0	0	0	0	3	-2

Rangers	GP	G	A	PTS	PIM	S	+\-
Graves	2	2	0	2	0	5	2
Kovalev	1	1	1	2	0	4	1
Tikkanen	2	1	1	2	2	4	1
Matteau	1	1	0	1	0	3	E
Noonan	1	1	0	1	4	1	2
Anderson	1	0	1	1	2	2	2
Beukeboom	2	0	1	1	2	5	2
Gilbert	2	0	1	1	2	4	E
Karpovtsev	2	0	1	1	4	1	2
Larmer	2	0	1	1	0	0	1
Leetch	2	0	1	1	0	10	4
Messier	2	0	1	1	2	6	1
Zubov	2	0	1	1	2	7	-1
Amonte	1	0	0	0	0	3	E
Gartner	1	0	0	0	0	3	E
Hudson	1	0	0	0	0	4	-1
MacTavish	1	0	0	0	0	0	E
Nemchinov	1	0	0	0	0	1	E
Olczyk	1	0	0	0	0	1	E
Kocur	2	0	0	0	5	1	E
Kypreos	2	0	0	0	2	0	E
Lowe	2	0	0	0	6	2	-1
Wells	2	0	0	0	6	1	E

GOALTENDING

	GP	MINS	GA	EN	AVG	W	L	T
Ranford	2	92	4	0	2.61	0	0	1
Brathwaite	1	33	2	0	3.64	0	1	0

	GP	MINS	GA	EN	AVG	W	L	T
Richter	2	125	4	0	1.92	1	0	1

Oilers Power Play: 2-11 (18.2%)
Power Play Goals: Arnott (2)
Shorthanded Goals: None
Game-Winning Goals: None
Game-Tying Goals: Beers
Goals by Period: 1st 2nd 3rd OT Total
Oilers   0   1   3   0   4
Rangers 2   2   2   0   6
Last Win at MSG: 3/17/93 (4-3)
Last Win at Edm: 12/7/90 (4-3)

Rangers Power Play: 1-9 (11.1%)
Power Play Goals: Matteau
Shorthanded Goals: None
Game Winning Goals: Noonan
Game Tying Goals: None
Shots by Period: 1st 2nd 3rd OT Total
Oilers   16 33 19   2   70
Rangers   24 22 18   2   66
Last Win at MSG: 2/7/90 (5-2)
Last Win at Edm: 3/23/94 (5-3)

Last Ranger trade with Edmonton: March 21, 1994, Oilers traded Craig MacTavish to the Rangers for Todd Marchant.

WHALERS vs. RANGERS, 1993-94

Overall Record: 3-1-0   at New York 2-0-0   at Hartford 1-1-0

	GP	W	L	T	GF	GA	PTS
Whalers	4	1	3	0	7	15	2
Rangers	4	3	1	0	15	7	6

Oct 30   Rangers 4, Whalers 1 at Hartford (Pietrangelo & Richter)
Dec.15   Rangers 5, Whalers 2 at New York (Burke & Richter)
Feb.19   Rangers 2, Whalers 4 at Hartford (Burke & Richter)
Mar.16   Rangers 4, Whalers 0 at New York (Burke & Richter)

SCORING

Whalers	GP	G	A	PTS	PIM	S	+\-
Cassels	3	2	1	3	2	4	-2
Verbeek	4	2	1	3	0	13	-3
Propp	3	1	1	2	0	5	2
Sanderson	4	1	1	2	2	12	-5
Patrick	1	0	2	2	2	0	1
Zalapski	2	0	2	2	0	3	-3
McCrimmon	3	1	0	1	6	2	E
Weinrich	1	0	1	1	0	1	E
Cunneyworth	3	0	1	1	2	4	3
Janssens	4	0	1	1	7	1	1
Crowley	1	0	0	0	0	0	-1
Drury	1	0	0	0	0	3	-2
Greig	1	0	0	0	7	3	-1
Houda	1	0	0	0	0	0	E
Keczmer	1	0	0	0	0	1	-1
Kucera	1	0	0	0	0	1	E
Lemieux	1	0	0	0	2	0	-1
Poulin	1	0	0	0	4	1	-1
Ranheim	1	0	0	0	2	3	-2
Sandlak	1	0	0	0	2	4	-1
Smyth	1	0	0	0	0	1	E
Chibirev	2	0	0	0	0	0	1
Godynyuk	2	0	0	0	4	9	-3
Harkins	2	0	0	0	0	0	-1
Marchment	2	0	0	0	19	2	E
McGill	2	0	0	0	2	1	-1
McKenzie	2	0	0	0	2	1	E
Petrovicky	2	0	0	0	2	0	E
Potvin	2	0	0	0	5	0	E
Burt	3	0	0	0	2	4	-4
Nylander	3	0	0	0	4	2	-2
Storm	3	0	0	0	0	2	E
Kron	4	0	0	0	0	9	-3
Pronger	4	0	0	0	8	12	2

Rangers	GP	G	A	PTS	PIM	S	+\-
Messier	4	2	4	6	2	13	1
Zubov	4	1	5	6	2	6	1
Larmer	3	2	3	5	2	11	4
Tikkanen	4	2	3	5	4	17	2
Graves	4	3	1	4	10	12	E
Kovalev	4	1	1	2	10	11	1
Gartner	4	0	2	2	6	11	1
Olczyk	1	1	0	1	0	2	E
Hudson	2	1	0	1	0	1	1
Beukeboom	3	1	0	1	4	2	3
Nemchinov	3	1	0	1	0	4	E
Norstrom	1	0	1	1	2	1	2
Turcotte	1	0	1	1	2	2	1
Lidster	2	0	1	1	2	0	1
Karpovtsev	3	0	1	1	0	2	E
Amonte	4	0	1	1	0	12	E
Gilbert	4	0	1	1	2	0	1
Leetch	4	0	1	1	0	8	1
Wells	4	0	1	1	7	3	1
Hiller	1	0	0	0	7	0	1
Bourque	2	0	0	0	0	0	1
Hartman	2	0	0	0	2	0	E
Kypreos	2	0	0	0	5	0	E
Kocur	3	0	0	0	2	0	1
Lowe	3	0	0	0	2	4	1

GOALTENDING

	GP	MINS	GA	EN	AVG	W	L	T
Burke	3	180	9	2	3.00	1	2	0
Pietrangelo	1	60	4	0	4.00	0	1	0

	GP	MINS	GA	EN	AVG	W	L	T
Richter	4	240	6	1	1.50	3	1	0

Whalers Power Play: 3-25 (12.0%)
Power Play Goals: Cassels, Sanderson, Verbeek
Shorthanded Goals: None
Game-Winning Goals: Cassels

Game-Tying Goals: None
Goals by Period:

	1st	2nd	3rd	OT	Total
Whalers	0	2	5	0	7
Rangers	6	4	5	0	15

Last Win at MSG: 4/5/93 (5-4)
Last Win at Hfd: 2/19/94 (4-2)

Rangers Power Play: 6-24 (25.0%)
Power Play Goals: Graves (3), Larmer, Zubov, Nemchinov
Shorthanded Goals: None
Game Winning Goals: Nemchinov, Messier, Larmer

Game Tying Goals: None
Shots by Period:

	1st	2nd	3rd	OT	Total
Whalers	36	32	36	0	104
Rangers	39	45	38	0	122

Last Win at MSG: 3/16/94 (4-0)
Last Win at Hfd: 10/30/93 (4-1)

Last Ranger trade with Hartford: November, 2 1993, Whalers traded Nick Kypreos, Steve Larmer, Barry Richter and a 1994 sixth round draft pick (Yuri Litvinov) to Rangers for Darren Turcotte and James Patrick.

PANTHERS vs. RANGERS, 1993-94

	Overall Record: 3-2-0		at New York 2-0-0		at Florida 1-2-0		
	GP	W	L	T	GF	GA	PTS
Panthers	5	2	3	0	11	13	4
Rangers	5	3	2	0	13	11	6

Nov. 16	Rangers 4, Panthers 2 at Florida (Vanbiesbrouck & Healy/Richter)
Dec. 22	Rangers 2, Panthers 3 at Florida (Vanbiesbrouck & Richter)
Jan. 3	Rangers 3, Panthers 2 at New York (Vanbiesbrouck & Richter)
Mar. 14	Rangers 1, Panthers 2 at Florida (Vanbiesbrouck & Richter)
Apr. 4	Rangers 3, Panthers 2 at New York (Vanbiesbrouck & Richter)

SCORING

Panthers	GP	G	A	PTS	PIM	S	+\-	Rangers	GP	G	A	PTS	PIM	S	+\-
Mellanby	5	3	3	6	12	13	E	Zubov	5	0	4	4	2	15	4
Belanger	5	0	5	5	0	8	-3	Larmer	5	2	1	3	2	8	2
Lomakin	5	2	1	3	6	8	-4	Nemchinov	5	2	1	3	4	8	3
Lowry	5	2	1	3	4	8	E	Leetch	5	1	2	3	6	20	1
Skrudland	5	0	3	3	8	6	1	Beukeboom	5	2	0	2	2	8	E
Hull	5	2	0	2	0	5	E	Graves	5	2	0	2	2	27	E
Hough	5	1	1	2	0	9	1	Amonte	4	1	1	2	9	15	E
Brown	3	1	0	1	2	5	-1	Gartner	4	0	2	2	2	15	E
Barnes	3	0	1	1	0	8	-2	Kovalev	5	0	2	2	12	13	3
Benning	3	0	1	1	4	3	-1	Hartman	3	1	0	1	0	3	1
Niedermayer	4	0	1	1	0	0	-1	Lowe	4	1	0	1	2	2	4
Fitzgerald	5	0	1	1	0	8	-1	Kocur	5	1	0	1	17	2	1
Andersson	1	0	0	0	0	1	-2	Matteau	1	0	1	1	0	2	1
Gilhen	1	0	0	0	0	3	E	Noonan	1	0	1	1	0	4	1
Kudelski	1	0	0	0	0	3	-1	Kypreos	2	0	1	1	4	1	1
Smyth	1	0	0	0	0	0	E	Olczyk	2	0	1	1	10	3	1
Hawgood	2	0	0	0	5	4	E	Gilbert	5	0	1	1	0	8	1
Cirella	3	0	0	0	4	3	-3	Tikkanen	5	0	1	1	4	10	3
Foligno	3	0	0	0	2	6	-2	Anderson	1	0	0	0	0	2	E
Laus	3	0	0	0	7	0	-1	MacTavish	1	0	0	0	0	3	1
Levins	3	0	0	0	2	8	-3	Hudson	2	0	0	0	0	1	-1
Smith	4	0	0	0	2	3	E	Lidster	2	0	0	0	0	1	E
Lindsay	5	0	0	0	0	5	-2	Norstrom	2	0	0	0	0	1	E
Murphy	5	0	0	0	0	6	-2	Karpovtsev	3	0	0	0	0	0	2
Severyn	5	0	0	0	13	8	-3	Messier	4	0	0	0	2	8	E

GOALTENDING

	GP	MINS	GA	EN	AVG	W	L	T		GP	MINS	GA	EN	AVG	W	L	T
Vanbiesbrouck	5	298	13	0	2.62	2	3	0	Healy	1	30	1	0	2.00	1	0	0
									Richter	5	268	10	0	2.24	2	2	0

Panthers Power Play: 7-23 (30.4%)
Power Play Goals: Mellanby (3), Lomakin (2), Lowry, Brown
Shorthanded Goals: None
Game-Winning Goals: Hull, Mellanby

Game-Tying Goals: None

Goals by Period:	1st	2nd	3rd	OT	Total
Panthers	5	4	2	0	11
Rangers	3	7	3	0	13

Last Win at MSG: None
Last Win at Fla: 3/14/94 (2-1)

Rangers Power Play: 3-17 (17.6%)
Power Play Goals: Leetch, Graves, Beukeboom
Shorthanded Goals: None
Game Winning Goals: Amonte, Graves, Larmer

Game Tying Goals: None

Shots by Period:	1st	2nd	3rd	OT	Total
Panthers	53	47	31	0	131
Rangers	64	65	55	0	184

Last Win at MSG: 4/4/94 (3-2)
Last Win at Fla: 11/16/93 (4-2)

Last Ranger trade with Panthers: March 21, 1994, Panthers traded a ninth round draft choice (Vitali Yeremeyev) in the 1994 NHL Entry Draft in exchange for Peter Andersson.

KINGS vs. RANGERS, 1993-94

	Overall Record: 2-0-0		at New York 1-0-0		at Los Angeles 1-0-0		
	GP	W	L	T	GF	GA	PTS
Kings	2	0	2	0	6	8	0
Rangers	2	2	0	0	8	6	4

Oct. 24	Rangers 3, Kings 2 at New York (Hrudey & Richter)
Jan. 27	Rangers 5, Kings 4 (OT) at Los Angeles (Hrudey & Richter)

SCORING

Kings	GP	G	A	PTS	PIM	S	+\-
Gretzky	2	2	1	3	0	7	1
Lang	1	1	1	2	0	1	1
Donnelly	2	1	1	2	0	2	1
Houda	1	1	0	1	2	1	2
Ward	1	1	0	1	6	2	1
Jay	1	0	1	1	0	0	-1
Zhitnik	1	0	1	1	0	0	-2
Blake	2	0	1	1	2	2	-4
Kurri	2	0	1	1	0	3	-2
Robitaille	2	0	1	1	2	4	E
Conacher	1	0	0	0	0	2	E
Druce	1	0	0	0	0	3	-2
McEachern	1	0	0	0	0	1	-2
Murphy	1	0	0	0	0	1	E
Potvin	1	0	0	0	0	1	E
Rychel	1	0	0	0	0	0	E
Taylor	1	0	0	0	0	0	-1
Thomlinson	1	0	0	0	0	2	-1
Thompson	1	0	0	0	5	2	E
Granato	2	0	0	0	2	3	E
Huddy	2	0	0	0	2	4	-1
Sandstrom	2	0	0	0	6	3	1
Shuchuk	2	0	0	0	0	0	-2
Sydor	2	0	0	0	0	1	2
Watters	2	0	0	0	2	2	E

Rangers	GP	G	A	PTS	PIM	S	+\-
Kovalev	2	2	1	3	4	6	2
Messier	2	1	2	3	0	6	1
Zubov	2	1	2	3	0	3	1
Nemchinov	2	1	1	2	0	5	2
Tikkanen	2	1	1	2	2	11	-2
Turcotte	1	1	0	1	0	2	1
Amonte	2	0	1	1	0	8	-1
Hartman	1	0	1	1	0	1	1
Hudson	1	0	1	1	0	3	-1
Kypreos	1	0	1	1	2	1	1
Gartner	2	0	1	1	2	6	1
Gilbert	2	0	1	1	0	2	-1
Graves	2	0	1	1	11	13	1
Kocur	2	0	1	1	2	1	E
Leetch	2	0	1	1	0	8	3
Beukeboom	1	0	0	0	0	0	-1
Bourque	1	0	0	0	0	0	E
Larmer	1	0	0	0	0	0	1
Lidster	1	0	0	0	0	0	E
Karpovtsev	2	0	0	0	6	1	2
Lowe	2	0	0	0	2	3	-1
Wells	2	0	0	0			

GOALTENDING

	GP	MINS	GA	EN	AVG	W	L	T
Hrudey	2	124	8	0	3.87	0	2	0

	GP	MINS	GA	EN	AVG	W	L	T
Richter	2	125	6	0	2.88	2	0	0

Kings Power Play: 1-9 (11.1%)
Power Play Goals: Gretzky
Shorthanded Goals: None
Game-Winning Goals: None

Game-Tying Goals: None
Goals by Period: 1st 2nd 3rd OT Total
Kings   2   3   1   0   6
Rangers   4   2   1   1   8
Last Win at MSG: 3/12/90 (6-2)
Last Win at LA: 11/12/91 (6-1)

Rangers Power Play: 1-7 (14.3%)
Power Play Goals: Kovalev
Shorthanded Goals: None
Game Winning Goals: Messier (OT), Tikkanen

Game Tying Goals: None
Shots by Period: 1st 2nd 3rd OT Total
Kings   17 15 15 1   48
Rangers   28 31 21 9   89
Last Win at MSG: 10/24/93 (3-2)
Last Win at LA: 1/27/94 (5-4)

Last Ranger trade with Los Angeles: March 22, 1993, Kings trade John McIntyre to Rangers for Mark Hardy and Ottawa's fifth round draft choice in 1993.

CANADIENS VS. RANGERS, 1993-94

Overall Record: 1-2-1 at New York 1-0-1 at Montreal 0-2-0

	GP	W	L	T	GF	GA	PTS
Canadiens	4	2	1	1	14	13	5
Rangers	4	1	2	1	13	14	3

Oct. 28	Rangers 3, Canadiens 3 at New York (Roy & Richter)
Nov. 23	Rangers 5, Canadiens 4 at New York (Roy & Richter)
Jan. 8	Rangers 2, Canadiens 3 at Montreal (Roy & Healy)
Feb. 9	Rangers 3, Canadiens 4 (OT) at Montreal (Roy & Healy)

SCORING

Canadiens	GP	G	A	PTS	PIM	S	+\-
Schneider	4	3	3	6	4	12	1
Keane	4	1	4	5	4	5	2
Desjardins	4	2	2	4	0	5	-2
Odelein	4	0	3	3	24	3	2
Carbonneau	4	2	0	2	4	6	E
Bellows	3	1	1	2	4	11	E
DiPietro	3	1	1	2	0	5	E
Muller	3	1	1	2	6	10	-1
Damphousse	4	1	1	2	12	6	-3
Dionne	4	1	1	2	4	12	1
LeClair	4	1	1	2	0	6	3
Daigneault	3	0	2	2	0	3	3
Brunet	2	0	1	1	0	3	1
Roberge	2	0	1	1	5	0	1
Brisebois	3	0	1	1	4	2	E
Wilson	4	0	1	1	2	3	1
Brashear	1	0	0	0	2	0	E
Petrov	1	0	0	0	0	2	-1
Ramage	1	0	0	0	0	1	-1
Sevigny	1	0	0	0	2	0	E
Lebeau	2	0	0	0	0	1	E
Popovic	2	0	0	0	0	1	1
Haller	3	0	0	0	10	6	-2
Leeman	3	0	0	0	0	7	-2
Ronan	3	0	0	0	2	3	E
Roy	4	0	0	0	2	0	E

Rangers	GP	G	A	PTS	PIM	S	+\-
Zubov	4	3	3	6	4	13	1
Graves	4	4	1	5	4	18	5
Messier	4	2	3	5	2	12	5
Leetch	4	0	5	5	0	18	E
Gartner	4	1	2	3	8	14	1
Tikkanen	4	1	2	3	14	21	-6
Kovalev	4	0	3	3	17	18	-1
Nemchinov	4	0	2	2	0	8	E
Olczyk	2	1	0	1	0	1	2
Beukeboom	3	1	0	1	10	1	1
Hudson	3	0	1	1	2	1	-2
Lowe	4	0	1	1	4	3	-2
Wells	4	0	1	1	0	1	1
Kypreos	1	0	0	0	2	1	-1
Turcotte	1	0	0	0	0	3	-1
Bourque	2	0	0	0	2	0	E
Hartman	2	0	0	0	7	2	-1
Larmer	2	0	0	0	2	4	-1
Lidster	2	0	0	0	9	1	-1
Gilbert	3	0	0	0	0	4	E
Karpovtsev	3	0	0	0	2	3	-2
Amonte	4	0	0	0	0	9	E
Kocur	4	0	0	0	9	0	E

GOALTENDING

	GP	MINS	GA	EN	AVG	W	L	T
Roy	4	246	13	0	3.17	2	1	1

	GP	MINS	GA	EN	AVG	W	L	T
Richter	2	124	7	0	3.39	1	0	1
Healy	2	121	7	0	3.49	0	2	0

Canadiens Power Play: 5-21 (23.8%)
Power Play Goals: Bellows, Schneider, Desjardins, Damphousse, Dionne
Shorthanded Goals: None
Game-Winning Goals: LeClair, Desjardins (OT)
Game-Tying Goals: None
Goals by Period:

	1st	2nd	3rd	OT	Total
Canadiens	3	7	3	0	14
Rangers	5	5	3	0	13

Last Win at MSG: 11/6/91 (4-1)
Last Win at Mtl.: 2/9/94 (4-3)

Rangers Power Play: 5-23 (21.7%)
Power Play Goals: Zubov (2), Graves (2), Tikkanen
Shorthanded Goals: None
Game Winning Goals: Olczyk
Game Tying Goals: Graves
Shots by Period:

	1st	2nd	3rd	OT	Total
Canadiens	41	39	29	4	113
Rangers	40	64	49	3	156

Last Win at MSG: 11/23/93 (5-4)
Last Win at Mtl.: 10/5/91 (2-1)

Last Ranger trade with Montreal: January 27, 1988, Canadiens traded Chris Nilan to Rangers in exchange for option to exchange first round draft picks in 1989.

DEVILS vs. RANGERS, 1993-94

	Overall Record: 6-0-0	at New York 2-0-0	at New Jersey 3-0-0	at Halifax 1-0-0	
	GP	W	L	T	GF	GA	PTS
Devils	6	0	6	0	9	24	0
Rangers	6	6	0	0	24	9	12

Oct. 31	Rangers 4, Devils 1 at Halifax (Brodeur/Terreri & Richter)
Nov. 30	Rangers 3, Devils 1 at New Jersey (Terreri & Richter)
Dec. 5	Rangers 2, Devils 1 at New York (Terreri & Richter)
Dec. 26	Rangers 8, Devils 3 at New York (Terreri/Brodeur & Healy)
Feb. 24	Rangers 3, Devils 1 at New Jersey (Terreri/Brodeur & Richter)
Apr. 2	Rangers 4, Devils 2 at New Jersey (Terreri/Brodeur & Richter)

SCORING

Devils	GP	G	A	PTS	PIM	S	+\-	Rangers	GP	G	A	PTS	PIM	S	+\-
MacLean	6	2	2	4	4	16	2	Gartner	5	5	4	9	6	20	5
Millen	6	2	2	4	6	7	E	Zubov	6	1	8	9	6	23	4
Zelepukin	6	1	2	3	11	9	E	Nemchinov	6	4	4	8	4	15	5
Stevens	6	0	3	3	8	14	-4	Leetch	6	3	3	6	4	16	5
Nicholls	4	1	1	2	8	7	2	Kovalev	4	2	4	6	0	9	4
Richer	6	0	2	2	2	14	E	Graves	6	3	1	4	10	16	3
Guerin	5	1	0	1	2	12	-2	Amonte	5	1	2	3	0	13	2
Chorske	6	1	0	1	0	8	-4	Messier	5	0	3	3	17	7	1
Lemieux	6	1	0	1	4	8	-4	Lowe	6	0	3	3	6	2	1
Modry	3	0	1	1	2	2	-1	Olczyk	3	1	1	2	0	6	2
Albelin	5	0	1	1	10	5	1	Larmer	5	0	2	2	0	14	-2
Holik	6	0	1	1	2	14	-2	Gilbert	6	1	1	2	2	5	1
Carpenter	6	0	1	1	0	4	-4	Tikkanen	6	0	2	2	10	16	E
Niedermayer	6	0	1	1	10	10	-1	MacTavish	1	1	0	1	0	1	2
Dowd	1	0	0	0	0	3	-1	Matteau	1	1	0	1	0	2	1
Fetisov	3	0	0	0	2	2	-2	Turcotte	1	0	0	0	0	1	E
Smith	3	0	0	0	0	7	-3	Beukeboom	5	0	0	0	14	6	4
Semak	3	0	0	0	0	7	-3	Anderson	1	0	0	0	4	0	E
Daneyko	5	0	0	0	2	5	-3	Bourque	1	0	0	0	0	0	-1
Driver	5	0	0	0	2	9	-3	Hiller	1	0	0	0	0	0	E
Peluso	5	0	0	0	14	2	-2	Kypreos	1	0	0	0	0	0	E
McKay	6	0	0	0	14	5	-4	Noonan	1	0	0	0	0	1	E
								Lidster	2	0	0	0	2	2	E
								Hartman	3	0	0	0	14	2	E
								Hudson	4	0	0	0	0	3	-1
								Wells	5	0	0	0	4	3	1
								Karpovtsev	6	0	0	0	10	6	1
								Kocur	6	0	0	0	4	1	-1

GOALTENDING

	GP	MINS	GA	EN	AVG	W	L	T		GP	MINS	GA	EN	AVG	W	L	T
Terreri	6	207	12	0	3.48	0	2	0	Richter	5	300	6	0	1.20	5	0	0
Brodeur	4	152	12	0	4.74	0	4	0	Healy	1	60	3	0	3.00	1	0	0

Devils Power Play: 1-28 (3.6%)
Power Play Goals: Zelepukin

Shorthanded Goals: None
Game-Winning Goals: None

Game-Tying Goals: None
Goals by Period: 1st 2nd 3rd OT Total
Devils   5   4   0   0   9
Rangers   4   13   7   0   24
Last Win at MSG: 12/23/92 (5-4)
Last Win at NJ: 4/7/93 (5-2)

Rangers Power Play: 8-29 (27.6%)
Power Play Goals: Gartner (2), Nemchinov, Leetch, Zubov, Kovalev, Larmer, Gilbert
Shorthanded Goals: Gartner
Game Winning Goals: Nemchinov (2), Leetch, Gartner, Graves, Kovalev
Game Tying Goals: None
Shots by Period: 1st 2nd 3rd OT Total
Devils   61   55   50   0   166
Rangers   57   67   64   0   188
Last Win at MSG: 12/26/93 (8-3)
Last Win at NJ: 4/2/94 (4-2)

Last Ranger trade with New Jersey: November 2, 1979, Rockies traded Barry Beck to Rangers for Bobby Crawford, Lucien DeBlois, Pat Hickey, Mike McEwen, and Dean Turner.

ISLANDERS vs. RANGERS, 1993-94

	Overall Record:	1-2-2	at New York 0-0-2		at Islanders 1-2-0		
	GP	W	L	T	GF	GA	PTS
Islanders	5	2	1	2	22	20	6
Rangers	5	1	2	2	20	22	4

Nov. 27	Rangers 4, Islanders 6 at Islanders (Hextall & Healy/Richter)
Feb. 2	Rangers 4, Islanders 4 at New York (Hextall & Richter)
Mar. 4	Rangers 3, Islanders 3 at New York (Hextall/McLennan & Richter)
Mar. 5	Rangers 5, Islanders 4 at Islanders (Hextall & Healy/Richter)
Apr. 10	Rangers 4, Islanders 5 at Islanders (Hextall & Healy)

SCORING

Islanders	GP	G	A	PTS	PIM	S	+\-	Rangers	GP	G	A	PTS	PIM	S	+\-
McInnis	5	4	3	7	0	12	3	Graves	5	5	5	10	20	17	6
Ferraro	5	3	3	6	2	10	E	Messier	5	2	7	9	15	12	5
King	5	3	3	6	2	7	4	Zubov	5	2	5	7	4	15	-2
Thomas	5	4	1	5	8	13	-5	Kovalev	5	1	3	4	4	11	E
Turgeon	4	1	4	5	2	17	-1	Larmer	5	1	3	4	0	10	-3
Green	5	1	4	5	4	16	1	Leetch	5	1	3	4	4	16	3
Hogue	5	3	1	4	6	12	-5	Amonte	4	2	0	2	4	10	-2
Flatley	4	0	4	4	4	7	2	Beukeboom	5	1	1	2	20	3	2
Kurvers	4	0	4	4	0	7	2	Tikkanen	5	1	1	2	4	13	-3
Malakhov	5	2	1	3	8	19	-1	Karpovtsev	4	0	2	2	4	10	1
Kasparaitis	5	0	3	3	12	3	-2	MacTavish	1	1	0	1	0	4	1
Krupp	2	1	1	2	0	6	-1	Kocur	2	1	0	1	6	2	E
Pilon	2	0	2	2	2	0	2	Gartner	4	1	0	1	4	17	-2
Maley	4	0	2	2	0	3	-1	Gilbert	4	0	1	1	5	3	E
Kaminsky	1	0	1	1	0	0	2	Matteau	1	0	1	1	0	0	-1
Lachance	5	0	1	1	4	0	E	Hudson	3	0	1	1	15	4	1
Vaske	5	0	1	1	16	6	E	Kypreos	4	0	1	1	21	2	-1
Day	1	0	0	0	9	1	1	Lowe	4	0	1	1	0	4	-5
Grieve	1	0	0	0	5	0	E	Nemchinov	5	0	1	1	0	7	-1
Plante	1	0	0	0	0	0	E	Wells	5	0	1	1	6	3	E
Chynoweth	2	0	0	0	16	0	E	Anderson	1	0	0	0	0	1	E
Dalgarno	4	0	0	0	2	3	-1	Andersson	1	0	0	0	0	0	E
Acton	5	0	0	0	14	1	E	Bourque	1	0	0	0	0	0	E
Hextall	5	0	0	0	6	0	E	Lacroix	1	0	0	0	0	0	E
Vukota	5	0	0	0	4	0	E	Lidster	1	0	0	0	2	0	E
								Noonan	1	0	0	0	2	1	E
								Olczyk	1	0	0	0	2	1	E
								Hartman	2	0	0	0	2	2	1

GOALTENDING

	GP	MINS	GA	EN	AVG	W	L	T		GP	MINS	GA	EN	AVG	W	L	T
Hextall	5	264	20	0	4.55	2	1	1	Richter	4	202	14	0	4.16	1	0	2
McLennan	1	45	0	0	0.00	0	0	1	Healy	3	108	8	0	4.44	0	2	0

Islanders Power Play: 7-24 (29.2%)
Power Play Goals: Thomas (3), Hogue (2), McInnis, Malakhov
Shorthanded Goals: Hogue
Game-Winning Goals: Thomas, Malakhov
Game-Tying Goals: Ferraro, King

Rangers Power Play: 5-28 (17.9%)
Power Play Goals: Zubov (2), Graves, Leetch, Amonte
Shorthanded Goals: None
Game Winning Goals: Zubov
Game-Tying Goals: None

Goals by Period:	1st	2nd	3rd	OT	Total
Islanders	6	11	5	0	22
Rangers	9	6	5	0	20

Last Win at MSG: 4/2/93 (3-2)
Last Win at NYI: 4/10/94 (5-4)

Shots by Period:	1st	2nd	3rd	OT	Total
Islanders	44	52	41	6	143
Rangers	49	54	61	5	169

Last Win at MSG: 2/12/93 (4-3)
Last Win at NYI: 3/5/94 (5-4)

Last Ranger trade with Islanders: November 14, 1973, Islanders sent cash to Rangers for Ron Stewart.

SENATORS vs. RANGERS, 1993-94

Overall Record: 4-0-0   at New York 2-0-0   at Ottawa 2-0-0

	GP	W	L	T	GF	GA	PTS
Senators	4	0	4	0	7	20	0
Rangers	4	4	0	0	20	7	8

Nov	24	Rangers 7, Senators 1 at Ottawa (Billington & Healy)
Dec.	19	Rangers 6, Senators 3 at New York (Billington & Richter)
Feb.	12	Rangers 4, Senators 3 (OT) at Ottawa (Madeley & Richter)
Feb.	18	Rangers 3, Senators 0 at New York (Billlington & Richter)

SCORING

Senators	GP	G	A	PTS	PIM	S	+\-	Rangers	GP	G	A	PTS	PIM	S	+\-
Daigle	4	1	2	3	0	13	-1	Zubov	4	2	6	8	2	11	2
McLlwain	4	1	2	3	4	9	-5	Graves	4	5	2	7	5	21	2
Yashin	4	1	2	3	0	10	-2	Gartner	4	3	2	5	2	11	E
McBain	3	0	2	2	2	2	1	Amonte	4	2	3	5	6	12	6
Davydov	2	1	0	1	2	1	1	Messier	4	2	3	5	2	13	6
Kudelski	2	1	0	1	0	5	-3	Nemchinov	4	2	3	5	0	6	4
Lamb	4	1	0	1	6	8	-1	Kovalev	3	2	2	4	2	6	5
Shaw	4	1	0	1	4	8	-6	Leetch	4	0	4	4	2	15	4
Archibald	1	0	1	1	0	1	-1	Larmer	4	1	2	3	0	7	2
Filimonov	1	0	1	1	0	0	2	Olczyk	2	0	2	2	0	2	1
Glynn	2	0	1	1	2	2	1	Karpovtsev	4	0	2	2	10	6	2
Kekalainen	2	0	1	1	0	1	E	Tikkanen	4	0	2	2	0	14	3
Dineen	4	0	1	1	2	2	-1	Lowe	4	1	0	1	4	3	5
Burakovsky	1	0	0	0	0	0	-1	Beukeboom	3	0	1	1	6	1	4
Hamr	1	0	0	0	0	0	-3	Andersson	1	0	0	0	0	0	-1
Levins	1	0	0	0	0	0	E	Lidster	1	0	0	0	0	1	-2
Raglan	1	0	0	0	0	0	E	Bourque	2	0	0	0	0	0	-1
Schneider	1	0	0	0	0	1	-2	Kocur	2	0	0	0	0	3	E
Huffman	2	0	0	0	0	2	-2	Kypreos	2	0	0	0	5	2	-1
Lammens	2	0	0	0	2	0	-4	Gilbert	4	0	0	0	0	1	-1
Lauer	2	0	0	0	2	2	-3	Hudson	4	0	0	0	4	4	-1
Ruzicka	2	0	0	0	0	1	-2	Wells	4	0	0	0	2	2	-1
Turgeon	2	0	0	0	0	1	1								
Huard	3	0	0	0	5	1	-1								
Maciver	3	0	0	0	2	2	-1								
Rumble	3	0	0	0	9	1	-1								
Vial	3	0	0	0	2	2	-1								
Loewen	4	0	0	0	2	3	E								
Mallette	4	0	0	0	2	2	-5								

GOALTENDING

	GP	MINS	GA	EN	AVG	W	L	T
Madeley	1	63	4	0	3.81	0	1	0
Billington	3	180	16	0	5.33	0	3	0

	GP	MINS	GA	EN	AVG	W	L	T
Healy	1	60	1	0	1.00	1	0	0
Richter	3	183	6	0	1.93	3	0	0

Senators Power Play: 1-21 (4.8%)
Power Play Goals: Yashin

Shorthanded Goals: None
Game-Winning Goals: None

Game-Tying Goals: None
Goals by Period:

	1st	2nd	3rd	OT	Total
Senators	2	4	1	0	7
Rangers	5	6	8	1	20

Last Win at MSG: 3/6/34 (5-4)
Last Win at OTT: 12/23/26 (1-0)

Rangers Power Play: 6-18 (33.3%)
Power Play Goals: Graves (3), Zubov (2), Messier

Shorthanded Goals: Larmer
Game Winning Goals: Larmer, Graves, Gartner (OT), Amonte

Game Tying Goals: None
Shots by Period:

	1st	2nd	3rd	OT	Total
Senators	27	32	20	1	80
Rangers	39	47	53	2	141

Last Win at MSG: 2/18/94 (3-0)
Last Win at OTT: 2/12/94 (4-3)

Last Ranger trade with Ottawa: March 21, 1994, Senators traded future considerations to Rangers for Phil Bourque.

FLYERS vs. RANGERS, 1993-94

	Overall Record: 3-1-1		at New York 2-0-1	at Philadelphia 1-1-0		
	GP	W	L	T	GF	GA	PTS
Flyers	5	1	3	1	12	18	3
Rangers	5	3	1	1	18	12	7

Oct. 16	Rangers 3, Flyers 4 at Philadelphia (Roussel & Healy)
Jan. 14	Rangers 5, Flyers 2 at New York (Soderstrom & Richter)
Feb. 28	Rangers 4, Flyers 1 at New York (Roussel & Richter)
Mar. 29	Rangers 4, Flyers 3 at Philadelphia (Soderstrom & Richter)
Apr. 14	Rangers 2, Flyers 2 at New York ((Roussel & Richter)

SCORING

Flyers	GP	G	A	PTS	PIM	S	+\-	Rangers	GP	G	A	PTS	PIM	S	+\-
Brind'Amour	5	4	2	6	2	16	3	Nemchinov	4	1	5	6	2	13	4
Fedyk	4	2	2	4	2	5	E	Leetch	5	3	2	5	6	17	2
Recchi	5	1	3	4	2	10	-2	Zubov	4	0	5	5	0	13	1
Galley	5	0	4	4	6	11	-1	Kovalev	5	3	1	4	2	12	2
Renberg	5	2	1	3	0	8	1	Graves	5	2	2	4	0	19	1
Lindros	4	1	2	3	2	6	-1	Larmer	3	1	3	4	4	9	2
DiMaio	2	1	1	2	0	6	E	Gartner	3	3	0	3	0	15	3
Beranek	5	1	0	1	0	5	E	Tikkanen	5	1	2	3	6	16	2
Hawgood	1	0	1	1	0	2	1	Messier	5	0	3	3	2	12	-2
Faust	3	0	1	1	0	4	E	Matteau	2	1	1	2	0	6	1
Malgunas	3	0	1	1	2	2	2	Wells	5	1	1	2	2	1	E
Racine	4	0	1	1	4	9	-5	Hudson	2	1	0	1	0	1	E
Boivin	1	0	0	0	2	0	-1	MacTavish	2	1	0	1	0	7	1
Brimanis	1	0	0	0	0	1	-1	Karpovtsev	4	0	1	1	2	6	E
Holan	1	0	0	0	0	0	E	Lowe	4	0	1	1	2	1	E
Kordic	1	0	0	0	0	0	E	Gilbert	5	0	1	1	0	1	-1
Ramage	1	0	0	0	0	1	-2	Bourque	1	0	0	0	0	0	E
Butsayev	2	0	0	0	2	2	-2	Hartman	1	0	0	0	0	0	E
Lamb	2	0	0	0	2	2	-2	Olczyk	1	0	0	0	0	0	E
McGill	2	0	0	0	6	5	-1	Patrick	1	0	0	0	0	2	-1
Bowen	3	0	0	0	2	7	2	Turcotte	1	0	0	0	2	0	E
Zettler	3	0	0	0	2	4	-3	Anderson	2	0	0	0	0	7	-1
Brown	4	0	0	0	0	2	-1	Noonan	2	0	0	0	4	2	-1
Finley	4	0	0	0	2	3	4	Amonte	3	0	0	0	0	6	E
Yushkevich	4	0	0	0	0	8	E	Kypreos	3	0	0	0	0	2	-2
Conroy	5	0	0	0	0	2	-1	Lidster	3	0	0	0	2	1	-2
Dineen	5	0	0	0	2	10	E	Beukeboom	4	0	0	0	2	2	3
Tippett	5	0	0	0	2	3	-1	Kocur	5	0	0	0	2	2	-1

GOALTENDING

	GP	MINS	GA	EN	AVG	W	L	T		GP	MINS	GA	EN	AVG	W	L	T
Roussell	3	185	9	0	2.92	1	1	1	Richter	4	245	8	0	1.96	3	0	1
Soderstrom	2	119	8	1	4.03	0	2	0	Healy	1	60	4	0	4.00	0	1	0

Flyers Power Play: 2-19 (10.5%)
Power Play Goals: Recchi, Brind'Amour

Shorthanded Goals: None
Game-Winning Goals: Brind'Amour
Game-Tying Goals: None
Goals by Period: 1st 2nd 3rd OT Total
Flyers 4 3 5 0 12
Rangers 5 7 6 0 18
Last Win at MSG: 3/24/93 (5-4)
Last Win at PHI: 10/16/93 (4-3)

Rangers Power Play: 6-21 (28.6%)
Power Play Goals: Leetch (2), Gartner, Graves, Kovalev, Nemchinov
Shorthanded Goals: Gartner
Game Winning Goals: Leetch, Kovalev
Game Tying Goals: MacTavish
Shots by Period: 1st 2nd 3rd OT Total
Flyers 37 45 48 4 134
Rangers 50 59 60 4 173
Last Win at MSG: 2/28/94 (4-1)
Last Win at PHI: 3/29/94 (4-3)

Last Ranger trade with Philadelphia: August 8, 1991, Flyers traded Don Biggs to the Rangers in exchange for future considerations.

PENGUINS vs. RANGERS, 1993-94

Overall Record: 2-2-0   at New York 2-0-0   at Pittsburgh 0-2-0

	GP	W	L	T	GF	GA	PTS
Penguins	4	2	2	0	15	13	4
Rangers	4	2	2	0	13	15	4

Oct. 9	Rangers 2, Penguins 3 at Pittsburgh (Wregget & Richter)
Jan. 31	Rangers 5, Penguins 3 at New York (Wregget & Richter)
Feb. 21	Rangers 4, Penguins 3 (OT) at New York (Barrasso & Richter)
Mar. 12	Rangers 2, Penguins 6 at Pittsburgh (Barrasso & Healy)

SCORING

Penguins	GP	G	A	PTS	PIM	S	+\-	Rangers	GP	G	A	PTS	PIM	S	+\-
Straka	4	5	1	6	0	7	4	Messier	4	2	3	5	4	13	-1
Jagr	3	2	4	6	2	13	3	Gartner	4	4	0	4	2	13	E
Lemieux	1	2	2	4	0	2	2	Zubov	3	0	4	4	7	8	-2
D. Brown	4	1	3	4	0	8	4	Graves	4	2	1	3	2	9	-1
Francis	4	0	4	4	4	2	-4	Leetch	4	1	2	3	2	14	-1
Murphy	4	0	4	4	2	6	-1	Nemchinov	4	1	1	2	2	8	E
Stevens	4	1	2	3	15	11	1	Larmer	3	0	2	2	2	6	-1
Mullen	4	1	1	2	2	8	2	Kovalev	3	0	2	2	4	7	E
K.Samuelsson	4	0	1	1	2	4	2	Hudson	3	1	0	1	10	8	2
Sandstrom	2	0	2	2	0	4	2	Wells	3	1	0	1	4	4	3
Taglianetti	2	0	2	2	0	1	2	Amonte	4	1	0	1	2	10	-3
McEachern	2	1	0	1	4	8	1	Beukeboom	3	0	1	1	21	4	-1
Stapleton	2	1	0	1	0	5	E	Gilbert	3	0	1	1	2	2	E
G. Brown	2	0	1	1	2	0	1	Karpovtsev	4	0	1	1	6	4	1
Tocchet	2	0	1	1	2	6	-1	Tikkanen	4	0	1	1	6	13	-4
U.Samuelsson	4	0	1	1	6	3	4	Andersson	1	0	0	0	0	0	-2
DePalma	1	0	0	0	0	0	E	Bourque	1	0	0	0	0	0	E
Karabin	1	0	0	0	0	0	E	Lacroix	1	0	0	0	0	0	E
Paek	1	0	0	0	0	0	-1	Lidster	1	0	0	0	2	1	E
Patterson	1	0	0	0	0	0	E	Norstrom	1	0	0	0	0	0	E
Tamer	1	0	0	0	0	0	E	Patrick	1	0	0	0	0	0	E
Trottier	1	0	0	0	2	1	E	Turcotte	1	0	0	0	0	1	E
Barrasso	2	0	0	0	2	0	E	Hartman	2	0	0	0	10	3	E
Jennings	2	0	0	0	5	2	-1	Kocur	3	0	0	0	9	3	1
McSorley	2	0	0	0	9	5	E	Kypreos	3	0	0	0	0	2	-1
Needham	2	0	0	0	0	0	E	Lowe	3	0	0	0	2	2	-2
Naslund	3	0	0	0	0	4	-2								
Daniels	4	0	0	0	0	3	-1								
Ramsey	4	0	0	0	6	2	-1								

GOALTENDING

	GP	MINS	GA	EN	AVG	W	L	T		GP	MINS	GA	EN	AVG	W	L	T
Barrasso	2	120	6	0	3.00	1	1	0	Richter	3	179	9	0	3.02	2	1	0
Wregget	2	119	7	0	3.50	1	1	0	Healy	1	60	6	0	6.00	0	1	0

Penguins Power Play: 6-25 (24.0%)
Power Play Goals: Straka, Mullen, Stapleton, Jagr, Lemieux, Stevens
Shorthanded Goals: None
Game-Winning Goals: Straka, Lemieux
Game-Tying Goals: None

Goals by Period:	1st	2nd	3rd	OT	Total
Penguins	4	5	6	0	15
Rangers	5	3	4	1	13

Last Win at MSG: 4/9/93 (10-4)
Last Win at Pit: 3/12/94 (6-2)

Rangers Power Play: 6-23 (26.1%)
Power Play Goals: Gartner (3), Graves (2), Leetch
Shorthanded Goals: Gartner
Game Winning Goals: Messier, Amonte (OT)
Game Tying Goals: None

Shots by Period:	1st	2nd	3rd	OT	Total
Penguins	35	39	29	0	103
Rangers	59	42	33	1	135

Last Win at MSG: 2/21/94 (4-3)
Last Win at Pit: 11/25/92 (11-3)

Last Ranger trade with Pittsburgh: Sept. 14, 1989, Penguins traded Lee Giffin to Rangers for future considerations.

NORDIQUES vs. RANGERS, 1993-94

Overall Record: 4-0-0 at New York 2-0-0   at Quebec 2-0-0

	GP	W	L	T	GF	GA	PTS
Nordiques	4	0	4	0	10	19	0
Rangers	4	4	0	0	19	10	8

Oct. 13	Rangers 6, Nordiques 4 at New York (Cloutier/Fiset & Richter/Healy)
Nov. 6	Rangers 4, Nordiques 2 at Quebec (Thibault & Richter)
Feb. 14	Rangers 4, Nordiques 2 at Quebec (Fiset & Richter)
Mar. 2	Rangers 5, Nordiques 2 at New York (Fiset & Richter)

SCORING

Nordiques	GP	G	A	PTS	PIM	S	+\-
Ricci	4	2	1	3	2	5	1
Gelinas	2	1	2	3	0	3	3
Sundin	4	1	2	3	6	5	-2
Sakic	4	0	3	3	3	12	-2
Gusarov	4	0	2	2	0	4	-1
Nolan	1	1	0	1	2	2	2
Bassen	2	1	0	1	2	3	-1
Kovalenko	2	1	0	1	0	3	1
Young	3	1	0	1	0	7	-1
Finn	4	1	0	1	2	7	2
Kamensky	4	1	0	1	8	7	E
Butcher	2	0	1	1	4	3	-3
Karpa	2	0	1	1	2	3	1
Sjodin	2	0	1	1	2	9	1
Twist	2	0	1	1	2	2	1
Fraser	1	0	0	0	0	0	E
Savage	1	0	0	0	0	0	E
Foote	2	0	0	0	4	3	1
Huffman	2	0	0	0	2	2	2
Lapointe	2	0	0	0	6	3	-1
Lindberg	2	0	0	0	4	2	E
McKee	2	0	0	0	0	1	1
Sutter	2	0	0	0	6	2	-1
Wolanin	2	0	0	0	6	4	E
MacDermid	3	0	0	0	0	0	-1
Rucinsky	3	0	0	0	4	7	-2
Leschyshyn	4	0	0	0	2	7	1
Simon	4	0	0	0	35	5	1

Rangers	GP	G	A	PTS	PIM	S	+\-
Messier	4	3	5	8	4	16	3
Leetch	4	2	6	8	2	15	3
Graves	4	3	4	7	7	13	1
Larmer	3	3	3	6	4	8	E
Tikkanen	4	2	2	4	2	12	-2
Gartner	4	2	1	3	2	7	E
Zubov	4	0	3	3	2	10	E
Andersson	2	1	1	2	2	4	1
Kypreos	2	1	1	2	11	4	2
Amonte	4	0	2	2	2	8	-3
Nemchinov	4	0	2	2	6	7	-1
Beukeboom	2	1	0	1	2	1	3
Karpovtsev	2	1	0	1	4	4	-1
Turcotte	1	0	1	1	5	0	-1
Lowe	2	0	1	1	12	0	E
Kovalev	3	0	1	1	21	3	-1
Norstrom	1	0	0	0	0	0	-2
Hudson	2	0	0	0	0	0	E
Olczyk	2	0	0	0	0	2	-2
Hartman	3	0	0	0	4	2	-1
Kocur	3	0	0	0	4	2	-1
Gilbert	4	0	0	0	2	6	-1
Lidster	4	0	0	0	4	6	-3
Wells	4	0	0	0	4	7	-3

GOALTENDING

Nordiques	GP	MINS	GA	EN	AVG	W	L	T
Thibault	1	59	4	0	4.10	0	1	0
Fiset	3	169	13	1	4.62	0	3	0
Cloutier	1	9	1	0	6.70	0	0	0

Rangers	GP	MINS	GA	EN	AVG	W	L	T
Healy	1	54	2	0	2.20	1	0	0
Richter	4	186	8	0	2.58	3	0	0

Nordiques Power Play: 1-30 (3.3%)
Power Play Goals: Ricci

Shorthanded Goals: Ricci

Game-Winning Goals: None

Game-Tying Goals: None

Goals by Period:

	1st	2nd	3rd	OT	Total
Nordiques	6	2	2	0	10
Rangers	6	8	5	0	19

Last Win at MSG: 3/28/93 (3-2)
Last Win at QUE: 3/6/93 (10-2)

Rangers Power Play: 11-30 (36.7%)
Power Play Goals: Leetch (2), Graves (2), Gartner (2), Larmer (2), Messier, Karpovtsev, Tikkanen

Shorthanded Goals: Tikkanen, Messier, Larmer, Andersson

Game Winning Goals: Messier, Karpovtsev, Kypreos, Andersson

Game Tying Goals: None

Shots by Period:

	1st	2nd	3rd	OT	Total
Nordiques	40	34	36	0	110
Rangers	51	51	35	0	137

Last Win at MSG: 3/2/94 (5-2)
Last Win at QUE: 2/14/94 (4-2)

Last Ranger trade with Quebec: September 9, 1993, Nordiques traded Alexander Karpovtsev to Rangers for Mike Hurlbut.

BLUES vs. RANGERS, 1993-94

	Overall Record: 2-0-0		at New York 1-0-0		at St. Louis 1-0-0		
	GP	W	L	T	GF	GA	PTS
Blues	2	0	2	0	4	8	0
Rangers	2	2	0	0	8	4	4

Dec. 29 Rangers 4, Blues 3 at St. Louis (Hrivnak & Richter)
Jan. 18 Rangers 4, Blues 1 at New York (Joseph & Richter)

SCORING

Blues	GP	G	A	PTS	PIM	S	+\-
Janney	2	0	2	2	0	1	E
Karamnov	2	0	2	2	0	3	3
Chase	1	1	0	1	2	2	1
Hull	2	1	0	1	0	7	-2
Montgomery	2	1	0	1	0	4	1
Prokhorov	2	1	0	1	2	4	E
Brown	1	0	1	1	0	5	E
Shanahan	2	0	1	1	0	13	2
Sutter	2	0	1	1	0	2	E
Butcher	1	0	0	0	0	1	-2
Korolev	1	0	0	0	0	2	E
La Fayette	1	0	0	0	0	2	-1
Laperierre	1	0	0	0	0	1	E
McRae	1	0	0	0	0	0	E
Zombo	1	0	0	0	2	0	1
Baron	2	0	0	0	2	2	-2
Bassen	2	0	0	0	4	6	-2
Bozon	2	0	0	0	4	5	-2
Crossman	2	0	0	0	0	1	2
Hedican	2	0	0	0	4	1	-2
Miller	2	0	0	0	0	4	-2
Tilley	2	0	0	0	0	0	-3

Rangers	GP	G	A	PTS	PIM	S	+\-
Larmer	2	0	4	4	0	3	3
Tikkanen	1	2	1	3	0	9	1
Zubov	2	0	3	3	0	6	3
Graves	2	2	0	2	0	10	E
Nemchinov	2	1	1	2	0	4	E
Amonte	2	0	2	2	2	7	2
Gartner	2	1	0	1	2	5	-1
Karpovtsev	2	1	0	1	4	3	E
Lowe	2	1	0	1	0	2	4
Messier	1	0	1	1	0	6	2
Beukeboom	2	0	1	1	8	1	-1
Leetch	2	0	1	1	2	4	-3
Bourque	1	0	0	0	0	2	E
Gilbert	1	0	0	0	0	1	1
Hartman	1	0	0	0	0	0	E
Kypreos	1	0	0	0	0	2	E
Hudson	2	0	0	0	4	1	-1
Kocur	2	0	0	0	0	0	E
Kovalev	2	0	0	0	2	3	-2
Olczyk	2	0	0	0	2	1	E
Wells	2	0	0	0	0	1	1

GOALTENDING

	GP	MINS	GA	EN	AVG	W	L	T
Hrivnak	1	60	4	0	4.00	0	1	0
Joseph	1	60	4	0	4.00	0	1	0

	GP	MINS	GA	EN	AVG	W	L	T
Richter	2	120	4	0	2.00	2	0	0

Blues Power Play: 0-13 (0.0%)
Power Play Goals: None
Shorthanded Goals: None
Game-Winning Goals: None
Game-Tying Goals: None
Goals by Period: 1st 2nd 3rd OT Total
Blues   1   1   2   0   4
Rangers   5   2   1   0   8
Last Win at MSG: 1/8/92 (5-3)
Last Win at St.L: 1/6/90 (4-3)

Rangers Power Play: 2-7 (28.6%)
Power Play Goals: Tikkanen, Graves
Shorthanded Goals: None
Game Winning Goals: Tikkanen, Nemchinov
Game Tying Goals: None
Shots by Period: 1st 2nd 3rd OT Total
Blues   24 17 25   0   66
Rangers   25 17 25   0   67
Last Win at MSG: 1/18/94 (4-1)
Last Win at St.L: 12/29/93 (4-3)

Last Ranger trade with St. Louis: July 24, 1994, Blues traded Petr Nedved to Rangers for Doug Lidster and Esa Tikkanen.

SHARKS vs. RANGERS, 1993-94

	Overall Record: 1-1-0		at New York 1-0-0		at San Jose 0-1-0		
	GP	W	L	T	GF	GA	PTS
Sharks	2	0	1	1	6	11	1
Rangers	2	1	0	1	11	6	3

Nov. 14 Rangers 3, Sharks 3 at New York (Irbe & Richter)
Jan. 25 Rangers 8, Sharks 3 at San Jose (Irbe/Waite & Richter)

SCORING

Sharks	GP	G	A	PTS	PIM	S	+\-
Garpenlov	2	1	2	3	0	6	1
Norton	2	0	3	3	2	3	E
Ozolinsh	2	2	0	2	0	3	1
Larionov	2	1	1	2	2	4	1
Odgers	2	1	1	2	2	5	-1
Falloon	2	1	0	1	0	6	E
Whitney	1	0	1	1	0	1	-1
Elik	2	0	1	1	4	5	E
Errey	2	0	1	1	8	3	-4
Gaudreau	2	0	1	1	0	5	-2
Craigwell	1	0	0	0	2	0	-1
Kroupa	1	0	0	0	0	0	-1
Maley	1	0	0	0	0	0	E
Baker	2	0	0	0	0	1	-3
Duchesne	2	0	0	0	0	1	-1
Makarov	2	0	0	0	0	1	1
Pederson	2	0	0	0	0	3	-2
Rathje	2	0	0	0	2	1	-2
Zettler	2	0	0	0	0	2	-2
Zmolek	2	0	0	0	8	1	-2

Rangers	GP	G	A	PTS	PIM	S	+\-
Larmer	2	2	3	5	0	6	3
Messier	2	2	2	4	4	6	3
Leetch	2	0	4	4	0	4	3
Zubov	2	0	4	4	2	2	1
Amonte	2	2	1	3	0	6	3
Tikkanen	2	0	3	3	4	1	1
Beukeboom	2	2	0	2	6	3	2
Graves	2	1	1	2	4	6	2
Lowe	2	0	2	2	2	0	1	E
Gartner	1	1	0	1	4	6	E
Nemchinov	2	1	0	1	0	4	E
Wells	2	0	1	1	2	0	1
Hudson	1	0	0	0	0	1	E
Karpovtsev	1	0	0	0	0	0	E
Lidster	1	0	0	0	4	0	E
Gilbert	2	0	0	0	0	0	2
Kocur	2	0	0	0	0	0	-1
Kovalev	2	0	0	0	4	5	1
Kypreos	2	0	0	0	0	2	-1
Olczyk	2	0	0	0	0	3	-2

GOALTENDING

	GP	MINS	GA	EN	AVG	W	L	T
Irbe	2	114	10	0	5.26	0	1	1
Waite	1	11	1	0	5.45	0	0	0

	GP	MINS	GA	EN	AVG	W	L	T
Richter	2	125	6	0	2.88	1	0	1

Sharks Power Play: 3-11 (27.3%)
Power Play Goals: Garpenlov, Ozolinsh, Odgers
Shorthanded Goals: None
Game-Winning Goals: None
Game-Tying Goals: Larionov

Goals by Period:	1st	2nd	3rd	OT	Total
Sharks	2	1	2	0	6
Rangers	4	2	5	0	11

Last Win at MSG: None
Last Win at SJ: None

Rangers Power Play: 4-10 (40.0%)
Power Play Goals: Larmer, Messier, Graves, Gartner
Shorthanded Goals: None
Game Winning Goals: Larmer
Game Tying Goals: None

Shots by Period:	1st	2nd	3rd	OT	Total
Sharks	15	22	13	1	51
Rangers	15	18	18	5	56

Last Win at MSG: 3/19/93 (8-1)
Last Win at SJ: 1/25/94 (8-3)

Last trade with San Jose: May 30, 1991, Sharks traded Tim Kerr to Rangers for Brian Mullen.

LIGHTNING vs. RANGERS, 1993-94

Overall Record: 3-2-0   at New York 2-1-0   at Tampa 1-1-0

	GP	W	L	T	GF	GA	PTS
Lightning	5	2	3	0	19	19	4
Rangers	5	3	2	0	19	19	6

Oct. 7	Rangers 5, Lightning 4 at New York (Jablonski & Healy)
Oct. 22	Rangers 1, Lightning 4 at Tampa Bay (Puppa & Richter)
Nov. 8	Rangers 6, Lightning 3 at New York (Puppa & Richter)
Nov. 19	Rangers 5, Lightning 3 at Tampa Bay (Puppa & Richter)
Jan. 10	Rangers 2, Lightning 5 at New York (Puppa & Healy/Richter)

SCORING

Lightning	GP	G	A	PTS	PIM	S	+\-	Rangers	GP	G	A	PTS	PIM	S	+\-
Gratton	5	1	5	6	0	11	E	Tikkanen	5	5	2	7	10	13	5
Bradley	4	2	3	5	2	11	-3	Graves	5	4	1	5	10	11	1
Klima	5	2	3	5	0	10	-4	Amonte	5	1	4	5	0	7	1
McDougall	4	2	2	4	0	6	1	Kovalev	5	1	4	5	21	17	-2
Andersson	5	2	2	4	17	14	4	Larmer	2	2	2	4	0	6	2
Savard	5	1	3	4	6	11	E	Messier	5	2	2	4	0	18	-1
Tucker	5	0	4	4	0	7	2	Zubov	4	0	4	4	0	10	1
Creighton	2	2	0	2	0	4	2	Leetch	5	2	1	3	15	19	-5
Beers	3	1	1	2	4	3	-3	Patrick	1	0	2	2	0	1	2
Bergevin	5	1	1	2	0	4	1	Hudson	3	0	2	2	0	5	3
Gallant	4	0	2	2	6	4	E	Lowe	5	0	2	2	6	5	4
Bureau	4	1	0	1	0	6	1	Kypreos	2	1	0	1	5	2	E
Dufresne	4	1	0	1	4	5	2	Nemchinov	5	1	0	1	2	12	-5
Zamuner	4	1	0	1	0	7	-2	Healy	2	0	1	1	2	0	E
Cole	5	1	0	1	2	7	E	Karpovtsev	3	0	1	1	2	9	1
Reekie	5	1	0	1	12	8	2	Lidster	3	0	1	1	0	4	-2
Joseph	2	0	1	1	6	6	-1	Wells	5	0	1	1	14	8	E
Elynuik	3	0	1	1	4	6	-1	Bourque	1	0	0	0	0	0	E
Poeschek	3	0	1	1	9	3	1	J. Messier	1	0	0	0	0	1	-1
Bergland	1	0	0	0	0	0	1	Hartman	2	0	0	0	0	0	E
Gretzky	1	0	0	0	0	0	E	Turcotte	2	0	0	0	0	1	-1
DiMaio	2	0	0	0	2	2	-2	Beukeboom	3	0	0	0	4	5	-2
Hamrlik	2	0	0	0	4	3	1	Olczyk	3	0	0	0	2	1	-2
Lipuma	2	0	0	0	2	1	E	Gartner	5	0	0	0	4	15	-3
Rochefort	2	0	0	0	6	2	1	Gilbert	5	0	0	0	2	1	-4
Chambers	3	0	0	0	2	2	1	Kocur	5	0	0	0	4	6	-1

GOALTENDING

	GP	MINS	GA	EN	AVG	W	L	T		GP	MINS	GA	EN	AVG	W	L	T
Puppa	4	240	14	0	3.50	2	2	0	Richter	4	193	12	0	3.73	2	1	0
Jablonski	1	59	5	0	5.10	0	1	0	Healy	2	107	7	0	3.93	1	1	0

Lightning Power Play: 4-21 (19.0%)
Power Play Goals: Beers, Bradley, Creighton, Klima
Shorthanded Goals: Gratton

Game-Winning Goals: Cole, Bergevin

Game-Tying Goals: None

Goals by Period:	1st	2nd	3rd	OT	Total
Lightning	11	4	4	0	19
Rangers	4	9	6	0	19

Last Win at MSG: 1/10/94 (5-2)
Last Win at T.B.: 10/22/93 (4-1)

Rangers Power Play: 5-18 (27.8%)
Power Play Goals: Leetch (2), Amonte, Graves, Nemchinov
Shorthanded Goals: Graves (2), Tikkanen, Larmer

Game Winning Goals: Leetch, Tikkanen, Messier

Game Tying Goals: None

Shots by Period:	1st	2nd	3rd	OT	Total
Lightning	52	48	43	0	143
Rangers	62	54	61	0	177

Last Win at MSG: 11/8/93 (6-3)
Last Win at T.B.: 11/19/93 (5-3)

Last Ranger trade with Lightning: June 25, 1993, Lightning traded Glenn Healy to Rangers in exchange for a return of Tampa Bay's 1993 third round draft choice.

MAPLE LEAFS vs. RANGERS, 1993-94

Overall Record: 2-0-0   at New York 1-0-0   at Toronto 1-0-0

	GP	W	L	T	GF	GA	PTS
Maple Leafs	2	0	2	0	6	9	0
Rangers	2	2	0	0	9	6	4

Dec. 4   Rangers 4, Maple Leafs 3 at Toronto (Potvin & Richter)
Apr. 8   Rangers 5, Maple Leafs 3 at New York (Potvin/Rhodes & Richter)

SCORING

Maple Leafs	GP	G	A	PTS	PIM	S	+\-
Clark	2	2	2	4	0	8	1
Cullen	1	1	2	3	0	1	1
Gartner	1	1	1	2	0	5	1
Macoun	2	0	2	2	0	2	-5
Borschevsky	1	1	0	1	0	2	E
Zezel	1	1	0	1	0	2	1
Osborne	1	0	1	1	2	0	1
Andreychuk	2	0	1	1	2	9	-3
Berg	2	0	1	1	4	2	E
Lefebvre	2	0	1	1	0	0	2
Potvin	2	0	1	1	0	0	E
Anderson	1	0	0	0	0	1	-2
Baumgartner	1	0	0	0	0	0	E
Berehowsky	1	0	0	0	0	2	2
Ellett	1	0	0	0	0	2	1
Gill	1	0	0	0	0	2	-1
Govedaris	1	0	0	0	0	0	E
Harlock	1	0	0	0	0	0	E
Krushelnyski	1	0	0	0	2	0	E
Larose	1	0	0	0	2	0	E
McRae	1	0	0	0	0	1	E
Mironov	1	0	0	0	2	1	-1
Eastwood	2	0	0	0	2	3	E
Gilmour	2	0	0	0	2	6	-6
Manderville	2	0	0	0	2	5	-1
Pearson	2	0	0	0	4	0	1
Rouse	2	0	0	0	0	0	-2

Rangers	GP	G	A	PTS	PIM	S	+\-
Kovalev	1	2	0	2	2	5	1
Tikkanen	2	2	0	2	0	10	3
Anderson	1	1	1	2	0	3	E
MacTavish	1	1	1	2	0	3	3
Larmer	2	1	1	2	15	3	2
Karpovtsev	2	0	2	2	0	1	2
Messier	2	0	2	2	0	9	1
Zubov	2	0	2	2	0	9	1
Gartner	1	1	0	1	0	5	-1
Graves	2	1	0	1	2	8	E
Noonan	1	0	1	1	2	2	2
Norstrom	1	0	1	1	0	0	E
Leetch	2	0	1	1	2	16	1
Amonte	1	0	0	0	2	3	E
Hartman	1	0	0	0	2	0	E
Hudson	1	0	0	0	2	0	E
Kocur	1	0	0	0	0	0	E
Kypreos	1	0	0	0	2	0	-1
Lowe	1	0	0	0	2	0	E
Matteau	1	0	0	0	0	1	E
Olczyk	1	0	0	0	0	1	E
Beukeboom	2	0	0	0	0	0	E
Gilbert	2	0	0	0	2	1	-2
Nemchinov	2	0	0	0	0	3	-3
Wells	1	0	0	0	2	1	-1

GOALTENDING

	GP	MINS	GA	EN	AVG	W	L	T
Rhodes	1	23	1	0	2.61	0	0	0
Potvin	2	96	8	0	5.00	0	2	0

	GP	MINS	GA	EN	AVG	W	L	T
Richter	2	120	6	0	3.00	2	0	0

Maple Leafs Power Play: 1-12 (8.3%)
Power Play Goals: Clark
Shorthanded Goals: None
Game-Winning Goals: None
Game-Tying Goals: None
Goals by Period: 1st 2nd 3rd OT Total
Maple Leafs   2   3   1   0   6
Rangers   0   7   2   0   9
Last Win at MSG: 12/19/90 (3-1)
Last Win at Tor: 1/30/93 (3-1)

Rangers Power Play: 2-11 (18.2%)
Power Play Goals: Graves, MacTavish
Shorthanded Goals: Tikkanen
Game Winning Goals: Gartner, MacTavish
Game Tying Goals: None
Shots by Period: 1st 2nd 3rd OT Total
Maple Leafs   19   19   16   0   54
Rangers   33   30   21   0   84
Last Win at MSG: 4/8/94 (5-3)
Last Win at Tor: 12/4/93 (4-3)

Last Ranger trade with Toronto: March 21, 1994 Maple Leafs traded Glenn Anderson, Scott Malone and a 1994 fourth round draft choice (Alexander Korobolin) to the Rangers in exchange for Mike Gartner.

CANUCKS vs. RANGERS, 1993-94

	Overall Record: 2-0-0	at New York 1-0-0	at Vancouver 1-0-0			
	GP	W	L	T	GF	GA	PTS
Canucks	2	0	2	0	5	11	0
Rangers	2	2	0	0	11	5	4

Nov. 3   Rangers 6, Canucks 3 at New York (Whitmore & Richter)
Mar. 25   Rangers 5, Canucks 2 at Vancouver (Whitmore & Richter)

SCORING

Canucks	GP	G	A	PTS	PIM	S	+\-	Rangers	GP	G	A	PTS	PIM	S	+\-
Courtnall	2	0	2	2	2	9	-3	Leetch	2	3	2	5	6	11	1
Charbonneau	1	1	0	1	0	1	1	Messier	2	0	4	4	0	4	1
Craven	1	1	0	1	0	1	1	Nemchinov	1	2	0	2	0	6	2
Linden	2	1	0	1	2	6	-4	Noonan	1	2	0	2	0	3	2
McIntyre	2	1	0	1	0	4	E	Larmer	2	2	0	2	2	3	2
Murzyn	2	1	0	1	4	4	1	Graves	2	1	1	2	2	3	1
Bure	1	0	1	1	2	4	-1	Amonte	1	0	2	2	0	2	1
Morin	1	0	1	1	0	3	1	Kovalev	2	0	2	2	4	2	1
Adams	2	0	1	1	2	5	E	Zubov	2	0	2	2	0	5	E
Antoski	2	0	1	1	13	2	E	Tikkanen	2	1	0	1	4	4	1
Lumme	2	0	1	1	2	8	-1	Gartner	1	1	0	1	0	3	1
Momesso	2	0	1	1	7	3	E	Gilbert	2	1	0	1	2	2	1
Odjick	2	0	1	1	14	2	E	Karpovtsev	2	0	1	1	0	0	3
Ronning	2	0	1	1	0	2	-5	Lowe	2	0	1	1	4	0	1
Babych	1	0	0	0	2	0	E	Anderson	1	0	0	0	0	0	-1
Brown	1	0	0	0	2	1	E	Beukeboom	1	0	0	0	15	1	E
Dirk	1	0	0	0	0	0	-3	Hartman	1	0	0	0	0	0	E
Hedican	1	0	0	0	0	2	1	Kypreos	1	0	0	0	5	1	-1
Hunter	1	0	0	0	26	0	E	Lidster	1	0	0	0	0	0	E
Lafayette	1	0	0	0	0	0	1	MacTavish	1	0	0	0	9	0	-1
Plavsic	1	0	0	0	0	2	E	Matteau	1	0	0	0	2	0	E
Ward	1	0	0	0	0	2	-1	Olczyk	1	0	0	0	0	4	E
Diduck	2	0	0	0	5	3	-3	Kocur	2	0	0	0	2	2	-1
Slegr	2	0	0	0	19	4	E	Wells	2	0	0	0	2	1	1

GOALTENDING

	GP	MINS	GA	EN	AVG	W	L	T		GP	MINS	GA	EN	AVG	W	L	T
Whitmore	2	120	11	0	5.50	0	2	0	Richter	2	120	5	0	2.50	2	0	0

Canucks Power Play: 1-12 (8.3%)
Power Play Goals: Linden

Shorthanded Goals: None
Game-Winning Goals: None
Game-Tying Goals: None
Goals by Period: 1st   2nd   3rd   OT   Total
Canucks   1   1   3   0   5
Rangers   6   5   0   0   11
Last Win at MSG: 2/21/88 (6-4)
Last Win at Van: 2/24/93 (5-4)

Rangers Power Play: 4-15 (26.7%)
Power Play Goals: Noonan (2), Leetch, Tikkanen

Shorthanded Goals: Leetch, Larmer
Game Winning Goals: Larmer, Noonan
Game Tying Goals: None
Shots by Period: 1st   2nd   3rd   OT   Total
Canucks   21   19   28   0   68
Rangers   20   23   14   0   57
Last Win at MSG: 11/3/93 (6-3)
Last Win at Van: 3/25/94 (5-2)

Last Ranger trade with Vancouver: June 20, 1993, Canucks traded Doug Lidster to Rangers for John Vanbiesbrouck.

CAPITALS vs. RANGERS, 1993-94

Overall Record: 5-1-0 at New York 2-1-0 at Washington 2-0-0 at Halifax 1-0-0

	GP	W	L	T	GF	GA	PTS
Capitals	6	1	5	0	12	19	2
Rangers	6	5	1	0	19	12	10

Oct. 11	Rangers 5, Capitals 2 at New York (Beaupre/Kolzig & Healy)
Nov. 13	Rangers 2, Capitals 0 at Washington (Tabaracci & Richter)
Nov. 28	Rangers 3, Capitals 1 at New York (Beaupre & Richter)
Dec. 23	Rangers 1, Capitals 0 at Washington (Tabaracci & Healy)
Feb. 7	Rangers 1, Capitals 4 at New York (Tabaracci & Healy/Richter)
Mar. 9	Rangers 7, Capitals 5 at Halifax (Kolzig & Healy)

SCORING

Capitals	GP	G	A	PTS	PIM	S	+\-	Rangers	GP	G	A	PTS	PIM	S	+\-
Hatcher	6	2	2	4	2	22	-4	Messier	5	3	5	8	2	11	2
Khristich	6	2	2	4	0	11	-1	Gartner	6	2	4	6	6	20	4
Hunter	4	2	1	3	0	4	E	Leetch	6	1	5	6	4	25	-1
Konowalchuk	4	2	1	3	2	6	4	Graves	6	3	1	4	11	16	E
Pivonka	6	2	1	3	4	11	-3	Nemchinov	6	3	1	4	2	14	1
Ridley	6	1	2	3	6	14	3	Zubov	6	0	4	4	2	8	E
Slaney	3	0	2	2	15	3	2	Tikkanen	6	1	2	3	10	18	3
Jones	5	0	2	2	21	2	-2	Kovalev	6	2	0	2	17	12	E
Bondra	4	1	0	1	2	7	-2	Larmer	5	1	1	2	2	12	E
Elynuik	1	0	1	1	0	2	1	Amonte	6	1	1	2	2	14	-1
Anderson	2	0	1	1	0	2	1	Karpovtsev	4	0	2	2	2	2	E
Peake	3	0	1	1	0	4	E	Lowe	5	0	2	2	4	3	3
Iafrate	5	0	1	1	4	14	-1	Kypreos	3	1	0	1	2	3	1
Krygier	5	0	1	1	2	7	-3	Hudson	4	1	0	1	2	1	-2
Burridge	6	0	1	1	4	7	E	Gilbert	5	0	1	1	2	6	2
Cote	6	0	1	1	4	13	-3	Bourque	1	0	0	0	0	0	E
Johnasson	6	0	1	1	4	14	-2	J. Messier	1	0	0	0	0	3	-1
Miller	6	0	1	1	4	4	E	Norstrom	1	0	0	0	0	0	E
Acton	1	0	1	1	0	0	-1	Turcotte	1	0	0	0	0	0	E
Kaminski	1	0	0	0	9	2	E	Hartman	2	0	0	0	0	0	-2
Woolley	1	0	0	0	2	0	1	Lidster	3	0	0	0	2	3	1
May	2	0	0	0	0	0	E	Kocur	4	0	0	0	9	1	-1
Ciccone	2	0	0	0	0	0	E	Olczyk	4	0	0	0	10	7	E
Curran	3	0	0	0	4	1	E	Beukeboom	5	0	0	0	16	1	-1
Berube	6	0	0	0	21	3	-3	Wells	6	0	0	0	4	5	2
Poulin	6	0	0	0	0	6	-3								

GOALTENDING

	GP	MINS	GA	EN	AVG	W	L	T
Tabaracci	3	177	4	0	1.36	1	2	0
Kolzig	2	112	8	1	4.29	0	1	0
Beaupre	2	67	6	0	5.37	0	2	0

	GP	MINS	GA	EN	AVG	W	L	T
Richter	3	200	4	0	1.50	2	1	0
Healy	4	160	8	0	2.40	3	0	0

Capitals Power Play: 3-27 (11.1%)
Power Play Goals: Khristich, Pivonka, Ridley

Shorthanded Goals: None
Game-Winning Goals: Pivonka

Game-Tying Goals: None
Goals by Period:

	1st	2nd	3rd	OT	Total
Capitals	3	4	5	0	12
Rangers	8	7	4	0	19

Last Win at MSG: 2/7/94 (4-1)
Last Win at Wsh.: 4/16/93 (4-2)

Rangers Power Play: 7-26 (26.9%)
Power Play Goals: Messier (2), Kovalev, Amonte, Tikkanen, Leetch, Larmer

Shorthanded Goals: Gartner
Game Winning Goals: Nemchinov, Tikkanen, Larmer, Graves, Hudson

Game Tying Goals: None
Shots by Period:

	1st	2nd	3rd	OT	Total
Capitals	51	44	62	0	157
Rangers	69	73	43	0	185

Last Win at MSG: 11/28/93 (3-1)
Last Win at Wsh.: 3/9/94 (7-5)

Last Ranger trade with Washington: August 27, 1987, Capitals traded a 1988 fifth round draft choice (Martin Bergeron) to Rangers for Peter Sundstrom.

JETS vs. RANGERS, 1993-94

Overall Record: 1-1-0   at New York 1-0-0   at Winnipeg 0-1-0

	GP	W	L	T	GF	GA	PTS
Jets	2	1	1	0	4	3	2
Rangers	2	1	1	0	3	4	2

Nov. 10 Rangers 2, Jets 1 at New York (Essensa & Richter)
Mar. 27 Rangers 1, Jets 3 at Winnipeg (Cheveldae & Healy)

SCORING

Jets	GP	G	A	PTS	PIM	S	+\-	Rangers	GP	G	A	PTS	PIM	S	+\-
Steen	2	0	2	2	0	6	1	Graves	2	1	1	2	2	5	1
Drake	1	1	0	1	0	4	1	Amonte	1	1	0	1	0	3	1
Selanne	1	1	0	1	0	2	E	Kovalev	1	1	0	1	0	3	1
Emerson	2	1	0	1	2	4	-2	Larmer	2	0	1	1	0	5	E
Tkachuk	2	1	0	1	14	3	E	Messier	2	0	1	1	10	10	1
Quintal	2	0	1	1	4	3	E	Tikkanen	2	0	1	1	12	7	-1
Darrin Shannon	2	0	1	1	2	2	-2	Zubov	2	0	1	1	0	10	E
Ulanov	2	0	1	1	6	1	1	Anderson	1	0	0	0	4	0	E
Barnes	1	0	0	0	0	1	E	Gartner	1	0	0	0	0	4	-1
Bautin	1	0	0	0	4	0	-1	Hartman	1	0	0	0	0	1	E
Eagles	1	0	0	0	2	0	E	Karpovtsev	1	0	0	0	0	0	E
Fisher	1	0	0	0	0	0	E	Lidster	1	0	0	0	0	1	E
LeBlanc	1	0	0	0	0	0	E	MacTavish	1	0	0	0	0	1	E
Manson	1	0	0	0	15	1	E	Matteau	1	0	0	0	0	4	E
McBean	1	0	0	0	2	0	E	Nemchinov	1	0	0	0	0	2	-1
Mironov	1	0	0	0	0	1	-1	Noonan	1	0	0	0	2	7	E
Numminen	1	0	0	0	0	2	E	Norstrom	1	0	0	0	4	0	E
Romaniuk	1	0	0	0	2	0	E	Olczyk	1	0	0	0	0	0	E
Darryl Shannon	1	0	0	0	2	1	E	Wells	1	0	0	0	8	0	E
Tomlinson	1	0	0	0	4	0	E	Beukeboom	2	0	0	0	2	1	E
Ysebaert	1	0	0	0	0	1	E	Gilbert	2	0	0	0	0	3	E
Zhamnov	1	0	0	0	0	5	E	Kocur	2	0	0	0	12	0	E
Borsato	2	0	0	0	0	1	E	Kypreos	2	0	0	0	12	0	E
Domi	2	0	0	0	0	2	E	Leetch	2	0	0	0	4	9	1
Kennedy	2	0	0	0	2	2	1	Lowe	2	0	0	0	2	0	-1
King	2	0	0	0	2	3	E								

GOALTENDING

	GP	MINS	GA	EN	AVG	W	L	T		GP	MINS	GA	EN	AVG	W	L	T
Essensa	1	59	2	0	2.03	0	1	0	Richter	1	60	1	0	1.00	1	0	0
Cheveldae	1	60	1	0	1.00	1	0	0	Healy	1	59	3	0	3.05	0	1	0

Jets Power Play: 2-16 (12.5%)
Power Play Goals: Emerson, Tkachuk
Shorthanded Goals: Drake
Game-Winning Goals: Drake
Game-Tying Goals: None
Goals by Period: 1st 2nd 3rd OT Total
Jets   0   3   1   0   4
Rangers   1   1   1   0   3
Last Win at MSG: 1/6/92 (4-2)
Last Win at WPG: 3/27/94 (3-1)

Rangers Power Play: 1-14 (7.1%)
Power Play Goals: Kovalev
Shorthanded Goals: Graves
Game Winning Goals: Amonte
Game Tying Goals: None
Shots by Period: 1st 2nd 3rd OT Total
Jets   14 22   9   0   45
Rangers   24 23 29   0   76
Last Win at MSG: 11/10/93 (2-1)
Last Win at WPG: 11/21/92 (5-4)

Last Ranger trade with Winnipeg: January 28, 1992, Jets traded Eddie Olczyk to Rangers for Tie Domi and Kris King.

How Chemical helped Hartz Mountain spread its wings around the world.

"In 1926, a penniless young man named Max Stern set sail from his native Germany with 5,000 canaries from the Harz Mountains in Bavaria and a dream of making it in the land of opportunity.

On his arrival in New York, a customer directed Max to a bank where the manager spoke German. The bank let Max open an account without the minimum balance—and the pet and pet supply business Max called Hartz Mountain was born.

Headed since 1959 by Max's son Leonard, Hartz has blossomed into an empire of widely successful ventures in real estate, publishing and, of course, pet products.

And Leonard happily reports that his two sons are now a big part of the company's future. Emanuel is a senior manager in the real estate group, while Edward is a senior manager in the pet supply business.

Tom Seaver's Business Hall of Fame

Leonard Stern, Chairman and CEO, the Hartz Group, with sons Emanuel and Edward Stern.

Which explains why Hartz is still using the bank where Max made that first deposit.

'Chemical stayed with us when my father bought out his partner,' says Leonard. 'They helped finance our expansion. They arranged the financing to help us reacquire 25% of the pet products company after it had gone public. And they put up the money when we bought the Meadowlands.'

It's all a part of Chemical's enduring commitment to growing businesses and the people who own them—a commitment that's made Chemical the leading bank for business in the tri-state area.

The Stern family knows how to aim for the top. That's why they're in Tom Seaver's Business Hall of Fame.

Because to make it in this town, you gotta have a dream. And you gotta have a bank that shares it."

CHEMICAL
The Business Bank

EXPECT MORE FROM US.®

©1994 Chemical Bank. Member FDIC.

STANLEY CUP PLAYOFFS

RANGERS 1994 FINAL PLAYOFF SCORING

POS	NO.	PLAYER	GP	G	A	PTS	+/-	PIM	PP	SH	GW	OT	S	PCTG
D	2	Brian Leetch	23	11	23	34	19	6	4	0	4	0	88	12.5
C	11	Mark Messier	23	12	18	30	14	33	2	1	4	0	75	16.0
C	27	Alexei Kovalev	23	9	12	21	5	18	5	0	2	0	71	12.7
D	21	Sergei Zubov	22	5	14	19	10	0	2	0	0	0	60	8.3
LW	9	Adam Graves	23	10	7	17	12	24	3	0	0	0	93	10.8
RW	28	Steve Larmer	23	9	7	16	8	14	3	0	0	0	54	16.7
RW	16	Brian Noonan	22	4	7	11	2	17	2	0	1	0	45	8.9
LW	32	Stephane Matteau	23	6	3	9	5	20	1	0	2	2	36	16.7
LW	10	Esa Tikkanen	23	4	4	8	1	34	0	0	1	0	56	7.1
C	13	Sergei Nemchinov	23	2	5	7	1	6	0	0	0	0	33	6.1
RW	36	Glenn Anderson	23	3	3	6	5	42	0	1	2	0	31	9.7
D	23	Jeff Beukeboom	22	0	6	6	17	50	0	0	0	0	22	.0
C	14	Craig MacTavish	23	1	4	5	0	22	0	0	0	0	15	6.7
LW	17	Greg Gilbert	23	1	3	4	2-	8	0	0	0	0	23	4.3
D	25	*A. Karpovtsev	17	0	4	4	6-	12	0	0	0	0	14	.0
D	6	Doug Lidster	9	2	0	2	4-	10	0	0	0	0	9	22.2
RW	26	Joe Kocur	20	1	1	2	1-	17	0	0	0	0	16	6.3
D	4	Kevin Lowe	22	1	0	1	6	20	0	0	0	0	15	6.7
C	12	Eddie Olczyk	1	0	0	0	1-	0	0	0	0	0	1	.0
G	30	Glenn Healy	2	0	0	0	0	0	0	0	0	0	0	.0
LW	19	Nick Kypreos	3	0	0	0	1-	2	0	0	0	0	0	.0
G	35	Mike Richter	23	0	0	0	0	2	0	0	0	0	0	.0
D	24	Jay Wells	23	0	0	0	6-	20	0	0	0	0	12	.0

GOALTENDING RECORDS

No.	GOALTENDER	GPI	MINS	AVG	W	L	EN	SO	GA	SA	SV%	G	A	PIM
30	Glenn Healy	2	68	.88	0	0	0	0	1	17	.941	0	0	0
35	Mike Richter	23	1417	2.07	16	7	0	4	49	623	.921	0	0	2
	NYR TOTALS	23	1485	2.02	16	7	0	4	50	640	.922			

*Indicates Rookie

PLAYOFF SCORING LEADERS

SCORING LEADERS

PLAYER	TEAM	GP	G	A	PTS
Brian Leetch	**NY RANGERS**	**23**	**11**	**23**	**34**
Pavel Bure	Vancouver	24	16	15	31
Mark Messier	**NY RANGERS**	**23**	**12**	**18**	**30**
Doug Gilmour	Toronto	18	6	22	28
Trevor Linden	Vancouver	24	12	13	25
Alexei Kovalev	**NY RANGERS**	**23**	**9**	**12**	**21**
Geoff Courtnall	Vancouver	24	9	10	19
Sergei Zubov	**NY RANGERS**	**22**	**5**	**14**	**19**
Claude Lemieux	New Jersey	20	7	11	18
Igor Larionov	San Jose	14	5	1	18
Dave Ellett	Toronto	18	3	15	18
Adam Graves	**NY RANGERS**	**23**	**10**	**7**	**17**
Wendel Clark	Toronto	18	9	7	16
Steve Larmer	**NY RANGERS**	**23**	**9**	**7**	**16**
John MacLean	New Jersey	20	6	10	16

PLAYOFF SCORING LEADERS

DEFENSEMEN SCORING LEADERS

PLAYER	TEAM	GP	G	A	PTS
Brian Leetch	NY RANGERS	23	11	23	34
Sergei Zubov	NY RANGERS	22	5	14	19
Dave Ellett	Toronto	18	3	15	18
Dimitri Mironov	Toronto	18	6	9	15
Jeff Brown	Vancouver	24	6	9	15
Jyrki Lumme	Vancouver	24	2	11	13
Scott Stevens	New Jersey	20	2	9	11
Ray Bourque	Boston	13	2	8	10
Sandis Ozolinsh	San Jose	14	0	10	10

GOALS

NAME	TEAM	GP	G
Pavel Bure	Vancouver	24	16
Mark Messier	NY RANGERS	23	12
Trevor Linden	Vancouver	24	12
Brian Leetch	NY RANGERS	23	11
Adam Graves	NY RANGERS	23	10
Wendel Clark	Toronto	18	9
Steve Larmer	NY RANGERS	23	9
Alexei Kovalev	NY RANGERS	23	9
Geoff Courtnall	Vancouver	24	9

ASSISTS

NAME	TEAM	GP	A
Brian Leetch	NY RANGERS	23	23
Doug Gilmour	Toronto	18	22
Mark Messier	NY RANGERS	23	18
Dave Ellett	Toronto	18	15
Pavel Bure	Vancouver	24	15
Sergei Zubov	NY RANGERS	22	14
Igor Larionov	San Jose	14	13
Trevor Linden	Vancouver	24	13
Alexei Kovalev	NY RANGERS	23	12

GOALTENDING LEADERS

GOALS AGAINST AVERAGE

GOALTENDER	TEAM	GPI	MINS	GA	AVG
Dominik Hasek	Buffalo	7	484	13	1.61
*Martin Brodeur	New Jersey	17	1171	38	1.95
Mike Richter	NY RANGERS	23	1417	49	2.07
Kirk McLean	Vancouver	24	1544	59	2.29
Felix Potvin	Toronto	18	1124	46	2.46

WINS

GOALTENDER	TEAM	GPI	MINS	W	L
Mike Richter	NY RANGERS	23	1417	16	7
Kirk McLean	Vancouver	24	1544	15	9
Felix Potvin	Toronto	18	1124	9	9
*Martin Brodeur	New Jersey	17	1171	8	9
Arturs Irbe	San Jose	14	806	7	7

SAVE PERCENTAGE

GOALTENDER	TEAM	GPI	MINS	GA	SA	SPCTG	W	L
Dominik Hasek	Buffalo	7	484	13	261	.950	3	4
Kirk McLean	Vancouver	24	1544	59	820	.928	15	9
*Martin Brodeur	New Jersey	17	1171	38	531	.928	8	9
Mike Richter	NY RANGERS	23	1417	49	623	.921	16	7
Felix Potvin	Toronto	18	1124	46	520	.911	9	9

SHUTOUTS

GOALTENDER	TEAM	GPI	MINS	SO	W	L
Mike Richter	NY RANGERS	23	1417	4	16	7
Kirk McLean	Vancouver	24	1544	4	15	9
Felix Potvin	Toronto	18	1124	3	9	9
Dominik Hasek	Buffalo	7	484	2	3	4

SPECIAL TEAMS SCORING BREAKDOWN

	Power Play			Shorthanded			Even Strength			Total		
	G	A	PTS	G	A	PTS	G	A	PTS	G	A	PTS
Anderson	0	0	0	1	0	1	2	3	5	3	3	6
Beukeboom	0	0	0	0	0	0	0	6	6	0	6	6
Gilbert	0	0	0	0	0	0	1	3	4	1	3	4
Graves	3	3	6	0	0	0	7	4	11	10	7	17
Hartman	0	0	0	0	0	0	0	0	0	0	0	0
Healy	0	0	0	0	0	0	0	0	0	0	0	0
Hudson	0	0	0	0	0	0	0	0	0	0	0	0
Karpovtsev	0	1	1	0	0	0	0	3	3	0	4	4
Kocur	0	0	0	0	0	0	1	1	2	1	1	2
Kovalev	5	4	9	0	0	0	4	8	12	9	12	21
Kypreos	0	0	0	0	0	0	0	0	0	0	0	0
Larmer	3	2	5	0	0	0	6	5	11	9	7	16
Leetch	4	10	14	0	0	0	7	13	20	11	23	34
Lidster	0	0	0	0	0	0	2	0	2	2	0	2
Lowe	0	0	0	0	0	0	1	0	1	1	0	1
MacTavish	0	0	0	0	0	0	1	4	5	1	4	5
Matteau	1	1	2	0	0	0	5	2	7	6	3	9
J. Messier	0	0	0	0	0	0	0	0	0	0	0	0
M. Messier	2	8	10	1	1	2	9	9	18	12	18	30
Nemchinov	0	0	0	0	0	0	2	5	7	2	5	7
Noonan	2	2	4	0	0	0	2	5	7	4	7	11
Norstrom	0	0	0	0	0	0	0	0	0	0	0	0
Olczyk	0	0	0	0	0	0	0	0	0	0	0	0
Richter	0	0	0	0	0	0	0	0	0	0	0	0
Tikkanen	0	0	0	0	0	0	4	4	8	4	4	8
Wells	0	0	0	0	0	0	0	0	0	0	0	0
Zubov	2	7	9	0	0	0	3	7	10	5	14	19

	HOME				ROAD			
	W	L	GF	GA	W	L	GF	GA
Conference Quarterfinals	2	0	12	0	2	0	10	3
Conference Semifinals	3	0	15	8	1	1	5	4
Conference Finals	2	2	10	9	2	1	8	7
Stanley Cup Finals	2	2	11	12	2	1	10	7
Playoff Totals	9	4	48	29	7	3	33	21

	Power Play			Penalty Killing		
	PPG	ATT	%	PPGA	TSH	%
Conference Quarterfinals	8	27	29.6	1	17	94.1
Conference Semifinals	4	24	16.7	2	25	92.0
Conference Finals	4	25	16	3	26	88.5
Stanley Cup Finals	6	28	21.4	3	34	91.2
Playoff Totals	22	104	21.2	9	102	91.2

SITUATIONAL GOALS FOR AND AGAINST

	Conference Quarterfinals		Conference Semifinals		Conference Finals		Stanley Cup Finals	
	GF	GA	GF	GA	GF	GA	GF	GA
Five-on-Five	12	2	14	7	12	12	12	15
Five-on-Four	8	0	4	1	4	1	6	0
Five-on-Three	0	0	0	0	0	0	0	0
Four-on-Four	2	0	2	2	1	0	2	1
Three-on-Three	0	0	0	0	0	0	0	0
Three-on-Four	0	0	0	0	0	0	0	0
Three-on-Five	0	0	0	1	0	0	0	0
Four-on-Five	0	1	0	1	1	3	1	3
Total	22	3	20	12	18	16	21	19

SCORING BREAKDOWN

	Home			Road			Total			Game-Winning		
	G	A	PTS	G	A	PTS	G	A	PTS	G	A	PTS
Anderson	2	3	5	1	0	1	3	3	6	2	0	2
Beukeboom	0	1	1	0	5	5	0	6	6	0	1	1
Gilbert	1	1	2	0	2	2	1	3	4	0	0	0
Graves	6	5	11	4	2	6	10	7	17	0	1	1
Hartman	0	0	0	0	0	0	0	0	0	0	0	0
Healy	0	0	0	0	0	0	0	0	0	0	0	0
Hudson	0	0	0	0	0	0	0	0	0	0	0	0
Karpovtsev	0	3	3	0	1	1	0	4	4	0	1	1
Kocur	1	1	2	0	0	0	1	1	2	0	0	0
Kovalev	3	9	12	6	3	9	9	12	21	2	1	3
Kypreos	0	0	0	0	0	0	0	0	0	0	0	0
Larmer	4	5	9	5	2	7	9	7	16	0	0	0
Leetch	6	10	16	5	13	18	11	23	34	4	4	8
Lidster	2	0	2	0	0	0	2	0	2	0	0	0
Lowe	1	0	1	0	0	0	1	0	1	0	0	0
MacTavish	1	3	4	0	1	1	1	4	5	0	1	1
Matteau	4	2	6	2	1	3	6	3	9	2	0	2
J. Messier	0	0	0	0	0	0	0	0	0	0	0	0
M. Messier	6	10	16	6	8	14	12	18	30	3	4	7
Nemchinov	2	3	5	0	2	2	2	5	7	0	1	1
Noonan	3	5	8	1	2	3	4	7	11	1	2	3
Norstrom	0	0	0	0	0	0	0	0	0	0	0	0
Olczyk	0	0	0	0	0	0	0	0	0	0	0	0
Richter	0	0	0	0	0	0	0	0	0	0	0	0
Tikkanen	3	3	6	1	1	2	4	4	8	1	1	2
Wells	0	0	0	0	0	0	0	0	0	0	0	0
Zubov	3	10	13	2	4	6	5	14	19	0	3	3

	Conference Quarterfinals			Conference Semifinals			Conference Finals			Stanley Cup Finals			Total		
	G	A	PTS	G	A	PTS	G	A	PTS	G	A	PTS	G	A	PTS
Anderson	0	1	1	0	1	1	1	0	1	2	1	3	3	3	6
Beukeboom	0	2	2	0	1	1	0	1	1	0	2	2	0	6	6
Gilbert	0	1	1	1	0	1	0	1	1	0	1	1	1	3	4
Graves	3	2	5	4	0	4	2	2	4	1	3	4	10	7	17
Hartman	0	0	0	0	0	0	0	0	0	0	0	0	0	0	0
Healy	0	0	0	0	0	0	0	0	0	0	0	0	0	0	0
Hudson	0	0	0	0	0	0	0	0	0	0	0	0	0	0	0
Karpovtsev	0	1	1	0	3	3	0	0	0	0	0	0	0	4	4
Kocur	0	0	0	1	1	2	0	0	0	0	0	0	1	1	2
Kovalev	4	3	7	0	4	4	1	2	3	4	3	7	9	12	21
Kypreos	0	0	0	0	0	0	0	0	0	0	0	0	0	0	0
Larmer	2	3	5	1	3	4	2	1	3	4	0	4	9	7	16
Leetch	2	6	8	3	6	9	1	5	6	5	6	11	11	23	34
Lidster	0	0	0	0	0	0	0	0	0	2	0	2	2	0	2
Lowe	0	1	1	0	0	0	0	0	0	0	0	0	1	0	1
MacTavish	1	1	2	0	2	2	0	0	0	0	1	1	1	4	5
Matteau	1	2	3	2	0	2	3	0	3	0	1	1	6	3	9
J. Messier	0	0	0	0	0	0	0	0	0	0	0	0	0	0	0
M. Messier	4	3	7	2	3	5	4	7	11	2	5	7	12	18	30
Nemchinov	0	1	1	0	2	2	2	0	2	0	2	2	2	5	7
Noonan	1	3	4	3	1	4	0	2	2	0	1	1	4	7	11
Norstrom	0	0	0	0	0	0	0	0	0	0	0	0	0	0	0
Olczyk	0	0	0	0	0	0	0	0	0	0	0	0	0	0	0
Richter	0	0	0	0	0	0	0	0	0	0	0	0	0	0	0
Tikkanen	1	1	2	2	1	3	1	1	2	0	1	1	4	4	8
Wells	0	0	0	0	0	0	0	0	0	0	0	0	0	0	0
Zubov	2	4	6	1	4	5	1	1	2	1	5	6	5	14	19

MISCELLANEOUS

GOALS BY PERIODS

	1st	2nd	3rd	OT	TOTALS
Rangers	24	28	27	2	81
Opponents	19	10	19	2	50

SHOTS BY PERIOD

	1st	2nd	3rd	OT	TOTALS
Rangers	245	251	213	60	769
Opponents	211	200	183	46	640

TEAM STATISTICS

Most Goals, Game– 6, (3 times) last–May 1, 1994 vs. Washington
Most Goals Allowed, Game– 6, (June 9, 1994 vs. Vancouver)
Most Goals, Period– 4, (twice) last– April 18, 1994 vs. NY Islanders, 2nd period
Most Goals Allowed, Period– 5, (June 9, 1994 vs. Vancouver, 3rd period)
Largest Margin of Victory– 6, (twice) last– April 18, 1994 vs. NY Islanders
Largest Margin of Defeat– 3, (3 times) last- June 11, 1994 @ Vancouver
Most Shots, Game– 54, (May 31, 1994 vs. Vancouver*)
Most Shots Allowed, Game– 48, (May 15, 1994 vs. New Jersey#)
Most Shots, Period– 19, (twice) last– (May 9, 1994 vs. Washington, 1st per.)
Most Shots Allowed, Period– 17, (June 9, 1994 vs. Vancouver, 3rd per.)
Least Shots, Game– 18, (April 21, 1994 @ NY Islanders)
Least Shots Allowed, Game– 16, (May 17, 1994 vs. New Jersey)
Least Shots, Period– 3, (twice) last– May 21, 1994 @ New Jersey, 1st period
Least Shots Allowed, Period– 0, (May 7, 1994 @ Washington, 3rd per.)
Most Power Play Goals, Game– 3, (April 21, 1994 @ NY Islanders)
Most Power Play Goals Allowed, Game– 1, (8 times) last– (June 11, 1994 @ Vancouver)
Most Shorthanded Goals, Game– 1, (twice) last- (June 2, 1994 vs. Vancouver)
Most Shorthanded Goals Allowed, Game– 1, (3 times) last– June 14, 1994 vs. Vancouver
Longest Winning Streak– 7, April 17 to May 5
Longest Losing Streak– 2, (twice) last- June 9 to June 11

* overtime
\# double overtime

INDIVIDUAL STATISTICS

Most Goals, Game– 3, Messier (May 25, 1994 @ New Jersey)
Most Assists, Game– 3, (3 times) last– Leetch (June 7, 1994 @. Vancouver)
Most Points, Game– 4, (4 times) last– Leetch (June 7, 1994 @ Vancouver)
Most Shots, Game– 10, Tikkanen (May 31, 1994 vs. Vancouver)
Most Shots, Period– 5, (3 times) last– Tikkanen (June 9, 1994 vs. Vancouver, 2nd period)
Most Penalty Minutes, Game– 17, Beukeboom (June 9, 1994 vs. Vancouver)
Longest Point Scoring Streak– 13, Messier (April 17 to May 21)
Longest Goal Scoring Streak– 4, Kovalev (April 17 to April 24)
Longest Assist Streak– 6, Messier (May 7 to May 21)

STATISTICS

RANGERS RECORD

	W	L
When Scoring First	11	3
When Allowing First Goal	5	4
When Leading After First Period	9	1
When Trailing After First Period	3	3
When Tied After First Period	4	3
When Leading After Second Period	13	2
When Trailing After Second Period	1	5
When Tied After Second Period	2	0
In Overtime	2	2
When Outshooting Opponents	11	3
When Outshot by Opponents	3	3
When Shots Are Even	2	1
When outscoring opponents on special teams	10	1
When outscored on special teams	1	1
When even on special teams	5	5
In Second Game of back–to back games	1	0
On Sundays	3	1
On Mondays	2	1
On Tuesdays	3	1
On Wednesdays	2	0
On Thursdays	4	1
On Fridays	1	0
On Saturdays	1	3
In One Goal Games	4	2
In Two Goal Games	3	2
In Three Goal Games	4	3
In Four Goal Games	3	0
In Five Goal Games	0	0
In Six Or More Goal Games	2	0

When Rangers Score

	W	L
0 Goals	–	0
1 Goal	0	3
2 Goals	1	2
3 Goals	4	2
4 Goals	4	0
5 Goals	4	0
6 Goals	3	0
7 Goals	0	0
8 Goals	0	0
9 or More Goals	0	0

When Opposition Scores

	W	L
0 Goals	4	–
1 Goal	3	1
2 Goals	6	0
3 Goals	2	2
4 Goals	1	3
5 Goals	0	0
6 Goals	0	1
7 Goals	0	0
8 Goals	0	0
9 or More Goals	0	0

EASTERN CONFERENCE QUARTERFINALS
ISLANDERS vs. RANGERS

Overall Record: 4-0   at New York 2-0   at Islanders 2-0

	GP	W	L	GF	GA
Islanders	4	0	4	3	22
Rangers	4	4	0	22	3

Apr. 17	Game One	Rangers 6, Islanders 0 at New York (Hextall/McLennan & Richter)
Apr. 18	Game Two	Rangers 6, Islanders 0 at New York (McLennan & Richter)
Apr. 21	Game Three	Rangers 5, Islanders 1 at Islanders (Hextall & Richter)
Apr. 24	Game Four	Rangers 5, Islanders 2 at Islanders (Hextall & Richter)

SCORING

Islanders	GP	G	A	PTS	PIM	S	+\-
Plante	1	1	0	1	2	3	E
Ferraro	4	1	0	1	6	8	-2
Thomas	4	1	0	1	8	9	-5
Hogue	4	0	1	1	4	5	-3
Dalgarno	4	0	1	1	4	8	-2
King	4	0	1	1	0	6	-3
Krupp	4	0	1	1	4	4	-3
Turgeon	4	0	1	1	0	7	-4
Vaske	4	0	1	1	2	0	-1
Chyzowski	2	0	0	0	0	3	-1
Chynoweth	2	0	0	0	2	0	-1
McLennan	2	0	0	0	0	0	E
Kaminsky	2	0	0	0	4	0	-1
Hextall	3	0	0	0	4	0	E
Kurvers	3	0	0	0	2	5	-4
Maley	3	0	0	0	0	3	-2
Lachance	3	0	0	0	0	3	-5
Acton	4	0	0	0	2	1	E
Vukota	4	0	0	0	17	1	E
Green	4	0	0	0	2	7	-5
Malakhov	4	0	0	0	6	7	-5
McInnis	4	0	0	0	0	7	-5
Kasparaitis	4	0	0	0	8	3	-6

Rangers	GP	G	A	PTS	PIM	S	+\-
Leetch	4	2	6	8	0	15	11
Messier	4	4	3	7	0	12	6
Kovalev	4	4	3	7	2	17	4
Zubov	4	2	4	6	0	12	3
Graves	4	3	2	5	2	19	6
Larmer	4	2	3	5	2	5	5
Noonan	4	1	3	4	6	8	3
Matteau	4	1	2	3	6	6	5
MacTavish	4	1	1	2	4	4	2
Tikkanen	4	1	1	2	2	8	1
Beukeboom	4	0	2	2	8	2	9
Lowe	4	1	0	1	2	2	2
Anderson	4	0	1	1	8	5	3
Gilbert	4	0	1	1	2	4	E
Karpovtsev	4	0	1	1	0	4	E
Nemchinov	4	0	1	1	0	3	E
Kocur	2	0	0	0	0	0	E
Kypreos	2	0	0	0	2	0	-1
Richter	4	0	0	0	0	0	E
Wells	4	0	0	0	6	1	-1

GOALTENDING

	GP	MINS	GA	EN	AVG	W	L
McLennan	2	82	6	0	4.39	0	1
Hextall	3	158	16	0	6.08	0	3

	GP	MINS	GA	EN	AVG	W	L
Richter	4	240	3	0	0.75	4	0

Islanders Power Play: 1-17 (5.9%)
Power Play Goals: Thomas

Shorthanded Goals: None
Game-Winning Goals: None

Goals by Period:

	1st	2nd	3rd	OT	Total
Islanders	2	1	0	-	3
Rangers	6	12	4	-	22

Rangers Power Play: 8-27 (29.6%)
Power Play Goals: Leetch (2), Kovalev (2), Noonan, Larmer, Graves, Zubov
Shorthanded Goals: None
Game Winning Goals: Leetch (2), Messier, Kovalev

Shots by Period:

	1st	2nd	3rd	OT	Total
Islanders	32	34	24	-	90
Rangers	42	51	34	-	127

EASTERN CONFERENCE

NEW YORK ISLANDERS

GAME ONE
Rangers 6, Islanders 0

Rangers open the playoffs with a 6-0 shutout as Mike Richter stops 21 shots while recording his third career playoff shutout. Mark Messier and Sergei Zubov lead the team with a goal and two assists while Alexei Kovalev, Adam Graves and Brian Leetch each collect a goal and an assist.

GAME TWO
Rangers 6, Islanders 0

Rangers post their second consecutive 6-0 shutout, becoming the first club to open the Stanley Cup Playoffs with back-to-back shutouts since the Buffalo Sabres in 1983. It also marks the first time the Rangers posted consecutive playoff shutouts since Dave Kerr blanked Boston, 1-0 and 1-0 on March 26 and 28, 1940. Kovalev tallies a goal and two assists, while Craig MacTavish and Brian Noonan each register a goal and an assist.

QUARTERFINALS

GAME THREE

Rangers 5, Islanders 1

Leetch, Graves and Kovalev tally power play goals as the Rangers go up three games to none in the series. Richter allows his first goal of the series at 15:28 of the second period after posting a career-high shutout streak of 155:28.

GAME FOUR

Rangers 5, Islanders 2

Rangers score five unanswered goals after trailing, 2-0, sweeping a four-game series for the first time since 1972 when they swept Chicago. Messier collects two goals, while Zubov and Steve Larmer each collect a goal and an assist. The Rangers set a club record for fewest goals allowed in a four-game series with three and post the second highest goal differential in a four-game series at 19.

NEW YORK RANGERS

EASTERN CONFERENCE SEMIFINALS
CAPITALS vs. RANGERS

Overall Record: 4-1 at New York 3-0 at Washington 1-1

	GP	W	L	GF	GA
Capitals	5	1	4	12	20
Rangers	5	4	1	20	12

May	1	Game One	Rangers 6, Capitals 3 at New York (Beaupre & Richter)
May	3	Game Two	Rangers 5, Capitals 2 at New York (Tabaracci & Richter)
May	5	Game Three	Rangers 3, Capitals 0 at Washington (Beaupre & Richter)
May	7	Game Four	Rangers 2, Capitals 4 at Washington (Beaupre & Richter/Healy)
May	9	Game Five	Rangers 4, Capitals 3 at New York (Beaupre/Tabaracci & Richter)

SCORING

Capitals	GP	G	A	PTS	PIM	S	+\-
Cote	5	1	6	7	4	19	E
Ridley	5	2	4	6	4	8	3
Hatcher	5	2	1	3	10	18	-4
Miller	5	1	2	3	0	4	-1
Krygier	4	2	0	2	10	5	-2
Juneau	5	1	1	2	0	8	-4
Hunter	5	0	2	2	10	5	-1
Pivonka	1	1	0	1	0	4	-1
Woolley	4	1	0	1	4	2	E
Anderson	5	1	0	1	2	9	-1
Bondra	3	0	1	1	2	7	-1
Burridge	5	0	1	1	0	3	-3
Jones	5	0	1	1	14	8	E
Khristich	5	0	1	1	2	4	E
Poulin	5	0	1	1	17	7	-2
Nelson	1	0	0	0	0	0	-2
Berube	3	0	0	0	7	0	-1
Beaupre	4	0	0	0	2	0	E
Peake	4	0	0	0	4	4	-3
Konowalchuk	5	0	0	0	4	4	-4
Reekie	5	0	0	0	21	3	E
Slaney	5	0	0	0	0	7	-4

Rangers	GP	G	A	PTS	PIM	S	+\-
Leetch	5	3	6	9	0	16	4
Messier	5	2	3	5	10	13	3
Zubov	5	1	4	5	0	11	4
Graves	5	4	0	4	4	19	3
Noonan	5	3	1	4	7	7	1
Larmer	5	1	3	4	6	9	2
Kovalev	5	0	4	4	6	11	1
Tikkanen	5	2	1	3	4	8	2
Karpovtsev	5	0	3	3	10	3	-1
Matteau	5	2	0	2	4	10	E
Kocur	5	1	1	2	9	5	1
MacTavish	5	0	2	2	8	2	2
Nemchinov	5	0	2	2	4	7	2
Gilbert	5	1	0	1	2	1	1
Beukeboom	5	0	1	1	6	4	2
Anderson	5	0	1	1	6	4	2
Lowe	5	0	0	0	2	1	3
Richter	5	0	0	0	2	0	E
Wells	5	0	0	0	4	2	E

GOALTENDING

	GP	MINS	GA	EN	AVG	W	L
Tabaracci	2	111	6	0	3.24	0	2
Beaupre	4	189	14	0	4.44	1	2

	GP	MINS	GA	EN	AVG	W	L
Healy	1	25	0	0	0.00	0	0
Richter	5	275	12	0	2.62	4	1

Capitals Power Play: 2-25 (8.0%)
Power Play Goals: Juneau, Miller

Shorthanded Goals: Hatcher
Game-Winning Goals: Woolley

Rangers Power Play: 4-25 (16.0%)
Power Play Goals: Leetch (2), Noonan, Messier

Shorthanded Goals: None
Game Winning Goals: Leetch (2), Noonan, Tikkanen

Goals by Period:	1st	2nd	3rd	OT	Total
Capitals	5	5	2	0	12
Rangers	9	5	6	0	20

Shots by Period:	1st	2nd	3rd	OT	Total
Capitals	40	52	37	0	129
Rangers	56	42	35	0	133

EASTERN CONFERENCE

WASHINGTON CAPITALS

GAME ONE
Rangers 6, Capitals 3

New York opens the second round with a 6-3 victory. Noonan tallies two goals, including the game-winner, and MacTavish, Kovalev and Zubov each register a pair of assists. Rangers tie club record with their fifth consecutive playoff victory.

GAME TWO
Rangers 5, Capitals 2

Esa Tikkanen notches a goal and an assist and Larmer adds two assists as the Rangers set a club record with their sixth consecutive playoff victory.

GAME THREE
Rangers 3, Capitals 0

Richter stops 21 shots while posting his fifth career playoff shutout, tying John Ross Roach for second place on the Rangers all-time playoff shutout list. Leetch tallies a goal and an assist as he, Messier and Kovalev extend their point scoring streaks to seven games.

SEMIFINALS

GAME FOUR
Capitals 4, Rangers 2

Rangers suffer their first defeat of the 1994 playoffs. Don Beaupre turns aside 25 shots while earning the victory. New York holds Washington without a shot in the third period. Leetch and Messier extend their scoring streaks to eight games.

GAME FIVE
Rangers 4, Capitals 3

Leetch tallies the game-winning goal with 3:28 remaining as New York advances to the Stanley Cup Semifinals for the first time since 1986. Graves tallies two goals, while Leetch and Zubov each add a pair of assists.

NEW YORK RANGERS

EASTERN CONFERENCE FINALS
DEVILS vs. RANGERS

Overall Record: 4-3-0   at New York 2-2-0   at New Jersey 2-1-0

	GP	W	L	GF	GA
Devils	7	3	4	16	18
Rangers	7	4	3	18	16

May 15	Game One	Rangers 3, Devils 4(2-OT) at New York (Brodeur & Richter)
May 17	Game Two	Rangers 4, Devils 0 at New York (Brodeur/Terreri & Richter)
May 19	Game Three	Rangers 3, Devils 2 (2-OT) at New Jersey (Brodeur & Richter)
May 21	Game Four	Rangers 1, Devils 3 at New Jersey (Brodeur & Richter/Healy)
May 23	Game Five	Rangers 1, Devils 4 at New York (Brodeur & Richter)
May 25	Game Six	Rangers 4, Devils 2 at New Jersey (Brodeur & Richter)
May 27	Game Seven	Rangers 2, Devils 1(2-OT) at New York (Brodeur & Richter)

SCORING

Devils	GP	G	A	PTS	PIM	S	+\-
Nicholls	6	2	3	5	20	15	4
Lemieux	7	2	3	5	30	17	1
Richer	7	2	2	4	6	24	1
MacLean	7	1	3	4	2	17	-1
Zelepukin	7	3	0	3	6	17	E
Guerin	7	2	0	2	14	20	E
Niedermayer	7	1	1	2	4	11	2
Albelin	7	0	2	2	6	6	3
Carpenter	7	0	2	2	2	12	-5
Driver	7	0	2	2	2	8	E
Chorske	7	1	0	1	0	10	-5
Fetisov	7	1	0	1	6	4	2
Peluso	7	1	0	1	17	3	1
Brodeur	7	0	1	1	0	0	E
Dowd	7	0	1	1	2	12	-2
Holik	7	0	1	1	2	6	2
McKay	7	0	1	1	0	7	1
Stevens	7	0	1	1	16	19	-3
Millen	1	0	0	0	0	1	
Daneyko	7	0	0	0	8	0	-6

Rangers	GP	G	A	PTS	PIM	S	+\-
Messier	7	4	7	11	6	25	5
Leetch	7	1	5	6	2	28	5
Graves	7	2	2	4	14	31	3
Matteau	7	3	0	3	4	13	1
Larmer	7	2	1	3	4	14	-2
Kovalev	7	1	2	3	8	19	4
Nemchinov	7	2	0	2	0	17	E
Tikkanen	7	1	1	2	16	16	E
Zubov	7	1	1	2	0	20	1
Noonan	6	0	2	2	4	15	E
Anderson	7	1	0	1	20	11	1
Beukeboom	6	0	1	1	11	8	3
Gilbert	7	0	1	1	2	11	-4
Olczyk	1	0	0	0	0	1	-1
Lidster	2	0	0	0	0	1	-1
Karpovtsev	6	0	0	0	2	7	-4
Kocur	7	0	0	0	6	6	-2
Lowe	7	0	0	0	10	8	1
MacTavish	7	0	0	0	4	5	-5
Wells	7	0	0	0	2	5	-3

GOALTENDING

	GP	MINS	GA	EN	AVG	W	L
Terreri	1	6	0	0	0.00	0	0
Brodeur	7	498	17	1	2.05	3	4

	GP	MINS	GA	EN	AVG	W	L
Healy	1	43	1	0	1.40	0	0
Richter	7	463	15	0	1.94	4	3

Devils Power Play: 3-26 (11.5%)
Power Play Goals: Zelepukin, Richer, Nicholls
Shorthanded Goals: Nicholls
Game-Winning Goals: Richer (2-OT), Guerin, Peluso

Goals by Period:
	1st	2nd	3rd	OT-1	OT-2	Total
Devils	7	1	7	0	1	16
Rangers	3	5	8	0	2	18

Rangers Power Play: 4-24 (16.7%)
Power Play Goals: Larmer (2), Graves, Matteau
Shorthanded Goals: Messier
Game Winning Goals: Messier (2), Matteau (2), (2-OT, 2-OT)

Shots by Period:
	1st	2nd	3rd	OT-1	OT-2	Total
Devils	65	53	53	24	13	208
Rangers	70	84	64	33	10	261

EASTERN CONFERENCE

NEW JERSEY DEVILS

GAME ONE
Devils 4, Rangers 3 (2 OT)

Devils rally and tie the game on Claude Lemieux's goal with 43 seconds remaining to force overtime. Srephane Richer tallies the game winning goal at 15:23 of the second overtime period.

GAME TWO
Rangers 4, Devils 0

Richter ties an NHL record, notching his fourth shutout of the playoffs, stopping 24 shots. He becomes the eighth goalie to acheive the mark and the first since Ken Dryden of Montreal in 1977. Messier extends his point scoring streak to 11 games with a goal and an assist..

GAME THREE
Rangers 3, Devils 2 (2 OT)

Stephane Matteau scores the game winner at 6:13 of the second overtime period, giving New York a two games to one lead. Graves registers a goal and an assist and Messier extends his point scoring streak to 12 games.

FINALS

GAME FOUR
Devils 3, Rangers 1

New Jersey evens the series at two, behind goals by Richer, Bill Guerin and Valeri Zelepukin. Messier assists on the lone Rangers goal, giving him a point in each of the 13 playoff mathces.

GAME FIVE
Devils 4, Rangers 2

Bernie Nicholls tallies two goals and Lemieux adds a pair of assists as New Jersey takes a three to two series lead. Messier's point scoring streak is halted at 13 games.

GAME SIX
Rangers 4, Devils 2

Messier guarantees victory, then delivers with a natural hat trick, collecting all three goals in the third period as New York overcomes a 2-0, second period deficit to even the series and force a seventh game. Messier also added an assist on Alexei Kovalev's goal late in the second period, while Richter stopped 30 shots in the victory.

NEW YORK RANGERS

GAME SEVEN
Rangers 2, Devils 1 (2 OT)

Leetch opens the scoring at 9:31 of the second period. Zelepukin ties the game at one with 7.7 seconds remaining to force overtime. Matteau tallies his second double overtime goal of the series at 4:24 of the second overtime period to give the Rangers the victory as they advance to the Stanley Cup Finals for the first time since 1979.

STANLEY CUP FINALS
CANUCKS vs. RANGERS

	Overall Record: 4-3		at New York 2-2		at Vancouver 2-1
	GP	W	L	GF	GA
Canucks	7	3	4	19	21
Rangers	7	4	3	21	19

May 31	Game One	Rangers 2, Canucks 3 (OT) at New York (McLean & Richter)
June 2	Game Two	Rangers 3, Canucks 1 at New York (McLean & Richter)
June 4	Game Three	Rangers 5, Canucks 1 at Vancouver (McLean & Richter)
June 7	Game Four	Rangers 4, Canucks 2 at Vancouver (McLean & Richter)
June 9	Game Five	Rangers 3, Canucks 6 at New York (McLean & Richter)
June 11	Game Six	Rangers 1, Canucks 4 at Vancouver (McLean & Richter)
June 14	Game Seven	Rangers 3, Canucks 2 at New York (McLean & Richter)

SCORING

Canucks	GP	G	A	PTS	PIM	S	+\-
Bure	7	3	5	8	15	30	E
Ronning	7	1	6	7	6	21	4
Courtnall	7	4	1	5	11	24	3
Linden	7	3	2	5	6	18	2
Brown	7	3	1	4	8	19	1
Hedican	7	1	3	4	4	8	5
Lumme	7	0	4	4	6	20	3
Adams	7	1	2	3	2	15	-3
La Fayette	7	0	3	3	0	7	4
Momesso	7	1	1	2	17	13	2
Craven	7	0	2	2	4	7	-1
Babych	7	1	0	1	2	8	-4
Gelinas	7	1	0	1	4	8	E
Antoski	7	0	1	1	8	2	-3
Diduck	7	0	1	1	6	6	-4
Glynn	7	0	1	1	0	3	2
Hunter	7	0	0	0	18	1	-3
McIntyre	7	0	0	0	6	3	-3

Rangers	GP	G	A	PTS	PIM	S	+\-
Leetch	7	5	6	11	4	29	-1
Kovalev	7	4	3	7	2	24	-4
Messier	7	2	5	7	17	25	E
Zubov	6	1	5	6	0	17	2
Larmer	7	4	0	4	2	26	3
Graves	7	1	3	4	4	24	E
Anderson	7	2	1	3	4	11	E
Lidster	7	2	0	2	10	8	-3
Beukeboom	7	0	2	2	25	8	3
Nemchinov	7	0	2	2	2	6	E
Gilbert	7	0	1	1	2	7	E
MacTavish	7	0	1	1	6	4	1
Matteau	7	0	1	1	6	7	-1
Noonan	7	0	1	1	0	15	-2
Tikkanen	7	0	1	1	12	24	-2
Kypreos	1	0	0	0	0	0	E
Karpovtsev	2	0	0	0	0	0	-1
Kocur	6	0	0	0	2	5	E
Lowe	6	0	0	0	6	4	E
Wells	7	0	0	0	8	4	-2

GOALTENDING

	GP	MINS	GA	EN	AVG	W	L
McLean	7	437	20	1	2.75	3	4

	GP	MINS	GA	EN	AVG	W	L
Richter	7	439	19	0	2.60	4	3

Canucks Power Play: 3-35 (8.6%)
Power Play Goals: Linden (2), Brown

Shorthanded Goals: Linden
Game-Winning Goals: Adams (OT), Courtnall, Babych

Goals by Period:	1st	2nd	3rd	OT	Total
Canucks	5	3	10	1	19
Rangers	6	6	9	0	21

Rangers Power Play: 6-28 (21.4%)
Power Play Goals: Kovalev (3), Zubov, Messier, Graves
Shorthanded Goals: Anderson
Game Winning Goals: Anderson (2), Kovalev, Messier

Shots by Period:	1st	2nd	3rd	OT	Total
Canucks	74	61	69	9	213
Rangers	77	74	80	17	248

STANLEY CUP

VANCOUVER CANUCKS

GAME ONE
Canucks 3, Rangers 2 (OT)

Kirk McLean stops 51 shots and lifts Vancouver to a 3-2 overtime victory. Greg Adams nets the game winner at 19:26 of overtime after Brian Leetch had hit the crossbar seconds earlier.

GAME TWO
Rangers 3, Canucks 1

Doug Lidster opens the scoring, while Glenn Anderson tallies the game winner while shorthanded. Brian Leetch adds his seventh goal of the post-season as New York evens the series at one.

GAME THREE
Rangers 5, Canucks 1

Leetch tallies a pair of goals and Anderson pots the game winner for the second consecutive game as New York goes up two games to one. Steve Larmer and Alexei Kovalev collect third period goals and Jeff Beukeboom adds two assists to help ensure the victory.

FINALS

GAME FOUR
Rangers 4, Canucks 2

Richter stops Pavel Bure's penalty shot attempt early in the second period to hold Vancouver lead at 2-1. Zubov, Kovalev and Larmer tally three unanswered goals to bring the Rangers to within one victory of the Stanley Cup.

GAME FIVE
Canucks 6, Rangers 3

Bure tallies his 15th goal of the playoffs at 2:48 of the third period to give Vancouver a 3-0 lead. New Yorks scores three unanswered goals, tying the game at three at 9:02 of the third. Dave Babych answers 29 seconds later and Geoff Courtnall and Bure add insurance goals to send the series back to Vancouver.

GAME SIX
Canucks 4, Rangers 1

McLean stops 28 shots, while Jeff Brown registers a pair of goals to give Vancouver a 4-1 victory and even the series at three. Kovalev scores New York's only goal on the power play, setting a club record for power play goals in a single post season.

GAME SEVEN
Rangers 3, Canucks 2

Leetch and Graves give New York a 2-0 lead after one period before Trevor Linden collects his first of two goals at 5:21 of the second period. Mark Messier tallies the Stanley Cup clinching goal at 13:29 of the second period on the power play to give the Rangers the Stanley Cup championship.

NEW YORK RANGERS

1994 STANLEY CUP PLAYOFFS

STANLEY CUP FINALS
Vancouver vs. New York
(New York wins series, 4-3)

Tue.	May 31	VAN	3	at NY	2	(OT)
Thu.	June 2	VAN	1	at NY	3	
Sat.	June 4	NY	5	at VAN	1	
Tue.	June 7	NY	4	at VAN	2	
Thu.	June 9	VAN	6	at NY	3	
Sat.	June 11	NY	1	at VAN	4	
Tue.	June 14	VAN	2	at NY	3	

CONFERENCE FINALS

EASTERN CONFERENCE
New Jersey vs. Rangers
(New York wins series, 4-3)

Sun.	May 15	NJ	4	at NYR	3	(2OT)
Tue.	May 17	NJ	0	at NYR	4	
Thu.	May 19	NYR	3	at NJ	2	(2OT)
Sat.	May 21	NYR	1	at NJ	3	
Mon.	May 23	NJ	4	at NYR	1	
Wed.	May 25	NYR	4	at NJ	2	
Fri.	May 27	NJ	1	at NYR	2	(2OT)

WESTERN CONFERENCE
Vancouver vs. Toronto
(Vancouver wins series, 4-1)

Mon.	May 16	VAN	2	at TOR	3	(OT)
Wed.	May 18	VAN	4	at TOR	3	
Fri.	May 20	TOR	0	at VAN	4	
Sun	May 22	TOR	0	at VAN	2	
Tue.	May 24	TOR	3	at VAN	4	(2OT)

CONFERENCE SEMIFINALS

EASTERN CONFERENCE
Washington vs. New York
(New York wins series, 4-1)

Sun.	May 1	WSH	3	at NYR	6
Tue.	May 3	WSH	2	at NYR	5
Thu.	May 5	NYR	3	at WSH	0
Sat.	May 7	NYR	2	at WSH	4
Mon.	May 9	WSH	3	at NYR	4

WESTERN CONFERENCE
San Jose vs. Toronto
(Toronto wins series, 4-3)

Mon.	May 2	SJ	3	at TOR	2	
Wed.	May 4	SJ	1	at TOR	5	
Fri.	May 6	TOR	2	at SJ	5	
Sun.	May 8	TOR	8	at SJ	3	
Tue.	May 10	TOR	2	at SJ	5	
Thu.	May 12	SJ	2	at TOR	3	(OT)
Sat.	May 14	SJ	2	at TOR	4	

Boston vs. New Jersey
(New Jersey wins series, 4-2)

Sun.	May 1	BOS	2	at NJ	1	
Tue.	May 3	BOS	6	at NJ	5	(OT)
Thu.	May 5	NJ	4	at BOS	2	
Sat.	May 7	NJ	5	at BOS	4	(OT)
Mon.	May 9	BOS	0	at NJ	2	
Wed.	May 11	NJ	5	at BOS	3	

Vancouver vs. Dallas
(Vancouver wins series, 4-1)

Mon.	May 2	VAN	6	at DAL	4	
Wed.	May 4	VAN	3	at DAL	0	
Fri.	May 6	DAL	4	at VAN	3	
Sun.	May 8	DAL	1	at VAN	2	(OT)
Tue.	May 10	DAL	2	at VAN	4	

CONFERENCE QUARTERFINALS

EASTERN CONFERENCE
Islanders vs. Rangers
(Rangers win series, 4-0)

Sun.	Apr. 17	NYI	0	at NYR	6
Mon.	Apr. 18	NYI	0	at NYR	6
Thu.	Apr. 21	NYR	5	at NYI	1
Sat.	Apr. 24	NYR	4	at NYI	2

WESTERN CONFERENCE
Chicago vs. Toronto
(Toronto wins series, 4-2)

Mon.	Apr. 18	CHI	1	at TOR	5	
Wed.	Apr. 20	CHI	0	at TOR	1	(OT)
Fri.	Apr. 22	TOR	4	at CHI	5	
Sun.	Apr. 24	TOR	3	at CHI	4	(OT)
Tue.	Apr. 26	CHI	0	at TOR	1	
Thu.	Apr. 28	TOR	1	at CHI	0	

Buffalo vs. New Jersey
(New Jersey wins series, 4-3)

Sun.	Apr. 17	BUF	2	at NJ	0	
Tue.	Apr. 19	BUF	1	at NJ	2	
Thu.	Apr. 21	NJ	2	at BUF	1	
Sat.	Apr. 23	NJ	3	at BUF	5	
Mon.	Apr. 25	BUF	3	at NJ	5	
Wed.	Apr. 27	NJ	0	at BUF	1	(4OT)
Fri.	Apr. 29	BUF	1	at NJ	2	

San Jose vs. Detroit
(San Jose wins series, 4-3)

Mon.	Apr. 18	SJ	5	at DET	4
Wed.	Apr. 20	SJ	0	at DET	4
Fri.	Apr. 22	DET	3	at SJ	2
Sat.	Apr. 23	DET	3	at SJ	4
Tue.	Apr. 26	DET	4	at SJ	6
Thu.	Apr. 28	SJ	1	at DET	7
Sat.	Apr. 30	SJ	3	at DET	2

Montreal vs. Boston
(Boston wins series, 4-3)

Sat.	Apr. 16	MTL	2	at BOS	3	
Mon.	Apr. 18	MTL	3	at BOS	2	
Thu.	Apr. 21	BOS	6	at MTL	3	
Sat.	Apr. 23	BOS	2	at MTL	5	
Mon.	Apr. 25	MTL	2	at BOS	1	(OT)
Wed.	Apr. 27	BOS	3	at MTL	2	
Fri.	Apr. 29	MTL	3	at BOS	5	

St. Louis vs. Dallas
(Dallas wins series, 4-0)

Sun.	Apr. 17	STL	3	at DAL	5	
Wed.	Apr. 20	STL	2	at DAL	4	
Fri.	Apr. 22	DAL	5	at STL	4	(OT)
Sun.	Apr. 24	DAL	2	at STL	1	

Washington vs. Pittsburgh
(Washington wins series, 4-2)

Sun.	Apr. 17	WSH	5	at PIT	3
Tue.	Apr. 19	WSH	1	at PIT	2
Thu.	Apr. 21	PIT	0	at WSH	2
Sat.	Apr. 23	PIT	1	at WSH	4
Mon.	Apr. 25	WSH	2	at PIT	3
Wed.	Apr. 27	PIT	3	at WSH	6

Vancouver at Calgary
(Vancouver wins series, 4-3)

Mon	Apr. 18	VAN	5	at CGY	0	
Wed	Apr. 20	VAN	5	at CGY	7	
Fri.	Apr. 22	CGY	2	at VAN	4	
Sun.	Apr. 24	CGY	3	at VAN	2	
Tue.	Apr. 26	VAN	2	at CGY	1	(OT)
Thu.	Apr. 28	CGY	2	at VAN	3	(OT)
Sat.	Apr. 30	VAN	4	at CGY	3	(2OT)

BINGHAMTON RANGERS COACHING STAFF

Al Hill
Head Coach

After completing his first season behind the bench as the head coach of the Binghamton Rangers, Al Hill enters his second season as head coach of the club.

Hill was named head coach on August 19, 1993 after spending the previous two and a half seasons as an assistant coach with Binghamton. He returned to the AHL after serving as an assistant coach in New York from January 4, 1993 through the remainder of the season.

Hill, 38, originally joined Binghamton as an assistant coach in August of 1990 after holding the same position with the Hershey Bears. He was teammates with former Binghamton coach John Paddock with the Philadelphia Flyers in 1979-80 and played on two AHL Calder Cup Championship teams in Maine and Hershey (1988).

A former NHL center, Hill played in 221 National Hockey League games, all with the Flyers. In his first game, he scored two goals and three assists in a 6-4 win over St. Louis on February 14, 1977. The five point total remains a record for most points by a player in his first NHL game. A native of Nanaimo, British Columbia, Hill also played in 655 AHL games with Springfield, Maine, Moncton, and Hershey.

Al and his wife, Deanna spend the off-season in Hershey, Pennsylvania with their children Justin and Jarrod.

Mike Busniuk
Assistant Coach

Mike Busniuk begins his second season with the Binghamton Rangers after being named assistant coach on September 2, 1993.

Busniuk, 44, joined the Rangers coaching staff last September after spending the previous two seasons as co-coach along with Bob McCammon of the Tri-City Americans of the Western Hockey League.

The native of Thunder Bay, Ontario played in 143 NHL matches with the Philadelphia Flyers from 1979-80 to 1980-81. He was originally drafted in 1971 by the Montreal Canadiens. Busniuk was a member of five Calder Cup Championship teams, two with the Nova Scotia Voyageurs in 1975-76 and 1976-77 and three with Maine in 1977-78, 1978-79 and 1983-84. A graduate of Denver University, Busniuk finished his playing career spending three seasons in Italy.

Mike and his wife Jan spend the off-season in Thunder Bay with their three children, Jake, Katie and Molly.

BINGHAMTON RANGERS DIRECTORY

President	James R. McCoy
Vice-President	Robert W. Carr Jr.
Secretary/Treasurer/Governor	Tom Mitchell
Managing Partner	Tom Mitchell
General Manager/Alternate Governor	Larry Pleau
Coach	All Hill
Assistant Coach	Mike Busniak
Medical Trainer	R. Christopher Felix
Equipment Manager	Mark Dumas
Vice-President Marketing/Public Relations	Patrick Snyder
Office Manager	Sandy Weber
Director of Merchandising/Promotions	Gary Foodim
Director of Broadcasting/Community Relations	David Miller
Director of Sales/Sponsorship	Ron Mitchell
Administrative Assistant	Darcie Kocan
Home Ice	Broome County Veterans Memorial Arena
Address	One Stuart Street
	Binghamton, NY 13901
Seating Capacity	4,803
NHL Affiliation	New York Rangers
Phone	(607) 723-8937
Fax Number	(607) 724-6892

1994-95 BINGHAMTON RANGERS SCHEDULE

September
Sept.	30	at Cornwall

October
Oct.	1	SYRACUSE
Oct.	7	at Providence
Oct.	8	at Portland
Oct.	9	at Worcester
Oct.	14	at Rochester
Oct.	15	ROCHESTER
Oct.	21	at Albany
Oct.	22	CORNWALL
Oct.	23	at Rochester
Oct.	26	at Worcester
Oct.	29	ROCHESTER
Oct.	31	at Syracuse

November
Nov.	4	ST. JOHN, NB
Nov.	5	ALBANY
Nov.	6	at Rochester
Nov.	11	CAPE BRETON
Nov.	12	CAPE BRETON
Nov.	18	ADIRONDACK
Nov.	19	P.E.I.
Nov.	23	at Albany
Nov.	24	HERSHEY
Nov.	26	at Cornwall
Nov.	27	SYRACUSE
Nov.	30	SPRINGFIELD

December
Dec.	2	HERSHEY
Dec.	3	PORTLAND
Dec.	4	at Hershey
Dec.	7	at Adirondack
Dec.	9	at Providence
Dec.	16	HERSHEY
Dec.	17	at Albany
Dec.	21	at Adirondack
Dec.	23	HERSHEY
Dec.	26	SOVIET WINGS
Dec.	27	at Hershey
Dec.	28	SYRACUSE
Dec.	30	at Portland
Dec.	31	PROVIDENCE

January
Jan.	6	ADIRONDACK
Jan.	8	at Syracuse
Jan.	11	at Hershey
Jan.	13	CORNWALL
Jan.	15	PORTLAND
Jan.	20	WORCESTER
Jan.	21	SPRINGFIELD
Jan.	24	at Cape Breton
Jan.	26	at Fredericton
Jan.	27	at P.E.I.
Jan.	28	at St.John'sNFLD
Jan.	30	at Cape Breton

February
Feb.	1	St. John's NB
Feb.	3	ROCHESTER
Feb.	4	ALBANY
Feb.	8	at Springfield
Feb.	10	SYRACUSE
Feb.	11	CORNWALL
Feb.	12	at Hershey
Feb.	17	at Rochester
Feb.	18	at Cornwall
Feb.	19	ROCHESTER
Feb.	22	CORNWALL
Feb.	25	at Springfield
Feb.	26	ALBANY

March
Mar.	4	at Hershey
Mar.	5	ADIRONDACK
Mar.	10	at Rochester
Mar.	11	WORCESTER
Mar.	12	at Syracuse
Mar.	17	FREDERICTON
Mar.	18	SYRACUSE
Mar.	22	at Hershey
Mar.	24	HERSHEY
Mar.	25	ST.JOHN'S NFLD
Mar.	26	at Syracuse
Mar.	31	PROVIDENCE

April
Apr.	1	at Syracuse
Apr.	2	at Adirondack
Apr.	5	at Cornwall
Apr.	7	HERSHEY
Apr.	8	ROCHESTER

AMERICAN HOCKEY LEAGUE
1993-94 FINAL STANDINGS

ATLANTIC DIVISION

Team	GP	W	L	T	GF	GA	PTS
St. John's	80	45	23	12	360	287	102
Saint John, NB	80	37	33	10	304	305	84
Moncton	80	37	36	7	310	303	81
Cape Breton	80	32	35	13	316	339	77
Fredericton	80	31	42	7	294	296	69
PEI Senators	80	23	49	8	269	356	54

NORTHERN DIVISION

Teams	GP	W	L	T	GF	GA	PTS
Adirondack	80	45	27	8	333	273	98
Portland	80	43	27	10	328	269	96
Albany	80	38	34	8	312	315	84
Springfield	80	29	38	13	309	327	71
Providence	80	28	39	13	283	319	69

SOUTHERN DIVISION

Team	GP	W	L	T	GF	GA	PTS
Hershey	80	38	31	11	306	298	87
Hamilton	80	36	37	7	302	305	79
Cornwall	80	33	36	11	294	295	77
Rochester	80	31	34	15	277	300	77
Binghamton	80	33	38	9	312	322	75

BINGHAMTON RANGERS FINAL SCORING

PLAYER	GP	G	A	PTS	+/-	PIM	PP	SH	GW
Ken Hodge	79	22	56	78	16	51	5	3	1
Shawn McCosh	75	31	44	75	-9	68	9	2	3
Eric Murano	75	35	37	72	-11	36	10	1	3
Craig Duncanson	70	25	44	69	5	83	12	1	2
Jean-Yves Roy	65	41	24	65	14	33	7	0	4
Jim Hiller	67	27	34	61	-3	61	0	0	0
Michael Stewart	79	8	42	50	16	75	4	0	0
Daniel Lacroix	59	20	23	43	2	278	1	1	1
Rob Kenny	63	27	14	41	-6	90	5	0	6
Dean Kolstad	68	7	26	33	4	92	1	1	1
Darcy Werenka	53	5	22	27	-17	10	2	0	1
Mike McLaughlin	56	11	13	24	E	33	1	1	3
Pete Florentino	68	7	15	22	-12	220	0	0	1
Dimitri Starostenko	41	12	9	21	-7	10	2	0	1
Fredric Jax	31	5	16	21	2	14	0	0	1
Joby Messier	42	6	14	20	10	58	5	0	2
Brad Tiley	29	6	10	16	7	6	2	0	0
Mattias Norstrom	55	1	9	10	-7	70	0	0	0
Ed Kastelic	44	3	6	9	2	119	0	0	0
Todd Marchant	8	2	2	9	-3	6	0	0	0
Darren Langdon	54	2	7	9	-7	327	0	0	1
Barry Richter	21	0	9	9	1	12	0	0	0
Bob Babcock	20	1	6	7	1	67	0	0	0
Andrei Kudinov	25	3	3	6	-5	6	0	0	1
Bruce Bell	13	1	5	6	-6	16	0	0	1
Roy Mitchell	11	1	3	4	4	18	1	0	0
Sergei Zubov	2	1	2	3	-2	2	0	0	0
Borin Rousson	62	0	2	2	-	12	-	-	-
Paval Komarov	1	1	0	1	1	2	0	0	0
Mike Vukonich	3	1	0	1	E	0	0	0	0
Eric Germain	3	0	0	0	-1	6	0	0	0
Corey Hirsch	10	0	0	0	-	0	-	-	-
Jon Hillebrandt	8	0	0	0	-	0	-	-	-
Mike Gilmore	8	0	0	0	-	0	-	-	-

GOALTENDING RECORDS

GOALTENDER	GPI	MINS	AVG	W	L	T	EN	SO	GA	SA	SPCTG
Boris Rousson	62	3598	3.87	26	26	8	6	0	232	1698	0.880
Corey Hirsch	10	610	3.73	5	4	1	1	0	38	306	0.890
Mike Gilmore	7	338	4.43	1	5	0	0	0	25	171	0.872
Jon Hillebrandt	7	294	3.67	1	3	0	2	0	18	138	0.885
Team Totals	**80**	**4840**	**3.87**	**33**	**38**	**9**	**9**	**0**	**313**	**2313**	**0.885**

RANGERS ALUMNI ASSOCIATION

With the motto of "Keeping in Touch with Tradition," the Rangers Alumni Association has become an increasingly more visible organization.

The association participates in various charity softball games and hockey games throughout the year, while many of the members of the RAA often represent the Rangers at golf outings and youth hockey clinics.

Last year the Rangers Alumni faced off against an NHL Legends All-Star team as part of the festivities for the 1994 NHL All-Star Game which will was held in Madison Square Garden on the weekend of January 21 and 22.

One of the association's most prestigious events is the annual RAA Golf Outing. At the golf outing held in September the Rangers honored Dave Maloney, Walt Tkaczuk and Lorne "Gump" Worsley.

Above, participants in the Heroes of Hockey Game at Madison Square Garden on January 21.

RYE PLAYLAND

OFFICIAL PRACTICE FACILITY OF THE NEW YORK RANGERS

For the past 15 seasons the New York Rangers have held their daily practices at Rye Playland's Ice Casino. Playland is one the summer's hottest attractions, an amusement park featuring the "Dragon Coaster." Several times each season the Rangers hold practices that are open to the public.

CAREER RECORDS

PLAYER CAREER RECORDS VS. NHL TEAMS

TEAM	Jeff Beukeboom GP	G	A	PTS	Glen Featherstone GP	G	A	PTS	Greg Gilbert GP	G	A	PTS	Adam Graves GP	G	A	PTS	Mike Hartman GP	G	A	PTS	Mike Hudson GP	G	A	PTS
Anaheim	1	0	1	1	1	0	1	1	1	0	0	0	2	0	1	1	1	0	0	0	1	0	0	0
Boston	18	0	1	1	5	0	2	2	29	7	3	10	17	4	3	7	32	4	4	8	12	2	3	5
Buffalo	21	0	8	8	12	1	2	3	29	5	6	11	21	6	6	12	6	0	1	1	11	1	1	2
Calgary	34	2	7	9	7	0	0	0	27	5	10	15	25	5	4	9	15	0	1	1	14	2	1	3
Chicago	16	1	4	5	17	1	3	4	17	3	5	8	19	10	1	11	16	1	1	2	1	0	0	0
Dallas	16	0	5	5	17	0	1	1	45	8	8	16	20	2	5	7	19	1	1	2	27	5	4	9
Detroit	20	0	2	2	22	2	5	7	44	12	14	26	13	6	2	8	17	4	4	8	26	2	8	10
Edmonton	5	0	1	1	8	0	2	2	26	2	5	7	9	3	0	3	17	2	2	4	14	1	2	3
Florida	5	2	0	2	3	0	0	0	5	0	1	1	5	2	0	2	3	1	0	1	2	0	0	0
Hartford	19	3	0	3	12	0	1	1	30	7	9	16	21	4	4	8	32	4	4	8	10	4	2	6
Los Angeles	35	2	7	9	5	0	0	0	29	3	7	10	23	3	3	6	16	6	2	8	14	1	5	6
Montreal	16	2	3	5	13	3	2	5	28	4	10	14	20	5	3	8	27	2	1	3	10	2	2	4
New Jersey	25	1	2	3	11	0	1	1	48	15	12	27	27	5	10	15	14	2	0	2	16	2	2	4
NY Islanders	25	2	4	6	9	1	0	1	13	3	3	6	25	14	8	22	15	0	1	1	11	0	3	3
Rangers	11	0	2	2	10	0	2	2	43	10	11	21	5	0	1	1	13	1	2	3	7	0	1	1
Ottawa	6	0	2	2	5	0	2	2	5	0	0	0	7	5	3	8	—	—	—	—	4	0	0	0
Philadelphia	26	0	1	1	9	0	1	1	54	9	21	30	27	8	9	17	12	1	1	2	11	1	5	6
Pittsburgh	25	0	5	5	9	0	0	0	55	7	23	30	28	8	10	18	17	2	1	3	12	3	4	7
Quebec	17	2	5	7	14	1	7	8	31	7	2	9	17	9	6	15	31	6	2	8	12	2	2	4
St. Louis	20	0	8	8	3	1	1	2	41	5	11	16	19	3	6	9	16	2	3	5	22	3	7	10
San Jose	8	2	1	3	2	0	0	0	7	1	1	2	7	7	5	12	10	0	0	0	6	1	2	3
Tampa Bay	6	0	3	3	6	1	0	1	12	0	1	1	8	5	2	7	2	0	0	0	7	0	2	2
Toronto	16	0	1	1	15	1	3	4	42	9	12	21	17	3	4	7	19	1	1	2	25	5	3	8
Vancouver	37	1	8	9	9	0	2	2	28	5	9	14	25	5	11	16	19	0	0	0	10	0	1	1
Washington	31	2	3	5	10	0	3	3	52	8	17	25	32	11	9	20	15	1	0	1	11	3	3	6
Winnipeg	31	1	8	9	9	0	1	1	33	4	12	16	26	4	10	14	12	2	3	5	14	2	3	5
Totals	490	23	92	115	243	12	42	54	774	139	213	352	465	137	126	263	396	43	35	78	310	42	66	108

PLAYER CAREER RECORDS VS. NHL TEAMS

TEAM	Alexander Karpovtsev				Joe Kocur				Alexei Kovalev				Nick Kypreos				Steve Larmer				Brian Leetch			
	GP	G	A	PTS	GP	G	A	PTS	GP	G	A	PTS	GP	G	A	PTS	GP	G	A	PTS	GP	G	A	PTS
Anaheim	2	0	0	0	2	0	0	0	2	0	2	2	1	0	0	0	1	0	0	0	2	1	1	2
Boston	3	0	0	0	20	2	3	5	6	5	0	5	17	1	1	2	36	16	23	39	17	2	15	17
Buffalo	4	1	1	2	24	3	1	4	6	2	1	3	19	1	2	3	35	13	11	24	18	1	15	16
Calgary	1	0	0	0	20	4	1	5	4	0	1	1	10	1	1	2	35	17	11	28	15	4	6	10
Chicago	1	0	0	0	47	7	6	13	4	1	3	4	11	0	0	0	2	1	1	2	16	1	14	15
Dallas	2	0	0	0	45	2	8	10	2	1	0	1	10	0	1	1	89	47	57	104	15	4	11	15
Detroit	2	0	0	0	7	3	0	3	3	1	0	1	10	2	0	2	91	28	55	83	16	6	10	16
Edmonton	2	0	1	1	18	3	3	6	3	1	1	2	10	2	4	6	36	19	27	46	15	3	9	12
Florida	3	0	0	0	5	1	0	1	5	0	2	2	2	0	1	1	5	2	1	3	5	1	2	3
Hartford	3	0	1	1	23	2	6	8	7	4	1	5	8	1	0	1	36	23	24	47	19	8	18	26
Los Angeles	2	0	0	0	25	1	2	3	3	1	2	3	10	3	1	4	36	13	16	29	14	3	10	13
Montreal	3	0	0	0	21	1	2	3	8	1	6	7	15	2	3	5	34	4	14	18	18	1	13	14
New Jersey	6	0	0	0	35	4	4	8	10	3	6	9	20	4	2	6	38	17	20	37	37	11	25	36
NY Islanders	4	0	2	2	24	3	1	4	12	3	4	7	21	4	4	8	37	25	19	44	34	8	21	29
Rangers	—	—	—	—	13	2	5	7	—	—	—	—	18	0	1	1	32	17	13	30	0	0	0	0
Ottawa	4	0	2	2	4	0	0	0	6	2	4	6	8	2	0	2	6	4	4	8	5	0	5	5
Philadelphia	4	0	1	1	26	3	2	5	10	3	1	4	24	2	3	5	35	10	19	29	35	10	24	34
Pittsburgh	4	0	1	1	28	1	1	2	8	1	2	3	17	1	2	3	34	16	26	42	32	10	34	44
Quebec	2	1	0	1	23	3	1	4	7	0	2	2	16	4	3	7	36	16	23	39	17	7	17	24
St. Louis	2	1	0	1	47	4	2	6	4	1	1	2	10	0	2	2	90	40	50	90	15	0	13	13
San Jose	1	0	0	0	6	1	1	2	5	3	0	3	6	0	2	2	8	3	6	9	5	2	5	7
Tampa Bay	3	0	1	1	6	0	0	0	8	3	4	7	4	2	0	2	9	4	6	10	8	2	5	7
Toronto	2	0	2	2	54	12	10	22	2	3	1	4	12	1	0	1	90	46	70	116	14	1	12	13
Vancouver	2	0	1	1	19	2	2	4	4	0	3	3	9	0	0	0	36	20	13	33	13	7	12	19
Washington	4	0	2	2	32	3	3	6	11	3	2	5	7	1	1	2	37	9	20	29	36	8	29	37
Winnipeg	1	0	0	0	18	1	2	3	1	1	0	1	11	4	0	4	35	17	27	44	16	2	17	19
Totals	67	3	15	18	592	68	66	134	141	43	51	94	306	38	34	72	959	427	556	983	437	103	343	446

177

PLAYER CAREER RECORDS VS. NHL TEAMS

TEAM	Kevin Lowe GP	G	A	PTS	Stephane Matteau GP	G	A	PTS	Joby Messier GP	G	A	PTS	Mark Messier GP	G	A	PTS	Petr Nedved GP	G	A	PTS	Sergei Nemchinov GP	G	A	PTS
Anaheim	1	0	0	0	3	1	0	1	—	—	—	—	2	2	0	2	7	—	—	—	2	0	0	0
Boston	43	1	11	12	9	1	3	4	1	0	2	2	41	8	29	37	7	1	3	4	10	1	3	4
Buffalo	44	4	12	16	9	1	0	1	1	0	0	0	43	19	34	53	8	3	2	5	11	5	7	12
Calgary	97	6	28	34	8	2	4	6	—	—	—	—	82	32	63	95	20	3	4	7	6	2	0	2
Chicago	43	4	16	20	3	1	0	1	—	—	—	—	41	17	38	55	11	6	5	11	6	2	1	3
Dallas	35	2	12	14	18	2	4	6	—	—	—	—	40	14	32	46	11	2	7	9	6	3	1	4
Detroit	41	7	11	18	17	5	3	8	—	—	—	—	39	24	35	59	9	2	0	2	7	2	2	4
Edmonton	4	0	0	0	18	5	1	6	—	—	—	—	6	3	3	6	18	7	6	13	5	1	0	1
Florida	4	1	0	1	3	0	1	1	—	—	—	—	4	0	0	0	1	0	1	1	5	2	1	3
Hartford	42	3	9	12	7	3	3	6	1	0	0	0	40	20	31	51	7	6	2	8	9	4	4	8
Los Angeles	94	5	32	37	16	1	3	4	—	—	—	—	86	43	67	110	24	9	8	17	6	2	4	6
Montreal	43	0	8	8	6	1	1	2	—	—	—	—	46	21	23	44	9	5	5	10	10	4	5	9
New Jersey	54	3	22	25	8	2	0	2	1	0	0	0	55	25	39	64	7	1	3	4	20	11	11	22
NY Islanders	45	1	16	17	9	2	3	5	2	0	0	0	52	19	36	55	9	3	3	6	18	3	3	6
Rangers	38	1	11	12	8	1	6	7	—	—	—	—	35	16	26	42	8	2	3	5	—	—	—	—
Ottawa	4	1	0	1	4	0	1	1	—	—	—	—	7	4	7	11	2	0	1	1	7	2	5	7
Philadelphia	43	3	7	10	8	4	3	7	2	0	0	0	54	20	31	51	8	0	3	3	17	6	10	16
Pittsburgh	47	4	21	25	8	2	2	4	2	0	0	0	52	21	54	75	7	2	0	2	17	6	4	10
Quebec	41	4	14	18	9	3	4	7	1	0	0	0	45	19	34	53	7	1	2	3	11	2	5	7
St. Louis	42	6	11	17	13	2	4	6	—	—	—	—	39	19	36	55	10	3	2	5	7	2	6	8
San Jose	11	0	3	3	10	1	3	4	—	—	—	—	7	3	5	8	15	5	5	10	7	4	5	9
Tampa Bay	5	0	2	2	6	1	4	5	1	0	0	0	8	4	4	8	4	0	3	3	8	2	1	3
Toronto	38	3	6	9	17	2	6	8	—	—	—	—	39	11	34	45	10	1	4	5	5	1	0	1
Vancouver	97	4	28	32	16	3	3	6	3	0	0	0	85	56	70	126	—	—	—	—	5	2	0	2
Washington	45	5	13	18	7	4	0	4	—	—	—	—	54	16	42	58	8	2	0	2	19	5	5	10
Winnipeg	85	13	30	43	18	5	2	7	—	—	—	—	79	42	65	107	21	5	3	8	6	1	3	4
Totals	1086	81	323	404	258	55	64	119	15	0	2	2	1081	478	838	1316	241	69	75	144	230	75	86	161

PLAYER CAREER RECORDS VS. NHL TEAMS

TEAM	Brian Noonan GP	G	A	PTS	Mattias Norstrom GP	G	A	PTS	Eddie Olczyk GP	G	A	PTS	Mark Osborne GP	G	A	PTS	Jay Wells GP	G	A	PTS	Sergei Zubov GP	G	A	PTS
Anaheim	5	0	0	0	—	—	—	—	2	0	0	0	3	0	0	0	2	0	0	0	1	0	0	0
Boston	13	3	3	6	—	—	—	—	23	7	5	12	28	8	7	15	45	2	8	10	5	2	4	6
Buffalo	10	1	4	5	—	—	—	—	26	5	5	10	31	4	8	12	37	1	6	7	6	1	4	5
Calgary	13	4	1	5	—	—	—	—	37	17	23	40	37	7	17	24	65	4	17	21	3	1	3	4
Chicago	0	0	0	0	1	0	0	0	34	12	22	34	68	15	27	42	35	5	8	13	4	0	2	2
Dallas	39	6	14	20	—	—	—	—	57	25	27	52	66	14	22	36	34	1	4	5	2	0	2	2
Detroit	32	7	9	16	—	—	—	—	61	26	26	52	48	10	17	27	36	0	4	4	3	1	3	4
Edmonton	14	3	5	8	—	—	—	—	35	15	19	34	40	8	13	21	68	4	21	25	3	0	2	2
Florida	2	0	2	2	2	0	0	0	2	0	1	1	3	0	0	0	4	0	0	0	5	0	4	4
Hartford	10	1	2	3	1	0	1	1	25	9	16	25	27	6	5	11	46	5	10	15	5	1	6	7
Los Angeles	13	3	5	8	—	—	—	—	34	15	19	34	38	14	11	25	12	0	2	2	4	1	2	3
Montreal	9	1	1	2	—	—	—	—	26	4	8	12	29	15	10	25	44	0	12	12	5	3	3	6
New Jersey	12	2	1	3	—	—	—	—	29	16	16	32	39	15	22	37	60	3	14	17	9	2	9	11
NY Islanders	12	1	1	2	—	—	—	—	29	11	15	26	45	11	10	21	45	1	9	10	9	2	7	9
Rangers	11	3	3	6	—	—	—	—	25	12	17	29	25	6	9	15	34	2	5	7	—	—	—	—
Ottawa	4	0	0	0	—	—	—	—	4	2	3	5	5	0	4	4	5	0	0	0	6	3	6	9
Philadelphia	14	6	1	7	—	—	—	—	28	12	14	26	41	2	9	11	41	4	7	11	8	0	7	7
Pittsburgh	12	2	2	4	1	0	0	0	28	4	14	18	46	15	20	35	50	3	10	13	8	1	5	6
Quebec	8	4	2	6	1	0	0	0	28	9	17	26	35	12	11	23	44	2	5	7	6	0	3	3
St. Louis	28	3	10	13	—	—	—	—	56	26	33	59	64	19	29	48	36	2	5	7	3	1	3	4
San Jose	9	4	2	6	—	—	—	—	11	6	6	12	10	0	0	0	3	0	1	1	5	0	6	6
Tampa Bay	5	1	1	2	—	—	—	—	4	0	1	1	11	3	2	5	8	0	2	2	6	0	4	4
Toronto	28	2	5	7	1	0	1	1	25	6	14	20	28	3	14	17	35	0	9	9	4	0	2	2
Vancouver	15	5	3	8	—	—	—	—	38	12	22	34	36	6	16	22	60	2	23	25	4	0	5	5
Washington	7	1	5	6	1	0	0	0	31	7	10	17	43	10	16	26	51	1	10	11	10	0	6	6
Winnipeg	16	4	5	9	1	0	0	0	20	5	10	15	36	8	17	25	58	3	14	17	3	1	2	3
Totals	341	67	87	154	9	0	2	2	718	263	363	626	882	211	316	527	958	45	206	251	127	20	100	120

CAREER BREAKDOWN OF CURRENT RANGERS GOALIES VS. OPPOSITION

	GLENN HEALY								COREY HIRSCH								MIKE RICHTER							
TEAM	GP	MINS	GA	SO	AVG	W	L	T	GP	MINS	GA	SO	AVG	W	L	T	GP	MINS	GA	SO	AVG	W	L	T
Anaheim	1	59	3	0	3.05	0	1	0	—	—	—	—	—	—	—	—	2	59	4	0	4.06	0	1	0
Boston	15	826	50	1	3.63	4	9	2	—	—	—	—	—	—	—	—	6	332	11	1	1.98	3	1	1
Buffalo	11	632	37	1	3.51	6	3	1	—	—	—	—	—	—	—	—	10	572	31	1	3.25	6	3	1
Calgary	14	721	50	0	4.16	6	6	1	—	—	—	—	—	—	—	—	8	408	28	0	4.11	1	3	2
Chicago	10	596	36	0	3.62	3	7	0	—	—	—	—	—	—	—	—	5	304	16	0	3.15	2	2	1
Dallas	11	559	37	0	3.97	5	4	0	—	—	—	—	—	—	—	—	7	429	14	1	1.95	4	1	2
Detroit	9	457	26	0	3.41	3	3	2	1	65	2	0	1.84	0	0	1	7	311	22	0	4.24	2	3	0
Edmonton	14	672	56	0	5	3	8	1	—	—	—	—	—	—	—	—	6	365	11	1	1.80	5	0	1
Florida	1	30	1	0	2	1	0	0	—	—	—	—	—	—	—	—	5	268	10	0	2.23	2	2	0
Hartford	8	474	32	0	4.05	3	3	1	—	—	—	—	—	—	—	—	13	783	38	1	2.91	9	3	1
Los Angeles	6	356	27	0	4.55	0	6	0	1	60	3	0	3.00	1	0	0	8	445	18	0	2.42	7	0	0
Montreal	8	447	22	0	2.95	2	5	1	—	—	—	—	—	—	—	—	5	302	19	0	3.77	2	1	1
New Jersey	19	1105	57	1	3.09	9	4	5	1	58	4	0	4.13	0	1	0	14	803	26	1	1.94	10	2	1
NY Islanders	6	289	20	0	4.15	1	4	0	—	—	—	—	—	—	—	—	17	873	51	0	3.50	4	6	4
Rangers	21	1193	72	0	3.62	11	7	1	—	—	—	—	—	—	—	—	—	—	—	—	—	—	—	—
Ottawa	3	179	8	0	2.68	2	1	0	—	—	—	—	—	—	—	—	5	308	10	1	1.94	5	0	0
Philadelphia	21	1171	71	0	3.63	8	9	3	—	—	—	—	—	—	—	—	16	928	48	0	3.10	9	4	2
Pittsburgh	16	892	65	0	4.37	4	9	2	1	40	5	0	7.50	0	1	0	16	872	61	0	4.19	4	10	1
Quebec	14	779	42	0	3.23	6	5	2	—	—	—	—	—	—	—	—	10	498	32	0	3.85	5	3	0
St. Louis	10	536	37	0	4.14	3	5	1	—	—	—	—	—	—	—	—	8	486	22	1	2.71	4	3	1
San Jose	3	180	7	1	2.33	3	0	0	—	—	—	—	—	—	—	—	4	246	10	0	2.43	3	0	1
Tampa Bay	3	167	8	0	2.87	2	1	0	—	—	—	—	—	—	—	—	5	253	17	0	4.03	2	2	0
Toronto	10	603	29	0	2.88	6	3	1	—	—	—	—	—	—	—	—	7	430	21	0	2.93	4	1	2
Vancouver	15	874	43	2	2.95	8	6	1	—	—	—	—	—	—	—	—	5	305	13	0	2.55	4	0	1
Washington	25	1326	85	1	3.84	10	12	1	—	—	—	—	—	—	—	—	22	1211	67	1	3.31	11	9	0
Winnipeg	14	680	45	0	3.97	4	7	1	—	—	—	—	—	—	—	—	4	239	8	0	2.00	3	1	0
Totals	288	15803	966	7	3.66	113	128	27	4	224	14	0	3.75	1	2	1	215	12030	608	9	3.03	111	61	23

LIFETIME SHUTOUTS OF CURRENT RANGER GOALIES

DATE		OPPONENT	SITE	SCORE	SAVES
GLENN HEALY					
(one with Los Angeles, four with Islanders, two with Rangers)					
Feb. 28,	1988	Vancouver	Vancouver	2-0	13
Jan. 16,	1990	Vancouver	Nassau Coliseum	3-0	51
Feb. 4,	1990	Buffalo	Buffalo	1-0	39
Apr. 15,	1992	New Jersey	Nassau Coliseum	7-0	22
Mar. 6,	1993	San Jose	San Jose	6-0	26
Dec. 23,	1993	Washington	Washington	1-0	20
Feb. 3,	1994	Boston	Boston	3-0	28
MIKE RICHTER					
Apr. 7,	1991	Washington (Play.)	Washington	6-0	37
Nov. 23,	1991	St. Louis	St. Louis	3-0	24
Dec. 8,	1991	Boston	MSG	4-0	30
Dec. 23,	1991	New Jersey	MSG	3-0	25
Apr. 25,	1992	New Jersey (Play.)	Meadowlands	3-0	33
Feb. 27,	1993	Edmonton	Edmonton	1-0	29
Nov. 13,	1993	Washington	Washington	2-0	21
Dec. 13,	1993	Buffalo	MSG	2-0	28
Feb. 18,	1994	Ottawa	MSG	3-0	24
Mar. 16,	1994	Hartford	MSG	4-0	27
Apr. 1,	1994	Dallas	MSG	3-0	28
Apr. 17,	1994	Islanders (Play.)	MSG	6-0	21
Apr. 18,	1994	Islanders (Play.)	MSG	6-0	29
May 5,	1994	Washington (Play.)	Washington	3-0	21
May 17,	1994	New Jersey (Play.)	MSG	3-0	16

Career Assists and Penalty Minutes of Current Rangers Goalies

	HEALY			RICHTER	
	ASSISTS	PIM		ASSISTS	PIM
1985-86	0	0	1989-90	3	0
1987-88	2	6	1990-91	1	4
1988-89	1	28	1991-92	0	6
1989-90	1	7	1992-93	5	2
1990-91	2	14	1993-94	0	2
1991-92	1	18	TOTALS	9	14
1992-93	2	2			
1993-94	2	2			
TOTALS	11	77			

Glenn Healy

Mike Richter

LIFETIME HAT TRICKS BY CURRENT RANGERS

DATE	OPPONENT	SITE	GOALTENDER
GREG GILBERT (2 with Islanders)			
Feb. 25, 1984	New Jersey	Nassau Coliseum	Ron Low
Feb. 16, 1988	Calgary	Nassau Colisum	Mike Vernon (2)
			Doug Dadswell (1)
ADAM GRAVES (1 with Detroit, 3 with Rangers)			
Dec. 14, 1989	Chicago	Chicago	Alain Chevrier
Feb. 14, 1992	Islanders	MSG	Mark Fitzpatrick
Nov. 25, 1992	Pittsburgh	Pittsburgh	Tom Barrasso (1)
			Ken Wregget (2)
Feb. 2, 1994	Islanders	MSG	Ron Hextall
ALEXEI KOVALEV			
Dec. 27, 1992	Boston	MSG	Andy Moog
STEVE LARMER (9 with Chicago)			
11/14/82	Minnesota	Chicago	Don Beaupre
12/18/82	Toronto	Toronto	Mike Palmateer
3/12/86	Buffalo	Buffalo	Tom Barrasso
3/28/88	Minnesota	Minnesota	Don Beaupre
			Jon Casey
10/13/90	Minnesota	Minnesota	Jon Casey
10/10/91	Vancouver	Chicago	Troy Gamble
12/08/91	Minnesota	Chicago	Jon Casey
			Darcy Wakaluk
11/28/92	Calgary	Calgary	Mike Vernon
12/23/92	Ottawa	Ottawa	Peter Sidorkiewicz
MARK MESSIER (16 with Edmonton, 4 with Rangers)			
Mar. 16, 1981	Pittsburgh	Edmonton	Greg Millen
Dec. 2, 1981	Quebec	Quebec	Dan Bouchard
Feb. 17, 1982	Minnesota	Edmonton	Don Beaupre
Dec. 19, 1982	Montreal (4 goals)	Edmonton	Richard Sevigny 3, ENG
Jan. 19, 1983	Vancouver	Edmonton	Richard Brodeur
*Apr. 14, 1983	Calgary (4 goals)	Edmonton	Rejean Lemelin
*April. 17, 1983	Calgary	Calgary	Rejean Lemelin (1)
			Don Edwards (2)
*Apr. 26, 1983	Chicago	Edmonton	Murray Bannerman
Feb. 25, 1984	Toronto	Edmonton	Allan Bester
Mar. 11, 1984	Vancouver	Edmonton	John Garrett
Feb. 26, 1986	Winnipeg	Winnipeg	Brian Hayward
Feb. 14, 1988	Vancouver	Edmonton	Frank Caprice
Feb. 21, 1989	Hartford (4 goals)	Edmonton	Mike Liut 3, ENG
Nov. 21, 1989	Vancouver	Edmonton	Kirk McLean
Jan. 17, 1990	Winnipeg	Edmonton	Bob Essensa
Mar. 3, 1990	Philadelphia (4 goals)	Edmonton	Ron Hextall
Nov. 19, 1991	Vancouver	Vancouver	Kirk McLean
Dec. 13, 1991	Washington	Washington	Don Beaupre 2, ENG
Mar. 22, 1992	New Jersey (4 goals)	MSG	Chad Erickson
*May 25, 1994	New Jersey	New Jersey	Martin Brodeur
SERGEI NEMCHINOV			
Jan. 29, 1993	Buffalo	Buffalo	Tom Draper
BRIAN NOONAN (4 with Chicago)			
12/05/91	Los Angeles	Chicago	Kelly Hrudey
12/27/91	Winnepeg	Chicago	Stephane Beauregard
12/29/91	Detroit (4 goals)	Chicago	Tim Cheveldae
*4/18/93	St. Louis	Chicago	Curtis Joseph
EDDIE OLCZYK (3 with Toronto, 1 with Rangers)			
*Apr. 12, 1988	Detroit	Toronto	Greg Stefan (2)
			Glen Hanlon (1)
Mar. 25, 1989	Detroit	Toronto	Glenn Hanlon
Jan. 27, 1990	Montreal	Toronto	Patrick Roy
Mar. 24, 1993	Philadelphia	MSG	Tommy Soderstrom
			Wendell Young (1)
MARK OSBORNE (1 with Detroit)			
Dec. 1, 1981	St. Louis	St.Louis	Mike Liut

*Playoff hat trick

ALL-STAR GAME APPEARANCES

(Current Rangers only)

ADAM GRAVES

Season	Club	GP	G	A	PTS
1993-94	Eastern All-Stars	1	0	2	2

STEVE LARMER

Season	Club	GP	G	A	PTS
1989-90	Campbell All-Stars	1	0	0	0
1990-91	Campbell All-Stars	1	0	2	2
	Totals	2	0	2	2

BRIAN LEETCH

Season	Club	GP	G	A	PTS
1989-90	Wales All-Stars	1	0	0	0
1990-91	Wales All-Stars	1	0	0	0
1991-92	Wales All-Stars	1	0	0	0
1992-93	Wales All-Stars	Injured			
1993-94	Eastern All-Stars	1	0	0	0
	Totals	4	0	0	0

KEVIN LOWE

Season	Club	GP	G	A	PTS
1983-84	Campbell All-Stars	1	0	0	0
1984-85	Campbell All-Stars	1	0	0	0
1985-86	Campbell All-Stars	1	0	0	0
1987-88	Campbell All-Stars	1	0	1	1
1988-89	Campbell All-Stars	1	0	0	0
1989-90	Campbell All-Stars	1	0	0	0
1992-93	Wales All-Stars	1	0	1	1
	Totals	7	0	2	2

MARK MESSIER

Season	Club	GP	G	A	PTS
1981-82	Campbell All-Stars	1	0	0	0
1982-83	Campbell All-Stars	1	0	3	3
1983-84	Campbell All-Stars	1	0	0	0
1985-86	Campbell All-Stars	1	0	0	0
1986-87	NHL All-Stars	1	1	0	1
1987-88	Campbell All-Stars	1	0	0	0
1988-89	Campbell All-Stars	1	1	1	2
1989-90	Campbell All-Stars	1	1	0	1
1990-91	Campbell All-Stars	1	0	1	1
1991-92	Wales All-Stars	1	0	1	1
1992-93	Wales All-Stars	Injured			
1993-94	Eastern All-Stars	1	1	2	3
	Totals	11	4	8	12

MIKE RICHTER

Season	Club	GP	MINS	GA	GAA
1991-92	Wales All-Stars	1	20	2	6.00
1993-94	Eastern All-Stars	1	20	2	6.00
	Totals	2	40	4	6.00

Adam Graves, Mark Messier, Mike Richter and Brian Leetch represented the Rangers in the 1994 All-Star game at Madison Square Garden.

CAREER GOAL BREAKDOWN AND SCORING STREAKS OF CURRENT RANGERS

JEFF BEUKEBOOM

SEASON	PPG	SHG	GWG
1986-87	1	0	1
1987-88	1	0	1
1988-89	0	0	0
1989-90	0	0	0
1990-91	0	0	0
1991-92	0	0	0
1992-93	0	0	0
1993-94	1	0	0
Totals	3	0	2

Last PPG: 1/3/94 vs. Fla. (Vanbiesbrouck)
Last SHG: None
Last GWG: 1/6/88 at Hfd. (Liut)
Longest Point Scoring Streak: 4, 1/11-1/18/88 (1 goals, 3 assists)
Longest Goal Scoring Streak: 2, 11/25-11/27/88 (2 goals)
Longest Assist Streak: 3, (many) last-10/29-11/2/92 (3 assists)

ADAM GRAVES

SEASON	PPG	SHG	GWG
1987-88	0	0	0
1988-89	0	0	1
1989-90	0	0	0
1990-91	2	0	1
1991-92	4	4	4
1992-93	12	1	6
1993-94	20	4	4
Totals	38	9	16

Last PPG: 3/16/94 vs. Hfd. (Burke)
Last SHG: 11/10/93 vs. Wpg. (Essensa)
Last GWG: 2/18/94 vs. Ott. (Billington)
Last 2-Goal Game: 3/23/93 at Edm. (Ranford)
Longest Point Scoring Streak: 5, (3 times) last-1/25-2/2/94 (4 goals, 4 assists)
Longest Goal Scoring Streak: 4, (4 times) last-11/16-11/24/93 (5 goals)
Longest Assist Streak: 4, (3 times) last-2/28-3/5/94 (4 assists)

GLEN FEATHERSTONE

SEASON	PPG	SHG	GWG
1988-89	1	0	0
1989-90	1	0	1
1990-91	0	0	0
1991-92	0	0	0
1992-93	1	0	0
1993-94	0	0	1
Totals	3	0	2

Last PPG: 1/25/93 at Mtl. (Roy)
Last SHG: None
Last GWG: 11/7/93 at Buf. (Fuhr)
Last 2-Goal Game: None
Longest Point Scoring Streak: 3, (twice) last-12/15-12/19/92 (1 goal, 2 assists)
Longest Goal Scoring Streak: One
Longest Assist Streak: 3, 12/20-12/26/89 (4 assists)

MIKE HARTMAN

SEASON	PPG	SHG	GWG
1987-88	0	0	1
1988-89	1	0	0
1989-90	2	0	3
1990-91	2	0	1
1991-92	0	0	1
1992-93	0	0	0
1993-94	0	0	0
Totals	5	0	6

Last PPG: 3/31/91 at Wpg. (Essensa)
Last SHG: None
Last GWG: 1/28/92 at Pit. (Barrasso)
Last 2-Goal Game: 11/5/89 vs. L.A. (Hrudey)
Longest Point Scoring Streak: 5, 12/14-12/23/88 (2 goals, 3 assists)
Longest Goal Scoring Streak: 3, 12/26-12/29/90 (3 goals)
Longest Assist Streak: 3, (3 times) last- 1/26-1/28/90 (2 assists)

GREG GILBERT

SEASON	PPG	SHG	GWG
1982-83	0	0	0
1983-84	6	0	2
1984-85	2	0	2
1985-86	1	0	2
1986-87	0	0	0
1987-88	1	1	0
1988-89	0	1	0
1989-90	0	0	3
1990-91	1	0	0
1991-92	0	0	1
1992-93	0	1	2
1993-94	1	0	0
Totals	12	3	12

Last PPG: 2/24/94 at. N.J. (Terreri)
Last SHG: 1/24/93 vs. Van. (McLean)
Last GWG: 1/16/93 vs. at Tor. (Fuhr)
Last 2-Goal Game: 11/17/92 at Det. (Cheveldae)
Longest Point Scoring Streak: 6, (twice) last-12/15-12/27/84 (5 goals, 7 assists)
Longest Goal Scoring Streak: 3, (6 times) last-2/14-2/16/88 (5 goals, 1 assist)
Longest Assist Streak: 4, (3 time) last- 2/18-2/27/93 (1 goal, 4 assists)

MIKE HUDSON

SEASON	PPG	SHG	GWG
1988-89	0	1	0
1989-90	0	0	3
1990-91	0	0	1
1991-92	2	1	2
1992-93	0	0	0
1993-94	0	0	1
Totals	2	2	7

Last PPG: 12/19/91 vs. Mtl. (Melanson or Racicot)
Last SHG: 10/13/91 vs. S.J. (Hayward or Hackett)
Last GWG: 3/1/94 vs. Wsh. at Halifax (Kolzig)
Last 2-Goal Game: 3/24/91 vs. Min. (Hayward)
Longest Point Scoring Streak: 3, (3 times) last-10/10-10/13/91 (2 goals, 3 assists)
Longest Goal Scoring Streak: 3, 1/26-2/1/90 (3 goals)
Longest Assist Streak: 3, 10/10-10/13/91 (4 assists)

CAREER GOAL BREAKDOWN AND SCORING STREAKS OF CURRENT RANGERS

ALEXANDER KARPOVTSEV

SEASON	PPG	SHG	GWG
1993-94	1	0	1
Totals	1	0	1

Last PPG: 10/13/93 vs. Que. (Fiset)
Last SHG: None
Last GWG: 10/13/94 vs. Que. (Fiset)
Last 2-Goal Game: None
Longest Point Scoring Streak: One
Longest Goal Scoring Streak: One
Longest Assist Streak: One

JOE KOCUR

SEASON	PPG	SHG	GWG
1984-85	0	0	0
1985-86	2	0	0
1986-87	2	0	2
1987-88	0	0	1
1988-89	1	0	1
1989-90	1	0	5
1990-91	0	0	0
1991-92	0	0	2
1992-93	1	0	0
1993-94	0	0	0
Totals	7	0	11

Last PPG: 12/2/92 vs. Det. (Cheveldae)
Last SHG: None
Last GWG: 11/23/91 at StL. (Joseph)
Last 2-Goal Game: 12/6/91 at Det. (Cheveldae)
Longest Point Scoring Streak: 3, (4 times) last-1/27-2/2/90 (4 goals, 3 assists)
Longest Goal Scoring Streak: 3, 1/27-2/2/90 (4 goals)
Longest Assist Streak: 2, (4 times) last-12/17-12/19/92 (3 assists)

ALEXEI KOVALEV

SEASON	PPG	SHG	GWG
1992-93	3	0	3
1993-94	7	0	3
Totals	10	0	6

Last PPG: 4/2/94 at N.J. (Brodeur)
Last SHG: None
Last GWG: 4/2/94 at N.J. (Brodeur)
Last 2-Goal Game: 4/8/94 vs. Tor. (Potvin)
Longest Point Scoring Streak: 11, 3/16-4/8/94 (10 goals, 5 assists)
Longest Goal Scoring Streak: 4, 3/27-4/2/94 (5 goals)
Longest Assist Streak: 4, (twice) last-3/18-3/25/94 (4 assists)

NICK KYPREOS

SEASON	PPG	SHG	GWG
1989-90	0	0	2
1990-91	0	0	3
1991-92	0	0	0
1992-93	0	0	2
1993-94	0	0	1
Totals	0	0	8

Last PPG: None
Last SHG: None
Last GWG: 2/14/94 at Que. (Fiset)
Last 2-Goal Game: 2/12/93 vs. Wpg. (Essensa)
Longest Point Scoring Streak: 3, (4 times) last-12/3-12/9/92 (2 goals, 1 assist)
Longest Goal Scoring Streak: 2, (6 times) last-3/16-3/19/93 (2 goals)
Longest Assist Streak: 2, 3/2-3/4/94 (2 assists)

STEVE LARMER

SEASON	PPG	SHG	GWG
1980-81	0	0	0
1981-82	0	0	0
1982-83	13	0	9
1983-84	13	0	3
1984-85	14	0	6
1985-86	13	1	3
1986-87	10	0	4
1987-88	21	7	0
1988-89	19	1	2
1989-90	8	2	4
1990-91	17	2	9
1991-92	11	2	3
1992-93	14	4	6
1993-94	6	4	7
Totals	159	23	56

Last PPG: 2/14/94 at Que. (Fiset)
Last SHG: 3/25/94 at Van. (Whitmore)
Last GWG: 4/4/94 vs. Fla. (Vanbiesbrouck)
Last 2-Goal Game: 2/14/94 at Que. (Fiset)
Longest Point Scoring Streak: 15, 10/11-11/11/87 (11 goals, 7 assists)
Longest Goal Scoring Streak: 7, 10/23-11/6/87 (8 goals)
Longest Assist Streak: 9, 12/6-12/23/89 (14 assists)

BRIAN LEETCH

SEASON	PPG	SHG	GWG
1987-88	1	0	1
1988-89	8	3	1
1989-89	5	0	2
1990-91	6	0	4
1991-92	10	1	3
1992-93	2	1	1
1993-94	17	1	4
Totals	49	6	16

Last PPG: 4/1/94 vs. Dal. (Moog)
Last SHG: 3/25/94 at Van. (Whitmore)
Last GWG: 4/1/94 vs. Dal. (Moog)
Last 2-Goal Game: 3/25/94 at Van. (Whitmore)
Longest Point Streak: 17, 11/23-12/31/91 (5 goals, 24 assists)
Longest Goal Scoring Streak: 3, (many) last-3/29-4/2/94 (3 goals)
Longest Assist Streak: 15, 11/29-12/31/91 (23 assists)

CAREER GOAL BREAKDOWN AND SCORING STREAKS OF CURRENT RANGERS

KEVIN LOWE

SEASON	PPG	SHG	GWG
1979-80	2	0	0
1980-81	4	0	2
1981-82	1	1	2
1982-83	1	0	0
1983-84	1	0	1
1984-85	1	0	1
1985-86	0	0	0
1986-87	2	2	1
1987-88	2	1	2
1988-89	0	0	1
1989-90	2	1	0
1990-91	0	0	0
1991-92	0	0	0
1992-93	0	0	0
1993-94	0	0	1
Totals	16	5	11

Last PPG: 11/11/90 at Wsh. (Beaupre)
Last SHG: 1/17/90 vs. Wpg. (Essensa)
Last GWG: 1/16/94 at Chi. (Belfour)
Last 2-Goal Game: None
Longest Point Scoring Streak: 7, (twice) last-1/28-2/8/87 (2 goals, 6 assists)
Longest Goals Scoring Streak: 2, (many) last-2/6-2/8/91 (2 goals)
Longest Assist Streak: 6, 1/28-2/6/87 (6 assists)

STEPHANE MATTEAU

SEASON	PPG	SHG	GWG
1990-91	0	1	1
1991-92	1	0	0
1992-93	2	0	4
1993-94	3	0	2
Totals	6	1	7

Last PPG: 3/23/94 at Edm. (Ranford)
Last SHG: 12/16/90 at Van. (Gamble)
Last GWG: 2/6/94 at Ana. (Hebert)
Last 2-Goal Game: 10/10/93 vs. Wpg. (Beauregard)
Longest Point Scoring Streak: 5, (twice) last- 3/26-4/12/92 (3 goals, 2 assists)
Longest Goal Scoring Streak: 3, 11/20-11/26/93 (3 goals)
Longest Assist Streak:3, 11/5-11/8/92 (3 assists)

JOBY MESSIER

SEASON	PPG	SHG	GWG
1992-93	0	0	0
1993-94	0	0	0
Totals	0	0	0

Last PPG: None
Last SHG: None
Last GWG: None
Last 2-Goal Game: None
Longest Point Scoring Streak: One
Longest Goal Scoring Streak: None
Longest Assist Streak: One

MARK MESSIER

SEASON	PPG	SHG	GWG
1979-80	1	1	1
1980-81	4	0	1
1981-82	10	0	3
1982-83	12	1	2
1983-84	7	4	7
1984-85	4	5	1
1985-86	10	5	7
1986-87	7	4	5
1987-88	12	3	7
1988-89	6	6	4
1989-90	13	6	3
1990-91	3	1	2
1991-92	12	4	6
1992-93	7	2	5
1993-94	6	2	5
Totals	114	44	56

Last PPG: 2/3/94 at Bos. (Riendeau)
Last SHG: 2/14/94 at Que. (Fiset)
Last GWG: 1/31/94 vs. Pit. (Wregget)
Last 2-Goal Game: 4/10/94 at NYI. (Hextall)
Longest Point Scoring Streak: 15, 2/5-3/7/92 (7 goals, 17 assists)
Longest Goal Scoring Streak: 6, 3/14-3/28/86 (7 goals)
Longest Assist Streak: 8, (twice) last-2/12-2/27/93 (11 assists)

PETR NEDVED

SEASON	PPG	SHG	GWG
1990-91	1	0	0
1991-92	5	0	1
1992-93	2	1	3
1993-94	2	0	0
Totals	10	1	4

Last PPG: 4/5/94 vs. Chi. (Belfour)
Last SHG: 3/20/93 vs. NYI (Fitzpatrick)
Last GWG: 2/24/93 vs. NYR (Vanbiesbrouck)
Last 2-Goal Game: 1/27/93 vs. Chi. (Waite)
Longest Point Scoring Streak: 15, 11/19-12/27/92 (15 goals, 9 assists)
Longest Goal Scoring Streak: 5, 11/26-12/9/92 (7 goals)
Longest Assist Streak: 4, (twice) last- 3/20-3/25/94 (5 assists)

SERGEI NEMCHINOV

SEASON	PPG	SHG	GWG
1991-92	2	0	5
1992-93	0	1	3
1993-94	4	0	6
Totals	6	1	14

Last PPG: 2/28/94 vs. Phi. (Roussel)
Lash SHG: 11/4/92 vs. Phi. (Beauregard)
Last GWG: 1/18/94 vs. Stl. (Joseph)
Last 2-Goal Game: 3/9/94 at Halifax vs. Wsh. (Kolzig)
Longest Point Scoring Streak: 11, 12/2-12/26/91 (9 goals, 4 assists)
Longest Goal Scoring Streak: 6, 12/12-12/14/91 (6 goals)
Longest Assist Streak: 4, (twice) last-3/7-3/14/92 (5 assists)

CAREER GOAL BREAKDOWN AND SCORING STREAKS OF CURRENT RANGERS

BRIAN NOONAN

SEASON	PPG	SHG	GWG
1987-88	3	0	2
1988-89	2	0	0
1989-90	0	0	0
1990-91	0	0	0
1991-92	4	0	0
1992-93	5	0	3
1993-94	10	0	6
Totals	24	0	11

Last PPG: 3/25/94 at Van. (Whitmore)
Last SHG: None
Last GWG: 4/12/94 vs. Buf. (Hasek)
Last 2-Goal Game: 3/25/94 at Van. (Whitmore)
Longest Point Scoring Streak: 5, 10/29-11/17/92 (4 goals, 3 assists)
Longest Goal Scoring Streak: 2, (10 times) last- 3/23-3/25/94 (3 goals)
Longest Assist Streak: 3, 2/14-2/17/89 (3 assists)

MATTIAS NORSTROM

SEASON	PPG	SHG	GWG
1993-94	0	0	0
Totals	0	0	0

Last PPG: None
Last SHG: None
Last GWG: None
Last 2-Goal Game: None
Longest Point Scoring Streak: None
Longest Goal Scoring Streak: None
Longest Assist Streak: None

EDDIE OLCZYK

SEASON	PPG	SHG	GWG
1984-85	1	1	2
1985-86	8	1	1
1986-87	2	1	2
1987-88	14	4	3
1988-89	11	2	4
1989-90	6	0	4
1990-91	14	0	5
1991-92	12	0	7
1992-93	2	0	1
1993-94	0	0	1
Totals	60	9	30

Last PPG: 11/14/92 at Stl. (Joseph)
Last SHG: 11/16/88 vs. Pit. (Barrasso)
Last GWG: 11/23/93 vs. Mtl. (Roy)
Last 2-Goal Game: 3/24/94 vs. Phi. (Soderstrom)
Longest Point Scoring Streak: 18, 12/2-1/8/90 (11 goals, 17 assists)
Longest Goal Scoring Streak: 4, 2/25-3/4/89 (4 goals)
Longest Assist Streak: 7, 1/31-2/17/87 (8 assists)

MARK OSBORNE

SEASON	PPG	SHG	GWG
1981-82	5	0	3
1982-83	3	0	3
1983-84	6	0	5
1984-85	0	0	0
1985-86	5	1	1
1986-87	6	0	2
1987-88	4	2	0
1988-89	5	0	1
1989-90	3	1	6
1990-91	1	1	2
1991-92	0	2	0
1992-93	0	2	2
1993-94	1	1	2
Totals	39	10	27

Last PPG: 12/17/93 at NYI (Hextall)
Last SHG: 4/10/94 vs.Wpg.(Cheveldae)
Last 2-Goal Game: 10/23/93 vs. T.B. (Puppa)
Longest Point Scoring Streak: 7, (twice) last- 1/13-1/31/90 (4 goals, 7 assists)
Longest Goal Scoring Streak: 5, 1/10-1/18/88 (5 goals)
Longest Assist Streak: 7, 1/13-1/31/90 (7 assists)

JAY WELLS

SEASON	PPG	SHG	GWG
1979-80	0	0	0
1980-81	0	0	1
1981-82	0	0	0
1982-83	0	0	1
1983-84	0	0	0
1984-85	0	0	0
1985-86	4	0	2
1986-87	6	0	2
1987-88	1	0	0
1988-89	0	0	0
1989-90	0	0	1
1990-91	0	0	0
1991-92	0	0	0
1992-93	0	0	0
1993-94	0	0	0
Totals	11	0	7

Last PPG: 10/10/87 vs. St.L. (Wamsley)
Last SHG: None
Last GWG: 11/14/89 at NYI (Healy)
Longest Point Scoring Streak: 3, (many) last-12/26-12/29/92 (3 assists)
Longest Goal Scoring Streak: 2, (many) last-10/19-10/22/87 (2 goals)
Longest Assist Streak: 3, (many) last- 12/26-12/29/92 (3 assists)

SERGEI ZUBOV

SEASON	PPG	SHG	GWG
1992-93	2	1	0
1993-94	9	0	1
Totals	11	1	1

Last PPG: 3/10/94 at Bos. (Casey)
Last SHG: 1/27/93 vs. Wpg. (Essensa)
Last GWG: 3/5/94 at NYI (Hextall)
Longest Point Scoring Streak: 8, 3/4-3/16/94 (3 goals, 6 assists)
Longest Goal Scoring Streak: 3, 12/17-12/19 (3 goals)
Longest Assist Streak: 5, (twice) last- 1/14-1/27/94 (8 assists)

RANGERS MILESTONES IN SIGHT

Jeff Beukeboom
10 games for 500

Glen Featherstone
57 games for 300

Greg Gilbert
26 games for 800
11 goals for 150

Adam Graves
35 games for 500
13 goals for 150
24 assists for 150
37 points for 300

Mike Hartman
4 games for 400
22 points for 100

Glen Healy
12 games for 300

Mike Hudson
40 games for 350

Alexander Karpovtsev
33 games for 100

Joe Kocur
69 PIM for 2200

Alexei Kovalev
6 points for 100
59 games for 200

Nick Kypreos
44 games for 350
52 PIM for 1000

Steve Larmer
41 games for 1000
17 points for 1000
44 assists for 600

Brian Leetch
54 points for 500
57 assists for 400
63 games for 500

Kevin Lowe
14 games for 1100

Stephane Matteau
48 games for 300

Mark Messier
22 goals for 500
62 assists for 900
84 points for 1400
19 games for 1100

Petr Nedved
51 games for 300
26 goals for 100
24 assists for 100

Sergei Nemchinov
60 games for 300
25 goals for 100
14 assists for 100
39 points for 200

Brian Noonan
59 games for 400
33 goals for 100
13 assists for 100
46 points for 200

Eddie Olczyk
24 points for 650

Mark Osborne
18 games for 900
23 points for 550
67 PIM for 1200

Mike Richter
45 games for 250
39 wins for 150

Jay Wells
42 games for 1000

Sergei Zubov
80 games for 100
80 points for 200

RANGERS GAME NIGHT STAFF

Game Director	Jeanie Baumgartner
Music Director	Ray Castoldi
Video\Matrix Operations	Rich Carlino
Press Box Attendants	Paul Clogher, Sal Frasca, Tommy Matthews
Press Room Attendants	Joe Pinto, John Arnone
Game Night Staff	Mike Manna, Jeorgie Ornstein, Brad Kolodny, Keith Soutar
Lockerroom Assistants	Joe Devanney, Tommy Horvath, Joe Vanness, Mike Vanness, Ed Whiteman
Video Staff	Rich Chapman, Ken Watnick
Interpreter	Irina Cytowicz
Public Address Announcer	Bob Galerstein

OFF-ICE OFFICIALS

Supervisor	Frank Koch
Timekeeper and Scoreboard Operator	Anthony Daddario
Goal Judge and Spare Official	Charles Joyce
Game Timekeeper and Scoreboard Operator	Frank Koch
Statistician and Spare Official	Stephen Devaney
Goal Judge and Spare Official	Adam Giever
Statistician and Spare Official	Joseph Leone
Goal Judge and Penalty Timekeeper	Charles O'Donnell
Scorer and Timekeeper	Mark Rubenfeld
Penalty Timekeeper and Spare Official	Bernard Ryan
Statistician and Spare Official	Jim Breidenbach
Goal Judge and Spare Official	Louis Venturino
Video Goal Judges	John Damante and Tim Rappleye

HOW THE RANGERS WERE BUILT

PLAYER	HOW ACQUIRED
Jeff Beukeboom	From the Edmonton Oilers for David Shaw as the future considerations of the Mark Messier trade on November 12, 1991.
Sylvain Blouin	Rangers fourth round choice, 104th overall, in the 1994 Entry Draft.
Eric Cairns	Rangers third round choice, 72nd overall, in the 1992 Entry Draft.
Craig Duncanson	Signed as a free agent on September 4, 1992.
Glen Featherstone	From the Boston Bruins for Daniel Lacroix on August 19, 1994.
Peter Fiorentino	Rangers 11th round choice, 215th overall, in 1988 Entry Draft.
Ken Gernander	Signed as a free agent on September 9, 1994.
Greg Gilbert	Signed as a free agent on July 29, 1993.
Adam Graves	Signed as a free agent from the Edmonton Oilers on September 3, 1991.
Mike Hartman	From the Tampa Bay Lightning for Randy Gilhen on March 22, 1993.
Glenn Healy	From the Tampa Bay Lightning for the return of Tampa Bay's third round choice in the 1993 Entry Draft on June 25, 1993.
Jim Hiller	Claimed off waivers from the Detroit Red Wings on October 12, 1993.
Jon Hillebrandt	Rangers 10th round choice, 202nd overall, in 1990 Entry Draft.
Corey Hirsch	Rangers eighth round choice, 169th overall, in 1991 Entry Draft.
Mike Hudson	Claimed from the Edmonton Oilers in the NHL waiver draft on October 3, 1993.
Alexander Karpovtsev	From the Quebec Nordiques in exchange for Mike Hurlbut on September 9, 1993.
Rob Kenny	Signed as a free agent on August 24, 1992.
Joe Kocur	From the Detroit Red Wings along with Per Djoos in exchange for Kevin Miller, Dennis Vial and Jim Cummins on March 5, 1991.
Alexei Kovalev	Rangers first round draft choice, 15th overall, in 1991 Entry Draft.
Andrei Kudinov	Rangers 10th round choice, 242nd overall, in the 1993 Entry Draft.
Nick Kypreos	From the Hartford Whalers with Steve Larmer, Barry Richter and a 1994 sixth round draft choice (Yuri Litvinov) in exchange for James Patrick and Darren Turcotte on November 2, 1993.
Darren Langdon	Signed as a free agent on August 16, 1993.
Steve Larmer	From the Hartford Whalers with Nick Kypreos, Barry Richter and a 1994 sixth round draft choice (Yuri Litvinov) in exchange for James Patrick and Darren Turcotte on November 2, 1993.
Brian Leetch	Rangers first round choice, ninth overall, in 1986 Entry Draft.
Kevin Lowe	From the Edmonton Oilers in exchange for Roman Oksyuta and Rangers' third round draft choice in 1993 Entry Draft on December 11, 1992.
Scott Malone	From the Toronto Maple Leafs with Glenn Anderson and a 1994 fourth round draft choice (Alexander Korobolin) in exchange for Mike Gartner on March 21, 1994.
Stephane Matteau	From the Chicago Blackhawks along with Brian Noonan in exchange for Tony Amonte and the rights to Matt Oates on March 21, 1994.
Shawn McCosh	Signed as a free agent on August 17, 1993.
Mike McLaughlin	Signed as a free agent on August 17, 1993.
Joby Messier	Rangers sixth round choice, 118th overall, in 1989 Entry Draft
Mark Messier	From the Edmonton Oilers along with future considerations (Jeff Beukeboom) in exchange for Bernie Nicholls, Steven Rice and Louie DeBrusk on October 4, 1991.
Petr Nedved	From the St. Louis Blues in exchange for Doug Lidster and Esa Tikkanen on July 24, 1994.
Jeff Neilsen	Rangers fourth round choice, 69th overall, in the 1990 Entry Draft.
Sergei Nemchinov	Rangers 12th round choice, 244th overall, in 1990 Entry Draft.
Brian Noonan	From the Chicago Blackhawks along with Stephane Matteau in exchange for Tony Amonte and the rights to Matt Oates on March 21, 1994.
Mattias Norstrom	Rangers second round choice, 48th overall, in 1992 Entry Draft.
Eddie Olczyk	From the Winnipeg Jets in exchange for Tie Domi and Kris King on December 28, 1992.
Mark Osborne	Signed as a free agent on September 6, 1994.
Jamie Ram	Rangers tenth round choice, 213th overall, in the 1991 Entry Draft.
Shawn Reid	Signed as a free agent on July 6, 1994.
Barry Richter	From the Hartford Whalers with Steve Larmer, Nick Kypreos and a 1994 sixth round draft choice (Yuri Litvinov) in exchange for James Patrick and Darren Turcotte on November 2, 1993.
Mike Richter	Rangers second round choice, 28th overall, in 1985 Entry Draft
Jean-Yves Roy	Signed as a free agent on July 20, 1992.
Andy Silverman	Rangers ninth round choice, 181st overall, in the 1990 Entry Draft.
Dave Smith	Signed as a free agent on September 9, 1994.
Dimitri Starostenko	Rangers fifth round choice, 120th overall, in 1992 Entry Draft.
Michael Stewart	Rangers first round choice, 13th overall, in 1990 Entry Draft.
Jay Wells	From the Buffalo Sabres for Randy Moller on March 9,1992.
Darcy Werenka	Rangers second round choice, 37th overall, in 1991 Entry Draft.
Sergei Zubov	Rangers fifth round choice, 85th overall, in 1990 Entry Draft.

IN THE PAST

RANGERS RECORD AGAINST ALL NATIONAL HOCKEY LEAGUE TEAMS SINCE 1926

OVERALL

New York Rangers vs.	GP	W	L	T	GF	GA	PTS
Chicago Blackhawks	557	228	233	96	1604	1638	552
Detroit Red Wings (a)	554	206	245	103	1541	1688	515
Boston Bruins	560	210	256	94	1631	1801	514
Toronto Maple Leafs	535	189	252	94	1513	1705	472
Montreal Canadiens	540	164	290	86	1405	1855	414
Pittsburgh Penguins	155	77	60	18	609	551	172
Philadelphia Flyers	168	68	67	33	528	537	169
St. Louis Blues	108	68	27	13	411	283	149
New Jersey Devils (K.C., Colo.)	119	67	40	12	496	391	146
Dallas Stars (Minn.)	107	62	27	18	399	310	142
Vancouver Canucks	92	66	18	8	402	261	140
New York Islanders	141	60	67	14	501	522	134
Los Angeles Kings	103	54	35	14	394	324	122
Washington Capitals	121	54	53	14	456	454	122
Buffalo Sabres	94	33	44	17	324	352	83
Calgary Flames (Atlanta)	87	29	44	14	290	356	72
Quebec Nordiques	49	26	17	6	209	176	58
Ottawa Senators (b)	39	24	6	9	124	75	57
Winnipeg Jets	45	24	17	4	191	173	52
Hartford Whalers	48	23	20	5	195	165	51
Edmonton Oilers	44	17	22	5	164	176	39
San Jose Sharks	7	6	0	1	37	16	13
Tampa Bay Lightning	8	5	3	0	31	33	10
Florida Panthers	5	3	2	0	13	11	6
Anaheim Mighty Ducks	2	0	2	0	4	7	0
Defunct Teams (c)	246	152	58	36	811	521	340
Totals	**4534**	**1915**	**1905**	**714**	**14283**	**14381**	**4544**

HOME

	GP	W	L	T	GF	GA	PTS
Detroit Red Wings (a)	276	131	87	58	852	710	320
Boston Bruins	282	122	106	54	857	792	298
Chicago Blackhawks	279	117	108	54	827	790	288
Toronto Maple Leafs	268	111	101	56	821	785	278
Montreal Canadiens	270	109	109	52	782	789	270
Philadelphia Flyers	85	39	26	20	285	246	98
New York Islanders	70	43	19	8	281	211	94
St. Louis Blues	53	42	6	5	228	120	89
Pittsburgh Penguins	78	41	30	7	320	273	89
New Jersey Devils (K.C., Colo.)	59	36	15	8	263	185	80
Dallas Stars (Minn.)	54	33	11	10	194	148	76
Vancouver Canucks	47	35	7	5	215	117	75
Los Angeles Kings	51	31	15	5	207	150	67
Washington Capitals	60	30	24	6	246	217	66
Buffalo Sabres	46	21	14	11	164	129	53
Calgary Flames (Atlanta)	44	19	20	5	156	160	43
Quebec Nordiques	24	16	5	3	103	66	35
Hartford Whalers	24	15	7	2	109	71	32
Winnipeg Jets	22	12	8	2	104	89	26
Ottawa Senators (b)	19	10	4	5	50	37	25
Edmonton Oilers	22	6	12	4	87	90	16
Tampa Bay Lightning	5	3	2	0	20	22	6
San Jose Sharks	3	2	0	1	15	7	5
Florida Panthers	2	2	0	0	6	4	4
Anaheim Mighty Ducks	1	0	1	0	2	4	0
Defunct Teams (c)	123	80	26	17	425	258	177
Totals	**2267**	**1106**	**763**	**398**	**7619**	**6470**	**2610**

ROAD

	GP	W	L	T	GF	GA	PTS
Chicago Blackhawks	278	111	125	42	777	848	264
Boston Bruins	278	88	150	40	774	1009	216
Detroit Red Wings (a)	278	75	158	45	689	978	195
Toronto Maple Leafs	267	78	151	38	692	920	194
Montreal Canadiens	270	55	181	34	623	1066	144
Pittsburgh Penguins	77	36	30	11	289	278	83
Philadelphia Flyers	83	29	41	13	243	291	71
Dallas Stars (Minn.)	53	29	16	8	205	162	66
Vancouver Canucks	45	31	11	3	187	144	65
New Jersey Devils (K.C., Colo.)	60	31	25	4	233	206	66
St. Louis Blues	55	26	21	8	183	163	60
Washington Capitals	61	24	29	8	210	237	56
Los Angeles Kings	52	23	20	9	187	174	55
New York Islanders	71	17	48	6	220	311	40
Ottawa Senators (b)	20	14	2	4	74	38	32
Buffalo Sabres	48	12	30	6	160	223	30
Calgary Flames (Atlanta)	43	10	24	9	134	196	29
Winnipeg Jets	23	12	9	2	87	84	26
Edmonton Oilers	22	11	10	1	77	86	23
Quebec Nordiques	25	10	12	3	106	110	23
Hartford Whalers	24	8	13	3	86	94	19
San Jose Sharks	4	4	0	0	22	9	8
Tampa Bay Lightning	3	2	1	0	11	11	4
Florida Panthers	3	1	2	0	7	7	2
Anaheim Mighty Ducks	1	0	1	0	2	3	0
Defunct Teams (c)	123	72	32	19	386	263	163
Totals	**2267**	**809**	**1142**	**316**	**6664**	**7911**	**1934**

(a) Includes records of Detroit Cougars and Detroit Falcons
(b) Includes records of Ottawa Senators
(c) Teams are: Brooklyn and New York Americans, Cleveland Barons (Calif.), Montreal Maroons, Philadelphia Quakers, Pittsburgh Pirates and St. Louis Eagles.

CURRENT STREAKS VS. NHL OPPONENTS

	AT GARDEN	ON ROAD	OVERALL
vs. ANAHEIM	0-1-0	0-1-0	0-2-0
vs. BOSTON	3-3-0	5-1-3	4-3-2
vs. BUFFALO	6-0-2	2-9-1	5-3-1
vs. CALGARY	5-2-1	0-6-3	0-2-3
vs. CHICAGO	5-3-3	3-0-0	5-2-0
vs. DALLAS	8-2-1	1-1-3	6-3-4
vs. DETROIT	5-4-1	1-8-3	2-6-2
vs. EDMONTON	4-5-3	5-1-0	6-3-3
vs. FLORIDA	2-0-0	1-2-0	3-2-0
vs. HARTFORD	8-1-0	3-6-1	11-5-1
vs. LOS ANGELES	5-0-0	5-1-0	10-1-0
vs. MONTREAL	7-3-4	3-7-0	7-9-2
vs. NEW JERSEY	8-1-0	3-0-0	6-0-0
vs. ISLANDERS	5-1-3	1-13-3	3-9-3
vs. OTTAWA	3-0-0	4-0-0	7-0-0
vs. PHILADELPHIA	13-1-2	2-5-0	11-6-2
vs. PITTSBURGH	6-4-0	4-6-0	4-7-0
vs. QUEBEC	10-2-0	6-3-0	4-0-0
vs. ST. LOUIS	13-3-2	8-1-1	14-4-2
vs. SAN JOSE	2-0-1	4-0-0	6-0-1
vs. TAMPA BAY	3-2-0	2-1-0	5-3-0
vs. TORONTO	4-1-1	5-5-1	10-6-3
vs. VANCOUVER	6-0-2	7-1-1	12-1-3
vs. WASHINGTON	5-7-1	7-4-0	9-6-1
vs. WINNIPEG	6-2-1	7-3-1	12-5-2

RECENT RECORDS VS. NHL OPPONENTS

	Last 5 Games	Last 10 Games	Last 15 Games	Last 20 Games
vs. ANAHEIM	0-2-0	- - -	- - -	- - -
vs. BOSTON	1-3-1	4-4-2	7-5-3	9-6-5
vs. BUFFALO	3-1-1	5-4-1	8-5-2	8-9-3
vs. CALGARY	0-2-3	2-4-4	4-7-4	5-11-4
vs. CHICAGO	3-2-0	5-5-0	8-5-2	11-5-4
vs. DALLAS	2-2-1	5-2-3	7-4-4	11-5-4
vs. DETROIT	2-2-1	2-6-2	4-8-3	5-11-4
vs. EDMONTON	3-1-1	5-3-2	7-5-3	8-9-3
vs. FLORIDA	3-2-0	- - -	- - -	- - -
vs. HARTFORD	3-2-0	6-3-1	9-5-1	12-7-1
vs. LOS ANGELES	5-0-0-	9-1-0	11-4-0	12-7-1
vs. MONTREAL	1-3-1	3-5-2	5-8-2	7-10-3
vs. NEW JERSEY	5-0-0	7-2-1	8-5-2	8-7-2
vs. ISLANDERS	1-2-2	2-5-3	3-8-4	6-10-4
vs. OTTAWA	5-0-0	7-0-0	- - -	- - -
vs. PHILADELPHIA	3-1-1	3-5-2	7-6-2	11-7-2
vs. PITTSBURGH	2-3-0	4-6-0	7-8-0	10-10-0
vs. QUEBEC	4-1-0	6-4-0	10-5-0	14-6-0
vs. ST. LOUIS	5-0-0	6-3-1	8-5-2	13-5-2
vs. SAN JOSE	4-0-1	6-0-1	- - -	- - -
vs. TAMPA BAY	3-2-0	5-3-0	- - -	- - -
vs. TORONTO	3-2-0	5-3-2	7-5-3	10-7-3
vs. VANCOUVER	2-1-2	6-1-3	11-1-3	14-3-3
vs. WASHINGTON	4-1-0	7-3-0	9-6-0	11-9-0
vs. WINNIPEG	4-1-0	7-3-0	9-5-1	12-6-2

RANGERS LAST SHUTOUT VS. NHL OPPONENTS

	BY RANGERS	VS. RANGERS
ANAHEIM	NONE	NONE
BOSTON	3-0, Feb. 3, 1994 at Bos. (Healy)	4-0, Mar. 20, 1983 at MSG (Peeters)
BUFFALO	2-0, Dec. 13, 1993 at MSG (Richter)	2-0, Mar. 8, 1989 at MSG (Malarchuk)
CALGARY	4-0, Nov. 4, 1991 at MSG (Vanbiesbrouck)	3-0, Dec. 15, 1992 at MSG (Vernon)
CHICAGO	3-0, Jan. 25, 1969 at MSG (Giacomin)	4-0, Nov. 30, 1983 at MSG (Bannerman)
DALLAS	3-0, Apr. 1, 1994 at MSG (Richter)	7-0, Oct. 10, 1981 at Minn. (Meloche)
DETROIT	5-0, Nov. 27, 1976 at Det. (Davidson)	4-0, Jan. 9, 1980 at Det. (Vachon)
EDMONTON	1-0, Feb. 27, 1993 at Edm. (Richter)	NONE
FLORIDA	NONE	NONE
HARTFORD	4-0, Mar. 16, 1994 at MSG (Richter)	5-0, Jan. 20, 1986 at MSG (Weeks)
LOS ANGELES	5-0, Oct. 25, 1985 at MSG (Vanbiesbrouck)	6-0, Dec. 2, 1989 at LA (Hayward)
MONTREAL	3-0, Oct. 12, 1990 at MSG (Vanbiesbrouck)	3-0, Jan. 16, 1993 at Mtl. (Roy)
NEW JERSEY	3-0, Dec. 21, 1992 at NJ (Vanbiesbrouck)	5-0, Oct. 10, 1988 at MSG (Burke)
ISLANDERS	0-0, Dec. 9, 1989 at Coliseum (Vanbiesbrouck)	0-0, Dec. 9, 1989 at Coliseum (Fitzpatrick)
OTTAWA	3-0, Feb. 18, 1994 at MSG (Richter)	0-0, Dec. 21, 1933 at MSG (Beveridge)
PHILADELPHIA	2-0, Apr. 5, 1981 at Phila. (Baker)	1-0, Apr. 12, 1993 at Phila. (Roussel)
PITTSBURGH	7-0, Nov. 18, 1973 at MSG (Giacomin)	3-0, Feb. 10, 1993 at MSG. (Barrasso)
ST. LOUIS	6-0, Mar. 14, 1992 at St.L. (Vanbiesbrouck)	NONE
SAN JOSE	4-0, Feb. 22, 1993 at SJ (Vanbiesbrouck)	NONE
TAMPA BAY	NONE	NONE
TORONTO	6-0, Dec. 6, 1992 at MSG (Vanbiesbrouck)	6-0, Feb. 15, 1967 at Tor. (Bower)
VANCOUVER	6-0, Jan. 2, 1985 at MSG (Vanbiesbrouck)	3-0, Nov. 20, 1977 at MSG (Maniago)
WASHINGTON	1-0, Dec. 23, 1993 at Wash. (Healy)	2-0, Apr. 14, 1993 at MSG (Tabaracci)
WINNIPEG	3-0, Jan. 12, 1980 at Winn. (Davidson)	NONE

RANGERS ALL-TIME WON-AND-LOST RECORD

Year	G	W	L	T	GF	GA	PTS	Finished*	Division Champion
1926-27	44	25	13	6	95	72	56	1st	**RANGERS
1927-28	44	19	16	9	94	79	47	2nd	Boston
1928-29	44	21	13	10	72	65	52	2nd	Boston
1929-30	44	17	17	10	136	143	44	3rd	Boston
1930-31	44	19	16	9	106	87	47	3rd	Boston
1931-32	48	23	17	8	134	112	54	1st	**RANGERS
1932-33	48	23	17	8	135	107	54	3rd	Boston
1933-34	48	21	19	8	120	113	50	3rd	Detroit
1934-35	48	22	20	6	137	139	50	3rd	Boston
1935-36	48	19	17	12	91	96	50	4th	Detroit
1936-37	48	19	20	9	117	106	47	3rd	Detroit
1937-38	48	27	15	6	149	96	60	2nd	Boston
1938-39	48	26	16	6	149	105	58	2nd	Boston
1939-40	48	27	11	10	136	77	64	2nd	Boston
1940-41	48	21	19	8	143	125	50	4th	Boston
1941-42	48	29	17	2	177	143	60	1st	**RANGERS
1942-43	50	11	31	8	161	253	30	6th	Detroit
1943-44	50	6	39	5	162	310	17	6th	Montreal
1944-45	50	11	29	10	154	247	32	6th	Montreal
1945-46	50	13	28	9	144	191	35	6th	Montreal
1946-47	60	22	32	6	167	186	50	5th	Montreal
1947-48	60	21	26	13	176	201	55	4th	Toronto
1948-49	60	18	31	11	133	172	47	6th	Detroit
1949-50	70	28	31	11	170	189	67	4th	Detroit
1950-51	70	20	29	21	169	201	61	5th	Detroit
1951-52	70	23	34	13	192	219	59	5th	Detroit
1952-53	70	17	37	16	152	211	50	6th	Detroit
1953-54	70	29	31	10	161	182	68	5th	Detroit
1954-55	70	17	35	18	150	210	52	5th	Detroit
1955-56	70	32	28	10	204	203	74	3rd	Montreal
1956-57	70	26	30	14	184	227	66	3rd	Detroit
1957-58	70	32	25	13	195	188	77	2nd	Montreal
1958-59	70	26	32	12	201	217	64	5th	Montreal
1959-60	70	17	38	15	187	247	49	6th	Montreal
1960-61	70	22	38	10	204	248	54	5th	Montreal
1961-62	70	26	32	12	195	207	64	4th	Montreal
1962-63	70	22	36	12	211	233	56	5th	Toronto
1963-64	70	22	38	10	186	242	54	5th	Montreal
1964-65	70	20	38	12	179	246	52	5th	Detroit
1965-66	70	18	41	11	195	261	47	6th	Montreal
1966-67	70	30	28	12	188	189	72	4th	Chicago
1967-68	74	39	23	12	226	183	90	2nd	Montreal
1968-69	76	41	26	9	231	196	91	3rd	Montreal
1969-70	76	38	22	16	246	189	92	4th	Chicago
1970-71	78	49	18	11	259	177	109	2nd	Boston
1971-72	78	48	17	13	317	192	109	2nd	Boston
1972-73	78	47	23	8	297	208	102	3rd	Montreal
1973-74	78	40	24	14	300	251	94	3rd	Boston
1974-75	80	37	29	14	319	276	88	2nd	Philadelphia
1975-76	80	29	42	9	262	333	67	4th	Philadelphia
1976-77	80	29	37	14	272	310	72	4th	Philadelphia
1977-78	80	30	37	13	279	280	73	4th	Islanders
1978-79	80	40	29	11	316	292	91	3rd	Islanders
1979-80	80	38	32	10	308	284	86	3rd	Philadelphia
1980-81	80	30	36	14	312	317	74	4th	Islanders
1981-82	80	39	27	14	316	306	92	2nd	Islanders
1982-83	80	35	35	10	306	287	80	4th	Philadelphia
1983-84	80	42	29	9	314	304	93	4th	Islanders
1984-85	80	26	44	10	295	345	62	4th	Philadelphia
1985-86	80	36	38	6	280	276	78	4th	Philadelphia
1986-87	80	34	38	8	307	323	76	4th	Philadelphia
1987-88	80	36	34	10	300	283	82	5th	Islanders
1988-89	80	37	35	8	310	307	82	3rd	Washington
1989-90	80	36	31	13	279	267	85	1st	RANGERS
1990-91	80	36	31	13	297	265	85	2nd	Pittsburgh
1991-92	80	50	25	5	321	246	105	1st	**RANGERS
1992-93	84	34	39	11	304	308	79	6th	Pittsburgh
1993-94	84	52	24	8	299	231	112	1st	**RANGERS

*From 1926-27 through 1937-38, listing refers to American Division only; from 1967-68 to 1973-74, listing refers to East Division only; from 1974-75, listing refers to Lester Patrick Division of Clarence Campbell Conferences; from 1981-82, listing refers to Patrick Divison of Prince of Wales Conference; from 1993-94, listing refers to Atlantic Division of Eastern Conference.
**Finished 1st overall in the league.

WON-AND-LOST RECORD—HOME AND AWAY

Year	G	W	L	Home T	GF	GA	PTS	G	W	L	Away T	GF	GA	PTS
1926-27	22	13	5	4	46	31	30	22	12	8	2	49	41	26
1927-28	22	10	8	4	47	36	24	22	9	8	5	47	43	23
1928-29	22	12	6	4	32	21	28	22	9	7	6	40	44	24
1929-30	22	11	5	6	79	54	28	22	6	12	4	57	89	16
1930-31	22	10	9	3	58	43	23	22	9	7	6	48	44	24
1931-32	24	13	7	4	66	54	30	24	10	10	4	68	58	24
1932-33	24	12	7	5	64	55	29	24	11	10	3	71	52	25
1933-34	24	11	7	6	58	47	28	24	10	12	2	62	66	22
1934-35	24	11	8	5	69	64	27	24	11	12	1	68	75	23
1935-36	24	11	6	7	49	42	29	24	8	11	5	42	54	21
1936-37	24	9	7	8	55	46	26	24	10	13	1	62	60	21
1937-38	24	15	5	4	79	50	34	24	12	10	2	70	46	26
1938-39	24	13	8	3	70	48	29	24	13	8	3	79	57	29
1939-40	24	17	4	3	82	33	37	24	10	7	7	54	44	27
1940-41	24	13	7	4	85	60	30	24	8	12	4	58	65	20
1941-42	24	15	8	1	97	72	31	24	14	9	1	80	71	29
1942-43	25	7	13	5	83	112	19	25	4	18	3	78	141	11
1943-44	25	4	17	4	78	137	12	25	2	22	1	84	173	5
1944-45	25	7	11	7	77	101	21	25	4	18	3	77	146	11
1945-46	25	8	12	5	72	85	21	25	5	16	4	72	106	14
1946-47	30	11	14	5	106	100	27	30	11	18	1	61	86	23
1947-48	30	11	12	7	90	96	29	30	10	14	6	86	105	26
1948-49	30	13	12	5	77	65	31	30	5	19	6	56	107	16
1949-50	35	19	12	4	89	73	42	35	9	19	7	81	116	25
1950-51	35	14	11	10	98	97	38	35	6	18	11	71	104	23
1951-52	35	16	13	6	112	97	38	35	7	21	7	80	122	21
1952-53	35	11	14	10	89	90	32	35	6	23	6	63	121	18
1953-54	35	18	12	5	95	90	41	35	11	19	5	66	92	27
1954-55	35	10	12	13	86	93	33	35	7	23	5	64	117	19
1955-56	35	20	7	8	122	78	48	35	12	21	2	82	125	26
1956-57	35	15	12	8	103	97	38	35	11	18	6	81	130	28
1957-58	35	14	15	6	92	93	34	35	18	10	7	103	95	43
1958-59	35	14	16	5	108	110	33	35	12	16	7	93	107	31
1959-60	35	10	15	10	103	105	30	35	7	23	5	84	142	19
1960-61	35	15	15	5	102	95	35	35	7	23	5	102	153	19
1961-62	35	16	11	8	105	91	40	35	10	21	4	90	116	24
1962-63	35	12	17	6	107	110	30	35	10	19	6	104	123	26
1963-64	35	14	13	8	97	102	36	35	8	25	2	89	140	18
1964-65	35	8	19	8	94	132	24	35	12	19	4	85	114	28
1965-66	35	12	16	7	95	104	31	35	6	25	4	100	157	16
1966-67	35	18	12	5	100	81	41	35	12	16	7	88	108	31
1967-68	37	22	8	7	118	87	51	37	17	15	5	108	96	39
1968-69	38	27	7	4	131	74	58	38	14	19	5	100	122	33
1969-70	38	22	8	8	125	84	52	38	16	14	8	121	105	40
1970-71	39	30	2	7	150	71	67	39	19	16	4	109	106	42
1971-72	39	26	6	7	173	88	59	39	22	11	6	144	104	50
1972-73	39	26	8	5	162	84	57	39	21	15	3	135	124	45
1973-74	39	26	7	6	166	102	58	39	14	17	8	134	149	36
1974-75	40	21	11	8	174	120	50	40	16	18	6	145	156	38
1975-76	40	16	16	8	134	136	40	40	13	26	1	128	197	27
1976-77	40	17	18	5	139	147	39	40	12	19	9	133	163	33
1977-78	40	18	15	7	157	138	43	40	12	22	6	122	142	30
1978-79	40	19	13	8	161	140	46	40	21	16	3	155	152	45
1979-80	40	22	10	8	168	129	52	40	16	22	2	140	155	34
1980-81	40	17	13	10	166	143	44	40	13	23	4	146	174	30
1981-82	40	19	15	6	162	154	44	40	20	12	8	154	152	48
1982-83	40	24	13	3	186	135	51	40	11	22	7	120	152	29
1983-84	40	27	12	1	169	145	55	40	15	17	8	145	159	38
1984-85	40	16	18	6	150	153	38	40	10	26	4	145	192	24
1985-86	40	20	18	2	147	123	42	40	16	20	4	133	153	36
1986-87	40	18	18	4	152	156	40	40	16	20	4	155	167	36
1987-88	40	22	13	5	160	125	49	40	14	21	5	140	158	33
1988-89	40	21	17	2	160	147	44	40	16	18	6	150	160	38
1989-90	40	20	11	9	147	119	49	40	16	20	4	132	148	36
1990-91	40	22	11	7	161	114	51	40	14	20	6	136	151	34
1991-92	40	28	8	4	170	106	60	40	22	17	1	151	140	45
1992-93	42	20	17	5	158	142	45	42	14	22	6	146	166	34
1993-94	42	28	8	6	153	111	62	42	24	16	2	146	120	50
Totals	2267	1107	763	397	7619	6470	2611	2267	808	1142	317	6664	7911	1933

RANGERS YEAR BY YEAR SCORING LEADERS

Year	Goals		Assists		Points	
1926-27	33	Bill Cook	15	Boucher	37	Bill Cook
1927-28	23	Boucher	14	Bun Cook	35	Boucher
1928-29	15	Bill Cook	16	Boucher	26	Boucher
1929-30	29	Bill Cook	36	Boucher	62	Boucher
1930-31	30	Bill Cook	27	Boucher	42	Bill Cook
1931-32	33	Bill Cook	23	Boucher	47	Bill Cook
1932-33	28	Bill Cook	28	Boucher	50	Bill Cook
1933-34	18	Bun Cook	30	Boucher	44	Boucher
1934-35	25	Dillon	32	Boucher	45	Boucher
1935-36	18	Dillon	18	Boucher	32	Dillon
1936-37	22	Keeling	18	N. Colville	31	Dillon
1937-38	21	Dillon	25	Watson	39	Dillon
1938-39	24	Shibicky	23	Heller	41	C. Smith
1939-40	24	Hextall	28	Watson	39	Hextall
1940-41	26	Hextall	28	N. Colville	44	Hextall
					44	Lynn Patrick
1941-42	32	Lynn Patrick	37	Watson	56	Hextall
1942-43	27	Hextall	39	Lynn Patrick	61	Lynn Patrick
1943-44	21	Hextall	33	Hextall	54	Hextall
1944-45	24	DeMarco	30	DeMarco	54	DeMarco
1945-46	20	DeMarco	27	DeMarco	47	DeMarco
1946-47	27	Leswick	25	Laprade	41	Leswick
1947-48	24	O'Connor	36	O'Connor	60	O'Connor
	24	Leswick				
1948-49	18	Laprade	24	O'Connor	35	O'Connor
1949-50	22	Laprade	25	Leswick	44	Laprade
			25	Raleigh	44	Leswick
1950-51	20	Mickoski	24	Raleigh	39	Raleigh
					39	Sinclair
1951-52	26	Hergesheimer	42	Raleigh	61	Raleigh
1952-53	30	Hergesheimer	38	Ronty	59	Hergesheimer
1953-54	27	Hergesheimer	33	Ronty	46	Ronty
1954-55	29	Lewicki	32	Raleigh	53	Lewicki
1955-56	24	Prentice	47	Bathgate	66	Bathgate
	24	Hebenton				
1956-57	27	Bathgate	50	Bathgate	77	Bathgate
1957-58	32	Henry	48	Bathgate	78	Bathgate
1958-59	40	Bathgate	48	Bathgate	88	Bathgate
1959-60	32	Prentice	48	Bathgate	74	Bathgate
1960-61	29	Bathgate	48	Bathgate	77	Bathgate
1961-62	28	Bathgate	56	Bathgate	84	Bathgate
1962-63	37	Henry	46	Bathgate	81	Bathgate
1963-64	29	Henry	41	Goyette	65	Goyette
1964-65	25	Gilbert	36	Gilbert	61	Gilbert
1965-66	29	Nevin	33	Nevin	62	Nevin
1966-67	28	Gilbert	49	Goyette	61	Goyette
1967-68	32	Ratelle	48	Gilbert	78	Ratelle
1968-69	32	Ratelle	49	Gilbert	78	Ratelle
1969-70	33	Balon	50	Tkaczuk	77	Tkaczuk
1970-71	36	Balon	49	Tkaczuk	75	Tkaczuk
1971-72	50	Hadfield	63	Ratelle	109	Ratelle
1972-73	41	Ratelle	59	Gilbert	94	Ratelle
1973-74	36	Gilbert	57	Park	82	Park
1974-75	41	Vickers	61	Gilbert	97	Gilbert
1975-76	36	Gilbert	53	Vickers	86	Gilbert
1976-77	34	Esposito	48	Gilbert	80	Esposito
1977-78	40	Hickey	48	Greschner	81	Esposito
1978-79	42	Esposito	45	Hedberg	78	Esposito
					78	Hedberg
1979-80	34	Esposito	50	Beck	78	Esposito
1980-81	30	Hedberg	41	Greschner	70	Hedberg
	30	Johnstone				
1981-82	40	Duguay	65	Rogers	103	Rogers
1982-83	37	Pavelich	53	Ruotsalainen	76	Rogers
1983-84	48	Larouche	53	Pavelich	82	Pavelich
1984-85	29	Sandstrom	45	Ruotsalainen	73	Ruotsalainen
1985-86	25	Sandstrom	43	Ridley	65	Ridley
1986-87	40	Poddubny	47	Poddubny	87	Poddubny
	40	Sandstrom				
1987-88	38	Poddubny	55	Kisio	88	Poddubny
1988-89	36	Granato	56	Sandstrom	88	Sandstrom
1989-90	43	Ogrodnick	45	Leetch	74	Ogrodnick
1990-91	49	Gartner	72	Leetch	88	Leetch
1991-92	40	Gartner	80	Leetch	107	Messier
1992-93	45	Gartner	66	Messier	91	Messier
1993-94	52	Graves	77	Zubov	89	Zubov

RANGERS ALL-TIME SCORING LIST

	PLAYER	GP	Goals	Assists	Points	PIM
1.	Rod Gilbert	1065	406	615	1021	508
2.	Jean Ratelle	862	336	481	817	192
3.	Andy Bathgate	719	272	457	729	444
4.	Walt Tkaczuk	945	227	451	678	556
5.	Ron Greschner	982	179	431	610	1226
6.	Steve Vickers	698	246	340	586	330
7.	Vic Hadfield	838	262	310	572	1036
8.	Don Maloney	653	195	307	502	739
9.	Camille Henry	637	256	222	478	78
10.	James Patrick	671	104	363	467	541
11.	Brian Leetch*	437	103	343	446	237
12.	Dean Prentice	666	186	236	422	263
13.	Frank Boucher	533	152	261	413	114
14.	Phil Esposito	422	184	220	404	263
15.	Anders Hedberg	465	172	225	397	144
16.	Tomas Sandstrom	407	173	207	380	563
17.	Brad Park	465	95	283	378	738
18.	Andy Hebenton	560	177	191	368	75
19.	Bill Cook	475	228	138	366	386
20.	Bryan Hextall	449	187	175	362	227
21.	Bill Fairbairn	536	138	224	362	161
22.	Phil Watson	546	127	233	360	471
23.	Harry Howell	1160	82	263	345	1147
24.	Bob Nevin	505	168	174	342	105
25.	Ron Duguay	499	164	176	340	370
26.	Lynn Patrick	455	145	190	335	240
27.	Phil Goyette	397	98	231	329	51
28.	Don Raleigh	535	101	219	320	96
29.	Mark Pavelich	341	133	185	318	326
30.	Pete Stemkowski	496	113	204	317	380
31.	Reijo Ruotsalainen	389	99	217	316	154
32.	Mike Rogers	316	117	191	308	142
33.	Kelly Kisio	336	110	195	305	415
34.	Jim Neilson	810	60	238	298	766
35.	Dave Maloney	605	70	225	295	1113
36.	Bun Cook	433	154	139	293	436
37.	Mike Gartner	322	173	113	286	231
38.	Mark Messier*	230	86	196	282	224
39.	Cecil Dillon	409	160	121	281	93
40.	Edgar Laprade	500	108	172	280	42
41.	Don Marshall	479	129	141	270	40
42.	Bill Gadsby	457	58	212	270	411
43.	Neil Colville	463	99	166	265	213
44.	Earl Ingarfield	527	122	142	264	198
45.	Pat Hickey	370	128	129	257	216
46.	Darren Turcotte	325	122	133	255	183
47.	John Ogrodnick	338	126	128	254	106
48.	Brian Mullen	307	100	148	248	188
49.	Rod Seiling	644	50	198	248	423
50.	Carol Vadnais	485	56	190	246	690
51.	Pierre Larouche	253	123	120	243	59
52.	Barry Beck	415	66	173	239	775
53.	Ed Johnstone	371	109	125	234	319
54.	Grant Warwick	293	117	116	233	179
55.	Ott Heller	647	55	176	231	465
56.	Jan Erixon	556	57	159	216	167
57.	Dave Balon	361	99	113	212	284
58.	Red Sullivan	322	59	150	209	300
59.	Adam Graves*	248	114	89	203	414
60.	Tony Leswick	368	113	89	202	420
61.	Larry Popein	402	75	127	202	150
62.	Alex Shibicky	322	110	91	201	161

* Active Rangers

RANGERS CAREER LEADERS

GOALS

Rod Gilbert	406
Jean Ratelle	336
Andy Bathgate	272
Vic Hadfield	262
Camille Henry	256
Steve Vickers	246
Bill Cook	228
Walt Tkaczuk	227
Don Maloney	195
Bryan Hextall	187
Dean Prentice	186
Phil Esposito	184
Ron Greschner	179
Andy Hebenton	177
Mike Gartner	173
Tomas Sandstrom	173
Anders Hedberg	172
Bob Nevin	168
Ron Duguay	164
Cecil Dillon	160
Bun Cook	154
Frank Boucher	152

GAMES

Harry Howell	1160
Rod Gilbert	1065
Rod Greschner	982
Walt Tkaczuk	945
Jean Ratelle	862
Vic Hadfield	838
Jim Neilson	810
Andy Bathgate	719
Steve Vickers	698
James Patrick	671
Dean Prentice	666
Don Maloney	653
Ott Heller	647
Rod Seiling	644
Camille Henry	637
Dave Maloney	605

WINS

Ed Giacomin	266
Lorne Worsley	204
John Vanbiesbrouck	200
Dave Kerr	157
Chuck Rayner	123
*Mike Richter	111
Gilles Villemure	96
John Davidson	93
John Ross Roach	80
Glen Hanlon	56

*Active Rangers

ASSISTS

Rod Gilbert	615
Jean Ratelle	481
Andy Bathgate	457
Walt Tkaczuk	451
Ron Greschner	431
James Patrick	363
*Brian Leetch	343
Steve Vickers	340
Vic Hadfield	310
Don Maloney	307
Brad Park	283
Harry Howell	263
Frank Boucher	261
Jim Neilson	238
Dean Prentice	236
Phil Watson	233
Phil Goyette	231
Anders Hedberg	225
Dave Maloney	225
Bill Fairbairn	224
Camille Henry	222
Phil Esposito	220
Don Raleigh	219
Reijo Ruotsalainen	217
Bill Gadsby	212
Tomas Sandstrom	207
Pete Stemkowski	204
*Mark Messier	196

PENALTY MINUTES

Ron Greschner	1226
Harry Howell	1147
Dave Maloney	1113
Vic Hadfield	1036
Nick Fotiu	970
Lou Fontinato	939
Ching Johnson	798
Barry Beck	775
Jim Neilson	766
Don Maloney	739
Brad Park	738
Kris King	733
Carol Vadnais	690
Jack Evans	670
Tomas Sandstrom	563
Tom Laidlaw	561
Troy Mallette	557
Walt Tkaczuk	556
Arnie Brown	545
Jame Patrick	541
Reg Fleming	540
Tie Domi	526
Rod Gilbert	508

SHUTOUTS

Ed Giacomin	49
Dave Kerr	40
John Ross Roach	30
Chuck Rayner	24
Lorne Worsley	24
Lorne Chabot	21
John Vanbiesbrouck	16
Gilles Villemure	13
Andy Aitkenhead	11
*Mike Richter	9

RANGERS SINGLE SEASON LEADERS

GOALS

*Adam Graves	1993-94	52
Vic Hadfield	1971-72	50
Mike Gartner	1990-91	49
Pierre Larouche	1983-84	48
Jean Ratelle	1971-72	46
Mike Gartner	1992-93	45
Rod Gilbert	1971-72	43
John Ogrodnick	1989-90	43
Phil Esposito	1978-79	42
Jean Ratelle	1972-73	41
Steve Vickers	1974-75	41
Andy Bathgate	1958-59	40
Pat Hickey	1977-78	40
Ron Duguay	1981-82	40
Walt Poddubny	1986-87	40
Tomas Sandstrom	1986-87	40
Mike Gartner	1991-92	40

POINTS

Jean Ratelle	1971-72	109
*Mark Messier	1991-92	107
Vic Hadfield	1971-72	106
Mike Rogers	1981-82	103
*Brian Leetch	1991-92	102
Rod Gilbert	1971-72	97
Rod Gilbert	1974-75	97
Jean Ratelle	1972-73	94
Jean Ratelle	1974-75	91
*Mark Messier	1992-93	91
Steve Vickers	1974-75	89
*Sergei Zubov	1993-94	89
Andy Bathgate	1958-59	88
Walt Poddubny	1987-88	88
Tomas Sandstrom	1988-89	88
*Brian Leetch	1990-91	88
Walt Poddubny	1986-87	87
Rod Gilbert	1975-76	86

ASSISTS

*Brian Leetch	1991-92	80
*Sergei Zubov	1993-94	77
*Brian Leetch	1990-91	72
*Mark Messier	1991-92	72
*Mark Messier	1992-93	66
Mike Rogers	1981-82	65
Jean Ratelle	1971-72	63
Rod Gilbert	1974-75	61
Rod Gilbert	1972-73	59
*Mark Messier	1993-94	58
Brad Park	1973-74	57
James Patrick	1991-92	57
Andy Bathgate	1961-62	56
Vic Hadfield	1971-72	56
Tomas Sandstrom	1988-89	56
*Brian Leetch	1993-94	56
Jean Ratelle	1974-75	55
Kelly Kisio	1987-88	55
Rod Gilbert	1971-72	54
Jean Ratelle	1972-73	53
Steve Vickers	1975-76	53
Reijo Ruotsalainen	1982-83	53
Mark Pavelich	1983-84	53
Andy Bathgate	1956-57	50
Walt Tkaczuk	1969-70	50
Rod Gilbert	1975-76	50
Walt Poddubny	1987-88	50

GOALS BY A ROOKIE

Tony Granato	1988-89	36
Tony Amonte	1991-92	35
Mark Pavelich	1981-82	33
Don Murdoch	1976-77	32
Darren Turcotte	1989-90	32
Steve Vickers	1972-73	30
Tomas Sandstrom	1984-85	29
Ulf Dahlen	1987-88	29
Wally Hergesheimer	1951-52	26
Mike Allison	1980-81	26

*Active Rangers

WINS

*Mike Richter	1993-94	42
Ed Giacomin	1968-69	37
Ed Giacomin	1967-68	36
Ed Giacomin	1969-70	35
Lorne Worsley	1955-56	32
John Vanbiesbrouck	1985-86	31
Ed Giacomin	1966-67	30
Ed Giacomin	1973-74	30
Jim Henry	1941-42	29
John Bower	1953-54	29
Chuck Rayner	1949-50	28
Glen Hanlon	1983-84	28
John Vanbiesbrouck	1988-89	28

PIM

Troy Mallette	1989-90	305
Kris King	1989-90	286
Troy Mallette	1990-91	252
Tie Domi	1991-92	246
Barry Beck	1980-81	231
Michel Petit	1987-88	223
Ed Hospodar	1980-81	214
Lou Fontinato	1955-56	202
Rudy Poeschek	1988-89	199
Nick Fotiu	1978-79	190
Dave Maloney	1979-80	186
Tie Domi	1990-91	185
Larry Melynk	1986-87	182
Chris Nilan	1988-89	177
Nick Fotiu	1976-77	174

GOALS BY A DEFENSEMAN

Brad Park	1973-74	25
Brad Park	1971-72	24
*Brian Leetch	1988-89	23
*Brian Leetch	1993-94	23
*Brian Leetch	1991-92	22
Ron Greschner	1977-78	21
Ron Greschner	1979-80	21
Ron Greschner	1980-81	20
Carol Vadnais	1975-76	20
Mike McEwen	1978-79	20
Reijo Ruotsalainen	1983-84	20

SHUTOUTS

John Ross Roach	1928-29	13
Lorne Chabot	1927-28	11
Lorne Chabot	1926-27	10
John Ross Roach	1931-32	9
Ed Giacomin	1966-67	9
Dave Kerr	1935-36	8
Dave Kerr	1937-38	8
Dave Kerr	1939-40	8
Ed Giacomin	1967-68	8
Ed Giacomin	1970-71	8

POWER PLAY GOALS

Vic Hadfield	1971-72	23
Marcel Dionne	1987-88	22
Mike Gartner	1990-91	22
Phil Esposito	1977-78	21
*Adam Graves	1993-94	20
Pierre Larouche	1983-84	19
John Ogrodnick	1989-90	19
*Brian Leetch	1993-94	17
Rod Gilbert	1973-74	16
Jean Ratelle	1974-75	16
Steve Vickers	1974-75	16
Phil Esposito	1975-76	16
Phil Esposito	1976-77	15
Darren Turcotte	1990-91	15
Mike Gartner	1991-92	15

SHORTHANDED GOALS

Don Maloney	1980-81	5
Mike Rogers	1982-83	5
Mike Gartner	1993-94	5
Ron Stewart	1969-70	4
Bill Fairbairn	1971-72	4
Greg Polis	1977-78	4
Tony Granato	1988-89	4
*Adam Graves	1991-92	4
*Mark Messier	1991-92	4
*Adam Graves	1993-94	4
*Steve Larmer	1993-94	4

RANGERS ALL-TIME LONGEST SCORING STREAKS

Longest All-Time Point Scoring Streaks

- **17   Brian Leetch, Nov. 23 to Dec. 31, 1991, (5 goals and 24 assists).**
- 16   Mike Rogers, Feb. 14 to Mar. 20, 1982, (10 goals and 18 assists).
- 15   Mark Messier, Feb. 5 to Mar. 7, 1992, (7 goals and 17 assists).
- 15   Walt Poddubny, Jan. 11 to Feb. 17, 1987, (11 goals and 8 assists).
- 14   Carey Wilson, Dec. 26 to Jan. 26, 1989, (7 goals and 17 assists).
- 14   Rod Gilbert, Oct. 7 to Nov. 8, 1972, (11 goals and 12 assists).
- 14   Brian Leetch, Oct. 7 to Nov. 4, 1991, (4 goals and 16 assists).
- 14   Reijo Ruotsalainen, Feb. 5 to Mar. 7, 1985, (9 goals and 11 assists).
- 13   Jean Ratelle, Feb. 3 to Feb. 27, 1972, (16 goals and 12 assists).
- 13   Walt Tkaczuk, Dec. 28 to Jan. 28, 1978, (9 goals and 12 assists).
- 13   Andy Bathgate, Dec. 9 to Jan. 5, 1963, (12 goals and 6 assists).
- 13   Rod Gilbert, Nov. 8 to Dec. 5, 1968, (5 goals and 12 assists).

Longest All-Time Goal Scoring Streaks

- **10   Andy Bathgate, Dec. 15 to Jan. 15, 1963, (11 goals).**
- 8   Jean Ratelle, Feb. 12 to Feb. 23, 1972, (12 goals).
- 8   Jean Ratelle, Feb. 15 to Mar. 4, 1973, (10 goals).
- 8   Phil Esposito, Mar. 22 to Mar. 29, 1978, (8 goals).
- 7   Rod Gilbert, Jan. 25 to Feb. 7, 1976, (12 goals).
- 7   Pierre Larouche, Feb. 5 to Feb. 24, 1986, (10 goals).
- 7   Andy Bathgate, Nov. 8 to Nov. 23, 1958, (9 goals).
- 7   Mike Gartner, Mar. 12 to Mar. 27, 1990, (8 goals).
- 7   Eddie Johnstone, Mar. 14 to Mar. 28, 1982, (8 goals).
- 7   Mike Gartner, Jan. 30 to Feb. 13, 1991, (7 goals).
- 7   Rod Gilbert, Dec. 12 to Jan. 23, 1964, (7 goals).
- 7   Bryan Hextall, Feb. 25 to Mar. 16, 1941, (7 goals).

Longest All-Time Assist Streaks

- **15   Brian Leetch, Nov. 29 to Dec. 31, 1991, (23 assists).**
- 10   Rod Gilbert, Mar. 5 to Mar. 26, 1969, (14 assists).
- 9   Darren Turcotte, Oct. 8 to Oct. 25, 1990, (11 assists).
- 9   Jean Ratelle, Oct. 25 to Nov. 8, 1972, (10 assists).
- 8   Don Maloney, Mar. 8 to Mar. 24, 1982, (12 assists).
- 8   Mark Messier, Feb. 12 to Feb 27, 1993, (11 assists).
- 8   Lynn Patrick, Jan. 1 to Jan. 21, 1943, (11 assists).
- 8   Mike Rogers, Mar. 4 to Mar. 20, 1982, (10 assists).
- 8   Babe Pratt, Jan. 6 to Feb. 1, 1942, (10 assists).
- 8   Earl Ingarfield, Jan. 22 to Feb. 5, 1961, (8 assists).

Seventeen players are tied with 7.

LONGEST GOAL SCORING STREAKS YEAR-BY-YEAR

(Since 1950)

Season	Player	Games	Dates	Goals
1993-94	Adam Graves	4	Oct. 11 to Oct. 16, 1993	(4 goals)
		4	Nov. 3 to Nov. 10, 1993	(4 goals)
		4	Nov. 16 to Nov. 24, 1993	(4 goals)
	Alexei Kovalev	4	Mar. 27 to Apr. 2, 1994	(4 goals)
	Mark Messier	4	Oct. 7 to Oct. 13, 1993	(4 goals)
		4	Jan. 25 to Jan. 31, 1994	(6 goals)
1992-93	Mike Gartner	6	Jan. 2 to Jan. 13, 1993	(9 goals)
	Darren Turcotte	6	Nov. 30 to Dec 11, 1992	(7 goals)
	Darren Turcotte	6	Oct. 31 to Nov 11, 1992	(7 goals)
1991-92	Sergei Nemchinov	6	Dec. 2 to Dec. 14, 1991	(6 goals)
1990-91	Mike Gartner	7	Jan. 30 to Feb. 13, 1991	(7 goals)
1989-90	Mike Gartner	7	Mar. 12 to Mar. 27, 1990	(8 goals)
1988-89	Tony Granato	6	Jan. 9 to Jan. 21, 1989	(10 goals)
1987-88	Walt Poddubny	5	Dec. 20 to Dec. 29, 1987	(7 goals)
	Ulf Dahlen	5	Dec. 31 to Jan. 8, 1988	(6 goals)
1986-87	Tomas Sandstrom	5	Jan. 14 to Jan. 26, 1987	(8 goals)
1985-86	Pierre Larouche	7	Feb. 5 to Feb. 24, 1986	(10 goals)
1984-85	Tomas Sandstrom	5	Dec. 30 to Jan. 9, 1985	(6 goals)
1983-84	Pierre Larouche	5	Dec. 12 to Dec. 30, 1983	(7 goals)
	Anders Hedberg	5	Mar. 22 to Mar. 31, 1984	(5 goals)
	Don Maloney	5	Nov. 13 to Nov. 23, 1983	(5 goals)
1982-83	Don Maloney	4	Jan. 3 to Jan. 9, 1983	(5 goals)
	Anders Hedberg	4	Oct. 20 to Oct. 27, 1982	(4 goals)
	Mark Pavelich	4	Oct. 24 to Oct. 31, 1982	(4 goals)
	Don Maloney	4	Nov. 10 to Nov. 17, 1982	(4 goals)
1981-82	Ed Johnstone	7	Mar. 4 to Mar. 28, 1982	(8 goals)
1980-81	Ron Greschner	5	Oct. 25 to Nov. 1, 1980	(5 goals)
1979-80	Phil Esposito	5	Jan. 22 to Feb. 2, 1980	(6 goals)
1978-79	Ron Duguay	6	Jan. 24 to Feb. 3, 1979	(7 goals)
1977-78	Phil Esposito	8	Mar. 22 to Mar. 29, 1978	(8 goals)
1976-77	Rod Gilbert	3	Nov. 22 to Nov. 27, 1976	(4 goals)
	Phil Esposito	3	Oct. 13 to Oct. 17, 1976	(3 goals)
1975-76	Rod Gilbert	7	Jan. 25 to Feb. 7, 1976	(12 goals)
1974-75	Steve Vickers	4	Mar. 19 to Mar. 23, 1975	(6 goals)
	Jean Ratelle	4	Jan. 23 to Jan. 28, 1975	(4 goals)
1973-74	Rod Gilbert	5	Dec. 16 to Dec. 26, 1973	(5 goals)
1972-73	Jean Ratelle	8	Feb. 15 to Mar. 4, 1973	(10 goals)
1971-72	Jean Ratelle	8	Feb. 12 to Feb. 23, 1972	(12 goals)
1970-71	Bruce MacGregor	5	Feb. 27 to Mar. 6, 1971	(6 goals)
	Rod Gilbert	5	Jan. 31 to Feb. 9, 1971	(5 goals)
1969-70	Dave Balon	5	Feb. 1 to Feb. 13, 1970	(7 goals)
1968-69	Reg Fleming	5	Dec. 21 to Dec. 28, 1968	(5 goals)
1967-68	Jean Ratelle	3	Feb. 11 to Feb. 18, 1968	(5 goals)
	Jean Ratelle	3	Feb. 24 to Feb. 29, 1968	(4 goals)
	Vic Hadfield	3	Oct. 21 to Oct. 25, 1967	(4 goals)
	Vic Hadfield	3	Mar. 2 to Mar. 6, 1968	(4 goals)
	Vic Hadfield	3	Dec. 30 to Jan. 3, 1968	(3 goals)
	Phil Goyette	3	Oct. 18 to Oct. 22, 1967	(4 goals)
	Phil Goyette	3	Jan. 13 to Jan. 19, 1968	(3 goals)
	Rod Gilbert	3	Dec. 31 to Jan. 6, 1968	(3 goals)
	Rod Gilbert	3	Feb. 4 to Feb. 11, 1968	(3 goals)
	Bob Nevin	3	Nov. 29 to Dec. 3, 1967	(3 goals)
1966-67	Rod Gilbert	5	Dec. 7 to Dec. 17, 1966	(7 goals)
1965-66	Jean Ratelle	3	Jan. 1 to Jan. 8, 1966	(4 goals)
	Don Marshall	3	Nov. 20 to Nov. 24, 1965	(3 goals)
	Don Marshall	3	Jan. 26 to Jan. 30, 1966	(3 goals)
	Rod Gilbert	3	Oct. 30 to Nov. 6, 1965	(3 goals)
	Rod Seiling	3	Nov. 13 to Nov. 17, 1965	(3 goals)
	Vic Hadfield	3	Jan. 30 to Feb. 5, 1966	(3 goals)
	Reg Fleming	3	Feb. 20 to Feb. 26, 1966	(3 goals)
1964-65	Rod Gilbert	4	Dec. 29 to Jan. 6, 1965	(4 goals)
1963-64	Rod Gilbert	7	Dec. 12 to Jan. 23, 1964	(7 goals)
1962-63	**ANDY BATHGATE**	**10**	**DEC. 15 TO JAN. 5, 1963**	**(11 GOALS)**
1961-62	Johnny Wilson	4	Feb. 15 to Feb. 21, 1962	(5 goals)
1960-61	Andy Hebenton	4	Jan. 8 to Jan. 15, 1961	4 goals)
	Camille Henry	4	Nov. 13 to Nov. 23, 1960	(4 goals)
1959-60	Andy Bathgate	4	Nov. 18 to Nov. 26, 1959	(6 goals)
	Dean Prentice	4	Nov. 28 to Dec. 5, 1959	(6 goals)
	Andy Hebenton	4	Dec. 27 to Jan. 3, 1960	(4 goals)
1958-59	Andy Bathgate	7	Nov. 8 to Nov. 23, 1958	(9 goals)
1957-58	Andy Bathgate	4	Feb. 23 to Mar. 2, 1958	(6 goals)
1956-57	Andy Hebenton	3	Jan. 9 to Jan. 12, 1957	(5 goals)
	Andy Bathgate	3	Nov. 28 to Dec. 2, 1956	(4 goals)
	Camille Henry	3	Feb. 7 to Feb. 10, 1957	(3 goals)
	Camille Henry	3	Feb. 14 to Feb. 20, 1957	(3 goals)
	Red Sullivan	3	Nov. 14 to Nov. 18, 1956	(3 goals)
1955-56	Andy Bathgate	5	Nov. 27 to Dec. 7, 1955	(6 goals)
1954-55	Danny Lewicki	3	Nov. 13 to Nov. 17, 1954	(5 goals)
	Dean Prentice	3	Dec. 25 to Dec. 30, 1954	(5 goals)
1953-54	Wally Hergesheimer	3	Jan. 17 to Jan. 23, 1954	(4 goals)
1952-53	Nick Mickoski	4	Dec. 28 to Jan. 7, 1953	(4 goals)
1951-52	Camille Henry	3	Nov. 4 to Nov. 11, 1951	(4 goals)
	Camille Henry	3	Dec. 9 to Dec. 12, 1951	(3 goals)
	Don Raleigh	3	Dec. 20 to Dec. 25, 1951	(3 goals)
1950-51	Nick Mickoski	3	Dec. 17 to Dec. 24, 1950	(6 goals)
	Tony Leswick	3	Jan. 13 to Jan. 17, 1951	(3 goals)

LONGEST ASSIST STREAKS YEAR-BY-YEAR

(Since 1950)

Season	Player	Games	Dates	Assists
1993-94	Brian Leetch	5	Nov. 14 to Nov. 24, 1993	(7 assists)
	Sergei Zubov	5	Oct. 22 to Oct. 31, 1993	(8 assists)
	Sergei Zubov	5	Jan. 14 to Jan. 27, 1994	(8 assists)
1992-93	Mark Messier	8	Feb. 12 to Feb. 27, 1993	(11 assists)
1991-92	**BRIAN LEETCH**	**15**	**NOV. 29 TO DEC. 31, 1991**	**(23 ASSISTS)**
1990-91	Darren Turcotte	9	Oct. 8 to Oct. 25, 1990	(11 assists)
1989-90	Brian Mullen	6	Feb. 21 to Mar. 3, 1990	(10 assists)
1988-89	Brian Leetch	7	Feb. 17 to Mar. 1, 1989	(11 assists)
	Carey Wilson	7	Jan. 9 to Jan. 23, 1989	(9 assists)
1987-88	Kelly Kisio	6	Jan. 19 to Feb. 4, 1988	(8 assists)
	Walt Poddubny	6	Feb. 29 to Mar. 12, 1988	(8 assists)
	Brian Leetch	6	Mar. 22 to Apr. 1, 1988	(7 assists)
1986-87	Pierre Larouche	5	Feb. 7 to Feb. 19, 1987	(7 assists)
	Curt Giles	5	Dec. 21 to Dec. 30, 1986	(6 assists)
1985-86	Mike Ridley	7	Feb. 8 to Feb. 25, 1986	(11 assists)
	Reijo Ruotsalainen	7	Oct. 25 to Mar. 9, 1985	(9 assists)
1984-85	Tomas Sandstrom	5	Dec. 30 to Jan. 9, 1985	(6 assists)
1983-84	Mikko Leinonen	6	Feb. 11 to Feb. 25, 1984	(7 assists)
1982-83	Dave Maloney	7	Nov. 11 to Dec. 12, 1982	(8 assists)
1981-82	Don Maloney	8	Mar. 8 to Mar. 24, 1982	(12 assists)
	Mike Rogers	8	Mar. 4 to Mar. 20, 1982	(10 assists)
1980-81	Tom Laidlaw	5	Feb. 19 to Feb. 28, 1981	(7 assists)
	Steve Vickers	5	Dec. 3 to Dec. 12, 1980	(5 assists)
1979-80	Don Maloney	7	Dec. 3 to Dec. 15, 1979	(6 assists)
1978-79	Ron Greschner	6	Oct. 28 to Nov. 8, 1978	(7 assists)
	Don Maloney	6	Mar. 4 to Mar. 15, 1979	(6 assists)
1977-78	Carol Vadnais	4	Oct. 25 to Oct. 30, 1977	(4 assists)
	Walt Tkaczuk	4	Mar. 8 to Mar. 18, 1978	(4 assists)
1976-77	Rod Gilbert	7	Nov. 28 to Dec. 8, 1976	(10 assists)
1975-76	Rod Gilbert	6	Oct. 8 to Oct. 19, 1975	(8 assists)
1974-75	Rod Gilbert	7	Nov. 27 to Dec. 12, 1974	(8 assists)
1973-74	Rod Gilbert	5	Dec. 1 to Dec. 9, 1973	(6 assists)
1972-73	Jean Ratelle	9	Oct. 25 to Nov. 8, 1972	(10 assists)
1971-72	Jean Ratelle	7	Nov. 28 to Dec. 12, 1971	(14 assists)
	Rod Gilbert	7	Feb. 13 to Feb. 23, 1972	(10 assists)
	Vic Hadfield	7	Oct. 31 to Nov. 14, 1971	(9 assists)
1970-71	Walt Tkaczuk	7	Dec. 19 to Dec. 29, 1970	(9 assists)
1969-70	Rod Gilbert	7	Nov. 22 to Dec. 10, 1969	(10 assists)
1968-69	Rod Gilbert	10	Mar. 5 to Mar. 26, 1969	(14 assists)
1967-68	Rod Gilbert	6	Feb. 4 to Feb. 17, 1968	(10 assists)
	Rod Gilbert	6	Feb. 24 to Mar. 6, 1968	(7 assists)
1966-67	Earl Ingarfield	5	Nov. 20 to Nov. 30, 1966	(6 assists)
	Phil Goyette	5	Feb. 8 to Feb. 26, 1967	(5 assists)
1965-66	Phil Goyette	5	Nov. 17 to Nov. 25, 1965	(7 assists)
1964-65	Rod Gilbert	7	Mar. 14 to Mar. 28, 1965	(10 assists)
1963-64	Phil Goyette	6	Jan. 15 to Jan. 25, 1964	(6 assists)
1962-63	Dean Prentice	5	Dec. 12 to Dec. 31, 1962	(6 assists)
	Andy Bathgate	5	Feb. 12 to Feb. 23, 1963	(5 assists)
1961-62	Andy Bathgate	6	Oct. 11 to Oct. 19, 1961	(8 assists)
	Andy Bathgate	6	Jan. 3 to Jan. 17, 1962	(7 assists)
1960-61	Earl Ingarfield	8	Jan. 22 to Feb. 5, 1961	(8 assists)
1959-60	Andy Hebenton	4	Oct. 24 to Nov. 1, 1959	(4 assists)
	Andy Bathgate	4	Dec. 5 to Dec. 13, 1959	(4 assists)
1958-59	Andy Bathgate	6	Jan. 14 to Jan. 28, 1959	(7 assists)
1957-58	Andy Bathgate	6	Feb. 14 to Feb. 26, 1958	(8 assists)
1956-57	Andy Bathgate	5	Feb. 10 to Feb. 20, 1957	(6 assists)
	Camille Henry	5	Feb. 7 to Feb. 16, 1957	(6 assists)
	Camille Henry	5	Feb. 20 to Mar. 2, 1957	(5 assists)
1955-56	Andy Bathgate	7	Dec. 25 to Jan. 11, 1956	(10 assists)
1954-55	Don Raleigh	6	Feb. 5 to Feb. 16, 1955	(7 assists)
1953-54	Paul Ronty	5	Feb. 14 to Feb. 24, 1954	(6 assists)
1952-53	Wally Hergesheimer	3	Dec. 17 to Dec. 20, 1952	(5 assists)
	Don Raleigh	3	Feb. 1 to Feb. 8, 1953	(4 assists)
	Hy Buller	3	Oct. 19 to Oct. 26, 1952	(3 assists)
	Hy Buller	3	Mar. 5 to Mar. 8, 1953	(3 assists)
	Wally Hergesheimer	3	Oct. 16 to Oct. 19, 1952	(3 assists)
	Paul Ronty	3	Mar. 14 to Mar. 18, 1953	(3 assists)
	Neil Strain	3	Dec. 14 to Dec. 18, 1952	(3 assists)
1951-52	Don Raleigh	4	Dec. 1 to Dec. 9, 1951	(7 assists)
	Steve Kraftcheck	4	Jan. 13 to Jan. 20, 1952	(4 assists)
1950-51	Reg Sinclair	5	Feb. 2 to Mar. 7, 1951	(7 assists)

RANGERS ALL-TIME POINT SCORING STREAKS YEAR-BY-YEAR

(Since 1950)

Season	Player	Games	Dates	(Goals and Assists)
1993-94	Alexei Kovalev	11	Mar. 16 to Apr. 8, 1994	(10 goals and 5 assists)
	Mark Messier	11	Jan. 14 to Feb. 9, 1994	(10 goals and 11 assists)
1992-93	Mark Messier	9	Oct. 12 to Oct. 29, 1992	(6 goals and 10 assists)
	Tony Amonte	9	Mar. 6 to Mar. 26, 1993	(3 goals and 11 assists)
1991-92	**BRIAN LEETCH**	**17**	**NOV. 23 TO DEC. 31, 1991**	**(5 GOALS AND 24 ASSISTS)**
1990-91	Darren Turcotte	11	Oct. 4 to Oct. 25, 1990	(6 goals and 13 assists)
1989-90	Brian Mullen	12	Feb. 14 to Mar. 10, 1990	(6 goals and 14 assists)
1988-89	Carey Wilson	14	Dec. 26 to Jan. 26, 1989	(7 goals and 17 assists)
1987-88	Walt Poddubny	11	Oct. 12 to Nov. 1, 1987	(9 goals and 9 assists)
1986-87	Walt Poddubny	15	Jan. 11 to Feb. 17, 1987	(11 goals and 8 assists)
1985-86	Pierre Larouche	9	Feb. 5 to Feb. 27, 1986	(10 goals and 4 assists)
1984-85	Reijo Ruotsalainen	14	Feb. 5 to Mar. 7, 1985	(9 goals and 11 assists)
1983-84	Mike Rogers	10	Oct. 10 to Oct. 30, 1983	(3 goals and 9 assists)
1982-83	Don Maloney	10	Nov. 6 to Nov. 27, 1982	(7 goals and 7 assists)
1981-82	Mike Rogers	16	Feb. 14 to Mar. 20, 1982	(10 goals and 18 assists)
1980-81	Don Maloney	7	Nov. 26 to Dec. 10, 1980	(4 goals and 5 assists)
1979-80	Don Maloney	7	Dec. 3 to Dec. 15, 1979	(3 goals and 6 assists)
1978-79	Mike McEwen	5	Oct. 12 to Oct. 21, 1978	(3 goals and 5 assists)
1977-78	Don Murdoch	8	Feb. 23 to Mar. 15, 1978	(7 goals and 6 assists)
1976-77	Rod Gilbert	10	Nov. 20 to Dec. 8, 1976	(7 goals and 11 assists)
1975-76	Rod Gilbert	8	Jan. 23 to Feb. 7, 1976	(12 goals and 3 assists)
1974-75	Rod Gilbert	7	Nov. 27 to Dec. 12, 1974	(7 goals and 8 assists)
1973-74	Rod Gilbert	5	Dec. 1 to Dec. 9, 1973	(5 goals and 6 assists)
1972-73	Rod Gilbert	14	Oct. 7 to Nov. 8, 1972	(11 goals and 12 assists)
1971-72	Jean Ratelle	13	Feb. 3 to Feb. 27, 1972	(16 goals and 12 assists)
1970-71	Rod Gilbert	10	Jan. 20 to Feb. 9, 1971	(9 goals and 3 assists)
1969-70	Walt Tkaczuk	13	Dec. 28 to Jan. 28, 1978	(9 goals and 12 assists)
1968-69	Rod Gilbert	13	Nov. 8 to Dec. 5, 1968	(5 goals and 12 assists)
1967-68	Rod Gilbert	10	Dec. 25 to Jan. 17, 1968	(6 goals and 11 assists)
1966-67	Earl Ingarfield	6	Nov. 19 to Nov. 30, 1966	(2 goals and 6 assists)
1965-66	Don Marshall	7	Feb. 19 to Mar. 3, 1966	(5 goals and 6 assists)
1964-65	Rod Gilbert	7	Mar. 14 to Mar. 28, 1965	(2 goals and 10 assists)
1963-64	Rod Gilbert	11	Dec. 29 to Jan. 23, 1964	(8 goals and 7 assists)
1962-63	Andy Bathgate	13	Dec. 9 to Jan. 5, 1963	(12 goals and 6 assists)
1961-62	Dean Prentice	9	Jan. 31 to Feb. 15, 1962	(5 goals and 7 assists)
1960-61	Red Sullivan	8	Jan. 4 to Feb. 18, 1961	(4 goals and 4 assists)
	Earl Ingarfield	8	Jan. 22 to Feb. 5, 1961	(8 assists)
1959-60	Dean Prentice	8	Mar. 6 to Mar. 20, 1960	(6 goals and 6 assists)
1958-59	Andy Bathgate	12	Jan. 10 to Feb. 7, 1959	(8 goals and 11 assists)
1957-58	Andy Bathgate	8	Feb. 14 to Mar. 2, 1958	(8 goals and 9 assists)
1956-57	Camille Henry	11	Feb. 7 to Mar. 2, 1957	(8 goals and 12 assists)
1955-56	Dave Creighton	8	Oct. 7 to Oct. 26, 1955	(4 goals and 8 assists)
1954-55	Danny Lewicki	6	Feb. 5 to Feb. 16, 1955	(4 goals and 5 assists)
	Don Raleigh	6	Feb. 5 to Feb. 16, 1955	(2 goals and 7 assists)
	Dean Prentice	6	Nov. 27 to Dec. 8, 1954	(2 goals and 5 assists)
1953-54	Paul Ronty	5	Feb. 14 to Feb. 24, 1954	(1 goal and 6 assists)
1952-53	Wally Hergesheimer	9	Dec. 7 to Dec. 28, 1952	(3 goals and 9 assists)
1951-52	Hy Buller	6	Jan. 9 to Jan. 20, 1952	(4 goals and 3 assists)
1950-51	Jack McLeod	6	Nov. 5 to Nov. 18, 1950	(3 goals and 4 assists)
	Buddy O'Connor	6	Feb. 1 to Feb. 15, 1951	(3 goals and 4 assists)

RANGERS LAST OVERTIME WIN & LOSS VS. NHL OPPONENTS

	WIN	**LOSS**
ANAHEIM	NONE	NONE
BOSTON	2-1, Oct. 7, 1991 at MSG (Gartner, :31)	2-3, Nov. 5, 1990 at MSG (B. Sweeney, 3:30)
BUFFALO	7-6, Nov. 2, 1992 at MSG (Turcotte, :58)	NONE
CALGARY	NONE	NONE
CHICAGO	NONE	4-5, Nov. 11, 1985 at MSG (B. Murray, :53)
DALLAS	NONE	3-4, Nov. 9, 1993 at Min. (Bjugstad, 2:04)
DETROIT	NONE	5-6, Dec. 6, 1991 at Det. (Fedyk, 4:23)
EDMONTON	NONE	3-4, Mar. 17, 1993 at MSG (MacTavish, 0:32)
FLORIDA	NONE	NONE
HARTFORD	NONE	3-4, Dec 21, 1986 at MSG (K. Dineen, 2:57)
LOS ANGELES	5-4, Jan. 27, 1994 at LA (Messier, 4:58)	NONE
MONTREAL	2-1, Oct. 5, 1991 at Mtl. (Nemchinov, 1:42)	3-4, Feb. 9, 1994 at Mtl. (Desjardins, 1:27)
NEW JERSEY	4-3, Feb. 19, 1990 at MSG (Mullen, 4:47)	4-5, Dec. 23, 1992 at MSG (Richer, 1:33)
ISLANDERS	4-3, Dec. 31, 1986 at MSG (Sandstrom, 4:37)	2-3, Apr. 3, 1993 at MSG (Turgeon, 3:41)
OTTAWA	4-3, Feb. 12, 1994 at Ott. (Gartner, 2:37)	NONE
PHILADELPHIA	2-1, Feb. 23, 1992 at MSG (Amonte, 4:21)	2-3, Feb. 19, 1984 at MSG (Kerr, 1:33)
PITTSBURGH	4-3, Feb. 21, 1994 at MSG (Amonte, 0:08)	4-5, Mar. 21, 1991 at Pit. (Stevens, :13)
ST. LOUIS	3-2, Jan. 5, 1991 at Stl. (Nicholls, 3:12)	NONE
SAN JOSE	4-3, Dec. 16, 1991 at MSG (Leetch, 0:23)	NONE
TAMPA BAY	NONE	NONE
TORONTO	NONE	NONE
VANCOUVER	5-4, Jan. 21, 1989 at Van. (Kisio, 1:59)	NONE
WASHINGTON	5-4, Feb. 7, 1987 at Wsh. (Sandstrom, 4:20)	3-4, Dec. 29, 1992 at Wsh. (Pivonka, 1:28)
WINNIPEG	6-5, Mar. 9, 1984 at Wpg. (Osborne, :43)	5-6, Jan. 9, 1985 at Wpg. (Hawerchuk, 3:50)

RANGERS MODERN DAY REGULAR SEASON OVERTIME HISTORY (1983-84—1986-87)

DATE	OPPONENT	SCORE / RESULT		GOAL SCORER	GOALTENDER	TIME OF GOAL
1983-84	**5-3-9**					
10-23-83	ISLANDERS	6-5	W	Sundstrom	Melanson	1:13
10-30-83	EDMONTON	4-5	L	Hughes	Weeks	1:18
11-2-83	@ Buffalo	3-3	T			
11-5-83	@ Quebec	4-4	T			
11-19-83	@ Boston	6-6	T			
11-20-83	QUEBEC	6-5	W	Andersson	Bouchard	:08
11-26-83	@ Hartford	3-4	L	Stoughton	Weeks	4:52
11-28-83	VANCOUVER	3-3	T			
1-2-84	@ Washington	2-2	T			
1-4-84	NEW JERSEY	4-3	W	Ruotsalainen	Resch	4:47
2-5-84	@ Los Angeles	3-3	T			
2-9-84	@ Minnesota	4-4	T			
2-11-84	@ Los Angeles	6-6	T			
2-19-84	PHILADELPHIA	2-3	L	Kerr	Hanlon	1:33
2-26-84	PITTSBURGH	4-3	W	Osborne	Herron	2:18
2-28-84	@ New Jersey	3-3	T			
3-9-84	@ Winnipeg	6-5	W	Osborne	Behrend	:43
1984-85	**2-5-10**					
10-11-84	HARTFORD	4-4	T			
11-9-84	ISLANDERS	5-4	W	Ruotsalainen	Melanson	:57
11-25-84	QUEBEC	2-3	L	Hunter	Hanlon	3:36
11-30-84	TORONTO	3-3	T			
12-5-84	CALGARY	4-4	T			
12-7-84	PITTSBURGH	3-4	L	Hillier	Hanlon	1:35
12-12-84	BOSTON	3-3	T			
12-23-84	MONTREAL	3-3	T			
1-5-85	@ Boston	3-3	T			
1-6-85	NEW JERSEY	5-4	W	Sandstrom	Resch	1:14
1-9-85	@ Winnipeg	5-6	L	Hawerchuk	Vanbiesbrouck	3:50
1-12-85	@ St. Louis	4-4	T			
1-16-85	BUFFALO	2-2	T			
2-9-85	@ Hartford	2-2	T			
2-21-85	HARTFORD	3-4	L	Cote	Hanlon	3:45
3-9-85	@ Edmonton	3-3	T			
3-11-85	CHICAGO	3-4	L	B. Wilson	Hanlon	1:36
1985-86	**0-7-6**					
10-13-85	NEW JERSEY	2-3	L	Preston	Kleisinger	3:41
11-2-85	@ New Jersey	5-6	L	Bridgman	Vanbiesbrouck	:50
11-9-85	@ Minnesota	3-4	L	Bjugstad	Scott	2:04
11-11-85	CHICAGO	4-5	L	B. Murray	Vanbiesbrouck	:53
11-16-85	@ Montreal	2-2	T			
11-17-85	EDMONTON	2-3	L	Napier	Vanbiesbrouck	2:06
11-24-85	ISLANDERS	3-4	L	Gilbert	Scott	1:57
12-20-85	ISLANDERS	2-2	T			
1-12-86	ST. LOUIS	2-2	T			
1-27-86	@ Quebec	6-6	T			
3-15-86	@ Pittsburgh	2-2	T			
4-5-86	@ Washington	4-4	T			
4-6-86	PITTSBURGH	4-5	L	Lemieux	Hanlon	:25
1986-87	**5-6-8**					
10-11-86	@ Pittsburgh	5-6	L	Bodger	Vanbiesbrouck	0:50
10-13-86	WASHINGTON	6-7	L	Gartner	Soetaert	3:20
10-15-86	@ Chicago	5-5	T			
10-19-86	ISLANDERS	2-2	T			
10-22-86	LOS ANGELES	5-4	W	Osborne	Eliot	4:34
10-25-86	@ Montreal	3-3	T			
10-26-86	TORONTO	3-3	T			
11-2-86	WINNIPEG	4-5	L	MacLean	Vanbiesbrouck	3:23
11-5-86	@ Detroit	4-5	L	Shedden	Soetaert	2:21
11-12-86	BUFFALO	2-1	W	Poddubny	Barrasso	2:01
11-19-86	@ Edmonton	4-5	L	Anderson	Vanbiesbrouck	1:05
11-29-86	@ Pittsburgh	5-5	T			
11-30-86	PITTSBURGH	2-2	T			
12-21-86	HARTFORD	3-4	L	Dineen	Vanbiesbrouck	2:57
12-31-86	ISLANDERS	4-3	W	Sandstrom	Hrudey	4:37
1-5-87	MINNESOTA	3-3	T			
1-19-87	@ Los Angeles	2-2	T			
2-7-87	@ Washington	5-4	W	Sandstrom	Mason	4:20
3-14-87	@ Pittsburgh	3-2	W	Sandstrom	Riggin	1:05

RANGERS MODERN DAY REGULAR SEASON OVERTIME HISTORY (1987-88—1991-92)

DATE	OPPONENT	SCORE / RESULT		GOAL SCORER	GOALTENDER	TIME OF GOAL
1987-88	**0-1-10**					
10-8-87	PITTSBURGH	4-4	T			
10-15-87	@ Pittsburgh	6-6	T			
10-26-87	PHILADELPHIA	2-2	T			
11-14-87	@ Pittsburgh	2-3	L	Mantha	Vanbiesbrouck	2:04
12-9-87	MONTREAL	2-2	T			
12-29-87	@ Islanders	3-3	T			
1-11-88	CHICAGO	2-2	T			
2-2-88	@ Islanders	2-2	T			
2-14-88	ISLANDERS	4-4	T			
3-26-88	@ Detroit	4-4	T			
4-1-88	@ Winnipeg	6-6	T			
1988-89	**1-1-8**					
10-6-88	@ Chicago	2-2	T			
11-11-88	BOSTON	4-4	T			
11-15-88	@ Philadelphia	3-3	T			
12-10-88	@ Boston	1-1	T			
12-23-88	@ Washington	2-2	T			
1-4-89	WASHINGTON	3-3	T			
1-14-89	@ Pittsburgh	4-4	T			
1-21-89	@ Vancouver	5-4	W	Kisio	McLean	1:59
1-28-89	@ Toronto	1-1	T			
2-1-89	WASHINGTON	3-4	L	Ridley	Vanbiesbrouck	1:51
1989-90	**2-2-13**					
10-17-89	CHICAGO	3-3	T			
10-25-89	EDMONTON	3-3	T			
10-27-89	ISLANDERS	5-5	T			
11-17-89	@ New Jersey	4-5	L	Muller	Vanbiesbrouck	3:37
11-20-89	WINNIPEG	3-3	T			
12-9-89	@ Islanders	0-0	T			
12-20-89	BUFFALO	2-2	T			
12-26-89	NEW JERSEY	4-4	T			
1-10-90	CHICAGO	2-2	T			
1-14-90	PHILADELPHIA	4-3	W	Leetch	Wregget	1:16
1-18-90	@ Pittsburgh	3-3	T			
1-31-90	ST. LOUIS	2-2	T			
2-14-90	PITTSBURGH	3-4	L	Loney	Richter	3:33
2-19-90	NEW JERSEY	4-3	W	Mullen	Burke	4:47
2-21-90	@ Detroit	4-4	T			
3-10-90	@ Minnesota	2-2	T			
3-21-90	TORONTO	5-5	T			
1990-91	**1-2-13**					
11-5-90	BOSTON	2-3	L	B. Sweeney	Vanbiesbrouck	3:30
11-11-90	CALGARY	4-4	T			
11-13-90	@ Philadelphia	1-1	T			
11-19-90	MINNESOTA	2-2	T			
11-21-90	@ Buffalo	5-5	T			
11-24-90	@ Islanders	2-2	T			
12-23-90	BOSTON	5-5	T			
12-30-90	NEW JERSEY	2-2	T			
1-5-91	@ St. Louis	3-2	W	Nicholls	Riendeau	3:12
1-15-91	EDMONTON	2-2	T			
1-31-91	@ Vancouver	3-3	T			
2-21-91	@ Philadelphia	4-4	T			
2-27-91	WASHINGTON	4-4	T			
2-28-91	@ St. Louis	4-4	T			
3-21-91	@ Pittsburgh	4-5	L	Stevens	Vanbiesbrouck	:13
3-26-91	NEW JERSEY	3-3	T			
1991-92	**5-1-5**					
10-5-91	@ Montreal	2-1	W	Nemchinov	Roy	1:42
10-7-91	BOSTON	2-1	W	Gartner	Delguidice	:31
11-8-91	TORONTO	3-3	T			
11-29-91	@ Buffalo	5-4	W	Messier	Draper	:43
12-6-91	@ Detroit	5-6	L	Fedyk	Vanbiesbrouck	4:23
12-16-91	SAN JOSE	4-3	W	Leetch	Hayward	:23
1-22-92	@ Calgary	4-4	T			
2-9-92	DETROIT	5-5	T			
2-17-92	VANCOUVER	3-3	T			
2-23-92	PHILADELPHIA	2-1	W	Amonte	Roussel	4:21
3-18-92	ISLANDERS	1-1	T			

RANGERS MODERN DAY REGULAR SEASON OVERTIME HISTORY (1992-93—1993-94)

DATE	OPPONENT	SCORE / RESULT		GOAL SCORER	GOALTENDER	TIME OF GOAL
1992-93	**2-4-11**					
10-23-92	MONTREAL	3-3	T			
10-24-92	@ Ottawa	3-2	W	Bourque	Sidorkiewicz	4:49
11-2-92	BUFFALO	7-6	W	Turcotte	Puppa	0:58
11-7-92	@ Boston	2-2	T			
11-27-92	@ Minnesota	4-4	T			
12-19-92	@ Hartford	4-4	T			
12-23-92	NEW JERSEY	4-5	L	Richer	Vanbiesbrouck	1:33
12-29-92	@ Washington	3-4	L	Pivonka	Vanbiesbrouck	1:28
1-4-93	NEW JERSEY	3-3	T			
1-11-93	VANCOUVER	3-3	T			
1-19-93	@ Detroit	2-2	T			
2-1-93	@ Islanders	4-4	T			
2-3-93	PHILADELPHIA	3-3	T			
2-26-93	@ Calgary	4-4	T			
3-3-93	BUFFALO	2-2	T			
3-17-93	EDMONTON	3-4	L	MacTavish	Vanbiesbrouck	0:32
4-2-93	ISLANDERS	2-3	L	Turgeon	Richter	3:41
1993-94	**3-1-8**					
10-28-93	MONTREAL	3-3	T			
11-14-93	SAN JOSE	3-3	T			
12-8-93	EDMONTON	1-1	T			
1-27-94	@ Los Angeles	5-4	W	Messier	Hrudey	4:58
2-9-94	@ Montreal	3-4	L	Desjardins	Healy	1:27
2-12-94	@ Ottawa	4-3	W	Gartner	Madeley	2:37
2-21-94	PITTSBURGH	4-3	W	Amonte	Barrasso	0:08
3-4-94	ISLANDERS	3-3	T			
3-10-94	@ Boston	2-2	T			
3-22-94	@ Calgary	4-4	T			
4-4-94	ISLANDERS	4-4	T			
4-14-94	PHILADELPHIA	2-2	T			

RANGERS MODERN DAY REGULAR SEASON OVERTIME RECORD
(Since 1983-84)

vs.	OVERALL	HOME	AWAY
Anaheim	0-0-0	0-0-0	0-0-0
Boston	1-1-8	1-1-3	0-0-5
Buffalo	3-0-5	2-0-3	1-0-2
Calgary	0-0-5	0-0-2	0-0-3
Chicago	0-2-5	0-2-3	0-0-2
Dallas	0-1-5	0-0-2	0-1-3
Detroit	0-2-4	0-0-1	0-2-3
Edmonton	0-4-4	0-3-3	0-1-1
Florida	0-0-0	0-0-0	0-0-0
Hartford	0-3-3	0-2-1	0-1-2
Los Angeles	2-0-3	1-0-0	1-0-3
Montreal	1-1-6	0-0-4	1-1-2
New Jersey	3-4-5	3-2-4	0-2-1
Islanders	3-2-12	3-2-7	0-0-5
Ottawa	2-0-0	0-0-0	2-0-0
Philadelphia	2-1-6	2-1-3	0-0-3
Pittsburgh	3-6-7	2-3-2	1-3-5
Quebec	1-1-2	1-1-0	0-0-2
St. Louis	1-0-4	0-0-2	1-0-2
San Jose	1-0-1	1-0-1	0-0-0
Tampa Bay	0-0-0	0-0-0	0-0-0
Toronto	0-0-5	0-0-4	0-0-1
Vancouver	1-0-4	0-0-3	1-0-1
Washington	1-3-5	0-2-2	1-1-3
Winnipeg	1-2-2	0-1-1	1-1-1
TOTALS	26-33-101	16-20-51	10-13-50

LIFETIME RANGERS SHUTOUTS

	Regular Season	Playoffs	Total
Giacomin	49	1	50
Kerr	40	7	47
Roach	30	5	35
Rayner	24	1	25
Worsley	24	0	24
Chabot	21	2	23
Vanbiesbrouck	16	2	18
Richter	9	6	15
Aitkenhead	11	3	14
Villemure	13	0	13
Davidson	7	1	8
Bower	5	0	5
Plante	5	0	5
Thomas	5	0	5
Henry	4	1	5
Baker	3	0	3
Healy	2	0	2
Maniago	2	0	2
Mio	2	0	2
Paille	2	0	2
Winkler	2	0	2
Hanlon	1	1	2
Beveridge	1	0	1
Froese	1	0	1
McAuley	1	0	1
McCartan	1	0	1
Sawchuk	1	0	1
Soetaert	1	0	1
Weeks	1	0	1
Miller	0	1	1
	284	31	315

MOST DECISIVE VICTORIES

HOME
- 12-1 — vs. California .... Nov. 21, 1971
- 10-0 — vs. California .... Nov. 17, 1974
- 9-0 — vs. Montreal ...... Feb. 4, 1940
- 9-0 — vs. Montreal ..... Jan. 30, 1949
- 9-0 — vs. Boston ...... Feb. 23, 1969
- 9-0 — vs. New Jersey... Mar. 31, 1986
- 11-2 — vs. Detroit .... Jan. 25, 1942
- 8-0 — vs. Los Angeles ... Jan. 9, 1972
- 9-1 — vs. St. Louis ..... Jan. 5, 1972
- 9-1 — vs. Pittsburgh.... Dec. 17, 1972
- 10-2 — vs. Chicago ..... Mar. 12, 1952
- 10-2 — vs. Edmonton .... Oct. 24, 1979
- 10-2 — vs. Detroit. ...... Dec. 23, 1985
- 11-3 — vs. Hartford ..... Feb. 23, 1983

ROAD
- 11-2 — at New Jersey.... Oct. 25, 1984
- 11-3 — at Pittsburgh. ... Nov. 25, 1992
- 7-0 — at NY Americans . Jan. 29, 1928
- 7-0 — at Montreal ...... Jan. 22, 1935
- 7-0 — at NY Americans .. Feb. 2, 1939
- 7-0 — at Toronto. ...... Mar. 22, 1958
- 8-1 — at Oakland .... Nov. 7, 1969
- 8-1 — at California ...... Nov. 5, 1971
- 8-1 — at Minnesota .... Dec. 30, 1974
- 9-2 — at Ottawa .... Jan. 28, 1933
- 9-2 — at Minnesota .... Feb. 15, 1975
- 11-4 — at Minnesota ..... Dec. 4, 1976
- 11-4 — at Washington ... Mar. 24, 1978

MOST DECISIVE DEFEATS

HOME
- 3-13 — vs. Boston. .... Jan. 2, 1944
- 0-9 — vs. Detroit. .... Dec. 6, 1950
- 1-10 — vs. Toronto...... Mar. 21, 1965
- 0-8 — vs. Toronto....... Mar. 9, 1944
- 0-8 — vs. Chicago. ...... Apr. 2, 1967

ROAD
- 0-15 — at Detroit. .... Jan. 23, 1944
- 1-14 — at Toronto ...... Mar. 16, 1957
- 3-14 — at Boston .... Jan. 21, 1945
- 2-12 — at Detroit .... Feb. 3, 1944

RANGERS AND OPPONENTS 10-GOAL GAMES SINCE 1950

RANGERS

Dec. 13, 1992	— 10-5 —	vs. Montreal at MSG
Nov. 25, 1992	— 11-3 —	vs. Pittsburgh at Pittsburgh
Dec. 23, 1985	— 10-2 —	vs. Detroit at MSG
Oct. 25, 1984	— 11-2 —	vs. New Jersey at New Jersey
Feb. 23, 1983	— 11-3 —	vs. Hartford at MSG
Oct. 24, 1979	— 10-2 —	vs. Edmonton at MSG
Mar. 24, 1978	— 11-4 —	vs. Washington at Washington
Dec. 4, 1976	— 11-4 —	vs. Minnesota at Minnesota
Oct. 12, 1976	— 10-4 —	vs. Minnesota at Minnesota
Feb. 18, 1976	— 11-4 —	vs. Washington at MSG
Nov. 17, 1974	— 10-0 —	vs. California at MSG
Nov. 21, 1971	— 12-1 —	vs. California at MSG
Mar. 29, 1967	— 10-5 —	vs. Detroit at MSG
Mar. 12, 1952	— 10-2 —	vs. Chicago at MSG

Opponents

Apr. 10, 1993	— 4-10 —	vs. Pittsburgh at MSG
Mar. 6, 1993	— 2-10 —	vs. Quebec at Quebec
Dec. 31, 1992	— 6-11 —	vs. Buffalo at Buffalo
Feb. 17, 1989	— 6-10 —	vs. Toronto at MSG
Dec. 4, 1988	— 6-10 —	vs. Edmonton at Edmonton
Mar. 7, 1985	— 5-11 —	vs. Calgary at Calgary
Feb. 25, 1985	— 5-12 —	vs. Winnipeg at MSG
Nov. 17, 1984	— 4-10 —	vs. Islanders at Nassau Coliseum
Nov. 13, 1979	— 5-10 —	vs. Islanders at Nassau Coliseum
Mar. 10, 1977	— 3-10 —	vs. Boston at Boston
Apr. 3, 1976	— 2-10 —	vs. Islanders at Nassau Coliseum
Dec. 19, 1974	— 3-11 —	vs. Boston at Boston
Nov. 15, 1973	— 2-10 —	vs. Boston at Boston
Mar. 21, 1965	— 1-10 —	vs. Toronto at MSG
Jan. 21, 1960	— 2-11 —	vs. Montreal at Montreal
Mar. 16, 1957	— 1-14 —	vs. Toronto at Toronto
Feb. 19, 1955	— 2-10 —	vs. Montreal at Montreal

RANGERS 0-0 GAMES SINCE 1950

Oct. 22, 1950 vs. Boston at Boston
  Goaltenders: Chuck Rayner and Jack Gelineau
Mar. 5, 1954 vs. Chicago at Chicago
  Goaltenders: Johnny Bower and Al Rollins
Jan. 12, 1955 vs. Toronto at Madison Square Garden
  Goaltenders: Lorne Worsley and Harry Lumley
Dec. 8, 1956 vs. Toronto at Toronto
  Goaltenders: Lorne Worsley and Ed Chadwick
Mar. 8, 1964 vs. Montreal at Madison Square Garden
  Goaltenders: Jacques Plante and Charlie Hodge
Mar. 8, 1970 vs. Pittsburgh at Madison Square Garden
  Goaltenders: Ed Giacomin and Al Smith
Mar. 30, 1981 vs. Philadelphia at Madison Square Garden
  Goaltenders: Steve Baker and Rick St. Croix
Dec. 9, 1989 vs. Islanders at Nassau Coliseum
  Goaltenders: John Vanbiesbrouck and Mark Fitzpatrick

RANGERS IN THE NHL ALL-STAR GAME

Season	Team	Player	G	A	Pts.
1947-48	NHL All-Stars	Edgar Laprade	0	1	1
	NHL All-Stars	Tony Leswick	0	0	0
	NHL All-Stars	Grant Warwick	1	0	1
1948-49	NHL All-Stars	Neil Colville	0	0	0
	NHL All-Stars	Edgar Laprade	0	0	0
	NHL All-Stars	Tony Leswick	0	0	0
1949-50	NHL All-Stars	Martin Egan	0	0	0
	NHL All-Stars	Edgar Laprade	0	1	1
	NHL All-Stars	Tony Leswick	0	0	0
	NHL All-Stars	Buddy O'Connor	0	0	0
	NHL All-Stars	Chuck Rayner	31:30, 0 GA		
1950-51	NHL All-Stars	Tony Leswick	0	0	0
	NHL All-Stars	Chuck Rayner	31:12, 3 GA		
	NHL All-Stars	Edgar Laprade	0	0	0
1951-52	First Team NHL	Frank Eddolls	0	0	0
	First Team NHL	Don Raleigh	0	1	1
	Second Team NHL	Chuck Rayner	29:28, 1 GA		
	First Team NHL	Reg Sinclair	0	0	0
	First Team NHL	Gaye Stewart	0	1	1
1952-53	Second Team NHL	Hy Buller	0	1	1
	First Team NHL	Leo Riese, Jr.	0	0	0
1953-54	NHL All-Stars	Wally Hergesheimer	2	0	2
	NHL All-Stars	Leo Riese, Jr.	0	0	0
	NHL All-Stars	Paul Ronty	0	1	1
1954-55	NHL All-Stars	Harry Howell	0	0	0
	NHL All-Stars	Don Raleigh	0	0	0
	NHL All-Stars	Paul Ronty	0	0	0
1955-56	NHL All-Stars	Dan Lewicki	0	0	0
1956-57	NHL All-Stars	David Creighton	0	0	0
	NHL All-Stars	Bill Gadsby	0	0	0
	NHL All-Stars	Red Sullivan	0	0	0
1957-58	NHL All-Stars	Andy Bathgate	1	1	2
	NHL All-Stars	Bill Gadsby	0	0	0
	NHL All-Stars	Dean Prentice	1	2	3
1958-59	NHL All-Stars	Andy Bathgate	2	0	2
	NHL All-Stars	Bill Gadsby	0	0	0
	NHL All-Stars	Camille Henry	0	1	1
	NHL All-Stars	Red Sullivan	0	1	1
1959-60	NHL All-Stars	Andy Bathgate	0	0	0
	NHL All-Stars	Bill Gadsby	0	0	0
	NHL All-Stars	Red Sullivan	0	0	0
1960-61	NHL All-Stars	Andy Bathgate	0	0	0
	NHL All-Stars	Bill Gadsby	0	0	0
	NHL All-Stars	Andy Hebenton	1	0	1
	NHL All-Stars	Red Sullivan	0	1	1
1961-62	NHL All-Stars	Andy Bathgate	0	1	1
	NHL All-Stars	Doug Harvey	0	0	0
	NHL All-Stars	Gump Worsley	30:00, 0 GA		
1962-63	NHL All-Stars	Andy Bathgate	0	0	0
	NHL All-Stars	Doug Harvey	0	0	0
	NHL All-Stars	Dean Prentice	0	0	0
	NHL All-Stars	Gump Worsley	20:00, 0 GA		
1963-64	NHL All-Stars	Andy Bathgate	0	0	0
	NHL All-Stars	Camille Henry	0	1	1
	NHL All-Stars	Harry Howell	0	0	0
1964-65	NHL All-Stars	Rod Gilbert	0	0	0
	NHL All-Stars	Camille Henry	0	0	0
	NHL All-Stars	Harry Howell	0	1	1
1965-66	NHL All-Stars	Rod Gilbert	0	0	0
	NHL All-Stars	Vic Hadfield	0	0	0
	NHL All-Stars	Harry Howell	0	0	0
1966-67	NHL All-Stars	Ed Giacomin	30:00, 1 GA		
	NHL All-Stars	Rod Gilbert	0	0	0
	NHL All-Stars	Harry Howell	0	0	0
	NHL All-Stars	Jim Neilson	0	0	0
	NHL All-Stars	Bob Nevin	0	0	0
1967-68	NHL All-Stars	Ed Giacomin	20:00, 1 GA		

RANGERS IN THE NHL ALL-STAR GAME

Season	Team	Player	G	A	Pts.
	NHL All-Stars	Harry Howell	0	0	
	NHL All-Stars	Don Marshall	0	0	0
1968-69	East	Ed Giacomin	40:00, 2 GA		
	East	Rod Gilbert	0	1	1
	East	Bob Nevin	1	0	1
1969-70	East	Ed Giacomin	30:00, 1 GA		
	East	Rod Gilbert	0	0	0
1969-70	East	Jim Neilson	0	0	0
(con't)	East	Brad Park	0	0	0
	East	Jean Ratelle	0	0	0
	East	Walt Tkaczuk	1	0	1
1970-71	East	Dave Balon	0	1	1
	East	Ed Giacomin	31:00, 2 GA		
	East	Jim Neilson	0	0	0
	East	Brad Park	0	0	0
	East	Jean Ratelle	0	0	0
	East	Gilles Villemure	29:00, 0 GA		
1971-72	East	Rod Gilbert	0	1	1
	East	Vic Hadfield	0	0	0
	East	Brad Park	0	1	1
	East	Jean Ratelle	1	0	1
	East	Rod Seiling	0	1	1
	East	Gilles Villemure	29:26, 0 GA		
1972-73	East	Ed Giacomin	30:44, 3 GA		
	East	Brad Park	0	1	1
	East	Jean Ratelle	0	0	0
	East	Gilles Villemure	29:16, 1 GA		
1973-74	East	Brad Park	0	0	0
1974-75	Campbell	Rod Gilbert	0	0	0
	Campbell	Brad Park	0	0	0
	Campbell	Steve Vickers	0	0	0
1975-76	Campbell	Carol Vadnais	0	0	0
	Campbell	Steve Vickers	1	0	1
1976-77	Campbell	Phil Esposito	1	0	1
	Campbell	Rod Gilbert	0	1	1
	Campbell	Don Murdoch	0	0	0
1977-78	Campbell	Phil Esposito	0	0	0
	Campbell	Carol Vadnais	0	0	0
1978-79	NHL (vs. USSR)	Anders Hedberg	0	0	0
	NHL (vs. USSR)	Ulf Nilsson	0	0	0
1979-80	Campbell	Phil Esposito	0	1	1
	Campbell	Ron Greschner	0	0	0
1980-81	Campbell	Ed Johnstone	0	2	2
1981-82	Wales	Barry Beck	0	1	1
	Wales	Ron Duguay	0	0	0
1982-83	Wales	Don Maloney	1	0	1
1983-84	Wales	Pierre Larouche	2	0	2
	Wales	Don Maloney (MVP)	1	3	4
1984-85	Wales	Anders Hedberg	1	0	1
1985-86	Wales	Reijo Ruotsalainen	0	0	0
1986-87	NHL (vs. USSR)	Tomas Sandstrom	0	0	0
1987-88	Wales	Tomas Sandstrom	1	0	1
1988-89	Wales	Brian Mullen	0	1	1
1989-90	Wales	Brian Leetch	0	0	0
1990-91	Wales	Brian Leetch	0	0	0
	Wales	Darren Turcotte	0	1	1
1991-92	Wales	Brian Leetch	0	0	0
	Wales	Mark Messier	0	1	1
	Wales	Mike Richter	20:00, 2 GA		
1992-93	Wales	Mike Gartner (MVP)	4	1	5
	Wales	Kevin Lowe	0	1	1
	Wales	Brian Leetch	Injured		
	Wales	Mark Messier	Injured		
1993-94	Eastern	Adam Graves	0	2	2
		Brian Leetch	0	0	0
		Mark Messier	1	2	3
		Mike Richter (MVP)	20:00, 2 GA		

RANGERS NHL ALL-STARS

FIRST TEAM

Bill Cook, right wing 1930-31
Lester Patrick, coach 1930-31
Bill Cook, right wing 1931-32
Ching Johnson, defense 1931-32
Lester Patrick, coach 1931-32
Frank Boucher, center 1932-33
Bill Cook, right wing 1932-33
Ching Johnson, defense 1932-33
Lester Patrick, coach 1932-33
Frank Boucher, center 1933-34
Lester Patrick, coach 1933-34
Frank Boucher, center 1934-35
Earl Seibert, defense............................1934-35
Lester Patrick, coach 1934-35
Lester Patrick, coach 1935-36
Cecil Dillon, right wing 1937-38
Lester Patrick, coach 1937-38
Bryan Hextall, right wing 1939-40
Dave Kerr, goal 1939-40
Bryan Hextall, right wing 1940-41

Bryan Hextall, right wing 1941-42
Lynn Patrick, left wing..........................1941-42
Frank Boucher, coach..........................1941-42
Bill Gadsby, defense.............................1955-56
Bill Gadsby, defense.............................1957-58
Bill Gadsby, defense.............................1958-59
Andy Bathgate, right wing...................1958-59
Andy Bathgate, right wing...................1961-62
Doug Harvey, defense..........................1961-62
Ed Giacomin, goal.................................1966-67
Harry Howell, defense..........................1966-67
Brad Park, defense................................1969-70
Ed Giacomin, goal.................................1970-71
Brad Park, defense................................1971-72
Rod Gilbert, right wing.........................1971-72
Brad Park, defense................................1973-74
John Vanbiesbrouck, goal 1985-86
Mark Messier, center............................1991-92
Brian Leetch, defense 1991-92

SECOND TEAM

Ching Johnson, defense......................1930-31
Frank Boucher, center 1930-31
Bun Cook, left wing...............................1930-31
Ching Johnson, defense......................1933-34
Bill Cook, right wing 1933-34
Cecil Dillon, right wing 1935-36
Cecil Dillon, right wing 1936-37
Dave Kerr, goal 1937-38
Art Coulter, defense..............................1937-38
Art Coulter, defense..............................1938-39
Neil Colville, center 1938-39
Art Coulter, defense..............................1939-40
Neil Colville, center 1939-40
Frank Boucher, coach..........................1939-40
Ott Heller, defense.................................1940-41
Phil Watson, center...............................1941-42
Bryan Hextall, right wing 1942-43
Lynn Patrick, left wing..........................1942-43
Buddy O'Connor, center 1947-48
Neil Colville, defense............................1947-48
Chuck Rayner, goal...............................1948-49
Chuck Rayner, goal...............................1949-50
Tony Leswick, left wing........................1949-50

Chuck Rayner, goal...............................1950-51
Hy Buller, defense 1951-52
Danny Lewicki, left wing......................1954-55
Bill Gadsby, defense.............................1956-57
Andy Bathgate, right wing...................1957-58
Camille Henry, left wing.......................1957-58
Dean Prentice, left wing.......................1959-60
Andy Bathgate, right wing...................1962-63
Don Marshall, left wing 1966-67
Ed Giacomin, goal.................................1967-68
Jim Neilson, defense............................1967-68
Rod Gilbert, right wing.........................1967-68
Ed Giacomin, goal.................................1968-69
Ed Giacomin, goal.................................1969-70
Brad Park, defense................................1970-71
Vic Hadfield, left wing 1971-72
Jean Ratelle, center...............................1971-72
Brad Park, defense................................1972-73
Steve Vickers, left wing 1974-75
Brian Leetch, defense 1990-91
Adam Graves, left wing 1993-94
Brian Leetch, defense 1993-94

RANGERS ALL-TIME LONGEST TEAM STREAKS

Overall

Winning Streak

10	12/19	—	1/13/40
10	1/19	—	2/10/73
8	2/16	—	3/6/74
8	12/27	—	1/11/15
7	1/18	—	2/5/42
7	12/11	—	12/23/70
7	2/20	—	3/5/72
7	10/22	—	11/5/78
7	10/16	—	10/30/88
7	12/13	—	12/26/91

Unbeaten Streak

19	11/23	—	1/13/40
16	2/6	—	3/11/72
16	1/7	—	2/11/73
14	11/7	—	12/10/69
14	10/16	—	11/14/71
14	10/24	—	11/24/93
13	1/3	—	2/5/35
11	12/10	—	1/5/32
11	2/20	—	3/14/71
11	11/17	—	12/5/63
10	2/10	—	3/6/74
10	11/7	—	11/26/90

Losing Streak

11	10/30	—	11/27/43
10	1/3	—	1/28/62
8	10/28	—	11/14/87
8	3/7	—	3/23/91
7	12/31	—	1/15/44
7	1/11	—	1/25/50
7	3/11	—	3/22/50
7	10/31	—	11/16/63
7	4/5	—	4/16/93

Winless Streak

21	1/23	—	3/19/44
19	12/31	—	2/20/43
15	10/30	—	12/11/43
15	10/19	—	11/19/50
14	12/1	—	12/26/54
11	11/25	—	12/18/65
11	12/9	—	12/31/89
10	10/28	—	11/21/56
10	1/14	—	2/3/60
10	1/3	—	1/28/62

Home

Winning Streak

14	12/19	—	2/25/40
9	2/10	—	3/14/71
9	11/10	—	12/15/71
8	12/13	—	1/14/32
8	12/31	—	2/15/70
8	2/20	—	3/16/80
8	10/8	—	10/31/90
7	1/5	—	2/8/69
7	2/9	—	3/5/72
7	2/6	—	3/10/74
7	11/17	—	12/15/82
7	12/21	—	1/18/84

Unbeaten Streak

24	10/14	—	1/31/71
18	11/28	—	2/25/40
18	1/5	—	3/30/69
18	10/17	—	12/29/71
16	10/24	—	1/5/94
13	11/25	—	2/5/42
12	12/28	—	2/25/70
11	11/7	—	12/12/73
11	1/6	—	3/10/74
11	1/14	—	3/1/92
10	11/2	—	12/10/69
10	10/11	—	11/15/72
10	1/7	—	2/28/73

Losing Streak

7	10/20	—	11/14/76
7	3/24	—	4/14/93
6	2/26	—	3/16/46
5	11/6	—	11/21/43
5	12/31	—	1/13/44
5	2/20	—	3/6/55
5	1/6	—	2/2/57
5	11/24	—	12/8/58

Winless Streak

10	1/30	—	3/19/44
9	12/31	—	2/18/43
9	11/29	—	1/3/65
8	11/12	—	12/27/44
8	12/1	—	12/26/54
7	2/23	—	3/16/46
7	10/28	—	11/25/56
7	12/25	—	1/29/58
7	3/3	—	3/28/65
7	10/20	—	11/14/76
7	3/24	—	4/14/93

Road

Winning Streak

7	1/12	—	2/12/35
7	10/28	—	11/29/78
6	10/30	—	11/24/93
5	1/19	—	2/10/73
4	(many times)		
	last 1/23 - 2/1/92		

Unbeaten Streak

11	11/5	—	1/13/40
10	11/12	—	1/3/31
10	12/20	—	2/10/73
9	2/8	—	3/22/58
8	2/3	—	3/9/68
8	12/2	—	1/15/82
8	12/23	—	1/23/89
7	1/12	—	2/12/35
7	10/28	—	11/29/78

Losing Streak

10	10/30	—	12/23/43
10	2/8	—	3/15/61
9	11/27	—	1/8/55
9	1/19	—	2/13/65
8	1/23	—	3/4/44
8	2/9	—	3/16/49
8	11/15	—	12/26/53
7	(10 times)		
	last 3/7 - 3/30/91		

Winless Streak

16	10/9	—	12/20/52
13	10/26	—	12/25/63
12	11/28	—	2/7/46
11	1/1	—	2/27/43
11	1/23	—	3/18/44
11	11/20	—	1/8/55
11	11/20	—	1/15/66
10	10/30	—	12/23/43
10	10/19	—	11/25/50
10	11/14	—	12/29/51
10	2/8	—	3/15/61
10	10/18	—	11/22/80

RANGERS LONGEST STREAKS

YEAR	WINNING STREAK		UNBEATEN STREAK		LOSING STREAK		WINLESS STREAK	
1926-27	5	3/15-3/25	7	3/5-3/25	3	12/23-12/28	3	(twice) last-3/1-3/13
1927-28	4	1/22-1/31	4	(twice) last-2/23-2/29	2	(3 times) last-3/6-3/8	5	2/4-2/16
1928-29	4	12/11-12/20	6	(twice) last-12/30-1/13	2	(3 times) last-3/5-3/10	4	(twice) last-2/5-2/14
1929-30	4	1/14-1/23	4	(twice) last-2/27-3/4	3	1/7-1/12	7	2/18-3/11
1930-31	3	12/23-12/28	5	12/20-12/30	4	1/18-1/29	8	1/11-1/31
1931-32	4	12/22-1/1	11	12/10-1/5	2	(5 times) last-3/15-3/17	5	2/9-2/21
1932-33	3	12/6-12/11	6	12/6-12/17	5	3/16-3/21	5	3/14-3/21
1933-34	3	(twice) last-1/23-1/28	6	12/14-12/28	2	(4 times) last-3/15-3/17	3	(twice) last-3/6-3/11
1934-35	5	1/27-2/5	13	1/3-2/5	4	(twice) last-2/26-3/7	5	2/24-3/7
1935-36	4	3/12-3/22	9	1/28-2/25	4	1/18-1/26	6	2/25-3/10
1936-37	3	12/20-12/29	5	1/24-2/4	3	(3 times) last-3/11-3/16	5	(twice) last-1/28-2/7
1937-38	5	(twice) last-2/1-2/13	7	12/5-12/23	3	(twice) last-2/17-2/22	4	11/21-12/2
1938-39	4	11/13-11/20	4	(3 times) last-1/31-2/5	3	2/26-3/5	4	2/26-3/7
1939-40	10	12/19-1/13	19	11/23-1/13	2	(twice) last-2/18-2/22	4	11/5-11/16
1940-41	5	2/18-3/1	5	2/18-3/1	2	2/11-2/16	4	2/11-2/16
1941-42	7	1/18-2/5	5	(twice) 1/18-2/5	4	(twice) last-2/10-2/17	4	(twice) last-2/10-2/17
1942-43	3	12/25-12/29	3	12/25-12/29	5	1/10-1/21	19	12/31-2/20
1943-44	2	(3 times) last-1/16-1/22	2	(3 times) last-1/16-1/22	11	10/30-11/27	21	1/23-3/19
1944-45	2	(twice) last-2/18-2/22	5	12/31-1/11	6	3/1-3/11	8	2/24-3/11
1945-46	2	3/13-3/17	4	12/30-1/6	5	11/6-1/26	6	(twice) last-12/13-12/26
1946-47	4	(twice) last-1/19-1/25	4	12/1-12/11	4	3/9-3/22	5	11/3-11/21
1947-48	4	11/16-11/30	7	12/6-12/17	5	11/6-11/15	7	(twice) last-3/3-3/16
1948-49	3	12/19-12/25	6	12/12-12/25	5	(twice) last-3/2-3/12	8	3/2-3/16
1949-50	4	(twice) 2/18-2/23	8	2/5-2/23	7	(twice) last-3/11-3/22	9	1/8-1/28
1950-51	3	(twice) last-2/11-2/15	6	12/10-12/24	3	3/14-3/21	15	10/19-11/19
1951-52	3	1/1-1/6	4	(twice) last-2/17-2/24	3	(3 times) last-3/1-3/4	4	(4 times) last-2/27-3/4
1952-53	2	(3 times) last-37-38	4	2/1-2/11	4	10/9-10/18	8	11/27-12/14
1953-54	4	1/1-1/10	4	(twice) last-2/14-2/21	3	(twice) last-12/26-12/29	7	12/2-12/13
1954-55	2	(3 times) last-3/12-3/13	8	2/9-2/16	4	(twice) last-2/27-3/6	14	12/1-12/26
1955-56	4	11/30-12/7	8	11/30-12/7	4	(twice) last-2/18-2/23	4	(4 times) last-2/18-2/23
1956-57	3	2/16-2/20	7	2/24-3/10	6	10/31-11/14	10	10/28-11/21
1957-58	3	(4 times) last-2/23-3/1	9	2/14-3/8	5	12/25-1/5	8	12/25-1/2
1958-59	5	11/8-11/19	6	11/8-11/22	6	2/7-2/18	7	2/7-2/21
1959-60	3	12/5-12/13	5	3/5-3/13	5	1/14-1/23	10	1/14-2/3

YEAR-BY-YEAR

YEAR	WINNING STREAK		UNBEATEN STREAK		LOSING STREAK		WINLESS STREAK	
1960-61	2	(5 times) last-2/19-2/22	5	1/8-1/18	5	(twice) last-12/28-1/7	8	10/27-11/13
1961-62	3	12/20-12/25	7	11/8-11/23	10	1/3-1/28	6	1/3-1/28
1962-63	3	11/18-11/22	5	12/27-1/5	3	(7 times) last-3/10-3/17	12	12/2-12/13
1963-64	4	1/1-1/9	5	1/25-2/2	7	10/31-11/16	9	11/28-12/14
1964-65	2	(5 times) last-2/27-2/28	3	(4 times) last-1/16-1/23	4	(4 times) last-2/13-2/20	7	(twice) last-3/6-3/21
1965-66	2	(twice) last-3/2-3/3	6	10/30-11/11	3	3/16-3/31	11	11/25-12/18
1966-67	5	12/7-12/17	5	(3 times) last-12/7-12/17	2	(9 times) last-4/1-4/2	4	2/26-3/18
1967-68	6	2/24-3/6	8	(twice) last-2/3-2/18	3	3/10-3/14	4	3/9-3/14
1968-69	5	1/23-1/30	8	3/2-3/19	3	(twice) last-2/12-2/15	8	12/5-12/21
1969-70	5	(twice) last-1/30-2/11	14	11/17-12/10	3	(twice) 3/11-3/15	9	2/26-3/15
1970-71	7	12/11-12/23	11	2/20-3/14	3	3/18-3/21	4	(twice) last-1/27-2/3
1971-72	7	2/20-3/5	6	2/6-3/11	2	(twice) last-4/1-4/2	6	3/25-4/2
1972-73	10	1/19-2/10	16	1/7-2/11	4	3/24-3/31	5	3/24-4/1
1973-74	3	2/16-3/6	10	(twice) last-2/10-3/6	4	10/20-10/28	5	10/20-10/28
1974-75	8	12/27-1/11	8	12/27-1/11	3	10/31-11/5	4	(twice) 2/16-2/22
1975-76	3	(twice) last-3/27-3/31	9	11/30-12/13	4	(twice) last-3/20-3/25	9	2/20-3/11
1976-77	3	3/19-3/23	9	11/22-12/8	4	2/26-3/5	5	1/5-1/13
1977-78	5	3/22-3/29	6	3/19-3/29	6	1/20-2/1	7	(twice) last-1/20-2/4
1978-79	7	10/22-11/5	7	10/22-11/5	2	(7 times) last-4/6-4/8	4	(twice) last-3/25-4/1
1979-80	5	2/24-3/5	7	12/1-12/12	3	(3 times) last-3/19-3/23	5	(3 times) last-3/19-3/28
1980-81	5	12/3-12/12	5	12/3-12/12	4	10/12-10/19	9	10/28-11/14
1981-82	5	3/17-3/26	9	3/8-3/26	3	(twice) last-10/25-10/31	5	11/21-11/29
1982-83	5	11/17-11/27	7	12/30-1/12	4	(twice) last-3/3-3/11	8	12/9-12/31
1983-84	5	10/5-10/13	6	2/4-2/15	4	2/29-3/7	11	1/12-1/27
1984-85	4	10/20-10/27	6	(twice) last-12/30-1/6	5	1/31-2/7	5	(3 times) last-2/28-3/7
1985-86	6	2/8-2/24	6	2/8-2/24	4	10/12-10/19	7	1/31-2/10
1986-87	4	1/31-2/7	6	10/15-10/26	4	3/15-3/21	4	(3 times) last-1/23-1/31
1987-88	4	(twice) last-2/25-3/2	6	12/26-1/6	8	10/28-11/14	5	10/25-11/5
1988-89	7	10/16-10/30	7	(twice) last-12/23-1/7	5	(twice) last-3/26-4/2	9	10/26-11/14
1989-90	4	2/23-3/2	8	10/15-10/28	4	12/10-12/17	5	(twice) last-3/26-4/2
1990-91	6	10/20-10/31	10	11/7-11/26	8	3/7-3/23	11	12/9-12/31
1991-92	7	12/13-12/26	8	(twice) last-3/11-3/24	3	(twice) last-3/4-3/9	8	3/7-3/23
1992-93	4	12/6-12/13	5	10/18-10/26	7	4/5-4/16	3	(twice) last-3/4-3/9
1993-94	7	10/30-11/13	14	10/24-11/24	3	(twice) last-1/5-1/10	7	4/5-4/16
							3	(3 times) last 3/10-3/14

217

RANGERS LONGEST HOME STREAKS

YEAR	WINNING STREAK		UNBEATEN STREAK		LOSING STREAK		WINLESS STREAK	
1926-27	3	(twice) last-3/20-3/25	6	1/6-1/23	2	2/22-2/24	3	2/22-3/13
1927-28	5	1/22-1/31	4	1/22-2/7	2	(twice) last-2/12-2/16	3	11/22-12/15
1928-29	5	11/25-12/20	5	(twice) last-12/30-1/22	1	(6 times) last-3/29	3	3/10-3/20
1929-30	4	(twice) last-1/14-1/28	7	1/14-2/13	2	2/18-2/23	4	2/18-3/11
1930-31	3	2/22-3/10	4	2/22-3/15	3	1/20-1/29	5	1/11-1/29
1931-32	8	12/13-1/14	8	12/13-1/14	2	1/28-2/2	3	2/16-2/25
1932-33	3	(twice) last-12/25-1/3	6	12/25-1/19	2	1/22-1/31	3	2/9-3/5
1933-34	6	1/2-1/28	8	1/2-2/6	3	3/6-3/15	4	12/7-12/21
1934-35	2	(3 times) last-2/14-2/19	10	12/25-2/3	3	2/28-3/17	4	2/24-3/17
1935-36	2	(4 times) last-3/12-3/17	8	11/19-12/31	3	1/2-1/12	4	2/16-3/8
1936-37	3	(3 times) last-2/18-3/23	9	11/19-1/5	3	3/7-3/16	4	1/28-2/14
1937-38	5	1/18-2/13	9	12/31-2/13	1	(6 times) last-3/13	2	(3 times) last-2/17-2/22
1938-39	5	12/31-1/22	5	12/31-1/22	2	(twice) last-2/26-3/2	4	2/26-3/12
1939-40	14	12/19-2/25	18	11/28-2/25	3	11/12-11/19	3	11/12-11/19
1940-41	5	2/23-3/16	5	(twice) last-2/23-3/16	3	(3 times) last-2/13-2/16	2	(4 times) last-2/13-2/16
1941-42	6	(twice) last-1/6-2/5	13	11/25-2/5	4	11/15-11/23	4	11/15-11/23
1942-43	2	(twice) last-2/21-2/25	12	(5 times) last-3/7-3/14	4	1/10-1/31	9	12/31-2/18
1943-44	3	12/12-12/26	3	12/12-12/26	5	(twice) 12/31-1/13	10	1/30-3/19
1944-45	3	2/15-2/22	4	(twice) last-2/15-2/25	3	(twice) last-3/1-3/11	8	11/12-12/27
1945-46	2	1/6-1/13	4	(twice) last-1/27-2/14	4	12/13-12/26	6	2/3-3/3
1946-47	6	1/12-2/19	7	1/12-2/23	6	2/26-3/16	5	2/23-3/16
1947-48	2	(3 times) last-2/29-3/2	4	12/7-12/17	3	3/14-3/21	5	1/18-2/18
1948-49	3	12/12-12/19	4	(twice) last-12/31-1/9	2	(twice) last-2/10-2/13	5	11/13-12/7
1949-50	5	(twice) last-12/21-1/4	6	(3 times) last-1/29-2/26	4	3/12-3/21	6	10/19-11/13
1950-51	2	12/24-1/7	3	12/13-1/7	4	(twice) last-3/14-3/21	6	10/25-11/19
1951-52	3	12/19-12/26	6	12/19-1/6	3	(twice) last-2/27-3-9	5	1/9-2/10
1952-53	2	(twice) last-2/25-3/1	3	11/19-11/26	2	(twice) last-3/18-3/22	4	(twice) last-3/11-3/22
1953-54	3	(3 times) last-2/17-2/28	5	(twice) last-2/10-2/28	5	(twice) last-12/27-12/29	4	12/2-12/13
1954-55	3	10/20-10/27	3	12/12-1/2	2	2/20-3/6	8	12/1-12/26
1955-56	4	2/26-3/11	7	11/9-12/7	2	2/19-2/22	2	(5 times) last-3/15-3/18
1956-57	5	2/6-2/24	8	(twice) last-2/6-3/10	5	1/6-2/2	7	10/28-11/25
1957-58	4	(twice) last-2/16-2/26	5	2/16-3/2	5	11/24-12/8	7	12/25-1/29
1958-59	3	(twice) last-12/21-12/31	4	(twice) last-2/22-3/8	3	3/11-3/22	4	(twice) last-3/11-3/22
1959-60	3	12/6-12/20	5	11/25-12/20	3	(twice) last-12/23-12/29	6	1/6-2/6

YEAR-BY-YEAR

YEAR	WINNING STREAK		UNBEATEN STREAK		LOSING STREAK		WINLESS STREAK	
1960-61	2	(4 times) last-3/1-3/5	5	2/1-2/22	3	(twice) last-12/28-1/4	5	11/27-12/21
1961-62	3	2/10-2/21	9	10/25-12/3	3	12/27-1/28	3	12/27-1/28
1962-63	2	(twice) last-3/20-3/24	4	2/6-2/20	3	(twice) last-1/27-2/3	5	(twice) last-1/6-2/3
1963-64	4	1/4-1/26	6	1/4-2/2	3	3/11-3/22	4	3/8-3/22
1964-65	3	10/28-11/11	3	10/28-11/11	4	12/16-12/29	9	11/29-1/3
1965-66	2	(3 times) last-3/9-3/13	6	2/23-3/13	3	3/16-3/27	6	11/27-12/12
1966-67	4	12/7-12/21	5	10/23-11/16	3	2/26-3/8	5	2/26-3/15
1967-68	4	2/25-3/6	7	12/27-1/28	2	3/10-3/13	3	12/23-12/30
1968-69	7	1/5-2/8	18	1/5-3/30	2	12/15-12/18	4	12/8-12/18
1969-70	8	12/31-2/15	12	12/28-2/25	3	3/15-3/25	6	3/1-3/25
1970-71	9	2/10-3/14	24	10/14-1/31	1	(twice) last-3/21	3	1/27-2/3
1971-72	9	11/10-12/15	18	10/17-12/29	1	(6 times) last-4-2	3	(twice) last-3/26-4/4
1972-73	6	(twice) last-10/25-11/15	10	(twice) last-1/7-2/28	2	3/25-3/28	3	3/25-4/1
1973-74	7	2/6-3/10	11	(twice) last-1/6-3/10	2	(twice) last-3/14-3/20	2	(3 times) last-3/27-3/31
1974-75	6	12/27-1/26	7	12/27-2/2	3	3/2-3/9	3	(twice) last-3/2-3/9
1975-76	3	3/28-4/4	4	2/29-3/17	3	2/4-2/13	5	(twice) last-2/22-3/7
1976-77	3	11/17-12/1	8	11/17-12/22	7	10/20-11/14	7	10/20-11/14
1977-78	2	(4 times) last-3/27-3/29	3	(5 times) last-3/8-3/15	4	1/9-2/1	6	12/28-2/1
1978-79	3	10/22-10/29	7	1/17-3/3	3	3/14-3/25	3	3/14-3/27
1979-80	8	2/20-3/16	8	2/20-3/16	2	11/21-11/25	5	11/21-12/5
1980-81	3	(twice) 2/18-2/25	6	2/18-3/8	3	(twice) last-12/22-12/31	4	3/1-3/11
1981-82	4	(twice) last-1/7-1/20	7	1/7-2/18	3	10/21-10/28	5	11/22-12/9
1982-83	7	11/17-12/15	7	11/17-12/15	4	1/16-1/30	5	1/12-1/30
1983-84	7	12/21-1/18	7	12/21-1/18	3	10/26-10/30	3	(twice) last-11/23-11/30
1984-85	4	1/24-2/17	5	1/16-2/17	3	2/21-2/28	6	11/25-12/7
1985-86	5	2/12-2/27	5	2/12-2/27	3	(twice) last-3/2-3/12	3	(4 times) last-3/2-3/12
1986-87	2	(5 times) last-2/15-2/17	3	(3 times) last-12/23-1/5	2	(5 times) last-4/1-4/5	3	(twice) last-1/5-1/9
1987-88	5	2/25-3/15	6	11/15-12/16	3	10/28-11/10	4	10/26-11/10
1988-89	6	10/16-11/9	7	10/16-11/11	2	(6 times) last-3/26-4/2	3	11/11-11/21
1989-90	5	2/19-3/5	7	10/11-10/27	3	12/10-12/17	6	12/10-12/31
1990-91	8	10/8-10/31	8	10/8-10/31	2	(4 times) last-3/13-3/17	3	(2 times) last-1/15-2/3
1991-92	5	12/2-12/23	11	1/14-3/1	3	3/4-3/9	3	(twice) last-3/4-3/9
1992-93	4	10/12-10/21	7	12/27-2/3	7	3/24-4/14	2	3/24-4/14
1993-94	4	(3 times) last-4/1-4/12	16	10/24-1/5	2	1/5-1/10	2	(3 times) last 3/4-3/7

219

RANGERS LONGEST ROAD STREAKS

YEAR	WINNING STREAK	UNBEATEN STREAK	LOSING STREAK	WINLESS STREAK
1926-27	4 1/27-2/12	6 1/27-2/27	3 12/15-12/26	3 12/15-12/26
1927-28	3 11/15-11/29	4 11/15-12/1	3 12/27-1/14	4 2/26-3/10
1928-29	2 (twice) last-1/24-2/3	6 12/6-1/10	3 2/7-2/23	4 (twice) last-2/7-2/28
1929-30	2 11/23-11/28	3 3/1-3/4	3 (twice) last-1/2-1/12	7 1/26-3/8
1930-31	2 2/5-2/10	5 (twice) last-1/31-2/15	2 12/4-12/6	3 (3 times) last-1/13-1/31
1931-32	4 11/12-11/29	10 11/12-1/3	2 3/6-3/22	4 3/6-3/22
1932-33	2 (4 times) last-2/26-3/12	3 (twice) last-1/24-2/2	4 (3 times) last-3/16-3/21	4 12/13-1/10
1933-34	4 12/2-12/24	4 12/2-12/24	4 11/11-11/25	4 11/11-11/25
1934-35	7 1/12-2/12	7 1/12-2/12	4 11/10-12/4	4 11/10-12/4
1935-36	2 3/15-3/22	3 (twice) last-3/10-3/22	3 1/18-1/26	4 (twice) last-2/25-3/10
1936-37	2 (twice) last-12/6-12/12	2 (3 times) last-1/26-2/4	3 2/11-3/4	3 2/11-3/4
1937-38	4 12/11-12/23	4 12/11-12/23	2 11/27-12/2	3 3/6-3/20
1938-39	3 (twice) last-2/2-2/12	3 (3 times) last-2/2-2/12	1 (8 times) last-3/18	4 1/5-1/19
1939-40	3 1/2-1/18	11 11/11-1/13	3 2/11-2/22	6 2/1-2/22
1940-41	3 2/18-3/1	3 2/18-3/1	3 12/13-12/28	5 12/13-1/4
1941-42	3 (3 times) last-1/20-2/3	3 (3 times) last-1/20-2/3	3 12/13-12/23	3 (twice) last-3/3-3/7
1942-43	3 12/25-12/29	3 12/19-12/29	6 1/24-2/7	11 1/1-2/27
1943-44	1 (twice) last-1/22	1 (3 times) last-3/12	10 10/30-12/23	11 1/23-3/18
1944-45	1 (4 times) last-1/24	1 (7 times) last-2/24	3 (4 times) last-3/7-3/10	9 1/27-3/10
1945-56	1 (5 times) last-3/13	3 2/16-2/27	7 1/12-2/27	12 11/28-2/7
1946-47	2 (4 times) last-1/22-1/25	4 (4 times) last-1/22-1/25	5 10/26-11/21	5 10/26-11/21
1947-48	3 11/19-11/30	6 11/19-12/13	5 10/19-11/9	8 2/4-3/13
1948-49	2 12/23-12/25	3 12/18-12/25	8 2/9-3/16	7 2/9-3/16
1949-50	3 2/9-2/23	4 2/5-2/23	4 1/14-1/25	8 1/14-2/5
1950-51	1 (6 times) last-3/1	2 2/4-2/15	3 3/10-3/17	10 10/19-11/25
1951-52	2 2/7-2/9	4 1/17-1/26	6 12/1-12/29	10 11/4-12/29
1952-53	1 (6 times) last-3/7	3 12/20-1/8	6 10/30-11/27	16 10/9-12/20
1953-54	2 (4 times) last-3/13-3/20	3 1/28-2/4	8 11/15-12/26	9 11/8-12/26
1954-55	1 (7 times) last-3/12	3 1/23-1/29	7 11/27-1/8	11 11/20-1/8
1955-56	2 (5 times) last-1/28-1/29	3 (twice) last-1/14-1/17	7 2/4-3/3	7 2/4-3/3
1956-57	2 (twice) last-1/26-1/27	3 (twice) last-3/2-3/9	5 10/14-11/8	6 10/14-11/18
1957-58	3 (twice) last-3/12-3/22	9 2/8-3/22	3 1/25-2/2	4 12/7-12/19
1958-59	3 1/26-2/5	3 (twice) last-1/26-2/5	3 (twice) last-2/8-2/18	7 10/8-11/4
1959-60	1 (7 times) last-3/12	2 (twice) last-3/10-3/12	5 1/14-1/23	7 (twice) last-1/14-1/30

YEAR-BY-YEAR

YEAR	WINNING STREAK	UNBEATEN STREAK	LOSING STREAK	WINLESS STREAK
1960-61	2 12/4-12/10	4 1/12-1/18	10 2/8-3/15	10 2/8-3/15
1961-62	2 12/25-1/1	2 (4 times) last-12/25-1/1	7 1/3-1/27	7 1/3-1/27
1962-63	2 2/26-2/28	2 (4 times) last-2/26-2/28	4 2/10-2/23	6 12/22-1/13
1963-64	2 1/1-1/9	2 (twice) last-1/25-1/30	7 10/26-11/28	13 10/26-12/25
1964-65	2 (twice) last-2/27-3/4	3 (3 times) last-1/16-1/23	7 1/24-2/24	8 1/23-2/24
1965-66	2 10/30-11/6	3 10/30-11/11	9 1/19-2/13	11 11/20-1/15
1966-67	2 (3 times) last-2/19-2/25	6 11/12-12/17	3 1/21-1/28	7 3/1-4/1
1967-68	4 2/15-2/29	8 2/3-3/9	4 (twice) last-12/7-12/16	4 (twice) last-12/7-12/16
1968-69	3 (twice) last-3/6-3/19	5 3/5-3/19	6 2/1-3/1	7 (twice) last-2/1-3/5
1969-70	3 11/7-11/15	5 11/7-11/22	3 3/6-3/14	8 2/13-3/14
1970-71	4 1/2-1/12	4 (3 times) last-2/20-3/10	3 2/9-2/17	4 1/15-1/30
1971-72	3 (4 times) last-2/22-3/11	8 10/9-11/6	2 11/20-11/27	3 3/23-4/1
1972-73	5 1/19-2/10	10 12/20-2/10	3 10/7-10/14	4 11/23-12/1
1973-74	4 2/16-3/2	5 2/14-3/2	4 12/23-1/10	7 10/20-11/15
1974-75	4 12/30-1/11	4 12/30-1/11	5 3/11-3/29	6 3/11-4/3
1975-76	3 12/5-12/13	4 12/4-12/13	4 (4 times) last-3/16-3/25	4 (4 times) last-3/16-3/25
1976-77	1 (12 times) last-3/19	5 11/22-12/4	4 (twice) last-2/26-3/12	5 (twice) last-1/19-2/3
1977-78	3 3/22-3/25	3 3/19-3/25	4 4/1-4/8	7 1/20-2/22
1978-79	7 10/28-11/29	7 10/28-11/29	3 (3 times) last-3/28-4/6	3 (3 times) last-3/28-4/6
1979-80	4 12/1-12/12	4 12/1-12/12	5 10/20-11/3	5 10/20-11/3
1980-81	4 (twice) last-1/23-1/31	4 (twice) last-1/23-1/31	7 2/5-3/10	10 10/18-11/22
1981-82	4 (twice) last-3/11-3/26	8 12/2-1/15	3 10/9-10/17	3 (4 times) last-2/4-2/10
1982-83	2 (3 times) last-3/29-3/31	3 1/29-2/5	4 10/16-11/5	6 (twice) last-11/28-12/26
1983-84	4 (4 times) last-3/9-3/10	5 2/4-2/11	3 2/29-3/7	8 2/9-3/7
1984-85	3 10/20-10/27	3 10/20-10/27	7 1/19-2/7	9 1/19-2/10
1985-86	4 1/14-1/22	5 1/14-1/27	4 10/12-11/2	4 10/12-11/2
1986-87	2 (4 times) last-3/12-3/14	3 10/15-10/25	3 11/9-11/19	4 (4 times) last-1/19-1/23
1987-88	3 1/22-1/30	3 1/22-2/2	6 10/31-11/19	6 10/31-11/19
1988-89	4 1/18-1/23	8 12/23-1/23	7 3/3-4/1	7 3/3-4/1
1989-90	2 (4 times) last-2/13-2/16	4 2/13-2/23	6 12/16-1/6	8 12/2-1/6
1990-91	3 2/28-1/5	6 11/9-11/24	6 1/30-2/28	6 1/30-2/28
1991-92	2 (twice) last-1/23-2/1	5 1/22-2/1	7 2/7-2/20	6 2/7-2/20
1992-93	3 3/11-4/4	4 12/11-12/21	3 12/26-1/16	7 12/26-1/19
1993-94	6 10/30-11/24	6 10/30-11/24	2 (4 times) last-3/12-3/14	4 3/10-3/22

221

ALL-TIME RANGERS AND OPPONENTS PENALTY SHOTS

PLAYER AND TEAM	DATE	SCORE	GOALTENDER	RESULT
Ebbie Goodfellow, Detroit	11/15/34	NYR 2 at Detroit 8	Percy Jackson	NO
Bun Cook, RANGERS	11/18/34	St. Louis 0 at NYR 5	Bill Beveridge	NO
Armand Mondou, Montreal	12/4/34	NYR 3 at Canadiens 5	Andy Aitkenhead	YES
Bun Cook, RANGERS	12/8/34	NYR 5 at Toronto 2	George Hainsworth	NO
Charlie Conacher, Toronto	12/11/34	Toronto 8 at NYR 4	Andy Aitkenhead	NO
Bert Connolly, RANGERS	1/24/35	Chicago 3 at NYR 3	Lorne Chabot	NO
Bert Connolly, RANGERS	1/31/35	NYR 3 at Toronto 2	George Hainsworth	NO
Bert Connolly, RANGERS	1/16/36	Toronto 0 at NYR 1	George Hainsworth	YES
Hap Emms, NY Americans	12/16/37	Americans 0 at NYR 2	Davey Kerr	NO
Neil Colville, RANGERS	12/16/37	Americans 0 at NYR 2	Earl Robertson	NO
Alex Shibicky, RANGERS	2/1/37	Chicago 1 at NYR 6	Mike Karakas	YES
Paul Thompson, Chicago	2/1/37	Chicago 1 at NYR 6	Davey Kerr	NO
Alex Shibicky, RANGERS	12/8/38	NYR 6 at Candiens 5	Claude Bourque	NO
Mac Colville, RANGERS	12/27/41	NYR 4 at Montreal 3	Paul Bibeault	YES
Sid Abel, Detroit	2/26/42	Detroit 4 at NYR 7	Jim Henry	YES
Bob Goldham, Toronto	3/7/42	NYR 2 at Toronto 4	Jim Henry	YES
Bud Poile, Toronto	11/19/42	Toronto 7 at NYR 3	Steve Buzinski	YES
Ray Getliffe, Montreal	2/20/43	NYR 1 at Canadiens 6	Bill Beveridge	NO
Ab DeMarco, Sr., RANGERS	2/19/44	NYR 2 at Canadiens 5	Bill Durnan	NO
Chuck Scherza, RANGERS	11/30/44	NYR 7 at Montreal 5	Bill Durnan	YES
Fred Thurier, RANGERS	1/18/45	NYR 3 at Detroit 7	Harry Lumley	YES
Alex Shibicky, RANGERS	11/25/45	NYR 4 at Detroit 1	Harry Lumley	YES
Ted Sloan, Toronto	2/17/51	NYR 0 at Toronto 2	Chuck Rayner	NO
Bernie Geoffrion, Montreal	10/16/52	NYR 1 at Montreal 3	Gump Worsley	YES
Gordie Howe, Detroit	3/5/53	NYR 1 at Detroit 7	Gump Worsley	YES
Danny Lewicki, RANGERS	10/24/56	Montreal 2 at NYR 3	Gerry McNeil	YES
Andy Bathgate, RANGERS	3/14/62	Detroit 2 at NYR 3	Hank Bassen	YES
Andy Hebenton, RANGERS	3/21/63	NYR 2 at Boston 2	Eddie Johnston	NO
Don Marshall, RANGERS	11/3/63	Montreal 5 at NYR 3	Charlie Hodge	NO
Rod Gilbert, RANGERS	11/27/63	Detroit 2 at NYR 3	Terry Sawchuk	YES
Bob Nevin, RANGERS	11/5/66	NYR 1 at Toronto 3	Terry Sawchuk	YES
Dallas Smith, Boston	12/21/66	Boston 1 at NYR 5	Ed Giacomin	NO
John Bucyk, Boston	2/4/67	NYR 4 at Boston 3	Ed Giacomin	YES
Ed Joyal, Los Angeles	10/31/67	NYR 6 at Los Angeles 1	Ed Giacomin	NO
Norm Ferguson, Oakland	11/24/68	Oakland 2 at NYR 3	Ed Giacomin	YES
Charlie Burns, Pittsburgh	2/5/69	NYR 2 at Pittsburgh 3	Ed Giacomin	NO
Keith McCreary, Pittsburgh	3/18/70	NYR 2 at Pittsburgh 4	Ed Giacomin	NO
Butch Goring, Los Angeles	2/13/72	Los Angeles 2 at NYR 4	Gilles Villemure	YES
Stan Mikita, Chicago	3/15/72	NYR 1 at Chicago 3	Ed Giacomin	NO
Ron Schock, Pittsburgh	3/10/73	NYR 5 at Pittsburgh 4	Ed Giacomin	NO
Jacques Lemaire, Montreal	3/31/73	NYR 1 at Montreal 5	Ed Giacomin	YES
Paul Henderson, Toronto	10/20/73	NYR 2 at Toronto 3	Gilles Villemure	NO
Yvan Cournoyer, Montreal	12/29/73	NYR 1 at Montreal 7	Ed Giacomin	NO
Greg Polis, RANGERS	2/1/76	Minnesota 2 at NYR 3	Cesare Maniago	NO
Don Murdoch, RANGERS	11/3/76	NYR 6 at Vancouver 2	Curt Ridley	YES
Bill Goldsworthy, RANGERS	11/14/76	Pittsburgh 5 at NYR 1	Dunc Wilson	NO
Don Murdoch, RANGERS	1/9/77	Los Angeles 5 at NYR 4	Rogie Vachon	NO
Don Murdoch, RANGERS	1/28/78	NYR 2 at Islanders 6	Glenn Resch	NO
Claude Larose, RANGERS	1/7/80	Hartford 2 at NYR 5	Al Smith	NO
Rolf Edberg, Washington	2/2/80	NYR 6 at Washington 3	Doug Soetaert	YES
Ron Greschner, RANGERS	10/28/80	NYR 4 at St. Louis 5	Mike Liut	YES
Mike Gartner, Washington	12/10/80	Washington 2 at NYR 6	Wayne Thomas	YES
Bobby MacMillan, Calgary	1/13/81	NYR 4 at Calgary 4	Doug Soetaert	NO
Mike Rogers, Hartford	2/22/81	NYR 5 at Hartford 5	Doug Soetaert	NO
Mike Rogers, RANGERS	12/5/81	NYR 2 at Colorado 1	Glenn Resch	NO
Pierre Larouche, RANGERS	2/16/86	Detroit 1 at NYR 3	Corrado Micalef	NO
Mike Ridley, RANGERS	2/16/86	Detroit 1 at NYR 3	Corrado Micalef	NO
Peter Sundstrom, RANGERS	3/2/86	Washington 4 at NYR 2	Al Jensen	YES
Petr Klima, Detroit	2/17/87	Detroit 2 at NYR 6	John Vanbiesbrouck	NO
Jan Erixon, RANGERS	10/24/87	NYR 5 at Philadelphia 3	Mark Laforest	YES
Pat Verbeek, New Jersey	3/27/88	NYR 2 at New Jersey 7	John Vanbiesbrouck	YES
Ray Bourque, Boston	11/11/88	Boston 4 at NYR 4	John Vanbiesbrouck	NO
Guy Lafleur, RANGERS	11/29/88	NYR 4 at Winnipeg 3	Eldon Reddick	NO
Kevin Dineen, Hartford	10/19/89	Hartford 3 at NYR 7	Mike Richter	NO
Lindy Ruff, RANGERS	11/26/89	Quebec 1 at NYR 3	Mario Brunetta	YES
Pelle Eklund, Philadelphia	1/14/90	Philadelphia 3 at NYR 4	Mike Richter	NO
Kelly Kisio, RANGERS	2/26/90	Boston 1 at NYR 6	Rejean Lemelin	NO
Keith Acton, Philadelphia	3/25/90	Philadelphia 3 at NYR 7	John Vanbiesbrouck	YES
Troy Murray, Winnipeg	11/27/91	NYR 2 at Winnipeg 3	Mike Richter	NO
Darren Turcotte, RANGERS	12/29/91	Pittsburgh 6 at NYR 3	Wendell Young	NO
Paul Broten, RANGERS	1/16/92	Calgary 4 at NYR 6	Mike Vernon	YES
Pavel Bure, Vancouver	2/17/92	Vancouver 3 at NYR 3	John Vanbiesbrouck	NO
Alexei Kovalev, RANGERS	10/5/93	Boston 4 at NYR 3	Jon Casey	NO
Steve Larmer, RANGERS	1/16/94	NYR 5 at Chicago 1	Ed Belfour	YES
Tony Amonte, RANGERS	1/27/94	NYR 5 at Los Angeles 4	Kelly Hrudey	NO

THE LAST TIME

RANGERS SHUTOUT OPPOSITION AT HOME: 4/1/94 Rangers 4, Dallas 0. Goaltender: Mike Richter.
RANGERS SHUTOUT OPPOSITION ON ROAD: 2/3/94 Rangers 3, Boston 0. Goaltender: Glenn Healy.
OPPOSITION SHUTOUT RANGERS AT HOME: 4/14/93, Rangers 0, Washington 2.
  Goaltender: Rick Tabaracci.
OPPOSITION SHUTOUT RANGERS ON ROAD: 4/12/93, Rangers 0, Philadelphia 1.
  Goaltender: Dominic Roussel.
RANGERS PLAYED A 0-0 GAME: 12/9/89 vs. Islanders at Nassau Coliseum.
  Goaltenders: John Vanbiesbrouck and Mark Fitzpatrick.
RANGERS WON A 1-0 GAME AT HOME: 3/14/71, Rangers 1, Toronto 0. Goaltender: Eddie Giacomin.
RANGERS LOST A 1-0 GAME AT HOME: 3/25/79, Rangers 0, Montreal 1. Goaltender: Michel Larocque.
RANGERS WON A 1-0 GAME ON ROAD: 12/23/93 Rangers 1, Washington 0. Goaltender Glenn Healy.
RANGERS LOST A 1-0 GAME ON ROAD: 4/12/93, Rangers 0, Philadelphia 1. Goaltender: Dominic Roussel.
RANGERS HAD TWO CONSECUTIVE SHUTOUTS: 1977 November 30 at St. Louis, Rangers 4, St. Louis 0.
  Goaltender: Wayne Thomas.
  December 3 at Minnesota, Rangers 4, Minnesota 0. Goaltender: John Davidson.
OPPOSITION HAD TWO CONSECUTIVE SHUTOUTS: 1993, April 12 at Piladelphia, Philadelphia 1 Rangers 0.
  Goaltender: Dominic Roussel.
  April 14 at Madison Square Garden, Washington 2, Rangers 0. Goaltender: Rick Tabaracci.
RANGERS HELD OPPOSITION SHOTLESS FOR ONE PERIOD: 2/25/79 Second period vs.
  New York Islanders at Madison Square Garden. Rangers won 3-2.
RANGERS DID NOT HAVE A PENALTY IN A GAME: 1/7/89 vs. Islanders at Nassau Coliseum.
  Rangers won 5-1. Referee Bob Myers.
RANGERS AND OPPONENT DID NOT HAVE A PENALTY IN A GAME: 3/13/76 vs. Vancouver Canucks
  at Vancouver. Rangers won 7-3. Referee Lloyd Gilmour.
RANGERS SCORED AT LEAST 10 GOALS IN A GAME: 12/13/92 vs. Montreal Canadiens at
  Madison Square Garden. Rangers won 10-3.
OPPOSITION SCORED AT LEAST 10 GOALS IN A GAME: 4/10/93 vs. Pittsburgh Penguins at
  Madison Square Garden. Penguins won 10-4.
RANGERS SCORED AT LEAST FIVE GOALS IN ONE PERIOD: 4/8/94 vs.Toronto Maple Leafs at MSG.
  Rangers scored five goals in the second period and won 5-3.
OPPOSITION SCORED AT LEAST FIVE GOALS IN ONE PERIOD: 4/9/93 vs. Pittsburghs Penguins at
  Madison Square Garden. Penguins scored five goals in the third period and won 10-4.
RANGERS HAD AT LEAST 50 SHOTS IN A GAME: 54, 4/14/94 vs. Philadelphia Flyers at
  Madison Square Garden. Rangers and Flyers tied 2-2.
OPPOSITION HAD AT LEAST 50 SHOTS IN A GAME: 51, 1/13/93 vs. Wahington Capitals at
  Madison Sqaure Garden. Rangers won 5-4.
RANGERS HAD AT LEAST 50 SHOTS IN CONSECUTIVE GAMES: 54, January 3, 1994 vs. Florida at MSG.
  53, January 5, 1994 vs. Calgary at MSG.
RANGERS HAD AT LEAST 25 SHOTS IN A PERIOD: 26, 11/12/89 vs. Islanders at Madison Square Garden.
  Rangers had 26 shots in second and won 4-2.
OPPOSITION HAD AT LEAST 25 SHOTS IN A PERIOD: 28, 1/31/91 vs. Vancouver Canucks at Vancouver.
  Canucks had 28 shots in third and game ended in 3-3 tie.
FOUR-GOAL GAME BY A RANGER AT GARDEN: 3/22/92 Mark Messier scored four goals vs.
  Chad Erickson of New Jersey Devils. Rangers won 6-3.
FOUR-GOAL GAME BY A RANGER ON THE ROAD: 11/21/86 Tony McKegney scored one goal vs.
  Richard Brodeur and three vs. Wendell Young of Vancouver Canucks. Rangers won 8-5.
OPPONENT HAD FOUR-GOAL GAME AT GARDEN: 1/8/90 Mario Lemieux of Pittsburgh Penguins scored
  two goals vs. Bob Froese and two vs. John Vanbiesbrouck. Pittsburgh Penguins won 7-5.
OPPONENT HAD FOUR-GOAL GAME ON THE ROAD: 11/21/86 Petri Skriko of Vancouver Canucks scored
  four goals vs. John Vanbiesbrouck. Rangers won 8-5.
FIVE-GOAL GAME BY A RANGER AT GARDEN: 2/23/83 Mark Pavelich scored five goals vs. Greg Millen of
  Hartford Whalers. Rangers won 11-3.
FIVE-GOAL GAME BY A RANGER ON THE ROAD: 10/12/76 Don Murdoch scored five goals against
  Gary Smith of Minnesota North Stars. Rangers won 10-4.
OPPONENT HAD FIVE-GOAL GAME AT GARDEN: 4/9/93 Mario Lemieux of Pittsburgh Penguins scored
  three goals vs. Corey Hirsch and two vs. Mike Richter. Pittsburgh won 10-4.
OPPONENT HAD FIVE-GOAL GAME ON THE ROAD: 12/23/78 Bryan Trottier of Islanders scored four goals
  vs. Wayne Thomas and one vs. John Davidson. Islanders won 9-4.
RANGERS GOALTENDER ASSISTED ON A GOAL: 10/15/93 Glenn Healy assisted on a goal by Mike Gartner
  at 7:21 of the first period against the Buffalo Sabres in Buffalo.. New York won 5-2.
RANGERS HAD TWO PENALTY SHOTS IN ONE GAME: 2/16/86 Pierre Larouche and Mike Rogers vs.
  Detroit at Madison Square Garden, against Corrado Micalef. Both missed, Rangers won 3-1.
RANGERS AND OPPONENT HAD A PENALTY SHOT IN ONE GAME: 2/1/37 Chicago vs. Rangers at
  Madison Square Garden. Alex Shibicky scored against Mike Karakulas and Paul Thompson missed against
  Davey Kerr. Rangers won 6-1.
RANGERS HAD TWO HAT TRICKS IN ONE GAME: Ron Duguay and Phil Esposito on March 24, 1978 at
  Washington. Rangers won 11-4.
RANGERS HAD HAT TRICKS IN CONSECUTIVE GAMES: Mike Gartner vs. Pittsburgh, at MSG on January
  31, 1994 and Adam Graves vs. Islanders, at MSG on February 2, 1994.

RANGERS REGULAR SEASON RECORDS

TEAM RECORDS

MOST VICTORIES, ONE SEASON: 52 1993-94. Home: 30, 1970-71 (39 games). Road: 24 1993-94.
FEWEST VICTORIES, ONE SEASON: 6 1943-44 (50-game schedule). Home: **4**, 1943-44 (25 games). Road: **2**, 1943-44 (25 games).
FEWEST VICTORIES, ONE SEASON (Minimum 70-game schedule): 17 1952-53, 1954-55, 1959-60. Home: **8**, 1964-65 (35 games). Road: **6**, 1950-51, 1952-53, 1965-66 (35 games).
FEWEST LOSSES, ONE SEASON: 11 1939-40 (48 games schedule). Home: **2**, 1970-71 (39 games). Road: **7**, 1928-29 (22 games), 1930-31 (22 games), 1939-40 (24 games).
FEWEST LOSSES, ONE SEASON (Minimum 70-game schedule): 17 1971-72. Home: **2**, 1970-71 (39 games). Road: **10**, 1957-58 (35 games).
MOST LOSSES, ONE SEASON: 44 1984-85 (80-game schedule). **39** 1943-44 (50-game schedule). Home: **17**, 1943-44 (25 games). **19**, 1964-65 (35 games). Road: **26**, 1975-76 (40 games), **26** 1984-85 (40 games).
MOST TIES, ONE SEASON: (Minimum 70-game schedule): 21 1950-51 (70-game schedule). Home: **13**, 1954-55 (35 games). Road: **11**, 1950-51 (35 games).
FEWEST TIES, ONE SEASON: (Minimum 70-game schedule): 5 1991-92 (80-game schedule). Home: **1**, 1983-84 (40 games). Road: **1**, 1991-92 & 1975-76 (40 games).
MOST POINTS, ONE SEASON: 112 1993-94. Home: 67, 1970-71 (39 games). Road: 50, (twice) 1971-72, 1993-94.
FEWEST POINTS, ONE SEASON: 17 1943-44 (50-game schedule). Home: **12**, 1943-44 (25 games). Road: **5**, 1943-44 (25 games).
FEWEST POINTS, ONE SEASON (Minimum 70-game schedule): 47 1965-66. Home: **24**, 1964-65 (35 games). Road: **16**, 1965-66 (35 games).
MOST GOALS ONE SEASON: 321 1991-92. Home: **186**, 1982-83 (40 games). Road: **155**, 1978-79, 1986-87 (40 games).
FEWEST GOALS , ONE SEASON: 72 1928-29 (44-game schedule). Home: **32**, 1928-29 (22 games). Road: **40**, 1928-29 (22 games).
FEWEST GOALS, ONE SEASON (Minimum 70-game schedule): 150 1954-55. Home: **86**, 1954-55 (35 games). Road: **63**, 1952-53 (35 games).
MOST ASSISTS, ONE SEASON: 540 1988-89.
FEWEST ASSISTS, ONE SEASON: 45 1926-27 (44-game schedule).
FEWEST GOALS AGAINST, ONE SEASON: 65 1928-29 (44-game schedule). Home: **21**, 1928-29 (22 games). Road: **41**, 1926-27 (22 games).
FEWEST GOALS AGAINST ONE SEASON (Minimum 70-game schedule): 177 1970-71. Home: **71**, 1970-71 (39 games). Road: **95**, 1957-58 (35 games).
MOST GOALS AGAINST, ONE SEASON: 345 1984-85 (80-game schedule). Home: **156**, 1986-87 (40 games). Road: **197**, 1975-76 (40 games).
MOST POWER PLAY GOALS, ONE SEASON: 111 1987-88.
MOST POWER PLAY GOALS, ONE GAME: 6 10/13/93 vs. Quebec at Madison Square Garden.
MOST POWER PLAY GOALS ALLOWED, ONE SEASON: 85 1988-89.
MOST SHORTHANDED GOALS, ONE SEASON: 20 1993-94.
MOST SHORTHANDED GOALS, ONE GAME: 3 10/5/83 vs. New Jersey at Madison Square Garden.
MOST SHORTHANDED GOALS ALLOWED, ONE SEASON: 18, 1992-93.
MOST 20-GOAL SCORERS, ONE SEASON: 9 1993-94.
MOST 30-GOAL SCORERS, ONE SEASON: 5 1991-92.
MOST 40-GOAL SCORERS, ONE SEASON: 3 1971-72.
MOST HAT TRICKS, ONE SEASON: 10 1986-87.
MOST PLAYERS USED, ONE SEASON: 46 1986-87.
MOST ROOKIES USED, ONE SEASON: 14 1988-89.
MOST ROOKIES USED, ONE GAME: 9 3/21/90, vs. Toronto and 3/27/90 vs. Quebec.
MOST SCORING POINTS (Goal and Assists), ONE SEASON: 854 1978-79.
FEWEST SCORING POINTS, ONE SEASON: 140 1926-27 (44-game schedule).
MOST PENALTY MINUTES, ONE SEASON: 2018 1989-90.
FEWEST PENALTY MINUTES, ONE SEASON: 253 1943-44 (50-game schedule).
MOST SHUTOUTS, ONE SEASON: 13 1928-29 (44-game schedule). Home: **8**, 1928-29 (22 games). Road: **7**, 1926-27 (22 games).
MOST TIMES SHUT OUT, ONE SEASON: 10 1928-29 (44-game schedule). Home: **5**, 1930-31 (22 games); 1938-39 (24 games). Road: **7**, 1952-53 (35 games).

RANGERS REGULAR SEASON RECORDS

(Team Records, cont.)

LONGEST WINNING STREAK: 10 1939-40. Began 12/19 with 5-2 victory over Montreal. Ended 1/14 when defeated by Chicago, 2-1. (Rangers then won next five games for overall record of 15 wins in 16 games). **10** 1972-73. Began 1/19 with 6-0 victory over California. Ended 2/11 with 2-2 tie against Montreal.

LONGEST WINNING STREAK AT START OF SEASON: 5 1983-84. Began 10/5 with 6-2 victory over New Jersey. Ended 10/15 when defeated by St. Louis, 6-5. (Rangers then won next four games for overall record of 9-1-0 in first 10 games of season.)

LONGEST HOME WINNING STREAK AT START OF SEASON: 8 1990-91. Began 10/8 with 6-3 victory over Minnesota. Ended 11/2 when defeated by Islanders, 3-2.

LONGEST LOSING STREAK AT START OF SEASON: 11 1943-44. Began October 30 with 5-2 loss to Toronto. Ended November 28 with a 2-2 tie with Montreal. (Rangers then lost next three games for overall record of 0-14-1 in first 15 games before defeating Boston 6-4 on December 12.)

LONGEST HOME WINNING STREAK: 14 1939-40. Began 12/19 with 5-2 victory over Montreal. Ended 2/29 when defeated by Chicago, 2-1.

LONGEST HOME LOSING STREAK AT START OF SEASON: 4 1940-41. Began 11/15 with 2-1 defeat to Boston. Ended with a 5-4 overtime victory over Chicago.

LONGEST ROAD WINNING STREAK: 7 1934-35. Began 1/12 with a 3-1 victory over Americans. Ended 2/16 when defeated by Toronto, 5-1. **7** 1978-79. Began 10/28 with a 2-1 victory over Montreal. Ended 12/2 when defeated by Toronto, 5-2.

LONGEST UNDEFEATED STREAK: 19 1939-40. Won 14 games and tied five. Began 11/23 with 1-1 tie against Montreal. Ended 1/14 when defeated by Chicago, 2-1. (Rangers then won next five games for overall record of 24 victories or ties in 25 games).

LONGEST HOME UNDEFEATED STREAK: 26 Won 19 games and tied seven. Began 3/29/70, with a 4-1 victory over Montreal. Ended 2/3/71, when defeated by Chicago, 4-2. The streak covered the final two games of the 1969-70 season and the first 24 games of the 1970-71 season.

LONGEST ROAD UNDEFEATED STREAK: 11 1939-40. Won six games and tied five. Began 11/5 with 1-1 tie against Detroit. Ended 1/14 when defeated by Chicago, 2-1.

MOST CONSECUTIVE TIE GAMES: 4 1929-30. Tied by Chicago, 1-1, on 2/27; by Toronto, 3-3, on 3/1; by Detroit, 2-2, on 3/2; by Chicago, 2-2 on 3/4. (All overtime games).

LONGEST LOSING STREAK: 11 1943-44. Began 10/30 with 5-2 defeat by Toronto. Ended 11/28 with 2-2 tie against Montreal.

LONGEST HOME LOSING STREAK: 7 1976-77. Began 10/20 with 4-2 defeat by Los Angeles. Ended 11/17 with 3-2 victory over Chicago. **7** 1992-93. Began 3/26 with a 3-1 defeat by Chicago. Continued to end of season.

LONGEST ROAD LOSING STREAK: 10 1943-44. Began 10/30 with 5-2 defeat by Toronto. Ended 12/25 with 5-3 victory over Toronto. **10** 1960-61. Began 2/8 with 5-3 defeat by at Toronto. Continued to end of season.

LONGEST WINLESS STREAK, ONE SEASON: 21 1943-44. Lost 17 games and tied four. Began 1/23 with 15-0 defeat by Detroit. Continued to end of season.

LONGEST HOME WINLESS STREAK, ONE SEASON: 10 1943-44. Lost seven games and tied three. Began 1/30 with 5-3 defeat by Montreal. Continued to end of season.

LONGEST ROAD WINLESS STREAK, ONE SEASON: 16 1952-53. Lost 12 games and tied four. Began 10/9 with 5-3 defeat by Detroit. Ended 12/25 with 2-1 victory over Boston.

MOST CONSECUTIVE SHUTOUTS: 4 1927-28. Rangers were not scored upon for a total of 297 minutes and 42 seconds. Defeated PIttsburgh, 3-0; Chicago, 1-0; tied Detroit, 0-0 (10 minutes overtime); defeated Toronto, 1-0. Streak started on 2/23 and ran until 2/28.

MOST CONSECUTIVE TIMES SHUT OUT: 4 1927-28. Rangers failed to score for 341 minutes and 42 seconds. Tied by Ottawa, 0-0 (twice); lost to Chicago, 3-0; Boston, 2-0. Streak ran 2/7-2/19.

LONGEST NON-SHUTOUT STREAK: 236 Began 12/20/89 with a 2-2 tie with Buffalo. Ended 12/15/92 vs. Calgary (Vernon).

MOST GOALS, ONE GAME: 12 Defeated California, 12-1 11/21/71, at Madison Square Garden.

MOST GOALS, ONE GAME, RANGERS AND OPPONENTS: 19 Defeated by Boston, 10-9, at Boston, 3/4/44.

MOST POINTS ONE GAME, RANGERS AND OPPONENTS: 46 Boston Bruins, at Boston, 3/4/44. Boston won, 10-9. Boston had 15 assists, Rangers 12.

MOST GOALS ALLOWED, ONE GAME: 15 Defeated by Detroit, 15-0, at Detroit, 1/23/44.

GREATEST WINNING MARGIN: 11 Defeated California, 12-1, 11/21/71, at Madison Square Garden.

GREATEST LOSING MARGIN: 15 Defeated by Detroit, 15-0 at Detroit, 1/23/44.

HIGHEST TIE SCORE: 7-7 Tied Minnesota on 3/19/78 at Minnesota. **7-7** Tied Quebec on 3/22/81 at Madison Square Garden.

MOST ASSISTS, ONE GAME: 23 11/21/71. Defeated California 12-1, at Madison Square Garden.

MOST POINTS, ONE GAME: 35 11/21/71. 12 goals and 23 assists.

MOST GOALS, ONE PERIOD: 8 11/21/71 (third period).

RANGERS REGULAR SEASON RECORDS

(Team Records, cont.)

MOST POINTS, ONE PERIOD: 23 11/21/71 (third period). Eight goals and 15 assists.
MOST ASSISTS, ONE PERIOD: 15 11/21/71 (third period).
MOST GOALS, ONE PERIOD, RANGERS AND OPPONENTS: 10 3/16/39 (third period). Rangers scored seven goals and Americans three, at Madison Square Garden. Rangers won game, 11-5.
MOST SHOTS, ONE GAME: 65 4/5/70. Defeated Detroit, 9-5, at Madison Square Garden.
LARGEST HOME ATTENDANCE, ONE SEASON: 738,968 1992-93.
FASTEST TWO GOALS BY RANGERS: 4 sec. Kris King at 19:45 and James Patrick at 19:49 of the third period against the Islanders at Madison Square Garden, 10/9/91 Rangers won 5-3.
FASTEST TWO GOALS BY RANGERS AND OPPONENTS: 4 sec. Denis Savard of Chicago at 19:23 of third period and Mark Pavelich of Rangers at 19:27, 2/24/82 at Madison Square Garden, Rangers won, 6-4.
FASTEST THREE GOALS BY RANGERS: 28 sec. Doug Sulliman at 7:52, Eddie Johnstone at 7:57 and Warren Miller at 8:20 of first period against Colorado at Madison Square Garden, 1/14/80. Game ended in a 6-6 tie.
FASTEST THREE GOALS vs. RANGERS: 21 sec. Bill Mosienko of Chicago scored all three goals at 6:09, 6:20 and 6:30 of third period, 2/23/52, at Madison Square Garden. Chicago won, 7-6.
FASTEST THREE GOALS BY RANGERS AND OPPONENTS: 15 sec. Mark Pavelich of Rangers at 19:18 of second period and Ron Greschner at 19:27 and Willi Plett of Minnesota at 19:33, 2/10/83, at Minnesota. Minnesota won game, 7-5.
FASTEST FOUR GOALS BY RANGERS: 1 min. 38 sec. Mark Pavelich at 15:53, Mike Rogers at 16:18, Ron Greschner at 16:51 and Mike Rogers at 17:31 of first period against Edmonton at Madison Square Garden, 2/15/85. Rangers won, 8-7.
FASTEST FOUR GOALS vs. RANGERS: 1 min. 20 sec. Bill Thoms of Boston at 6:34 of second period, Frank Mario at 7:08 and 7:27, and Ken Smith at 7:54, 1/21/45, at Boston. Boston won 14-3.
FASTEST FOUR GOALS BY RANGERS AND OPPONENTS: 1 min. 1 sec. Doug Sulliman of Rangers at 7:52 of first period, Eddie Johnstone at 7:57, Warren Miller at 8:20 and Rob Ramage of Colorado at 8:53, 1/14/80, at Madison Square Garden. Game ended in 6-6 tie.
FASTEST FIVE GOALS BY RANGERS: 3 min. 22 sec. Mark Pavelich at 15:53, Mike Rogers at 16:18, Ron Greschner at 16:51, Mike Rogers at 17:31 and Grant Ledyard at 19:15 of first period against Edmonton at Madison Square Garden, 2/15/85. Rangers won, 8-7.
FASTEST FIVE GOALS vs. RANGERS: 2 min. 55 sec. Bobby Schmautz of Boston at 19:13 of first period, Ken Hodge at 0:18, Phil Esposito at 0:43, Don Marcotte at 0:58 and John Bucyk at 2:08 of second period, 12/19/74, at Boston. Boston won, 11-3.
MOST PENALTY MINUTES, ONE GAME BY RANGERS: 134 Rangers vs. Pittsburgh, 10/30/88 at Madison Square Garden.
MOST PENALTY MINUTES, ONE GAME BY RANGERS AND OPPONENT: 292 Rangers vs. Pittsburgh, 10/30/88 at Madison Square Garden.
MOST PENALTY MINUTES, ONE PERIOD BY RANGERS: 126 Rangers vs. Pittsburgh, 10/30/88 at Madison Square Garden (third period).
MOST PENALTY MINUTES, ONE PERIOD BY RANGERS AND OPPONENT: 272 Rangers vs. Pittsburgh, 10/30/88 at Madison Square Garden (third period).

Doug Sulliman, Eddie Johnstone and Warren Miller combined for the fastest three goals in Rangers history when they scored three goals in 28 seconds on January 14, 1980 in a 6-6 tie vs. Colorado.

RANGERS REGULAR SEASON RECORDS

INDIVIDUAL PLAYER RECORDS

MOST GOALS, ONE SEASON: 52 Adam Graves, 1993-94.
MOST ASSISTS, ONE SEASON: 88 Brian Leetch, 1991-92.
MOST POINTS, ONE SEASON: 109 Jean Ratelle, 1971-72.
MOST GOALS BY A CENTER, ONE SEASON: 48 Pierre Larouche, 1983-84.
MOST ASSISTS BY A CENTER, ONE SEASON: 72 Mark Messier, 1991-92.
MOST POINTS BY A CENTER, ONE SEASON: 109 Jean Ratelle, 1971-72.
MOST GOALS BY A LEFT WING, ONE SEASON: 52 Adam Graves, 1993-94.
MOST ASSISTS BY A LEFT WING, ONE SEASON: 56 Vic Hadfield, 1971-72.
MOST POINTS BY A LEFT WING, ONE SEASON: 106 Vic Hadfield, 1971-72.
MOST GOALS BY A RIGHT WING, ONE SEASON: 49 Mike Gartner, 1990-91.
MOST ASSISTS BY A RIGHT WING, ONE SEASON: 61 Rod Gilbert, 1974-75.
MOST POINTS BY A RIGHT WING, ONE SEASON: 97 Rod Gilbert, 1971-72, 1974-75
MOST POWER PLAY GOALS, ONE SEASON: 23 Vic Hadfield, 1971-72.
MOST SHORTHANDED GOALS, ONE SEASON: 5 Mike Gartner, 1993-94. Don Maloney, 1980-81. Mike Rogers, 1982-83.
HIGHEST SHOOTING PERCENTAGE, ONE SEASON: 29.6 Steve Vickers, 1979-80 (29 goals on 98 shots).
MOST GAME-WINNING GOALS, ONE SEASON: 9 Don Maloney, 1980-81.
MOST POINTS BY A LINE, ONE SEASON*: 302 Vic Hadfield (97)-Jean Ratelle (109)-Rod Gilbert (96) 1971-72.
MOST GOALS BY A LINE, ONE SEASON*: 133 Vic Hadfield (45)-Jean Ratelle (46)-Rod Gilbert (42) 1971-72.
MOST GOALS, ONE GAME: 5 Don Murdoch, 10/12/76 against Minnesota at Minnesota; Mark Pavelich, 2/23/83 against Hartford at Madison Square Garden.
MOST POWER PLAY GOALS, ONE GAME: 3 Mark Messier, March 22, 1992 against New Jersey at Madison Square Garden.
MOST SHORTHANDED GOALS, ONE GAME: 2 Greg Polis, November 4, 1977 against Vancouver at Vancouver. Ron Duguay, January 22, 1980 against Los Angeles at Los Angeles. Don Maloney, February 21, 1981 against Washington at Madison Square Garden. Don Maloney, October 5, 1983 against New Jersey at Madison Square Garden. Don Maloney, January 14, 1987 against Calgary at Calgary.
MOST GOALS, ONE PERIOD: 3 Many: Last time: Adam Graves, November 25, 1992 in third period vs. Pittsburgh at Pittsburgh.
MOST ASSISTS, ONE PERIOD: 4 Phil Goyette. First period on October 20, 1963 against Boston at Madison Square Garden.
MOST ASSISTS, ONE GAME: 5 Walt Tkaczuk on Feb. 12, 1972 against Pittsburgh at Pittsburgh. Rod Gilbert on March 2, 1975 against Pittsburgh at Madison Square Garden and October 8, 1976 against Colorado at Colorado. Don Maloney on January 3, 1987 against Quebec at Quebec.
MOST POINTS, ONE GAME: 7 Steve Vickers. Three goals and four assists on Feb. 18, 1976 against Washington at Madison Square Garden.
MOST HAT TRICKS, ONE SEASON: 4 Tomas Sandstrom, 1986-87.
MOST CONSECUTIVE HAT TRICKS: 2 Steve Vickers scored hat tricks against Los Angeles on November 12, 1972 and against Philadelphia on Nov. 15, 1972.
MOST SHOTS ON GOAL, ONE GAME: 16 Rod Gilbert, February 24, 1968 against Montreal at Montreal.
MOST SHOTS ON GOAL, ONE SEASON: 344 Phil Esposito, 1976-77.

*These records computed on basis of having at least two members of line on ice at time of each goal.

RANGERS REGULAR SEASON RECORDS

(Player Records, cont.)

LONGEST CONSECUTIVE GOAL SCORING STREAK: 10 Andy Bathgate. Dec. 15, 1962 to Jan. 5, 1963 (11 goals during streak).

LONGEST CONSECUTIVE ASSIST SCORING STREAK: 15 Brian Leetch, Nov. 29 to December 31, 1991 (23 assists during the streak).

LONGEST CONSECUTIVE POINT SCORING STREAK: 17 Brian Leetch, Nov. 23 to December 31, 1991 (five goals and 24 assists during the streak).

FASTEST GOAL AT START OF GAME: 9 sec. Ron Duguay, April 6, 1980 at Philadelphia and Jim Wiemer, March 27, 1985, at Buffalo.

FASTEST TWO GOALS: 8 sec. Pierre Jarry. Scored at 11:03 and 11:11 of third period against California on November 21, 1971 at Madison Square Garden. Don Maloney. Scored at 12:48 and 12:56 of third period against Philadelphia on March 12, 1987 at Philadelphia.

FASTEST THREE GOALS: 2 min. 30 sec. Don Maloney scored at 16:41, 18:37 and 19:11 of second period on February 21, 1981 against Washington at Madison Square Garden.

FASTEST THREE ASSISTS: 1 min. 21 sec. Don Raleigh at 5:23; 5:43 and 6:44 of first period on November 16, 1947 against Montreal at Madison Square Garden.

MOST PENALTY MINUTES, ONE GAME: 35 Chris Nilan, October 8, 1989 against Chicago at Chicago.

MOST PENALTY MINUTES, ONE SEASON: 305 Troy Mallette, 1989-90.

MOST GOALS WITH THE RANGERS: 406 Rod Gilbert.

MOST ASSISTS WITH THE RANGERS: 615 Rod Gilbert.

MOST POINTS WITH THE RANGERS: 1,021 Rod Gilbert.

MOST PENALTY MINUTES WITH THE RANGERS: 1,226 Ron Greschner.

MOST GAMES WITH THE RANGERS: 1,160 Harry Howell.

MOST SEASONS WITH THE RANGERS: 18 Rod Gilbert, 1960-61 - 1977-78.

MOST CONSECUTIVE GAMES WITH THE RANGERS: 560 Andy Hebenton. Including playoff games, 19, Hebenton appeared in 582 consecutive games with the Rangers (1955-56 - 1962-63).

MOST 20-GOAL SEASONS WITH THE RANGERS: 12 Rod Gilbert.

MOST 20-ASSIST SEASONS WITH THE RANGERS: 13 Walt Tkaczuk, Rod Gilbert.

MOST 30-POINT SEASONS WITH THE RANGERS: 14 Rod Gilbert.

MOST 30-GOAL SEASONS WITH THE RANGERS: 6 Jean Ratelle.

Jean Ratelle posted 6, 30-goal seasons with the Rangers.

RANGERS REGULAR SEASON RECORDS

INDIVIDUAL ROOKIE RECORDS

MOST GOALS, ONE SEASON: 36 Tony Granato, 1988-89.
MOST ASSISTS, ONE SEASON: 48 Brian Leetch, 1988-89.
MOST POINTS, ONE SEASON: 76 Mark Pavelich, 1981-82.
MOST GOALS BY A DEFENSEMAN, ONE SEASON: 23 Brian Leetch, 1988-89.
MOST ASSISTS BY A DEFENSEMAN, ONE SEASON: 48 Brian Leetch, 1988-89.
MOST POINTS BY A DEFENSEMAN, ONE SEASON: 71 Brian Leetch, 1988-89.
MOST GOALS, ONE GAME: 5 Don Murdoch, October 12, 1976 against Minnesota at Minnesota.
MOST ASSISTS, ONE GAME: 4 Brad Park, February 2, 1969 against Pittsburgh at Madison Square Garden; Walt Tkaczuk, February 26, 1969 against Chicago at Madison Square Garden; Mark Heaslip, March 12, 1978 against Washington at Madison Square Garden; Brian Leetch, February 17, 1989 against Toronto at Madison Square Garden.
MOST POINTS ONE GAME: 5 Rick Middleton, November 17, 1974 against California at Madison Square Garden; Don Murdoch, October 12, 1976 against Minnesota at Minnesota; Brian Leetch, February 17, 1989 against Toronto at Madison Square Garden.
LONGEST GOAL SCORING STREAK: 7 Darren Turcotte, October 15, 1989-October 28, 1989 (Scored eight goals during streak.)
MOST POWER PLAY GOALS, ONE SEASON: 15 Camille Henry, 1953-54.
MOST SHORTHANDED GOALS, ONE SEASON: 4 Tony Granato, 1988-89.
MOST SHOTS, ONE SEASON: 268 Brian Leetch, 1988-89.
MOST HAT TRICKS, ONE SEASON: 3 Tony Granato, 1988-89.
MOST PENALTY MINUTES, ONE SEASON: 305 Troy Mallette, 1989-90.

INDIVIDUAL DEFENSEMEN RECORDS

MOST GOALS, ONE SEASON: 25 Brad Park, 1973-74.
MOST ASSISTS, ONE SEASON: 88 Brian Leetch, 1991-92.
MOST POINTS, ONE SEASON: 102 Brian Leetch, 1991-92.
MOST GOALS, ONE GAME: 3 Many. Last time: Reijo Ruotsalainen, March 17, 1982 against Philadelphia at Madison Square Garden.
MOSTS ASSISTS, ONE GAME: 4 Many. Last time: Sergei Zubov, January 25, 1994 against San Jose at Madison Square Garden.
MOST POINTS, ONE GAME: 5 Brian Leetch, February 17, 1989 against Toronto at Madison Square Garden.
MOST POWER PLAY GOALS, ONE SEASON: 17 Brian Leetch, 1993-94.
MOST SHORTHANDED GOALS, ONE SEASON: 3 Brian Leetch, 1988-89.
MOST SHOTS, ONE SEASON: 328 Brian Leetch, 1993-94.
MOST SHOTS, ONE GAME: 13 Brian Leetch, January 4, 1989 against Washington at Madison Square Garden.
MOST PENALTY MINUTES, ONE SEASON: 231 Barry Beck, 1980-81.
LONGEST CONSECUTIVE ASSIST SCORING STREAK: 15 Brian Leetch, Nov. 29 to December 31, 1991 (23 assists during the streak).
LONGEST CONSECUTIVE POINT SCORING STREAK: 17 Brian Leetch, Nov. 23 to December 31, 1991 (5 goals and 24 assists over the span).

INDIVIDUAL GOALTENDER RECORDS

MOST GAMES, ONE SEASON: 70 Johnny Bower, 1953-54. Ed Giacomin, 1968-69 and 1969-70.
MOST WINS, ONE SEASON: 42 Mike Richter, 1993-94.
MOST WINS, ONE SEASON (Including Playoffs): 58 Mike Richter, 1993-94.
LOWEST GOAL-AGAINST AVERAGE: 1.48 John Ross Roach, 1928-29.
MOST SHUTOUTS, ONE SEASON: 13 John Ross Roach, 1928-29.
MOST ASSISTS, ONE SEASON: 5 John Vanbiesbrouck, 1984-85 and 1987-88. Mike Richer, 1992-93.
MOST PENALTY MINUTES, ONE SEASON: 56 Bob Froese, 1986-87.
HIGHEST SAVE PERCENTAGE, ONE SEASON: .910 John Vanbiesbrouck, 1991-92. Mike Richter, 1993-94.
MOST SAVES, ONE GAME: 59 Mike Richter, January 31, 1991 vs. Vancouver at Vancouver. Game ended in 3-3 tie.
MOST ASSISTS ONE GAME: 2 Ed Giacomin, March 19, 1972 vs. Toronto at Madison Square Garden. John Vanbiesbrouck, January 8, 1985 vs. Winnipeg at Winnipeg. Mike Richter, February 23, 1990 vs. Washington at Washington, and October 29, 1992 vs. Quebec at MSG.
MOST ASSISTS, CAREER: 22 John Vanbiesbrouck.
MOST SHUTOUTS, CAREER: 49 Ed Giacomin.
MOST WINS, CAREER: 266 Ed Giacomin.

RANGERS PLAYOFF RECORDS

TEAM RECORDS

MOST VICTORIES, ONE YEAR: 16 1993-94 (23 games).
MOST LOSSES, ONE YEAR: 8 1985-86 (16 games).
MOST TIES, ONE YEAR: 2 1934-35 (4 games).
MOST GOALS SCORED, ONE YEAR: 81 1993-94 (23 games).
MOST GOALS ALLOWED, ONE YEAR: 56 1980-81 (14 games).
MOST ASSISTS, ONE YEAR: 121 1993-94 (23 games).
MOST SCORING POINTS, ONE YEAR: 202 1993-94 (23 games).
MOST PENALTY MINUTES, ONE YEAR: 426 1985-86 (16 games).
MOST SHUTOUTS, ONE YEAR: 4 (twice) 1993-94 (23 games) and 1936-37 (9 games).
MOST SHUTOUTS AGAINST, ONE YEAR: 2 1927-28 (9 games); 1928-29 (6 games); 1930-31 (4 games); 1936-37 (9 games); 1986-87 (6 games).
MOST GOALS SCORED, ONE GAME: 10 April 11, 1981, Rangers defeated Los Angeles, 10-3, at Madison Square Garden.
MOST GOALS ALLOWED, ONE GAME: 8 (5 times) last-April 9, 1987, Philadelphia won game 8-3 in Philadelphia.
MOST GOALS SCORED, ONE PERIOD: 6 April 24, 1979 vs. Philadelphia at Philadelphia. Rangers scored six goals in third period and won game 8-3.
MOST GOALS ALLOWED, ONE PERIOD: 5 (7 times) last-June 9, 1994 by Vancouver at MSG. Canucks scored five goals in the third period and won the game 6-3.
MOST GOALS BY RANGERS AND OPPONENT, ONE PERIOD: 9 April 24, 1979 vs. Philadelphia in the third period at Philadelphia. Rangers scored six goals and the Flyers three.
MOST GOALS THREE-GAMES SERIES: 18 1982-83. Rangers defeated Philadelphia, 3 games to 0.
MOST GOALS FOUR-GAME SERIES: 23 1980-81, Rangers defeated Los Angeles, 3 games to 1.
MOST GOALS FIVE-GAME SERIES: 28 1978-79. Rangers defeated Philadelphia, 4 games to 1.
MOST GOALS SIX-GAME SERIES: 29 1980-81, Rangers defeated St. Louis, 4 games to 2.
MOST GOALS SEVEN-GAME SERIES: 28 1991-92, Rangers defeated New Jersey, 4 games to 3.
MOST SHOTS, ONE GAME: 49 April 9, 1989 vs. Pittsburgh at Madison Square Garden. Pittsburgh won game 4-3.
MOST SHOTS, ONE GAME (OVERTIME): 54 May 31, 1994 vs. Vancouver at Madison Square Garden. Canucks won game 3-2.
MOST SHOTS ALLOWED, ONE GAME: 55 April 11, 1991 vs. Washington at Madison Square Garden. Washington won game 5-4 in overtime.
MOST PENALTY MINUTES, ONE GAME: 142 April 9, 1981 at Los Angeles. Los Angeles had 125 minutes for a total of 267 minutes.
MOST PENALTY MINUTES, ONE PERIOD: 125 April 9, 1981 in first period at Los Angeles. Los Angeles had 104 minutes for a total of 229 minutes.
MOST PENALTIES, ONE GAME: 31 April 9, 1981 at Los Angeles. Los Angeles had 28 penalities for a total of 59 penalties.
MOST PENALTIES, ONE PERIOD: 24 April 9, 1981 in first period at Los Angeles. Los Angeles had 19 penalites for a total of 43.
MOST PENALTY MINUTES, ONE SERIES: 214 1988-89 vs. Pittsburgh (4 games). Pittsburgh had 210 penalty minutes for a total of 424 minutes.
MOST PENALTIES, ONE SERIES: 65 1991-92 vs. New Jersey (7 games). New Jersey had 64 penalities for a total of 129 penalties.

SPECIALTY TEAMS

MOST POWER PLAY GOALS, ONE GAME: 4 April 8, 1982 vs. Philadelphia at Madison Square Garden.
MOST POWER PLAY GOALS, ONE SERIES: 10 1989-90 vs. Islanders.
MOST POWER PLAY GOALS, ONE YEAR: 22 1993-94 8 vs. Islanders, 4 vs. Washington, 4 vs. New Jersey and 6 vs. Vancouver.
MOST SHORTHANDED GOALS, ONE GAME: 2 (5 times) last-May 1, 1992 vs. New Jersey at New York.
MOST SHORTHANDED GOALS, ONE SERIES: 5 1978-79 vs. Philadelphia.
MOST SHORTHANDED GOALS, ONE YEAR: 6 1978-79. 5 vs. Philadelphia and 1 vs. Montreal.

OVERTIME

ALL-TIME OVERTIME RECORD: 26 Wins and 30 Losses, 10-14 at home and 16-16 on road.
LONGEST HOME OVERTIME PLAYED BY RANGERS: 59 min. 25 sec. Mel Hill of the Boston Bruins scored at 19.25 of the third overtime, March 21, 1939. Bruins won 2-1.
LONGEST ROAD OVERTIME PLAYED BY RANGERS: 68 min. 52 sec. Gus Rivers of the Montreal Canadiens scored at 8:52 of the fourth overtime, March 28, 1930 at Montreal. Canadiens won, 2-1.
SHORTEST HOME OVERTIME PLAYED BY RANGERS: 11 sec. J.P. Parise of the New York Islanders scored at 0:11 of the first overtime, April 11, 1975. Islanders won, 4-3.
SHORTEST ROAD OVERTIME PLAYED BY THE RANGERS: 34 sec. Rod Langway of the Washington Capitals scored at 0:34 of the first overtme, April 25, 1990 at Washington. Capitals won, 4-3.
FASTEST GOAL FROM START OF GAME: 27 sec. Ed Hospodar on April 9, 1981 vs. Los Angeles at Los Angeles.
FASTEST GOAL FROM START OF GAME BY OPPONENT: 13 sec. Claude Larose of Montreal on April 11, 1967 at Madison Square Garden.
FASTEST TWO GOALS: 6 sec. Rod Gilbert at 9:32 and 9:38 of second period against Chicago in Quarter-Finals at Chicago, April 11, 1968.
FASTEST THREE GOALS: 38 sec. Jim Wiemer at 12:29, Bob Brooke at 12:43, Ron Greschner at 13:07 of third period against Philadelphia in Division Semi-Finals at Madison Square Garden, April 12, 1986.
LATEST DATE OF PLAYOFF GAME: June 14, 1994 vs. Vancouver.

RANGERS PLAYOFF RECORDS

PLAYER RECORDS

MOST GOALS, ONE GAME: 3 (10 times), last-Mark Messier, May 25, 1994 at New Jersey. Frank Boucher, 1932, Bryan Hextall, 1940, Pentti Lund, 1950, Vic Hadfield, 1971, Steve Vickers, 1973, Ron Duguay, 1980, Mike Gartner, 1990, Bernie Nicholls, 1990, Mike Gartner, 1992, Mark Messier, 1994.
MOST ASSISTS, ONE GAME: 6 Mikko Leinonen, April 8, 1982 against Philadelphia.
MOST POINTS, ONE GAME: 6 Mikko Leinonen, April 8, 1982 against Philadelphia.
MOST GOALS, ONE YEAR: 12 Mark Messier, 1993-94.
MOST ASSISTS, ONE YEAR: 23 Brian Leetch, 1993-94.
MOST POINTS, ONE YEAR: 34 Brian Leetch, 1993-94.
MOST GOALS, ONE PERIOD: 3 Mark Messier, May 25, 1994 at New Jersey in the third period.
MOST ASSISTS, ONE PERIOD: 3 Brian Leetch, May 9 vs. Washington at Madison Square Garden in the first period. Jean Ratelle, April 22, 1971 vs. Chicago at Madison Square Garden in the first period. Mike Leinonen, April 8, 1982 vs. Philadelphia at Madison Square Garden in the first period.
MOST POINTS BY A ROOKIE, ONE YEAR: 20 Don Maloney, 1978-79.
MOST GOALS BY A DEFENSEMAN, ONE YEAR: 11 Brian Leetch, 1993-94.
MOST ASSISTS BY A DEFENSEMAN, ONE YEAR: 23 Brian Leetch, 1993-94.
MOST POINTS BY A DEFENSEMAN, ONE YEAR: 34 Brian Leetch, 1993-94.
MOST POINTS BY A DEFENSEMAN, ONE GAME: 4 Brian Leetch, May 9, 1994 vs. Washington at Madison Square Garden (one goal, three assists). Brian Leetch, June 7, 1994 vs. Vancouver at Madison Square Garden (one goal, three assists). Brad Park, May 4, 1972 vs. Boston at Madison Square Garden (two goals, two assists). Dave Maloney, April 9, 1983 vs. Philadelphia at Madison Square Garden (four assists).
MOST POWER PLAY GOALS, ONE PERIOD: 2 Mac Colville, March 22, 1942 vs. Toronto at Madison Square Garden in the third period. Brad Park, May 4, 1972 vs. Boston at Madison Square Garden in the first period.
MOST POWER PLAY GOALS, ONE GAME: 2 Mac Colville, March 22, 1942 vs. Toronto at Madison Square Garden. Brad Park, May 4, 1972 vs. Boston at Madison Square Garden. Ron Duguay, April 20, 1980 vs. Philadelphia at Madison Square Garden. Robbie Ftorek, April 11, 1982 vs. Philadelphia at Madison Square Garden. Mike Ridley, April 9, 1986 vs. Philadelphia at Philadelphia. Mike Gartner, April 13, 1990 vs. Islanders at New York.
MOST POWER PLAY GOALS: ONE YEAR: 5 Alexei Kovalev, 1993-94.
MOST GAME-WINNING GOALS, ONE YEAR: 4 Brian Leetch and Mark Messier, 1993-94.
MOST PENALTY MINUTES, ONE GAME: 39 Ed Hospodar, April 9, 1981 at Los Angeles.
MOST PENALTY MINUTES, ONE YEAR: 93 Ed Hospodar, 1980-81.
MOST WINS BY A GOALTENDER, ONE YEAR: 16 Mike Richter, 1993-94.
MOST SHUTOUTS, ONE YEAR: 4 Mike Richter 1993-94, Dave Kerr, 1936-37.
FASTEST OVERTIME GOAL BY A RANGER: 33 sec. Steve Vickers scored at 0:33 of the first overtime against the Atlanta Flames at Madison Square Garden, April 8, 1980. Rangers won, 2-1.
MOST SHORTHANDED GOALS, ONE GAME: 2 Mark Messier, April 21, 1992 against New Jersey at New York.

CAREER PLAYER RECORDS

MOST GOALS: 34 Rod Gilbert; 28 Ron Duguay; 24 Steve Vickers.
MOST ASSISTS: 39 Brian Leetch, 35 Don Maloney, 33 Rod Gilbert, Jean Ratelle, 32 Brad Park, Walt Tkaczuk, Ron Greschner.
MOST POINTS: 67 Rod Gilbert, 10 playoffs; 58, Brian Leetch, four playoffs; 57 Don Maloney, 9 playoffs; 51 Walt Tkaczuk, 10 playoffs.
MOST POINTS BY A DEFENSEMAN: 58 Brian Leetch, four playoffs; 44 Brad Park, 7 playoffs; 37 Ron Greschner, 12 playoffs; 32 Barry Beck, 6 playoffs.
MOST GAMES: 93 Walt Tkaczuk, 85 Don Maloney, 84 Ron Greschner, 79 Rod Gilbert.
MOST POWER PLAY GOALS: 10 Rod Gilbert.
MOST PENALTY MINUTES: 159 Ching Johnson.
MOST SHUTOUTS BY A GOALTENDER: 7 Dave Kerr.
PARTICIPATED IN THE MOST PLAYOFFS: 12 Ron Greschner.

PLAYOFF SCORING LEADERS IN RANGERS HISTORY

No.	Player	GP	G	A	PTS
1.	Rod Gilbert	79	34	33	67
2.	*Brian Leetch	46	19	39	58
3.	Don Maloney	85	22	35	57
4.	Walt Tkaczuk	93	19	32	51
5.	Steve Vickers	68	24	25	49
6.	Ron Greschner	84	17	32	49
7.	Ron Duguay	69	28	19	47
8.	Anders Hedberg	58	22	24	46
9.	*Mark Messier	34	19	25	44
10.	Brad Park	64	12	32	44
11.	Jean Ratelle	65	9	33	42
12.	Vic Hadfield	61	22	19	41

* Active Rangers

RANGERS PLAYOFF OVERTIME GAMES

DATE	PLACE	OPP.	GAME/ SERIES	FINAL SCORE	GOAL SCORER	TIME	SERIES WINNER
4-7-28	Mont.	Maroons	2/F	2-1	Frank Boucher	7:05	Rangers
3-21-29	N.Y.	Americans	2/Q	1-0	Butch Keeling	29:50	Rangers
3-26-29	Tor.	Maple Leafs	2/S	2-1	Frank Boucher	2:03	Rangers
3-28-30	Mont.	Canadiens	1/S	1-2	Gus Rivers	68:52	Canadiens
3-26-32	Mont.	Canadiens	2/S	4-3	Bun Cook	59:32	Rangers
4-13-33	Tor.	Maple Leafs	4/S	1-0	Bill Cook*	7:33	Rangers
3-25-37	N.Y.	Maple Leafs	2/Q	2-1	Babe Pratt	13:05	Rangers
3-22-38	N.Y.	Americans	1/Q	1-2	Johnny Sorrell	21:25	Americans
3-27-38	N.Y.	Americans	3/Q	2-3	Lorne Carr	40:40	Americans
3-21-39	N.Y.	Bruins	1/S	1-2	Mel Hill	59:25	Bruins
3-23-39	Bost.	Bruins	2/S	2-3	Mel Hill	8:24	Bruins
3-30-39	Bost.	Bruins	5/S	2-1	Snuffy Smith	17:19	Bruins
4-2-39	Bost.	Bruins	7/S	1-2	Mel Hill	48:00	Bruins
4-2-40	N.Y.	Maple Leafs	1/F	2-1	Alf Pike	15:30	Rangers
4-11-40	Tor.	Maple Leafs	5/F	2-1	Muzz Patrick	11:43	Rangers
4-13-40	Tor.	Maple Leafs	6/F	3-2	Bryan Hextall*	2:07	Rangers
3-20-41	Det.	Red Wings	1/Q	1-2	Gus Giesebrecht	12:01	Red Wings
4-4-50	Mont.	Canadiens	4/S	2-3	Elmer Lach	15:19	Rangers
4-18-50	Det.	Red Wings	4/F	4-3	Don Raleigh	8:34	Red Wings
4-20-50	Det.	Red Wings	5/F	2-1	Don Raleigh	1:38	Red Wings
4-23-50	Det.	Red Wings	7/F	3-4	Pete Babando*	28:31	Red Wings
3-28-57	N.Y.	Canadiens	2/S	4-3	Andy Hebenton	13:38	Canadiens
4-4-57	Mont.	Canadiens	5/S	3-4	Maurice Richard	1:11	Canadiens
3-27-58	N.Y.	Bruins	2/S	3-4	Jerry Toppazzini	4:46	Bruins
4-5-62	Tor.	Maple Leafs	5/S	2-3	Red Kelly	24:23	Maple Leafs
4-13-67	N.Y.	Canadiens	4/S	1-2	John Ferguson	6:28	Canadiens
4-15-71	Tor.	Maple Leafs	6/Q	2-1	Bob Nevin	9:07	Rangers
4-18-71	Chi.	Blackhawks	1/S	2-1	Pete Stemkowski	1:37	Blackhawks
4-27-71	Chi.	Blackhawks	5/S	2-3	Bobby Hull	6:35	Blackhawks
4-29-71	N.Y.	Blackhawks	6/S	3-2	Pete Stemkowski	41:29	Blackhawks
4-16-74	Mont.	Canadiens	5/Q	3-2	Ron Harris	4:07	Rangers
4-28-74	N.Y.	Flyers	4/S	2-1	Rod Gilbert	4:20	Flyers
4-11-75	N.Y.	Islanders	3/P	3-4	J.P. Parise	0:11	Islanders
4-13-78	N.Y.	Sabres	2/P	4-3	Don Murdoch	1:37	Sabres
4-12-79	L.A.	Kings	2/P	2-1	Phil Esposito	6:11	Rangers
4-16-79	Phil.	Flyers	1/Q	2-3	Ken Linseman	0:44	Rangers
4-28-79	Nass.	Islanders	2/SF	3-4	Denis Potvin	8:02	Rangers
5-3-79	N.Y.	Islanders	4/SF	2-3	Bob Nystrom	3:40	Rangers
5-19-79	N.Y.	Canadiens	4/F	3-4	Serge Savard	7:25	Canadiens
4-8-80	N.Y.	Flames	1/P	2-1	Steve Vickers	0:33	Rangers
4-18-82	N.Y.	Islanders	3/DF	3-4	Bryan Trottier	3:00	Islanders
4-10-84	Nass.	Islanders	5/DSF	2-3	Ken Morrow	8:56	Islanders
4-10-85	Phil.	Flyers	1/DSF	4-5	Mark Howe	8:01	Flyers
4-17-86	Wash.	Capitals	1/DF	4-3	Brian MacLellan	1:16	Rangers
4-23-86	N.Y.	Capitals	4/DF	6-5	Bob Brooke	2:40	Rangers
5-5-86	N.Y.	Canadiens	3/CF	3-4	Claude Lemieux	9:41	Canadiens
4-9-90	Nass.	Islanders	3/DSF	3-4	Brent Sutter	20:59	Rangers
4-25-90	Wash.	Capitals	4/DF	3-4	Rod Langway	0:34	Capitals
4-27-90	N.Y.	Capitals	5/DF	1-2	John Druce	6:48	Capitals
4-11-91	N.Y.	Capitals	5/DSF	4-5	Dino Ciccarelli	6:44	Capitals
5-7-92	Pit.	Penguins	3/DF	6-5	Kris King	1:29	Penguins
5-9-92	Pit.	Penguins	4/DF	4-5	Ron Francis	2:47	Penguins
5-15-94	N.Y.	Devils	1/CF	3-4	Stephane Richer	35:23	Rangers
5-19-94	N.J.	Devils	3/CF	3-2	Stephane Matteau	26:13	Rangers
5-27-94	N.Y.	Devils	7/CF	2-1	Stephane Matteau	24:24	Rangers
5-31-94	N.Y.	Canucks	1/F	2-3	Greg Adams	19:26	Rangers

P: Preliminaries; Q: Quarter-finals; DSF: Division Semi-Finals; DF: Division-Finals;
CF: Conference-Finals; S: Semi-finals; F: Finals.)
*Goal decided Stanley Cup.

RANGERS PLAYOFF RECORD YEAR BY YEAR

Year	Opponent	W-L-T	GF/GA
1926-27	Boston	0-1-1	1/ 3
1927-28	Pittsburgh	1-1-0	6/ 4
	Boston	1-0-1	5/ 2
	Maroons	3-2-0	5/ 6
1928-29	Americans	1-0-1	1/ 0
	Toronto	2-0-0	3/ 1
	Boston	0-2-0	1/ 4
1929-30	Ottawa	1-0-1	6/ 3
	Canadiens	0-2-0	1/ 4
1930-31	Maroons	2-0-0	8/ 1
	Chicago	0-2-0	0/ 3
1931-32	Canadiens	3-1-0	13/ 9
	Toronto	0-3-0	10/18
1932-33	Canadiens	1-0-1	8/ 5
	Detroit	2-0-0	6/ 3
	Toronto	3-1-0	11/ 5
1933-34	Maroons	0-1-1	1/ 2
1934-35	Canadiens	1-0-1	6/ 5
	Maroons	0-1-1	4/ 5
1936-37	Toronto	2-0-0	5/ 1
	Maroons	2-0-0	5/ 0
	Detroit	2-3-0	8/ 9
1937-38	Americans	1-2-0	7/ 8
1938-39	Boston	3-4-0	12/14
1939-40	Boston	4-2-0	15/ 9
	Toronto	4-2-0	14/11
1940-41	Detroit	1-2-0	6/ 6
1941-42	Toronto	2-4-0	12/13
1947-48	Detroit	2-4-0	12/17
1949-50	Montreal	4-1-0	15/ 7
	Detroit	3-4-0	17/22
1955-56	Montreal	1-4-0	9/24
1956-57	Montreal	1-4-0	12/22
1957-58	Boston	2-4-0	16/28
1961-62	Toronto	2-4-0	15/22
1966-67	Montreal	0-4-0	8/14
1967-68	Chicago	2-4-0	12/18
1968-69	Montreal	0-4-0	7/16
1969-70	Boston	2-4-0	16/25
1970-71	Toronto	4-2-0	16/15
	Chicago	3-4-0	14/21
1971-72	Montreal	4-2-0	19/14
	Chicago	4-0-0	17/ 9
	Boston	2-4-0	16/18
1972-73	Boston	4-1-0	22/11
	Chicago	1-4-0	11/15
1973-74	Montreal	4-2-0	21/17
	Philadelphia	3-4-0	17/22
1974-75	Islanders	1-2-0	13/10
1977-78	Buffalo	1-2-0	6/11
1978-79	Los Angeles	2-0-0	9/ 2
	Philadelphia	4-1-0	28/ 8
	Islanders	4-2-0	18/13
	Montreal	1-4-0	11/19
1979-80	Atlanta	3-1-0	14/ 8
	Philadelphia	1-4-0	7/14
1980-81	Los Angeles	3-1-0	23/12
	St. Louis	4-2-0	29/22
	Islanders	0-4-0	8/22
1981-82	Philadelphia	3-1-0	19/15
	Islanders	2-4-0	20/27
1982-83	Philadelphia	3-0-0	18/ 9
	Islanders	2-4-0	15/28
1983-84	Islanders	2-3-0	14/13
1984-85	Philadelphia	0-3-0	10/14
1985-86	Philadelphia	3-2-0	18/15
	Washington	4-2-0	20/25
	Montreal	1-4-0	9/15
1986-87	Philadelphia	2-4-0	13/22
1988-89	Pittsburgh	0-4-0	11/19
1989-90	Islanders	4-1-0	22/13
	Washington	1-4-0	15/22
1990-91	Washington	2-4-0	16/16
1991-92	New Jersey	4-3-0	28/25
	Pittsburgh	2-4-0	19/24
1993-94	Islanders	4-0-0	22/3
	Washington	4-1-0	20/12
	New Jersey	4-3-0	18/16
	Vancouver	4-3-0	21/19

Totals	W-L-T	GF/GA
Preliminary Round	35-28-0	256/207
Quarter-Finals	44-45-0	286/298
Semi-Finals	62-76-8	350/386
Finals	22-25-0	94/113
Overall	163-174-8	986/1004

RANGERS PLAYOFF RECORDS

STANLEY CUP WINNING GOALS BY RANGERS

1928	Frank Boucher vs. Montreal Maroons	(at Montreal)
1933	Bill Cook vs. Toronto Maple Leafs	(at Toronto)
1940	Bryan Hextall, Sr. vs. Toronto Maple Leafs	(at Toronto)
1994	Mark Messier vs. Vancouver	(at Madison Square Garden)

AGAINST RANGERS

1929	Bill Carson — Boston Bruins	(at Madison Square Garden)
1932	Ace Bailey — Toronto Maple Leafs	(at Toronto)
1937	Marty Barry — Detroit Red Wings	(at Detroit)
1950	Pete Babando — Detroit Red Wings	(at Detroit)
1972	Bobby Orr — Boston Bruins	(at Madison Square Garden)
1979	Jacques Lemaire — Montreal Canadiens	(at Montreal)

RANGER PLAYOFF HAT TRICKS

Frank Boucher vs. Toronto, 4/9/32 at Toronto, Finals Game 3, 6-4 Maple Leafs, Opposing Goalie: Lorne Chabot.

Bryan Hextall vs. Toronto, 4/3/40 at New York, Finals Game 2, 6-2 Rangers, Opposing Goalie: Turk Broda.

Pentti Lund vs. Montreal, 4/2/50 at New York, Semifinals Game 3, 4-1 Rangers, Opposing Goalie: Bill Durnan.

Vic Hadfield vs. Chicago, 4/22/71 at New York, Semifinals Game 3, 4-1 Rangers, Opposing Goalie: Tony Esposito.

Steve Vickers vs. Boston, 4/10/73 at Boston, Quarterfinals Game 5, 6-3 Rangers, Opposing Goalies: Ross Brooks & Eddie Johnston.

Ron Duguay vs. Philadelphia, 4/20/80 at New York, Quarterfinals Game 4, 4-2 Rangers, Opposing Goalie: Pete Peeters.

Mike Gartner vs. Islanders, 4/13/90 at New York, Division Semifinals Game 5, 6-5 Rangers, Opposing Goalie: Mark Fitzpatrick.

Bernie Nicholls vs. Washington, 4/19/90 at New York, Division Finals Game 1, 7-3 Rangers, Opposing Goalie: Mike Liut.

Mike Gartner vs. New Jersey, 4/27/92 at New York, Division Semifinals Game 5, 8-5 Rangers, Opposing Goalie: Chris Terreri.

Mark Messier vs. New Jersey, 5/27/94 at New Jersey, Conference Finals Game 6, 4-2 Rangers, Opposing Goalie: Martin Brodeur.

Mark Messier celebrates after scoring the Stanley Cup winning goal against the Vancouver Canucks.

RANGERS PLAYOFF RECORDS

RANGERS PLAYOFF SHUTOUTS

Lorne Chabot, vs. Boston Bruins, 4/2/27 at Boston, Semifinals Game 1, 0-0.
Lorne Chabot, vs. Pittsburgh Pirates, 3/27/28 at New York, Quarterfinals Game 1, 4-0.
Joe Miller, vs. Montreal Maroons, 4/12/28 at Montreal, Finals Game 4, 1-0.
John Ross Roach, vs. New York Americans, 3/19/29 at New York, Quarterfinals Game 1, 0-0.
John Ross Roach, vs. New York Americans, 3/21/29 at New York, Quarterfinals Game 2, 1-0.
John Ross Roach, vs. Toronto Maple Leafs, 3/24/29 at New York, Semifinals Game 1, 1-0.
John Ross Roach, vs. Montreal Maroons, 3/26/31 at Montreal, Quarterfinals Game 2, 3-0.
John Ross Roach, vs. Montreal Canadiens, 3/27/32 at New York, Semifinals Game 3, 1-0.
Andy Aitkenhead, vs. Detroit Red Wings, 3/30/33 at New York, Semifinals Game 1, 2-0.
Andy Aitkenhead, vs. Toronto Maple Leafs, 4/13/33 at Toronto, Finals Game 4, 1-0.
Andy Aitkenhead, vs. Montreal Maroons, 3/20/34 at Montreal, Quarterfinals Game 1, 0-0.
Dave Kerr, vs. Toronto Maple Leafs, 3/23/37 at Toronto, Quarterfinals Game 1, 3-0.
Dave Kerr, vs. Montreal Maroons, 4/1/37 at New York, Semifinals Game 1, 1-0.
Dave Kerr, vs. Montreal Maroons, 4/3/37 at Montreal, Semifinals Game 2, 4-0.
Dave Kerr, vs. Detroit Red Wings, 4/11/37 at New York, Finals Game 3, 1-0.
Dave Kerr, vs. Boston Bruins, 3/19/40 at New York, Semifinals Game 1, 4-0.
Dave Kerr, vs. Boston Bruins, 3/26/40 at New York, Semifinals Game 4, 1-0.
Dave Kerr, vs. Boston Bruins, 3/28/40 at Boston, Semifinals Game 5, 1-0.
Jim Henry, vs. Toronto Maple Leafs, 3/24/42 at New York, Semifinals Game 3, 3-0.
Chuck Rayner, vs. Montreal Canadiens, 4/6/50 at Montreal, Semifinals Game 6, 3-0.
Eddie Giacomin, vs. Boston Bruins, 4/8/73 at New York, Quarterfinals Game 4, 4-0.
John Davidson, vs. Philadelphia Flyers, 4/22/79 at New York, Quarterfinals Game 4, 6-0.
Glen Hanlon, vs. New York Islanders, 4/5/84 at Nassau Coliseum, Division Semifinals Game 2, 3-0.
John Vanbiesbrouck, vs. Montreal Canadiens, 5/7/86 at New York, Conference Finals Game 4, 2-0.
John Vanbiesbrouck, vs. Philadelphia Flyers, 4/8/87 at Philadelphia, Division Semifinals Game 1, 3-0.
Mike Richter, vs. Washington Capitals, 4/7/91 at Washington, Division Semifinals Game 3, 6-0.
Mike Richter, vs. New Jersey Devils, 4/25/92 at New Jersey, Division Semifinals Game 4, 3-0.
Mike Richter, vs. New York Islanders, 4/17/94 at Madison Square Garden, Conference Quarterfinals Game 1, 6-0.
Mike Richter, vs. New York Islanders, 4/18/94 at Madison Square Garden, Conference Quarterfinals Game 2, 6-0.
Mike Richter, vs. Washington Capitals, 5/5/94 at Washington Conference Semifinals, Game 3, 3-0.
Mike Richter, vs. New Jersey Devils, 5/17/94 at Madison Square Garden Conference Finals, Game 2, 3-0.

Mike Richter recorded four shutouts in the 1994 playoffs.

NEW YORK RANGERS
STANLEY CUP CHAMPIONS

1927-28 — Standing (Left to Right)-Ching Johnson, Bill Boyd, Paul Thompson, Lorne Chabot, Lester Patrick (sub-goaltender, manager and coach), Bill Cook, Taffy Abel, Joe Miller (sub-goaltender), Bun Cook. Bottom Row (Left to Right)-Harry Westerby (trainer), Murray Murdoch, Art Chapman, Leo Bourgault, Patsy Gallighen, (unknown), Frank Boucher, Alex Gray.

1932-33 — Standing (Left to Right)-Jimmy Arnott, Gordon Pettinger, Bill Cook, Earl Seibert, Ossie Asmundsen, Lester Patrick (Manager), Babe Siebert, Ching Johnson, Bun Cook, Butch Keeling, Murray Murdoch, Ott Heller, Doug Brennan. Bottom row (Left to Right)-Wilfie Starr, Carl Voss, Cecil Dillon, Harry Westerby (Trainer), Artie Somers, Andy Aitkenhead.

1939-40 — Standing(Left to Right)-Frank Boucher(Coach), Lynn Patrick, Neil Colville, Ott Heller, Art Coulter(Captain), Babe Pratt, Muzz Patrick, Alf Pike, Lester Patrick (Manager). Bottom row (Left to Right)-Alex Shibicky, Phil Watson, Kilby MacDonald, Bryan Hextall, Dave Kerr, Mac Colville, Clint Smith, Dutch Miller, Harry Westerby(Trainer).

NEW YORK RANGERS
1993-94 STANLEY CUP CHAMPIONS

First Row (left to right): Mike Richter, Kevin Lowe, Steve Larmer, Dick Todd - Assistant Coach, Neil Smith - President and General Manager, Mark Messier - Captain, Mike Keenan - Head Coach, Colin Campbell - Associate Coach, Brian Leetch, Adam Graves, Glenn Healy. Second Row: Mike Folga - Trainer, Joe Murphy - Trainer, Glenn Anderson, Joe Kocur, Alexei Kovalev, Craig MacTavish, Sergei Nemchinov, Sergei Zubov, Dave Smith - Trainer, Bruce Lifrieri - Trainer. Third Row: Esa Tikkanen, Greg Gilbert, Jay Wells, Stephane Matteau, Jeff Beukeboom, Doug Lidster, Brian Noonan. Top Row: Mike Hartman, Mike Hudson, Alexander Karpovtsev, Eddie Olczyk, Nick Kypreos.

RANGERS MANAGEMENT

Rangers Presidents

John S. Hammond	(1926 thru 1931-32)
William F. Carey	(1932-33)
John Reed Kilpatrick	(1933-34)
John S. Hammond	(1934-35)
John Reed Kilpatrick	(1935-36 thru 1959-60)
John J. Bergen	(1960-61 thru 1961-62)
William M. Jennings	(1962-63 thru 1980-81)
John H. Krumpe	(1981-82 thru Dec. 31, 1986)
Richard H. Evans	(Jan. 1, 1987 to June 28, 1990)
John C. Diller	(June 29, 1990 to April 22, 1991)
Neil Smith	(June 19, 1992 to present)

Rangers General Managers

Lester Patrick	(1926-27 thru 1945-46)
Frank Boucher	(1946-47 thru 1954-55)
Muzz Patrick	(1955-56 thru 1963-64)
Emile Francis	(1964-65 to Jan. 6, 1976)
John Ferguson	(Jan. 7, 1976 to June 2, 1978)
Fred Shero	(June 2, 1978 to Nov. 21, 1980)
Craig Patrick	(Nov. 21, 1980 to July 14, 1986)
Phil Esposito	(July 14, 1986 to May 24, 1989)
Neil Smith	(July 17, 1989 to present)

Rangers Coaches & Records

Coach	GC	W	L	T	PCT.
Lester Patrick (1926-27 thru 1938-39)	604	281	216	107	.554
Frank Boucher (1939-40 - 12/21/48)	486	166	243	77	.412
Lynn Patrick (12/21/48 thru 1949-50)	107	40	51	16	.449
Neil Colville (1950-51 - 12/6/51)	93	26	41	26	.419
Bill Cook (12/6/51 thru 1952-53)	117	34	59	24	.393
Frank Boucher (1953-54 - 1/6/54)	39	13	20	6	.410
Muzz Patrick (1/6/54 thru 1954-55)	105	35	47	23	.443
Phil Watson (1955-56 - 11/12/59)	294	118	124	52	.490
Alf Pike (11/18/59 thru 1960-61)	123	36	66	21	.378
Doug Harvey (5/30/61 thru 1961-62)	70	26	32	12	.457
Muzz Patrick (9/7/62 - 12/28/62)	34	11	19	4	.382
Red Sullivan (12/28/62 - 12/5/65)	196	58	103	35	.385
Emile Francis (12/5/65 - 6/4/68)	193	81	82	30	.497
Bernie Geoffrion (6/4/68 - 1/17/69)	43	22	18	3	.547
Emile Francis (1/17/69 - 6/4/73)	344	202	88	54	.666
Larry Popein (6/4/73 - 1/11/74)	41	18	14	9	.549
Emile Francis (1/11/74 - 5/19/75)	117	59	39	19	.585
Ron Stewart (5/19/75 - 1/7/76)	39	15	20	4	.436
John Ferguson (1/7/76 - 8/22/77)	121	43	59	19	.434
Jean-Guy Talbot (8/22/77 - 6/2/78)	80	30	37	13	.456
Fred Shero (6/2/78 - 11/22/80)	180	82	74	24	.522
Craig Patrick (11/22/80 - 6/4/81)	60	26	23	11	.525
Herb Brooks (6/4/81 - 1/21/85)	285	131	113	41	.532
Craig Patrick (1/21/85 - 6/19/85)	35	11	22	2	.343
Ted Sator (6/19/85 - 11/21/86)	99	41	48	10	.465
*Phil Esposito (1986-87)	43	24	19	0	.558
*Tom Webster (1986-87)	16	5	7	4	.474
*Wayne Cashman/Ed Giacomin (1986-87)	2	0	2	0	.000
Michel Bergeron (6/18/87 to 4/1/89)	158	73	67	18	.518
Phil Esposito (4/1/89 - 5/24/89)	2	0	2	0	.000
Roger Neilson (8/15/89 - 1/4/93)	280	141	104	35	.566
Ron Smith (1/4/93 - 4/16/93)	44	15	22	7	.421
Mike Keenan (4/17/93-7/24/94)	84	52	24	8	.667

*(Due to illness to Tom Webster, head coaching situation changed several times during season.)

CAPTAINS / COACHING RECORDS

Rangers Captains

Vic Hadfield served as the Rangers captain from 1971-72 through 1973-74.

Bill Cook	(1926-27 thru 1936-37)
Art Coulter	(1937-38 thru 1941-42)
Ott Heller	(1942-43 thru 1944-45)
Neil Colville	(1945-46 thru Dec. 21, 1948)
Buddy O'Connor	(1949-50)
Frank Eddolls	(1950-51 to Dec. 6, 1951)
Allan Stanley	(Dec. 20, 1951 to Nov. 3, 1953)
Don Raleigh	(Nov. 4, 1953 thru 1954-55)
Harry Howell	(1955-56 thru 1956-57)
George Sullivan	(1957-58 thru 1960-61)
Andy Bathgate	(1961-62 to Feb. 22, 1964)
Camille Henry	(Feb. 23, 1964 to Feb. 4, 1965)
Bob Nevin	(Feb. 5, 1965 thru 1970-71)
Vic Hadfield	(1971-72 thru 1973-74)
Brad Park	(1974-75 to Nov. 7, 1975)
Phil Esposito	(Nov. 12, 1975 to Oct. 10, 1978)
Dave Maloney	(Oct. 11, 1978 to Dec. 6, 1980)
Walt Tkaczuk	(Dec. 7, 1980 to Feb. 3, 1981)
Barry Beck	(Feb. 4, 1981 to May 9, 1986)
Ron Greschner	(Oct. 9, 1986 to Dec. 3, 1987)
Kelly Kisio	(Dec. 24, 1987 to May 30, 1991)
Mark Messier	(Oct. 7, 1991 to present)

Rangers Coaching Records

Games Coached
Emile Francis	654
Lester Patrick	604
Frank Boucher	525
Phil Watson	294
Herb Brooks	285
Roger Neilson	280
Red Sullivan	196

Wins
Emile Francis	342
Lester Patrick	281
Frank Boucher	179
Roger Neilson	141
Herb Brooks	131
Phil Watson	118

Losses
Frank Boucher	243
Lester Patrick	216
Emile Francis	209
Phil Watson	124
Herb Brooks	113
Roger Neilson	104

Winning Percentage (minimum 100 games)
Emile Francis	.602
Roger Neilson	.566
Herb Brooks	.532
Fred Shero	.522
Lester Patrick	.554
Michel Bergeron	.519

Fred Shero ranks fourth among Rangers coaches with a .522 winning percentage.

A Brief History of
The New York Rangers

The Rangers' Official Emblem

The New York Rangers have thrilled fans for 68 seasons with exciting hockey and notable achievements, most recently the club's proudest moment — the dramatic 1993-94 Stanley Cup championship.

After finishing atop the NHL during the regular season, the Rangers defeated the New York Islanders and Washington Capitals in the first two playoff rounds, then came from behind to win the Eastern Conference championship on Mark Messier's third period hat trick in Game Six and Stephane Matteau's double overtime goal in Game Seven against the New Jersey Devils. They defeated the Vancouver Canucks in another seven game thriller, with captain Mark Messier scoring the Stanley Cup-winning goal.

The Rangers' fourth Cup and the numerous franchise records set last season continued a long, distinguished history marked by outstanding team and individual performances. In the past five years, those performances have included three division titles and two Presidents' Trophy seasons for the NHL's best regular season record. But success is not new for the Rangers. From the outset, the club was among the best in the NHL.

The NHL granted Madison Square Garden a franchise to operate its own team for the 1926-27 season, following the initial success of the New York Americans, who began play in the Garden for the 1925-26 season and would become the Rangers first arch-rivals. Garden president G.L. "Tex" Rickard chose University of Toronto's Conn Smythe to build his team and Smythe assembled a talented roster, including future Hall of Famers Frank Boucher and Bill Cook, who with Cook's brother Bun formed hockey's top line; Hall of Fame defenseman Ivan "Ching" Johnson, who effectively teamed with Taffy Abel; and second line winger Murray Murdoch, who would become hockey's first "iron man," playing 508 consecutive games. Sportswriters dubbed the team "Tex's Rangers" and that was the origin of the club's name.

Prior to the start of their first season, however, disagreements with the Garden management caused Smythe's exit. On the eve of the club's first season, the task of guiding the Rangers was handed to one of professional hockey's pioneers, Lester Patrick, who grew to be the Big Apple's most visible and quotable hockey man. Patrick directed the Rangers to a first place finish in their opening season (with Bill Cook winning the league scoring title) and, led by Boucher's scoring heroics, their first Stanley Cup in 1927-28. It was the last time an NHL team has won the Cup as quickly as its sophomore campaign. During Game Two of the 1928 Finals against the Montreal Maroons, the 44-year old Patrick substituted for injured goaltender Lorne Chabot in one of hockey's legendary moments.

With hard, clean play and innovative tactics, the Rangers became known as ìthe classiest team in hockey,î going to the Finals four times in six years. Regularly among the leaders in assists, Boucher epitomized the club's style, winning the Lady Byng Trophy so frequently, the league allowed him to keep the original silverware and struck a new award. Bill Cook won a second scoring title in 1932-33 and in April, his overtime goal in Game Four of the Finals gave the Rangers a 1-0 win over Toronto and their second Stanley Cup title. Cecil Dillon's scoring and Andy Aitkenhead's goaltending led the way for Patrick's club.

In their first 16 seasons, the Rangers missed the playoffs only once, and only twice did they fall lower than third place. New York won three regular-season championships in that span, finished second five times and third on six other occasions. The Garden became the place to be on nights the Rangers played, attracting a "dinner-jacket" crowd which often included other sports figures, Broadway entertainers, New York's society elite and City Hall politicians. The Rangers built an empire and New Yorkers loved it.

The Original Rangers gave way to a new group of stars in the late 1930s. Patrick acquired goalie Davey Kerr from the Maroons in 1934 and defenseman Art Coulter from Chicago in 1936 and they became the backbone of the next great Rangers team, which lost a five game Final to Detroit in 1937. Three seasons later, Boucher succeeded Patrick as coach and the Rangers won the Cup again. The 1940 Rangers were led by the dangerous line of Hall of Famer Neil Colville, his brother Mac and Alex Shibicky. Hall of Famer Bryan Hextall, Phil Watson, Dutch Hiller, Alf Pike, Clint Smith, Kilby MacDonald and Lester's son Lynn gave Boucher great depth up front. Lester's other son Muzz helped form a solid defense corps with captain Coulter, Babe Pratt and Ott Heller. Hextall's overtime goal against Toronto in Game Six of the 1940 Finals was the decisive tally in the Rangers third Cup championship.

Two years later, the Rangers finished atop the league with the Watson-Patrick-Hextall line dominating league scoring. But World War II had already begun breaking up this collection of Ranger All-Stars. In the years that followed, the club struggled. In the next 13 seasons, the club only made the playoffs twice. Still the Rangers featured outstanding individual talents. Buddy O'Connor became the first Ranger to win the Hart Trophy as NHL MVP in 1947-48 and goalie Chuck Rayner won the Hart in 1949-50, the year the Rangers lost a seven game overtime Stanley Cup Final to the Red Wings. Edgar Laprade, Hy Buller and Bones Raleigh were standouts in the late Forties and early Fifties.

In the 1950s, a fertile farm system and some deft trades improved the team's fortunes. Hall of Famers Andy Bathgate, Dean Prentice, Harry Howell, Bill Gadsby and Gump Worsley, along with Camille Henry, Andy Hebenton and "Leapin' Louie" Fontinato helped the team back into the playoffs in mid-decade. Bathgate, who became the club's captain and all-time leading scorer, won the Hart Trophy for the 1958-59 season. Hebenton played 560 consecutive games as a Ranger and Howell became recognized as one of hockey's best defensemen and was awarded the Norris Trophy in 1966-67.

A Rangers Renaissance began in 1960s, directed by coach and general manager Emile Francis. Beginning in 1966-67, the club made the playoffs nine consecutive seasons, the only NHL team of the period to accomplish that feat. Led by Rod Gilbert, who eclipsed Bathgate's club scoring records, and his linemates Jean Ratelle and Vic Hadfield, the Rangers were again an NHL powerhouse. All three became All-Stars during the period as did defenseman Brad Park and goalie Ed Giacomin. Reliable two-way players like Pete Stemkowski, Steve Vickers and Walt Tkaczuk helped round out the team. In 1971-72, Hadfield became the first Ranger to score 50 goals in a season and that year the Rangers faced Boston in the Stanley Cup Finals, losing a tough six-game series.

Following a two-year absence from post-season play in the mid-1970s, a new group of Rangers emerged led by stars Anders Hedberg, Ulf Nilsson, Barry Beck, Ron Greschner, Phil Esposito, John Davidson, and the Maloney brothers, Dave and Don. The Rangers dramatically marched to the Stanley Cup Finals in 1979, defeating their new arch-rivals, New York Islanders in the semi-finals before bowing to the Montreal Canadiens in a five game Final. While the Rangers would not reach the Finals again until 1994, they built a good team and it took the best teams to defeat them. Beginning in 1979, the clubs that eliminated the Rangers in the playoffs over each of the next nine seasons all went to the Finals or won the Stanley Cup.

The hiring of Neil Smith as general manager of the Rangers in 1989 began the process which led to the 1994 Stanley Cup championship. Smith acquired center Mark Messier from Edmonton for the 1991-92 season and Messier led the club to the top of the league and was recognized for his efforts by winning the Hart Trophy that season. Messier became the driving force that propelled the Rangers to the Stanley Cup. Through timely trades, keen drafting and opportunistic free agent signings, Smith pieced together as talented a club as the Rangers ever had. The emergence of new superstars like Brian Leetch, Mike Richter and Adam Graves, who broke Hadfield's 50 goal mark in 1993-94 as well as a wealth of potential superstars like Sergei Zubov and Alexei Kovalev make the future of the New York Rangers brighter than ever.

RANGERS POWER PLAY AND PENALTY KILLING SINCE EXPANSION (1967-68)

Year	Power Play					Penalty Killing			
	PPG	ADV	PCT.	SHG	PPGA	TSH	PCT.	SHGA	
1967-68	46	217	21.2	1	42	223	81.2	7	
1968-69	56	275	20.4	4	35	223	84.3	9	
1969-70	52	295	17.6	7	40	269	85.1	7	
1970-71	60	234	25.6	5	41	253	83.8	3	
1971-72	60	257	23.3	14	44	282	84.4	10	
1972-73	54	238	22.7	5	39	250	84.4	5	
1973-74	66	222	29.7	9	45	239	81.2	2	
1974-75	84	296	28.4	6	54	295	81.7	7	
1975-76	67	323	20.7	3	68	277	75.5	11	
1976-77	60	290	20.7	6	55	268	79.5	16	
1977-78	78	279	28.0	10	48	244	80.3	6	
1978-79	75	306	24.5	9	78	311	74.9	12	
1979-80	79	304	26.0	8	54	303	82.2	7	
1980-81	63	351	17.9	14	83	392	78.8	12	
1981-82	68	306	22.2	7	75	319	76.5	12	
1982-83	71	317	22.4	12	75	312	76.0	8	
1983-84	74	295	25.1	12	76	347	78.1	11	
1984-85	72	305	23.6	9	64	333	80.8	8	
1985-86	73	362	20.2	9	81	365	77.8	4	
1986-87	75	375	20.0	12	71	379	81.3	15	
1987-88	111	491	22.6	6	82	423	80.6	11	
1988-89	85	457	18.6	13	85	371	77.1	17	
1989-90	103	442	23.3	7	77	362	78.7	8	
1990-91	91	389	23.4	9	73	362	79.8	10	
1991-92	81	387	20.9	14	60	395	84.8	12	
1992-93	77	420	18.3	12	84	446	81.2	18	
1993-94	96	417	23.0	20	67	435	84.6	5	

Recent Manpower Games Lost Due to Injuries

Year	Games Lost
1979-80	139
1980-81	296
1981-82	539
1982-83	348
1983-84	139
1984-85	480
1985-86	290
1986-87	339
1987-88	262
1988-89	367
1989-90	334
1990-91	249
1991-92	245
1992-93	208
1993-94	99

RANGERS YEAR-BY-YEAR SCORING STATISTICS

Year-By-Year Scoring
1926-27—1930-31

1926-27	GP	G	A	PTS	PIM	Playoffs GP	G	A	PTS	PIM
Bill Cook	44	33	4	37	58	2	1	0	1	10
Frank Boucher	44	13	15	28	17	2	0	0	0	4
Bun Cook	44	14	9	23	42	2	0	0	0	6
Taffy Abel	44	8	4	12	78	2	0	1	1	8
Paul Thompson	43	7	3	10	12	2	0	0	0	0
Murray Murdoch	44	6	4	10	12	2	0	0	0	0
Stan Brown	24	6	2	8	14	2	0	0	0	0
Billy Boyd	41	4	1	5	40	—	—	—	—	—
Ching Johnson	27	3	2	5	66	2	0	0	0	8
Leo Bourgault	20	1	1	2	28	2	0	0	0	4
Lester Patrick	1	0	0	0	2	—	—	—	—	—
Ollie Reinikka	16	0	0	0	0	—	—	—	—	—
Reg Mackey	34	0	0	0	16	1	0	0	0	0

1927-28	GP	G	A	PTS	PIM	Playoffs GP	G	A	PTS	PIM
Frank Boucher	44	23	12	35	14	9	7	1	8	2
Bun Cook	44	14	14	28	45	9	2	1	3	8
Bill Cook	43	18	6	24	42	9	2	3	5	26
Ching Johnson	43	10	6	16	146	9	1	1	2	46
Murray Murdoch	44	7	3	10	14	9	2	1	3	12
Paul Thompson	41	4	4	8	22	8	0	0	0	30
Leo Bourgault	37	7	0	7	72	9	0	0	0	10
Alex Gray	43	7	0	7	30	9	1	0	1	0
Billy Boyd	43	4	0	4	11	9	0	0	0	4
Taffy Abel	22	0	1	1	28	9	1	0	1	14
Laurie Scott	23	0	1	1	6	—	—	—	—	—
Patsy Callighen	36	0	0	0	32	9	0	0	0	0

1928-29	GP	G	A	PTS	PIM	Playoffs GP	G	A	PTS	PIM
Frank Boucher	44	10	16	26	8	6	1	0	1	0
Bill Cook	43	15	8	23	41	6	0	0	0	6
Bun Cook	43	13	5	18	70	6	1	0	1	12
Paul Thompson	44	10	7	17	38	6	0	2	2	6
Murray Murdoch	44	8	6	14	18	6	0	0	0	2
Butch Keeling	43	6	3	9	35	6	3	0	3	2
Leo Bourgault	44	2	3	5	59	6	0	0	0	0
Sparky Vail	18	3	0	3	16	6	0	0	0	2
Taffy Abel	44	2	1	3	41	6	0	0	0	8
Myles Lane	24	2	0	2	24	—	—	—	—	—
Russ Oatman	27	1	1	2	10	6	0	0	0	0
Ching Johnson	9	0	0	0	14	6	0	0	0	26
Jerry Carson	10	0	0	0	5	5	0	0	0	0
Billy Boyd	11	0	0	0	5	—	—	—	—	—

1929-30	GP	G	A	PTS	PIM	Playoffs GP	G	A	PTS	PIM
Frank Boucher	42	26	36	62	16	3	1	1	2	0
Bill Cook	44	29	30	59	56	4	0	1	1	11
Bun Cook	43	24	18	42	55	4	2	0	2	10
Butch Keeling	44	19	7	26	34	4	0	3	3	8
Murray Murdoch	44	13	13	26	22	4	3	0	3	6
Paul Thompson	44	7	12	19	36	4	0	0	0	2
Leo Bourgault	44	7	6	13	54	3	1	1	2	6
Ching Johnson	30	3	3	6	82	4	0	0	0	14
Roy Goldsworthy	44	4	1	5	16	4	0	0	0	2
Leo Quenneville	25	0	3	3	10	3	0	0	0	0
Ralph Taylor	24	2	0	2	28	4	0	0	0	10
Sparky Vail	32	1	1	2	2	4	0	0	0	0
Orville Heximer	19	1	0	1	4	—	—	—	—	—
Leo Reise	14	0	1	1	8	4	0	0	0	16
Bill Regan	10	0	0	0	4	4	0	0	0	0
Harry Foster	31	0	0	0	10	—	—	—	—	—

1930-31	GP	G	A	PTS	PIM	Playoffs GP	G	A	PTS	PIM
Bill Cook	44	30	12	42	39	4	3	0	3	4
Frank Boucher	44	12	27	39	20	4	0	2	2	0
Bun Cook	44	18	17	35	72	4	0	0	0	2
Butch Keeling	44	13	9	22	35	4	1	1	2	0
Murray Murdoch	44	7	7	14	8	4	0	2	2	0
Paul Thompson	44	7	7	14	36	4	3	0	3	2
Joe Jerwa	33	4	7	11	72	4	0	0	0	4

Year-By-Year Scoring
1930-31—1934-35

1930-31 (cont'd.)	GP	G	A	PTS	PIM	Playoffs GP	G	A	PTS	PIM
Ching Johnson	44	2	6	8	77	4	1	0	1	17
Henry Maracle	11	1	3	4	2	4	0	0	0	2
Frank Waite	17	1	3	4	4	–	–	–	–	–
Bill Regan	42	2	1	3	49	4	0	0	0	2
Eddie Rodden	24	0	3	3	8	–	–	–	–	–
Gene Carrigan	33	2	0	2	13	–	–	–	–	–
Leo Bourgault	10	0	1	1	6	–	–	–	–	–
Sam McAdam	4	0	0	0	0	–	–	–	–	–
Ernie Kenny	6	0	0	0	0	–	–	–	–	–
Frank Peters	44	0	0	0	59	4	0	0	0	2

1931-32	GP	G	A	PTS	PIM	Playoffs GP	G	A	PTS	PIM
Bill Cook	48	33	14	47	33	7	3	3	6	2
Cecil Dillon	48	23	15	38	22	7	2	1	3	4
Frank Boucher	48	12	23	35	18	7	3	6	9	0
Bun Cook	45	14	20	34	43	7	6	2	8	12
Art Somers	48	11	15	26	45	7	0	1	1	0
Murray Murdoch	48	5	16	21	32	7	0	2	2	2
Butch Keeling	48	17	3	20	38	7	2	1	3	12
Ching Johnson	47	3	10	13	106	7	2	0	2	24
Norman Gainor	46	3	9	12	9	7	0	0	0	2
Earl Seibert	44	4	6	10	88	7	1	2	3	14
Doug Brennan	38	4	3	7	40	7	1	0	1	10
Vic Desjardins	48	3	3	6	16	6	0	0	0	0
Ott Heller	21	2	2	4	9	7	3	1	4	8
Hib Milks	45	0	4	4	12	6	0	0	0	0

1932-33	GP	G	A	PTS	PIM	Playoffs GP	G	A	PTS	PIM
Bill Cook	48	28	22	50	51	8	3	2	5	4
Bun Cook	48	22	15	37	35	8	2	0	2	4
Frank Boucher	46	7	28	35	4	8	2	2	4	6
Cecil Dillon	48	21	10	31	12	8	8	2	10	6
Art Somers	48	7	15	22	28	8	1	4	5	8
Babe Siebert	42	9	10	19	38	8	1	0	1	12
Ching Johnson	48	8	9	17	127	8	1	0	1	14
Murray Murdoch	48	5	11	16	23	8	3	4	7	2
Ozzie Asmundson	48	5	10	15	20	8	0	2	2	4
Butch Keeling	47	8	6	14	22	8	0	2	2	8
Ott Heller	40	5	7	12	31	8	3	0	3	10
Doug Brennan	48	5	4	9	94	8	0	0	0	11
Earl Seibert	45	2	3	5	92	8	1	0	1	14
Carl Voss	10	2	1	3	4	–	–	–	–	–
Gordon Pettinger	35	1	2	3	18	8	0	0	0	0

1933-34	GP	G	A	PTS	PIM	Playoffs GP	G	A	PTS	PIM
Frank Boucher	48	14	30	44	4	2	0	0	0	0
Cecil Dillon	48	13	26	39	10	2	0	1	1	2
Bun Cook	48	18	15	33	36	2	0	0	0	2
Murray Murdoch	48	17	10	27	29	2	0	0	0	0
Bill Cook	48	13	13	26	21	2	0	0	0	2
Earl Seibert	48	13	10	23	66	2	0	0	0	4
Butch Keeling	48	15	5	20	20	2	0	0	0	0
Vic Ripley	35	5	12	17	10	2	1	0	1	4
Ozzie Asmundson	46	2	6	8	8	1	0	0	0	0
Ching Johnson	48	2	6	8	86	2	0	0	0	4
Ott Heller	48	2	5	7	29	2	0	0	0	0
Dan Cox	15	5	0	5	2	–	–	–	–	–
Art Somers	8	1	2	3	5	2	0	0	0	0
Duke Dutkowski	29	0	3	3	16	2	0	0	0	0
Jean Pusie	19	0	2	2	17	–	–	–	–	–
Babe Siebert	13	0	1	1	18	–	–	–	–	–
Albert Leduc	7	0	0	0	6	–	–	–	–	–
Lorne Carr	14	0	0	0	0	–	–	–	–	–
Doug Brennan	37	0	0	0	18	1	0	0	0	0

1934-35	GP	G	A	PTS	PIM	Playoffs GP	G	A	PTS	PIM
Frank Boucher	48	13	32	45	2	4	0	3	3	0
Bill Cook	48	21	15	36	23	4	1	2	3	7
Cecil Dillon	48	25	9	34	4	4	2	1	3	0
Bun Cook	48	13	21	34	26	4	2	0	2	0
Murray Murdoch	48	14	15	29	14	4	0	2	2	4
Earl Seibert	48	6	19	25	86	4	0	0	0	6
Lynn Patrick	48	9	13	22	17	4	2	2	4	0
Bert Connolly	47	10	11	21	23	4	1	0	1	0
Butch Connolly	47	15	4	19	14	4	2	1	3	0
Charlie Mason	46	5	9	14	14	4	0	1	1	0
Ott Heller	47	3	11	14	31	4	0	1	1	4

Year-By-Year Scoring
1934-35—1938-39

1934-35 (cont'd)

	GP	G	A	PTS	PIM	Playoffs GP	G	A	PTS	PIM
Ching Johnson	26	2	3	5	34	3	0	0	0	2
Art Somers	41	0	5	5	4	2	0	0	0	2
Alex Levinsky	21	0	4	4	6	–	–	–	–	–
Vic Ripley	4	0	2	2	2	–	–	–	–	–
Bill MacKenzie	20	1	0	1	10	3	0	0	0	0
Harold Starr	30	0	0	0	26	4	0	0	0	2

1935-36

	GP	G	A	PTS	PIM	Playoffs GP	G	A	PTS	PIM
Cecil Dillon	48	18	14	32	12					
Frank Boucher	48	11	18	29	2					
Lynn Patrick	48	11	14	25	29					
Butch Keeling	47	13	5	18	22					
Bill Cook	44	7	10	17	16					
Glenn Brydson	30	4	12	16	7					
Ott Heller	43	2	11	13	40					
Murray Murdoch	48	2	9	11	9					
Bun Cook	26	4	5	9	12					
Ching Johnson	47	5	3	8	58					
Howie Morenz	19	2	5	7	6					
Alex Shibicky	18	4	2	6	6					

1935-36 (cont'd)

	GP	G	A	PTS	PIM
Ant Coulter	23	1	5	6	26
Charlie Mason	28	1	5	6	30
Earl Seibert	17	2	3	5	6
Mac Colville	18	1	4	5	6
Bert Connolly	25	2	2	4	10
Thomas Ayres	28	0	4	4	38
Babe Pratt	17	1	1	2	16
Phil Watson	24	0	2	2	24
Neil Colville	1	0	0	0	0
Joe Cooper	1	0	0	0	0
Harold Starr	15	0	0	0	12

*Did not qualify for playoffs

1936-37

	GP	G	A	PTS	PIM	Playoffs GP	G	A	PTS	PIM
Cecil Dillon	48	20	11	31	13	9	0	3	3	0
Phil Watson	48	11	17	28	22	9	0	2	2	9
Neil Colville	45	10	18	28	33	9	3	3	6	0
Butch Keeling	48	22	4	26	18	9	3	2	5	2
Lynn Patrick	45	8	16	24	23	9	3	0	3	2
Alex Shibicky	47	14	8	22	30	9	1	4	5	0
Frank Boucher	44	7	13	20	5	9	2	3	5	0
Mac Colville	46	7	12	19	10	9	1	2	3	2
Ott Heller	48	5	12	17	42	9	0	0	0	11
Babe Pratt	47	8	7	15	23	9	3	1	4	11
Murray Murdoch	48	0	14	14	16	9	1	1	2	0
Art Coulter	47	1	5	6	27	9	0	3	3	15
Bill Cook	21	1	4	5	6	–	–	–	–	–
Joe Cooper	48	0	3	3	42	9	1	1	2	12
Eddie Wares	2	2	0	2	0	–	–	–	–	–
Clint Smith	2	1	0	1	0	–	–	–	–	–
Bryan Hextall	3	0	1	1	0	–	–	–	–	–
Joe Krol	1	0	0	0	0	–	–	–	–	–
Ching Johnson	34	0	0	0	2	9	0	1	1	4

1937-38

	GP	G	A	PTS	PIM	Playoffs GP	G	A	PTS	PIM
Cecil Dillon	48	21	18	39	6	3	1	0	1	0
Clint Smith	48	14	23	37	0	3	2	0	2	0
Neil Colville	45	17	19	36	11	2	0	1	1	0
Alex Shibicky	48	17	18	35	26	3	2	0	2	2
Lynn Patrick	48	15	19	34	24	3	0	1	1	2
Phil Watson	48	7	25	32	52	3	0	2	2	0
Mac Colville	48	14	14	28	18	3	0	2	2	0
Bryan Hextall	48	17	4	21	6	3	2	0	2	0
Babe Pratt	47	5	14	19	56	2	0	0	0	2
Butch Keeling	39	8	9	17	12	3	0	1	1	2
Ott Heller	48	2	14	16	68	3	0	1	1	2
Art Coulter	43	5	10	15	80	–	–	–	–	–
Bobby Kirk	39	4	8	12	14	–	–	–	–	–
Joe Cooper	46	3	2	5	56	3	0	0	0	4
Muzz Patrick	1	0	2	2	0	3	0	0	0	2
Dutch Hiller	9	0	1	1	2	1	0	0	0	0
Frank Boucher	18	0	1	1	2	–	–	–	–	–
Larry Molyneaux	2	0	0	0	2	3	0	0	0	8
Jonny Sherf						1	0	0	0	0

1938-39

	GP	G	A	PTS	PIM	Playoffs GP	G	A	PTS	PIM
Clint Smith	48	21	20	41	2	7	1	2	3	0
Neil Colville	47	18	19	37	12	7	0	2	2	2
Phil Watson	48	15	22	37	42	7	1	1	2	7
Bryan Hextall	48	20	15	35	18	7	0	1	1	4
Alex Shibicky	48	24	9	33	24	7	3	1	4	2
Dutch Hiller	48	10	19	29	22	7	1	0	1	9
Lynn Patrick	35	8	21	29	25	7	1	1	2	0
Mac Colville	48	7	21	28	26	7	1	2	3	4
Cecil Dillon	48	12	15	27	6	1	0	0	0	0
Ott Helle	48	0	23	23	42	7	0	1	1	10
Babe Pratt	48	2	19	21	20	7	1	2	3	9
George Allen	19	6	6	12	10	7	0	0	0	4
Art Coulter	4	4	8	12	58	7	1	1	2	6
Muzz Patrick	48	1	10	11	64	7	1	0	1	17

Year-By-Year Scoring
1938-39—1942-43

1938-39 (cont'd.)	GP	G	A	PTS	PIM	Playoffs GP	G	A	PTS	PIM
Joe Krol	1	1	1	2	0	—	—	—	—	—
Bill Carse	1	0	1	1	0	6	1	1	2	0
Larry Molyneaux	43	0	1	1	18	7	0	0	0	0

1939-40	GP	G	A	PTS	PIM	Playoffs GP	G	A	PTS	PIM
Bryan Hextall	48	24	15	39	52	12	4	3	7	11
Neil Colville	48	19	19	38	22	12	2	7	9	18
Phil Watson	48	7	28	35	42	12	3	6	9	16
Alex Shibicky	43	11	21	32	33	11	2	5	7	4
Dutch Hiller	48	13	18	31	57	12	2	4	6	2
Kilby MacDonald	44	15	13	28	19	12	0	2	2	4
Lynn Patrick	48	12	16	28	34	12	2	2	4	4
Clint Smith	41	8	16	24	2	12	1	3	4	2
Mac Colville	47	7	14	21	12	12	3	2	5	6
Ott Heller	47	5	14	19	26	12	0	3	3	12
Alfie Pike	47	8	9	17	38	12	3	1	4	6
Babe Pratt	48	4	13	17	61	12	3	1	4	18
Art Coulter	48	1	9	10	68	12	1	0	1	21
Muzz Patrick	46	2	4	6	44	12	3	0	3	13
Johnny Polich	1	0	0	0	0	—	—	—	—	—
Stan Smith	1	0	0	0	0	1	0	0	0	0
Cliff Barton	3	0	0	0	0	—	—	—	—	—

1940-41	GP	G	A	PTS	PIM	Playoffs GP	G	A	PTS	PIM
Bryan Hextall	48	26	18	44	16	3	0	1	1	0
Lynn Patrick	48	20	24	44	12	3	1	0	1	14
Neil Colville	48	14	28	42	28	3	1	1	2	0
Phil Watson	40	11	25	36	49	3	0	2	2	9
Mac Colville	47	14	17	31	18	3	1	1	2	2
Clint Smith	48	14	11	25	0	3	0	0	0	0
Alex Shibicky	40	10	14	24	14	3	1	0	1	2
Babe Pratt	47	3	17	20	52	3	1	1	2	6
Alfie Pike	48	6	13	19	23	3	0	1	1	2
Art Coulter	35	5	14	19	42	3	0	0	0	14
Dutch Hiller	45	8	10	18	20	3	0	0	0	0
Ott Heller	48	2	16	18	42	3	0	1	1	4
Kilby MacDonald	47	5	6	11	12	3	1	0	1	0
Muzz Patrick	47	2	8	10	21	3	0	0	0	2
Stan Smith	8	2	1	3	0	—	—	—	—	—
Herb Foster	4	1	0	1	5	—	—	—	—	—
Bill Allum	1	0	1	1	0	—	—	—	—	—
Johnny Polich	2	0	1	1	0	—	—	—	—	—
Bill Juzda	5	0	0	0	2	—	—	—	—	—

1941-42	GP	G	A	PTS	PIM	Playoffs GP	G	A	PTS	PIM
Bryan Hextall	48	24	32	56	30	6	1	1	2	4
Lynn Patrick	47	32	22	54	18	6	1	0	1	0
Phil Watson	48	15	37	52	58	6	1	4	5	6
Alex Shibicky	45	20	14	34	16	6	3	2	5	2
Clint Smith	47	10	24	34	4	5	0	0	0	0
Grant Warwick	44	16	17	33	36	6	0	1	1	2
Neil Colville	48	8	25	33	37	6	0	5	5	6
Mac Colville	46	14	16	30	26	6	3	1	4	0
Babe Pratt	47	4	24	28	65	6	1	3	4	24
Alfie Pike	34	8	19	27	16	6	1	0	1	4
Alan Kuntz	31	10	11	21	10	6	1	0	1	2
Art Coulter	47	1	16	17	31	6	0	1	1	4
Bill Juzda	45	4	8	12	29	6	0	1	1	4
Ott Heller	35	6	5	11	22	6	0	0	0	0
Hub Macey	9	3	5	8	0	1	0	0	0	0
Norman Tustin	18	2	4	6	0	—	—	—	—	—
Norman Burns	11	0	4	4	2	—	—	—	—	—

1942-43	GP	G	A	PTS	PIM	1942-43 (cont'd)	GP	G	A	PTS	PIM
Lynn Patrick	50	22	39	61	28	Felix Mancuso	21	6	8	14	13
Bryan Hextall	50	27	32	59	28	Joe Shack	20	5	9	14	6
Phil Watson	46	14	28	42	44	Joe Bell	15	2	5	7	6
Grant Warwick	50	17	18	35	31	Hub Macey	9	3	3	6	0
Clint Smith	47	12	21	33	4	Gordon Davidson	35	2	3	5	4
Bob Kirkpatrick	49	12	12	24	6	Lin Bend	8	3	1	4	2
Hank Goldup	36	11	20	21	33	Billy Gooden	12	0	3	3	0
Alfie Pike	41	6	16	22	48	Dudley Garrett	23	1	1	2	18
Angus Cameron	35	8	11	19	0	Babe Pratt	4	0	2	2	6
Ott Heller	45	4	14	18	14	Billy Warwick	1	0	1	1	4
Vic Myles	45	6	9	15	57	Spence Tatchell	1	0	0	0	0

*Did not qualify for playoffs

Year-By-Year Scoring
1943-44—1947-48

1943-44

Player	GP	G	A	PTS	PIM
Bryan Hextall	50	21	33	54	41
Dutch Hiller	50	18	22	40	15
Ott Heller	50	8	27	35	29
Ab DeMarco	36	14	19	33	2
John Mahaffy	28	9	20	29	0
Oscar Aubuchon	38	15	12	27	4
Fern Gauthier	33	14	10	24	0
John McDonald	43	10	9	19	6
Billy Gooden	41	9	8	17	15
Grant Warwick	18	8	9	17	14
Kilby MacDonald	24	7	9	16	4
Bob Dill	28	6	10	16	66
Frank Boucher	15	4	10	14	2
Bob McDonald	39	5	6	11	14
Billy Warwick	13	3	2	5	12
Chuck Scherza	24	3	2	5	13

1943-44 (cont'd)

Player	GP	G	A	PTS	PIM
Dan Raleigh	15	2	2	4	2
Gordon Davidson	16	1	3	4	4
Roger Leger	7	1	2	3	2
Aldo Palazzari	12	2	0	2	0
Tommy Dewar	9	0	2	2	4
Chuck Sands	9	0	2	2	0
Hank D'Amore	4	1	0	1	2
Jimmy Jamieson	1	0	1	1	0
Archie Fraser	3	0	1	1	0
Tony Demers	1	0	0	0	0
Hank Dyck	1	0	0	0	0
Bob McDonald	1	0	0	0	0
Lloyd Mohns	1	0	0	0	0
Jack Mann	3	0	0	0	0
Max Labovitch	5	0	0	0	0
Art Strobel	7	0	0	0	0

*Did not qualify for playoffs

1944-45

Player	GP	G	A	PTS	PIM
Ab DeMarco	50	24	30	54	10
Grant Warwick	52	20	22	42	25
Hank Goldup	48	17	25	42	25
Fred Thurier	50	16	19	35	14
Fred Hunt	44	13	9	22	6
Joe Shack	50	4	18	22	14
Ants Atanas	49	13	8	21	40
Phil Watson	45	11	8	19	24
Ott Heller	45	7	12	19	26
Kilby MacDonald	36	9	6	15	12
Bob Dill	48	9	5	14	69

1944-45 (cont'd)

Player	GP	G	A	PTS	PIM
Bucko McDonald	40	2	9	11	0
Jack Mann	6	3	4	7	0
Bill Moe	35	2	4	6	14
Chuck Scherza	22	2	3	5	18
Guy Labrie	27	2	2	4	14
Neil Colville	4	0	1	1	2
Alex Ritson	1	0	0	0	0
Len Wharton	1	0	0	0	0
Jim Drummond	2	0	0	0	0
Hal Cooper	8	0	0	0	2

*Did not qualify for playoffs

1945-46

Player	GP	G	A	PTS	PIM
Ab DeMarco	50	20	27	47	20
Grant Warwick	45	19	18	37	19
Edgar Laprade	49	15	19	34	0
Phil Watson	49	12	14	26	43
Tony Leswick	50	15	9	24	26
Alfie Pike	33	7	9	16	18
Alex Shibicky	33	10	5	15	12
Lynn Patrick	38	8	6	14	30
Mac Colville	39	7	6	13	8
Cal Gardner	16	8	2	10	2
Neil Colville	49	5	4	9	25
Bill Moe	48	4	4	8	14

1945-46 (cont'd)

Player	GP	G	A	PTS	PIM
Rene Trudell	16	3	5	8	4
Hank Goldup	19	6	1	7	11
Ott Heller	34	2	3	5	14
Bill Juzda	32	1	3	4	17
Church Russell	17	0	5	5	2
Hal Brown	13	2	1	3	2
Muzz Patrick	24	0	2	2	4
Hal Laycoe	17	0	2	2	6
Bryan Hextall	3	0	1	1	0
Alan Kuntz	14	0	1	1	2
Chuck Rayner	40	0	0	0	6

*Did not qualify for playoffs

1946-47

Player	GP	G	A	PTS	PIM
Tony Leswick	59	27	14	41	51
Grant Warwick	54	20	20	40	24
Edgar Laprade	58	15	25	40	9
Bryan Hextall	60	20	10	30	18
Carl Gardner	52	13	16	29	30
Church Russell	54	20	8	28	8
Rene Trudell	59	8	16	24	38
Neil Colville	60	4	16	20	16
Ab DeMarco	44	9	10	19	4
Alfie Pike	31	7	11	18	2
Phil Watson	48	6	12	18	17
Bill Moe	59	4	10	14	44
Hal Laycoe	58	1	12	13	25

1946-47 (cont'd)

Player	GP	G	A	PTS	PIM
Joe Bill	47	6	4	10	12
Joe Cooper	59	2	8	10	38
Bill Juzda	45	3	5	8	60
Joe Levandoski	8	1	1	2	0
Jean Paul Lamirande	14	1	1	2	14
Harry Bell	1	0	1	1	0
Jean Paul Denis	6	0	1	1	0
Jack Lancien	1	0	0	0	0
Norm Larson	1	0	0	0	0
Sherman White	1	0	0	0	0
Mel Read	6	0	0	0	8
Mac Colville	14	0	0	0	8

*Did not qualify for playoffs

1947-48

Player	GP	G	A	PTS	PIM	Playoffs GP	G	A	PTS	PIM
Buddy O'Connor	60	24	36	60	8	6	1	4	5	0
Edgar Laprade	59	13	34	47	7	6	1	4	50	0
Tony Leswick	60	24	16	40	76	6	3	2	5	8
Phil Watson	54	18	15	33	54	5	2	3	5	2
Don Raleigh	52	15	18	33	2	6	2	0	2	2
Eddie Kullman	51	15	17	32	32	6	1	0	1	2
Grant Warwick	40	17	12	29	30	—	—	—	—	—
Cal Gardner	58	7	18	25	71	5	0	0	0	0
Bryan Hextall	43	8	14	22	18	6	1	3	4	0
Rene Trudell	54	13	7	20	30	5	0	0	0	2
Frank Eddolls	58	6	13	19	16	2	0	0	0	0
Neil Colville	55	4	12	16	25	6	1	0	1	6
Bill Moe	59	1	15	16	31	1	0	0	0	0
Bill Juzda	60	3	9	12	70	6	0	0	0	9
Ed Slowinski	38	6	5	11	2	4	0	0	0	0
Church Russell	19	0	3	3	2	—	—	—	—	—
Ronnie Rowe	5	1	0	1	0	—	—	—	—	—
Fred Shero	19	1	0	1	2	6	0	1	1	6
Jean Lamirande	18	0	1	1	6	6	0	0	0	4

Year-By-Year Scoring
1947-48—1950-51

1947-48 (cont'd)	GP	G	A	PTS	PIM	Playoffs GP	G	A	PTS	PIM
Herb Foster	1	0	0	0	0	–	–	–	–	–
Larry Kwong	1	0	0	0	0	–	–	–	–	–
Hub Anslow	2	0	0	0	0	–	–	–	–	–
Bing Juckes	2	0	0	0	0	–	–	–	–	–
Fern Perrault	2	0	0	0	0	–	–	–	–	–
Billy Taylor	2	0	0	0	0	–	–	–	–	–
Ken Davies	–	–	–	–	–	1	0	0	0	0
Duncan Fisher	–	–	–	–	–	1	0	1	1	0
Jack Lancien	–	–	–	–	–	2	0	0	0	2
Nick Mickoski	–	–	–	–	–	2	0	1	1	0

1948-49	GP	G	A	PTS	PIM
Buddy O'Connor	46	11	24	35	0
Alex Kaleta	56	12	19	31	18
Edgar Laprade	56	18	12	30	12
Penti Lund	59	14	16	30	16
Tony Leswick	60	13	14	27	70
Don Raleigh	41	10	16	26	8
Dunc Fisher	60	9	16	25	40
Nick Mickoski	54	13	9	22	20
Clint Albright	59	14	5	19	19
Jack Gordon	31	3	9	12	0
Allan Stanley	40	2	8	10	22
Ed Kullman	18	4	5	9	14
Fred Shero	59	3	6	9	64
Wally Stanowski	60	1	8	9	16

*Did not qualify for playoffs

1948-49 (cont'd)	GP	G	A	PTS	PIM
Bill Moe	60	0	9	9	60
Frank Eddolis	34	4	2	6	10
Neil Colville	14	0	5	5	2
Wes Trainor	17	1	2	3	6
Ed Slowinski	20	1	1	2	2
Ray Manson	1	0	1	1	0
Red Staley	1	0	1	1	0
Elwin Morris	18	0	1	1	8
Dick Kotanen	1	0	0	0	0
Bucky Buchanan	2	0	0	0	0
Val DeLory	1	0	0	0	0
Odie Lowe	1	0	0	0	0
Jack Evans	3	0	0	0	4
Chuck Rayner	58	0	0	0	2

1949-50	GP	G	A	PTS	PIM	Playoffs GP	G	A	PTS	PIM
Edgar Laprade	60	22	22	44	2	12	3	5	8	4
Tony Leswick	69	19	25	44	85	12	2	4	6	12
Ed Slowinski	63	14	23	37	12	12	2	6	8	6
Don Raleigh	70	12	25	37	11	12	4	5	9	4
Duncan Fisher	70	12	21	33	42	12	3	3	6	14
Buddy O'Connor	66	11	22	33	4	12	4	2	6	4
Alex Kaleta	67	17	14	31	40	10	0	3	3	0
Pentti Lund	64	18	9	27	16	12	6	5	11	0
Nick Mickoski	47	10	10	20	10	12	1	5	6	2
Pat Egan	70	5	11	16	50	12	3	1	4	6
Jack McLeod	38	6	9	15	2	7	0	0	0	0
Fred Shero	67	2	8	10	71	7	0	1	1	2
Bud Poile	28	3	6	9	8	–	–	–	–	–
Allan Stanley	55	4	4	8	58	12	2	5	7	10
Gus Kyle	70	3	5	8	143	12	1	2	3	30
Frank Eddolls	58	2	6	8	20	11	0	1	1	4
Jean Lamirande	16	4	3	7	6	2	0	0	0	0
Jack Lancien	43	1	4	5	27	4	0	1	1	0
Bing Juckes	14	2	1	3	6	–	–	–	–	–
Odie Lowe	3	1	1	2	0	–	–	–	–	–
Don Smith	10	1	1	2	0	1	0	0	0	0
Wally Stanowski	37	1	1	2	10	–	–	–	–	–
Sherman White	3	0	2	2	0	–	–	–	–	–
Doug Adam	4	0	1	1	0	–	–	–	–	–
Jean Denis	4	0	1	1	2	–	–	–	–	–
Jack Gordon	1	0	0	0	0	9	1	1	2	7
Fern Perrault	1	0	0	0	0	–	–	–	–	–
Bill Kyle	2	0	0	0	0	–	–	–	–	–
Jack Evans	3	0	0	0	2	–	–	–	–	–
Bill McDonagh	4	0	0	0	2	–	–	–	–	–
Chick Webster	14	0	0	0	4	–	–	–	–	–
Chuck Rayner	69	0	0	0	6	12	0	0	0	0

1950-51	GP	G	A	PTS	PIM
Reg Sinclair	70	18	21	39	70
Don Raleigh	64	15	24	39	18
Buddy O'Connor	66	16	20	36	0
Nick Mickoski	64	20	15	35	12
Ed Slowinski	69	14	18	32	15
Ed Kullman	70	14	18	32	88
Zellio Toppanazzi	55	14	13	27	27
Tony Leswick	70	15	11	26	112
Edgar Laprade	42	10	13	23	0
Al Stanley	70	7	14	21	75
Pentti Lund	59	4	16	20	6
Jack McLeod	41	5	10	15	2
Pat Egan	70	5	10	15	70
Frank Eddolis	68	3	8	11	24

*Did not qualify for playoffs

1950-51 (cont'd)	GP	G	A	PTS	PIM
Alex Kaleta	58	3	4	7	26
Wally Stanowski	49	1	5	6	28
Gus Kyle	64	2	3	5	92
Bill Kyle	1	0	3	3	0
Vic Howe	3	1	0	1	0
Ed Harrison	4	1	0	1	2
Jack Evans	49	1	0	1	95
Jack Gordon	4	0	1	1	0
Jack Lancien	19	0	1	1	8
Dick Kotanen	1	0	0	0	0
Bob Wood	1	0	0	0	0
Bill Wylie	1	0	0	0	0
Dunc Fisher	12	0	0	0	0
Chuck Rayner	66	0	0	0	6

Year-By-Year Scoring
1951-52—1955-56

1951-52	GP	G	A	PTS	PIM
Don Raleigh	70	19	42	61	14
Ed Slowinski	64	21	22	43	18
Paul Ronty	65	12	31	43	16
Gaye Stewart	69	15	25	40	22
Wally Hergesheimer	68	26	12	38	6
Edgar Laprade	70	9	29	38	8
Hy Buller	68	12	23	35	96
Reg Sinclair	69	20	10	30	33
Herb Dickenson	37	14	13	27	8
Eddie Kullman	64	11	10	21	59
Nick Mickoski	43	7	13	20	20
Al Stanley	50	5	14	19	52

*Did not qualify for playoffs

1951-52 (cont'd)	GP	G	A	PTS	PIM
Steve Kraftcheck	58	8	9	17	30
Jim Ross	51	2	9	11	25
Frank Eddolis	42	3	5	8	18
Jack Evans	52	1	6	7	83
Jack Stoddard	20	4	2	6	2
Jack McLeod	13	2	3	5	2
Zellio Toppazzini	16	1	1	2	4
Clare Martin	15	0	1	1	8
Jim Conacher	16	0	1	1	2
Lloyd Ailsby	3	0	0	0	2
Chuck Rayner	53	0	0	0	4

1952-53	GP	G	A	PTS	PIM
Wally Hergesheimer	70	30	29	59	10
Paul Ronty	70	16	38	54	20
Nick Mickoski	70	19	16	35	39
Jack Stoddard	60	12	13	25	29
Hy Buller	70	7	18	25	73
Neil Strain	52	11	13	24	12
Don Raleigh	55	4	18	22	2
Leo Reise	61	4	15	19	53
Ed Kullman	70	8	10	18	61
Allan Stanley	70	5	12	17	52
Harry Howell	67	3	8	11	46
Steve Kraftcheck	69	2	9	11	45
Dean Prentice	55	6	3	9	20
Pete Babando	30	4	5	9	8
Herb Dickenson	11	4	4	8	2
Aldo Guidolin	30	4	4	8	24
Ed Slowinski	37	2	5	7	14

*Did not qualify for playoffs

1952-53 (cont'd)	GP	G	A	PTS	PIM
George Senick	13	2	3	5	8
Jim Conacher	17	1	4	5	2
Ron Murphy	15	3	1	4	0
Edgar Laprade	11	3	2	1	3	2
Gaye Steward	18	1	2	3	8
Jim Ross	11	0	2	2	4
Kelly Burnett	3	1	0	1	0
Dolph Kukulowicz	3	1	0	1	0
Gordie Haworth	2	0	1	1	0
Andy Bathgate	18	0	1	1	6
Frank Bathgate	2	0	0	0	2
Michel Labadie	3	0	0	0	0
Jack McLeod	3	0	0	0	2
Ian Mackintosh	4	0	0	0	4
Chuck Rayner	20	0	0	0	2
Lorne Worsley	50	0	0	0	2

1953-54	GP	G	A	PTS	PIM
Paul Ronty	70	13	33	46	18
Don Raleigh	70	15	30	45	16
Wally Hergesheimer	66	27	16	43	42
Camille Henry	66	24	15	39	10
Nick Micoski	68	19	16	35	22
Max Bentley	57	14	18	32	15
Dean Prentice	52	4	13	17	18
Hy Buller	41	3	14	17	40
Harry Howell	67	7	9	16	58
Ed Kullman	70	4	10	14	44
Ivan Irwin	56	2	12	14	109
Ike Hildebrand	31	6	7	13	12
Doug Bentley	20	2	10	12	2
Bob Chrystal	64	5	5	10	44

*Did not qualify for playoffs

1953-54 (cont'd)	GP	G	A	PTS	PIM
Jack Evans	44	4	4	8	73
Leo Reise	70	3	5	8	71
Aldo Guidolin	68	3	2	6	8	51
Edgar Laprade	35	1	6	7	2
Andy Bathgate	20	1	2	3	4	18
Ron Murphy	27	1	3	4	20
Glen Sonmor	15	1	2	3	0	17
Billy Dea	14	1	1	2	2
Allan Stanley	10	0	2	2	11
Bill Chalmers	1	0	0	0	0
Vic Howe	1	0	0	0	0
Dolph Kukulowicz	1	0	0	0	0
Bill McCreary	1	0	0	0	0

1954-55	GP	G	A	PTS	PIM
Danny Lewicki	70	29	24	53	8
Andy Bathgate	70	20	20	40	37
Don Raleigh	69	8	32	40	19
Dean Prentice	70	16	15	31	20
Ron Murphy	66	14	16	30	36
Larry Popein	70	11	17	28	27
Nick Mickoski	18	0	19	19	6
Pete Conacher	52	10	7	17	10
Bill Gadsby	52	8	8	16	42
Harry Howell	70	2	14	16	87
Bob Chrystal	68	6	9	15	68
Paul Ronty	54	4	11	15	10
Edgar Laprade	60	3	11	14	0
Ivan Irwin	60	0	13	12	85

*Did not qualify for playoffs

1954-55 (cont'd)	GP	G	A	PTS	PIM
Camille Henry	21	5	2	7	4
Aldo Guidolin	70	5	2	5	7	34
Wally Hergesheimer	14	4	2	6	4
Vic Howe	29	4	2	6	10
Jack Evans	47	0	5	5	91
Bill Ezinicki	16	2	2	4	22
Lou Fontinato	28	2	2	4	60
Jackie McLeod	11	1	1	2	2
Bill McCreary	8	0	2	2	0
Allan Stanley	12	0	2	1	2
Dick Bouchard	1	0	0	0	0
Ron Howell	3	0	0	0	4
Glen Sonmor	13	0	0	0	0
Lorne Worsley	65	0	0	0	2

1955-56	GP	G	A	PTS	PIM	Playoffs GP	G	A	PTS	PIM
Andy Bathgate	70	19	47	66	59	5	1	2	3	2
Dave Creighton	70	20	31	51	43	5	0	0	0	4
Bill Gadsby	70	9	42	51	84	5	1	3	4	4
Danny Lewicki	70	18	27	45	26	5	0	3	3	0
Ron Murphy	66	16	28	44	71	5	0	1	1	2
Dean Prentice	70	24	18	42	44	5	1	0	1	2
Wally Hergesheimer	70	22	18	40	26	5	0	1	1	0
Larry Popein	64	14	25	39	37	5	0	1	1	2
Andy Hebenton	70	24	14	38	8	5	1	0	1	2
Bronco Horvath	66	12	17	29	40	5	1	2	3	4
Pete Conacher	41	11	11	22	10	5	0	0	0	0
Lou Fontinato	70	3	15	18	202	4	0	0	0	6
Harry Howell	70	3	15	18	77	5	0	1	1	4
Don Raleigh	29	2	12	13	4	—	—	—	—	—
Guy Gendron	63	5	7	12	38	5	2	1	3	2
Jack Evans	70	2	9	11	104	5	1	0	1	18

Year-By-Year Scoring
1956-57—1960-61

1956-57

	GP	G	A	PTS	PIM	Playoffs GP	G	A	PTS	PIM
Andy Bathgate	70	27	50	77	60	5	2	0	2	7
Andy Hebenton	70	21	23	44	10	5	2	0	2	2
Dean Prentice	68	19	23	42	38	5	0	2	2	4
Bill Gadsby	70	4	37	41	72	5	1	2	3	2
Dave Creighton	70	18	21	39	42	5	2	2	4	2
Danny Lewicki	70	18	20	38	47	5	0	1	1	2
Larry Popein	67	11	19	30	20	5	0	3	3	0
Camille Henry	36	14	15	29	2	5	2	3	5	0
Red Sullivan	42	6	17	23	36	5	1	2	3	4
Ron Murphy	33	7	12	19	14	5	0	0	0	0
Gerry Foley	69	7	9	16	48	3	0	0	0	0
Guy Gendron	70	9	6	15	40	5	0	1	1	6
Parker MacDonald	45	7	8	15	24	1	1	1	2	0
Lou Fontinato	70	3	12	15	139	5	0	0	0	7
Harry Howell	65	2	10	12	70	5	1	0	1	6
Larry Cahan	61	5	4	9	65	3	0	0	0	2
Jack Evans	70	3	6	9	110	5	0	1	1	4
Bruce Cline	30	2	3	5	10	—	—	—	—	—
Bronco Horvath	7	1	2	3	4	—	—	—	—	—

1957-58

	GP	G	A	PTS	PIM	Playoffs GP	G	A	PTS	PIM
Andy Bathgate	65	30	48	78	42	6	5	3	8	6
Camille Henry	70	32	24	56	2	6	1	4	5	5
Dave Creighton	70	17	35	52	40	6	3	3	6	2
Bill Gadsby	65	14	32	46	48	6	0	3	3	4
Red Sullivan	70	11	35	46	61	1	0	0	0	0
Andy Hebenton	70	21	24	45	17	6	2	3	5	4
Larry Popein	70	12	22	34	22	6	1	0	1	4
Danny Lewicki	70	11	19	30	26	6	0	0	0	6
Guy Gendron	70	10	17	27	68	6	1	0	1	11
Dean Prentice	38	13	9	22	14	6	1	3	4	4
Parker MacDonald	70	8	10	18	30	6	1	2	3	2
Jack Evans	70	4	8	12	108	6	0	0	0	17
Harry Howell	70	4	7	11	62	6	1	0	1	8
Lou Fontinato	70	3	8	11	152	6	0	1	1	6
Hank Ciesla	60	2	6	8	16	6	0	2	2	0
Gerry Foley	68	2	5	7	43	6	0	1	1	2
Larry Cahan	34	1	1	2	20	5	0	0	0	4

1958-59

	GP	G	A	PTS	PIM
Andy Bathgate	70	40	48	88	48
George Sullivan	70	21	42	63	56
Andy Hebenton	70	33	29	62	8
Camille Henry	70	23	35	58	2
Bill Gadsby	70	5	46	51	56
Dean Prentice	70	17	33	50	11
Larry Popein	61	13	21	34	28
Eddie Schack	67	7	14	21	109
James Bartlett	70	11	9	20	118
Hank Diesla	69	6	14	20	21
Harry Howell	70	4	10	14	101
Lou Fontinato	64	7	6	13	149
Les Colwill	69	7	6	13	16
John Hanna	70	1	10	11	83
Wally Hergesheimer	22	3	0	3	6
Jack Bownass	35	1	2	3	20
Earl Ingarfield	35	1	2	3	10
Larry Cahan	16	1	0	1	8

*Did not qualify for playoffs

1959-60

	GP	G	A	PTS	PIM
Andy Bathgate	70	26	48	74	28
Dean Prentice	70	32	34	66	43
Andy Hebenton	70	19	27	46	4
Red Sullivan	70	12	25	37	81
Larry Popein	66	14	22	36	16
Bill Gadsby	65	9	22	31	60
Ken Schinkel	69	13	16	29	27
Brian Cullen	64	8	21	29	6
Camille Henry	49	12	15	27	6
Eddie Shack	62	8	10	18	110
Bob Kabel	44	5	11	16	32
Harry Howell	67	7	6	13	58
Lou Fontinato	64	2	11	13	137
Jim Bartlett	44	8	4	12	48
John Hanna	61	4	8	12	87
Art Stratton	18	2	5	7	2
Jack Bownass	37	2	5	7	34
Mel Pearson	23	1	5	6	13
Earl Ingarfield	20	1	2	3	2
Irv Spencer	32	1	2	3	20
Bill Sweeney	4	1	0	1	0
Ian Cushenan	17	0	1	1	22
Dave Balon	3	0	0	0	0
Parker MacDonald	4	0	0	0	0
Noel Price	6	0	0	0	0

*Did not qualify for playoffs

1960-61

	GP	G	A	PTS	PIM
Andy Bathgate	70	29	48	77	22
Andy Hebenton	70	26	28	54	10
Camille Henry	53	28	25	53	8
Dean Prentice	56	20	25	45	17
George Sullivan	70	9	31	40	66
Bill Gadsby	65	9	26	35	49
Earl Ingarfield	66	13	21	34	18
Brian Cullen	42	11	19	30	6
Johnny Wilson	56	14	12	26	24
Pat Hannigan	53	11	9	20	24
Ted Hampson	69	6	14	20	4
Harry Howell	70	7	10	17	62
Floyd Smith	29	5	9	14	0
John Hanna	46	1	8	9	34
Irv Spencer	56	1	8	9	30
Ken Schinkel	38	2	6	8	18
Don Johns	63	1	7	8	34
Jim Morrison	19	1	6	7	6
Lou Fontinato	53	2	3	5	100
Jean Ratelle	3	2	1	3	0
Len Ronson	13	2	1	3	10
Eddie Shack	12	1	2	3	17
Dave Balon	13	1	2	3	8
Danny Belisle	4	2	0	2	0
Bob Kabel	4	0	2	2	0
Al Lebrun	4	0	2	2	4
Rod Gilbert	1	0	1	1	2
Bob Cunningham	3	0	1	1	0

Year-By-Year Scoring
1960-61—1964-65

1960-61 (cont'd)	GP	G	A	PTS	PIM
Larry Popein	4	0	1	1	0
Noel Price	1	0	0	0	2
Wayne Hall	4	0	0	0	0

1960-61 (cont'd)	GP	G	A	PTS	PIM
Phil Latreille	4	0	0	0	2
Ron Hutchinson	9	0	0	0	0

*Did not qualify for playoffs

1961-62	GP	G	A	PTS	PIM	GP	G	A	PTS	PIM
Andy Bathgate	70	28	56	84	44	6	1	2	3	4
Dean Prentice	68	22	38	60	20	3	0	2	2	0
Earl Ingarfield	70	26	31	57	18	6	3	2	5	2
Andy Hebenton	70	18	24	42	10	6	1	2	3	0
Camille Henry	60	23	15	38	8	5	0	0	0	0
Doug Harvey	69	6	24	30	42	6	0	1	1	2
Ken Schinkel	65	7	21	28	17	2	1	0	1	0
Ted Hampson	68	4	24	28	10	6	0	1	1	0
Guy Gendron	69	14	11	25	71	6	3	1	4	2
Albert Langlois	69	7	18	25	90	6	0	1	1	2
Pat Hannigan	56	8	14	22	34	4	0	0	0	2
Harry Howell	66	6	15	21	89	6	0	1	1	8
Dave Balon	30	4	11	15	11	6	2	3	5	2
John Wilson	40	11	3	14	14	6	2	2	4	4
Jean Ratelle	31	4	8	12	4	–	–	–	–	–
Irv Spencer	43	2	10	12	31	1	0	0	0	2
Larry Cahan	57	2	7	9	85	6	0	0	0	10
Vic Hadfield	44	3	1	4	22	4	0	0	0	2
Pete Goegan	7	0	2	2	6	–	–	–	–	–
Bob Cunningham	1	0	0	0	0	–	–	–	–	–
Rod Gilbert	1	0	0	0	0	4	2	3	5	4
Mel Pearson	3	0	0	0	2	–	–	–	–	–
Jack Bownass	4	0	0	0	4	–	–	–	–	–

1962-63	GP	G	A	PTS	PIM
Andy Bathgate	70	35	46	81	54
Camille Henry	60	37	23	60	8
Dean Prentice	68	19	34	53	22
Earl Ingarfield	69	19	24	43	40
Doug Harvey	68	4	35	39	92
Andy Hebenton	70	15	22	37	8
Rod Gilbert	70	11	20	31	20
Harry Howell	70	5	20	25	55
Dave Balon	70	11	13	24	72
Don McKenney	21	8	16	24	4
Bronco Horvath	41	7	15	22	34
Jean Ratelle	48	11	9	20	8

1962-63 (cont'd)	GP	G	A	PTS	PIM
Larry Cahan	56	6	14	20	47
Jim Neilson	69	5	11	16	38
Albert Langlois	60	2	14	16	62
Ken Schinkel	69	6	9	15	15
Vic Hadfield	36	5	6	11	32
Leon Rochefort	23	5	4	9	6
Ted Hampson	46	4	2	6	2
Don Johns	6	0	4	4	6
Bryan Hextall	21	0	2	2	10
Mel Pearson	5	1	0	1	6
Daune Rupp	2	0	0	0	0

*Did not qualify for playoffs

1963-64	GP	G	A	PTS	PIM
Phil Goyette	67	24	41	65	15
Rod Gilbert	70	24	40	64	62
Andy Bathgate	56	16	43	59	26
Camille Henry	68	29	26	55	8
Harry Howell	70	5	31	36	75
Jim Neilson	69	5	24	29	93
Earl Ingarfield	63	16	11	26	26
Don McKenney	55	9	17	26	6
Vic Hadfield	68	14	11	25	151
Val Fonteyne	69	7	18	25	4
Don Marshall	70	11	12	23	8
Al Langlois	61	5	8	13	45
Larry Cahan	53	4	8	12	80
Don Johns	57	1	9	10	20

1963-64 (cont'd)	GP	G	A	PTS	PIM
Bob Nevin	14	5	4	9	9
Richard Duff	14	4	4	8	2
Richard Meissner	35	3	5	8	0
Jean Ratelle	15	0	7	7	6
David Richardson	34	3	1	4	21
Ronald Ingram	16	1	3	4	8
Doug Harvey	14	0	2	2	10
Marc Dufour	10	1	0	1	2
Howie Glover	25	1	0	1	9
Rod Seiling	2	0	1	1	0
Mike McMahon	18	0	1	1	16
Donald McGregor	2	0	0	0	2
Kenneth Schinkel	4	0	0	0	0
Gordon Labossiere	15	0	0	0	12

*Did not qualify for playoffs

1964-65	GP	G	A	PTS	PIM
Rod Gilbert	70	25	36	61	52
Phil Goyette	52	12	34	46	6
Vic Hadfield	70	18	20	38	102
Camille Henry	48	21	15	36	20
Don Marshall	69	20	15	35	2
Jean Ratelle	54	14	21	35	14
Bob Nevin	64	16	14	30	28
Earl Ingarfield	69	15	13	28	40
Rod Seiling	68	4	22	26	44
Doug Robinson	21	8	14	22	2
Harry Howell	68	2	20	22	63
Lou Angotti	70	9	8	17	20
Bill Hicke	40	6	11	17	26
Jim Nielson	62	0	13	13	58
Dick Duff	29	3	9	12	20
Arnie Brown	58	1	11	12	145
Wayne Hillman	22	1	8	9	26
John Brenneman	22	3	3	6	6

1964-65 (cont'd)	GP	G	A	PTS	PIM
Larry Cahan	26	0	5	5	32
Jim Mikol	30	1	3	4	6
Dave Richardson	7	0	1	1	4
Don Johns	22	0	1	1	4
Val Fonteyne	27	0	1	1	2
Trevor Fahey	1	0	0	0	0
Jim Johnson	1	0	0	0	0
Gord Laboissiere	1	0	0	0	0
Mike McMahon	1	0	0	0	0
Dick Meissner	1	0	0	0	0
Marc Dufour	2	0	0	0	0
Billy Taylor	2	0	0	0	0
Ron Ingram	3	0	0	0	2
Sandy Fitzpatrick	4	0	0	0	2
Ulf Sterner	4	0	0	0	0
Ted Taylor	4	0	0	0	4
Mel Pearson	4	0	0	0	0
Bob Plager	10	0	0	0	18

*Did not qualify for playoffs

Year-By-Year Scoring
1965-66—1968-69

1965-66	GP	G	A	PTS	PIM
Bob Nevin	69	29	33	62	10
Don Marshall	69	26	28	54	6
Jean Ratelle	67	21	30	51	10
Phil Goyette	60	11	31	42	6
Earl Ingarfield	68	20	16	36	35
Vic Hadfield	67	16	19	35	112
Harry Howell	70	4	29	33	92
Bill Hicke	49	9	18	27	21
Rod Gilbert	34	10	15	25	20
Reggie Fleming	35	10	14	24	122
Jim Neilson	65	4	19	23	84
Doug Robinson	51	8	12	20	8
Wayne Hillman	68	3	17	20	70
Lou Angotti	51	6	12	18	14
Rod Seiling	52	5	10	15	24

*Did not qualify for playoffs

1965-66 (cont'd)	GP	G	A	PTS	PIM
Mike McMahon	41	0	12	12	34
John McKenzie	35	6	5	11	36
Gary Peters	63	7	3	10	42
Arnie Brown	64	1	7	8	106
Bob Plager	18	0	5	5	22
Ray Cullen	8	1	3	4	0
Paul Andrea	4	1	1	2	0
Jim Johnson	5	1	0	1	0
Ted Taylor	4	0	1	1	2
Al Lebrun	2	0	0	0	0
Dunc McCallum	2	0	0	0	2
Allan Hamilton	4	0	0	0	2
Larry Mickey	7	0	0	0	2
John Brenneman	11	0	0	0	14

1966-67	GP	G	A	PTS	PIM	GP	G	A	PTS	PIM
Phil Goyette	70	12	49	61	6	4	1	0	1	0
Rod Gilbert	64	28	18	46	12	4	2	2	4	6
Don Marshall	70	24	22	46	4	4	0	1	1	2
Bob Nevin	67	20	24	44	6	4	0	3	3	2
Bernie Geoffrion	58	17	25	42	42	4	2	0	2	0
Harry Howell	70	12	28	40	54	4	0	0	0	4
Orland Kurtenbach	60	11	25	36	58	3	0	2	2	0
Earl Ingarfield	67	12	22	34	12	4	1	0	1	2
Vic Hadfield	69	13	20	33	80	4	1	0	1	17
Reg Fleming	61	15	16	31	146	4	0	2	2	11
Jim Neilson	61	4	11	15	65	4	1	0	1	0
Wayne Hillman	67	2	12	14	43	4	0	0	0	2
Arnie Brown	69	2	10	12	61	4	0	0	0	6
Jean Ratelle	41	6	5	11	4	4	0	0	0	2
Bill Hicke	48	3	4	7	11	—	—	—	—	—
Red Berenson	30	0	5	5	2	4	0	1	1	2
Al MacNeil	58	0	4	4	44	4	0	0	0	2
Rod Seiling	12	1	1	2	6	—	—	—	—	—
Larry Mickey	4	0	2	2	0	—	—	—	—	—

1967-68	GP	G	A	PTS	PIM	GP	G	A	PTS	PIM
Jean Ratelle	74	32	46	78	18	6	0	4	4	2
Rod Gilbert	73	29	48	77	12	6	5	0	5	4
Phil Goyette	73	25	40	65	10	6	0	1	1	4
Bob Nevin	74	28	30	58	20	6	0	3	3	4
Don Marshall	70	19	30	49	2	6	2	1	3	0
Vic Hadfield	59	20	19	39	45	6	1	2	3	6
Orland Kurtenbach	73	15	20	35	82	6	1	0	1	26
Jim Neilson	67	6	29	35	60	6	1	1	2	4
Harry Howell	74	5	24	29	62	6	0	1	1	0
Arnie Brown	74	1	25	26	83	6	0	1	1	8
Reg Fleming	73	17	7	24	132	6	0	2	2	4
Bernie Geoffrion	59	5	16	21	11	1	0	1	1	0
Camille Henry	36	8	12	20	0	6	0	0	0	0
Rod Seiling	71	5	11	16	44	6	0	2	2	4
Ron Stewart	55	7	7	14	19	6	1	1	2	2
Larry Jeffrey	47	2	4	6	15	3	0	0	0	0
Wayne Hillman	62	0	5	5	46	6	0	0	0	0
Red Berenson	19	2	1	3	2	—	—	—	—	—
Larry Mickey	4	0	2	2	0	—	—	—	—	—
Allan Hamilton	2	0	0	0	0	—	—	—	—	—
Walt Tkaczuk	2	0	0	0	0	—	—	—	—	—

1968-69	GP	G	A	PTS	PIM	GP	G	A	PTS	PIM
Jean Ratelle	75	32	46	78	26	4	1	0	1	0
Rod Gilbert	66	28	49	77	22	4	1	0	1	2
Vic Hadfield	73	26	40	66	108	4	2	1	3	2
Bob Nevin	71	31	25	56	14	4	0	2	2	0
Phil Goyette	67	13	32	45	8	3	0	0	0	4
Jim Neilson	76	10	34	44	95	4	0	3	3	5
Don Marshall	74	20	19	39	12	4	1	0	1	0
Walt Tkaczuk	71	12	24	36	28	4	0	1	1	6
Dave Balon	75	10	21	31	57	4	1	0	1	6
Ron Stewart	75	18	11	29	20	4	0	1	1	0
Brad Park	54	3	23	26	70	4	0	2	2	7
Arnie Brown	74	10	12	22	48	4	0	1	1	0
Rod Sieling	73	4	17	21	73	4	1	0	1	2
Reg Fleming	72	8	12	20	138	3	0	0	0	7
Harry Howell	56	4	7	11	36	2	0	0	0	0
Larry Jeffrey	75	1	6	7	12	4	0	0	0	2
Dennis Hextall	13	1	4	5	25	—	—	—	—	—
Bill Fairbairn	1	0	0	0	0	—	—	—	—	—
Bob Jones	2	0	0	0	0	—	—	—	—	—

Year-By-Year Scoring
1968-69—1971-72

1968-69 (cont'd)	GP	G	A	PTS	PIM	Playoffs GP	G	A	PTS	PIM
Orland Kurtenbach	2	0	0	0	2	—	—	—	—	—
Guy Trottier	2	0	0	0	0	—	—	—	—	—
Wayne Rivers	4	0	0	0	0	—	—	—	—	—
Bob Blackburn	11	0	0	0	0	—	—	—	—	—
Al Hamilton	16	0	0	0	8	1	0	0	0	0

1969-70	GP	G	A	PTS	PIM	Playoffs GP	G	A	PTS	PIM
Walt Tkaczuk	76	27	50	77	38	6	2	1	3	17
Jean Ratelle	75	32	42	74	28	6	1	3	4	0
Dave Balon	76	33	37	70	100	6	1	1	2	32
Bill Fairbairn	76	23	33	56	23	6	0	1	1	10
Vic Hadfield	71	20	34	54	69	—	—	—	—	—
Rod Gilbert	72	16	37	53	22	6	4	5	9	0
Bob Nevin	68	18	19	37	8	6	1	1	2	2
Brad Park	60	11	26	37	98	5	1	2	3	11
Arnie Brown	73	15	21	36	78	4	0	4	4	9
Rod Seiling	76	5	21	26	68	2	0	0	0	0
Ron Stewart	76	14	10	24	14	6	0	0	0	2
Don Marshall	57	9	15	24	6	1	0	0	0	0
Jim Neilson	62	3	20	23	75	6	0	1	1	8
Orland Kurtenbach	53	4	10	14	47	6	1	2	3	24
Tim Horton	15	1	5	6	16	6	1	1	2	28
Allan Hamilton	59	0	5	5	54	5	0	0	0	2
Jack Egers	6	3	0	3	2	5	3	1	4	10
Don Luce	12	1	2	3	8	5	0	1	1	4
Larry Brown	15	0	3	3	8	—	—	—	—	—
Ted Irvine	17	0	3	3	10	6	1	2	3	8
Don Blackburn	3	0	0	0	0	1	0	0	0	0
Ab DeMarco	3	0	0	0	0	5	0	0	0	2
Mike Robitaille	4	0	0	0	8	—	—	—	—	—

1970-71	GP	G	A	PTS	PIM	Playoffs GP	G	A	PTS	PIM
Walter Tkaczuk	77	26	49	75	48	13	1	5	6	14
Jean Ratelle	78	26	46	72	14	13	2	9	11	8
Rod Gilbert	78	30	31	61	65	13	4	6	10	8
Dave Balon	78	36	24	60	32	13	3	2	5	4
Bob Nevin	78	21	25	46	10	13	5	3	8	0
Pete Stemkowski	68	16	29	45	61	13	3	2	5	6
Vic Hadfield	63	22	22	44	38	13	8	5	13	46
Brad Park	68	7	37	44	114	13	0	4	4	42
Ted Irvine	76	20	18	38	137	12	1	2	3	28
Jim Neilson	77	8	24	32	69	13	0	3	3	30
Bill Fairbairn	56	7	23	30	32	4	0	0	0	0
Rod Seiling	68	5	22	27	34	13	1	0	1	12
Bruce MacGregor	27	12	13	25	4	13	0	4	4	2
Tim Horton	78	2	18	20	57	13	1	4	5	14
Jack Egers	60	7	10	17	50	3	0	0	0	2
Arnie Brown	48	3	12	15	24	—	—	—	—	—
Ron Stewart	76	5	6	11	19	13	1	0	1	0
Dale Rolfe	14	0	7	7	23	13	0	1	1	14
Andre Dupont	7	1	2	3	21	—	—	—	—	—
Syl Apps	31	1	2	3	11	—	—	—	—	—
Glen Sather	31	2	0	2	52	13	0	1	1	18
Mike Robitaille	11	1	1	2	7	—	—	—	—	—
Larry Brown	31	1	1	2	16	11	0	1	1	0
Jim Krulicki	27	0	2	2	6	—	—	—	—	—
Ab DeMarco	2	0	1	1	0	—	—	—	—	—
Don Luce	9	0	1	1	0	—	—	—	—	—
Don Blackburn	1	0	0	0	0	—	—	—	—	—

1971-72	GP	G	A	PTS	PIM	Playoffs GP	G	A	PTS	PIM
Jean Ratelle	63	46	63	109	4	6	0	1	1	0
Vic Hadfield	78	50	56	106	142	16	7	9	16	22
Rod Gilbert	73	43	54	97	64	16	7	8	15	11
Brad Park	75	24	49	73	130	16	4	7	11	21
Walter Tkaczuk	76	24	42	66	65	16	4	6	10	35
Bill Fairbairn	78	22	37	59	53	16	5	7	12	11
Bobby Rousseau	78	21	36	57	12	16	6	11	17	7
Rod Seiling	78	5	36	41	62	16	1	4	5	10
Bruce MacGregor	75	19	21	40	22	16	2	6	8	4
Jim Neilson	78	7	30	37	56	10	0	3	3	8
Ted Irvine	78	15	21	36	66	16	4	5	9	19
Pete Stemkowski	59	11	17	28	53	16	4	8	12	5
Gene Carr	59	8	8	16	25	16	1	3	4	21
Dale Rolfe	68	2	14	16	67	16	4	3	7	16
Glen Sather	75	5	9	14	77	16	0	1	1	22
Ab DeMarco	48	4	7	11	4	4	0	1	1	0
Gary Doak	49	1	11	12	12	12	0	0	0	46
Dave Balon	16	4	5	9	2	—	—	—	—	—

Year-By-Year Scoring
1971-72—1974-75

						Playoffs				
1971-72 (cont'd)	**GP**	**G**	**A**	**PTS**	**PIM**	**GP**	**G**	**A**	**PTS**	**PIM**
Pierre Jarry	34	3	3	6	20	—	—	—	—	—
Phil Goyette	8	1	4	5	0	13	1	3	4	2
Jack Egers	17	2	1	3	14	—	—	—	—	—
Ron Stewart	13	0	2	2	2	8	2	1	3	0
Norm Gratton	3	0	1	1	0	—	—	—	—	—
Jim Dorey	1	0	0	0	0	1	0	0	0	0
Mike McMahon	1	0	0	0	0	—	—	—	—	—
Tom Williams	3	0	0	0	2	—	—	—	—	—
Jim Lorentz	7	0	0	0	0	—	—	—	—	—
Steve Andrascik						1	0	0	0	2

						Playoffs				
1972-73	**GP**	**G**	**A**	**PTS**	**PIM**	**GP**	**G**	**A**	**PTS**	**PIM**
Jean Ratelle	78	41	53	94	12	10	2	7	9	0
Rod Gilbert	76	25	59	84	25	10	5	1	6	0
Walt Tkaczuk	76	27	39	66	59	10	7	2	9	8
Bill Fairbairn	78	30	33	63	23	10	1	8	9	2
Vic Hadfield	63	28	34	62	60	9	2	2	4	11
Pete Stemkowski	78	22	37	59	71	10	4	2	6	6
Steve Vickers	61	30	23	53	37	10	5	4	9	4
Brad Park	52	10	43	53	51	10	2	5	7	8
Bobby Rousseau	78	8	37	45	14	10	2	4	6	2
Rod Seiling	72	9	33	42	36	—	—	—	—	—
Dale Rolfe	72	7	25	32	74	9	0	5	5	4
Bruce MacGregor	52	14	12	26	12	10	2	2	4	2
Glen Sather	77	11	15	26	64	9	0	0	0	7
Ted Irvine	53	8	12	20	54	10	1	3	4	20
Jim Neilson	52	4	16	20	35	10	0	4	4	2
Gene Carr	50	9	10	19	50	1	0	1	1	0
Ab DeMarco	51	3	13	16	15	—	—	—	—	—
Ron Harris	45	3	10	13	17	10	0	3	3	2
Mike Murphy	15	4	4	8	5	10	0	0	0	0
Randy Legge	12	0	2	2	2	—	—	—	—	—
Bill Heindl	4	1	0	1	0	—	—	—	—	—
Jerry Butler	8	1	0	1	4	—	—	—	—	—
Larry Sacharuk	8	1	0	1	0	—	—	—	—	—
Sheldon Kannegeisser	3	0	1	1	0	1	0	0	0	2
Tom Williams	8	0	1	1	0	—	—	—	—	—
Ron Stewart	11	0	1	1	0	—	—	—	—	—
Curt Bennett	16	0	1	1	11	—	—	—	—	—
Bert Marshall	8	0	0	0	14	—	—	—	—	—

						Playoffs				
1973-74	**GP**	**G**	**A**	**PTS**	**PIM**	**GP**	**G**	**A**	**PTS**	**PIM**
Brad Park	78	25	57	82	148	13	4	8	12	38
Rod Gilbert	75	36	41	77	20	13	3	5	8	4
Pete Stemkowski	78	25	45	70	74	13	6	6	12	35
Jean Ratelle	68	28	39	67	16	13	2	4	6	0
Walt Tkaczuk	71	21	42	63	58	13	0	5	5	22
Bill Fairbairn	78	18	44	62	12	13	3	5	8	6
Steve Vickers	75	34	24	58	18	11	4	4	8	17
Vic Hadfield	77	27	28	55	75	6	1	0	1	0
Bobby Rousseau	72	10	41	51	4	12	1	8	9	4
Ted Irvine	75	26	20	46	105	13	3	5	8	16
Bruce MacGregor	66	17	27	44	6	13	6	2	8	2
Rod Seiling	68	7	23	30	32	13	0	2	2	19
Gilles Marotte	46	2	17	19	28	12	0	1	1	6
Jerry Butler	26	6	10	16	24	12	0	2	2	25
Dale Rolfe	48	3	12	15	56	13	1	8	9	23
Ron Harris	63	2	12	14	25	11	3	0	3	14
Jim Neilson	72	4	7	11	38	12	0	1	1	4
Larry Sacharuk	23	2	4	6	4	—	—	—	—	—
Gene Carr	29	1	5	6	15	—	—	—	—	—
Sheldon Kannegeisser	12	1	3	4	6	—	—	—	—	—
Jack Egers	28	1	3	4	6	8	1	0	1	4
Mike Murphy	16	2	1	3	0	—	—	—	—	—
Tom Williams	14	1	2	3	4	—	—	—	—	—
Bert Wilson	5	1	1	2	2	—	—	—	—	—
Glen Sather	2	0	0	0	2	—	—	—	—	—
Real Lemieux	7	0	0	0	0	—	—	—	—	—

						Playoffs				
1974-75	**GP**	**G**	**A**	**PTS**	**PIM**	**GP**	**G**	**A**	**PTS**	**PIM**
Rod Gilbert	76	36	61	97	22	3	1	3	4	2
Jean Ratelle	79	36	55	91	26	3	1	5	6	2
Steve Vickers	80	41	48	89	64	3	2	4	6	6
Bill Fairbairn	80	24	37	61	10	3	4	0	4	13
Pete Stemkowski	77	24	35	59	63	3	1	0	1	10
Brad Park	65	13	44	57	104	3	1	4	5	2
Derek Sanderson	75	25	25	50	106	3	0	0	0	0
Ron Greschner	70	8	37	45	93	3	0	1	1	2
Greg Polis	76	26	15	41	55	3	0	1	0	6

Year-By-Year Scoring
1974-75—1977-78

1974-75 (cont'd)

Player	GP	G	A	PTS	PIM	Playoffs GP	G	A	PTS	PIM
Rick Middleton	47	22	18	40	19	3	0	0	0	2
Walt Tkaczuk	62	11	25	36	34	3	1	2	3	5
Gilles Marotte	77	4	32	36	69	3	0	1	1	4
Ted Irvine	79	17	17	34	66	3	0	1	1	11
Jerry Butler	78	17	16	33	102	3	1	0	1	16
Nick Beverley	54	3	15	18	19	3	0	1	1	0
John Bednarski	35	1	10	11	37	1	0	0	0	17
Dale Rolfe	42	1	8	9	30	—	—	—	—	—
Ron Harris	34	1	7	8	22	3	1	0	1	9
Bert Wilson	61	5	1	6	66	—	—	—	—	—
Bobby Rousseau	8	2	2	4	0	—	—	—	—	—
Bob MacMillan	22	1	2	3	4	—	—	—	—	—
Dave Maloney	4	0	2	2	0	—	—	—	—	—
Joe Zanussi	8	0	2	2	4	—	—	—	—	—
Jerry Holland	1	1	0	1	0	—	—	—	—	—
Rod Seiling	4	0	1	1	0	—	—	—	—	—
Hartland Monahan	6	0	1	1	4	—	—	—	—	—

1975-76

Player	GP	G	A	PTS	PIM
Rod Gilbert	70	36	50	86	32
Steve Vickers	80	30	53	83	40
Phil Esposito	62	29	38	67	28
Rick Middleton	77	24	26	50	14
Carol Vadnais	64	20	30	50	104
Wayne Dillon	79	21	24	45	10
Pete Stemkowski	75	13	28	41	49
Gerg Polis	79	15	21	36	77
Pat Hickey	70	14	22	36	36
Walt Tkaczuk	78	8	28	36	56
Bill Fairbairn	80	13	15	28	8
Ron Greschner	77	6	21	27	93
Giles Marotte	57	4	17	21	34
Jean Ratelle	13	5	10	15	2

1975-76 (cont'd)

Player	GP	G	A	PTS	PIM
Larry Sacharuk	42	6	7	13	14
Jerry Holland	36	7	4	11	6
John Bednarski	59	1	8	9	77
Nick Beverley	63	1	8	9	46
Bill Collins	50	4	4	8	38
Brad Park	6	2	4	6	23
Dave Maloney	21	1	3	4	66
Doug Jarrett	45	0	4	4	19
Eddie Johnstone	10	2	1	3	4
Ron Harris	3	0	1	1	0
Greg Holst	2	0	0	0	0
Dale Lewis	8	0	0	0	0
Derek Sanderson	8	0	0	0	4

*Did not qualify for playoffs

1976-77

Player	GP	G	A	PTS	PIM
Phil Esposito	80	34	46	80	52
Rod Gilbert	77	27	48	75	50
Ken Hodge	78	21	41	62	43
Don Murdoch	59	32	24	56	47
Steve Vickers	75	22	31	53	26
Walt Tkaczuk	80	12	38	50	38
Carol Vadnais	74	11	37	48	131
Ron Greschner	80	11	36	47	89
Wayne Dillon	78	17	29	46	33
Mike McEwen	80	14	29	43	38
Pat Hickey	80	23	17	40	35
Greg Polis	77	16	23	39	44
Bill Goldsworthy	61	10	12	22	43

1976-77 (cont'd)

Player	GP	G	A	PTS	PIM
Dave Maloney	66	3	18	21	100
Dave Farrish	80	2	17	19	102
Dan Newman	41	9	8	17	37
Pete Stemkowski	61	2	13	15	8
Nick Fotiu	70	4	8	12	174
Bill Fairbairn	9	1	2	3	0
Mark Heaslip	19	1	0	1	31
Larry Huras	1	0	0	0	0
Larry Sacharuk	2	0	0	0	0
John Bednarski	5	0	0	0	0
Greg Holst	5	0	0	0	0
Nick Beverley	9	0	0	0	2
Doug Jarrett	9	0	0	0	4

*Did not qualify for playoffs

1977-78

Player	GP	G	A	PTS	PIM	Playoffs GP	G	A	PTS	PIM
Phil Esposito	79	38	43	81	53	3	0	1	1	5
Pat Hickey	80	40	33	73	47	3	2	0	2	0
Ron Greschner	78	24	48	72	100	3	0	0	0	2
Walt Tkaczuk	80	26	40	66	30	3	0	2	2	0
Steve Vickers	79	19	44	63	30	3	2	1	3	0
Don Murdoch	66	27	28	55	41	3	1	3	4	4
Carol Vadnais	80	6	40	46	115	3	0	2	2	16
Ron Duguay	71	20	20	40	43	3	1	1	2	2
Lucien DeBlois	71	22	8	30	27	3	0	0	0	2
Ed Johnstone	53	13	13	26	44	3	0	0	0	2
Greg Polis	37	7	16	23	12	3	1	2	3	5
Dave Maloney	56	2	19	21	63	3	0	0	0	11
Dave Farrish	80	2	17	19	102	3	0	0	0	0
Mike McEwen	57	5	13	18	52	3	1	0	1	16
Wayne Dillon	59	5	13	18	52	3	0	1	1	0
Dan Newman	59	5	13	18	22	3	0	0	0	4
Mark Heaslip	29	5	10	15	31	3	0	0	0	0
Rod Gilbert	19	2	7	9	6	—	—	—	—	—
Nick Fotiu	59	2	7	9	105	3	0	0	0	5
Don Awrey	78	2	8	8	38	3	0	0	0	6
Ken Hodge	18	2	4	6	8	—	—	—	—	—
Dallas Smith	29	1	4	5	23	1	0	1	1	0
Jerry Byers	7	2	1	3	0	—	—	—	—	—
Mario Marois	8	1	1	2	15	1	0	0	0	5
Bill Goldsworthy	7	0	1	1	12	—	—	—	—	—
Greg Hickey	1	0	0	0	0	—	—	—	—	—
Mike Keating	1	0	0	0	0	—	—	—	—	—
Bud Stefanski	1	0	0	0	0	—	—	—	—	—
Greg Holst	4	0	0	0	0	—	—	—	—	—
Benoit Gosselin	7	0	0	0	33	—	—	—	—	—

Year-By-Year Scoring
1978-79—1980-81

1978-79

	GP	G	A	PTS	PIM	Playoffs GP	G	A	PTS	PIM
Phil Esposito	80	42	36	78	37	18	8	12	20	20
Anders Hedberg	80	33	45	78	33	18	4	5	9	12
Pat Hickey	80	34	41	75	56	18	1	7	8	6
Ulf Nilsson	59	27	39	66	21	2	0	0	0	2
Ron Duguay	79	27	36	63	35	18	5	4	9	11
Mike McEwen	80	20	38	58	35	18	2	11	13	8
Ron Greschner	60	17	36	53	6	18	7	5	12	16
Steve Vickers	66	13	34	47	24	18	5	3	8	13
Carol Vadnais	77	8	37	45	86	18	2	9	11	13
Walt Tkaczuk	77	15	27	42	38	18	4	7	11	10
Don Murdoch	40	15	22	37	6	18	7	5	12	12
Pierre Plante	70	6	25	31	37	18	0	6	6	20
Mario Marois	71	5	26	31	153	18	0	6	6	29
Dean Talafous	68	13	16	29	29	—	—	—	—	—
Lucien DeBlois	62	11	17	28	26	9	2	0	2	4
Dave Maloney	76	11	17	28	151	17	3	4	7	45
Don Maloney	28	9	17	26	39	18	7	13	20	19
David Farrish	71	1	19	20	61	7	0	2	2	14
Ed Johnstone	30	5	3	8	27	17	5	0	5	10
Nick Fotiu	71	3	5	8	190	4	0	0	0	6
Dan Clark	4	0	1	1	6	—	—	—	—	—
Mike Korney	18	0	1	1	18	—	—	—	—	—
Tim Bothwell	1	0	0	0	2	—	—	—	—	—
Mike McDougal	1	0	0	0	0	—	—	—	—	—
Dean Turner	1	0	0	0	0	—	—	—	—	—
Frank Beaton	2	0	0	0	0	—	—	—	—	—
Andre Dore	2	0	0	0	0	—	—	—	—	—
Bobby Sheehan	—	—	—	—	—	15	4	3	7	8

1979-80

	GP	G	A	PTS	PIM	Playoffs GP	G	A	PTS	PIM
Phil Esposito	80	34	44	78	73	9	3	3	6	8
Don Maloney	79	25	48	73	97	9	0	4	4	10
Anders Hedberg	80	32	39	71	21	9	3	2	5	7
Steve Vickers	75	29	33	62	38	9	2	2	4	4
Barry Beck	61	14	45	59	98	9	1	4	5	6
Ron Greschner	76	21	37	58	103	9	0	6	6	10
Ulf Nilsson	50	14	44	58	20	9	3	2	5	7
Ron Duguay	73	28	22	50	37	9	5	2	7	11
Walt Tkaczuk	76	12	25	37	36	7	0	1	1	2
Dave Maloney	77	12	25	37	186	8	1	2	3	8
Eddie Johnstone	78	14	21	35	60	9	0	1	1	25
Mario Marois	79	8	23	31	142	9	0	2	2	8
Dean Talafous	55	10	20	30	26	5	1	2	3	9
Carol Vadnais	66	3	20	23	118	9	1	2	3	6
Warren Miller	55	7	6	13	17	6	1	0	1	0
Claude Larose	25	4	7	11	2	—	—	—	—	—
Doug Sulliman	31	4	7	11	2	—	—	—	—	—
Tim Bothwell	45	4	6	10	20	9	0	0	0	8
Jocelyn Guevremont	20	2	5	7	6	—	—	—	—	—
Pat Conacher	17	0	5	5	4	3	0	1	1	2
Cam Conner	12	0	3	3	37	2	0	0	0	2
Ray Markham	14	1	1	2	21	7	1	0	1	24
Frank Beaton	23	1	1	2	43	—	—	—	—	—
Ed Hospodar	20	0	1	1	76	7	0	1	1	42
Andre Dore	2	0	0	0	0	—	—	—	—	—
Dave Silk	2	0	0	0	0	—	—	—	—	—
Jim Mayer	4	0	0	0	0	—	—	—	—	—
Bill Lochead	7	0	0	0	4	—	—	—	—	—

1980-81

	GP	G	A	PTS	PIM	Playoffs GP	G	A	PTS	PIM
Anders Hedberg	80	30	40	70	52	14	8	8	16	6
Ed Johnstone	80	30	38	68	100	8	2	2	4	4
Ron Greschner	74	27	41	68	112	14	4	8	12	17
Mike Allison	75	26	38	64	83	14	3	1	4	20
Steve Vickers	73	19	39	58	40	12	4	7	11	14
Don Maloney	61	29	23	52	99	13	1	6	7	13
Dave Maloney	79	11	36	47	132	2	0	2	2	9
Ulf Nilsson	51	14	25	39	42	14	8	8	16	23
Ron Duguay	50	17	21	38	83	14	8	9	17	16
Barry Beck	75	11	23	34	231	14	5	8	13	32
Dean Talafous	50	13	17	30	28	14	3	5	8	2
Tom Laidlaw	80	6	23	29	100	14	1	4	5	18
Walt Tkaczuk	43	6	22	28	28	1	0	0	0	0
Dave Silk	59	14	12	26	58	—	—	—	—	—
Lance Nethery	33	11	12	23	12	14	5	3	8	9
Carol Vadnais	74	3	20	23	91	14	1	3	4	26
Jere Gillis	35	10	10	20	4	14	2	5	7	2
Ed Hospodar	61	5	14	19	214	12	2	0	2	93
Chris Kotsopoulos	54	4	12	16	153	14	0	3	3	63
Nick Fotiu	27	5	6	11	91	2	0	0	0	4
Peter Wallin	12	1	5	6	2	14	2	6	8	6
Doug Sulliman	32	4	1	5	32	3	1	0	1	0
Dan McCarthy	5	4	0	4	4	—	—	—	—	—

Year-By-Year Scoring
1980-81—1983-84

1980-81 (cont'd)	GP	G	A	PTS	PIM	Playoffs GP	G	A	PTS	PIM
Gary Burns	11	2	2	4	18	1	0	0	0	2
Cam Connor	15	1	3	4	44	–	–	–	–	–
Andre Dore	15	1	3	4	15	–	–	–	–	–
Mario Marois	8	1	2	3	46	–	–	–	–	–
Jeff Bandura	2	0	1	1	0	–	–	–	–	–
Tim Bothwell	3	0	1	1	0	–	–	–	–	–
Mike McDougal	2	0	0	0	0	–	–	–	–	–
John Hughes	–	–	–	–	–	3	0	1	1	6

1981-82	GP	G	A	PTS	PIM	Playoffs GP	G	A	PTS	PIM
Mike Rogers	80	38	65	103	43	9	1	6	7	2
Ron Duguay	72	40	36	76	82	10	5	1	6	31
Mark Pavelich	79	33	43	76	67	6	1	5	6	0
Ed Johnstone	68	30	28	58	57	10	2	6	8	25
Don Maloney	54	22	36	58	73	10	5	5	10	10
Reijo Ruotsalainen	78	18	38	56	27	10	4	5	9	2
Dave Maloney	64	13	36	49	105	10	1	4	5	6
Barry Beck	60	9	29	38	108	10	1	5	6	14
Dave Silk	64	15	20	35	39	9	2	4	6	4
Robbie Ftorek	30	8	25	33	24	10	7	4	11	11
Mikko Leinonen	53	11	19	30	18	7	1	6	7	20
Pat Hickey	53	15	14	29	32	–	–	–	–	–
Mike Allison	48	7	15	22	74	10	1	3	4	18
Tom Laidlaw	79	3	18	21	104	10	0	3	3	14
Andre Dore	56	4	16	20	64	10	1	1	2	16
Nick Fotiu	70	8	10	18	151	10	0	2	2	6
Ron Greschner	29	5	11	16	16	–	–	–	–	–
Rob McClanahan	22	5	9	14	10	10	2	5	7	2
Dean Talafous	29	6	7	13	8	–	–	–	–	–
Jere Gillis	26	3	9	12	16	–	–	–	–	–
Ed Hospodar	41	3	8	11	152	–	–	–	–	–
Peter Wallin	40	2	9	11	12	–	–	–	–	–
Tom Younghans	47	3	5	8	17	2	0	0	0	0
Tim Bothwell	13	0	3	3	10	–	–	–	–	–
Mark Morrison	9	1	1	2	0	–	–	–	–	–
Mike Backman	3	0	2	2	4	1	0	0	0	2
Anders Hedberg	4	0	1	1	0	–	–	–	–	–
Lance Nethery	5	0	0	0	0	–	–	–	–	–
Gary Burns	–	–	–	–	–	4	0	0	0	0
Cam Connor	–	–	–	–	–	10	4	0	4	4

1982-83	GP	G	A	PTS	PIM	Playoffs GP	G	A	PTS	PIM
Mike Rogers	71	29	47	76	28	1	0	0	0	0
Mark Pavelich	78	37	38	75	52	9	4	5	9	12
Don Maloney	78	29	40	69	88	5	0	1	1	0
Reijo Ruotsalainen	77	16	53	69	22	9	4	2	6	6
Anders Hedberg	78	25	34	59	12	9	4	8	12	4
Mikko Leinonen	78	17	34	51	23	7	1	3	4	4
Dave Maloney	78	8	42	50	132	7	1	6	7	10
Rob McClanahan	78	22	26	48	46	9	2	5	7	12
Ron Duguay	72	19	25	44	58	9	2	2	4	28
Ed Johnstone	52	15	21	36	27	9	4	1	5	19
Barry Beck	66	12	22	34	112	9	2	4	6	8
Robbie Ftorek	61	12	19	31	41	4	1	0	1	0
Kent-Erik Andersson	71	8	20	28	14	9	0	0	0	0
Nick Fotiu	72	8	13	21	90	5	0	1	1	6
Vaclav Nedomansky	35	12	8	20	0	–	–	–	–	–
Mike Allison	39	11	9	20	37	8	0	5	5	10
Bill Baker	70	4	14	18	64	2	0	0	0	0
Chris Kontos	44	8	7	15	33	–	–	–	–	–
Scot Kleinendorst	30	2	9	11	8	6	0	2	2	2
Tom Laidlaw	80	0	10	10	75	9	1	1	2	10
Ron Greschner	10	3	5	8	0	8	2	2	4	12
Ulf Nilsson	10	2	4	6	2	–	–	–	–	–
Rick Chartraw	26	2	2	4	37	9	0	2	2	6
Mike Backman	7	1	3	4	6	9	2	2	4	0
Dave Silk	16	1	1	2	15	–	–	–	–	–
Pat Conacher	5	0	1	1	4	1	0	0	0	0
Cam Connor	1	0	0	0	0	–	–	–	–	–
Graeme Nicolson	10	0	0	0	9	–	–	–	–	–
George McPhee	–	–	–	–	–	9	3	3	6	6

1983-84	GP	G	A	PTS	PIM	Playoffs GP	G	A	PTS	PIM
Mark Pavelich	77	29	53	82	96	5	2	4	6	0
Pierre Larouche	77	48	33	81	22	5	3	1	4	2
Anders Hedberg	79	32	35	67	16	5	1	0	1	0
Don Maloney	79	24	42	66	62	5	1	4	5	0
Mike Rogers	78	23	38	61	45	1	0	0	0	0
Reijo Ruotsalainen	74	20	39	59	26	5	1	1	2	2
Ron Greschner	77	12	44	56	117	2	1	0	1	2
Mark Osborne	73	23	28	51	88	5	0	1	1	7

Year-By-Year Scoring
1983-84—1985-86

1983-84 (cont'd)	GP	G	A	PTS	PIM	Playoffs GP	G	A	PTS	PIM
Peter Sundstrom	77	22	22	44	24	5	1	3	4	0
Barry Beck	72	9	27	36	134	4	1	0	1	6
Dave Maloney	68	7	26	33	168	1	0	0	0	2
Jan Erixon	75	5	25	30	16	5	2	0	2	4
Mikko Leinonen	28	3	23	26	28	5	0	2	2	4
Willie Huber	42	9	14	23	60	4	1	1	2	9
Mike Allison	45	8	12	20	64	5	0	1	1	6
Kent-Erik Andersson	63	5	15	20	8	5	0	1	1	0
Tom Laidlaw	79	3	15	18	62	5	0	0	0	8
Rob McClanahan	41	6	8	14	21	—	—	—	—	—
Nick Fotiu	40	7	6	13	115	—	—	—	—	—
Mike Blaisdell	36	5	6	11	31	—	—	—	—	—
James Patrick	12	1	7	8	2	5	0	3	3	2
Blaine Stoughton	14	5	2	7	4	—	—	—	—	—
Steve Richmond	26	2	5	7	110	4	0	0	0	12
Rob Ftorek	31	3	2	5	22	—	—	—	—	—
Bob Brooke	9	1	2	3	4	5	0	0	0	7
Larry Patey	9	1	2	3	4	4	0	1	1	6
George McPhee	9	1	1	2	11	—	—	—	—	—
Scot Kleinendorst	23	0	2	2	35	—	—	—	—	—
Mike Backman	8	0	1	1	8	—	—	—	—	—
Chris Kontos	46	0	1	1	38	—	—	—	—	—
Mark Morrison	1	0	0	0	0	—	—	—	—	—
Rick Chartraw	4	0	0	0	4	—	—	—	—	—
Dave Barr	6	0	0	0	2	—	—	—	—	—

1984-85	GP	G	A	PTS	PIM	Playoffs GP	G	A	PTS	PIM
Reijo Ruotsalainen	80	28	45	73	32	3	2	0	2	6
Mike Rogers	78	26	38	64	24	3	0	4	4	4
Pierre Larouche	65	24	36	60	8	—	—	—	—	—
Tomas Sandstrom	74	29	29	58	51	3	0	2	2	0
Anders Hedberg	64	20	31	51	10	3	2	1	3	2
Ron Greschner	48	16	29	45	42	2	0	3	3	12
Mark Pavelich	48	14	31	45	29	3	0	3	3	2
Peter Sundstrom	76	18	25	43	34	3	0	0	0	0
James Patrick	75	8	28	36	71	3	0	0	0	4
Steve Patrick	43	11	18	29	63	1	0	0	0	0
Jan Erixon	66	7	22	29	33	2	0	0	0	2
George McPhee	49	12	15	27	139	3	1	0	1	7
Don Maloney	37	11	16	27	32	3	4	0	4	2
Barry Beck	56	7	19	26	75	3	0	1	1	11
Mike Allison	31	9	15	24	17	—	—	—	—	—
Grant Ledyard	42	8	12	20	53	3	0	2	2	4
Robbie Ftorek	48	9	10	19	35	—	—	—	—	—
Bob Brooke	72	7	9	16	79	3	0	0	0	8
Willie Huber	49	3	11	14	55	2	1	0	1	2
Dave Gagner	38	6	6	12	16	—	—	—	—	—
Chris Kontos	28	4	8	12	24	—	—	—	—	—
Tom Laidlaw	61	1	11	12	52	3	0	2	2	4
Nick Fotiu	46	4	7	11	54	—	—	—	—	—
Mark Osborne	23	4	4	8	33	3	0	0	0	4
Jim Wiemer	22	4	3	7	30	1	0	0	0	0
Andre Dore	25	0	7	7	35	—	—	—	—	—
Randy Heath	12	2	3	5	15	—	—	—	—	—
Steve Richmond	34	0	5	5	90	—	—	—	—	—
Dave Maloney	16	2	1	3	10	—	—	—	—	—
Kelly Miller	5	0	2	2	2	3	0	0	0	2
Mike Blaisdell	12	1	0	1	11	—	—	—	—	—
Larry Patey	7	0	1	1	12	1	0	0	0	0
Simo Saarinen	8	0	0	0	8	—	—	—	—	—

1985-86	GP	G	A	PTS	PIM	Playoffs GP	G	A	PTS	PIM
Mike Ridley	80	22	43	65	69	16	6	8	14	26
Reijo Ruotsalainen	80	17	42	59	47	16	0	8	8	6
Tomas Sandstrom	73	25	29	54	109	16	4	6	10	20
Ron Greschner	78	20	28	48	104	5	3	1	4	11
Bob Brooke	79	24	20	44	111	16	6	9	15	28
James Patrick	75	14	29	43	88	16	1	5	6	34
Mark Pavelich	59	20	20	40	82	—	—	—	—	—
Mark Osborne	62	16	24	40	80	15	2	3	5	26
Raimo Helminen	66	10	30	40	10	2	0	0	0	0
Kelly Miller	74	13	20	33	52	16	3	4	7	4
Brian MacLellan	51	11	21	32	47	16	2	4	6	15
Don Maloney	68	11	17	28	56	16	2	1	3	31
Pierre Larouche	28	20	7	27	4	16	8	9	17	2
Peter Sundstrom	53	8	15	23	12	1	0	0	0	2
Jan Erixon	31	2	17	19	4	12	0	1	1	4
Tom Laidlaw	68	6	12	18	103	7	0	2	2	12
Willie Huber	70	7	8	15	85	16	3	2	5	16
Mike Allison	28	2	13	15	22	7	0	2	2	38
Barry Beck	25	4	8	12	7	—	—	—	—	—
Dave Gagner	32	4	6	10	19	4	1	2	3	2
Larry Melnyk	46	1	8	9	65	16	1	2	3	46

Year-By-Year Scoring
1985-86—1988-89

1985-86 (cont'd)	GP	G	A	PTS	PIM	Playoffs GP	G	A	PTS	PIM
George McPhee	30	4	4	8	63	11	0	0	0	32
Wilf Paiement	8	1	6	7	13	16	5	5	10	45
Rob Whistle	32	4	2	6	10	3	0	0	0	2
Chris Jensen	9	1	3	4	0	—	—	—	—	—
Jim Wiemer	7	3	0	3	2	8	1	0	1	6
Bob Crawford	11	1	2	3	10	7	0	1	1	8
Randy Heath	1	0	1	1	0	—	—	—	—	—
Kjell Samuelsson	9	0	0	0	10	9	0	1	1	8
Tony Feltrin	10	0	0	0	21	—	—	—	—	—

1986-87	GP	G	A	PTS	PIM	Playoffs GP	G	A	PTS	PIM
Walt Poddubny	75	40	47	87	49	6	0	0	0	8
Tomas Sandstrom	64	40	34	74	60	6	1	2	3	20
Kelly Kisio	70	24	40	64	73	4	0	1	1	2
Pierre Larouche	73	28	35	63	12	6	3	2	5	4
Don Maloney	72	19	38	57	117	6	2	1	3	6
James Patrick	78	10	45	55	62	6	1	2	3	2
Tony McKegney	64	29	17	46	56	—	—	—	—	—
Ron Greschner	61	6	34	40	62	6	0	5	5	0
Willie Huber	66	8	22	30	70	6	0	2	2	6
Jan Erixon	68	8	18	26	24	6	1	0	1	0
Ron Duguay	34	9	12	21	9	6	2	0	2	4
Curt Giles	61	2	17	19	50	5	0	0	0	6
Larry Melnyk	73	3	12	15	182	6	0	0	0	4
Terry Carkner	52	2	13	15	120	1	0	0	0	0
Chris Jensen	37	6	7	13	21	—	—	—	—	—
Lucien DeBlois	40	3	8	11	27	2	0	0	0	2
Marcel Dionne	14	4	6	10	6	6	1	1	2	2
George McPhee	21	4	4	8	34	6	1	0	1	28
Jeff Jackson	9	5	1	6	15	6	1	1	2	16
Dave Gagner	10	1	4	5	12	—	—	—	—	—
Jay Caufield	13	2	1	3	45	3	0	0	0	12
Mike Donnelly	5	1	1	2	0	—	—	—	—	—
Pat Price	13	0	2	2	37	—	—	—	—	—
Gord Walker	1	1	0	1	2	—	—	—	—	—
Don Jackson	22	1	0	1	91	—	—	—	—	—
Norm Maciver	3	0	1	1	0	—	—	—	—	—
Jim Leavins	4	0	1	1	4	—	—	—	—	—
Mike Siltala	1	0	0	0	0	—	—	—	—	—
Stu Kulak	3	0	0	0	0	3	0	0	0	2
Ron Talakoski	3	0	0	0	24	—	—	—	—	—
Paul Fenton	8	0	0	0	0	—	—	—	—	—

1987-88	GP	G	A	PTS	PIM
Walt Poddubny	77	38	50	88	76
Kelly Kisio	77	23	55	78	88
Tomas Sandstrom	69	28	40	68	95
Marcel Dionne	67	31	34	65	54
James Patrick	70	17	45	62	52
Brian Mullen	74	25	29	54	42
John Ogrodnick	64	22	32	54	16
Ulf Dahlen	70	29	23	52	26
Don Maloney	66	12	21	33	60
Michel Petit	64	9	24	33	223
David Shaw	68	7	25	32	100
Lucien DeBlois	74	9	21	30	103
Jan Erixon	70	7	19	26	33
Norm Maciver	37	9	15	24	14
Paul Cyr	40	4	13	17	41
Jari Gronstrand	62	3	11	14	63
Brian Leetch	17	2	12	14	0
Pierre Larouche	10	3	9	12	13

*Did not qualify for playoffs

1987-88 (cont'd)	GP	G	A	PTS	PIM
Ron Duguay	48	4	4	8	23
Chris Nilan	22	3	5	8	96
Ron Greschner	51	1	5	6	82
Gord Walker	18	1	4	5	17
Mike Donnelly	17	2	2	4	8
Mark Hardy	19	2	2	4	31
Dave Pichette	6	1	3	4	4
Joe Paterson	21	1	2	3	65
Bruce Bell	13	1	2	3	8
Mark Tinordi	24	1	2	3	50
Steve Nemeth	12	2	0	2	2
Jeff Brubaker	31	2	0	2	78
Simon Wheeldon	5	0	2	2	4
Ron Talakoski	6	0	1	1	12
Chris Jensen	7	0	1	1	2
Mark Janssens	1	0	0	0	0
Rudy Poeschek	1	0	0	0	2
Curt Giles	13	0	0	0	10

1988-89	GP	G	A	PTS	PIM	Playoffs GP	G	A	PTS	PIM
Tomas Sandstrom	79	32	56	88	148	4	3	2	5	12
Brian Leetch	68	23	48	71	50	4	3	2	5	2
Brian Mullen	78	29	35	64	60	3	0	1	1	4
Tony Granato	78	36	27	63	140	4	1	1	2	21
Kelly Kisio	70	26	36	62	91	4	0	0	0	9
Carey Wilson	41	21	34	55	45	4	1	2	3	2
James Patrick	68	11	36	47	41	4	0	1	1	2
Guy Lafleur	67	18	27	45	12	4	1	0	1	0
Ulf Dahlen	56	24	19	43	50	4	0	0	0	0
John Ogrodnick	60	13	29	42	14	3	2	0	2	0
Lucien DeBlois	73	9	24	33	107	4	0	0	0	4
Michel Petit	69	8	25	33	154	4	0	2	2	27
Jason Lafreniere	38	8	16	24	6	3	0	0	0	17
Marcel Dionne	37	7	16	23	20	—	—	—	—	—
Brian Lawton	30	7	10	17	39	—	—	—	—	—
David Shaw	63	6	11	17	88	4	0	2	2	30
Jan Erixon	44	4	11	15	27	4	0	1	1	2
Chris Nilan	38	7	7	14	177	4	0	1	1	28

Year-By-Year Scoring
1988-89—1990-91

1988-89 (cont'd)

	GP	G	A	PTS	PIM	GP	G	A	PTS	PIM
						\multicolumn{5}{c	}{Playoffs}

	GP	G	A	PTS	PIM	GP	G	A	PTS	PIM
Mark Hardy	45	2	12	14	45	4	0	1	1	31
Don Maloney	31	4	9	13	16	—	—	—	—	—
Ron Greschner	58	1	10	11	94	4	0	1	1	6
Darren Turcotte	20	7	3	10	4	1	0	0	0	0
Norm Maciver	26	0	10	10	14	—	—	—	—	—
Kevin Miller	24	3	5	8	2	—	—	—	—	—
Normand Rochefort	11	1	5	6	18	—	—	—	—	—
Lindy Ruff	13	0	5	5	31	2	0	0	0	17
Rudy Poeschek	52	0	2	2	199	—	—	—	—	—
Miloslav Horava	6	0	1	1	0	—	—	—	—	—
Simon Wheeldon	6	0	1	1	2	—	—	—	—	—
Joe Paterson	20	0	1	1	84	—	—	—	—	—
Stephane Brochu	1	0	0	0	0	—	—	—	—	—
Paul Cyr	1	0	0	0	2	—	—	—	—	—
Jim Latos	1	0	0	0	0	—	—	—	—	—
Jayson More	1	0	0	0	0	—	—	—	—	—
Mark Janssens	5	0	0	0	0	—	—	—	—	—
Jeff Bloemberg	9	0	0	0	0	1	0	0	0	0
Peter Laviolette	12	0	0	0	6	—	—	—	—	—

1989-90

	GP	G	A	PTS	PIM	GP	G	A	PTS	PIM
John Ogrodnick	80	43	31	74	44	10	6	3	9	0
Brian Mullen	76	27	41	68	42	10	2	2	4	8
Darren Turcotte	76	32	34	66	32	10	1	6	7	4
Kelly Kisio	68	22	44	66	105	10	2	8	10	8
James Patrick	73	14	43	57	50	10	3	8	11	0
Brian Leetch	72	11	45	56	26	—	—	—	—	—
Bernie Nicholls	32	12	25	37	20	10	7	5	12	16
Troy Mallette	79	13	16	29	305	10	2	2	4	81
Carey Wilson	41	9	17	26	57	10	2	1	3	0
Mike Gartner	12	11	5	16	6	10	5	3	8	12
Mark Hardy	54	0	15	15	94	3	0	1	1	2
Miloslav Horava	45	4	10	14	26	2	0	1	1	0
Kris King	68	6	7	13	286	10	0	1	1	30
Mark Janssens	80	5	8	13	161	9	2	1	3	10
Jan Erixon	58	4	9	13	8	10	1	0	1	2
Randy Moller	60	1	12	13	139	10	1	6	7	32
David Shaw	22	2	10	12	22	—	—	—	—	—
Ron Greschner	55	1	9	10	53	10	0	0	0	16
Lindy Ruff	56	3	6	9	77	8	0	3	3	12
Paul Broten	32	3	5	8	26	6	1	1	2	2
Jeff Bloemberg	28	3	3	6	25	7	0	3	3	5
David Archibald	19	2	3	5	6	—	—	—	—	—
Kevin Miller	16	0	5	5	2	1	0	0	0	0
Normand Rochefort	31	3	1	4	24	10	2	1	3	26
Chris Nilan	25	1	2	3	59	4	0	1	1	19
Ric Bennett	6	0	3	1	5	—	—	—	—	—
Corey Millen	4	0	0	0	2	—	—	—	—	—
Todd Charlesworth	7	0	0	0	6	—	—	—	—	—
Rudy Poeschek	15	0	0	0	55	—	—	—	—	—

1990-91

	GP	G	A	PTS	PIM	GP	G	A	PTS	PIM
Brian Leetch	80	16	72	88	42	6	1	3	4	0
Bernie Nicholls	71	25	48	73	96	5	4	3	7	8
Mike Gartner	79	49	20	69	53	6	1	1	2	0
Darren Turcotte	74	26	41	67	37	6	1	2	3	0
Brian Mullen	79	19	43	62	43	6	0	2	2	0
James Patrick	74	10	49	59	58	6	0	0	0	6
John Ogrodnck	79	31	23	54	10	4	0	0	0	0
Ray Sheppard	59	24	23	47	21	—	—	—	—	—
Kevin Miller	63	17	27	44	63	—	—	—	—	—
Kelly Kisio	51	15	20	35	58	—	—	—	—	—
Kris King	72	11	14	25	156	6	2	0	2	36
Jan Erixon	53	7	18	25	8	6	1	2	3	0
Randy Moller	61	4	19	23	161	6	0	0	0	11
Troy Mallette	71	12	10	22	252	5	0	0	0	18
Mark Janssens	69	9	7	16	172	6	3	0	3	6
Jody Hull	47	5	8	13	10	—	—	—	—	—
David Shaw	77	2	10	12	89	6	0	0	0	11
Paul Broten	28	4	6	10	10	5	0	0	0	2
Normand Rochefort	44	3	7	10	35	—	—	—	—	—
Miloslav Horava	29	1	6	7	12	—	—	—	—	—
Mark Hardy	70	1	5	6	89	6	0	1	1	30
Corey Millen	4	3	1	4	0	6	1	2	3	0
Steven Rice	11	1	1	2	4	2	2	1	3	6
Jeff Bloemberg	3	0	2	2	0	—	—	—	—	—
Joe Cirella	19	1	0	1	52	6	0	2	2	26
Tie Domi	28	1	0	1	185	—	—	—	—	—
Lindy Ruff	14	0	1	1	27	—	—	—	—	—
Brian McReynolds	1	0	0	0	0	—	—	—	—	—
Joey Kocur	5	0	0	0	36	6	0	2	2	21
Eric Bennett	6	0	0	0	6	—	—	—	—	—
Dennis Vial	21	0	0	0	61	—	—	—	—	—

Year-By-Year Scoring
1990-91—1992-93

1990-91 (cont'd)	GP	G	A	PTS	PIM	Playoffs GP	G	A	PTS	PIM
Tony Amonte	–	–	–	–	–	2	0	2	2	2
Doug Weight	–	–	–	–	–	1	0	0	0	0

1991-92	GP	G	A	PTS	PIM	Playoffs GP	G	A	PTS	PIM
Mark Messier	79	35	72	107	76	11	7	7	14	6
Brian Leetch	80	22	80	102	26	13	4	11	15	4
Mike Gartner	76	40	41	81	55	13	8	8	16	4
James Patrick	80	14	57	71	54	13	0	7	7	12
Tony Amonte	79	35	34	69	55	13	3	6	9	2
Adam Graves	80	26	33	59	139	10	5	3	8	22
Sergei Nemchinov	73	30	28	58	15	13	1	4	5	8
Darren Turcotte	71	30	23	53	57	8	4	0	4	6
John Ogrodnick	55	17	13	30	22	3	0	0	0	0
Doug Weight	53	8	22	30	23	7	2	2	4	0
Kris King	79	10	9	19	224	13	4	1	5	14
Per Djoos	50	1	18	19	40	–	–	–	–	–
Tim Kerr	32	7	11	18	12	8	1	0	1	0
Jan Erixon	46	8	9	17	4	13	2	3	5	2
Joe Cirella	67	3	12	15	121	13	0	4	4	23
Randy Gilhen	40	7	7	14	14	13	1	2	3	2
Joey Kocur	51	7	4	11	121	12	1	1	2	38
Jeff Beukeboom	56	1	10	11	122	13	2	3	5	47
Paul Broten	28	4	6	10	18	13	1	2	3	10
Randy Moller	32	2	7	9	78	–	–	–	–	–
Mark Hardy	52	1	8	9	65	13	0	3	3	31
Tie Domi	42	2	4	6	246	6	1	1	2	32
Corey Millen	11	1	4	5	44	–	–	–	–	–
Rob Zamuner	9	1	2	3	2	–	–	–	–	–
Normand Rochefort	26	0	2	2	31	–	–	–	–	–
Eric Bennett	3	0	1	1	2	–	–	–	–	–
Jeff Bloemberg	3	0	1	1	0	–	–	–	–	–
David Shaw	10	0	1	1	15	–	–	–	–	–
Peter Fiorentino	1	0	0	0	0	–	–	–	–	–
Bernie Nichols	1	0	0	0	0	–	–	–	–	–
Jody Hull	3	0	0	0	2	–	–	–	–	–
Mark Janssens	4	0	0	0	5	–	–	–	–	–
Jay Wells	11	0	0	0	24	13	0	2	2	10

1992-93	GP	G	A	PTS	PIM
Mark Messier	75	25	66	91	72
Tony Amonte	83	33	43	76	49
Mike Gartner	84	45	23	68	59
Adam Graves	84	36	29	65	148
Sergei Nemchinov	81	23	31	54	34
Darren Turcotte	71	25	28	53	40
Alexei Kovalev	65	20	18	38	79
Brain Leetch	36	6	30	36	26
Sergei Zubov	49	8	23	31	4
Eddie Olczyk	46	13	16	29	26
James Patrick	60	5	21	26	61
Phil Bourque	55	6	14	20	39
Jeff Beudeboom	82	2	17	19	153
Jan Erixon	45	5	11	16	10
Peter Andersson	31	4	11	15	18
Kevin Lowe	49	3	12	15	58
Paul Broten	60	5	9	14	48
Steven King	24	7	5	12	16
Jay Wells	53	1	9	10	107
Joe Cirella	55	3	6	9	85
Joe Kocur	65	3	6	9	131
Mike Hurlbut	23	1	8	9	16
Esa Tikkanen	15	2	5	7	18
Mike Richter	38	0	5	5	2
Per Djoos	6	1	1	2	2
John McIntyre	11	1	0	1	4
Craig Duncanson	3	0	1	1	0
John Vanbiesbrouck	48	0	1	1	18
Dave Marcinyshyn	2	0	0	0	2
Mike Hartman	3	0	0	0	6
Corey Hirsch	4	0	0	0	0
Joby Messier	11	0	0	0	6

* Did not qualify for playoffs

YEAR-BY-YEAR GOALTENDING STATISTICS

Regular Season

Year	Goaltender	G	W	L	T	GA	AVG	Shutouts
1926-27	Hal Winkler	8	3	4	1	16	2.00	2
	Lorne Chabot	36	22	9	5	56	1.56	10
1927-28	Lorne Chabot	44	19	16	9	79	1.80	11
1928-29	John Ross Roach	44	21	13	10	65	1.48	13
1929-30	John Ross Roach	44	17	17	10	143	3.25	1
1930-31	John Ross Roach	44	19	16	9	87	1.98	7
1931-32	John Ross Roach	48	23	17	8	112	2.33	9
1932-33	Andy Aitkenhead	48	23	17	8	107	2.23	3
1933-34	Andy Aitkenhead	48	21	19	8	113	2.35	7
1934-35	Andy Aitkenhead	10	3	7	0	37	3.70	1
	Percy Jackson	1	0	1	0	8	8.00	0
	Dave Kerr	37	19	12	6	94	2.54	4
1935-36	Dave Kerr	47	18	17	12	95	2.02	8
	Bert Gardiner	1	1	0	0	1	1.00	0
1936-37	Dave Kerr	48	19	20	9	106	2.21	4
1937-38	Dave Kerr	48	27	15	6	96	2.00	8
1938-39	Dave Kerr	48	26	16	6	105	2.19	6
1939-40	Dave Kerr	48	27	11	10	77	1.60	8
1940-41	Dave Kerr	48	21	19	8	125	2.60	2
1941-42	Jim Henry	48	29	17	2	143	2.98	1
1942-43	Jimmy Franks	23	5	14	4	103	4.48	0
	Bill Beveridge	17	4	10	3	89	5.24	1
	Steve Buzinski	9	2	6	1	55	6.11	0
	Lionel Bouvrette	1	0	1	0	6	6.00	0
1943-44	Ken McAuley*	50	6	39	5	310	6.20	0
1944-45	Ken McAuley	46	10	26	10	227	4.94	1
	Doug Stevenson	4	1	3	0	20	5.00	0
1945-46	Chuck Rayner	41	12	21	7	150	3.75	1
	Jim Henry	11	1	7	2	41	4.10	1
1946-47	Chuck Rayner	58	22	30	6	177	3.05	5
	Jim Henry	2	0	2	0	9	4.50	0
1947-48	Jim Henry	48	17	18	13	153	3.19	2
	Chuck Rayner	12	4	8	0	42	3.65	0
	Bob DeCourcy	1	0	0	0	6	6.00	0
1948-49	Chuck Rayner	58	16	31	11	168	2.90	7
	Emile Francis	2	2	0	0	4	2.00	0
1949-50	Chuck Rayner	69	28	30	11	181	2.62	6
	Emile Francis	1	0	1	0	8	8.00	0
1950-51	Chuck Rayner	66	19	27	20	187	2.83	2
	Emile Francis	5	1	2	1	14	2.80	0
1951-52	Chuck Rayner	53	18	25	10	159	3.00	2
	Emile Francis	14	4	7	3	42	3.00	0
	Lorne Anderson	3	1	2	0	18	6.00	0
1952-53	Chuck Rayner	20	4	9	7	58	2.90	1
	Lorne Worsley	50	13	28	9	153	3.06	2
1953-54	Johnny Bower	70	29	31	10	182	2.60	5
1954-55	Lorne Worsley	65	15	33	17	197	3.03	4
	Johnny Bower	5	2	2	1	13	2.60	0
1955-56	Lorne Worsley	70	32	28	10	203	2.90	4
1956-57	Lorne Worsley	68	26	28	14	220	3.24	3
	Johnny Bower	2	0	2	0	7	3.50	0
1957-58	Lorne Worsley	37	21	10	14	86	2.32	4
	Marcel Paille	33	11	15	7	102	3.09	0
1958-59	Lorne Worsley	67	26	9	12	205	3.07	2
	Marcel Paille	1	0	0	1	4	4.00	0
	Bruce Gamble	2	0	2	0	6	3.00	0
	Julian Klymkiw	1	0	0	0	2	6.32	0
1959-60	Lorne Worsley	41	8	25	8	137	3.57	0
	Marcel Paille	17	6	9	2	67	3.94	0
	Al Rollins	8	1	3	4	31	3.88	1
	Jack McCartan	4	2	1	1	7	1.75	0
	Joe Schaefer	1	0	0	0	5	7.69	0
1960-61	Lorne Worsley	59	0	0	0	193	3.29	1
	Marcel Paille	4	0	0	0	16	4.00	0
	Jack McCartan	7	0	0	0	36	4.91	1
	Joe Schaefer	1	0	1	0	3	3.83	0
1961-62	Lorne Worsley	60	22	27	9	174	2.97	2
	Marcel Paille	10	4	4	2	28	2.80	0
	Danny Olesevich	1	0	0	1	2	3.00	0
	Dave Dryden	1	0	1	0	3	4.50	0
1962-63	Lorne Worsley	67	22	34	9	219	3.30	2
	Marcel Paille	3	0	1	2	10	3.33	0
	Marcel Pelletier	2	0	1	1	4	6.00	0
1963-64	Jacques Plante	65	22	35	8	220	3.38	3
	Gilles Villemure	5	0	3	2	18	3.60	0
1964-65	Jacques Plante	33	10	17	5	109	3.37	2
	Marcel Paille	39	10	21	7	135	3.58	0
1965-66	Ed Giacomin	36	8	19	7	128	3.66	0
	Cesare Maniago	28	9	16	3	94	3.50	2
	Don Simmons	11	3	6	3	37	4.52	0

Year	Goaltender	G	W	L	T	GA	AVG	Shutouts
1966-67	Ed Giacomin	68	30	25	11	173	2.61	9
	Cesare Maniago	6	0	3	1	14	3.84	0
1967-68	Ed Giacomin	66	36	20	10	160	2.44	8
	Gilles Villemure	4	1	2	0	8	2.40	0
	Don Simmons	5	2	1	2	13	2.60	0
1968-69	Ed Giacomin	70	37	23	7	175	2.55	7
	Gilles Villemure	4	0	1	0	9	2.25	0
	Don Simmons	5	2	2	1	8	2.33	0
1969-70	Ed Giacomin	70	35	21	14	163	2.36	6
	Terry Sawchuk	8	3	1	2	20	2.91	1
1970-71	Ed Giacomin	45	27	10	7	95	2.16	8
	Gilles Villemure	34	22	8	4	78	2.30	4
1971-72	Ed Giacomin	44	24	10	9	115	2.70	1
	Gilles Villemure	37	24	7	4	74	2.09	3
1972-73	Ed Giacomin	43	26	11	6	125	2.91	4
	Gilles Villemure	34	20	12	2	78	2.29	3
	Peter McDuffe	1	1	0	0	1	1.00	0
1973-74	Ed Giacomin	56	30	15	10	168	3.07	5
	Gilles Villemure	21	7	7	3	62	3.53	0
	Peter McDuffe	6	3	2	1	18	3.18	0
1974-75	Ed Giacomin	37	13	12	8	120	3.48	1
	Gilles Villemure	45	22	14	6	130	3.16	2
	Dunc Wilson	3	1	2	0	13	4.33	0
	Curt Ridley	2	1	1	0	7	5.19	0
1975-76	Ed Giacomin	4	0	3	1	19	4.75	0
	John Davidson	56	22	28	5	212	3.97	3
	Dunc Wilson	20	5	9	3	76	4.22	0
	Doug Soetaert	8	2	2	0	24	5.27	0
1976-77	John Davidson	39	14	14	6	125	3.54	1
	Doug Soetaert	12	3	4	1	58	2.95	1
	Gilles Gratton	41	11	18	7	143	4.22	0
	Dave Tataryn	2	1	1	0	10	7.50	0
1977-78	John Davidson	34	14	13	4	98	3.18	1
	Doug Soetaert	6	2	2	2	20	3.33	0
	Hardy Astrom	4	2	2	0	14	3.50	0
	Wayne Thomas	42	12	20	7	141	3.60	4
1978-79	John Davidson	39	14	13	4	98	3.18	1
	Doug Soetaert	6	2	2	2	20	3.33	0
	Hardy Astrom	4	2	2	0	14	3.50	0
	Wayne Thomas	2	12	20	7	141	3.60	4
1979-80	John Davidson	41	20	15	4	122	3.17	2
	Steve Baker	27	9	8	6	79	3.41	1
	Wayne Thomas	12	4	7	0	44	3.95	0
	Doug Soetaert	8	5	2	0	33	4.55	0
1980-81	Doug Soetaert	39	16	16	7	152	3.93	0
	Steve Baker	21	10	6	5	73	3.48	2
	Wayne Thomas	10	3	6	1	34	3.40	0
	John Davidson	10	1	7	1	48	5.14	0
	Steve Weeks	1	0	1	0	2	2.00	0
1981-82	John Davidson	1	1	0	0	1	1.00	0
	Ed Mio	25	13	6	5	89	3.56	0
	Steve Weeks	49	23	16	9	179	3.77	1
	Steve Baker	6	1	5	0	33	6.03	0
	John Vanbiesbrouck	1	1	0	0	1	1.00	0
1982-83	Ed Mio	41	16	18	6	136	3.45	2
	John Davidson	2	1	1	0	50	2.50	0
	Steve Baker	3	0	1	0	50	2.94	0
	Glen Hanlon	21	9	10	1	670	3.43	0
	Steve Weeks	18	9	5	3	680	3.92	0
1983-84	Glen Hanlon	50	28	14	4	166	3.51	1
	Steve Weeks	26	10	11	2	90	3.97	0
	Ron Scott	9	2	3	3	29	3.59	0
	John Vanbiesbrouck	3	2	1	0	10	3.33	0
1984-85	Glen Hanlon	44	14	20	7	175	4.18	0
	John Vanbiesbrouck	42	12	24	3	166	4.22	1
1985-86	John Vanbiesbrouck	61	31	21	5	184	3.32	3
	Glen Hanlon	23	5	12	1	65	3.33	0
	Ron Scott	4	0	3	0	11	4.23	0
	Terry Kleisinger	4	0	2	0	14	4.40	0
1986-87	Bob Froese	28	14	11	0	92	3.74	0
	John Vanbiesbrouck	50	18	20	5	161	3.63	0
	Ron Scott	1	0	0	1	5	4.62	0
	Doug Soetaert	13	2	7	2	58	3.99	0
1987-88	John Vanbiesbrouck	56	27	22	7	187	3.38	2
	Bob Froese	25	8	11	3	85	2.53	0
	Ron Scott	2	1	1	0	6	4.00	0
1988-89	John Vanbiesbrouck	56	28	21	4	197	3.69	0
	Bob Froese	30	9	14	4	102	3.78	1
1989-90	Mike Richter	23	12	5	5	66	3.00	0
	Bob Froese	15	5	7	1	45	3.33	0
	John Vanbiesbrouck	80	36	31	13	267	3.38	1
1990-91	Mike Richter	45	21	13	7	135	3.12	0
	John Vanbiesbrouck	40	15	18	6	126	3.35	3
1991-92	John Vanbiesbrouck	45	27	13	3	120	2.85	2
	Mike Richter	41	23	12	2	119	3.11	3
1992-93	John Vanbiesbrouck	48	20	18	7	152	3.31	4
	Corey Hirsch	4	1	2	1	14	3.75	0
	Mike Richter	38	13	19	3	134	3.82	1
1993-94	Mike Richter	68	42	12	6	159	2.57	5
	Glenn Healy	29	10	12	2	69	3.03	2

* Harry Lumley, spare Detroit goaltender, substituted for McAuley in one period of one game when McAuley was injured. Lumley allowed no goals.

YEAR-BY-YEAR GOALTENDING STATISTICS

Playoffs

Year	Goaltender	G	W	L	T	GA	AVG	Shutouts
1933-34	Andy Aitkenhead	2	0	1	1	2	1.00	1
1934-35	Dave Kerr	4	1	1	2	10	2.50	0
1936-37	Dave Kerr	9	6	3	0	10	1.11	4
1937-38	Dave Kerr	3	1	2	0	8	2.67	0
1938-39	Dave Kerr	1	0	1	0	2	2.00	0
	Bert Gardiner	6	3	3	0	12	2.00	0
1939-40	Dave Kerr	12	8	4	0	20	1.67	3
1940-41	Dave Kerr	3	1	2	0	6	2.00	0
1941-42	Jim Henry	6	2	4	0	13	2.16	1
1947-48	Chuck Rayner	6	2	4	0	17	2.83	0
1949-50	Chuck Rayner	12	7	5	0	29	2.42	1
1955-56	Lorne Worsley	5	1	4	–	22	4.40	0
1956-57	Lorne Worsley	5	1	4	–	22	4.18	0
1957-58	Lorne Worsley	6	2	4	–	28	4.60	0
1961-62	Lorne Worsley	6	2	4	–	22	3.44	0
1966-67	Ed Giacomin	4	0	4	–	14	3.41	0
1967-68	Ed Giacomin	6	2	4	–	18	3.00	0
1968-69	Ed Giacomin	3	0	3	–	10	3.33	0
	Gilles Villemure	1	0	1	–	4	4.00	0
1969-70	Ed Giacomin	5	2	3	–	19	4.13	0
	Terry Sawchuk	3	0	1	–	6	4.50	0
1970-71	Ed Giacomin	12	7	5	–	28	2.21	0
	Gilles Villemure	2	0	1	–	6	4.50	0
1971-72	Ed Giacomin	10	6	4	–	27	2.70	0
	Gilles Villemure	6	4	2	–	14	2.33	0
1972-73	Ed Giacomin	10	5	4	–	23	2.56	1
	Gilles Villemure	2	0	1	–	2	1.93	0
1973-74	Ed Giacomin	13	7	6	–	37	2.82	0
	Gilles Villemure	1	0	0	–	0	0.00	0
1974-75	Ed Giacomin	2	0	2	–	6	2.79	0
	Gilles Villemure	2	1	0	–	6	2.93	0
1977-78	John Davidson	2	1	1	–	7	3.44	0
	Wayne Thomas	1	0	1	–	4	4.00	0
1978-79	John Davidson	18	11	7	–	42	2.28	1
1979-80	John Davidson	9	4	5	–	21	2.33	0
1980-81	Steve Baker	14	7	7	–	55	4.00	0
	Steve Weeks	1	0	0	–	1	4.29	0
1981-82	John Davidson	1	0	0	–	3	5.45	0
	Ed Mio	8	4	3	–	28	3.79	0
	Steve Weeks	4	1	2	–	9	4.25	0
1982-83	Glen Hanlon	2	0	1	–	5	5.00	0
	Ed Mio	8	5	3	–	32	4.00	0
1983-84	Glen Hanlon	5	2	3	–	13	2.53	1
	John Vanbiesbrouck	1	0	0	–	0	0.00	0
1984-85	Glen Hanlon	3	0	3	–	14	5.00	0
	John Vanbiesbrouck	1	0	0	–	0	0.00	0
1985-86	John Vanbiesbrouck	16	8	8	–	49	3.27	1
	Glen Hanlon	3	0	0	–	6	4.80	0
1986-87	Bob Froese	4	1	1	–	10	3.64	0
	John Vanbiesbrouck	4	1	3	–	11	3.38	1
1988-89	Bob Froese	2	0	2	–	8	6.67	0
	Mike Richter	1	0	1	–	4	4.14	0
	John Vanbiesbrouck	2	0	1	–	6	3.36	0
1989-90	Mike Richter	6	3	2	–	19	3.45	0
	John Vanbiesbrouck	6	2	3	–	15	3.02	0
1990-91	Mike Richter	6	2	4	–	14	2.68	1
	John Vanbiesbrouck	1	0	0	–	1	1.15	0
1991-92	John Vanbiesbrouck	7	2	5	–	23	3.75	0
	Mike Richter	7	4	2	–	24	3.50	1
1993-94	Mike Richter	23	16	7	–	49	2.07	4
	Glenn Healy	2	0	0	–	1	0.88	0

ALL TIME RANGERS GAME-BY-GAME RESULTS 1926-27 TO 1992-93

1926-27–1928-29

1926-27

Game No.	Date	Opponent	Score	Result
1	11-16	Maroons	1-0	W
2	11-20	at Toronto	5-1	W
3	11-25	at Pittsburgh	0-2	L
4	11-27	at Canadiens	2-0	W
5	11-30	Chicago	4-3*	W
6	12-4	at Detroit	0-1	L
7	12-7	at Boston	1-0	W
8	12-12	Boston	2-1	W
9	12-15	at Chicago	2-6	L
10	12-19	Detroit	1-1	T
11	12-21	Pittsburgh	1-0	W
12	12-23	at Ottawa	0-1	L
13	12-26	at Americans	2-5	L
14	12-28	Ottawa	2-3*	L
15	1-1	at Chicago	4-0	W
16	1-6	Canadiens	1-0	W
17	1-9	Detroit	4-1	W
18	1-11	at Maroons	3-2	W
19	1-15	Toronto	1-1	T
20	1-16	Chicago	5-4	W
21	1-18	at Boston	3-7	L
22	1-20	Boston	2-2	T
23	1-23	Americans	2-0	W
24	1-27	at Canadiens	3-2	W
25	1-29	at Detroit	2-0	W
26	2-1	Canadiens	0-1*	L
27	2-6	Pittsburgh	2-1*	W
28	2-10	at Toronto	3-2	W
29	2-12	at Pittsburgh	3-2	W
30	2-15	at Ottawa	2-2	T
31	2-17	Maroons	1-4	L
32	2-20	Boston	3-1	W
33	2-22	Toronto	2-3*	L
34	2-24	Ottawa	0-1*	L
35	2-27	at Americans	4-1	W
36	3-1	at Chicago	0-3	L
37	3-5	at Maroons	0-0	T
38	3-13	Detroit	2-2	T
39	3-15	at Pittsburgh	5-0	W
40	3-17	at Detroit	2-0	W
41	3-20	Americans	2-1	W
42	3-22	Pittsburgh	4-1	W
43	3-25	Chicago	4-0	W
44	3-26	at Boston	3-4	L

*Overtime

1927-28

Game No.	Date	Opponent	Score	Result
1	11-15	at Toronto	4-2	W
2	11-17	Ottawa	3-2	W
3	11-20	at Americans	2-1	W
4	11-22	Maroons	3-4	L
5	11-27	Boston	1-1	T
6	11-29	at Ottawa	2-1	W
7	12-1	at Maroons	1-1	T
8	12-3	at Chicago	2-4	L
9	12-4	at Detroit	3-1	W
10	12-6	at Pittsburgh	2-2	T
11	12-11	Canadiens	0-2	L
12	12-13	at Boston	3-2	W
13	12-15	Detroit	1-2	L
14	12-20	Pittsburgh	2-0	W
15	12-25	Chicago	2-0	W
16	12-27	at Boston	0-2	L
17	12-29	Americans	3-3	T
18	12-31	at Canadiens	0-1	L
19	1-3	Detroit	2-4	L
20	1-8	Chicago	5-0	W
21	1-12	Boston	2-2	T
22	1-14	at Toronto	1-6	L
23	1-15	at Detroit	2-1	W
24	1-17	Toronto	1-2	L
25	1-22	Pittsburgh	4-1	W
26	1-26	Detroit	3-0	W
27	1-29	at Americans	7-0	W
28	1-31	Maroons	3-1	W
29	2-4	at Pittsburgh	2-4	L
30	2-7	Ottawa	0-0	T
31	2-8	at Ottawa	0-0	T
32	2-12	Chicago	0-3	L
33	2-16	Boston	0-2	L
34	2-23	Pittsburgh	3-0	W
35	2-25	at Chicago	1-0	W
36	2-26	at Detroit	0-0	T
37	2-28	Toronto	1-0	W
38	3-6	at Maroons	1-3	L
39	3-8	at Canadiens	4-3	L
40	3-10	at Boston	3-3	T
41	3-13	Canadiens	1-4	L
42	3-18	Americans	7-3	W
43	3-21	at Chicago	6-1	W
44	3-24	at Pittsburgh	2-4	L

*Overtime

1928-29

Game No.	Date	Opponent	Score	Result
1	11-15	at Detroit	2-0	W
2	11-18	at Americans	1-1	T
3	11-20	Maroons	0-1	L
4	11-22	at Chicago	2-1	W
5	11-25	Pittsburgh	2-0	W
6	11-29	Chicago	2-1*	W
7	12-1	at Maroons	0-3	L
8	12-4	at Boston	0-2	L
9	12-6	at Pittsburgh	0-0	T
10	12-9	at Detroit	2-2	T
11	12-11	Toronto	3-2	W
12	12-13	at Canadiens	3-2*	W
13	12-16	Detroit	3-0	W
14	12-20	Ottawa	1-0	W
15	12-25	Americans	0-1	L
16	12-30	Boston	2-0	W
17	1-1	at Toronto	3-2	W
18	1-3	Pittsburgh	2-2	T
19	1-6	at Americans	0-0	T
20	1-10	at Ottawa	9-3	W
21	1-13	Detroit	1-0	W
22	1-15	at Boston	1-4	L
23	1-17	Chicago	1-0	W
24	1-19	at Canadiens	0-0	T
25	1-22	Toronto	1-0	W
26	1-24	at Pittsburgh	3-1	W
27	1-27	Boston	1-2	L
28	1-31	Americans	2-1	W
29	2-3	at Chicago	3-2	W
30	2-5	Maroons	1-1	T
31	2-7	at Ottawa	1-2	L
32	2-10	Canadiens	3-3	T
33	2-14	at Toronto	1-3	L
34	2-17	Pittsburgh	2-1	W
35	2-21	Detroit	0-1	L
36	2-23	at Maroons	1-9	L
37	2-26	Ottawa	2-0	W
38	2-28	at Chicago	0-0	T
39	3-3	at Detroit	3-2	W
40	3-5	at Boston	1-2	L
41	3-10	Boston	2-3	L
42	3-14	Chicago	1-1	T
43	3-17	at Pittsburgh	4-3	W
44	3-20	Canadiens	0-1	L

*Overtime

Game-By-Game Results
1929-30—1931-32

1929-30

Game No.	Date	Opponent	Score	Result
1	11-14	at Maroons	2-1	W
2	11-17	Detroit	5-5	T
3	11-19	at Boston	2-3	L
4	11-21	Maroons	2-1	W
5	11-23	at Pittsburgh	5-3	W
6	11-25	Toronto	3-4	L
7	11-28	at Canadiens	3-2	W
8	12-1	at Detroit	3-4	L
9	12-8	Pittsburgh	5-1	W
10	12-12	Canadiens	8-3	W
11	12-14	at Toronto	6-7*	L
12	12-17	Americans	6-2	W
13	12-19	at Canadiens	2-7	L
14	12-22	Chicago	3-1	W
15	12-25	Boston	2-4	L
16	12-28	at Ottawa	3-1	W
17	12-31	Ottawa	1-1	T
18	1-2	at Americans	1-7	L
19	1-5	Pittsburgh	8-3	W
20	1-7	at Boston	0-3	L
21	1-9	Maroons	4-5	L
22	1-12	at Chicago	1-2	L
23	1-14	Detroit	3-0	W
24	1-18	at Pittsburgh	6-5	W
25	1-19	Chicago	4-1	W
26	1-23	Ottawa	6-3	W
27	1-26	at Detroit	3-7	L
28	1-28	Americans	4-3*	W
29	2-2	Boston	3-3	T
30	2-4	at Americans	3-5	L
31	2-6	Detroit	1-1	T
32	2-8	at Ottawa	2-2	T
33	2-11	at Maroons	2-5	L
34	2-13	Pittsburgh	4-1	W
35	2-18	Toronto	1-5	L
36	2-23	Boston	2-3	L
37	2-27	Chicago	1-1	T
38	3-1	at Toronto	3-3	T
39	3-2	at Detroit	2-2	T
40	3-4	at Chicago	2-2	T
41	3-8	at Canadiens	0-6	L
42	3-11	Canadiens	3-3	T
43	3-15	at Pittsburgh	4-3*	W
44	3-18	at Boston	2-9	L

*Overtime

1930-31

Game No.	Date	Opponent	Score	Result
1	11-11	at Philadelphia	3-0	W
2	11-13	at Detroit	0-1	L
3	11-16	at Chicago	1-1	T
4	11-18	Americans	0-0	T
5	11-23	Philadelphia	5-2	W
6	11-25	at Maroons	2-5	L
7	11-27	Chicago	0-4	L
8	11-29	at Philadelphia	6-3	W
9	12-4	at Canadiens	4-5	L
10	12-6	at Toronto	2-4	L
11	12-9	Ottawa	3-2	W
12	12-14	Detroit	3-0	W
13	12-18	Boston	2-4	L
14	12-20	at Boston	2-2	T
15	12-23	Canadiens	5-1	W
16	12-25	at Ottawa	4-1	W
17	12-28	Philadelphia	4-2	W
18	12-30	at Americans	2-2	T
19	1-1	Boston	3-4*	L
20	1-6	Maroons	5-1	W
21	1-8	at Detroit	1-0	W
22	1-11	Chicago	0-2	L
23	1-13	at Boston	2-2	T
24	1-15	Toronto	1-1	T
25	1-18	at Chicago	1-2	L
26	1-20	Canadiens	2-3*	L
27	1-25	Detroit	0-1	L
28	1-29	Boston	3-4	L
29	1-31	at Maroons	2-2	T
30	2-3	Montreal	3-0	W
31	2-5	at Americans	2-0	W
32	2-8	Chicago	2-3	L
33	2-10	at Philadelphia	3-1	W
34	2-12	at Detroit	1-1	T
35	2-15	at Chicago	2-1	W
36	2-17	Ottawa	4-5	L
37	2-22	Philadelphia	6-1	W
38	2-26	Toronto	4-1	W
39	3-3	at Boston	1-4	L
40	3-5	at Canadiens	2-1	W
41	3-7	at Toronto	2-5	L
42	3-10	Detroit	3-2	W
43	3-15	Americans	0-0	T
44	3-17	at Ottawa	3-1	W

*Overtime

1931-32

Game No.	Date	Opponent	Score	Result
1	11-12	at Canadiens	4-1	W
2	11-15	Detroit	1-2	L
3	11-17	at Americans	3-0	W
4	11-19	Boston	2-1	W
5	11-21	at Toronto	5-3	W
6	11-24	Chicago	1-1	T
7	11-29	at Chicago	5-0	W
8	12-3	at Detroit	1-1	T
9	12-8	Toronto	2-4	L
10	12-10	at Maroons	3-2	W
11	12-13	Americans	2-1	W
12	12-15	at Boston	2-2	T
13	12-17	Maroons	5-4*	W
14	12-19	at Canadiens	2-2	T
15	12-22	Canadiens	6-2	W
16	12-25	at Americans	6-0	W
17	12-27	Chicago	3-1	W
18	1-1	Detroit	3-0	W
19	1-3	at Chicago	1-1	T
20	1-5	Maroons	2-0	W
21	1-7	at Maroons	3-4	L
22	1-10	Toronto	2-0	W
23	1-12	at Boston	5-3	W
24	1-14	Boston	3-1	W
25	1-17	at Detroit	2-4	L
26	1-19	Canadiens	3-5	L
27	1-24	Detroit	4-3	W
28	1-28	Boston	1-4	L
29	1-30	at Toronto	3-6*	L
30	1-31	at Chicago	3-0	W
31	2-2	Canadiens	1-4	L
32	2-7	Chicago	1-0	W
33	2-9	at Boston	1-2	L
34	2-13	at Canadiens	1-3	L
35	2-16	Detroit	2-2	T
36	2-18	at Toronto	3-5	L
37	2-21	Americans	2-3	L
38	2-23	at Boston	2-0*	W
39	2-25	Boston	3-3*	T
40	3-3	at Detroit	2-1	W
41	3-6	at Chicago	3-4*	L
42	3-8	Chicago	6-1	W
43	3-10	at Americans	1-5	L
44	3-13	Maroons	4-4	T
45	3-15	at Maroons	3-4	L
46	3-17	Toronto	3-6	L
47	3-20	Americans	4-2	W
48	3-22	at Detroit	4-5	L

*Overtime

Game-By-Game Results
1932-33—1934-35

Game No.	Date	Opponent	Score	Result
1932-33				
1	11-10	at Maroons	4-2	W
2	11-12	at Toronto	2-4	L
3	11-20	Toronto	7-0	W
4	11-24	Chicago	1-1	T
5	11-29	at Boston	6-4	W
6	12-1	at Detroit	4-2	W
7	12-4	at Chicago	3-4	L
8	12-6	Canadiens	5-3	W
9	12-8	at Americans	3-1	W
10	12-11	Boston	3-1	W
11	12-13	at Canadiens	1-1	T
12	12-15	Americans	3-2	W
13	12-17	at Ottawa	2-2	T
14	12-20	Detroit	1-4	L
15	12-25	Maroons	2-0	W
16	12-29	Ottawa	4-2	W
17	12-31	at Maroons	2-4	L
18	1-3	Toronto	4-2	W
19	1-8	Americans	2-2	T
20	1-10	at Toronto	2-3	L
21	1-12	Boston	3-1	W
22	1-15	at Chicago	5-0	W
23	1-17	at Detroit	0-2	L
24	1-19	Canadiens	2-1	W
1932-33 (cont'd)				
25	1-22	Maroons	0-5	L
26	1-24	at Americans	3-2	W
27	1-26	Chicago	1-3	L
28	1-28	at Ottawa	9-2	W
29	1-31	Detroit	1-2	L
30	2-2	at Americans	2-2	T
31	2-5	Americans	4-1	W
32	2-7	at Boston	1-2	L
33	2-9	Ottawa	3-3	T
34	2-11	at Toronto	1-2	L
35	2-14	at Ottawa	3-1	W
36	2-16	Toronto	2-5	L
37	2-18	at Canadiens	3-1	W
38	2-21	Chicago	2-2	T
39	2-23	at Detroit	0-3	L
40	2-26	at Chicago	4-1	W
41	3-5	Boston	1-2	L
42	3-9	Detroit	3-2	W
43	3-12	at Americans	8-2	W
44	3-14	Ottawa	3-3	T
45	3-16	at Canadiens	1-2	L
46	3-19	Maroons	3-6	L
47	3-21	at Boston	2-3	L
48	3-23	Canadiens	4-2	W

*Overtime

Game No.	Date	Opponent	Score	Result
1933-34				
1	11-11	at Toronto	3-4	L
2	11-12	at Chicago	0-1	L
3	11-16	Detroit	2-1	W
4	11-19	at Detroit	1-4	L
5	11-21	Toronto	1-1	T
6	11-25	at Maroons	0-1	L
7	12-2	at Boston	3-0	W
8	12-3	Chicago	1-0*	W
9	12-7	Canadiens	0-0	T
10	12-9	at Canadiens	4-2	W
11	12-12	Americans	0-3	L
12	12-14	at Ottawa	4-3	W
13	12-17	Boston	2-2	T
14	12-21	Ottawa	0-0	T
15	12-24	at Americans	3-1	W
16	12-25	Maroons	3-0	W
17	12-28	Toronto	2-2	T
18	12-31	Americans	1-3	L
19	1-2	Canadiens	3-2	W
20	1-4	at Detroit	1-3	L
21	1-7	at Chicago	1-1	T
22	1-9	Detroit	2-1	W
23	1-11	at Ottawa	5-3	W
24	1-14	Maroons	3-1	W
1933-34 (cont'd)				
25	1-16	at Americans	1-2	L
26	1-18	Chicago	5-0	W
27	1-20	at Canadiens	4-5	L
28	1-23	Ottawa	5-2	W
29	1-25	at Ottawa	6-3	W
30	1-28	Boston	5-2	W
31	1-30	at Boston	1-2	L
32	2-1	Toronto	5-5	T
33	2-3	at Maroons	4-2	W
34	2-6	Canadiens	3-0	W
35	2-11	Americans	3-4	L
36	2-13	at Boston	6-4	W
37	2-15	at Canadiens	2-5	L
38	2-18	Chicago	1-2	L
39	2-22	Detroit	3-1	W
40	2-24	at Toronto	3-8	L
41	2-27	at Detroit	1-5	L
42	3-1	at Chicago	3-1	W
43	3-6	Ottawa	4-5*	L
44	3-8	at Maroons	2-2	T
45	3-11	Maroons	3-7*	L
46	3-13	at Americans	2-1	W
47	3-15	Boston	2-3	L
48	3-17	at Toronto	2-3	L

*Overtime

Game No.	Date	Opponent	Score	Result
1934-35				
1	11-10	at St. Louis	2-4	L
2	11-15	at Detroit	2-8	L
3	11-18	St. Louis	5-0	W
4	11-22	Detroit	4-3*	W
5	11-25	at Americans	1-3	L
6	11-27	Canadiens	2-3	L
7	12-1	Maroons	2-5	L
8	12-4	at Canadiens	3-5	L
9	12-8	at Toronto	5-2	W
10	12-9	at Chicago	0-4	L
11	12-11	Toronto	4-8	L
12	12-16	Boston	2-1	W
13	12-18	at Boston	3-5	L
14	12-20	Chicago	1-4	L
15	12-22	at Maroons	2-1	W
16	12-25	Americans	3-1	W
17	12-30	Boston	0-0	T
18	1-1	at Boston	2-5	L
19	1-3	Detroit	3-2	W
20	1-8	Maroons	1-1	T
21	1-12	at Americans	3-1	W
22	1-13	St. Louis	3-2	W
23	1-15	Americans	1-1	T
24	1-20	Canadiens	7-1	W
1934-35 (cont'd)				
25	1-22	at Canadiens	7-0	W
26	1-24	Chicago	3-3	T
27	1-27	at Americans	4-2	W
28	1-29	Toronto	7-5	W
29	1-31	at Toronto	3-2	W
30	2-3	Detroit	5-3	W
31	2-5	at Maroons	5-4	W
32	2-7	Americans	4-6	L
33	2-10	at Chicago	2-1	W
34	2-12	at St. Louis	5-1	W
35	2-14	Toronto	3-0	W
36	2-16	at Toronto	1-5	L
37	2-17	at Detroit	5-3	W
38	2-19	St. Louis	2-1	W
39	2-24	Boston	0-0	T
40	2-26	at Maroons	1-3	L
41	2-28	Maroons	2-5	L
42	3-5	at Boston	1-3	L
43	3-7	at Detroit	1-6	L
44	3-9	at St. Louis	5-1	W
45	3-10	at Chicago	1-1	T
46	3-12	Canadiens	3-4	L
47	3-14	at Canadiens	4-5	L
48	3-17	Chicago	2-5	L

*Overtime

Game-By-Game Results
1935-36—1937-38

Game No.	Date	Opponent	Score	Result
1935-36				
1	11-10	at Detroit	1-1	T
2	11-12	at Canadiens	2-1*	W
3	11-14	Toronto	0-1	L
4	11-16	at Toronto	2-3	L
5	11-17	at Chicago	0-3	L
6	11-19	Detroit	2-2	T
7	11-24	Boston	1-0	W
8	11-25	at Americans	1-0	W
9	11-28	Chicago	2-1	W
10	12-1	at Boston	0-2	L
11	12-8	Maroons	3-3	T
12	12-12	Americans	5-2*	W
13	12-14	at Maroons	6-2	W
14	12-15	at Detroit	2-4	L
15	12-17	Canadiens	1-1	T
16	12-22	Boston	3-1	W
17	12-25	at Boston	3-2	W
18	12-28	at Toronto	3-9	L
19	12-29	at Chicago	1-3	L
20	12-31	Maroons	1-0	W
21	1-2	Americans	3-6	L
22	1-5	at Americans	0-0	T
23	1-7	Detroit	1-2	L
24	1-12	Boston	3-6	L

*Overtime

Game No.	Date	Opponent	Score	Result
1935-36 (cont'd)				
25	1-14	at Maroons	2-1	W
26	1-16	Toronto	1-0	W
27	1-18	at Canadiens	1-3	L
28	1-21	Chicago	0-1	L
29	1-23	at Detroit	2-4	L
30	1-26	at Chicago	1-2	L
31	1-28	Canadiens	3-2*	W
32	2-2	Maroons	4-2	W
33	2-4	Detroit	4-4	T
34	2-9	Boston	2-0	W
35	2-11	at Canadiens	1-1	T
36	2-16	Canadiens	1-1	T
37	2-20	Chicago	1-1	T
38	2-23	at Boston	4-3	W
39	2-25	at Toronto	2-2	T
40	2-27	at Detroit	2-4	L
41	3-1	at Chicago	1-2	L
42	3-3	Toronto	0-0	T
43	3-8	Americans	0-1	L
44	3-10	at Maroons	0-0	T
45	3-12	Detroit	4-3*	W
46	3-15	at Americans	2-1	W
47	3-17	Chicago	4-2	W
48	3-22	at Boston	3-1	W

Game No.	Date	Opponent	Score	Result
1936-37				
1	11-8	at Detroit	2-5	L
2	11-10	at Maroons	4-1	W
3	11-15	Americans	1-2	L
4	11-17	at Boston	6-1	W
5	11-19	Detroit	1-0	W
6	11-21	at Canadiens	1-3*	L
7	11-24	Toronto	5-1	W
8	11-26	at Americans	3-1	W
9	11-28	Boston	2-2	T
10	12-3	at Detroit	0-2	L
11	12-6	at Chicago	2-1	W
12	12-8	Chicago	0-0	T
13	12-12	at Toronto	5-3	W
14	12-15	Maroons	2-2	T
15	12-19	at Canadiens	2-4*	L
16	12-20	Canadiens	5-3*	W
17	12-27	Chicago	1-0	W
18	12-29	at Americans	5-1	W
19	12-31	Boston	2-2	T
20	1-3	at Boston	2-3	L
21	1-5	Americans	7-1	W
22	1-9	at Maroons	3-2	W
23	1-10	Montreal	2-5	L
24	1-14	Detroit	0-2	L

*Overtime

Game No.	Date	Opponent	Score	Result
1936-37 (cont'd)				
25	1-19	Canadiens	1-1	T
26	1-21	at Chicago	0-2	L
27	1-23	at Toronto	0-4	L
28	1-24	Toronto	4-2	W
29	1-26	at Boston	3-0	W
30	1-28	Boston	1-1	T
31	2-2	Detroit	4-4	T
32	2-4	at Detroit	2-2	T
33	2-6	at Maroons	2-4	L
34	2-7	Maroons	1-1	T
35	2-9	at Toronto	5-1	W
36	2-11	at Chicago	2-5	L
37	2-14	Americans	4-5	L
38	2-16	at Boston	2-3	L
39	2-18	Chicago	2-1	W
40	2-23	Toronto	2-1	W
41	2-28	at Chicago	3-4	L
42	3-4	at Detroit	1-2	L
43	3-7	Boston	0-1	L
44	3-9	at Americans	7-8	W
45	3-11	Detroit	2-4	L
46	3-13	at Canadiens	0-1	L
47	3-16	Chicago	3-4	L
48	3-21	Canadiens	3-1	W

Game No.	Date	Opponent	Score	Result
1937-38				
1	11-7	at Detroit	3-0	W
2	11-11	Chicago	1-3	L
3	11-14	at Boston	2-3	L
4	11-16	Americans	1-0	W
5	11-20	at Maroons	3-0	W
6	11-21	Maroons	3-3	T
7	11-25	Toronto	1-3	L
8	11-27	at Canadiens	1-2	L
9	12-2	at Chicago	1-2	L
10	12-5	Boston	4-0	W
11	12-11	at Toronto	6-3	W
12	12-12	at Detroit	5-2	W
13	12-14	Detroit	3-1	W
14	12-16	at Americans	2-0	W
15	12-19	Canadiens	2-2	T
16	12-23	at Maroons	4-0	W
17	12-26	Chicago	1-3	L
18	12-28	at Boston	2-3	L
19	12-31	Boston	5-3	W
20	1-4	Americans	5-5	T
21	1-6	at Chicago	4-1	W
22	1-8	at Toronto	2-3	L
23	1-9	Detroit	4-1	W
24	1-13	Detroit	3-3	T

*Overtime

Game No.	Date	Opponent	Score	Result
1937-38 (cont'd)				
25	1-16	at Americans	4-0	W
26	1-18	Canadiens	3-1*	W
27	1-23	Maroons	8-2	W
28	1-25	at Boston	3-2	W
29	1-27	at Canadiens	2-4	L
30	1-30	at Chicago	2-2	T
31	2-1	Chicago	6-1	W
32	2-6	Toronto	2-1	W
33	2-10	at Detroit	4-0	W
34	2-12	at Maroons	5-3	W
35	2-13	Maroons	4-1	W
36	2-17	Boston	2-3*	L
37	2-20	at Boston	2-3*	L
38	2-22	Canadiens	1-2	L
39	2-24	Chicago	6-3	W
40	2-26	at Toronto	4-2	W
41	2-27	at Chicago	4-1	W
42	3-3	Detroit	4-3	W
43	3-6	at Americans	1-3	L
44	3-8	Toronto	4-3	W
45	3-13	Boston	1-2	L
46	3-17	Americans	5-3	W
47	3-19	at Canadiens	1-1	T
48	3-20	at Detroit	3-4	L

Game-By-Game Results
1938-39—1940-41

1938-39

Game No.	Date	Opponent	Score	Result
1	11-13	at Detroit	3-4	W
2	11-15	Detroit	2-0	W
3	11-17	at Chicago	1-0	W
4	11-20	Canadiens	2-1	W
5	11-22	at Boston	2-4	L
6	11-24	Toronto	6-2	W
7	11-27	Chicago	0-1	L
8	12-4	at Americans	6-1	W
9	12-8	at Canadiens	6-5	W
10	12-11	Boston	0-3	L
11	12-15	Americans	1-1	T
12	12-17	at Toronto	3-2	W
13	12-18	at Chicago	0-5	L
14	12-20	Detroit	6-2	W
15	12-22	at Canadiens	5-2	W
16	12-25	at Boston	1-0	W
17	12-28	Toronto	0-2	L
18	12-31	Boston	2-1*	W
19	1-2	Detroit	3-0	W
20	1-5	at Canadiens	2-2	T
21	1-8	Americans	5-2	W
22	1-10	at Americans	0-1*	L
23	1-12	Chicago	6-0	W
24	1-15	at Chicago	1-1	T

*Overtime

1938-39 (cont'd)

Game No.	Date	Opponent	Score	Result
25	1-19	at Detroit	3-4	L
26	1-22	Canadiens	7-3	W
27	1-26	Americans	0-1	L
28	1-31	Chicago	3-2	W
29	2-2	at Americans	7-0	W
30	2-4	at Toronto	4-2	W
31	2-5	Toronto	5-5	T
32	2-9	Boston	2-4	L
33	2-12	at Boston	3-2	W
34	2-16	Americans	2-1	W
35	2-18	at Toronto	1-2	L
36	2-21	Detroit	7-3	W
37	2-23	at Detroit	4-2	W
38	2-25	at Canadiens	1-1	T
39	2-26	Canadiens	0-3	L
40	3-2	Chicago	1-3	L
41	3-5	at Boston	3-5*	L
42	3-7	Canadiens	2-2	T
43	3-9	at Chicago	8-3	W
44	3-12	Boston	2-4	L
45	3-14	at Detroit	2-3	L
46	3-16	at Americans	11-5	W
47	3-18	at Toronto	1-2	L
48	3-19	Toronto	6-2	W

1939-40

Game No.	Date	Opponent	Score	Result
1	11-5	at Detroit	1-1	T
2	11-11	at Toronto	1-1	T
3	11-12	Toronto	0-1	L
4	11-16	Chicago	2-3	L
5	11-18	at Americans	3-1	W
6	11-19	Canadiens	1-2*	L
7	11-23	at Canadiens	1-1	T
8	11-26	at Boston	2-2	T
9	11-28	Detroit	4-1	W
10	11-30	at Chicago	7-2	W
11	12-2	Americans	1-1	T
12	12-10	Boston	3-2	W
13	12-14	Detroit	2-2	T
14	12-16	at Canadiens	4-2	W
15	12-17	at Detroit	0-0	T
16	12-19	Canadiens	5-2	W
17	12-23	Chicago	7-1	W
18	12-25	Toronto	4-1	W
19	12-29	Boston	4-0	W
20	12-31	Americans	5-2	W
21	1-2	at Boston	6-4	W
22	1-4	at Americans	6-2	W
23	1-7	Detroit	3-0	W
24	1-11	Chicago	5-3	W

*Overtime

1939-40 (cont'd)

Game No.	Date	Opponent	Score	Result
25	1-13	at Toronto	4-1	W
26	1-14	at Chicago	1-2	L
27	1-18	at Canadiens	1-0	W
28	1-21	Boston	4-2	W
29	1-23	at Americans	5-3	W
30	1-25	Toronto	3-0	W
31	1-28	Americans	4-2	W
32	2-1	at Detroit	0-2	L
33	2-4	Canadiens	9-0	W
34	2-6	at Boston	2-6	L
35	2-8	Toronto	2-1	W
36	2-10	at Toronto	4-4	T
37	2-11	at Chicago	0-3	L
38	2-15	Detroit	3-1	W
39	2-18	at Detroit	0-2	L
40	2-22	at Americans	0-1*	L
41	2-24	at Canadiens	2-0	W
42	2-25	Canadiens	6-2	W
43	2-29	Chicago	1-2	L
44	3-2	at Toronto	1-1	T
45	3-3	at Chicago	2-1	W
46	3-10	Americans	4-2	W
47	3-12	at Boston	1-2	L
48	3-14	Boston	0-0	T

1940-41

Game No.	Date	Opponent	Score	Result
1	11-2	at Toronto	4-1	W
2	11-10	at Detroit	2-2	T
3	11-16	Detroit	3-3	T
4	11-19	Americans	3-2	W
5	11-23	Boston	1-2	L
6	11-26	Toronto	2-4	L
7	11-28	at Americans	1-2	L
8	11-30	Canadiens	6-1	W
9	12-1	at Chicago	1-4	L
10	12-5	at Canadiens	3-2	W
11	12-8	Detroit	1-3	L
12	12-10	at Boston	2-6	L
13	12-13	at Detroit	2-3*	L
14	12-15	Americans	6-3	W
15	12-19	Boston	5-3	W
16	12-22	at Chicago	1-3*	L
17	12-25	Chicago	3-3	T
18	12-28	at Toronto	2-3	L
19	12-29	Toronto	3-2	W
20	12-31	at Boston	2-2	T
21	1-1	Canadiens	1-2	L
22	1-4	at Canadiens	3-3	T
23	1-5	at Americans	6-2	W
24	1-7	Chicago	2-3	L

*Overtime

1940-41 (cont'd)

Game No.	Date	Opponent	Score	Result
25	1-9	at Toronto	2-3*	L
26	1-12	Americans	3-1	W
27	1-14	Detroit	3-3	T
28	1-16	Boston	2-2	T
29	1-19	at Detroit	2-1	W
30	1-21	at Boston	3-4*	L
31	1-26	at Chicago	1-4	L
32	2-2	Canadiens	2-1	W
33	2-4	at Americans	2-2	T
34	2-6	Chicago	6-2	W
35	2-9	at Chicago	2-1	W
36	2-11	at Canadiens	2-6	L
37	2-13	Boston	3-5	L
38	2-15	at Toronto	3-4	L
39	2-16	Toronto	1-4	L
40	2-18	at Americans	5-2	W
41	2-23	Chicago	4-1	W
42	2-25	at Boston	2-0	W
43	2-27	Canadiens	5-2	W
44	3-1	at Canadiens	3-1	W
45	3-2	at Detroit	2-4*	L
46	3-4	Detroit	6-0	W
47	3-9	Toronto	8-5	W
48	3-16	Americans	6-3	W

Game-By-Game Results
1941-42—1943-44

1941-42

Game No.	Date	Opponent	Score	Result
1	11-1	at Toronto	4-3	W
2	11-9	at Detroit	3-1	W
3	11-15	Boston	1-2	L
4	11-16	at Boston	1-2	L
5	11-18	Toronto	6-8	L
6	11-20	Americans	1-4	L
7	11-22	at Canadiens	7-2	W
8	11-23	Canadiens	4-6	L
9	11-25	Chicago	5-4*	W
10	11-29	Detroit	4-1	W
11	11-30	at Chicago	5-1	W
12	12-7	Boston	5-4	W
13	12-11	at Americans	5-3	W
14	12-13	at Toronto	1-2	L
15	12-16	Americans	3-2*	W
16	12-18	at Chicago	1-5	L
17	12-21	Canadiens	4-3*	W
18	12-23	at Boston	2-3	L
19	12-25	Chicago	5-2	W
20	12-27	at Canadiens	4-2	W
21	12-28	at Detroit	3-1	W
22	12-31	at Americans	4-3	W
23	1-1	Toronto	3-3	T
24	1-6	Detroit	3-2	W

*Overtime

1941-42 (cont'd)

Game No.	Date	Opponent	Score	Result
25	1-13	Americans	9-2	W
26	1-17	at Americans	2-6	L
27	1-18	Canadiens	5-4*	W
28	1-20	at Boston	4-2	W
29	1-24	at Detroit	3-2	W
30	1-25	Detroit	11-2	W
31	2-1	Toronto	7-2	W
32	2-3	at Americans	3-2	W
33	2-5	Boston	4-1	W
34	2-7	at Toronto	4-6	L
35	2-8	at Chicago	4-3	W
36	2-10	Chicago	2-5	L
37	2-14	at Canadiens	3-5	L
38	2-15	Americans	1-5	L
39	2-17	Canadiens	1-2*	L
40	2-22	Chicago	3-2	W
41	2-24	at Boston	4-3	W
42	2-26	Detroit	7-4	W
43	3-3	at Americans	4-4	T
44	3-5	at Detroit	2-5	L
45	3-7	at Toronto	2-4	L
46	3-8	Toronto	2-0	W
47	3-12	Boston	1-2	L
48	3-15	at Chicago	5-1	W

1942-43

Game No.	Date	Opponent	Score	Result
1	10-31	at Toronto	2-7	L
2	11-5	at Detroit	5-12	L
3	11-7	Canadiens	4-3	W
4	11-8	at Canadiens	4-10	L
5	11-10	Chicago	5-3*	W
6	11-14	at Boston	3-5	L
7	11-15	Boston	3-4	L
8	11-19	Toronto	3-7	L
9	11-22	Detroit	4-4	T
10	11-26	at Chicago	2-1	W
11	11-28	at Toronto	6-8	L
12	11-29	Boston	3-2	W
13	12-3	at Chicago	1-3	L
14	12-6	at Boston	4-5	L
15	12-13	Canadiens	3-7	L
16	12-17	Boston	3-7	L
17	12-19	at Canadiens	1-1	T
18	12-20	Toronto	2-8	L
19	12-25	at Detroit	3-1	W
20	12-27	Toronto	3-1	W
21	12-29	at Boston	5-3	W
22	12-31	Detroit	0-2	L
23	1-1	at Chicago	5-6	L
24	1-3	Chicago	3-3	T
25	1-7	at Detroit	2-2	T

*Overtime

1942-43 (cont'd)

Game No.	Date	Opponent	Score	Result
26	1-10	Canadiens	4-7	L
27	1-14	Detroit	1-4	L
28	1-16	at Boston	5-7	L
29	1-17	Boston	3-6	L
30	1-21	at Toronto	4-7	L
31	1-23	at Canadiens	5-5	T
32	1-24	at Detroit	0-7	L
33	1-28	at Chicago	1-10	L
34	1-31	Boston	2-7	L
35	2-4	Chicago	1-1	T
36	2-6	at Toronto	2-3	L
37	2-7	at Chicago	4-8	L
38	2-14	Toronto	4-4	T
39	2-18	Detroit	4-5	L
40	2-20	at Canadiens	1-6	L
41	2-21	Canadiens	6-1	W
42	2-25	Chicago	7-4	W
43	2-27	at Detroit	1-7	L
44	2-28	Detroit	1-5	L
45	3-2	at Toronto	4-0	W
46	3-4	Canadiens	2-7	L
47	3-7	Toronto	5-5	T
48	3-14	Chicago	7-5	W
49	3-16	at Boston	5-11	L
50	3-18	at Canadiens	3-6	L

1943-44

Game No.	Date	Opponent	Score	Result
1	10-30	at Toronto	2-5	L
2	10-31	at Detroit	3-8	L
3	11-2	at Canadiens	1-2	L
4	11-6	Chicago	3-4	L
5	11-7	Toronto	4-7	L
6	11-13	Boston	2-6	L
7	11-14	at Chicago	5-10	L
8	11-18	Detroit	1-3	L
9	11-21	Toronto	2-5	L
10	11-25	at Boston	2-6	L
11	11-27	at Canadiens	3-6	L
12	11-28	Canadiens	2-2	T
13	12-4	at Toronto	4-11	L
14	12-5	at Chicago	6-7	L
15	12-11	at Boston	6-9	L
16	12-12	Boston	6-4	W
17	12-19	Detroit	6-2	W
18	12-23	at Detroit	3-5	L
19	12-25	at Toronto	5-3	W
20	12-26	Chicago	7-6	W
21	12-31	Toronto	0-4	L
22	1-2	Boston	3-13	L
23	1-6	Detroit	0-5	L
24	1-8	at Canadiens	2-8	L
25	1-9	Canadiens	5-6	L

1943-44 (cont'd)

Game No.	Date	Opponent	Score	Result
26	1-13	Chicago	2-5	L
27	1-15	at Boston	5-7	L
28	1-16	Boston	8-6	W
29	1-22	at Toronto	5-1	W
30	1-23	at Detroit	0-15	L
31	1-27	at Chicago	4-6	L
32	1-30	Canadiens	3-5	L
33	2-3	at Detroit	2-12	L
34	2-5	at Boston	2-7	L
35	2-6	Chicago	4-4	T
36	2-10	Detroit	3-8	L
37	2-13	Toronto	3-6	L
38	2-19	at Canadiens	2-5	L
39	2-20	Canadiens	2-7	L
40	2-22	Chicago	4-8	L
41	2-24	Detroit	3-3	T
42	2-27	at Chicago	2-4	L
43	3-2	at Detroit	5-6	L
44	3-4	at Boston	9-10	L
45	3-5	Boston	4-4	T
46	3-9	Toronto	0-5	L
47	3-11	at Toronto	0-5	L
48	3-12	at Chicago	4-4	T
49	3-18	at Canadiens	2-11	L
50	3-19	Canadiens	1-6	L

Game-By-Game Results
1944-45—1946-47

Game No.	Date	Opponent	Score	Result
1944-45				
1	10-28	at Toronto	1-2	L
2	11-1	at Chicago	3-8	L
3	11-2	at Detroit	3-10	L
4	11-9	Toronto	3-6	L
5	11-11	Detroit	5-3	W
6	11-12	Boston	5-5	T
7	11-18	Detroit	2-2	T
8	11-19	Canadiens	2-6	L
9	11-23	at Chicago	4-4	T
10	11-26	at Boston	4-8	L
11	11-30	at Canadiens	7-5	W
12	12-2	at Toronto	3-4	L
13	12-7	Detroit	2-3	L
14	12-10	Chicago	1-1	T
15	12-12	at Boston	5-7	L
16	12-17	Canadiens	1-4	L
17	12-20	at Chicago	3-1	W
18	12-21	at Detroit	3-11	L
19	12-24	Chicago	3-3	T
20	12-27	Toronto	2-8	L
21	12-30	at Canadiens	1-4	L
22	12-31	Boston	3-2	W
23	1-4	Detroit	4-4	T
24	1-7	Chicago	0-0	T
25	1-9	at Toronto	5-4	W
1944-45 (cont'd)				
26	1-11	Boston	5-1	W
27	1-14	Canadiens	2-6	L
28	1-18	at Detroit	3-7	L
29	1-20	at Canadiens	2-5	L
30	1-21	at Boston	3-14	L
31	1-24	at Chicago	4-3	W
32	1-27	at Toronto	0-3	L
33	1-28	Toronto	0-7	L
34	2-4	at Boston	3-3	T
35	2-8	at Canadiens	4-9	L
36	2-11	Canadiens	3-4	L
37	2-14	at Detroit	2-4	L
38	2-15	Chicago	6-2	W
39	2-17	at Boston	1-6	L
40	2-18	Boston	2-1	W
41	2-22	Detroit	5-3	W
42	2-24	at Toronto	4-4	T
43	2-25	Boston	4-4	T
44	3-1	Chicago	3-5	L
45	3-4	Toronto	3-6	L
46	3-7	at Chicago	3-6	L
47	3-8	at Detroit	3-7	L
48	3-10	at Canadiens	3-7	L
49	3-11	Canadiens	5-11	L
50	3-18	Toronto	6-5	W
1945-46				
1	10-31	at Chicago	1-5	L
2	11-3	at Toronto	4-1	W
3	11-4	at Detroit	1-4	L
4	11-8	Chicago	4-5	L
5	11-10	Detroit	2-0	W
6	11-11	Boston	1-7	L
7	11-15	at Canadiens	0-2	L
8	11-17	Canadiens	3-7	L
9	11-18	Toronto	1-3	L
10	11-22	at Chicago	3-3	T
11	11-24	at Toronto	3-4	L
12	11-25	at Detroit	4-1	W
13	11-28	at Boston	1-5	L
14	12-1	at Canadiens	3-4	L
15	12-9	Toronto	2-1	W
16	12-13	Chicago	4-7	L
17	12-16	Canadiens	2-4	L
18	12-19	at Boston	7-8	L
19	12-22	at Toronto	5-5	T
20	12-23	Toronto	3-4	L
21	12-26	Detroit	2-3	L
22	12-30	Chicago	3-2	W
23	12-31	Canadiens	0-0	T
24	1-3	at Detroit	3-3	T
25	1-6	Boston	4-2	W
1945-46 (cont'd)				
26	1-12	at Canadiens	3-9	L
27	1-13	Chicago	3-2	W
28	1-16	at Boston	2-3	L
29	1-17	Boston	2-4	L
30	1-19	at Toronto	1-3	L
31	1-20	at Chicago	1-9	L
32	1-26	at Canadiens	3-5	L
33	1-27	Detroit	5-2	W
34	2-3	Toronto	6-6	T
35	2-6	at Chicago	2-6	L
36	2-7	at Detroit	2-4	L
37	2-10	Chicago	2-2	T
38	2-14	Boston	2-2	T
39	2-16	at Boston	6-2	W
40	2-17	Canadiens	4-5	L
41	2-21	Detroit	2-2	T
42	2-24	at Chicago	2-2	T
43	2-27	at Toronto	6-4	W
44	2-28	at Detroit	1-4	L
45	3-3	Toronto	2-5	L
46	3-6	at Canadiens	3-7	L
47	3-10	Detroit	3-2	W
48	3-12	Boston	2-3	L
49	3-13	at Boston	5-3	W
50	3-17	Canadiens	8-5	W
1946-47				
1	10-17	at Canadiens	0-3	L
2	10-20	at Detroit	3-1	W
3	10-23	at Canadiens	4-1	W
4	10-26	at Boston	1-3	L
5	10-30	Boston	3-3	T
6	11-2	Detroit	7-4	W
7	11-3	at Detroit	1-3	L
8	11-6	at Chicago	2-6	L
9	11-9	at Toronto	2-4	L
10	11-10	Boston	0-4	L
11	11-13	Canadiens	4-4	T
12	11-16	Chicago	2-6	L
13	11-17	Toronto	4-5	L
14	11-21	at Detroit	1-3	L
15	11-23	at Canadiens	3-2	W
16	11-24	at Chicago	5-1	W
17	11-27	at Boston	2-5	L
18	12-1	at Chicago	2-1	W
19	12-4	Canadiens	2-1	W
20	12-8	at Boston	6-4	W
21	12-11	Detroit	1-1	T
22	12-14	at Toronto	2-3	L
23	12-15	Canadiens	3-5	L
24	12-18	at Boston	2-3	L
25	12-22	Toronto	1-3	L
26	12-25	Canadiens	2-0	W
27	12-28	at Detroit	2-2	T
28	12-29	Boston	2-2	T
29	12-31	Detroit	4-5	L
30	1-1	at Boston	1-3	L
1946-47 (cont'd)				
31	1-2	Toronto	4-5	L
32	1-4	at Toronto	2-0	W
33	1-5	Chicago	9-0	W
34	1-8	Boston	1-3	L
35	1-12	Toronto	3-2	W
36	1-15	Detroit	4-3	W
37	1-18	at Canadiens	2-6	L
38	1-19	Chicago	5-3	W
39	1-22	at Chicago	4-2	W
40	1-25	at Toronto	1-0	W
41	2-1	at Canadiens	1-2	L
42	2-2	Canadiens	7-1	W
43	2-5	at Chicago	3-2	W
44	2-9	at Detroit	2-5	L
45	2-12	at Boston	1-10	L
46	2-16	Toronto	6-2	W
47	2-19	Boston	6-0	W
48	2-22	at Toronto	0-2	L
49	2-23	Detroit	2-2	T
50	2-26	Chicago	7-9	L
51	3-2	Boston	2-3	L
52	3-3	Chicago	4-9	L
53	3-5	at Chicago	3-1	W
54	3-9	Toronto	2-4	L
55	3-12	Detroit	2-4	L
56	3-15	at Chicago	0-1	L
57	3-16	Canadiens	3-4	L
58	3-19	at Detroit	0-2	L
59	3-22	at Toronto	3-5	L
60	3-23	Chicago	4-3	W

Game-By-Game Results
1947-48—1948-49

Game No.	Date	Opponent	Score	Result
1947-48				
1	10-16	at Canadiens	2-1	W
2	10-19	at Boston	1-3	L
3	10-22	at Toronto	1-3	L
4	10-29	Boston	1-3	L
5	11-1	Detroit	4-3	W
6	11-2	Toronto	7-4	W
7	11-6	at Detroit	1-2	L
8	11-8	at Toronto	2-7	L
9	11-9	at Chicago	5-8	L
10	11-12	Boston	2-8	L
11	11-15	Chicago	3-5	L
12	11-16	Canadiens	4-2	W
13	11-19	at Detroit	6-5	W
14	11-22	at Canadiens	5-3	W
15	11-30	at Chicago	6-2	W
16	12-3	Toronto	1-4	L
17	12-6	at Boston	5-5	T
18	12-7	Detroit	3-1	W
19	12-10	Canadiens	4-4	T
20	12-11	at Canadiens	4-2	W
21	12-13	at Toronto	4-1	W
22	12-14	Detroit	1-1	T
23	12-17	Boston	5-2	W
24	12-21	Canadiens	3-4	L
25	12-23	at Chicago	1-7	L
26	12-25	at Detroit	2-0	W
27	12-28	Toronto	1-1	T
28	12-31	Boston	7-3	W
29	1-1	at Boston	1-4	L
30	1-3	at Toronto	5-5	T
1947-48 (cont'd)				
31	1-4	Chicago	1-4	L
32	1-7	at Detroit	0-6	L
33	1-10	at Canadiens	1-1	T
34	1-11	Canadiens	3-1	W
35	1-14	Chicago	4-2	W
36	1-18	Toronto	2-2	T
37	1-21	Detroit	3-4	L
38	1-25	at Boston	4-6	L
39	1-28	at Chicago	3-2	W
40	1-31	at Canadiens	4-2	W
41	2-1	Chicago	2-2	T
42	2-4	at Detroit	4-4	T
43	2-7	at Toronto	0-3	L
44	2-8	at Chicago	2-2	T
45	2-14	at Boston	4-4	T
46	2-15	Toronto	4-4	T
47	2-18	Detroit	1-3	L
48	2-22	Boston	4-1	W
49	2-25	Chicago	4-7	L
50	2-29	Canadiens	5-3	W
51	3-2	Toronto	1-0	W
52	3-3	at Detroit	2-4	L
53	3-6	at Toronto	1-2	L
54	3-7	Detroit	2-2	T
55	3-10	at Boston	3-6	L
56	3-13	at Canadiens	2-3	L
57	3-14	Canadiens	3-6	L
58	3-16	Boston	2-6	L
59	3-17	at Chicago	5-2	W
60	3-21	Chicago	3-4	L

Game No.	Date	Opponent	Score	Result
1948-49				
1	10-14	at Canadiens	1-1	T
2	10-17	at Detroit	0-7	L
3	10-24	at Boston	1-4	L
4	10-27	Detroit	2-3	L
5	10-31	Boston	2-0	W
6	11-6	at Toronto	3-3	T
7	11-7	at Chicago	2-4	L
8	11-10	Chicago	4-3	W
9	11-13	Canadiens	1-3	L
10	11-14	Toronto	4-4	T
11	11-17	at Boston	4-4	T
12	11-21	at Boston	4-1	W
13	11-25	at Chicago	4-6	L
14	11-27	at Toronto	0-3	L
15	11-30	Chicago	2-4	L
16	12-4	at Canadiens	1-3	L
17	12-5	Detroit	1-3	L
18	12-7	Boston	2-2	T
19	12-11	at Detroit	3-5	L
20	12-12	Detroit	2-0	W
21	12-15	Toronto	3-1	W
22	12-18	at Toronto	3-3	T
23	12-19	Canadiens	3-2	W
24	12-23	at Chicago	3-2	W
25	12-25	at Canadiens	2-0	W
26	12-26	Chicago	1-2	L
27	12-31	Boston	2-2	T
28	1-1	at Boston	1-4	L
29	1-2	Toronto	4-2	W
30	1-5	Chicago	3-1	W
1948-49 (cont'd)				
31	1-9	Canadiens	1-1	T
32	1-12	Detroit	1-4	L
33	1-15	at Toronto	1-1	L
34	1-16	Toronto	4-0	W
35	1-19	Boston	2-5	L
36	1-20	at Canadiens	1-2	L
37	1-23	at Chicago	2-2	T
38	1-26	at Detroit	5-1	W
39	1-30	Canadiens	9-0	W
40	2-2	at Boston	3-5	L
41	2-5	at Toronto	1-1	T
42	2-6	at Chicago	2-0	W
43	2-9	at Detroit	0-8	L
44	2-10	Chicago	1-3	L
45	2-12	at Boston	2-4	L
46	2-13	Toronto	0-3	L
47	2-16	Detroit	4-0	W
48	2-19	at Canadiens	1-3	L
49	2-20	Canadiens	3-2	W
50	2-23	Boston	2-3	L
51	2-27	Detroit	3-2	W
52	3-2	at Chicago	2-5	L
53	3-5	at Toronto	1-7	L
54	3-6	Toronto	3-4	L
55	3-9	at Boston	1-8	L
56	3-12	at Canadiens	0-3	L
57	3-13	Canadiens	1-1	T
58	3-15	Boston	2-4	L
59	3-16	at Detroit	2-6	L
60	3-20	Chicago	5-1	W

Game-By-Game Results
1949-50—1950-51

1949-50

Game No.	Date	Opponent	Score	Result
1	10-15	at Canadiens	1-3	L
2	10-16	at Boston	2-2	T
3	10-19	Detroit	1-6	L
4	10-22	Toronto	2-2	T
5	10-25	at Chicago	2-1	W
6	10-26	at Boston	5-2	W
7	10-29	at Chicago	0-2	L
8	10-30	Toronto	2-4	L
9	11-2	at Toronto	3-3	T
10	11-6	at Detroit	0-7	L
11	11-9	Canadiens	2-2	T
12	11-12	Canadiens	3-5	L
13	11-13	Detroit	1-1	T
14	11-16	Boston	2-1	W
15	11-20	at Chicago	5-2	W
16	11-23	at Detroit	3-4	L
17	11-26	at Canadiens	1-5	L
18	11-27	at Boston	1-1	T
19	11-30	Canadiens	5-2	W
20	12-3	at Toronto	0-2	L
21	12-4	Chicago	4-0	W
22	12-7	Chicago	2-1	W
23	12-10	at Detroit	1-0	W
24	12-11	Detroit	2-1	W
25	12-14	at Chicago	3-5	L
26	12-17	at Boston	3-1	W
27	12-18	Toronto	0-2	L
28	12-21	Canadiens	4-1	W
29	12-24	at Canadiens	0-0	T
30	12-25	Toronto	3-1	W
31	12-28	Chicago	3-2	W
32	12-31	Boston	4-1	W
33	1-1	at Boston	0-6	L
34	1-4	Detroit	2-1	W
35	1-7	at Canadiens	3-1	W
36	1-8	Chicago	1-1	T
37	1-11	Toronto	1-2	L
38	1-14	at Detroit	2-4	L
39	1-15	Detroit	0-1	L
40	1-18	Boston	2-4	L
41	1-21	at Toronto	1-2	L
42	1-22	at Chicago	3-4	L
43	1-25	at Toronto	1-5	L
44	1-28	at Boston	2-2	T
45	1-29	Canadiens	2-0	W
46	2-1	at Boston	2-3	L
47	2-2	at Canadiens	2-4	L
48	2-5	at Detroit	5-5	T
49	2-9	at Chicago	5-3	W
50	2-12	Detroit	4-0	W
51	2-15	Boston	2-2	T
52	2-18	at Canadiens	4-2	W
53	2-19	Toronto	2-1	W
54	2-22	Chicago	3-0	W
55	2-23	at Chicago	7-3	W
56	2-25	at Toronto	2-4	L
57	2-26	Boston	4-3	W
58	3-1	Detroit	2-5	L
59	3-4	at Boston	1-5	L
60	3-5	Toronto	5-2	W
61	3-8	at Chicago	4-2	W
62	3-9	Detroit	3-1	W
63	3-11	at Toronto	0-4	L
64	3-12	Canadiens	1-5	L
65	3-15	Boston	1-4	L
66	3-18	at Canadiens	3-5	L
67	3-19	Canadiens	2-4	L
68	3-21	Chicago	3-6	L
69	3-22	at Detroit	7-8	L
70	3-26	Toronto	5-3	W

1950-51

Game No.	Date	Opponent	Score	Result
1	10-11	at Detroit	2-3	L
2	10-15	at Chicago	3-2	W
3	10-19	at Canadiens	0-4	L
4	10-21	at Toronto	0-5	L
5	10-22	at Boston	0-0	T
6	10-25	Boston	1-1	T
7	10-28	at Canadiens	1-5	L
8	10-29	Canadiens	2-2	T
9	11-2	at Detroit	2-2	T
10	11-4	at Toronto	2-2	T
11	11-5	at Chicago	1-3	L
12	11-8	Toronto	3-5	L
13	11-11	at Canadiens	1-1	T
14	11-12	Chicago	1-4	L
15	11-15	Boston	3-4	L
16	11-18	at Toronto	4-5	L
17	11-19	Detroit	3-3	T
18	11-22	Canadiens	3-2	W
19	11-25	at Boston	3-3	T
20	11-26	Toronto	2-3	L
21	11-29	Chicago	1-1	T
22	12-2	at Boston	3-2	W
23	12-3	Boston	3-5	L
24	12-6	Detroit	0-9	L
25	12-9	at Detroit	0-5	L
26	12-10	at Chicago	3-3	T
27	12-13	Canadiens	3-2	W
28	12-16	at Canadiens	1-1	T
29	12-17	Detroit	3-3	T
30	12-20	Boston	4-4	T
31	12-24	Chicago	6-1	W
32	12-25	at Detroit	1-4	L
33	12-27	Toronto	3-1	W
34	12-31	Boston	3-0	W
35	1-1	at Boston	2-3	L
36	1-3	Detroit	5-3	W
37	1-6	at Toronto	4-2	W
38	1-7	Chicago	3-2	W
39	1-10	Canadiens	0-3	L
40	1-13	at Detroit	2-4	L
41	1-14	Toronto	2-1	W
42	1-17	Boston	3-3	T
43	1-20	at Canadiens	2-2	T
44	1-21	at Boston	1-5	L
45	1-25	at Chicago	2-1	W
46	1-27	at Toronto	1-2	L
47	1-28	Detroit	5-3	W
48	2-1	at Detroit	2-3	L
49	2-4	at Chicago	4-4	T
50	2-7	at Boston	2-2	T
51	2-11	Canadiens	3-1	W
52	2-14	Chicago	5-1	W
53	2-15	at Chicago	7-3	W
54	2-17	at Toronto	0-2	L
55	2-18	Toronto	2-5	L
56	2-21	Boston	2-2	T
57	2-24	at Canadiens	2-6	L
58	2-25	Detroit	6-2	W
59	3-1	at Chicago	4-1	W
60	3-3	at Boston	3-3	T
61	3-4	Canadiens	2-2	T
62	3-7	Chicago	3-1	W
63	3-10	at Detroit	2-3	L
64	3-11	Canadiens	5-5	T
65	3-14	Toronto	1-3	L
66	3-15	at Canadiens	3-5	L
67	3-17	at Toronto	1-3	L
68	3-18	Toronto	1-4	L
69	3-21	Detroit	1-4	L
70	3-25	Chicago	5-2	W

Game-By-Game Results
1951-52—1952-53

Game No.	Date	Opponent	Score	Result
1951-52				
1	10-14	at Chicago	2-3	L
2	10-18	at Canadiens	2-3	L
3	10-20	at Toronto	3-2	W
4	10-21	at Boston	1-1	T
5	10-24	Boston	1-3	L
6	10-28	Canadiens	2-1	W
7	10-29	at Canadiens	1-6	L
8	11-1	at Chicago	2-4	L
9	11-3	at Toronto	2-1	W
10	11-4	at Detroit	2-4	L
11	11-7	Detroit	4-4	T
12	11-11	Chicago	3-2	W
13	11-14	Toronto	2-2	T
14	11-17	at Canadiens	2-3	L
15	11-18	Detroit	2-5	L
16	11-21	Boston	3-3	T
17	11-22	at Detroit	1-2	L
18	11-25	Canadiens	2-1	W
19	11-27	at Boston	1-1	T
20	11-28	Chicago	6-3	W
21	12-1	at Toronto	2-8	L
22	12-2	at Chicago	4-6	L
23	12-5	Boston	2-3	L
24	12-9	Toronto	7-2	W
25	12-11	at Boston	2-4	L
26	12-12	Boston	6-3	W
27	12-15	at Toronto	1-4	L
28	12-16	Detroit	1-3	L
29	12-19	Canadiens	4-2	W
30	12-23	Chicago	3-2	W
31	12-25	at Detroit	1-2	L
32	12-26	Detroit	1-0	W
33	12-29	at Canadiens	2-7	L
34	12-30	Toronto	2-2	T
35	1-1	at Boston	4-2	W

Game No.	Date	Opponent	Score	Result
1951-52 (cont'd)				
36	1-2	Detroit	1-0	W
37	1-6	Chicago	3-2	W
38	1-9	Toronto	1-2	L
39	1-10	at Detroit	2-5	L
40	1-13	Canadiens	2-2	T
41	1-16	Chicago	4-6	L
42	1-17	at Chicago	6-6	T
43	1-20	at Detroit	3-2	W
44	1-22	at Boston	3-3	T
45	1-26	at Toronto	3-3	T
46	1-27	Canadiens	3-5	L
47	1-31	at Canadiens	0-1	L
48	2-3	at Detroit	3-4	L
49	2-7	at Chicago	3-1	W
50	2-9	at Boston	4-2	W
51	2-10	Toronto	3-4	L
52	2-13	Boston	6-2	W
53	2-16	at Canadiens	1-5	L
54	2-17	Canadiens	3-2	W
55	2-19	at Toronto	3-3	T
56	2-20	Detroit	1-1	T
57	2-24	Boston	5-2	W
58	2-27	Toronto	1-3	L
59	2-28	at Chicago	2-2	T
60	3-1	at Canadiens	1-3	L
61	3-2	Detroit	4-6	L
62	3-4	at Boston	1-4	L
63	3-6	at Chicago	5-3	W
64	3-9	Canadiens	0-2	L
65	3-12	Chicago	10-2	W
66	3-15	at Toronto	2-5	L
67	3-16	Toronto	2-4	L
68	3-19	Boston	6-4	W
69	3-20	at Detroit	3-7	L
70	3-23	Chicago	6-7	L

Game No.	Date	Opponent	Score	Result
1952-53				
1	10-9	at Detroit	3-5	L
2	10-12	at Chicago	0-2	L
3	10-16	at Canadiens	1-3	L
4	10-18	at Toronto	3-4	L
5	10-19	at Boston	2-2	T
6	10-22	Boston	3-3	T
7	10-26	Detroit	3-2	W
8	10-29	Chicago	1-3	L
9	10-30	at Chicago	3-8	L
10	11-1	at Canadiens	1-4	L
11	11-2	Canadiens	2-2	T
12	11-5	at Toronto	1-4	L
13	11-9	at Detroit	1-3	L
14	11-12	Chicago	5-2	W
15	11-13	at Chicago	2-6	L
16	11-16	Toronto	3-6	L
17	11-19	Detroit	2-2	T
18	11-23	Canadiens	2-2	T
19	11-26	Toronto	4-2	W
20	11-27	at Boston	1-3	L
21	11-30	at Chicago	1-1	T
22	12-3	Chicago	3-5	L
23	12-4	at Detroit	3-5	L
24	12-6	at Toronto	2-2	T
25	12-7	Canadiens	2-2	T
26	12-10	Boston	1-4	L
27	12-14	Toronto	2-2	T
28	12-17	Boston	5-0	W
29	12-18	at Canadiens	2-6	L
30	12-20	at Detroit	1-1	T
31	12-21	Detroit	2-5	L
32	12-25	at Boston	2-1	W
33	12-28	Chicago	3-6	L
34	12-31	Toronto	3-3	T
35	1-4	Boston	5-2	W

Game No.	Date	Opponent	Score	Result
1952-53 (cont'd)				
36	1-7	Chicago	4-6	L
37	1-8	at Canadiens	4-4	T
38	1-11	Canadiens	7-0	W
39	1-14	Detroit	3-2	W
40	1-17	at Toronto	0-1	L
41	1-18	at Chicago	0-2	L
42	1-22	at Detroit	8-2	W
43	1-24	at Boston	0-9	L
44	1-25	at Boston	2-1	W
45	1-28	Canadiens	1-2	L
46	1-29	at Canadiens	2-5	L
47	1-31	at Toronto	0-4	L
48	2-1	at Chicago	1-0	W
49	2-5	at Detroit	3-3	T
50	2-8	Canadiens	1-1	T
51	2-11	Detroit	2-2	T
52	2-14	at Boston	4-5	L
53	2-15	Toronto	1-2	L
54	2-18	Boston	4-2	W
55	2-19	at Chicago	4-2	W
56	2-21	at Canadiens	1-4	L
57	2-22	Detroit	1-2	L
58	2-25	Boston	2-1	W
59	2-28	at Toronto	0-3	L
60	3-1	Toronto	4-2	W
61	3-4	Chicago	1-4	L
62	3-5	at Detroit	1-7	L
63	3-7	at Boston	2-1	W
64	3-8	Canadiens	4-3	W
65	3-11	Detroit	0-2	L
66	3-14	at Canadiens	2-3	L
67	3-15	Toronto	1-1	T
68	3-18	Boston	1-2	L
69	3-21	at Toronto	0-5	L
70	3-22	Chicago	1-3	L

Game-By-Game Results
1953-54—1954-55

Game No.	Date	Opponent	Score	Result
1953-54				
1	10-8	at Detroit	1-4	L
2	10-11	at Chicago	5-3	W
3	10-15	at Canadiens	1-6	L
4	10-17	at Toronto	1-1	T
5	10-18	at Boston	2-3	L
6	10-22	Boston	4-3	W
7	10-25	Canadiens	1-2	L
8	10-28	Chicago	1-6	L
9	10-31	at Toronto	1-4	L
10	11-1	Toronto	2-2	T
11	11-5	at Canadiens	3-4	L
12	11-7	at Chicago	3-1	W
13	11-8	at Detroit	2-2	T
14	11-11	Chicago	3-2	W
15	11-14	Detroit	2-3	L
16	11-15	at Detroit	1-4	L
17	11-18	Chicago	3-1	W
18	11-21	at Toronto	0-1	L
19	11-22	Detroit	2-3	L
20	11-25	Boston	5-3	W
21	11-26	at Boston	2-5	L
22	11-29	Canadiens	2-1	W
23	12-2	Chicago	3-3	T
24	12-3	at Detroit	0-4	L
25	12-5	at Chicago	1-2	L
26	12-6	Toronto	3-3	T
27	12-9	Detroit	3-3	T
28	12-12	at Canadiens	2-7	L
29	12-13	Toronto	1-2	L
30	12-16	Boston	4-3	W
31	12-19	at Toronto	2-3	L
32	12-20	Canadiens	3-1	W
33	12-23	Detroit	2-1	W
34	12-26	at Canadiens	0-2	L
35	12-27	Chicago	1-4	L

Game No.	Date	Opponent	Score	Result
1953-54 (cont'd)				
36	12-29	Boston	2-6	L
37	1-1	at Boston	2-1	W
38	1-3	Canadiens	4-3	W
39	1-6	Chicago	4-3	W
40	1-10	Toronto	4-1	W
41	1-13	Detroit	1-3	L
42	1-14	at Chicago	2-0	W
43	1-16	at Toronto	0-4	L
44	1-17	at Detroit	3-2	W
45	1-20	Boston	8-3	W
46	1-23	at Boston	4-3	W
47	1-24	at Boston	1-2	L
48	1-28	at Detroit	3-3	T
49	1-30	at Canadiens	2-1	W
50	2-4	at Chicago	3-2	W
51	2-6	at Canadiens	3-4	L
52	2-7	Canadiens	1-4	L
53	2-10	Detroit	3-2	W
54	2-13	at Boston	0-1	L
55	2-14	Toronto	3-3	T
56	2-17	Boston	2-1	W
57	2-19	at Chicago	3-0	W
58	2-21	Toronto	6-1	W
59	2-24	Boston	3-5	L
60	2-27	at Canadiens	0-5	L
61	2-28	Canadiens	2-0	W
62	3-3	at Toronto	3-3	T
63	3-5	at Chicago	0-0	T
64	3-7	Toronto	0-4	L
65	3-10	Chicago	4-2	W
66	3-11	at Boston	0-1	L
67	3-13	at Detroit	5-2	W
68	3-14	Detroit	2-0	W
69	3-20	at Toronto	5-2	W
70	3-21	Canadiens	1-3	L

Game No.	Date	Opponent	Score	Result
1954-55				
1	10-9	at Detroit	0-4	L
2	10-10	at Chicago	2-1	W
3	10-14	at Boston	3-5	L
4	10-16	at Toronto	4-2	W
5	10-20	Boston	6-2	W
6	10-23	at Canadiens	1-7	L
7	10-24	Canadiens	4-2	W
8	10-27	Detroit	5-2	W
9	10-30	at Toronto	1-3	L
10	10-31	Chicago	1-1	T
11	11-4	at Chicago	1-3	L
12	11-7	at Detroit	0-1	L
13	11-10	Toronto	1-2	L
14	11-13	Chicago	3-5	L
15	11-14	at Chicago	5-0	W
16	11-17	Boston	2-2	T
17	11-20	at Canadiens	1-4	L
18	11-21	Toronto	2-2	T
19	11-24	Boston	3-1	W
20	11-25	at Boston	2-2	T
21	11-27	at Toronto	1-3	L
22	11-28	Canadiens	4-1	W
23	12-1	Detroit	1-6	L
24	12-4	at Boston	3-6	L
25	12-5	Canadiens	3-3	T
26	12-8	Chicago	1-2	L
27	12-9	at Detroit	2-3	L
28	12-11	at Detroit	1-4	L
29	12-12	Toronto	1-1	T
30	12-15	Detroit	3-3	T
31	12-16	at Canadiens	1-5	L
32	12-18	at Toronto	1-3	L
33	12-19	Toronto	3-3	T
34	12-22	Detroit	2-2	T
35	12-25	at Canadiens	1-4	L

Game No.	Date	Opponent	Score	Result
1954-55 (cont'd)				
36	12-26	Chicago	4-4	T
37	12-30	Boston	6-1	W
38	1-1	at Boston	0-4	L
39	1-2	Boston	3-3	T
40	1-5	Chicago	2-3	L
41	1-8	at Toronto	0-5	L
42	1-9	Canadiens	1-7	L
43	1-12	Toronto	0-0	T
44	1-14	at Chicago	6-2	W
45	1-16	at Detroit	0-3	L
46	1-19	Detroit	2-0	W
47	1-22	at Boston	1-3	L
48	1-23	at Boston	2-0	W
49	1-27	at Detroit	3-3	T
50	1-29	at Toronto	3-1	W
51	1-30	at Chicago	2-4	L
52	2-5	at Canadiens	1-3	L
53	2-6	Canadiens	3-7	L
54	2-9	Chicago	2-2	T
55	2-12	at Boston	5-5	T
56	2-13	Canadiens	4-1	W
57	2-16	Boston	2-2	T
58	2-19	at Canadiens	2-10	L
59	2-20	Detroit	0-5	L
60	2-23	Toronto	1-3	L
61	2-25	at Chicago	2-2	T
62	2-27	Canadiens	1-7	L
63	3-2	Boston	1-2	L
64	3-5	at Detroit	2-6	L
65	3-6	Detroit	1-2	L
66	3-12	at Toronto	2-1	W
67	3-13	Chicago	5-2	W
68	3-16	at Chicago	1-1	T
69	3-19	at Canadiens	2-4	L
70	3-20	Toronto	3-2	W

Game-By-Game Results
1955-56—1956-57

1955-56

Game No.	Date	Opponent	Score	Result
1	10-7	at Chicago	7-4	W
2	10-9	at Detroit	3-2	W
3	10-15	at Canadiens	1-4	L
4	10-16	at Boston	1-4	L
5	10-19	Toronto	6-2	W
6	10-22	at Toronto	2-3	L
7	10-23	Chicago	5-4	W
8	10-26	Detroit	6-2	W
9	10-29	Boston	0-1	L
10	11-3	at Detroit	1-1	T
11	11-5	at Toronto	5-0	W
12	11-6	at Chicago	4-2	W
13	11-9	Canadiens	1-1	T
14	11-10	at Boston	1-5	L
15	11-13	Toronto	4-1	W
16	11-16	Detroit	3-3	T
17	11-19	at Canadiens	1-6	L
18	11-20	Canadiens	1-1	T
19	11-23	Boston	4-0	W
20	11-24	at Boston	5-0	W
21	11-27	Canadiens	3-3	T
22	11-30	Chicago	6-1	W
23	12-2	at Chicago	2-1	W
24	12-4	Detroit	7-3	W
25	12-7	Toronto	3-1	W
26	12-10	at Toronto	1-6	L
27	12-11	at Detroit	0-2	L
28	12-14	Chicago	1-4	L
29	12-15	at Canadiens	0-2	L
30	12-18	Toronto	4-0	W
31	12-21	Boston	3-3	T
32	12-25	Canadiens	5-1	W
33	12-29	Chicago	2-4	L
34	12-31	Boston	6-2	W
35	1-1	at Boston	4-2	W

1955-56 (cont'd)

Game No.	Date	Opponent	Score	Result
36	1-4	Detroit	5-4	W
37	1-8	Chicago	3-5	L
38	1-11	Canadiens	6-1	W
39	1-12	at Detroit	0-6	L
40	1-14	at Toronto	6-5	W
41	1-15	at Chicago	2-0	W
42	1-17	at Chicago	2-2	T
43	1-21	at Canadiens	1-3	L
44	1-22	at Boston	1-3	L
45	1-26	at Detroit	1-3	L
46	1-28	at Toronto	3-1	W
47	1-29	at Chicago	6-2	W
48	2-1	Toronto	5-2	W
49	2-4	at Boston	1-7	L
50	2-5	Canadiens	3-3	T
51	2-8	Boston	3-3	T
52	2-11	at Toronto	0-5	L
53	2-12	Detroit	2-1	W
54	2-14	at Detroit	3-5	L
55	2-15	Chicago	5-1	W
56	2-18	at Canadiens	4-9	L
57	2-19	Boston	0-3	L
58	2-22	Toronto	2-4	L
59	2-23	at Canadiens	2-5	L
60	2-26	Detroit	3-2	W
61	2-28	at Detroit	1-4	L
62	2-29	Boston	4-2	W
63	3-3	Boston	2-5	L
64	3-4	Chicago	3-2	W
65	3-8	at Chicago	6-4	W
66	3-10	at Toronto	2-5	L
67	3-11	Toronto	4-2	W
68	3-15	Detroit	2-2	T
69	3-17	at Canadiens	2-7	L
70	3-18	Canadiens	1-3	L

1956-57

Game No.	Date	Opponent	Score	Result
1	10-12	at Chicago	3-0	W
2	10-14	at Detroit	1-2	L
3	10-17	Boston	2-0	W
4	10-20	at Canadiens	0-5	L
5	10-21	Chicago	4-1	W
6	10-24	Canadiens	3-2	W
7	10-28	Toronto	1-1	T
8	10-31	at Toronto	2-7	L
9	11-4	at Boston	1-4	L
10	11-7	Boston	2-4	L
11	11-8	at Canadiens	2-4	L
12	11-10	Detroit	4-6	L
13	11-14	Canadiens	3-5	L
14	11-17	Boston	4-4	T
15	11-18	at Chicago	2-2	T
16	11-21	Toronto	3-3	T
17	11-22	at Boston	4-3	W
18	11-24	at Canadiens	1-6	L
19	11-25	Canadiens	1-1	T
20	11-28	Boston	2-1	W
21	11-29	at Detroit	1-4	L
22	12-2	Toronto	4-2	W
23	12-5	Chicago	2-2	T
24	12-8	at Toronto	0-0	T
25	12-9	Detroit	4-2	W
26	12-13	at Detroit	1-2	L
27	12-15	at Toronto	1-2	L
28	12-16	Canadiens	4-2	W
29	12-21	at Chicago	3-2	W
30	12-23	Toronto	1-3	L
31	12-25	at Detroit	1-8	L
32	12-27	Chicago	3-2	W
33	12-29	at Canadiens	3-6	L
34	12-31	Detroit	0-1	L
35	1-1	at Boston	3-5	L

1956-57 (cont'd)

Game No.	Date	Opponent	Score	Result
36	1-5	Chicago	4-1	W
37	1-6	Canadiens	2-3	L
38	1-9	Toronto	3-4	L
39	1-11	at Chicago	7-4	W
40	1-12	at Detroit	5-4	W
41	1-13	Detroit	2-3	L
42	1-19	at Canadiens	0-5	L
43	1-20	at Detroit	2-5	L
44	1-23	at Toronto	4-4	T
45	1-26	at Boston	5-3	W
46	1-27	at Chicago	3-2	W
47	1-30	Chicago	2-7	L
48	2-2	Detroit	4-5	L
49	2-3	at Boston	1-4	L
50	2-6	Boston	3-2	W
51	2-7	at Chicago	4-4	T
52	2-9	at Toronto	4-4	T
53	2-10	Canadiens	5-4	W
54	2-14	at Detroit	2-3	L
55	2-16	at Canadiens	2-1	W
56	2-17	Toronto	3-2	W
57	2-20	Boston	5-2	W
58	2-23	at Canadiens	1-4	L
59	2-24	Canadiens	4-3	W
60	2-27	Chicago	6-6	T
61	3-2	at Boston	3-2	W
62	3-3	Detroit	1-1	T
63	3-7	at Chicago	2-2	T
64	3-9	at Toronto	2-1	W
65	3-10	Detroit	4-1	W
66	3-13	Boston	1-2	L
67	3-16	at Toronto	1-4	L
68	3-17	Toronto	3-5	L
69	3-23	at Boston	4-2	W
70	3-24	Chicago	4-4	T

Game-By-Game Results
1957-58—1958-59

Game No.	Date	Opponent	Score	Result
1957-58				
1	10-10	at Detroit	3-2	W
2	10-12	at Canadiens	2-2	T
3	10-13	at Boston	1-3	L
4	10-16	Boston	2-6	L
5	10-20	Chicago	6-1	W
6	10-23	Toronto	3-0	W
7	10-26	at Toronto	0-3	L
8	10-27	Canadiens	4-1	W
9	10-30	Detroit	0-4	L
10	10-31	at Boston	3-0	W
11	11-2	Boston	5-0	W
12	11-3	at Chicago	3-2	W
13	11-5	at Detroit	1-1	T
14	11-6	at Toronto	4-2	W
15	11-9	at Chicago	0-5	L
16	11-13	Chicago	2-2	T
17	11-16	at Canadiens	4-2	W
18	11-17	Canadiens	4-2	W
19	11-20	Detroit	1-1	T
20	11-22	at Chicago	4-2	W
21	11-24	Toronto	1-5	L
22	11-27	Boston	2-5	L
23	11-28	at Boston	0-1	L
24	11-30	Detroit	1-3	L
25	12-1	at Detroit	5-1	W
26	12-4	Chicago	0-2	L
27	12-7	at Toronto	3-3	T
28	12-8	Toronto	1-2	L
29	12-12	at Canadiens	2-3	L
30	12-14	at Detroit	4-4	T
31	12-15	Detroit	4-2	W
32	12-18	Canadiens	5-4	W
33	12-19	at Boston	3-3	T
34	12-21	at Canadiens	4-2	W
35	12-22	Toronto	5-2	W
1957-58 (cont'd)				
36	12-25	Chicago	1-3	L
37	12-28	at Toronto	1-6	L
38	12-29	Canadiens	3-4	L
39	1-4	Boston	4-7	L
40	1-5	Canadiens	0-4	L
41	1-8	Toronto	5-5	T
42	1-11	at Canadiens	3-9	L
43	1-12	Detroit	2-3	L
44	1-16	at Boston	3-2	W
45	1-18	at Chicago	3-2	W
46	1-19	at Detroit	6-1	W
47	1-25	at Toronto	1-7	L
48	1-26	at Chicago	3-4	L
49	1-29	Boston	1-1	T
50	2-1	Chicago	3-2	W
51	2-2	at Boston	3-4	L
52	2-8	at Detroit	5-2	W
53	2-9	Canadiens	1-3	L
54	2-14	at Chicago	3-1	W
55	2-16	Boston	3-2	W
56	2-19	Chicago	3-2	W
57	2-22	at Canadiens	2-2	T
58	2-23	Toronto	4-2	W
59	2-26	Chicago	4-3	W
60	3-1	at Toronto	5-4	W
61	3-2	Detroit	4-4	T
62	3-8	at Canadiens	3-2	W
63	3-9	Detroit	2-4	L
64	3-11	at Detroit	2-2	T
65	3-12	at Chicago	3-2	W
66	3-15	at Boston	4-0	W
67	3-16	Canadiens	2-3	L
68	3-19	Boston	1-1	T
69	3-22	at Toronto	7-0	W
70	3-23	Toronto	3-2	W

Game No.	Date	Opponent	Score	Result
1958-59				
1	10-8	at Chicago	1-1	T
2	10-11	at Boston	4-4	T
3	10-12	at Detroit	0-3	L
4	10-15	Boston	4-4	T
5	10-18	at Canadiens	2-2	T
6	10-19	Canadiens	3-5	L
7	10-25	Chicago	6-2	W
8	10-26	Toronto	3-2	W
9	10-29	Boston	2-2	T
10	10-30	at Detroit	1-4	L
11	11-1	at Toronto	3-4	L
12	11-2	Detroit	1-2	L
13	11-4	at Chicago	2-4	L
14	11-8	at Canadiens	6-5	W
15	11-9	at Boston	5-1	W
16	11-15	Boston	4-2	W
17	11-16	Canadiens	2-1	W
18	11-19	Toronto	7-4	W
19	11-22	at Toronto	2-2	T
20	11-23	Detroit	1-3	L
21	11-26	Canadiens	5-3	W
22	11-27	at Boston	1-3	L
23	11-29	Boston	1-3	L
24	11-30	at Chicago	2-2	T
25	12-3	Chicago	4-2	W
26	12-6	at Canadiens	0-6	L
27	12-7	Toronto	0-2	L
28	12-10	Detroit	1-2	L
29	12-13	at Toronto	4-4	T
30	12-14	Chicago	3-3	T
31	12-18	at Detroit	2-0	W
32	12-21	Toronto	5-1	W
33	12-25	at Canadiens	1-4	L
34	12-28	Canadiens	5-3	W
35	12-31	Boston	4-3	W
1958-59 (cont'd)				
36	1-1	at Boston	5-2	W
37	1-3	at Canadiens	1-5	L
38	1-4	Toronto	2-4	L
39	1-7	Chicago	0-4	L
40	1-10	Detroit	3-3	T
41	1-11	at Chicago	4-3	W
42	1-14	at Toronto	3-2	W
43	1-17	at Chicago	1-7	L
44	1-18	at Detroit	4-2	W
45	1-24	at Canadiens	1-3	L
46	1-26	at Boston	8-3	W
47	1-28	Chicago	1-3	L
48	1-31	at Toronto	5-2	W
49	2-1	Detroit	5-4	W
50	2-5	at Detroit	5-0	W
51	2-7	Chicago	3-6	L
52	2-8	at Boston	1-4	L
53	2-11	Boston	3-5	L
54	2-12	at Detroit	0-1	L
55	2-15	Canadiens	1-5	L
56	2-18	at Chicago	2-4	L
57	2-21	at Toronto	1-1	T
58	2-22	Canadiens	5-1	W
59	2-25	Detroit	6-3	W
60	2-28	at Canadiens	1-6	L
61	3-1	Toronto	1-1	T
62	3-7	at Chicago	6-1	W
63	3-8	Detroit	4-2	W
64	3-11	Chicago	3-5	L
65	3-12	at Boston	4-5	L
66	3-14	at Toronto	0-5	L
67	3-15	Toronto	5-6	L
68	3-18	Boston	3-5	L
69	3-21	at Detroit	5-2	W
70	3-22	Canadiens	2-4	L

Game-By-Game Results
1959-60—1960-61

1959-60

Game No.	Date	Opponent	Score	Result
1	10-7	at Chicago	2-5	L
2	10-10	at Boston	4-6	L
3	10-11	at Detroit	2-4	L
4	10-14	Boston	3-4	L
5	10-17	at Canadiens	4-2	W
6	10-18	Canadiens	5-6	L
7	10-21	Toronto	2-3	L
8	10-24	at Toronto	1-1	T
9	10-25	Chicago	3-1	W
10	10-28	Detroit	3-3	T
11	11-1	Canadiens	1-3	L
12	11-4	at Toronto	1-4	L
13	11-5	at Canadiens	2-8	L
14	11-8	at Detroit	3-3	T
15	11-11	Boston	6-3	W
16	11-14	Detroit	0-4	L
17	11-15	Toronto	2-2	T
18	11-18	at Chicago	3-5	L
19	11-22	Detroit	3-5	L
20	11-25	Boston	3-3	T
21	11-26	at Boston	3-4	L
22	11-28	at Chicago	2-6	L
23	11-29	Chicago	2-2	T
24	12-3	at Canadiens	7-4	W
25	12-5	at Toronto	3-6	L
26	12-6	Toronto	6-0	W
27	12-12	at Boston	4-3	W
28	12-13	Boston	4-3	W
29	12-19	at Canadiens	3-5	L
30	12-20	Canadiens	6-5	W
31	12-23	Chicago	0-3	L
32	12-25	at Detroit	5-2	W
33	12-26	at Toronto	0-4	L
34	12-27	Toronto	3-6	L
35	12-29	Boston	3-4	L
36	1-1	at Boston	3-7	L
37	1-3	Canadiens	8-3	W
38	1-6	Chicago	1-2	L
39	1-9	Detroit	3-3	T
40	1-10	at Detroit	4-3	W
41	1-14	at Boston	0-6	L
42	1-16	at Toronto	1-3	L
43	1-17	at Chicago	1-3	L
44	1-21	at Canadiens	2-11	L
45	1-23	at Chicago	1-2	L
46	1-24	at Detroit	2-2	T
47	1-27	Canadiens	2-2	T
48	1-30	at Toronto	2-3	L
49	1-31	Detroit	3-3	T
50	2-3	Toronto	2-4	L
51	2-4	at Detroit	3-1	W
52	2-6	Chicago	1-5	L
53	2-7	Canadiens	4-1	W
54	2-10	at Chicago	1-5	L
55	2-14	at Boston	0-3	L
56	2-17	Chicago	1-5	L
57	2-20	at Canadiens	3-3	T
58	2-21	Boston	7-2	W
59	2-24	Detroit	2-2	T
60	2-27	at Canadiens	2-3	L
61	2-28	Toronto	3-5	L
62	3-5	at Chicago	0-5	L
63	3-6	Detroit	3-1	W
64	3-9	Chicago	1-1	T
65	3-10	at Boston	3-3	T
66	3-12	at Toronto	4-1	W
67	3-13	Toronto	2-2	T
68	3-16	Boston	2-3	L
69	3-19	at Detroit	3-6	L
70	3-20	Canadiens	3-1	W

1960-61

Game No.	Date	Opponent	Score	Result
1	10-5	Boston	2-1	W
2	10-8	at Toronto	5-2	W
3	10-9	at Chicago	2-3	L
4	10-11	Canadiens	2-3	L
5	10-15	at Canadiens	4-8	L
6	10-16	Toronto	2-7	L
7	10-19	Chicago	2-0	W
8	10-23	Canadiens	2-4	L
9	10-26	Detroit	4-3	W
10	10-27	at Boston	4-6	L
11	10-30	Toronto	1-3	L
12	11-2	at Chicago	4-4	T
13	11-5	at Toronto	3-7	L
14	11-6	at Detroit	2-5	L
15	11-9	Detroit	3-4	L
16	11-10	at Canadiens	7-9	L
17	11-13	Canadiens	1-2	L
18	11-16	Boston	4-3	W
19	11-20	Detroit	3-4	L
20	11-23	Boston	6-3	W
21	11-24	at Boston	5-3	W
22	11-27	Chicago	3-3	T
23	12-3	at Toronto	2-5	L
24	12-4	at Detroit	4-1	W
25	12-7	Detroit	1-3	L
26	12-10	at Boston	3-0	W
27	12-11	Boston	2-2	T
28	12-14	at Chicago	0-4	L
29	12-15	at Detroit	1-1	T
30	12-17	at Canadiens	0-2	L
31	12-18	Toronto	2-3	L
32	12-21	Chicago	2-2	T
33	12-25	Canadiens	4-1	W
34	12-28	Detroit	3-4	L
35	12-31	at Toronto	1-2	L
36	1-1	Toronto	1-4	L
37	1-4	Chicago	2-3	L
38	1-7	at Canadiens	3-6	L
39	1-8	Canadiens	4-2	W
40	1-12	at Boston	4-4	T
41	1-14	at Detroit	2-2	T
42	1-15	at Chicago	3-1	W
43	1-18	at Toronto	4-4	T
44	1-21	at Chicago	3-5	L
45	1-22	at Detroit	5-3	W
46	1-25	Boston	2-1	W
47	1-29	Toronto	1-4	L
48	2-1	Chicago	3-1	W
49	2-2	at Canadiens	5-7	L
50	2-4	at Boston	2-1	W
51	2-5	Boston	5-2	W
52	2-8	at Toronto	3-5	L
53	2-9	at Detroit	2-4	L
54	2-11	Canadiens	3-3	T
55	2-12	at Boston	3-8	L
56	2-15	at Chicago	2-5	L
57	2-18	at Canadiens	4-7	L
58	2-19	Toronto	4-2	W
59	2-22	Chicago	4-2	W
60	2-26	Canadiens	1-3	L
61	3-1	Boston	3-1	W
62	3-2	at Chicago	1-7	L
63	3-4	at Toronto	4-5	L
64	3-5	Detroit	8-3	W
65	3-8	Chicago	3-4	L
66	3-9	at Canadiens	1-6	L
67	3-12	Detroit	7-3	W
68	3-14	at Detroit	2-5	L
69	3-15	at Boston	2-6	L
70	3-19	Toronto	2-2	T

Game-By-Game Results
1961-62—1962-63

Game No.	Date	Opponent	Score	Result
1961-62				
1	10-11	at Boston	6-2	W
2	10-12	Boston	6-3	W
3	10-14	at Canadiens	1-3	L
4	10-15	Toronto	2-1	W
5	10-18	Canadiens	2-5	L
6	10—19	at Chicago	4-2	W
7	10-21	at Detroit	4-4	T
8	10-22	Detroit	4-5	L
9	10-25	Chicago	1-1	T
10	10-28	at Toronto	1-5	L
11	10-29	Toronto	4-2	W
12	10-31	at Chicago	4-2	W
13	11-2	at Detroit	0-1	L
14	11-4	at Canadiens	3-3	T
15	11-8	Boston	4-4	T
16	11-12	Chicago	4-1	W
17	11-18	Canadiens	4-4	T
18	11-19	Toronto	5-3	W
19	11-22	Detroit	4-0	W
20	11-23	at Boston	4-3	W
21	11-25	at Toronto	0-6	L
22	11-26	Canadiens	2-2	T
23	12-2	at Boston	1-3	L
24	12-3	Boston	3-1	W
25	12-6	Chicago	3-8	L
26	12-7	at Detroit	3-3	T
27	12-9	at Canadiens	2-2	T
28	12-10	Toronto	2-3	L
29	12-16	at Toronto	2-4	L
30	12-17	at Chicago	1-3	L
31	12-20	Detroit	6-1	W
32	12-23	Chicago	7-3	W
33	12-25	at Detroit	6-4	W
34	12-27	Canadiens	0-3	L
35	12-31	Boston	4-7	L

Game No.	Date	Opponent	Score	Result
1961-62 (cont'd)				
36	1-1	at Boston	4-2	W
37	1-3	at Chicago	1-2	L
38	1-6	at Canadiens	1-5	L
39	1-7	Toronto	3-4	L
40	1-13	at Chicago	2-4	L
41	1-14	at Detroit	1-2	L
42	1-17	at Toronto	2-4	L
43	1-21	at Chicago	1-3	L
44	1-24	Detroit	0-3	L
45	1-27	at Canadiens	1-5	L
46	1-28	Chicago	0-3	L
47	1-31	Boston	5-0	W
48	2-1	at Boston	5-3	W
49	2-3	at Toronto	1-4	L
50	2-4	Canadiens	2-1	W
51	2-7	Detroit	2-2	T
52	2-10	Chicago	2-1	W
53	2-11	at Boston	5-3	W
54	2-14	at Chicago	3-4	L
55	2-15	at Detroit	3-4	L
56	2-17	at Toronto	3-5	L
57	2-18	Toronto	6-2	W
58	2-21	Boston	4-2	W
59	2-24	at Canadiens	2-4	L
60	2-25	Canadiens	3-3	T
61	2-28	Boston	2-2	T
62	3-3	at Toronto	1-3	L
63	3-4	Detroit	2-4	L
64	3-6	at Detroit	5-4	W
65	3-11	Canadiens	1-2	L
66	3-14	Detroit	3-2	W
67	3-17	at Canadiens	0-2	L
68	3-18	Toronto	2-2	T
69	3-22	at Boston	4-3	W
70	3-25	Chicago	4-1	W

Game No.	Date	Opponent	Score	Result
1962-63				
1	10-11	Detroit	1-2	L
2	10-13	at Canadiens	3-6	L
3	10-14	Toronto	5-3	W
4	10-17	Chicago	1-5	L
5	10-21	Canadiens	3-3	T
6	10-27	at Toronto	5-1	W
7	10-28	Chicago	3-5	L
8	10-30	at Chicago	3-5	L
9	11-1	at Detroit	0-4	L
10	11-3	at Canadiens	3-3	T
11	11-4	at Boston	4-3	W
12	11-7	Toronto	1-5	L
13	11-10	at Toronto	3-5	L
14	11-11	Detroit	2-3	L
15	11-14	Boston	6-2	W
16	11-17	Chicago	3-4	L
17	11-18	Toronto	3-1	W
18	11-21	Boston	4-2	W
19	11-22	at Boston	7-1	W
20	11-24	at Toronto	1-4	L
21	11-25	Canadiens	1-3	L
22	11-29	at Detroit	5-0	W
23	12-2	at Chicago	1-5	L
24	12-5	Detroit	3-3	T
25	12-8	at Boston	3-3	T
26	12-9	Boston	2-4	L
27	12-12	at Chicago	3-4	L
28	12-13	at Detroit	2-3	L
29	12-15	at Canadiens	4-2	W
30	12-16	Detroit	5-2	W
31	12-22	at Toronto	2-4	L
32	12-23	Chicago	1-3	L
33	12-25	at Boston	2-6	L
34	12-27	Boston	9-3	W
35	12-30	Canadiens	4-4	T

Game No.	Date	Opponent	Score	Result
1962-63 (cont'd)				
36	12-31	at Detroit	1-1	T
37	1-2	Toronto	3-2	W
38	1-5	at Canadiens	2-2	T
39	1-6	Canadiens	0-6	L
40	1-12	at Chicago	1-3	L
41	1-13	at Detroit	2-4	L
42	1-19	at Boston	5-3	W
43	1-20	at Chicago	2-6	L
44	1-23	Chicago	3-3	T
45	1-26	at Canadiens	4-2	W
46	1-27	Toronto	2-4	L
47	1-30	Detroit	1-6	L
48	2-2	at Toronto	2-2	T
49	2-3	Boston	4-6	L
50	2-6	Canadiens	6-3	W
51	2-9	Chicago	3-3	T
52	2-10	at Chicago	2-4	L
53	2-12	at Boston	3-6	L
54	2-16	at Toronto	2-4	L
55	2-17	Toronto	4-1	W
56	2-20	Boston	3-3	T
57	2-23	at Canadiens	3-6	L
58	2-24	Detroit	2-3	L
59	2-26	at Detroit	4-3	W
60	2-28	at Chicago	6-1	W
61	3-2	at Toronto	3-4	L
62	3-3	Detroit	2-3	L
63	3-6	Chicago	5-2	W
64	3-9	at Canadiens	5-2	W
65	3-10	Canadiens	1-5	L
66	3-14	at Detroit	4-9	L
67	3-17	Toronto	1-2	L
68	3-20	Boston	5-1	W
69	3-21	at Boston	2-2	T
70	3-24	Canadiens	5-0	W

Game-By-Game Results
1963-64—1964-65

1963-64

Game No.	Date	Opponent	Score	Result
1	10-9	at Chicago	1-3	L
2	10-12	at Canadiens	2-6	L
3	10-16	Detroit	3-0	W
4	10-20	Boston	5-1	W
5	10-24	at Boston	2-0	W
6	10-26	at Toronto	4-6	L
7	10-27	Chicago	1-4	L
8	10-30	Boston	4-3	W
9	10-31	at Detroit	1-4	L
10	11-3	Canadiens	3-5	L
11	11-5	at Chicago	2-3	L
12	11-7	at Detroit	0-1	L
13	11-9	at Canadiens	2-4	L
14	11-14	Toronto	4-5	L
15	11-16	at Toronto	4-5	L
16	11-17	Detroit	5-2	W
17	11-20	Boston	1-1	T
18	11-24	Toronto	3-3	T
19	11-27	Detroit	3-2	W
20	11-28	at Boston	3-5	L
21	11-30	Chicago	2-3	L
22	12-1	at Chicago	3-3	T
23	12-5	at Canadiens	2-4	L
24	12-7	at Boston	6-8	L
25	12-8	Boston	2-2	T
26	12-11	Chicago	2-6	L
27	12-12	at Canadiens	4-6	L
28	12-14	at Toronto	3-5	L
29	12-15	Canadiens	4-2	W
30	12-18	Detroit	1-1	T
31	12-22	Toronto	1-1	T
32	12-25	at Detroit	3-4	L
33	12-27	Chicago	4-2	W
34	12-29	Canadiens	2-6	L
35	1-1	at Chicago	5-2	W
36	1-4	Detroit	5-2	W
37	1-5	Toronto	3-2	W
38	1-9	at Boston	5-3	W
39	1-12	at Detroit	3-5	L
40	1-15	at Toronto	5-4	W
41	1-18	at Chicago	1-6	L
42	1-19	at Detroit	3-1	W
43	1-22	Boston	6-4	W
44	1-23	at Canadiens	2-4	L
45	1-25	at Toronto	1-1	T
46	1-26	Detroit	3-2	W
47	1-30	at Boston	3-1	W
48	2-1	Chicago	2-2	T
49	2-2	Chicago	4-2	W
50	2-5	Boston	2-3	L
51	2-6	at Boston	0-4	L
52	2-8	Canadiens	2-8	L
53	2-9	at Detroit	2-4	L
54	2-12	at Chicago	2-5	L
55	2-16	Toronto	4-2	W
56	2-19	Chicago	2-7	L
57	2-22	at Toronto	2-5	L
58	2-23	Toronto	3-4	L
59	2-27	at Boston	4-2	W
60	2-29	at Canadiens	0-4	L
61	3-1	Detroit	2-2	T
62	3-4	Chicago	4-3	W
63	3-7	at Canadiens	3-2	W
64	3-8	Canadiens	0-0	T
65	3-11	Boston	3-5	L
66	3-14	at Toronto	3-7	L
67	3-15	Toronto	1-3	L
68	3-17	at Chicago	0-4	L
69	3-19	at Detroit	3-9	L
70	3-22	Canadiens	1-2	L

1964-65

Game No.	Date	Opponent	Score	Result
1	10-12	at Boston	6-2	W
2	10-13	Canadiens	0-3	L
3	10-17	at Canadiens	2-2	T
4	10-18	Toronto	3-3	T
5	10-21	Detroit	0-1	L
6	10-24	at Toronto	1-1	T
7	10-25	Chicago	2-5	L
8	10-28	Boston	3-1	W
9	11-1	Canadiens	3-1	W
10	11-3	at Chicago	1-2	L
11	11-5	at Detroit	1-3	L
12	11-7	at Toronto	1-0	W
13	11-11	Boston	4-2	W
14	11-15	Detroit	2-6	L
15	11-17	at Chicago	2-1	W
16	11-22	Detroit	3-3	T
17	11-25	Toronto	6-3	W
18	11-26	at Boston	1-6	L
19	11-28	at Toronto	4-1	W
20	11-29	Canadiens	2-5	L
21	12-2	Chicago	3-3	T
22	12-5	at Boston	3-3	T
23	12-6	at Chicago	4-1	W
24	12-9	Chicago	1-6	L
25	12-12	at Canadiens	1-7	L
26	12-13	Toronto	3-3	T
27	12-16	Detroit	3-7	L
28	12-19	at Toronto	3-6	L
29	12-20	Boston	2-3	L
30	12-23	at Canadiens	0-2	L
31	12-25	at Boston	3-0	W
32	12-26	Boston	0-2	L
33	12-27	at Detroit	1-3	L
34	12-29	Chicago	2-4	L
35	1-1	at Chicago	1-2	L
36	1-3	Toronto	3-3	T
37	1-6	Boston	5-2	W
38	1-9	at Canadiens	6-5	W
39	1-10	Toronto	0-6	L
40	1-14	at Boston	2-5	L
41	1-16	at Chicago	6-3	W
42	1-17	at Detroit	4-2	W
43	1-23	at Toronto	1-1	T
44	1-24	at Chicago	2-7	L
45	1-27	Boston	5-2	W
46	1-30	at Canadiens	1-5	L
47	1-31	Detroit	1-4	L
48	2-3	Chicago	1-4	L
49	2-6	at Boston	2-3	L
50	2-7	Boston	8-3	W
51	2-13	Chicago	0-3	L
52	2-14	at Detroit	2-6	L
53	2-17	at Chicago	4-5	L
54	2-20	at Detroit	2-3	L
55	2-21	Canadiens	2-2	T
56	2-24	at Canadiens	1-6	L
57	2-27	at Toronto	4-3	W
58	2-28	Toronto	6-2	W
59	3-3	Boston	1-6	L
60	3-4	at Boston	4-3	W
61	3-6	at Canadiens	1-2	L
62	3-7	Detroit	5-6	L
63	3-10	Chicago	1-1	T
64	3-14	Canadiens	4-6	L
65	3-19	Detroit	6-6	T
66	3-20	at Toronto	1-4	L
67	3-21	Toronto	1-10	L
68	3-23	at Chicago	3-2	W
69	3-25	at Detroit	4-7	L
70	3-28	Canadiens	3-5	L

Game-By-Game Results
1965-66—1966-67

Game No.	Date	Opponent	Score	Result
1965-66				
1	10-24	Canadiens	3-4	L
2	10-27	at Canadiens	3-4	L
3	10-30	at Boston	8-2	W
4	11-3	Toronto	2-2	T
5	11-6	at Toronto	4-2	W
6	11-7	Detroit	3-2	W
7	11-10	Boston	2-2	T
8	11-11	at Detroit	3-3	T
9	11-13	at Toronto	3-5	L
10	11-14	at Chicago	4-2	W
11	11-17	Chicago	3-5	L
12	11-20	at Canadiens	3-9	L
13	11-21	Detroit	3-3	T
14	11-24	Boston	4-1	W
15	11-25	at Boston	2-6	L
16	11-27	Chicago	0-1	L
17	11-28	Toronto	2-4	L
18	12-1	Toronto	2-2	T
19	12-4	at Canadiens	3-4	L
20	12-5	Chicago	2-6	L
21	12-8	at Chicago	2-2	T
22	12-9	at Detroit	3-7	L
23	12-11	Detroit	2-4	L
24	12-12	Toronto	1-1	T
25	12-18	at Toronto	4-8	L
26	12-19	Canadiens	3-2	W
27	12-22	at Chicago	3-4	L
28	12-23	at Detroit	2-4	L
29	12-25	at Boston	2-4	L
30	12-26	Boston	6-4	W
31	12-29	Chicago	0-3	L
32	1-1	at Canadiens	1-5	L
33	1-2	Canadiens	3-6	L
34	1-8	Chicago	6-4	W
35	1-9	Boston	1-3	L
36	1-15	at Detroit	4-4	T
37	1-16	at Chicago	6-5	W
38	1-19	at Toronto	2-6	L
39	1-22	at Boston	3-5	L
40	1-23	at Detroit	1-5	L
41	1-26	Detroit	4-3	W
42	1-29	at Canadiens	2-6	L
43	1-30	Toronto	8-4	W
44	2-2	at Chicago	3-4	L
45	2-5	at Boston	3-5	L
46	2-6	Canadiens	0-4	L
47	2-9	at Toronto	0-3	L
48	2-10	at Detroit	2-6	L
49	2-12	Boston	9-2	W
50	2-13	at Chicago	1-6	L
51	2-16	Chicago	2-5	L
52	2-19	at Toronto	3-1	W
53	2-20	Canadiens	3-5	L
54	2-23	Detroit	5-0	W
55	2-26	at Canadiens	3-4	L
56	2-27	Toronto	2-2	T
57	3-2	Boston	5-3	W
58	3-3	at Boston	5-4	W
59	3-6	Detroit	1-1	T
60	3-9	Chicago	1-0	W
61	3-12	at Chicago	2-4	L
62	3-13	Canadiens	3-2	W
63	3-16	Boston	1-3	L
64	3-19	at Canadiens	2-6	L
65	3-20	at Boston	3-4	L
66	3-23	Detroit	1-2	L
67	3-27	Toronto	1-5	L
68	3-31	at Detroit	3-5	L
69	4-2	at Toronto	3-3	T
70	4-3	Canadiens	4-1	W

Game No.	Date	Opponent	Score	Result
1966-67				
1	10-19	Chicago	3-6	L
2	10-22	at Toronto	4-4	T
3	10-23	Toronto	1-0	W
4	10-27	at Detroit	3-5	L
5	10-29	at Canadiens	0-3	L
6	11-3	at Boston	7-1	W
7	11-5	at Toronto	1-3	L
8	11-6	Toronto	3-3	T
9	11-8	at Chicago	1-3	L
10	11-9	Boston	3-3	T
11	11-12	at Canadiens	6-3	W
12	11-13	Detroit	5-2	W
13	11-16	Chicago	2-2	T
14	11-19	at Boston	3-3	T
15	11-20	Canadiens	1-2	L
16	11-23	Boston	5-4	W
17	11-26	Chicago	4-1	W
18	11-27	Toronto	5-0	W
19	11-30	at Chicago	5-0	W
20	12-3	at Boston	2-2	T
21	12-4	Canadiens	1-3	L
22	12-7	Boston	4-2	W
23	12-8	at Detroit	4-2	W
24	12-11	Canadiens	4-2	W
25	12-14	Detroit	4-1	W
26	12-17	at Toronto	3-1	W
27	12-18	at Detroit	0-5	L
28	12-21	Boston	5-1	W
29	12-24	at Canadiens	4-3	W
30	12-25	at Chicago	1-0	W
31	12-27	Chicago	2-3	L
32	12-29	Detroit	4-2	W
33	12-31	at Canadiens	0-3	L
34	1-1	Toronto	1-2	L
35	1-4	at Toronto	1-1	T
36	1-8	Canadiens	2-1	W
37	1-12	at Boston	3-0	W
38	1-14	at Chicago	3-5	L
39	1-15	at Detroit	2-0	W
40	1-21	at Boston	2-6	L
41	1-22	at Detroit	2-7	L
42	1-25	Boston	2-1	W
43	1-28	at Canadiens	2-3	L
44	1-29	Detroit	2-4	L
45	2-4	at Boston	4-3	W
46	2-5	Toronto	4-1	W
47	2-8	Boston	1-2	L
48	2-11	at Detroit	3-6	L
49	2-12	Canadiens	4-4	T
50	2-15	at Toronto	0-6	L
51	2-18	Chicago	4-1	W
52	2-19	at Chicago	3-2	W
53	2-22	Detroit	1-0	W
54	2-25	at Canadiens	5-0	W
55	2-26	Toronto	2-4	L
56	3-1	at Chicago	1-6	L
57	3-4	at Boston	4-4	T
58	3-5	Canadiens	0-2	L
59	3-8	Detroit	1-3	L
60	3-11	at Toronto	2-2	T
61	3-12	Canadiens	2-2	T
62	3-15	Chicago	1-3	L
63	3-18	at Canadiens	2-4	L
64	3-19	Boston	3-1	W
65	3-22	at Chicago	3-3	T
66	3-23	at Detroit	1-4	L
67	3-26	Toronto	4-0	W
68	3-29	Detroit	10-5	W
69	4-1	at Toronto	1-5	L
70	4-2	Chicago	0-8	L

Game-By-Game Results
1967-68—1968-69

Game No.	Date	Opponent	Score	Result
1967-68				
1	10-11	at Chicago	6-3	W
2	10-15	at Detroit	2-3	L
3	10-18	Canadiens	2-2	T
4	10-21	at Toronto	5-3	W
5	10-22	Pittsburgh	6-4	W
6	10-25	Chicago	2-2	T
7	10-26	at Canadiens	1-1	T
8	10-29	Toronto	3-2	W
9	10-31	at Los Angeles	6-1	W
10	11-1	at California	2-0	W
11	11-4	at Toronto	2-4	L
12	11-8	Boston	3-6	L
13	11-12	Oakland	5-3	W
14	11-16	at Philadelphia	2-3	L
15	11-18	at Boston	1-3	L
16	11-19	Minnesota	5-2	W
17	11-22	Chicago	1-7	L
18	11-23	at Boston	2-4	L
19	11-26	St. Louis	1-0	W
20	11-29	Detroit	1-3	L
21	12-2	at Pittsburgh	4-1	W
22	12-3	Los Angeles	4-2	W
23	12-6	Detroit	3-3	T
24	12-7	at Boston	1-3	L
25	12-9	at Detroit	2-3	L
26	12-10	Canadiens	3-2	W
27	12-13	at Chicago	2-5	L
28	12-16	at Toronto	2-4	L
29	12-17	St. Louis	5-3	W
30	12-20	Detroit	2-0	W
31	12-23	Boston	0-4	L
32	12-25	at Philadelphia	3-1	W
33	12-27	Minnesota	3-3	T
34	12-30	Chicago	3-3	T
35	12-31	Toronto	4-0	W
36	1-3	Boston	5-5	T
37	1-6	at Canadiens	2-5	L
1967-68 (cont'd)				
38	1-7	Toronto	6-2	W
39	1-10	at Chicago	3-3	T
40	1-13	at St. Louis	3-1	W
41	1-17	at Chicago	4-2	W
42	1-19	at Los Angeles	2-5	L
43	1-20	at Oakland	3-0	W
44	1-24	Boston	2-1	W
45	1-27	at St. Louis	3-4	L
46	1-28	Oakland	4-2	W
47	1-31	Chicago	2-3	L
48	2-1	at Canadiens	2-5	L
49	2-3	at Boston	3-3	T
50	2-4	Canadiens	3-0	W
51	2-8	at Detroit	3-2	W
52	2-10	at Pittsburgh	2-2	T
53	2-11	Detroit	3-3	T
54	2-15	at Minnesota	6-2	W
55	2-17	at Toronto	3-2	W
56	2-18	Philadelphia	3-1	W
57	2-21	Canadiens	2-7	L
58	2-24	at Canadiens	6-1	W
59	2-25	Toronto	3-1	W
60	2-29	at Detroit	4-2	W
61	3-2	Philadelphia	4-0	W
62	3-3	Chicago	4-0	W
63	3-6	Detroit	6-1	W
64	3-9	at Minnesota	1-1	T
65	3-10	Los Angeles	3-4	L
66	3-13	Boston	1-2	L
67	3-14	at Canadiens	1-3	L
68	3-17	Pittsburgh	3-0	W
69	3-20	at Chicago	5-3	W
70	3-23	at Toronto	1-3	L
71	3-24	Toronto	4-2	W
72	3-28	at Boston	5-4	W
73	3-30	at Detroit	3-1	W
74	3-31	Canadiens	4-2	W

Game No.	Date	Opponent	Score	Result
1968-69				
1	10-13	at Chicago	2-5	L
2	10-16	Philadelphia	3-1	W
3	10-17	at Detroit	2-7	L
4	10-20	Los Angeles	7-0	W
5	10-23	Oakland	6-1	W
6	10-26	at Minnesota	3-0	W
7	10-27	Toronto	3-5	L
8	10-30	Pittsburgh	7-3	W
9	10-31	at Philadelphia	2-1	W
10	11-3	Minnesota	2-1	W
11	11-6	at Los Angeles	0-2	L
12	11-8	at Oakland	3-2	W
13	11-10	at Chicago	4-2	W
14	11-13	St. Louis	1-3	L
15	11-16	at Pittsburgh	2-1	W
16	11-17	Montreal	3-2	W
17	11-20	Los Angeles	4-2	W
18	11-23	at Boston	1-5	L
19	11-24	Oakland	3-2	W
20	11-27	Chicago	2-4	L
21	11-30	at Boston	4-1	W
22	12-1	Toronto	3-1	W
23	12-4	at Montreal	4-2	W
24	12-5	at Detroit	2-4	L
25	12-7	at Toronto	2-5	L
26	12-8	Detroit	2-5	L
27	12-11	Boston	2-2	T
28	12-14	at Minnesota	1-4	L
29	12-15	Philadelphia	1-3	L
30	12-18	Chicago	1-3	L
31	12-21	at St. Louis	2-2	T
32	12-22	Minnesota	4-2	W
33	12-25	at Philadelphia	2-2	T
34	12-26	Oakland	3-1	W
35	12-28	at Montreal	3-5	L
36	12-29	Montreal	3-1	W
37	1-2	Boston	2-4	L
38	1-4	at Toronto	3-5	L
1968-69 (cont'd)				
39	1-5	Minnesota	5-1	W
40	1-9	at Philadelphia	3-1	W
41	1-11	at Detroit	2-3	L
42	1-14	at Los Angeles	1-3	L
43	1-17	at Oakland	3-1	W
44	1-18	at St. Louis	2-2	T
45	1-23	Los Angeles	3-1	W
46	1-25	Chicago	3-0	W
47	1-26	Montreal	3-2	W
48	1-29	Detroit	2-0	W
49	1-30	at St. Louis	4-3	W
50	2-1	at Montreal	2-6	L
51	2-2	Pittsburgh	7-3	W
52	2-5	at Pittsburgh	2-3	L
53	2-8	St. Louis	2-0	W
54	2-9	Philadelphia	3-3	T
55	2-12	at Oakland	2-3	L
56	2-13	at Los Angeles	1-4	L
57	2-15	at Toronto	2-6	L
58	2-16	Toronto	4-2	W
59	2-19	Detroit	1-1	T
60	2-23	Boston	9-0	W
61	2-26	Chicago	5-3	W
62	3-1	at Boston	5-8	L
63	3-2	St. Louis	2-1	W
64	3-5	at Chicago	4-4	T
65	3-6	at Detroit	4-1	W
66	3-8	at Pittsburgh	5-3	W
67	3-9	Montreal	2-2	T
68	3-12	Pittsburgh	4-3	W
69	3-16	Detroit	6-4	W
70	3-19	at Minnesota	4-2	W
71	3-22	at Montreal	1-3	L
72	3-23	Boston	4-2	W
73	3-26	at Chicago	4-6	L
74	3-27	at Boston	3-3	T
75	3-29	at Toronto	4-2	W
76	3-30	Toronto	4-0	W

Game-By-Game Results
1969-70—1970-71

Game No.	Date	Opponent	Score	Result
1969-70				
1	10-12	at Boston	1-2	L
2	10-15	Minnesota	4-3	W
3	10-18	at Montreal	3-7	L
4	10-19	Toronto	1-0	W
5	10-22	Chicago	1-1	T
6	10-25	at Detroit	4-1	W
7	10-26	Montreal	3-8	L
8	10-29	at Pittsburgh	3-1	W
9	10-30	at Philadelphia	3-3	T
10	11-1	at Toronto	3-2	W
11	11-2	St. Louis	6-4	W
12	11-5	at Chicago	1-3	L
13	11-7	at Oakland	8-1	W
14	11-8	at Los Angeles	4-1	W
15	11-12	Detroit	4-2	W
16	11-15	at Boston	6-5	W
17	11-16	St. Louis	4-2	W
18	11-19	at Chicago	1-1	T
19	11-22	at St. Louis	5-0	W
20	11-23	Oakland	5-2	W
21	11-26	Boston	3-0	W
22	11-29	Philadelphia	2-2	T
23	11-30	Minnesota	2-2	T
24	12-3	Chicago	3-3	T
25	12-7	Montreal	6-3	W
26	12-10	Boston	5-2	W
27	12-11	at Boston	1-2	L
28	12-13	at Minnesota	5-2	W
29	12-14	Toronto	1-3	L
30	12-17	Philadelphia	2-2	T
31	12-20	at Toronto	5-2	W
32	12-21	Oakland	3-1	W
33	12-26	Pittsburgh	2-3	L
34	12-28	Los Angeles	3-3	T
35	12-31	Chicago	2-1	W
36	1-3	at Minnesota	3-3	T
37	1-4	Oakland	5-2	W
38	1-7	at Pittsburgh	5-3	W
1969-70 (cont'd)				
39	1-11	at Montreal	1-4	L
40	1-14	at Toronto	7-1	W
41	1-15	at Philadelphia	4-4	T
42	1-17	at Minnesota	3-1	W
43	1-22	at St. Louis	3-4	L
44	1-24	Boston	8-1	W
45	1-25	Los Angeles	3-2	W
46	1-28	at Los Angeles	4-5	L
47	1-30	at Oakland	2-1	W
48	2-1	Pittsburgh	6-0	W
49	2-4	Detroit	5-1	W
50	2-8	Los Angeles	5-1	W
51	2-11	at Los Angeles	6-2	W
52	2-13	at Oakland	2-4	L
53	2-15	Montreal	2-0	W
54	2-18	Philadelphia	3-3	T
55	2-19	at Detroit	3-3	T
56	2-21	at Chicago	2-4	L
57	2-22	Toronto	5-3	W
58	2-25	St. Louis	2-1	W
59	2-26	at Boston	3-5	L
60	2-28	at Detroit	3-3	T
61	3-1	Chicago	1-3	L
62	3-4	Detroit	0-2	L
63	3-6	at St. Louis	1-3	L
64	3-8	Pittsburgh	0-0	T
65	3-11	at Montreal	3-5	L
66	3-14	at Chicago	4-7	L
67	3-15	Minnesota	2-4	L
68	3-18	at Pittsburgh	2-0	W
69	3-19	at Philadelphia	2-2	T
70	3-22	Toronto	2-5	L
71	3-25	Boston	1-3	L
72	3-28	at Montreal	1-1	T
73	3-29	Montreal	4-1	W
74	4-1	at Toronto	2-1	W
75	4-4	at Detroit	2-6	L
76	4-5	Detroit	9-5	W

Game No.	Date	Opponent	Score	Result
1970-71				
1	10-10	at St. Louis	1-3	L
2	10-14	Buffalo	3-0	W
3	10-17	at Toronto	6-2	W
4	10-18	Montreal	1-0	W
5	10-21	Toronto	3-2	W
6	10-24	at Minnesota	4-1	W
7	10-25	California	2-2	T
8	10-28	Detroit	4-1	W
9	10-31	at Boston	0-6	L
10	11-1	Chicago	5-2	W
11	11-4	at California	1-3	L
12	11-7	at Los Angeles	6-2	W
13	11-11	Pittsburgh	3-3	T
14	11-14	at Chicago	1-2	L
15	11-15	Toronto	4-2	W
16	11-18	at Los Angeles	5-3	W
17	11-21	at Montreal	5-4	W
18	11-22	Minnesota	2-0	W
19	11-25	at Philadelphia	1-3	L
20	11-26	at Buffalo	2-2	T
21	11-28	Boston	3-3	T
22	11-29	Pittsburgh	6-2	W
23	12-2	St. Louis	4-2	W
24	12-5	at Toronto	1-0	W
25	12-6	Vancouver	4-1	W
26	12-8	at Vancouver	1-4	L
27	12-9	Los Angeles	2-2	T
28	12-11	at California	2-1	W
29	12-13	Los Angeles	4-0	W
30	12-16	Buffalo	4-0	W
31	12-19	at Minnesota	5-3	W
32	12-20	Vancouver	5-1	W
33	12-22	at Buffalo	7-2	W
34	12-23	Pittsburgh	6-1	W
35	12-26	at Detroit	4-7	L
36	12-27	St. Louis	4-4	L
37	12-29	California	3-2	W
38	1-2	at Pittsburgh	3-1	W
39	1-3	Montreal	6-5	W
1970-71 (cont'd)				
40	1-9	at Minnesota	1-0	W
41	1-10	at St. Louis	4-2	W
42	1-12	at Vancouver	4-2	W
43	1-15	at California	1-3	L
44	1-17	at Chicago	3-4	L
45	1-20	Philadelphia	3-3	T
46	1-21	at Buffalo	5-5	T
47	1-24	Minnesota	6-2	W
48	1-27	Boston	2-2	T
49	1-30	at Philadelphia	2-5	L
50	1-31	Los Angeles	2-2	T
51	2-3	Chicago	2-4	L
52	2-4	at Detroit	1-0	W
53	2-6	at Vancouver	5-4	W
54	2-9	at Boston	3-6	L
55	2-10	Minnesota	4-3	W
56	2-13	at St. Louis	1-2	L
57	2-14	St. Louis	2-1	W
58	2-17	at Montreal	0-3	L
59	2-20	at Pittsburgh	2-0	W
60	2-21	Detroit	4-1	W
61	2-24	Philadelphia	4-2	W
62	2-27	at Pittsburgh	4-0	W
63	2-28	Vancouver	4-2	W
64	3-3	California	8-1	W
65	3-6	at Detroit	2-2	T
66	3-7	Los Angeles	4-2	W
67	3-10	at Chicago	4-2	W
68	3-12	Philadelphia	7-2	W
69	3-14	Toronto	1-0	W
70	3-18	at Philadelphia	1-2	L
71	3-20	at Toronto	1-3	L
72	3-21	Montreal	2-6	L
73	3-23	Buffalo	7-2	W
74	3-27	at Boston	6-3	W
75	3-28	Boston	2-1	W
76	3-31	Chicago	4-2	W
77	4-3	at Montreal	2-7	L
78	4-4	Detroit	6-0	W

Game-By-Game Results
1971-72—1972-73

1971-72

Game No.	Date	Opponent	Score	Result
1	10-9	at Montreal	4-4	T
2	10-10	at Boston	4-1	W
3	10-13	Boston	1-6	L
4	10-16	at Toronto	5-3	W
5	10-17	Montreal	8-4	W
6	10-20	Chicago	3-1	W
7	10-23	at St. Louis	4-3	W
8	10-24	Pittsburgh	1-1	T
9	10-27	Detroit	7-4	W
10	10-30	at Pittsburgh	1-1	T
11	10-31	Toronto	3-3	T
12	11-3	at Los Angeles	7-1	W
13	11-5	at California	8-1	W
14	11-6	at Vancouver	3-1	W
15	11-10	Los Angeles	7-1	W
16	11-13	Buffalo	5-2	W
17	11-14	Vancouver	6-1	W
18	11-20	at Minnesota	1-4	L
19	11-21	California	12-1	W
20	11-24	St. Louis	8-3	W
21	11-27	at Detroit	1-3	L
22	11-28	at Philadelphia	4-2	W
23	12-1	Buffalo	7-2	W
24	12-4	at Pittsburgh	2-4	L
25	12-5	Vancouver	6-3	W
26	12-8	at Chicago	2-2	T
27	12-9	at Philadelphia	5-0	W
28	12-12	Pittsburgh	6-1	W
29	12-15	Philadelphia	6-2	W
30	12-16	at Boston	1-8	L
31	12-18	at St. Louis	5-2	W
32	12-19	Minnesota	1-1	T
33	12-22	Pittsburgh	4-2	W
34	12-25	at Minnesota	2-1	W
35	12-26	Montreal	5-1	W
36	12-29	Philadelphia	5-1	W
37	1-2	Boston	1-4	L
38	1-5	St. Louis	9-1	W
39	1-9	Los Angeles	8-0	W
40	1-12	at Chicago	5-5	T
41	1-13	at Buffalo	5-2	W
42	1-15	at Toronto	3-4	L
43	1-19	at Los Angeles	5-1	W
44	1-21	at California	5-0	W
45	1-22	at Vancouver	2-5	L
46	1-26	Buffalo	5-1	W
47	1-29	at Minnesota	2-4	L
48	1-30	Minnesota	1-1	T
49	2-2	Boston	0-2	L
50	2-3	at Buffalo	4-2	W
51	2-5	at St. Louis	5-6	L
52	2-6	Toronto	2-2	T
53	2-9	Chicago	4-1	W
54	2-12	at Pittsburgh	8-3	W
55	2-13	Los Angeles	4-2	W
56	2-15	at Vancouver	5-1	W
57	2-17	at Los Angeles	6-4	W
58	2-18	at California	2-2	T
59	2-20	Detroit	4-3	W
60	2-22	at Montreal	7-3	W
61	2-23	Philadelphia	4-3	W
62	2-27	St. Louis	4-2	W
63	3-1	California	4-1	W
64	3-2	at Buffalo	4-3	W
65	3-5	Vancouver	6-1	W
66	3-8	Chicago	3-3	T
67	3-11	at Detroit	4-2	W
68	3-12	California	3-7	L
69	3-15	at Chicago	1-3	L
70	3-16	at Detroit	2-1	W
71	3-18	at Philadelphia	5-3	W
72	3-19	Toronto	5-3	W
73	3-23	at Boston	1-4	L
74	3-25	at Montreal	3-3	T
75	3-26	Minnesota	0-5	L
76	3-29	Detroit	2-2	T
77	4-1	at Toronto	1-2	L
78	4-2	Montreal	5-6	L

1972-73

Game No.	Date	Opponent	Score	Result
1	10-7	at Detroit	3-5	L
2	10-8	at Chicago	1-5	L
3	10-11	Vancouver	5-3	W
4	10-14	at Montreal	1-6	L
5	10-15	Minnesota	6-2	W
6	10-18	Boston	7-1	W
7	10-21	at Islanders	2-1	W
8	10-22	Montreal	1-1	T
9	10-25	Philadelphia	6-1	W
10	10-29	Chicago	7-1	W
11	11-1	at Chicago	3-2	W
12	11-4	at Pittsburgh	4-6	L
13	11-5	at Philadelphia	3-2	W
14	11-8	Vancouver	5-2	W
15	11-11	California	7-2	W
16	11-12	Los Angeles	5-1	W
17	11-15	Philadelphia	7-3	W
18	11-18	at St. Louis	3-1	W
19	11-19	Pittsburgh	3-5	L
20	11-21	at Atlanta	3-1	W
21	11-23	at Buffalo	3-5	L
22	11-26	Toronto	7-4	W
23	11-28	at Vancouver	1-2	L
24	11-29	at Los Angeles	2-2	T
25	12-1	at California	3-3	T
26	12-3	Atlanta	3-2	W
27	12-6	Buffalo	2-3	L
28	12-9	at Islanders	4-1	W
29	12-10	Islanders	4-1	W
30	12-13	at Toronto	4-3	W
31	12-14	at Boston	2-4	L
32	12-16	at Minnesota	1-5	L
33	12-17	Pittsburgh	9-1	W
34	12-20	at St. Louis	5-4	W
35	12-21	Atlanta	2-5	L
36	12-24	Detroit	5-0	W
37	12-27	Buffalo	1-4	L
38	12-31	St. Louis	6-1	W
39	1-3	Los Angeles	3-0	W
40	1-6	Buffalo	1-4	L
41	1-7	Pittsburgh	3-0	W
42	1-11	at Buffalo	4-2	W
43	1-13	at St. Louis	5-3	W
44	1-14	at Philadelphia	5-2	W
45	1-17	at Los Angeles	4-4	T
46	1-19	at California	6-0	W
47	1-20	at Vancouver	4-3	W
48	1-24	Boston	4-2	W
49	1-27	at Detroit	6-3	W
50	1-28	Toronto	5-2	W
51	1-31	California	3-1	W
52	2-3	at Boston	7-3	W
53	2-4	Atlanta	6-0	W
54	2-7	Islanders	6-0	W
55	2-10	at Islanders	6-0	W
56	2-11	Montreal	2-2	T
57	2-14	at Montreal	3-6	L
58	2-15	at Buffalo	1-4	L
59	2-18	Islanders	3-2	W
60	2-21	at Los Angeles	4-3	W
61	2-23	at California	3-5	L
62	2-25	Minnesota	6-5	W
63	2-28	Chicago	3-3	T
64	3-3	at Detroit	6-3	W
65	3-4	Vancouver	3-4	L
66	3-7	Philadelphia	2-2	T
67	3-10	at Pittsburgh	5-4	W
68	3-11	Toronto	4-2	W
69	3-14	at Chicago	2-4	L
70	3-17	at Toronto	5-7	L
71	3-18	St. Louis	3-1	W
72	3-20	at Minnesota	6-1	W
73	3-22	at Atlanta	4-1	W
74	3-24	at Boston	0-3	L
75	3-25	Minnesota	1-2	L
76	3-28	Boston	3-6	L
77	3-31	at Montreal	1-5	L
78	4-1	Detroit	3-3	T

Game-By-Game Results
1973-74—1974-75

Game No.	Date	Opponent	Score	Result
1973-74				
1	10-10	Detroit	4-1	W
2	10-13	at Pittsburgh	8-2	W
3	10-14	Los Angeles	1-1	T
4	10-17	St. Louis	4-0	W
5	10-20	at Toronto	2-3	L
6	10-21	Montreal	2-3	L
7	10-27	at Islanders	2-3	L
8	10-28	Pittsburgh	2-7	L
9	10-30	at Vancouver	3-3	T
10	11-1	at Los Angeles	1-2	L
11	11-4	at Chicago	1-4	L
12	11-7	Boston	7-3	W
13	11-9	at Atlanta	3-3	T
14	11-11	Islanders	5-2	W
15	11-14	Chicago	4-4	T
16	11-15	at Boston	2-10	L
17	11-17	at Minnesota	6-3	W
18	11-18	Pittsburgh	7-0	W
19	11-21	California	3-0	W
20	11-22	at Buffalo	7-6	W
21	11-24	Los Angeles	5-5	T
22	11-25	Vancouver	5-0	W
23	11-29	at Philadelphia	2-2	T
24	12-1	at St. Louis	4-4	T
25	12-2	Toronto	6-4	W
26	12-5	St. Louis	5-1	W
27	12-6	at Buffalo	4-8	L
28	12-9	California	6-3	W
29	12-12	Buffalo	1-1	T
30	12-15	at Toronto	2-2	T
31	12-16	Chicago	1-6	L
32	12-20	Detroit	5-2	W
33	12-22	at Pittsburgh	4-1	W
34	12-23	at Atlanta	1-3	L
35	12-26	Philadelphia	2-1	W
36	12-29	at Montreal	1-7	L
37	12-30	Minnesota	4-3	W
38	1-3	at Philadelphia	2-4	L
39	1-4	Boston	2-4	L
40	1-6	Atlanta	5-2	W
41	1-10	at Buffalo	2-7	L
42	1-12	at Vancouver	6-1	W
43	1-13	at California	7-2	W
44	1-16	at Detroit	4-4	T
45	1-17	at St. Louis	2-3	L
46	1-19	at Chicago	3-2	W
47	1-23	Atlanta	4-1	W
48	1-27	Los Angeles	5-3	W
49	1-30	at Pittsburgh	4-2	W
50	2-2	at Minnesota	3-1	W
51	2-3	Minnesota	5-5	T
52	2-6	Islanders	6-0	W
53	2-9	at Montreal	2-9	L
54	2-10	St. Louis	4-2	W
55	2-14	at Philadelphia	4-4	T
56	2-16	at Vancouver	9-4	W
57	2-21	at Los Angeles	5-3	W
58	2-22	at California	4-3	W
59	2-24	Philadelphia	3-2	W
60	2-27	Vancouver	4-2	W
61	3-2	at Minnesota	3-1	W
62	3-3	California	8-2	W
63	3-6	Montreal	9-2	W
64	3-9	at Montreal	2-4	L
65	3-10	Islanders	4-2	W
66	3-14	Chicago	2-5	L
67	3-16	at Islanders	3-1	W
68	3-17	at Boston	2-5	L
69	3-20	Vancouver	5-7	L
70	3-21	at Atlanta	5-5	T
71	3-23	at Detroit	2-5	L
72	3-24	Buffalo	5-3	W
73	3-27	Boston	2-3	L
74	3-30	at Toronto	3-7	L
75	3-31	Toronto	3-3	T
76	4-3	Detroit	5-3	W
77	4-6	at Detroit	3-8	L
78	4-7	Montreal	6-4	W
1974-75				
1	10-9	Washington	6-3	W
2	10-12	at Toronto	3-7	L
3	10-16	California	5-5	T
4	10-19	at Islanders	4-2	W
5	10-20	Vancouver	0-1	L
6	10-23	St. Louis	5-1	W
7	10-26	at Pittsburgh	5-4	W
8	10-27	Atlanta	4-1	W
9	10-30	Islanders	1-1	T
10	10-31	at Philadelphia	1-5	L
11	11-3	Buffalo	3-4	L
12	11-5	at Vancouver	1-2	L
13	11-6	at California	7-3	W
14	11-9	at Los Angeles	2-2	T
15	11-13	Philadelphia	2-3	L
16	11-16	at Montreal	4-4	T
17	11-17	California	10-0	W
18	11-20	at Detroit	5-4	W
19	11-23	Boston	2-5	L
20	11-24	Pittsburgh	7-5	W
21	11-27	Toronto	4-1	W
22	11-29	at Atlanta	2-3	L
23	12-1	St. Louis	4-4	T
24	12-4	Detroit	4-2	W
25	12-7	at Chicago	7-4	W
26	12-8	Montreal	3-3	T
27	12-12	at Washington	6-6	T
28	12-14	at St. Louis	2-6	L
29	12-15	Los Angeles	3-3	T
30	12-18	Minnesota	7-0	W
31	12-19	at Boston	3-11	L
32	12-22	Atlanta	3-4	L
33	12-27	Buffalo	9-5	W
34	12-29	Kansas City	2-1	W
35	12-30	at Minnesota	8-1	W
36	1-1	Chicago	6-2	W
37	1-4	at Islanders	5-3	W
38	1-5	Vancouver	6-2	W
39	1-8	at Kansas City	6-1	W
40	1-11	at St. Louis	5-3	W
41	1-12	at Chicago	2-4	L
42	1-15	at Minnesota	5-3	W
43	1-17	at California	4-4	T
44	1-18	at Vancouver	3-2	W
45	1-23	Atlanta	5-2	W
46	1-25	at Pittsburgh	2-5	L
47	1-26	Los Angeles	3-2	W
48	1-28	at Los Angeles	2-5	L
49	1-30	at Buffalo	3-6	L
50	2-1	at Chicago	4-1	W
51	2-2	Detroit	5-5	T
52	2-5	Philadelphia	3-4	L
53	2-6	at Philadelphia	3-1	W
54	2-8	at Montreal	1-7	L
55	2-9	Washington	7-3	W
56	2-11	at Washington	4-7	L
57	2-15	at Minnesota	9-2	W
58	2-16	Toronto	5-5	T
59	2-18	at Kansas City	2-2	T
60	2-19	Chicago	2-2	T
61	2-22	at Toronto	2-5	L
62	2-23	Philadelphia	2-1	W
63	2-26	St. Louis	5-1	W
64	3-2	Pittsburgh	6-8	L
65	3-5	Buffalo	3-6	L
66	3-7	at Kansas City	5-2	W
67	3-9	Montreal	3-5	L
68	3-11	at Boston	3-6	L
69	3-12	Islanders	5-3	W
70	3-14	at Atlanta	0-1	L
71	3-19	Vancouver	3-0	W
72	3-20	at Buffalo	3-6	L
73	3-22	at Detroit	4-7	L
74	3-23	Boston	7-5	W
75	3-26	Minnesota	2-4	L
76	3-29	at Islanders	4-6	L
77	3-30	Kansas City	8-2	W
78	4-3	at Philadelphia	1-1	T
79	4-4	at Atlanta	3-2	W
80	4-6	Islanders	4-6	L

Game-By-Game Results
1975-76—1976-77

1975-76

Game No.	Date	Opponent	Score	Result
1	10-8	Chicago	2-2	T
2	10-10	at Atlanta	2-1	W
3	10-12	Los Angeles	4-6	L
4	10-15	Atlanta	3-1	W
5	10-18	at Toronto	1-4	L
6	10-19	Vancouver	8-1	W
7	10-22	at Buffalo	1-9	L
8	10-25	at Islanders	1-7	L
9	10-26	Philadelphia	2-7	L
10	10-29	St. Louis	3-1	W
11	11-1	at Montreal	0-4	L
12	11-2	Detroit	4-6	L
13	11-4	at Vancouver	4-2	W
14	11-7	at California	5-7	L
15	11-8	at Los Angeles	1-3	L
16	11-11	at St. Louis	3-5	L
17	11-12	Chicago	4-4	T
18	11-15	at Minnesota	5-2	W
19	11-16	Detroit	3-0	W
20	11-19	Kansas City	4-6	L
21	11-22	at Philadelphia	2-4	L
22	11-23	California	3-2	W
23	11-26	Boston	4-6	L
24	11-29	at Pittsburgh	3-8	L
25	11-30	St. Louis	5-2	W
26	12-4	at Buffalo	6-6	T
27	12-5	at Kansas City	3-2	W
28	12-7	Washington	5-2	W
29	12-10	Buffalo	2-2	T
30	12-11	at Boston	5-1	W
31	12-13	at Detroit	5-2	W
32	12-14	Toronto	1-6	L
33	12-17	Islanders	0-3	L
34	12-19	at Atlanta	3-8	L
35	12-21	Minnesota	2-0	W
36	12-23	Pittsburgh	4-3	W
37	12-31	Atlanta	1-8	L
38	1-4	Toronto	6-8	L
39	1-6	at St. Louis	2-5	L
40	1-10	at Kansas City	8-4	W

1975-76 (cont'd)

Game No.	Date	Opponent	Score	Result
41	1-11	at Chicago	6-2	W
42	1-14	at Vancouver	1-5	L
43	1-16	at California	0-7	L
44	1-18	at Pittsburgh	3-8	L
45	1-21	Chicago	3-3	T
46	1-23	at Washington	5-7	L
47	1-25	Los Angeles	1-4	L
48	1-28	Buffalo	3-3	T
49	1-29	at St. Louis	6-3	W
50	1-31	at Toronto	4-6	L
51	2-1	Minnesota	3-2	W
52	2-4	Islanders	5-6	L
53	2-7	at Detroit	5-4	W
54	2-8	Montreal	0-3	L
55	2-12	at Philadelphia	1-6	L
56	2-13	Philadelphia	3-5	L
57	2-15	Kansas City	5-1	W
58	2-17	at Islanders	3-1	W
59	2-18	Washington	11-4	W
60	2-20	at Montreal	3-5	L
61	2-22	Boston	2-5	L
62	2-25	California	4-6	L
63	2-28	at Minnesota	3-5	L
64	2-29	Montreal	1-1	T
65	3-3	Vancouver	3-3	T
66	3-5	at Atlanta	3-8	L
67	3-7	Atlanta	6-6	T
68	3-11	at Los Angeles	3-4	L
69	3-13	at Vancouver	7-3	W
70	3-16	at Washington	2-5	L
71	3-17	Minnesota	3-1	W
72	3-20	at Boston	1-8	L
73	3-21	Pittsburgh	2-4	L
74	3-24	at Buffalo	3-7	L
75	3-25	at Philadelphia	1-4	L
76	3-27	at Chicago	6-5	W
77	3-28	Kansas City	4-2	W
78	3-31	Islanders	3-1	W
79	4-3	at Islanders	2-10	L
80	4-4	Philadelphia	2-0	W

1976-77

Game No.	Date	Opponent	Score	Result
1	10-6	Minnesota	6-5	W
2	10-8	at Colorado	5-3	W
3	10-9	at St. Louis	1-2	L
4	10-12	at Minnesota	10-4	W
5	10-13	Boston	1-5	L
6	10-16	at Montreal	4-7	L
7	10-17	Colorado	4-3	W
8	10-20	Los Angeles	2-4	L
9	10-24	Vancouver	4-5	L
10	10-26	at Cleveland	5-2	W
11	10-27	Boston	3-4	L
12	10-30	at Pittsburgh	2-2	T
13	10-31	Detroit	5-6	L
14	11-3	at Vancouver	6-1	W
15	11-6	at Los Angeles	3-3	T
16	11-10	Washington	5-7	L
17	11-13	Buffalo	2-6	L
18	11-14	Pittsburgh	1-5	L
19	11-17	Chicago	3-2	W
20	11-20	at St. Louis	1-3	L
21	11-22	at Vancouver	3-2	W
22	11-24	at Philadelphia	2-2	T
23	11-27	at Detroit	5-0	W
24	11-28	Minnesota	4-1	W
25	11-30	at Atlanta	2-2	T
26	12-1	Washington	4-1	W
27	12-4	at Minnesota	11-4	W
28	12-5	Toronto	5-5	T
29	12-8	St. Louis	4-4	T
30	12-11	at Toronto	1-4	L
31	12-12	Montreal	5-2	W
32	12-14	at Islanders	4-4	T
33	12-16	at Buffalo	2-7	L
34	12-18	at Chicago	3-3	T
35	12-19	Cleveland	3-2	W
36	12-22	Philadelphia	3-3	T
37	12-23	at Boston	3-3	T
38	12-26	Islanders	1-2	L
39	12-28	at Washington	5-2	W
40	12-31	Atlanta	2-4	L

1976-77 (cont'd)

Game No.	Date	Opponent	Score	Result
41	1-2	Vancouver	5-3	W
42	1-5	Philadelphia	4-4	T
43	1-7	at Colorado	4-4	T
44	1-9	Los Angeles	4-5	L
45	1-12	at Atlanta	1-6	L
46	1-13	at Buffalo	5-7	L
47	1-16	at Chicago	5-2	W
48	1-19	at Cleveland	3-3	T
49	1-22	at Los Angeles	0-6	L
50	1-23	at Vancouver	2-6	L
51	1-27	Pittsburgh	0-3	L
52	1-30	St. Louis	5-2	W
53	2-1	at Colorado	2-5	L
54	2-3	at Islanders	3-6	L
55	2-6	Islanders	4-0	W
56	2-9	Buffalo	1-2	L
57	2-10	at Detroit	5-4	W
58	2-13	Toronto	8-3	W
59	2-17	at Philadelphia	1-7	L
60	2-19	at Islanders	2-5	L
61	2-20	Detroit	3-2	W
62	2-23	at Toronto	5-4	W
63	2-26	at Chicago	1-2	L
64	2-27	Montreal	1-8	L
65	3-3	Boston	1-4	L
66	3-5	at Montreal	2-7	L
67	3-6	Cleveland	4-3	W
68	3-9	Minnesota	6-4	W
69	3-10	at Boston	3-10	L
70	3-12	at Atlanta	3-6	L
71	3-13	Atlanta	3-5	L
72	3-16	Philadelphia	4-4	T
73	3-19	at Pittsburgh	5-2	W
74	3-20	St. Louis	5-3	W
75	3-23	Colorado	5-3	W
76	3-25	at Washington	2-7	L
77	3-27	Chicago	3-5	L
78	3-30	Atlanta	4-3	W
79	4-2	at Philadelphia	1-4	L
80	4-3	Islanders	2-5	L

Game-By-Game Results
1977-78—1978-79

1977-78

Game No.	Date	Opponent	Score	Result
1	10-12	Vancouver	6-3	W
2	10-15	at Montreal	0-5	L
3	10-16	Islanders	4-2	W
4	10-19	Pittsburgh	3-3	T
5	10-22	at Islanders	2-7	L
6	10-23	Montreal	2-6	L
7	10-25	at Cleveland	5-0	W
8	10-26	St. Louis	6-2	W
9	10-29	at Atlanta	3-4	L
10	10-30	Los Angeles	3-5	L
11	11-2	at Colorado	2-6	L
12	11-4	at Vancouver	5-1	W
13	11-5	at Los Angeles	1-3	L
14	11-9	Buffalo	8-4	W
15	11-12	at Detroit	1-3	L
16	11-13	Atlanta	2-5	L
17	11-16	Chicago	5-2	W
18	11-19	at Pittsburgh	5-5	T
19	11-20	Vancouver	0-3	L
20	11-23	Colorado	6-3	W
21	11-26	at Boston	2-3	L
22	11-27	at Buffalo	2-3	L
23	11-30	at St. Louis	4-0	W
24	12-3	at Minnesota	4-0	W
25	12-4	Minnesota	4-4	T
26	12-7	Philadelphia	3-3	T
27	12-8	at Philadelphia	4-7	L
28	12-11	Boston	2-8	L
29	12-14	at Chicago	2-2	T
30	12-15	at Detroit	5-5	T
31	12-17	at Cleveland	2-4	L
32	12-18	Detroit	6-2	W
33	12-21	Washington	5-5	T
34	12-23	Cleveland	5-4	W
35	12-28	Philadelphia	3-4	L
36	12-30	at Washington	3-3	T
37	12-31	Buffalo	2-2	T
38	1-4	at Minnesota	5-3	W
39	1-7	at Colorado	1-3	L
40	1-9	Pittsburgh	3-5	L
41	1-10	at Boston	3-2	W
42	1-14	at Philadelphia	1-4	L
43	1-17	at Vancouver	5-4	W
44	1-18	at Los Angeles	3-0	W
45	1-20	at Atlanta	3-5	L
46	1-22	at Pittsburgh	1-3	L
47	1-25	Toronto	3-4	L
48	1-28	at Islanders	2-6	L
49	1-29	Los Angeles	1-4	L
50	2-1	Islanders	6-7	L
51	2-4	at St. Louis	2-2	T
52	2-5	Colorado	6-3	W
53	2-8	Minnesota	3-0	W
54	2-9	at Buffalo	0-2	L
55	2-11	at Toronto	2-3	L
56	2-12	Montreal	3-5	L
57	2-15	Vancouver	6-3	W
58	2-19	Colorado	4-4	T
59	2-22	at Chicago	2-3	L
60	2-23	Chicago	6-2	W
61	2-25	at Montreal	6-3	W
62	2-27	Atlanta	3-5	L
63	3-1	Detroit	3-2	W
64	3-5	Toronto	1-4	L
65	3-8	Cleveland	6-1	W
66	3-12	Washington	8-2	W
67	3-15	Philadelphia	2-2	T
68	3-18	Boston	3-6	L
69	3-19	at Minnesota	7-7	T
70	3-22	at St. Louis	6-1	W
71	3-24	at Washington	11-4	W
72	3-25	at Toronto	5-2	W
73	3-27	St. Louis	5-2	W
74	3-29	Islanders	5-1	W
75	4-1	at Atlanta	0-6	L
76	4-2	at Boston	3-8	L
77	4-5	Atlanta	2-4	L
78	4-6	at Philadelphia	0-3	L
79	4-8	at Islanders	2-7	L
80	4-9	Chicago	3-2	W

1978-79

Game No.	Date	Opponent	Score	Result
1	10-12	Philadelphia	3-3	T
2	10-15	Colorado	4-1	W
3	10-18	Detroit	3-3	T
4	10-19	at Detroit	2-2	T
5	10-21	at Islanders	3-5	L
6	10-22	Toronto	5-2	W
7	10-25	Vancouver	6-2	W
8	10-28	at Montreal	2-1	W
9	10-29	Pittsburgh	3-2	W
10	11-2	at Colorado	3-0	W
11	11-4	at Los Angeles	7-3	W
12	11-5	at Vancouver	5-2	W
13	11-8	Minnesota	3-5	L
14	11-11	at Pittsburgh	2-1	W
15	11-12	Islanders	3-5	L
16	11-15	Chicago	8-1	W
17	11-18	at Minnesota	7-2	W
18	11-19	Atlanta	1-3	L
19	11-22	Toronto	3-3	T
20	11-26	Washington	9-4	W
21	11-29	at Atlanta	5-3	W
22	12-2	at Toronto	2-5	L
23	12-3	Boston	2-3	L
24	12-6	St. Louis	7-4	W
25	12-7	at Philadelphia	5-2	W
26	12-9	at Detroit	4-5	L
27	12-10	Philadelphia	0-4	L
28	12-13	Los Angeles	8-7	W
29	12-16	at Boston	1-4	L
30	12-17	Boston	1-4	L
31	12-20	Buffalo	6-3	W
32	12-22	Detroit	4-2	W
33	12-23	at Islanders	4-9	L
34	12-26	at Atlanta	5-3	W
35	12-28	at Philadelphia	5-6	L
36	12-30	at Chicago	5-4	W
37	12-31	Atlanta	5-6	L
38	1-3	Montreal	6-2	W
39	1-5	Vancouver	6-4	W
40	1-9	at St. Louis	5-3	W
41	1-10	at Colorado	5-3	W
42	1-14	at Atlanta	6-4	W
43	1-15	Minnesota	1-8	L
44	1-17	Islanders	5-3	W
45	1-20	at St. Louis	2-3	L
46	1-21	Philadelphia	5-5	T
47	1-24	at Washington	1-5	L
48	1-25	at Buffalo	5-4	W
49	1-27	at Islanders	7-2	W
50	1-30	at Vancouver	5-3	W
51	1-31	at Colorado	4-5	L
52	2-3	at Los Angeles	2-4	L
53	2-14	Boston	5-1	W
54	2-15	at Buffalo	3-4	L
55	2-17	at Philadelphia	4-2	W
56	2-18	Washington	6-6	T
57	2-21	St. Louis	7-3	W
58	2-24	at Toronto	4-2	W
59	2-25	Islanders	3-2	W
60	2-27	at St. Louis	1-4	L
61	2-28	at Minnesota	4-4	T
62	3-3	Buffalo	2-2	T
63	3-4	Toronto	2-4	L
64	3-7	Colorado	5-3	W
65	3-10	at Montreal	6-3	W
66	3-11	Chicago	5-2	W
67	3-14	Atlanta	4-6	L
68	3-15	at Boston	7-4	W
69	3-17	at Islanders	2-5	L
70	3-18	Pittsburgh	1-5	L
71	3-20	at Washington	2-2	T
72	3-21	at Chicago	7-6	W
73	3-25	Montreal	0-1	L
74	3-27	Philadelphia	4-4	T
75	3-28	at Pittsburgh	1-7	L
76	4-1	at Philadelphia	3-7	L
77	4-2	Los Angeles	5-4	W
78	4-4	Atlanta	3-3	T
79	4-6	at Atlanta	2-9	L
80	4-8	Islanders	2-5	L

Game-By-Game Results
1979-80—1980-81

1979-80

Game No.	Date	Opponent	Score	Result
1	10-10	at Toronto	6-3	W
2	10-14	Washington	3-5	L
3	10-18	Vancouver	6-3	W
4	10-20	at Montreal	4-5	L
5	10-21	Pittsburgh	6-3	W
6	10-24	Edmonton	10-2	W
7	10-25	at Philadelphia	2-5	L
8	10-27	at Minnesota	2-7	L
9	10-28	Hartford	2-2	T
10	11-1	at Los Angeles	2-4	L
11	11-3	at Colorado	2-7	L
12	11-4	at Vancouver	4-2	W
13	11-7	Los Angeles	8-4	W
14	11-10	Quebec	5-4	W
15	11-11	Pittsburgh	1-4	L
16	11-13	at Islanders	5-10	L
17	11-14	Detroit	3-2	W
18	11-16	at Atlanta	2-4	L
19	11-18	St. Louis	5-3	W
20	11-21	Winnipeg	4-6	L
21	11-24	at Pittsburgh	3-5	L
22	11-25	Toronto	3-4	L
23	11-28	Minnesota	4-4	T
24	11-29	at Buffalo	1-2	L
25	12-1	at St. Louis	2-0	W
26	12-3	Montreal	3-3	T
27	12-5	Chicago	3-3	T
28	12-7	at Hartford	7-4	W
29	12-9	Islanders	5-4	W
30	12-11	at Detroit	2-1	W
31	12-12	at Chicago	5-2	W
32	12-15	at Washington	4-5	L
33	12-16	Philadelphia	1-1	T
34	12-19	Vancouver	5-3	W
35	12-22	at Pittsburgh	4-3	W
36	12-23	Boston	3-4	L
37	12-30	Washington	5-2	W
38	1-2	at Quebec	3-3	T
39	1-4	Philadelphia	3-5	L
40	1-6	Atlanta	5-5	T
41	1-7	Hartford	5-2	W
42	1-9	at Detroit	0-4	L
43	1-11	at Edmonton	6-2	W
44	1-12	at Washington	3-0	W
45	1-14	Colorado	6-6	T
46	1-16	Winnipeg	4-1	W
47	1-19	at Boston	3-6	L
48	1-20	Chicago	1-2	L
49	1-22	at Los Angeles	5-4	W
50	1-23	at Vancouver	6-4	W
51	1-27	at Colorado	3-3	T
52	1-31	at Buffalo	2-6	L
53	2-2	at Washington	6-3	W
54	2-3	at Quebec	4-5	L
55	2-10	Quebec	3-1	W
56	2-13	at Chicago	1-3	L
57	2-17	Toronto	4-6	L
58	2-18	at Hartford	4-6	L
59	2-20	Edmonton	4-1	W
60	2-23	at Minnesota	3-6	L
61	2-24	Islanders	8-2	W
62	2-27	Los Angeles	5-4	W
63	2-28	at Boston	5-2	W
64	3-2	Boston	2-1	W
65	3-5	Buffalo	4-2	W
66	3-8	at Montreal	2-5	L
67	3-9	Minnesota	4-2	W
68	3-12	Colorado	6-0	W
69	3-15	at Toronto	8-4	W
70	3-16	St. Louis	5-2	W
71	3-19	at Edmonton	2-4	L
72	3-21	at Winnipeg	2-4	L
73	3-23	Montreal	1-6	L
74	3-25	Buffalo	3-3	T
75	3-28	at Atlanta	2-4	L
76	3-29	at St. Louis	4-3	W
77	3-31	Detroit	7-5	W
78	4-2	Atlanta	3-7	L
79	4-5	at Islanders	1-2	L
80	4-6	at Philadelphia	8-3	W

1980-81

Game No.	Date	Opponent	Score	Result
1	10-9	at Boston	2-7	L
2	10-11	at Toronto	8-3	W
3	10-12	Pittsburgh	3-6	L
4	10-15	St. Louis	1-2	L
5	10-18	at Washington	2-8	L
6	10-19	Edmonton	2-4	L
7	10-22	Vancouver	3-2	W
8	10-25	at Detroit	2-4	L
9	10-26	Detroit	7-6	W
10	10-28	at St. Louis	4-5	L
11	10-30	at Philadelphia	3-3	T
12	11-1	at Montreal	4-7	L
13	11-2	Los Angeles	3-6	L
14	11-5	at Chicago	3-3	T
15	11-8	at Vancouver	4-6	L
16	11-10	at Los Angeles	1-4	L
17	11-11	at Calgary	3-7	L
18	11-14	Pittsburgh	3-3	T
19	11-16	Hartford	7-3	W
20	11-19	Philadelphia	1-5	L
21	11-22	at Islanders	4-6	L
22	11-23	Vancouver	2-2	T
23	11-26	Boston	6-4	W
24	11-29	at Pittsburgh	4-2	W
25	12-1	Minnesota	3-5	L
26	12-3	at Winnipeg	4-3	W
27	12-5	at Edmonton	5-1	W
28	12-7	Chicago	5-4	W
29	12-10	Washington	6-2	W
30	12-12	at Colorado	4-3	W
31	12-14	at Chicago	1-2	L
32	12-17	Winnipeg	8-2	W
33	12-20	at Minnesota	3-3	T
34	12-22	Calgary	2-3	L
35	12-26	at Washington	3-7	L
36	12-28	Montreal	2-5	L
37	12-30	at Quebec	6-3	W
38	12-31	Colorado	4-6	L
39	1-2	Islanders	3-1	W
40	1-4	Quebec	2-2	T
41	1-9	Buffalo	3-3	T
42	1-11	Toronto	3-5	L
43	1-13	at Calgary	4-4	T
44	1-15	at Colorado	3-4	L
45	1-18	at Buffalo	0-4	L
46	1-19	Calgary	6-3	W
47	1-21	at Winnipeg	1-5	L
48	1-23	at Edmonton	7-4	W
49	1-24	at Vancouver	7-5	W
50	1-28	at Los Angeles	6-2	W
51	1-31	at Minnesota	7-3	W
52	2-2	Los Angeles	2-3	L
53	2-4	Islanders	9-3	W
54	2-5	at Boston	3-6	L
55	2-8	Minnesota	3-3	T
56	2-12	Winnipeg	8-6	W
57	2-14	at Toronto	3-6	L
58	2-15	St. Louis	4-5	L
59	2-18	Toronto	8-3	W
60	2-19	at Detroit	3-7	L
61	2-21	Washington	6-4	W
62	2-22	at Hartford	5-6	L
63	2-25	Buffalo	6-3	W
64	2-28	at Pittsburgh	4-6	L
65	3-1	Montreal	4-4	T
66	3-4	Edmonton	5-5	T
67	3-7	at St. Louis	2-7	L
68	3-8	Detroit	4-4	T
69	3-10	at Quebec	4-6	L
70	3-11	Colorado	3-4	L
71	3-14	Hartford	6-2	W
72	3-18	Boston	3-2	W
73	3-21	at Hartford	6-4	W
74	3-22	Quebec	7-7	T
75	3-25	at Buffalo	2-4	L
76	3-28	at Montreal	6-2	W
77	3-30	Philadelphia	0-0	T
78	4-2	at Islanders	1-2	L
79	4-3	Chicago	3-1	W
80	4-5	at Philadelphia	2-0	W

Game-By-Game Results
1981-82—1982-83

1981-82

Game No.	Date	Opponent	Score	Result
1	10-6	Detroit	2-5	L
2	10-9	at Winnipeg	3-8	L
3	10-10	at Minnesota	0-7	L
4	10-14	Vancouver	2-1	W
5	10-17	at Islanders	4-5	L
6	10-18	St. Louis	5-3	W
7	10-21	Los Angeles	2-5	L
8	10-24	at Toronto	5-3	W
9	10-25	Montreal	2-4	L
10	10-28	Edmonton	3-5	L
11	10-31	at Boston	3-7	L
12	11-1	Calgary	4-2	W
13	11-4	at Pittsburgh	3-6	L
14	11-5	at Philadelphia	6-2	W
15	11-7	at Washington	3-1	W
16	11-11	Buffalo	7-3	W
17	11-13	at Buffalo	3-3	T
18	11-15	Edmonton	3-5	L
19	11-18	Philadelphia	5-2	W
20	11-21	at Islanders	3-4	L
21	11-22	Islanders	2-7	L
22	11-25	Toronto	3-3	T
23	11-28	at Quebec	4-7	L
24	11-29	Quebec	4-4	T
25	12-2	at Los Angeles	4-3	W
26	12-5	at Colorado	2-1	W
27	12-6	Hartford	3-5	L
28	12-9	Boston	3-4	L
29	12-12	at Philadelphia	5-3	W
30	12-14	Pittsburgh	5-4	W
31	12-16	Philadelphia	3-7	L
32	12-19	at Pittsburgh	3-3	T
33	12-20	Washington	2-3	W
34	12-23	Winnipeg	5-2	W
35	12-26	at Washington	4-4	T
36	12-27	Pittsburgh	5-3	W
37	12-30	Islanders	6-4	W
38	1-2	at Montreal	6-5	W
39	1-3	Washington	3-4	L
40	1-7	Vancouver	4-1	W

1981-82 (cont'd)

Game No.	Date	Opponent	Score	Result
41	1-9	Chicago	7-5	W
42	1-11	Minnesota	5-3	W
43	1-13	at Minnesota	2-0	W
44	1-15	at Winnipeg	4-4	T
45	1-18	at Toronto	2-6	L
46	1-20	Islanders	3-2	W
47	1-23	at Islanders	1-6	L
48	1-24	Washington	4-4	T
49	1-27	at Washington	5-4	W
50	1-29	at Colorado	5-2	W
51	1-31	at Los Angeles	6-3	W
52	2-2	at Vancouver	4-3	W
53	2-4	at Calgary	4-4	T
54	2-7	at Edmonton	4-8	L
55	2-10	at St. Louis	3-3	T
56	2-13	at Hartford	3-2	W
57	2-14	Quebec	5-2	W
58	2-17	at Pittsburgh	5-3	W
59	2-18	Colorado	4-4	T
60	2-21	Montreal	2-4	L
61	2-24	Chicago	6-4	W
62	2-27	at Boston	6-4	W
63	2-28	Pittsburgh	2-4	L
64	3-3	Calgary	4-2	W
65	3-4	at Philadelphia	4-4	T
66	3-6	at Islanders	4-6	L
67	3-8	Detroit	6-3	W
68	3-10	Philadelphia	5-5	T
69	3-11	at Detroit	4-1	W
70	3-14	Washington	5-5	T
71	3-17	Philadelphia	5-2	W
72	3-20	at Washington	4-3	W
73	3-21	St. Louis	8-5	W
74	3-24	at Pittsburgh	7-2	W
75	3-26	at Buffalo	8-5	W
76	3-28	at Philadelphia	1-3	L
77	3-29	Islanders	3-7	L
78	3-31	at Chicago	4-1	W
79	4-2	Pittsburgh	5-7	L
80	4-3	at Hartford	3-3	T

1982-83

Game No.	Date	Opponent	Score	Result
1	10-6	Washington	4-5	L
2	10-8	at New Jersey	2-3	L
3	10-9	at Pittsburgh	5-3	W
4	10-11	Islanders	3-4	L
5	10-13	Philadelphia	5-2	W
6	10-16	at Montreal	2-8	L
7	10-17	Los Angeles	3-5	L
8	10-20	Vancouver	6-5	W
9	10-23	at Islanders	2-5	L
10	10-24	Minnesota	4-2	W
11	10-27	Calgary	7-4	W
12	10-30	at Quebec	4-5	L
13	10-31	Pittsburgh	6-2	W
14	11-5	at Edmonton	1-5	L
15	11-6	at Calgary	2-2	T
16	11-10	St. Louis	5-4	W
17	11-11	at Philadelphia	3-7	L
18	11-14	Edmonton	2-7	L
19	11-17	Toronto	6-1	W
20	11-20	at Toronto	6-3	W
21	11-21	Islanders	7-3	W
22	11-24	Minnesota	8-5	W
23	11-27	at Islanders	3-0	W
24	11-28	at Buffalo	3-7	L
25	12-1	Hartford	6-1	W
26	12-4	at Hartford	2-5	L
27	12-5	Toronto	6-5	W
28	12-8	at Chicago	2-7	L
29	12-10	at Washington	4-4	T
30	12-12	New Jersey	4-0	W
31	12-15	Los Angeles	7-1	W
32	12-17	Islanders	2-5	L
33	12-18	at Detroit	3-3	T
34	12-20	Pittsburgh	6-3	W
35	12-22	Buffalo	1-3	L
36	12-26	at Pittsburgh	3-4	L
37	12-30	at New Jersey	5-2	W
38	1-1	at Washington	7-2	W
39	1-3	Detroit	6-2	W
40	1-5	Buffalo	3-3	T

1982-83 (cont'd)

Game No.	Date	Opponent	Score	Result
41	1-7	Quebec	5-1	W
42	1-9	New Jersey	4-3	W
43	1-12	Winnipeg	5-5	T
44	1-15	at Boston	0-2	L
45	1-16	Philadelphia	0-4	L
46	1-18	at Vancouver	3-3	T
47	1-21	at Winnipeg	1-4	L
48	1-23	at Philadelphia	1-3	L
49	1-24	Boston	1-3	L
50	1-27	Montreal	1-4	L
51	1-29	at Pittsburgh	2-1	W
52	1-30	Chicago	4-5	L
53	2-1	at Los Angeles	5-5	T
54	2-5	at St. Louis	2-2	T
55	2-6	at Chicago	1-4	L
56	2-10	at Minnesota	5-7	L
57	2-12	at Montreal	3-2	W
58	2-16	Washington	5-4	W
59	2-19	at Philadelphia	5-8	L
60	2-20	Winnipeg	9-4	W
61	2-23	Hartford	11-3	W
62	2-26	at Quebec	3-6	L
63	2-28	Pittsburgh	9-3	W
64	3-1	at Pittsburgh	3-3	T
65	3-3	Washington	3-4	L
66	3-6	New Jersey	4-6	L
67	3-8	at Vancouver	3-7	L
68	3-11	at Edmonton	1-3	L
69	3-12	at Calgary	4-1	W
70	3-14	Philadelphia	8-2	W
71	3-16	Islanders	2-1	W
72	3-20	Boston	0-4	L
73	3-21	at New Jersey	2-4	L
74	3-23	at Detroit	7-1	W
75	3-26	at Islanders	2-3	L
76	3-27	Washington	5-4	W
77	3-29	at St. Louis	4-3	W
78	3-31	at Philadelphia	4-1	W
79	4-1	New Jersey	3-3	T
80	4-3	at Washington	0-3	L

Game-By-Game Results
1983-84—1984-85

Game No.	Date	Opponent	Score	Result
1983-84				
1	10-5	New Jersey	6-2	W
2	10-7	at New Jersey	3-1	W
3	10-8	at Pittsburgh	6-1	W
4	10-10	Los Angeles	2-1	W
5	10-13	Washington	4-3	W
6	10-15	at St. Louis	5-6	L
7	10-16	Philadelphia	5-4	W
8	10-19	Calgary	3-1	W
9	10-22	at Islanders	6-3	W
10	10-23	Islanders	6-5*	W
11	10-26	Winnipeg	5-7	L
12	10-28	Toronto	3-5	L
13	10-30	Edmonton	4-5*	L
14	11-2	at Buffalo	3-3	T
15	11-5	at Quebec	4-4	T
16	11-8	at New Jersey	5-1	W
17	11-9	Calgary	4-3	W
18	11-12	at Washington	4-7	L
19	11-13	Detroit	6-3	W
20	11-16	Washington	4-1	W
21	11-19	at Boston	6-6	T
22	11-20	Quebec	6-5*	W
23	11-23	Buffalo	4-6	L
24	11-25	at Washington	1-3	L
25	11-26	at Hartford	3-4*	L
26	11-28	Vancouver	3-3	T
27	11-30	Chicago	0-4	L
28	12-3	at Detroit	4-2	W
29	12-4	Minnesota	6-4	W
30	12-7	Washington	7-5	W
31	12-12	New Jersey	3-7	L
32	12-14	Edmonton	4-9	L
33	12-17	at Islanders	1-7	L
34	12-21	Pittsburgh	6-1	W
35	12-23	Chicago	3-2	W
36	12-26	at Pittsburgh	4-7	L
37	12-28	at Chicago	7-4	W
38	12-30	Philadelphia	6-3	W
39	12-31	at Buffalo	3-2	W
40	1-2	at Washington	2-2	T
1983-84 (cont'd)				
41	1-4	New Jersey	4-3*	W
42	1-7	at Boston	2-5	L
43	1-8	Islanders	5-4	W
44	1-12	at Philadelphia	2-1	W
45	1-14	at Islanders	2-4	L
46	1-16	Detroit	8-5	W
47	1-18	St. Louis	6-2	W
48	1-20	Pittsburgh	3-6	L
49	1-21	at Toronto	6-3	W
50	1-25	at Pittsburgh	6-3	W
51	1-26	Montreal	2-4	L
52	1-29	St. Louis	3-2	W
53	2-2	at Calgary	1-8	L
54	2-4	at Vancouver	5-4	W
55	2-5	at Los Angeles	3-3	T
56	2-8	at Winnipeg	3-1	W
57	2-9	at Minnesota	4-4	T
58	2-11	at Los Angeles	6-6	T
59	2-15	Islanders	3-2	W
60	2-18	at Islanders	3-4	L
61	2-19	Philadelphia	2-3*	L
62	2-23	Quebec	4-2	W
63	2-25	at Montreal	4-7	L
64	2-26	Pittsburgh	4-3*	W
65	2-28	at New Jersey	3-3	T
66	2-29	at Toronto	1-3	L
67	3-3	at Washington	1-5	L
68	3-4	Vancouver	4-5	L
69	3-7	at Minnesota	3-6	L
70	3-9	at Winnipeg	6-5*	W
71	3-10	at Edmonton	3-2	W
72	3-14	Philadelphia	6-3	W
73	3-17	at Philadelphia	4-6	L
74	3-20	Boston	4-6	L
75	3-22	at New Jersey	5-3	W
76	3-24	at Philadelphia	5-6	L
77	3-25	Montreal	3-2	W
78	3-29	Pittsburgh	6-4	W
79	3-31	at Hartford	3-5	L
80	4-1	Hartford	2-0	W

*Overtime

Game No.	Date	Opponent	Score	Result
1984-85				
1	10-11	Hartford	4-4	T
2	10-13	at Minnesota	1-3	L
3	10-14	Minnesota	1-3	L
4	10-20	at Washington	6-5	W
5	10-21	Islanders	6-5	W
6	10-25	at New Jersey	11-2	W
7	10-27	at Quebec	5-2	W
8	10-28	Boston	4-6	L
9	10-30	at Islanders	3-7	L
10	11-3	at Pittsburgh	7-5	W
11	11-7	Washington	4-3	W
12	11-9	Islanders	5-4*	W
13	11-11	Los Angeles	2-4	L
14	11-14	at Chicago	4-6	L
15	11-17	at Islanders	4-10	L
16	11-18	New Jersey	0-6	L
17	11-21	Buffalo	3-2	W
18	11-24	at Quebec	3-8	L
19	11-25	Quebec	2-3*	L
20	11-28	Washington	1-2	L
21	11-30	Toronto	3-3	T
22	12-1	at Toronto	4-1	W
23	12-3	Philadelphia	2-6	L
24	12-5	Calgary	4-4	T
25	12-7	Pittsburgh	3-4*	L
26	12-8	at Philadelphia	2-4	L
27	12-10	Los Angeles	4-2	W
28	12-12	Boston	3-3	T
29	12-15	at Washington	2-4	L
30	12-16	Washington	3-6	L
31	12-19	Winnipeg	4-5	L
32	12-22	at New Jersey	5-3	W
33	12-23	Montreal	3-3	T
34	12-26	at Detroit	2-5	L
35	12-29	at Montreal	3-7	L
36	12-30	St. Louis	6-2	W
37	1-2	Vancouver	6-0	W
38	1-5	at Boston	3-3	T
39	1-6	New Jersey	5-4*	W
40	1-9	at Winnipeg	5-6*	L
1984-85 (cont'd)				
41	1-12	at St. Louis	4-4	T
42	1-14	New Jersey	1-2	L
43	1-16	Buffalo	2-2	T
44	1-18	at New Jersey	9-6	W
45	1-19	at Washington	1-7	L
46	1-24	Detroit	3-1	W
47	1-26	at Montreal	2-3	L
48	1-27	Minnesota	3-2	W
49	1-31	at Calgary	2-7	L
50	2-2	at Edmonton	1-5	L
51	2-3	at Vancouver	1-4	L
52	2-5	at Los Angeles	5-7	L
53	2-7	at Islanders	5-7	L
54	2-9	at Hartford	2-2	T
55	2-10	at Philadelphia	2-3	L
56	2-15	Edmonton	8-7	W
57	2-17	Islanders	9-3	W
58	2-21	Hartford	3-4*	L
59	2-22	at Pittsburgh	8-3	W
60	2-25	Winnipeg	5-12	L
61	2-28	Washington	4-5	L
62	3-2	at Pittsburgh	4-5	L
63	3-3	Pittsburgh	7-3	W
64	3-6	at Vancouver	6-3	W
65	3-7	at Calgary	5-11	L
66	3-9	at Edmonton	3-3	T
67	3-11	Chicago	3-4*	L
68	3-13	Philadelphia	2-5	L
69	3-16	at Pittsburgh	0-5	L
70	3-17	New Jersey	7-3	W
71	3-21	at Philadelphia	4-8	L
72	3-22	at Detroit	3-5	L
73	3-24	Islanders	2-5	L
74	3-26	Pittsburgh	5-4	W
75	3-27	at Buffalo	2-3	L
76	3-30	at Philadelphia	0-3	L
77	3-31	Toronto	7-5	W
78	4-2	Philadelphia	1-2	L
79	4-4	at St. Louis	5-4	W
80	4-7	at Chicago	1-3	L

*Overtime

Game-By-Game Results
1985-86—1986-87

Game No.	Date	Opponent	Score	Result
1985-86				
1	10-10	Washington	4-2	W
2	10-12	at Hartford	2-8	L
3	10-13	New Jersey	2-3*	L
4	10-16	at Los Angeles	3-4	L
5	10-19	at Islanders	4-5	L
6	10-20	Vancouver	4-3	W
7	10-23	New Jersey	5-1	W
8	10-25	Los Angeles	5-0	W
9	10-27	Boston	2-1	W
10	11-2	at New Jersey	5-6*	L
11	11-4	at Pittsburgh	4-2	W
12	11-6	Philadelphia	2-5	L
13	11-8	at Winnipeg	7-3	W
14	11-9	at Minnesota	3-4*	L
15	11-11	Chicago	4-5*	L
16	11-13	Montreal	5-2	W
17	11-16	at Montreal	2-2	T
18	11-17	Edmonton	2-3*	L
19	11-20	Toronto	7-3	W
20	11-23	at Islanders	5-0	W
21	11-24	Islanders	3-4*	L
22	11-27	Calgary	2-5	L
23	11-29	at Washington	5-2	W
24	11-30	at Pittsburgh	4-5	L
25	12-2	Pittsburgh	0-6	L
26	12-4	Winnipeg	7-4	W
27	12-7	at Philadelphia	0-4	L
28	12-8	Philadelphia	3-1	W
29	12-11	at New Jersey	4-2	W
30	12-14	at Boston	2-4	L
31	12-15	Pittsburgh	2-5	L
32	12-18	Buffalo	4-5	L
33	12-20	Islanders	2-2	T
34	12-21	at Islanders	5-4	W
35	12-23	Detroit	10-2	W
36	12-26	at Buffalo	1-6	L
37	12-28	at Minnesota	1-3	L
38	12-29	Washington	6-5	W
39	1-1	at Washington	0-3	L
40	1-5	Quebec	4-5	L
1985-86 (cont'd)				
41	1-10	Montreal	6-4	W
42	1-12	St. Louis	2-2	T
43	1-14	at Vancouver	2-1	W
44	1-15	at Los Angeles	4-3	W
45	1-18	at Edmonton	5-4	W
46	1-20	Hartford	0-5	L
47	1-22	at Toronto	4-2	W
48	1-23	Quebec	0-4	L
49	1-27	at Quebec	6-6	T
50	1-29	at Chicago	4-5	L
51	1-31	at Buffalo	3-5	L
52	2-1	at Hartford	3-1	W
53	2-5	at St. Louis	3-4	L
54	2-8	at Boston	3-2	W
55	2-12	Vancouver	5-2	W
56	2-14	at Detroit	7-5	W
57	2-16	Detroit	3-1	W
58	2-20	St. Louis	3-2	W
59	2-24	Minnesota	5-1	W
60	2-25	at Toronto	3-7	L
61	2-27	Pittsburgh	8-3	W
62	3-1	at Washington	0-4	L
63	3-2	Washington	2-4	L
64	3-5	at Winnipeg	1-4	L
65	3-6	at Calgary	5-2	W
66	3-9	Philadelphia	1-4	L
67	3-11	at New Jersey	6-3	W
68	3-12	Calgary	2-3	L
69	3-15	at Pittsburgh	2-2	T
70	3-16	Islanders	3-1	W
71	3-18	at Islanders	2-6	L
72	3-22	at Philadelphia	2-4	L
73	3-23	Chicago	3-5	L
74	3-25	at New Jersey	5-4	W
75	3-28	Edmonton	4-2	W
76	3-29	at Philadelphia	2-8	L
77	3-31	New Jersey	9-0	W
78	4-2	Philadelphia	2-3	L
79	4-5	at Washington	4-4	T
80	4-6	Pittsburgh	4-5*	L

*Overtime

Game No.	Date	Opponent	Score	Result
1986-87				
1	10-9	New Jersey	3-5	L
2	10-11	at Pittsburgh	5-6*	L
3	10-13	Washington	6-7*	L
4	10-15	at Chicago	5-5	T
5	10-18	at Islanders	3-2	W
6	10-19	Islanders	2-2	T
7	10-22	Los Angeles	5-4*	W
8	10-25	at Montreal	3-3	T
9	10-26	Toronto	3-3	T
10	10-29	at St. Louis	2-7	L
11	11-2	Winnipeg	4-5*	L
12	11-5	at Detroit	4-5*	L
13	11-8	at Philadelphia	3-2	W
14	11-9	at Quebec	5-6	L
15	11-12	Buffalo	2-1*	W
16	11-14	Philadelphia	2-1	W
17	11-16	Edmonton	6-8	L
18	11-17	at New Jersey	2-3	L
19	11-19	at Edmonton	4-5*	L
20	11-21	at Vancouver	8-5	W
21	11-22	at Calgary	5-8	L
22	11-26	Quebec	4-2	W
23	11-29	at Pittsburgh	5-5	T
24	11-30	Pittsburgh	2-2	T
25	12-2	at New Jersey	5-8	L
26	12-5	at Winnipeg	6-3	W
27	12-10	Los Angeles	5-4	W
28	12-11	at Montreal	2-6	L
29	12-14	at Washington	3-1	W
30	12-15	Minnesota	3-4	L
31	12-17	Washington	6-1	W
32	12-20	at Islanders	2-5	L
33	12-21	Hartford	3-4*	L
34	12-23	New Jersey	8-5	W
35	12-26	at New Jersey	7-4	W
36	12-27	at St. Louis	2-3	L
37	12-30	at Pittsburgh	5-3	W
38	12-31	Islanders	4-3*	W
39	1-3	at Quebec	5-2	W
40	1-5	Minnesota	3-3	T
1986-87 (cont'd)				
41	1-7	Philadelphia	3-6	L
42	1-9	Islanders	1-2	L
43	1-11	Vancouver	8-3	W
44	1-12	at Boston	1-4	L
45	1-14	at Calgary	8-5	W
46	1-19	at Los Angeles	2-2	T
47	1-21	at Vancouver	3-5	L
48	1-23	at Edmonton	4-7	L
49	1-26	New Jersey	6-3	W
50	1-28	Winnipeg	1-2	L
51	1-31	at Philadelphia	3-1	W
52	2-1	Boston	5-4	W
53	2-4	Washington	3-2	W
54	2-7	at Washington	5-4*	W
55	2-8	Toronto	4-5	L
56	2-15	Pittsburgh	4-1	W
57	2-17	Detroit	6-2	W
58	2-19	at Chicago	2-5	L
59	2-20	Buffalo	3-6	L
60	2-22	Pittsburgh	2-4	L
61	2-24	at Buffalo	6-3	W
62	2-25	at Toronto	4-2	W
63	2-28	at Detroit	1-4	L
64	3-1	at Washington	3-7	L
65	3-4	Islanders	7-5	W
66	3-8	Calgary	4-7	L
67	3-11	Boston	3-2	W
68	3-12	at Philadelphia	6-1	W
69	3-14	at Pittsburgh	3-2*	W
70	3-15	Philadelphia	2-5	L
71	3-17	at Philadelphia	1-4	L
72	3-18	Hartford	3-5	L
73	3-21	at Islanders	3-4	L
74	3-22	Chicago	5-3	W
75	3-25	New Jersey	2-8	L
76	3-27	St. Louis	6-4	W
77	3-30	at Minnesota	6-5	W
78	4-1	Washington	1-5	L
79	4-4	at Hartford	3-5	L
80	4-5	Montreal	2-8	L

*Overtime

Game-By-Game Results
1987-88—1988-89

1987-88

Game No.	Date	Opponent	Score	Result
1	10-8	Pittsburgh	4-4	T
2	10-10	at Hartford	6-2	W
3	10-12	Minnesota	4-2	W
4	10-15	at Pittsburgh	6-6	T
5	10-17	at Washington	3-4	L
6	10-19	Washington	2-4	L
7	10-21	Calgary	4-5	L
8	10-23	Chicago	7-3	W
9	10-24	at Philadelphia	5-3	W
10	10-26	Philadelphia	2-2	T
11	10-28	Los Angeles	3-4	L
12	10-31	at NY Islanders	2-8	L
13	11-1	Edmonton	6-7	L
14	11-3	at Calgary	3-5	L
15	11-4	at Edmonton	2-7	L
16	11-7	at Los Angeles	4-5	L
17	11-10	New Jersey	2-3	L
18	11-14	at Pittsburgh	2-3*	L
19	11-15	Winnipeg	6-4	W
20	11-19	at Minnesota	3-4	L
21	11-20	at Winnipeg	4-3	W
22	11-25	Toronto	5-3	W
23	11-28	at NY Islanders	4-5	L
24	11-29	NY Islanders	3-1	W
25	12-3	at Boston	3-4	L
26	12-5	at St. Louis	3-2	W
27	12-9	Montreal	2-2	T
28	12-10	at Philadelphia	3-5	L
29	12-12	at Toronto	3-4	L
30	12-14	Detroit	4-3	W
31	12-16	New Jersey	9-3	W
32	12-19	at Pittsburgh	3-4	L
33	12-20	Pittsburgh	4-8	L
34	12-22	Philadelphia	4-6	L
35	12-26	at New Jersey	5-3	W
36	12-27	Boston	4-1	W
37	12-29	at NY Islanders	3-3	T
38	12-31	Quebec	6-1	W
39	1-2	at Minnesota	5-3	W
40	1-4	St. Louis	6-2	W
41	1-6	Vancouver	4-2	W
42	1-8	at Washington	4-8	L
43	1-10	at Buffalo	3-4	L
44	1-11	Chicago	2-2	T
45	1-13	Detroit	4-7	L
46	1-16	at Montreal	3-4	L
47	1-17	Philadelphia	1-2	L
48	1-19	at Los Angeles	3-6	L
49	1-22	at Vancouver	6-3	W
50	1-28	at Philadelphia	5-2	W
51	1-30	at Boston	4-2	W
52	2-2	at NY Islanders	2-2	T
53	2-4	at Quebec	2-3	L
54	2-6	at Washington	3-0	W
55	2-7	Pittsburgh	6-3	W
56	2-11	Washington	3-5	L
57	2-14	NY Islanders	4-4	T
58	2-15	Montreal	3-1	W
59	2-17	Calgary	5-3	W
60	2-19	at New Jersey	3-6	L
61	2-21	Vancouver	4-6	L
62	2-25	Pittsburgh	2-1	W
63	2-26	at New Jersey	2-1	W
64	2-29	St. Louis	5-2	W
65	3-2	NY Islanders	3-1	W
66	3-4	at Buffalo	3-6	L
67	3-5	at Hartford	1-3	L
68	3-8	New Jersey	7-4	W
69	3-12	at Washington	4-2	W
70	3-15	Philadelphia	3-1	W
71	3-16	Washington	4-8	L
72	3-19	at Toronto	4-3	W
73	3-20	Hartford	2-1	W
74	3-22	Buffalo	2-3	L
75	3-24	Edmonton	6-1	W
76	3-26	at Detroit	4-4	T
77	3-27	at New Jersey	2-7	L
78	3-30	at Chicago	4-3	W
79	4-1	at Winnipeg	6-6	T
80	4-3	Quebec	3-0	W

*Overtime

1988-89

Game No.	Date	Opponent	Score	Result
1	10-6	at Chicago	2-2	T
2	10-8	at St. Louis	4-2	W
3	10-10	New Jersey	0-5	L
4	10-12	Hartford	3-4	L
5	10-16	Vancouver	3-2	W
6	10-19	Washington	5-1	W
7	10-21	at Washington	4-1	W
8	10-23	Quebec	8-2	W
9	10-26	Philadelphia	4-3	W
10	10-29	at Philadelphia	6-5	W
11	10-30	Pittsburgh	9-2	W
12	11-2	at Buffalo	4-6	L
13	11-6	at New Jersey	5-6	L
14	11-8	at NY Islanders	3-4	L
15	11-9	Philadelphia	5-3	W
16	11-11	Boston	4-4	T
17	11-13	Detroit	3-5	L
18	11-15	at Philadelphia	3-3	T
19	11-17	at Los Angeles	6-5	W
20	11-19	at Minnesota	4-1	W
21	11-21	Montreal	2-4	L
22	11-23	at Pittsburgh	2-8	L
23	11-26	at NY Islanders	6-4	W
24	11-27	NY Islanders	5-3	W
25	11-29	at Winnipeg	4-3	W
26	12-1	at Calgary	3-6	L
27	12-4	at Edmonton	6-10	L
28	12-6	at Vancouver	5-3	W
29	12-8	at Hartford	5-4	L
30	12-10	at Boston	1-1	T
31	12-12	Los Angeles	2-5	L
32	12-14	NY Islanders	2-1	W
33	12-17	at Montreal	3-6	L
34	12-19	Washington	3-1	W
35	12-21	Buffalo	2-5	L
36	12-23	at Washington	2-2	T
37	12-26	New Jersey	5-1	W
38	12-27	at New Jersey	7-5	W
39	12-31	Chicago	4-1	W
40	1-2	Hartford	5-4	W
41	1-4	Washington	3-3	T
42	1-7	at NY Islanders	5-1	W
43	1-9	New Jersey	4-5	L
44	1-14	at Pittsburgh	4-4	T
45	1-15	Pittsburgh	6-4	W
46	1-18	at Chicago	6-4	W
47	1-19	at St. Louis	5-0	W
48	1-21	at Vancouver	5-4*	W
49	1-23	at Edmonton	3-2	W
50	1-26	at Calgary	3-5	L
51	1-28	at Toronto	1-1	T
52	1-30	NY Islanders	7-3	W
53	2-1	Washington	3-4*	L
54	2-4	at Montreal	5-7	L
55	2-5	Minnesota	3-5	L
56	2-9	Winnipeg	4-3	W
57	2-12	Edmonton	1-3	L
58	2-14	at Philadelphia	1-3	L
59	2-17	Toronto	6-10	L
60	2-18	at Pittsburgh	5-3	W
61	2-20	New Jersey	7-4	W
62	2-22	Philadelphia	4-6	L
63	2-25	at Quebec	7-2	W
64	2-27	Los Angeles	6-4	W
65	3-1	Toronto	7-4	W
66	3-3	at New Jersey	3-6	L
67	3-5	Boston	0-5	L
68	3-8	Buffalo	0-2	L
69	3-9	at Detroit	2-3	L
70	3-11	at Washington	2-4	L
71	3-13	Calgary	4-3	W
72	3-15	Winnipeg	3-6	L
73	3-18	at Quebec	3-8	L
74	3-20	St. Louis	7-4	W
75	3-22	Minnesota	3-1	W
76	3-26	at Philadelphia	1-6	L
77	3-26	Pittsburgh	4-6	L
78	3-29	at Detroit	3-4	L
79	4-1	at Pittsburgh	2-5	L
80	4-2	NY Islanders	4-6	L

*Overtime

Game-By-Game Results
1989-90—1990-91

1989-90

Game No.	Date	Opponent	Score	Result
1	10-6	at Winnipeg	4-1	W
2	10-8	at Chicago	5-3	W
3	10-11	Calgary	5-4	W
4	10-13	at Washington	4-7	L
5	10-15	Pittsburgh	4-2	W
6	10-17	Chicago	3-3	T
7	10-19	Hartford	7-3	W
8	10-21	at Philadelphia	3-1	W
9	10-23	Vancouver	5-3	W
10	10-25	Edmonton	3-3	T
11	10-27	Islanders	5-5	T
12	10-28	at Islanders	4-1	W
13	10-30	Philadelphia	1-3	L
14	11-2	Quebec	6-1	W
15	11-4	at Montreal	2-3	L
16	11-6	Detroit	6-1	W
17	11-8	Montreal	2-3	L
18	11-12	Islanders	4-2	W
19	11-14	at Pittsburgh	0-6	L
20	11-17	at New Jersey	4-5*	L
21	11-18	at Hartford	3-2	W
22	11-20	Winnipeg	3-3	T
23	11-22	at Buffalo	1-4	L
24	11-25	at Toronto	4-7	L
25	11-26	Quebec	3-1	W
26	11-29	at Winnipeg	4-5	L
27	12-1	at Vancouver	4-3	W
28	12-2	at Los Angeles	0-6	L
29	12-6	New Jersey	5-3	W
30	12-9	at Islanders	0-0	T
31	12-10	Philadelphia	2-4	L
32	12-13	St. Louis	1-3	L
33	12-16	at Islanders	3-4	L
34	12-17	Montreal	0-2	L
35	12-20	Buffalo	2-2	T
36	12-23	at Washington	2-3	L
37	12-26	New Jersey	4-4	T
38	12-27	at Pittsburgh	4-7	L
39	12-29	at New Jersey	2-3	L
40	12-31	Pittsburgh	4-5	L

1989-90 (cont'd)

Game No.	Date	Opponent	Score	Result
41	1-3	Washington	2-1	W
42	1-4	at Minnesota	2-8	L
43	1-6	at St. Louis	3-4	L
44	1-8	Pittsburgh	5-7	L
45	1-10	Chicago	2-2	T
46	1-13	at Boston	3-2	W
47	1-14	Philadelphia	4-3*	W
48	1-18	at Pittsburgh	3-3	T
49	1-23	at Edmonton	4-3	W
50	1-25	at Calgary	5-8	L
51	1-27	at Los Angeles	3-1	W
52	1-31	St. Louis	2-2	T
53	2-3	at Boston	2-1	W
54	2-4	Minnesota	4-3	W
55	2-7	Edmonton	5-2	W
56	2-9	at Buffalo	2-3	L
57	2-11	Calgary	2-5	L
58	2-13	at Philadelphia	4-3	W
59	2-14	Pittsburgh	3-4*	L
60	2-16	at New Jersey	3-2	W
61	2-19	New Jersey	4-3*	W
62	2-21	at Detroit	4-4	T
63	2-23	at Washington	6-3	W
64	2-26	Boston	6-1	W
65	2-28	Washington	3-2	W
66	3-2	Islanders	6-3	W
67	3-3	at Hartford	4-6	L
68	3-5	Detroit	3-2	W
69	3-8	at Philadelphia	7-5	W
70	3-10	at Minnesota	2-2	T
71	3-12	Los Angeles	2-6	L
72	3-14	at Toronto	8-2	W
73	3-17	at Islanders	3-6	L
74	3-18	Vancouver	4-2	W
75	3-21	Toronto	5-5	T
76	3-25	Philadelphia	7-3	W
77	3-27	at Quebec	7-4	W
78	3-29	at New Jersey	4-6	L
79	3-31	at Washington	1-2	L
80	4-1	Washington	2-3	L

*Overtime

1990-91

Game No.	Date	Opponent	Score	Result
1	10-4	at Chicago	3-4	L
2	10-6	at Hartford	4-5	L
3	10-8	Minnesota	6-3	W
4	10-10	Washington	4-2	W
5	10-12	Montreal	3-0	W
6	10-13	at Washington	5-2	W
7	10-17	Winnipeg	5-3	W
8	10-19	at New Jersey	2-3	L
9	10-20	at Pittsburgh	4-3	W
10	10-22	Toronto	5-1	W
11	10-25	Philadelphia	5-3	W
12	10-27	at Quebec	4-1	W
13	10-29	Quebec	5-0	W
14	10-31	Los Angeles	9-4	W
15	11-2	Islanders	2-3	L
16	11-3	at Pittsburgh	1-3	L
17	11-5	Boston	2-3*	L
18	11-7	Buffalo	6-2	W
19	11-9	at New Jersey	3-2	W
20	11-11	Calgary	4-4	T
21	11-13	at Philadelphia	1-1	T
22	11-15	at Minnesota	4-2	W
23	11-16	at Winnipeg	6-4	W
24	11-19	Minnesota	2-2	T
25	11-21	at Buffalo	5-5	T
26	11-24	at Islanders	2-2	T
27	11-26	Buffalo	5-0	W
28	11-28	Washington	3-6	L
29	11-30	at Philadelphia	1-5	L
30	12-1	at Boston	5-4	W
31	12-3	Pittsburgh	4-9	L
32	12-5	at Calgary	1-4	L
33	12-7	at Edmonton	3-4	L
34	12-11	at Los Angeles	6-4	W
35	12-14	at Vancouver	5-3	W
36	12-17	Washington	5-3	W
37	12-19	Toronto	1-4	L
38	12-22	at Montreal	1-3	L
39	12-23	Boston	5-5	T
40	12-28	at Washington	5-3	W

1990-91 (cont'd)

Game No.	Date	Opponent	Score	Result
41	12-30	New Jersey	2-2	T
42	1-2	Los Angeles	4-1	W
43	1-3	at Pittsburgh	7-5	W
44	1-5	at St. Louis	3-2*	W
45	1-7	Philadelphia	3-2	W
46	1-9	St. Louis	2-3	L
47	1-11	at Detroit	3-6	L
48	1-13	Hartford	4-3	W
49	1-15	Edmonton	2-2	T
50	1-17	Chicago	2-3	L
51	1-22	at Islanders	2-3	L
52	1-25	at Edmonton	4-3	W
53	1-30	at Calgary	1-5	L
54	1-31	at Vancouver	3-3	T
55	2-3	Winnipeg	3-4	L
56	2-6	Islanders	5-2	W
57	2-8	Vancouver	8-1	W
58	2-9	at Montreal	4-6	L
59	2-13	New Jersey	6-3	W
60	2-15	Hartford	5-3	W
61	2-18	Islanders	4-5	L
62	2-21	at Philadelphia	4-4	T
63	2-22	at Washington	2-3	L
64	2-24	New Jersey	5-2	W
65	2-27	Washington	4-4	T
66	2-28	at St. Louis	4-4	T
67	3-2	at Toronto	4-4	W
68	3-4	Philadelphia	6-2	W
69	3-7	at Quebec	2-4	L
70	3-9	at Islanders	4-6	L
71	3-10	at Chicago	2-5	L
72	3-13	Detroit	1-4	L
73	3-15	at New Jersey	2-5	L
74	3-17	Pittsburgh	2-4	L
75	3-21	at Pittsburgh	4-5*	L
76	3-23	at Philadelphia	4-7	L
77	3-24	Islanders	3-1	W
78	3-26	New Jersey	3-3	T
79	3-30	at Detroit	5-6	L
80	3-31	Pittsburgh	6-3	W

*Overtime

Game-By-Game Results
1991-92—1992-93

1991-92

Game No.	Date	Opponent	Score	Result
1	10-3	at Boston	3-5	L
2	10-5	at Montreal	2-1	W
3	10-7	Boston	2-1	W
4	10-9	Islanders	5-3	W
5	10-11	at Washington	1-5	L
6	10-12	at Hartford	2-5	L
7	10-14	Washington	3-5	L
8	10-16	New Jersey	4-2	W
9	10-19	at Pittsburgh	5-4	W
10	10-20	Edmonton	3-4	L
11	10-23	Los Angeles	7-2	W
12	10-26	at Quebec	5-3	W
13	10-29	Minnesota	3-2	W
14	10-31	Quebec	5-4	W
15	11-2	at Philadelphia	4-2	W
16	11-4	Calgary	4-0	W
17	11-6	Montreal	1-4	L
18	11-8	Toronto	3-3	T
19	11-11	Pittsburgh	3-1	W
20	11-13	Washington	3-5	L
21	11-16	at Islanders	2-4	L
22	11-19	at Vancouver	4-3	W
23	11-21	at Los Angeles	1-6	L
24	11-23	at St. Louis	3-0	W
25	11-27	at Winnipeg	2-3	L
26	11-29	at Buffalo	5-4	W
27	12-2	Philadelphia	4-2	W
28	12-6	at Detroit	5-6	L
29	12-8	Boston	4-0	W
30	12-10	at Pittsburgh	3-5	L
31	12-13	at Washington	5-3	W
32	12-14	at Hartford	6-2	W
33	12-16	San Jose	4-3	W
34	12-18	Philadelphia	6-3	W
35	12-21	at Pittsburgh	7-5	W
36	12-23	New Jersey	3-0	W
37	12-26	at Washington	8-6	W
38	12-28	at Islanders	4-5	L
39	12-29	Pittsburgh	3-6	L
40	12-31	at Winnipeg	5-2	W
41	1-2	at Chicago	4-3	W
42	1-4	at New Jersey	4-6	L
43	1-6	Winnipeg	4-2	W
44	1-8	St. Louis	3-5	L
45	1-11	at Quebec	7-2	W
46	1-12	at Buffalo	3-6	L
47	1-14	Buffalo	6-2	W
48	1-16	Calgary	6-4	W
49	1-22	at Calgary	4-4	T
50	1-23	at Edmonton	3-1	W
51	1-28	San Jose	4-2	W
52	1-30	at Los Angeles	4-1	W
53	2-1	at Minnesota	2-1	W
54	2-5	Pittsburgh	4-3	W
55	2-7	at Washington	2-6	L
56	2-9	Detroit	5-5	T
57	2-12	Vancouver	5-2	W
58	2-14	Islanders	9-2	W
59	2-16	at New Jersey	2-4	L
60	2-17	Vancouver	3-3	T
61	2-20	at Islanders	2-6	L
62	2-21	Minnesota	5-4	W
63	2-23	Philadelphia	2-1	W
64	2-25	Chicago	4-1	W
65	3-1	Hartford	9-4	W
66	3-2	at New Jersey	7-1	W
67	3-4	New Jersey	4-5	L
68	3-7	at Philadelphia	4-5	L
69	3-9	Washington	2-5	L
70	3-11	Chicago	3-2	W
71	3-14	at St. Louis	6-0	W
72	3-16	Montreal	4-1	W
73	3-18	Islanders	1-1	T
74	3-20	at Detroit	4-2	W
75	3-22	New Jersey	6-3	W
76	3-23	at Philadelphia	4-3	W
77	3-24	Philadelphia	4-1	W
78	3-28	at Islanders	1-4	L
79	4-15	at Toronto	2-4	L
80	4-16	Pittsburgh	7-1	W

1992-93

Game No.	Date	Opponent	Score	Result
1	10/9	at Washington	4-2	W
2	10/10	at New Jersey	2-4	L
3	10/12	Hartford	6-2	W
4	10/14	New Jersey	6-1	W
5	10/17	at Islanders	3-6	L
6	10/18	Islanders	4-3	W
7	10/21	Washington	2-1	W
8	10/23	Montreal	3-3	T
9	10/24	at Ottawa	3-2	W
10	10/26	Philadelphia	8-4	W
11	10/29	Quebec	3-6	L
12	10/31	at Montreal	3-4	L
13	11/2	Buffalo	7-6	W
14	11/4	Philadelphia	3-1	W
15	11/7	at Boston	2-2	T
16	11/9	Tampa Bay	1-5	L
17	11/11	Washington	4-7	L
18	11/14	at Quebec	3-6	L
19	11/19	at Philadelphia	3-7	L
20	11/21	at Winnipeg	5-4	W
21	11/23	Pittsburgh	2-5	L
22	11/25	at Pittsburgh	11-3	W
23	11/27	at Minnesota	4-4	T
24	11/30	Minnesota	2-4	L
25	12/2	Detroit	5-3	W
26	12/4	at Washington	4-8	L
27	12/6	Toronto	6-0	W
28	12/9	Tampa Bay	6-5	W
29	12/11	at Tampa Bay	5-4	W
30	12/13	Montreal	10-5	W
31	12/15	Calgary	0-3	L
32	12/17	at St. Louis	4-3	W
33	12/19	at Hartford	4-4	T
34	12/21	at New Jersey	3-0	W
35	12/23	New Jersey	4-5	L
36	12/26	at Islanders	4-6	L
37	12/27	Boston	6-5	W
38	12/29	at Washington	3-4	L
39	12/31	at Buffalo	6-11	L
40	1/2	at Pittsburgh	2-5	L
41	1/4	New Jersey	3-3	T
42	1/6	Ottawa	6-2	W
43	1/9	at Philadelphia	3-4	L
44	1/11	Vancouver	3-3	T
45	1/13	Washington	5-4	W
46	1/16	at Montreal	0-3	L
47	1/19	at Detroit	2-2	T
48	1/23	at Los Angeles	8-3	W
49	1/27	Winnipeg	5-2	W
50	1/29	at Buffalo	4-6	L
51	1/30	at Toronto	1-3	L
52	2/1	at Islanders	4-4	T
53	2/3	Philadelphia	2-2	T
54	2/8	at New Jersey	4-5	L
55	2/10	Pittsburgh	0-3	L
56	2/12	Islanders	4-3	W
57	2/13	at Islanders	2-5	L
58	2/15	St. Louis	4-1	W
59	2/20	at San Jose	6-4	W
60	2/22	at San Jose	4-0	W
61	2/24	at Vancouver	4-5	L
62	2/26	at Calgary	4-4	T
63	2/27	at Edmonton	1-0	W
64	3/3	Buffalo	2-2	T
65	3/5	Pittsburgh	3-1	W
66	3/6	at Quebec	2-10	L
67	3/9	Los Angeles	4-3	W
68	3/11	at Chicago	4-1	W
69	3/15	Boston	1-3	L
70	3/17	Edmonton	3-4	L
71	3/19	San Jose	8-1	W
72	3/22	at Ottawa	5-4	W
73	3/24	Philadelphia	4-5	L
74	3/26	Chicago	1-3	L
75	3/28	Quebec	2-3	L
76	4/2	Islanders	2-3	L
77	4/4	at Washington	4-0	W
78	4/5	Hartford	4-5	L
79	4/7	at New Jersey	2-5	L
80	4/9	Pittsburgh	4-10	L
81	4/10	at Pittsburgh	2-4	L
82	4/12	at Philadelphia	0-1	L
83	4/14	Washington	0-2	L
84	4/16	at Washington	2-4	L

STEVEN McDONALD AWARD

Following the 1987-88 season, the Rangers, in conjunction with Mitsubishi Motors, established a new award dedicated to paralyzed New York City police officer Steven McDonald. The award was named the Steven McDonald "Extra Effort Award", and is presented annually to the Rangers player "who goes above and beyond the call of duty," as Steven did as a New York City police officer. The winner is chosen by Rangers fans who vote on the award from February through April.

McDonald, a lifelong Rangers fan, was shot in the line of duty on July 12, 1986, in Central Park. He spent 18 months in the hospital and watched video tapes of each Rangers game during his recovery. Several Rangers players visited him in the hospital and presented him with a jersey.

He grew up listening to Rangers games on the radio and watching on television but had never been to a game in person. His heroes included Eddie Giacomin, Brad Park, and Jean Ratelle. He now attends a good number of games during the season, sitting at ice level in the zamboni entrance.

The inaugural winner of the award was Jan Erixon in 1987-88. NHL rookie-of-the-year finalist Tony Granato captured the award in 1988-89 before Kelly Kisio and John Vanbiesbrouck were named co-winners in 1989-90. Jan Erixon became the first repeat winner of the award in 1990-91.

For the third consecutive year, Adam Graves captured the prestigious award. Graves has now won the award in each of his first three seasons with the Rangers.

Along with the trophy, Graves received a 1994 Mitsubishi Galant, courtesy of Mitsubishi Motors, while Mitsubishi also presented their annual check for $15,000 to the Steven McDonald Foundation.

Adam Graves receives his third Steven McDonald Award. Pictured left to right are Patty Ann McDonald, the McDonald's son Conor, Steven and Adam Graves.

LARS-ERIK SJOBERG AWARD

For the sixth consecutive year, the New York Rangers, in conjunction with the Professional Hockey Writer's Association, presented the Lars-Erik Sjoberg Award, symbolic of the best rookie in training camp.

Sjoberg a, 180-pound defenseman, came to North America in 1974 after a distinguished nine-year career in Sweden, along with fellow countrymen Anders Hedberg and Ulf Nilsson. The trio were three of an unprecedented six Europeans signed by the Winnipeg Jets of the World Hockey Association, that year helping blaze the trail for Europeans to play in the NHL. Sjoberg, who served as Jets team captain for five seasons, led the Jets to three WHA Championships during the 1970's. "Pound-for-pound, he was one of the best defensemen who has ever played the game," said Jets teammate Bobby Hull.

Sjoberg joined the Rangers staff on July 22, 1980 when he was named as the team's European Scout. He held that position until he passed away in October of 1987. In his time with New York, the Rangers drafted several European players who went on to play in the National Hockey League including, Reijo Ruotsalainen, Jan Erixon, Peter Sundstrom, Tomas Sandstrom, Kjell Samuelsson and Ulf Dahlen.

The 1993 recepient of the award was defenseman Mattias Norstrom. The native of Stockholm, Sweden was appearing in his second training camp with the Rangers after being selected in the second round, 48th overall in the 1992 NHL Entry Draft.

Previous winners of the award include Peter Andersson in 1992, Tony Amonte 1991, Steven Rice in 1990 and Troy Mallette in 1989. The inaugural winner of the award was Mike Richter in 1988.

Frank Brown of the New York Daily News presents Mattias Norstrom with the Lars-Erik Sjoberg award symbolic of the best rookie in training camp.

RANGERS AWARD WINNERS

NHL AWARDS

LADY BYNG TROPHY
Frank Boucher 1927-28
Frank Boucher 1928-29
Frank Boucher 1929-30
Frank Boucher 1930-31
Frank Boucher 1932-33
Frank Boucher 1933-34
Frank Boucher 1934-35
Clint Smith 1938-39
Buddy O'Connor 1947-48
Edgar Laprade 1949-50
Camille Henry 1957-58
Jean Ratelle 1971-72

NORRIS TROPHY
Doug Harvey 1961-62
Harry Howell 1966-67
Brian Leetch 1991-92

HART TROPHY
Buddy O'Connor 1947-48
Chuck Rayner 1949-50
Andy Bathgate 1958-59
Mark Messier 1991-92

KING CLANCY TROPHY
Adam Graves 1993-94

CONN SMYTHE TROPHY
Brian Leetch 1994

CALDER TROPHY
Kilby MacDonald 1939-40
Grant Warwick 1941-42
Edgar Laprade 1945-46
Pentti Lund 1948-49
Lorne Worsley 1952-53
Camille Henry 1953-54
Steve Vickers 1972-73
Brian Leetch 1988-89

VEZINA TROPHY
Dave Kerr 1939-40
Ed Giacomin, Gilles Villemure 1970-71
John Vanbiesbrouck 1985-86

ROSS TROPHY
Bill Cook 1926-27
Bill Cook 1932-33
Bryan Hextall 1941-42

PATRICK TROPHY
William Jennings 1971
Phil Esposito 1978
Fred Shero 1980
Rod Gilbert 1991

MASTERTON TROPHY
Jean Ratelle 1970-71
Rod Gilbert 1975-76
Anders Hedberg 1984-85

NHL Commissioner Gary Bettman presents Brian Leetch with the Conn Smythe Trophy as the MVP in the 1994 Stanley Cup Playoffs.

RANGERS AWARD WINNERS

WEST SIDE ASSN. TROPHY AS RANGERS' MVP

Lynn Patrick	1941-42
Lynn Patrick	1942-43
Ott Heller and	
Bryan Hextall	1943-44
Ab DeMarco	1944-45
Chuck Rayner	1945-46
Chuck Rayner	1946-47
Buddy O'Connor	1947-48
Edgar Laprade and	
Chuck Rayner	1948-49
Edgar Laprade	1949-50
Don Raleigh	1950-51
Hy Buller	1951-52
Paul Ronty	1952-53
Wally Hergesheimer	1953-54
Danny Lewicki	1954-55
Bill Gadsby	1955-56
Andy Bathgate	1956-57
Andy Bathgate	1957-58
Andy Bathgate	1958-59
Dean Prentice	1959-60
Lorne Worsley	1960-61
Andy Bathgate	1961-62
Lorne Worsley	1962-63
Harry Howell	1963-64
Don Marshall	1964-65
Bob Nevin	1965-66
Ed Giacomin	1966-67
Rod Gilbert	1967-68
Ed Giacomin	1968-69
Walter Tkaczuk	1969-70
Ed Giacomin	1970-71
Jean Ratelle	1971-72
Jean Ratelle	1972-73
Brad Park	1973-74
Rod Gilbert	1974-75
Rod Gilbert	1975-76
Dave Maloney	1976-77
Walter Tkaczuk	1977-78
Phil Esposito	1978-79
Anders Hedberg	1979-80
Eddie Johnstone	1980-81
Barry Beck and	
Mike Rogers	1981-82
Mark Pavelich	1982-83
Barry Beck	1983-84
Tomas Sandstrom	1984-85
John Vanbiesbrouck	1985-86
Walt Poddubny	1986-87
James Patrick	1987-88
Brian Leetch	1988-89
John Ogrodnick	1989-90
Brian Leetch	1990-91
Mark Messier	1991-92
Adam Graves	1992-93
Adam Graves	1993-94

WEST SIDE ASSOCIATION PLAYERS' PLAYER AWARD

Andy Hebenton	1958-59
Red Sullivan and	
Andy Hebenton	1959-60
Andy Hebenton	1960-61
Earl Ingarfield	1961-62
Andy Bathgate	1962-63
Rod Gilbert and	
Phil Goyette	1963-64
Harry Howell	1964-65
Wayne Hillman and	
Don Marshall	1965-66
Harry Howell	1966-67
Jean Ratelle	1967-68
Jean Ratelle	1968-69
Jean Ratelle	1969-70
Jean Ratelle	1970-71
Vic Hadfield	1971-72
Walter Tkaczuk	1972-73
Ted Irvine	1973-74
Jean Ratelle	1974-75
John Davidson	1975-76
John Davidson and	
Phil Esposito	1976-77
John Davidson and	
Ron Greschner	1977-78
Ulf Nilsson	1978-79
Don Maloney	1979-80
Don Maloney	1980-81
Tom Laidlaw and	
Mark Pavelich	1981-82
Tom Laidlaw	1982-83
Glen Hanlon	1983-84
Reijo Ruotsalainen	1984-85
John Vanbiesbrouck	1985-86
Don Maloney	1986-87
James Patrick	1987-88
Guy Lafleur	1988-89
Kelly Kisio	1989-90
Mike Richter	1990-91
Adam Graves	1991-92
Adam Graves	1992-93
Eddie Olczyk	1993-94

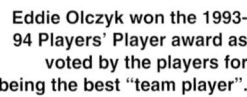

Eddie Olczyk won the 1993-94 Players' Player award as voted by the players for being the best "team player".

RANGERS AWARD WINNERS

RANGERS FAN CLUB'S FRANK BOUCHER TROPHY

Don Raleigh	1951-52
Wally Hergesheimer	1952-53
Johnny Bower	1953-54
Edgar Laprade	1954-55
Lorne Worsley	1955-56
Andy Bathgate	1956-57
Andy Bathgate	1957-58
Andy Bathgate	1958-59
Dean Prentice	1959-60
Lorne Worsley	1960-61
Andy Bathgate	1961-62
Lorne Worsley	1962-63
Rod Gilbert	1963-64
Harry Howell	1964-65
Harry Howell	1965-66
Harry Howell	1966-67
Rod Gilbert	1967-68
Ed Giacomin	1968-69
Walter Tkaczuk	1969-70
Dave Balon	1970-71
Jean Ratelle	1971-72
Jean Ratelle	1972-73
Brad Park	1973-74
Rod Gilbert	1974-75
Rod Gilbert	1975-76
Rod Gilbert	1976-77
Pat Hickey	1977-78
Phil Esposito	1978-79
Phil Esposito	1979-80
Eddie Johnstone	1980-81
Nick Fotiu	1981-82
Mark Pavelich	1982-83
Barry Beck and Nick Fotiu	1983-84
Anders Hedberg and Mike Rogers	1984-85
John Vanbiesbrouck	1985-86
Walt Poddubny	1986-87
Walt Poddubny	1987-88
Guy Lafleur	1988-89
Brian Mullen	1989-90
Mike Richter	1990-91
Mark Messier	1991-92
Mike Gartner	1992-93
Adam Graves	1993-94

STEVEN McDONALD EXTRA EFFORT AWARD

Jan Erixon	1987-88
Tony Granato	1988-89
John Vanbiesbrouck and Kelly Kisio	1989-90
Jan Erixon	1990-91
Adam Graves	1991-92
Adam Graves	1992-93
Adam Graves	1993-94

RANGERS GOOD GUY AWARD, FOR COOPERATION WITH MEDIA AS VOTED BY THE PROFESSIONAL HOCKEY WRITERS ASSOCIATION

Ted Irvine	1974-75
Ron Harris	1975-76
John Davidson	1976-77
Rod Gilbert	1977-78
Dave Maloney	1978-79
Anders Hedberg	1979-80
Don Maloney	1980-81
Barry Beck	1981-82
Rob McClanahan	1982-83
Pierre Larouche	1983-84
John Vanbiesbrouck	1984-85
Ron Greschner	1985-86
James Patrick	1986-87
Bob Froese	1987-88
Tony Granato	1988-89
Kelly Kisio	1989-90
Mike Richter	1990-91
Mark Messier	1991-92
Adam Graves	1992-93
Neil Smith	1993-94

RANGERS FAN CLUB ROOKIE OF THE YEAR

John Vanbiesbrouck	1984-85
Mike Ridley	1985-86
Terry Carkner	1986-87
Ulf Dahlen	1987-88
Brian Leetch and Tony Granato	1988-89
Darren Turcotte	1989-90
Mike Richter	1990-91
Tony Amonte	1991-92
Sergei Zubov	1992-93
Alexander Karpovtsev	1993-94

LARS-ERIK SJOBERG AWARD (BEST ROOKIE OF TRAINING CAMP)

Mike Richter	1988
Troy Mallette	1989
Steven Rice	1990
Tony Amonte	1991
Peter Andersson	1992
Mattias Norstrom	1993

Neil Smith is the 1993-94 recipient of the Rangers Good Guy award, as voted by the PHWA.

RANGERS MILESTONE WINNERS / HALL OF FAMERS

RANGERS NHL MILESTONE WINNERS

Andy Bathgate	624 assists	Rod Gilbert	406 goals
	1069 games		615 assists
Marcel Dionne	731 goals		1021 points
	1040 assists		1065 games
	1771 points	Vic Hadfield	1002 games
Phil Esposito	717 goals	Harry Howell	1411 games
	873 assists	Kevin Lowe	1086 games
	1590 points	Mark Messier	478 goals
	1282 games		838 assists
Mike Gartner	611 goals		1316 points
	548 assists		1081 games
	1159 points	Jim Neilson	1023 games
	1160 games	Bob Nevin	1128 games
Ed Giacomin	54 shutouts	Dean Prentice	1378 games
	610 games	Chuck Rayner	25 shutouts

RANGERS IN U.S. HOCKEY HALL OF FAME

Robert E. Dill William M. Jennings
Victor Des Jardins John W. McCartan

RANGERS IN HOCKEY HALL OF FAME
PLAYERS (33)

Howie Morenz ....(April, 1945)	Art Coulter ....(August, 1974)
Lester Patrick ....(April, 1945)	Andy Bathgate ....(September, 1978)
Bill Cook ....(August, 1952)	Jacques Plante ....(September, 1978)
Frank Boucher......................(April, 1958)	Harry Howell ....(September, 1979)
Ching Johnson ....(April, 1958)	Lynn Patrick ....(September, 1980)
Babe Siebert ....(June, 1961)	Gump Worsley ....(September, 1980)
Earl Seibert ....(June, 1963)	Rod Gilbert.................(September, 1982)
Doug Bentley ....(June, 1964)	Phil Esposito ....(September, 1984)
Max Bentley.....................(August, 1966)	Jean Ratelle ....(September, 1985)
Babe Pratt ....(August, 1966)	Ed Giacomin ....(June, 1987)
Neil Colville ....(September, 1967)	Guy Lafleur ....(September, 1988)
Bryan Hextall ....(June, 1969)	Buddy O'Connor ....(September, 1988)
Bill Gadsby...........................(June, 1970)	Brad Park ....(September, 1988)
Terry Sawchuk ....(August, 1971)	Clint Smith..................(September, 1991)
Bernie Geoffrion ....(August, 1972)	Marcel Dionne............(September, 1992)
Doug Harvey ....(August, 1973)	Edgar Laprade ....(September, 1993)
Chuck Rayner...................(August, 1973)	

RANGERS ALL-TIME DRAFT

1963

Round/Overall	Name	Pos.	Team, League
1/4	Al Osborne	RW	Weston, Jr. B
2/10	Terry Jones	C	Weston, Midg.
3/15	Mike Cummings	LW	Georgetown, OHL Midget
4/20	Campbell Alleson	D	Portage La Praire, Jr. B

1964

Round/Overall	Name	Pos.	Team, League
1/3	Robert Graham	D	Toronto, Midget
2/9	Tim Ecclestone	C	Etobicoke, Jr. B
3/15	Gordon Lowe	D	Toronto, Midget
4/21	Syl. Apps Jr.	C	Kingston, Midget

1965

Round/Overall	Name	Pos.	Team, League
1/1	Andre Veilleux	RW	Montreal, Jr. B
2/6	George Surmay	G	Winnipeg, MJHL
3/10	Michel Parizeau	LW	Montreal, Jr. B

1966

Round/Overall	Name	Pos.	Team, League
1/2	Brad Park	D	Toronto, OHA
2/8	Joey Johnston	C	Peterborough, OHA
3/14	Don Luce	C	Kitchener, OHA
4/20	Jack Egers	LW	Kitchener, Jr. B

1967

Round/Overall	Name	Pos.	Team, League
1/6	Robert Dickson	LW	Chatham, OHL
2/15	Brian Tosh	D	Smith Falls, Jr. A

1968

Round/Overall	Name	Pos.	Team, League
3/19	Bruce Buchanan	D	Weyburn, WHL

1969

Round/Overall	Name	Pos.	Team, League
1/8	Andre Dupont	D	Montreal, OHA
2/12	Pierre Jarry	C	Ottawa, OHA
3/23	Bert Wilson	LW	London, OHA
4/35	Kevin Morrison	RW	St. Jerome, QMJHL
5/47	Bruce Hellemond	D	Moose Jaw, WHL
6/59	Gordon Smith	D	Cornwall, QMJHL

1970

Round/Overall	Name	Pos.	Team, League
1/11	Normand Gratton	RW	Montreal, OHA
2/25	Mike Murphy	RW	Toronto, OHA
3/39	Wendell Bennett	RW	Weyburn, SJHL
4/53	Andre St. Pierre	D	Drummondville, QMJHL
5/67	Gary Coalter	RW	Hamilton, OHA
6/81	Duane Wylie	C	St. Catharines, OHA
7/94	Wayne Bell	G	Estevan, WHL
8/106	Pierre Brind'Amour	LW	Montreal, OHA

1971

Round/Overall	Name	Pos.	Team, League
1/10	Steve Vickers	LW	Toronto, OHA
1/13	Steve Durbano	D	Toronto, OHA
2/27	Tom Williams	LW	Hamilton, OHA
3/41	Terry West	C	London, OHA
4/55	Jerry Butler	RW	Hamilton, OHA
5/69	Fraser Robertson	D	Lethbridge, AJHL
6/83	Wayne Wood	G	Montreal, OHA
7/96	Doug Keeler	C	Ottawa, OHA
7/97	Jean-Denis Royal	D	St. Jerome, QMJHL
9/109	Eugene Sobchuk	D	Regina, WHL
10/109	Jim Ivison	D	Brandon, WHL
11/111	Andre Peloffy	C	Rosemount, QMJHL
12/112	Elston Evoy	C	Sault Ste. Marie, OHA
13/114	Gerald Lacompte	D	Sherbrooke, QMJHL
14/115	Wayne Forsey	LW	Swift Current, WHL
15/116	Bill Forrest	D	Hamilton, OHA

1972

Round/Overall	Name	Pos.	Team, League
1/10	Al Blanchard	RW	Kitchener, OHA
1/15	Bob MacMillan	C	St. Catharines, OHA
2/21	Larry Sacharuk	D	Saskatoon, WHL
2/31	Rene Villemure	LW	Shawinigan, QMJHL
3/48	Gerry Teeple	C	Cornwall , QMJHL
4/63	Doug Horbul	LW	Calgary, WHL
5/78	Marty Gateman	D	Hamilton, OHA
6/95	Ken Ireland	C	New Westminster, WHL
7/111	Jeff Hunt	RW	Winnipeg, WHL
8/127	Yvon Blais	LW	Cornwall, QMJHL
9/137	Pierre Archambault	D	St. Jerome, QMJHL

1973

Round/Overall	Name	Pos.	Team, League
1/14	Rick Middleton	RW	Oshawa, OHA
2/30	Pat Hickey	RW	Hamilton, OHA
3/46	John Campbell	LW	Sault Ste. Marie, OHA
4/62	Brian Movik	D	Calgary, WHL
5/78	Pierre Laganiere	RW	Sherbrooke, QMJHL
6/94	Dwayne Pentland	D	Brandon, WHL

1974

Round/Overall	Name	Pos.	Team, League
1/14	Dave Maloney	D	Kitchener, OHA
2/32	Ron Greschner	D	New Westminster, WHL
3/50	Jerry Holland	LW	Calgary, WHL
4/68	Boyd Anderson	LW	Medicine Hat, WHL
5/86	Dennis Olmstead	C	Univ. of Wisc., WCHA
6/104	Eddie Johnstone	RW	Medicine Hat, WHL
7/122	John Memryk	G	Winnipeg, WHL
8/139	Greg Holst	C	Kingston, OHA
9/156	Claude Arvisais	C	Shawinigan, QMJHL
10/171	Ken Dodd	LW	New Westminster, WHL
11/186	Ralph Krentz	LW	Brandon, WHL
12/198	Larry Jacques	RW	Ottawa, OHA
13/208	Tom Gastle	LW	Peterborough, OHA
14/218	Eric Brubacher	C	Kingston, OHA
15/224	Russell Hall	RW	Winnipeg, WHL
16/227	Bill Kriski	G	Winnipeg, WHL
17/230	Kevin Treacy	RW	Cornwall, QMJHL
18/233	Ken Gassoff	D	Medicine Hat, WHL
19/236	Clifford Bast	D	Medicine Hat, WHL
20/239	Jim Mayer	RW	Mich. Tech, WCHA
21/241	Warren Miller	RW	Univ. of Minn., WCHA
22/243	Kevin Walker	D	Cornell University, ECAC
23/245	Jim Warner	RW	Minnesota, Midwest Jr.

RANGERS ALL-TIME DRAFT

1975

Round/Overall	Name	Pos.	Team, League
1/12	Wayne Dillon	C	Toronto, WHA
2/30	Doug Soetaert	G	Edmonton, WHL
3/48	Greg Hickey	LW	Hamilton, OHA
4/66	Bill Cheropita	G	St. Catharines, OHA
5/84	Larry Huras	D	Kitchener, OHA
6/102	Randy Koch	LW	Univ. of Vermont, ECAC
7/120	Claude Larose	LW	Sherbrooke, QMJHL
8/138	Bill Hamilton	RW	St. Catherine's, OHA
9/154	Bud Stefanski	C	Oshawa, OHA
10/169	Dan Beaulieu	LW	Quebec, QMJHL
11/184	John McMorrow	C	Providence Coll., ECAC
12/195	Tom McNamara	G	Univ. of Vermont, ECAC
13/200	Steve Roberts	D	Providence Coll., ECAC
13/201	Paul Dionne	D	Princeton Univ., ECAC
14/205	Cecil Luckern	RW	U. of New Hamp., ECAC
15/209	John Corriveau	RW	U. of New Hamp., ECAC
16/212	Tom Funke	LW	Fargo, Midwest Jr.

1976

Round/Overall	Name	Pos.	Team, League
1/6	Don Murdoch	RW	Medicine Hat, WHL
2/24	Dave Farrish	D	Sudbury, OHA
3/42	Mike McEwen	D	Toronto, OHA
4/60	Claude Periard	LW	Trois Rivieres, QMJHL
5/78	Doug Gaines	C	St. Catharines, OHA
6/96	Barry Scully	RW	Kingston, OHA
7/112	Remi Levesque	LW	Quebec, QMJHL

1977

Round/Overall	Name	Pos.	Team, League
1/8	Lucien DeBlois	RW	Sorel, QMJHL
1/13	Ron Duguay	C	Sudbury, OHA
2/26	Mike Keating	LW	St. Catharines, OHA
3/44	Steve Baker	G	Union College, Ind.
4/62	Mario Marois	D	Quebec, QMJHL
5/80	Benoit Gosselin	LW	Trois Rivieres, QMJHL
6/98	John Bethel	LW	Boston University, ECAC
7/116	Robert Sullivan	C	Chicoutimi, QMJHL
8/131	Lance Nethery	LW	Cornell University, ECAC
9/146	Alex Jeans	RW/C	Univ. of Toronto, OUAA
10/157	Peter Raps	LW	West. Mich. Univ., CCHA
11/164	Mike Brown	RW	West. Mich. Univ., CCHA
12/171	Mark Miler	LW	Univ. of Michigan, WCHA

1978

Round/Overall	Name	Pos.	Team, League
2/26	Don Maloney	LW	Kitchener, OHA
3/43	Ray Markham	C	Flin Flon, WHL
3/44	Dean Turner	D	Univ. of Michigan, WCHA
4/59	Dave Silk	RW	Boston University, ECAC
4/60	Andre Dore	D	Quebec, OHL
5/76	Mike McDougal	RW	Port Huron, IHL
6/93	Tom Laidlaw	D	North. Mich Univ., CCHA
7/110	Dan Clark	D	Milwaukee, IHL
8/127	Greg Kostenko	D	Ohio State Univ., CCHA
8/144	Brian McDavid	D	Sudbury, OHA
9/161	Mark Rodrigues	G	Yale University, ECAC
10/176	Steve Weeks	G	North. Mich. Univ., CCHA
11/192	Pierre Daigneault	LW	St. Laurent Coll., QUAA
12/206	Chris McLaughlin	D	Dartmouth Coll., ECAC
13/217	Todd Johnson	C	Boston University, ECAC
13/223	Dan McCarthy	C	Sudbury, OHA

1979

Round/Overall	Name	Pos.	Team, League
1/13	Doug Sulliman	LW	Kitchener, OHA
2/34	Ed Hospodar	D	Ottawa, OHA
4/76	Pat Conacher	C	Saskatoon, WHL
5/97	Dan Makuch	RW	Clarkson College, ECAC
6/118	Stan Adams	C	Niagara Falls, OHA

1980

Round/Overall	Name	Pos.	Team, League
1/14	Jim Malone	C	Toronto, OHA
2/35	Mike Allison	C	Sudbury, OHA
4/77	Kurt Kleinendorst	C	Providence Coll., ECAC
5/98	Scot Kleinendorst	D	Providence Coll., ECAC
6/119	Reijo Ruotsalainen	D	Karpat Finnish
7/140	Bob Scurfield	C	West. Mich. Univ., CCHA
8/161	Bart Wilson	D	Toronto, OHA
9/182	Chris Wray	RW	Boston College, ECAC
10/203	Anders Backstrom	D	Brynas, Swedish

1981

Round/Overall	Name	Pos.	Team, League
1/9	James Patrick	D	Prince Albert, SJHL
2/30	Jan Erixon	RW	Skelleftea, Swedish
3/50	Peter Sundstrom	LW	Bjorkloven, Swedish
3/51	Mark Morrison	C	Victoria, WHL
4/72	John Vanbiesbrouck	G	Sault Ste. Marie, OHA
6/114	Eric Magnuson	D	RPI, ECAC
7/135	Mike Guentzel	D	Coleraine H.S., (MN)
8/156	Ari Lahtenmaki	RW	IFK Helsinki, Finnish
9/177	Paul Reifenberger	RW/C	Anoka H.S., (MN)
10/198	Mario Proulx	G	Providence Coll., ECAC

1982

Round/Overall	Name	Pos.	Team, League
1/15	Chris Kontos	C	Toronto, OHL
2/36	Tomas Sandstrom	RW	Farjestads, Swedish
3/57	Corey Millen	C	Cloquet H.S., (MN)
4/78	Chris Jensen	C	Kelowna, BCJHL
6/120	Tony Granato	C	Northwood Prep, (NY)
7/141	Sergei Kapustin	LW	Central Red Army, USSR
8/160	Brian Glynn	C	Buffalo, NAJHL
8/162	Jan Karlsson	D	Kiruna, Swedish
9/183	Kelly Miller	C	Mich. St. Univ., CCHA
10/193	Simo Saarinen	D	IFK Helsinki, Finnish
10/204	Bob Lowes	C	Prince Albert, SJHL
11/225	Andy Otto	D	Northwood Prep, (NY)
12/246	Dwayne Robinson	D	U. of N. Hamp., Hockey E.

1983

Round/Overall	Name	Pos.	Team, League
1/12	Dave Gagner	C	Brantford, OHL
2/33	Randy Heath	LW	Portland, WHL
3/49	Vesa Salo	D	Lukko, Finnish
3/53	Gordon Walker	LW	Portland, WHL
4/73	Peter Andersson	D	Orebo IK, Swedish
5/93	Jim Andonoff	RW	Belleville, OHL
6/113	Bob Alexander	D	Rosemount H.S., (MN)
7/133	Steve Orth	C	St. Cloud Tech H.S., (MN)
8/153	Peter Marcov	LW	Welland, Ont. Jr. B
9/173	Paul Jerrard	D/RW	Notre Dame H.S., (Sask.)
11/213	Bryan Walker	D	Portland, WHL
12/233	Ulf Nilsson	G	Skelleftea, Sweden

RANGERS ALL-TIME DRAFT

1984

Round/Overall	Name	Pos.	Team, League
1/14	Terry Carkner	D	Peterborough, OHL
2/35	Raimo Helminen	C	Ilves, Finnish
4/77	Paul Broten	C	Roseau H.S., (MN)
5/98	Clark Donatelli	LW	Stratford, Ont. Jr. B
6/119	Kjell Samuelsson	D	Leksand, Swedish
7/140	Tom Hussey	LW	St. Andrew's H.S., (Ont.)
8/161	Brian Nelson	C	Wilmar H.S., (MN)
9/182	Ville Kentala	LW	IFK Helsinki, Finnish
9/188	Heinz Ehlers	C	Leksand, Swedish
10/202	Kevin Miller	C	Redford, NAJHL
11/223	Tom Lorentz	C	Brady H.S., (MN)
12/243	Scott Brower	G	Lloydminster, SJHL

1985

Round/Overall	Name	Pos.	Team, League
1/7	Ulf Dahlen	C	Ostersund, Swedish
2/28	Mike Richter	G	Northwood Prep, (NY)
3/49	San Lindstahl	G	Sodertalje, Swedish
4/70	Pat Janostin	D	Notre Dame H.S., (Sask.)
5/91	Brad Stepan	LW	Hastings H.S., (MN)
6/112	Brian McReynolds	D	Orillia, OHL
7/133	Neil Pilon	D	Kamloops, WHL
8/154	Larry Bernard	LW	Seattle, WHL
9/175	Stephane Brochu	D	Quebec, QMJHL
10/196	Steve Nemeth	C	Lethbridge, WHL
11/217	Robert Burakovski	LW	Leksand, Swedish
12/238	Rudy Poeschek	D	Kamloops, WHL

1986

Round/Overall	Name	Pos.	Team, League
1/9	Brian Leetch	D	Avon Old Farms HS, (CT)
3/51	Bret Walter	C	Univ. of Alberta, CWUAA
3/53	Shaun Clouston	RW	Univ. of Alberta, CWUAA
4/72	Mark Janssens	C	Regina, WHL
5/93	Jeff Bloemberg	D	North Bay, OHL
6/114	Darren Turcotte	D	North Bay, OHL
7/135	Robb Graham	RW	Guelph, OHL
8/156	Barry Chyzowski	C	St. Albert, AJHL
9/177	Pat Scanlon	LW/C	Cretin H.S., (MN)
10/198	Joe Ranger	D	London, OHL
11/219	Russell Parent	D	S. Winnipeg, MJHL
12/240	Soren True	LW	Skobakken, Denmark

1987

Round/Overall	Name	Pos.	Team, League
1/10	Jayson More	D	New Westminster, WHL
2/31	Daniel Lacroix	LW	Granby, QMJHL
3/46	Simon Gagne	RW	Laval, QMJHL
4/69	Michael Sullivan	C	Boston Univ., Hockey E.
5/94	Erik O'Borsky	C	Yale University, ECAC
6/115	Ludek Cajka	D	Dukla Jihlava, Czech.
7/136	Clint Thomas	D	RPI, ECAC
8/157	Chuck Wiegand	C	Essex Junction HS, (VT)
9/178	Eric Burrill	RW	Tartan H.S., (MN)
10/199	David Porter	LW	North. Mich. U., WCHA
11/205	Bret Barnett	RW	Wexford, Ont. Jr. B
11/220	Lance Marciano	D	Choate H.S., (CT)

1988

Round/Overall	Name	Pos.	Team, League
2/22	Troy Mallette	C	Sault Ste. Marie, OHL
2/26	Murray Duval	D	Spokane, WHL
4/68	Tony Amonte	RW	Thayer Academy, (MA)
5/99	Martin Bergeron	C	Drummondville, QMJHL
6/110	Dennis Vial	D	Hamilton, OHL
7/131	Mike Rosati	G	Hamilton, OHL
8/152	Eric Couvrette	LW	St. Jean, QMJHL
9/173	Patrick Forrest	D	St. Cloud State
10/194	Paul Cain	C	Cornwall, OHL
10/202	Eric Fenton	C	N. Yarmouth Prep, (MA).
11/215	Peter Fiorentino	D	Sault Ste. Marie, OHL
12/236	Keith Slifstein	RW	Choate H.S., (CT)

1989

Round/Overall	Name	Pos.	Team, League
1/20	Steven Rice	RW	Kitchene, OHL
2/40	Jason Prosofsky	RW	Medicine Hat, WHL
3/45	Rob Zamuner	C	Guelph, OHL
3/49	Louie DeBrusk	LW	London, OHL
4/67	Jim Cummins	RW	Michigan State, CCHA
5/88	Aaron Miller	D	Niagara Scenics, NAHL
6/118	Joby Messier	D	Michigan State, CCHA
7/139	Greg Leahy	C	Portland, WHL
8/160	Greg Spenrath	LW	Tri-City, WHL
9/181	Mark Bavis	C	Cushing Academy, USS
10/202	Roman Oksyuta	RW	Khimik Voskresensk, Rus.
11/223	Steve Locke	LW	Niagara Falls, OHL
12/244	Ken MacDermid	LW	Hull, QMJHL

1990

Round/Overall	Name	Pos.	Team, League
1/13	Michael Stewart	D	Michigan State, CCHA
2/34	Doug Weight	C	Lake Superior St., CCHA
3/55	John Vary	D	North Bay, OHL
4/69	Jeff Nielsen	RW	Grand Rapids H.S., (MN)
4/76	Rick Willis	LW	Pingree Prep, (MA)
5/85	Sergei Zubov	D	CSKA, Sov. Elite
5/99	Lubos Rob	C	Budejovice, Czech.
6/118	Jason Weinrich	D	Springfield H.S., (MA)
7/139	Bryan Lonsinger	D	Choate H.S., (CT)
8/160	Todd Hedlund	RW	Roseau H.S., (MN)
9/181	Andrew Silverman	D	Beverly H.S., (MA)
10/202	Jon Hillebrandt	G	Monona Grove H.S., (WI)
11/223	Brett Lievers	C	Wayzata H.S., (MN)
12/244	Sergei Nemchinov	C	Soviet Wings, Sov. Elite

1991

Round/Overall	Name	Pos.	Team, League
1/15	Alexei Kovalev	LW	Dynamo Moscow, USSR
2/37	Darcy Werenka	D	Lethbridge, WHL
5/96	Corey Machanic	D	U. of Vermont, USC
6/125	Fredrik Jax	RW	Leksand, Swe.
6/128	Barry Young	D	Sudbury, OHL
7/147	John Rushin	C	Kennedy, USS
8/169	Corey Hirsch	G	Kamloops, WHL
9/191	Vjateslav Uvaev	D	Spartkak Moscow, USSR
10/213	Jamie Ram	G	Mich. Tech Univ., USC
11/235	Vitali Chinakov	C	Torpedo Jaroslav, USSR
12/257	Brian Wiseman	C	Univ. of Michigan, USC

RANGERS ALL-TIME DRAFT

1992

Round/Overall	Name	Pos.	Team, League
1/24	Peter Ferraro	C/R	Waterloo, USJHL
2/48	Mattias Norstrom	D/L	AIK, Swe. El.
3/72	Eric Cairns	D/L	Detroit, OHL
4/85	Chris Ferraro	RW/R	Waterloo, USJHL
5/120	Dimitri Starostenko	RW/L	CSKA Moscow, CIS
6/144	Davide Dal Grande	D/L	Ottawa, Tier 2,
7/168	Matt Oates	LW/L	Miami of Ohio, WCHA
8/192	Mickey Elick	D	Univ. of Wisc., WCHA
9/216	Dan Brierley	D/L	Choate H.S., (CT)
10/240	Vladimir Vorobiev	RW/L	Met. Cherepovets, CIS

1993

Round/Overall	Name	Pos.	Team, League
1/8	Niklas Sundstrom	C	Modo, Swe. El.
2/34	Lee Sorochan	D	Lethbridge, WHL
3/61	Maxim Galanov	D	Lada Togilatti, CIS
4/86	Sergei Olympijev	C	Dynamo Minsk, CIS
5/112	Gary Roach	D	Sault Ste. Marie, OHL
6/138	Dave Trofimenkoff	G	Lethbridge, WHL
7/162	Serei Kondrashkin	RW	Cheropovets, CIS
7/164	Todd Marchant	C	Clarkson Univ., ECAC
8/190	Eddy Campbell	D	Omaha Jr. A, Tier 2
9/216	Ken Shepard	G	Oshawa, OHL
10/242	Andrei Kudinov	C	Chelyabinsk, CIS
11/261	Pavel Komarov	D	Nizhni Novgorod, CIS
11/268	Maxim Smelnitski	C	Chelyabinsk, CIS

1994

Round/Overall	Name	Pos.	Team, League
1/26	Dan Cloutier	G	Sault Ste. Marie, OHL
2/52	Rudolf Vercik	LW	Slovan Bratislava, Slovakia
3/78	Adam Smith	D	Tacoma, WHL
4/100	Alexander Korobolin	D	Chelyabinsk, Rus. El.
4/104	Sylvain Blouin	D	Laval, QMJHL
5/130	Martin Ethier	D	Beauport, QMJHL
6/135	Yuri Litvinov	C	Krylja Sovetov, Rus. El.
6/156	David Brosseau	C	Shawinigan, QMJHL
7/182	Alexei Lazarenko	W	CSKA, Rus. El.
8/208	Craig Anderson	D	Park Center H.S., MN
9/209	Vitali Yeremeyev	G	Ust-Kamenogorsk, Rus.
10/260	Radoslav Kropac	RW	Slovan Bratislava, Slovakia
11/267	Jamie Butt	LW	Tacoma, WHL
11/286	Kim Johnsson	D	Malmo, Swe. El.

Larry Pleau and the Rangers scouting staff at the 1994 NHL Entry Draft in Hartford.

RANGERS ALL-TIME REGISTER

(A complete listing of everyone who has played for the New York Rangers from 1926-27 through 1993-94)

Number	Name & Position	Yrs. Played	GP	G	A	PTS	PIM
A							
4	Taffy Abel (D)	1926-27—1928-29	110	10	6	16	147
19	Doug Adam (LW)	1949-50	4	0	1	1	0
17	Lloyd Ailsby (D)	1951-52	3	0	0	0	2
15	Clint Albright (C)	1948-49	59	14	5	19	19
17	George Allen (D)	1938-39	19	6	6	12	10
14	Mike Allison (C)	1980-81—1985-86	266	63	102	165	297
18	Bill Allum (D)	1940-41	1	0	1	1	0
33, 31	Tony Amonte (RW)	1991-92—1993-94	234	84	99	183	135
36	Glenn Anderson (RW)	1993-94	12	4	2	6	12
24	Kent-Erik Andersson (RW)	1982-83—1983-84	134	13	35	48	22
5	Peter Andersson (D)	1992-93—1993-94	39	5	12	17	20
25	Steve Andrascik**(RW)	1971-72	**1	0	0	0	0
18	Paul Andrea (RW)	1965-66	4	1	1	2	0
17	Lou Angotti (C)	1964-65—1965-66	91	11	10	21	22
20	Hub Anslow (LW)	1947-48	2	0	0	0	0
6	Syl Apps (C)	1970-71	31	1	2	3	11
10	Dave Archibald (C)	1989-90	19	2	3	5	6
16	Oscar Asmundson (C)	1932-33—1933-34	94	7	16	23	28
9	Walt Atanas (RW)	1944-45	49	13	8	21	40
24	Ron Attwell (C)	1967-68	4	0	0	0	2
10	Oscar Aubuchon (LW)	1943-44	38	16	12	28	4
6	Don Awrey (D)	1977-78	78	2	8	10	38
2	Thomas Ayres (D)	1935-36	28	0	4	4	38
B							
15	Pete Babando (LW)	1952-53	29	4	4	8	4
21	Mike Backman (RW)	1981-82—1983-84	18	1	6	7	18
6	Bill Baker (D)	1982-83	70	4	14	18	64
11, 22, 8, 17	Dave Balon (LW)	1959-60—1962-63; 1968-69—1971-72	361	99	113	212	284
25	Jeff Bandura (D)	1980-81	2	0	1	1	0
11	Dave Barr (C)	1983-84	6	0	0	0	2
22, 14, 17	Jimmy Bartlett (LW)	1955-56; 1958-59—1959-60	126	19	14	33	174
	Cliff Barton (RW)	1939-40	3	0	0	0	0
12, 10, 9, 16,	Andy Bathgate (RW)	1952-53—1963-64	719	272	457	729	444
16	Frank Bathgate (C)	1952-53	2	0	0	0	2
21	Frank Beaton (LW)	1978-79—1979-80	25	1	1	2	43
5, 3	Barry Beck (D)	1979-80—1985-86	415	66	173	239	775
23	John Bednarski (D)	1974-75—1976-77	99	2	18	20	114
19	Danny Belisle (RW)	1960-61	4	2	0	2	0
29	Bruce Bell (D)	1987-88	13	1	2	3	8
2	Harry Bell (D)	1946-47	1	0	1	1	0
20, 5	Joe Bell (LW)	1942-43; 1946-47	62	8	9	17	18
15	Lin Bend (C)	1942-43	8	3	1	4	2
20	Curt Bennett (C)	1972-73	16	0	1	1	11
17, 27	Ric Bennett (LW)	1989-90—1991-92	15	1	1	2	13
14	Doug Bentley (LW)	1953-54	20	2	10	12	2
22, 10	Max Bentley (C)	1953-54	57	14	18	32	15
24	Gordon Berenson (C)	1966-67—1967-68	49	2	6	8	4
23	Jeff Beukeboom (D)	1991-92—1993-94	206	11	35	46	445
25	Nick Beverley (D)	1974-75—1976-77	126	4	23	27	67
6	Bob Blackburn (D)	1968-69	11	0	0	0	0
23	Don Blackburn (LW)	1969-70—1970-71	4	0	0	0	0
18	Mike Blaisdell (RW)	1983-84—1984-85	48	6	6	12	42
38	Jeff Bloemberg (D)	1988-89—1991-92	43	3	6	9	25
6, 3	Tim Bothwell (D)	1978-79—1981-82	62	4	10	14	32
21	Dick Bouchard (RW)	1954-55	1	0	0	0	0
17, 7	Frank Boucher (C)	1926-27—1937-38; 1943-44	533	152	261	413	114
2, 12	Leo Bourgault (D)	1926-27—1930-31	155	17	11	28	219
29	Phil Bourque	1992-93—1993-94	71	6	15	21	47
27	Paul Boutilier	1987-88	4	0	1	1	6

**Denotes playoff statistics

RANGERS ALL-TIME REGISTER

Number	Name & Position	Yrs. Played	GP	G	A	PTS	PIM
15, 2	Jack Bownass (D)	1958-59—1959-60; 1961-62	76	3	7	10	58
8	William Boyd (RW)	1926-27—1928-29	95	8	1	9	56
15	Doug Brennan (D)	1931-32—1933-34	123	9	7	16	152
18	John Brenneman (LW)	1964-65—1965-66	33	3	3	6	20
32	Stephane Brochu (D)	1988-89	1	0	0	0	0
13	Bob Brooke (C)	1983-84—1986-87	175	35	36	71	214
37	Paul Broten (RW)	1989-90—1992-93	194	27	33	60	194
4	Arnie Brown (D)	1964-65—1970-71	460	33	98	131	545
16	Harold Brown (RW)	1945-46	13	2	1	3	2
4, 21	Larry Brown (D)	1969-70—1970-71	46	1	4	5	18
14	Stanley Brown (LW)	1926-27	24	6	2	8	14
17, 24	Jeff Brubaker (LW)	1987-88	31	2	0	2	78
12	Glenn Brydson (RW)	1935-36	30	4	12	16	9
19	Bucky Buchanan (C)	1948-49	2	0	0	0	0
4	Hy Buller (D)	1951-52—1953-54	179	22	55	77	209
14	Kelly Burnett (C)	1952-53	3	1	0	1	0
24, 27	Gary Burns (LW)	1980-81—1981-82	11	2	2	4	18
15	Norman Burns (C)	1941-42	11	0	4	4	2
17, 20	Jerry Butler (RW)	1972-73—1974-75	112	24	26	50	130
15	Jerry Byers (LW)	1977-78	7	2	1	3	0

C

Number	Name & Position	Yrs. Played	GP	G	A	PTS	PIM
5, 2	Larry Cahan (D)	1956-57—1958-59; 1961-62—1964-65	303	19	39	58	337
14	Patsy Callighen (D)	1927-28	36	0	0	0	32
14	Angus Cameron (C)	1942-43	35	8	11	19	0
38	Terry Carkner (D)	1986-87	52	2	13	15	120
11	Bob Carpenter (C)	1986-87	28	2	8	10	20
9, 20	Gene Carr (C)	1971-72—1973-74	138	18	23	41	90
11	Lorne Carr (RW)	1933-34	14	0	0	0	0
14	Gene Carrigan (C)	1930-31	33	2	0	2	13
18	Bill Carse (C)	1938-39	1	0	1	1	0
	Gerald Carson (C)	1928-29	14	0	0	0	5
26	Jay Caufield (RW)	1986-87	13	2	1	3	45
	Bill Chalmers (C)	1953-54	1	0	0	0	0
36	Todd Charlesworth (D)	1989-90	7	0	0	0	6
11	Rick Chartraw (D)	1982-83—1983-84	30	2	2	4	41
6	Bob Crystal (D)	1953-54—1954-55	132	11	14	25	112
15	Hank Ciesla (C)	1957-58—1958-59	129	8	20	28	37
18, 6	Joe Cirella (D)	1990-91—1992-93	141	7	18	25	258
32	Dan Clark (D)	1978-79	4	0	1	1	6
6	Bruce Cline (RW)	1956-57	30	2	3	5	10
15	Bill Collins (RW)	1975-76	50	4	4	8	38
5, 16	Mac Colville (RW)	1935-36—1941-42; 1945-46—1946-47	353	71	104	175	132
6	Neil Colville (C)	1935-36—1941-42; 1944-45—1948-49	464	99	166	265	213
16	Les Colwill (RW)	1958-59	69	7	6	13	16
15, 5	Jim Conacher (C)	1951-52—1952-53	33	2	5	7	4
6, 16	Charles Conacher, Jr. (LW)	1954-55—1955-56	93	21	18	39	22
28	Pat Conacher (C)	1979-80; 1982-83	22	0	6	6	8
15	Bert Connolly (LW)	1934-35—1935-36	72	12	13	25	33
20	Cam Connor (RW)	1979-80—1982-83	28	1	6	7	81
5	Bill Cook (RW)	1926-27—1936-37	475	228	138	366	386
6	Fred "Bun" Cook (LW)	1926-27—1935-36	433	154	139	293	436
10	Hal Cooper (RW)	1944-45	8	0	0	0	2
11, 12	Joe Cooper (D)	1935-36—1937-38; 1946-47	154	5	13	18	136
2, 17	Art Coulter (D)	1935-36—1941-42	287	18	67	85	332
18	Danny Cox (LW)	1933-34	15	5	0	5	2
32	Bob Crawford (RW)	1985-86—1986-87	14	1	2	3	12
16	Dave Creighton (C)	1955-56—1957-58	210	55	87	142	125
14	Brian Cullen (C)	1959-60—1960-61	106	19	40	59	12
17	Ray Cullen (C)	1965-66	8	1	3	4	0
19	Bob Cunningham (C)	1960-61—1961-62	4	0	1	1	0
2	Ian Cushenan (D)	1959-60	17	0	1	1	12
22	Paul Cyr (LW)	1987-88—1988-89	41	4	13	17	43

RANGERS ALL-TIME REGISTER

Number	Name & Position	Yrs. Played	GP	G	A	PTS	PIM
		D					
16, 9	Ulf Dahlen (LW)	1987-88—1989-90	189	71	60	131	106
5	Hank DiAmore (C)	1943-44	4	1	0	1	2
4	Gordon Davidson (D)	1942-43—1943-44	51	3	6	9	8
8	Ken Davies** (C)	1947-48	**1	0	0	0	0
16	Billy Dea (LW)	1953-54	14	1	1	2	2
35, 23, 23, 32	Lucien DeBlois (RW)	1977-78—1979-80; 1986-97—1988-89	326	57	79	136	297
16	Val Delory (LW)	1948-49	1	0	0	0	0
24	Ab DeMarco, Jr. (D)	1969-70—1972-73	104	8	21	29	19
15	Ab DeMarco, Sr. (D)	1943-44—1946-47	182	67	86	153	36
5	Tony Demers (RW)	1943-44	1	0	0	0	0
14	Jean Paul Denis (RW)	1946-47; 1949-50	10	0	2	2	2
11	Victor Desjardins (C)	1931-32	48	3	3	6	16
2	Tommy Dewar (D)	1943-44	9	0	2	2	4
14	Herb Dickenson (LW)	1951-52—1952-53	48	18	17	35	10
4	Bob Dill (D)	1943-44—1944-45	76	15	15	30	135
8, 15	Cecil Dillon (RW)	1930-31—1938-39	409	160	121	281	93
9, 11	Wayne Dillon (C)	1975-76—1977-78	216	43	66	109	58
16	Marcel Dionne (C)	1986-87—1988-89	118	42	56	98	80
44	Per Djoos (D)	1991-92—1992-93	56	2	19	21	42
3	Gary Doak (D)	1971-72	49	1	10	11	2
28	Tie Domi (RW)	1990-91—1992-93	82	5	4	9	526
22	Mike Donnelly (LW)	1986-87—1987-88	22	3	3	6	8
27, 2, 33	Andre Dore (D)	1978-79—1982-83; 1984-85	139	8	38	46	153
8	Jim Dorey (D)	1971-72	1	0	0	0	0
16	Jim Drummond (D)	1944-45	2	0	0	0	0
9	Dick Duff (LW)	1963-64—1964-65	43	7	13	20	22
6	Marc Dufour (LW)	1963-64—1964-65	12	1	0	1	2
44, 10	Ron Duguay (C)	1977-78—1982-83; 1986-87—1987-88	499	164	176	340	370
19	Craig Duncanson (RW)	1992-93	3	0	1	1	0
25	Andre Dupont (D)	1970-71	7	1	2	3	21
18	Duke Dutkowski (D)	1933-34	29	0	3	3	16
	Henry Dyck (LW)	1943-44	1	0	0	0	0
		E					
2	Frank Eddolis (D)	1947-48—1951-52	260	18	34	52	88
6	Pat Egan (D)	1949-50—1950-51	140	10	21	31	120
20	Jack Egers (RW)	1969-70—1971-72; 1973-74	111	13	14	27	72
20	Jan Erixon (LW)	1983-84—1992-93	556	57	159	216	167
77, 12, 5	Phil Esposito (C)	1975-76—1980-81	422	184	220	404	263
5, 30, 3	Jack Evans (D)	1948-49—1951-52; 1953-54—1957-58	407	15	38	53	670
5	Bill Ezinicki (RW)	1954-55	16	2	2	4	22
		F					
24	Trevor Fahey (LW)	1964-65	1	0	0	0	0
10, 14	Bill Fairbairn (RW)	1968-69—1976-77	536	138	224	362	161
3	Dave Farrish (D)	1976-77—1978-79	217	6	41	47	225
32	Tony Feltrin (D)	1985-86	10	0	0	0	21
42, 25	Paul Fenton (LW)	1986-87	8	0	0	0	2
41	Peter Fiorentino (D)	1991-92	1	0	0	0	0
12	Dunc Fisher (RW)	1947-48—1950-51	142	21	37	58	82
6	Sandy Fitzpatrick (C)	1964-65	4	0	0	0	2
9	Reg Fleming (LW)	1965-66—1968-69	241	50	49	99	540
18	Gerry Foley (RW)	1956-57—1957-58	137	9	14	23	91
14	Val Fonteyne (LW)	1963-64—1964-65	96	7	19	26	6
8	Lou Fontinato (D)	1954-55—1960-61	418	22	57	79	939
4	Harry "Yip" Foster (D)	1929-30	31	0	0	0	10
18	Herb Foster (LW)	1940-41; 1947-48	5	1	0	1	5
22	Nick Fotiu (LW)	1976-77—1978-79; 1980-81—1984-85	455	41	62	103	970
6	Archie Fraser (C)	1943-44	3	0	1	1	0
8, 38	Robbie Ftorek (C)	1981-82—1984-85	170	32	55	87	112

**Denotes playoff statistics

RANGERS ALL-TIME REGISTER

Number	Name & Position	Yrs. Played	GP	G	Statistics A	PTS	PIM
		G					
4	Bill Gadsby (D)	1954-55—1960-61	457	58	212	270	411
9	Dave Gagner (C)	1984-85—1986-87	80	11	16	27	47
8	Dutch Gainor (D)	1931-32	46	3	9	12	9
17, 12	Cal Gardner (C)	1945-46—1947-48	126	28	36	64	103
15	Dudley Garrett (D)	1942-43	23	1	1	2	18
22	Mike Gartner (RW)	1989-90—1993-94	322	173	113	286	231
9	Fern Gauthier (RW)	1943-44	33	14	10	24	0
7, 10	Guy Gendron (LW)	1955-56—1957-58; 1961-62	272	38	41	79	217
5	Bernie Geoffrion (RW)	1966-67—1967-68	117	22	41	63	53
17	Greg Gilbert (LW)	1993-94	76	4	11	15	29
6	Curt Giles (D)	1986-87—1987-88	74	2	17	19	60
7, 16	Rod Gilbert (RW)	1960-61—1977-78	1065	406	615	1021	508
16	Randy Gilhen (C)	1991-92—1992-93	73	10	9	19	22
6	Jere Gillis (LW)	1980-81—1981-82	61	13	19	32	20
8	Howie Glover (RW)	1963-64	25	1	0	1	9
19	Pete Geogan (D)	1961-62	7	0	2	2	6
12	Bill Goldsworthy (RW)	1976-77—1977-78	68	10	13	23	55
14	Leroy Goldsworthy (D)	1929-30	44	4	1	5	16
11	Hank Goldup (LW)	1942-43—1945-46	103	34	46	80	69
16	Billy Gooden (LW)	1942-43—1943-44	53	9	11	20	15
19, 16	Jack Gordon (RW)	1948-49—1950-51	36	3	10	13	0
11	Benoit Gosselin (LW)	1977-78	7	0	0	0	33
9, 20	Phil Goyette (C)	1963-64—1968-69; 1971-72	397	98	231	329	51
18, 39	Tony Granato (RW)	1988-89—1989-90	115	43	45	88	217
23	Norm Gratton (LW)	1971-72	3	0	1	1	0
9, 11	Adam Graves (LW)	1991-92—1993-94	248	114	89	203	414
2	Alex Gray (RW)	1927-28	43	7	0	7	28
4	Ron Greschner (D)	1974-75—1989-90	982	179	431	610	1226
5	Jari Gronstrand (D)	1987-88	62	3	11	14	63
2	Jocelyn Guevremont (D)	1979-80	20	2	5	7	6
20, 12	Aldo Guidolin (D)	1952-53—1955-56	182	9	15	24	117
		H					
11	Vic Hadfield (LW)	1961-62—1973-74	839	262	310	572	1036
19	Wayne Hall (LW)	1960-61	4	0	0	0	0
6, 25	Allan Hamilton (D)	1965-66; 1967-68—1969-70	81	0	5	5	54
6	Ken Hammond (D)	1988-89	3	0	0	0	0
22	Ted Hampson (C)	1960-61—1962-63	183	14	40	54	16
2, 6	John Hanna (D)	1958-59—1960-61	177	6	26	32	204
6	Pat Hannigan (RW)	1960-61—1961-62	109	19	23	42	58
14	Mark Hardy (D)	1987-88—1992-93	284	7	52	59	409
3	Ron Harris (D)	1972-73—1975-76	146	6	30	36	64
17	Ed Harrison (LW)	1950-51	4	1	0	1	2
18	Mike Hartman (RW)	1992-93—1993-94	38	1	1	2	76
2	Doug Harvey (D)	1961-62—1963-64	151	10	61	71	144
12	Gordie Haworth (C)	1952-53	2	0	1	1	0
19	Mark Heaslip (RW)	1976-77—1977-78	48	6	10	16	65
26, 40	Randy Heath (LW)	1984-85—1985-86	13	2	4	6	15
12	Andy Hebenton (RW)	1956-57—1962-63	560	177	191	368	75
15	Anders Hedberg (RW)	1978-79—1984-85	465	172	225	397	144
23	Bill Heindl (LW)	1972-73	4	1	0	1	0
3, 14	Ott Heller (D)	1931-32—1945-46	647	55	176	231	465
23	Raimo Helminen (C)	1985-86—1986-87	87	12	34	46	12
21	Camille Henry (C)	1953-54—1954-55; 1956-57—1964-65; 1967-68	637	256	222	478	78
18	Wally Hergesheimer (RW)	1951-52—1955-56; 1958-59	310	112	77	189	94
15	Orville Heximer (LW)	1929-30	19	1	0	1	4
6	Bryan Hextall, Jr. (C)	1962-63	21	0	2	2	10
12, 19	Bryan Hextall, Sr. (RW)	1936-37—1943-44; 1945-46—1947-48	449	187	175	362	227
21	Dennis Hextall (C)	1967-68—1968-69	13	1	4	5	25
17, 12	Bill Hicke (RW)	1964-65—1966-67	137	18	33	51	58
28	Greg Hickey (LW)	1977-78	1	0	0	0	0

RANGERS ALL-TIME REGISTER

Number	Name & Position	Yrs. Played	GP	G	A	PTS	PIM
16, 14	Pat Hickey (LW)	1975-76—1979-80;					
24		1981-82	370	128	129	257	216
14	Ike Hildebrand (RW)	1953-54	31	6	7	13	12
8, 18	Dutch Hiller (LW)	1937-38—1940-41;					
		1943-44	200	49	70	119	116
16	Jim Hiller (RW)	1993-94	2	0	0	0	7
2	Wayne Hillman (D)	1964-65—1967-68	219	6	42	48	185
88	Ken Hodge (RW)	1976-77—1977-78	96	23	45	68	51
22	Jerry Holland (LW)	1974-75—1975-76	37	8	4	12	6
17	Greg Holst (C)	1975-76—1977-78	11	0	0	0	0
6	Miloslav Horava (D)	1988-89—1990-91	79	5	17	22	38
3	Tim Horton (D)	1969-70—1970-71	93	3	23	26	73
6, 11	Bronco Horvath (C)	1955-56—1956-57;					
		1962-63	114	20	34	54	78
23	Ed Hospodar (D)	1979-80—1980-81	122	8	23	31	442
16, 11	Vic Howe (RW)	1950-51;					
		1953-54—1954-55	33	3	4	7	10
3	Harry Howell (D)	1952-53—1968-69	1160	82	263	345	1147
21, 5	Ron Howell (D-F)	1954-55—1955-56	4	0	0	0	4
27	Willie Huber (D)	1983-84—1987-88	238	28	58	86	284
15	Mike Hudson (C)	1993-94	48	4	7	11	47
28	John Hughes** (D)	1980-81	**3	0	1	1	6
21	Jody Hull (RW)	1990-91—1991-92	50	5	8	13	12
5	Fred Hunt (RW)	1944-45	44	13	9	22	6
25	Larry Huras (D)	1976-77	1	0	0	0	0
32	Mike Hurlbut (D)	1992-93	23	1	8	9	16
11	Ron Hutchinson (C)	1960-61	9	0	0	0	0

I

Number	Name & Position	Yrs. Played	GP	G	A	PTS	PIM
10	Earl Ingarfield (C)	1958-59—1966-67	527	122	142	264	201
4	Ron Ingram (D)	1963-64—1964-65	19	1	3	4	10
27	Ted Irvine (LW)	1969-70—1974-75	378	86	91	177	438
2	Ivan Irwin (D)	1953-54—1955-56;					
		1957-58	151	2	26	28	214

J

Number	Name & Position	Yrs. Played	GP	G	A	PTS	PIM
29	Don Jackson (D)	1986-87	22	1	0	1	91
14	Jeff Jackson (LW)	1986-87	9	5	1	6	15
14	Jimmy Jamieson (D)	1943-44	1	0	1	1	0
15, 47, 27	Mark Janssens (C)	1987-88—1991-92	157	14	15	29	338
28	Doug Jarrett (D)	1975-76—1976-77	54	0	4	4	23
8	Pierre Jarry (LW)	1971-72	34	3	3	6	20
10, 17	Larry Jeffrey (LW)	1967-68—1968-69	122	3	10	13	27
15, 39	Chris Jensen (RW)	1985-86—1987-88	53	7	11	18	23
2	Joe Jerwa (D)	1930-31	33	4	7	11	72
6, 5	Don Johns (D)	1960-61;					
		1962-63—1964-65	148	2	21	23	70
3	Ching Johnson (D)	1926-27—1936-37	403	38	48	86	798
24	Jim Johnson (C)	1964-65—1966-67	8	1	0	1	0
17, 14	Ed Johnstone (RW)	1975-76;					
		1977-78—1982-83	371	109	125	234	319
6	Bob Jones (LW)	1968-69	2	0	0	0	0
16	Bing Juckes (LW)	1947-48; 1949-50	16	2	1	3	6
19	Bill Juzda (D)	1940-41—1941-42;					
		1945-46—1947-48	187	11	25	36	178

K

Number	Name & Position	Yrs. Played	GP	G	A	PTS	PIM
11, 15	Bob Kabel (C)	1959-60—1960-61	48	5	13	18	34
17	Alex Kaleta (LW)	1948-49—1950-51	181	32	37	69	84
26	Sheldon Kannegiesser (D)	1972-73—1973-74	12	1	3	4	6
25	Alexander Karpovtsev (D)	1993-94	67	3	15	18	58
21	Mike Keating (LW)	1977-78	1	0	0	0	0
10, 11	Butch Keeling (LW)	1928-29—1937-38	455	136	55	191	250
6	Ralph Keller (D)	1962-63	3	1	0	1	6
6	Dean Kennedy (D)	1988-89	16	0	1	1	40
16	Bill Kenny (D)	1930-31	6	0	0	0	0
12	Tim Kerr (RW)	1991-92	32	7	11	18	12
19, 12	Kris King (LW)	1989-90—1992-93	249	27	33	60	733
25	Steven King (RW)	1992-93	24	7	5	12	16

RANGERS ALL-TIME REGISTER

Number	Name & Position	Yrs. Played	GP	G	A	PTS	PIM
16	Bobby Krik (RW)	1937-38	39	4	8	12	14
6	Bob Kirkpatrick (C)	1942-43	49	12	12	24	6
11, 16	Kelly Kisio (C)	1986-87—1990-91	336	110	195	305	415
3	Scot Kleinendorst (D)	1982-83—1983-84	53	2	11	13	43
26	Joe Kocur (RW)	1990-91—1993-94	192	12	11	23	417
23	Chris Kontos (C)	1982-83—1984-85	78	12	16	28	65
6	Mike Korney (RW)	1978-79	18	0	1	1	18
16	Dick Kotanen (D)	1948-49; 1950-51	2	0	0	0	0
24	Chris Kotsopoulos (D)	1980-81	54	4	12	16	153
27	Alexei Kovalev (RW)	1992-93—1993-94	141	43	51	94	233
6	Steve Kraftcheck (D)	1951-52—1952-53	127	10	18	28	75
12	Joe Krol (LW)	1936-37; 1938-39	2	1	1	2	0
22	Jim Krulicki (LW)	1970-71	27	0	2	2	6
15	Dolph Kukulowicz (C)	1952-53—1953-54	4	1	0	1	0
18	Stu Kulak (RW)	1986-87	3	0	0	0	0
19, 14	Eddie Kullman (RW)	1947-48—1948-49; 1950-51—1953-54	343	56	70	126	298
17	Alan Kuntz (LW)	1941-42; 1945-46	45	10	12	22	12
25	Orland Kurtenbach (C)	1960-61; 1966-67—1969-70	198	30	61	91	191
	Larry Kwong	1947-48	1	0	0	0	0
19	Bill Kyle (C)	1949-50—1950-51	3	0	3	3	0
156	Gus Kyle (D)	1949-50—1950-51	134	5	8	13	235
19	Nick Kypreos (LW)	1993-94	46	3	5	8	102

L

Number	Name & Position	Yrs. Played	GP	G	A	PTS	PIM
15	Michel Labadie (RW)	1952-53	3	0	0	0	0
18, 19	Gordon Labossiere (C)	1963-64—1964-65	16	0	0	0	12
17	Max Labovitch (RW)	1943-44	5	0	0	0	4
20	Guy Labrie (D)	1944-45	27	2	2	4	14
32	Daniel Lacroix (C)	1993-94	4	0	0	0	0
10	Guy Lafleur (RW)	1988-89	67	18	29	45	12
15	Jason Lafreneiere (C)	1988-89	38	8	16	24	6
2	Tom Laidlaw (D)	1980-81—1986-87	510	20	99	119	561
14	Lane Lambert (RW)	1986-87	18	2	2	4	33
21, 16, 22	Jean Paul Lamirande (D)	1946-47—1947-48; 1949-50	48	5	5	10	26
16	Jack Lancien (D)	1946-47—1947-48; 1949-50—1950-51	63	1	5	6	35
12	Myles Lane (D)	1928-29	24	2	0	2	24
4	Al Langlois (D)	1961-62—1963-64	173	13	34	47	184
10	Edgar Laprade (C)	1945-46—1954-55	500	108	172	280	42
28	Steve Larmer (RW)	1993-94	68	21	39	60	41
20	Claude Larose (LW)	1979-80—1981-82	25	4	7	11	2
10, 24, 10	Pierre Larouche (RW)	1983-84—1987-88	253	123	120	243	59
19	Norm Larson (RW)	1946-47	1	0	0	0	0
44	Jim Latos (RW)	1988-89	1	0	0	0	0
18	Phil Latreille (RW)	1960-61	4	0	0	0	2
39	Peter Laviolette (D)	1988-89	12	0	0	0	6
17	Brian Lawton (C)	1988-89	30	7	10	17	39
2	Hal Laycoe (D)	1945-46—1946-47	75	1	14	15	31
24	Jim Leavins (D)	1986-87	4	0	1	1	4
18	Al Lebrun (D)	1960-61; 1965-66	6	0	2	2	4
18	Albert Leduc (D)	1933-34	10	0	0	0	6
30	Grant Ledyard (D)	1984-85—1985-86	69	10	21	31	73
2	Brian Leetch (D)	1987-88—1993-94	437	103	343	446	237
5	Roger Leger (D)	1943-44	7	1	2	3	2
4	Randy Legge (D)	1972-73	12	0	2	2	2
28	Mikko Leinonen (C)	1981-82—1983-84	159	31	77	108	69
14, 9	Real Lemieux (LW)	1969-70; 1973-74	62	4	6	10	51
18	Tony Leswick (LW)	1945-46—1950-51	368	113	89	202	420
14	Joe Levandoski (RW)	1946-47	8	1	1	2	0
11	Alex Levinsky (D)	1934-35	21	0	4	4	6
22	Danny Lewicki (LW)	1954-55—1957-58	280	76	90	166	107
27	Dale Lewis (LW)	1975-76	8	0	0	0	0
26	Igor Liba (LW)	1988-89	10	2	5	7	15
6	Doug Lidster (D)	1993-94	34	0	2	2	33
28	Bill Lochead (LW)	1979-80	7	0	0	0	4
25	Jim Lorentz (C)	1971-72	5	0	0	0	0
4	Kevin Lowe (D)	1992-93—1993-94	120	8	26	34	128

RANGERS ALL-TIME REGISTER

Number	Name & Position	Yrs. Played	GP	G	A	PTS	PIM
19	Odie Lowe (C)	1948-49—1949-50	4	1	1	2	0
14	Don Luce (C)	1969-70—1970-71	21	1	3	4	8
9	Pentti Lund (RW)	1948-49—1950-51	182	36	41	77	38

M

Number	Name & Position	Yrs. Played	GP	G	A	PTS	PIM
2, 8, 14	Kilby MacDonald (LW)	1939-40—1940-41; 1943-44—1944-45	151	36	34	70	47
14	Parker MacDonald (LW)	1956-57—1957-58; 1959-60	119	15	18	33	54
19, 17	Hub Macey (LW)	1941-42—1942-43	18	6	8	14	0
12, 14	Bruce MacGregor (RW)	1970-71—1973-74	220	62	73	135	44
37	Norm Maciver (D)	1986-87—1988-89	66	9	26	35	28
11	Bill MacKenzie (D)	1934-35	20	1	0	1	10
2	Reg Mackey (D)	1926-27	34	0	0	0	16
14	Mickey Mackintosh (F)	1952-53	4	0	0	0	4
26	Brian MacLellan (LW)	1985-86	51	11	21	32	47
12	Bob MacMillan (RW)	1974-75	22	1	2	3	4
6	Al MacNeil (D)	1966-67	58	0	4	4	44
14	Craig MacTavish (C)	1993-94	12	4	2	6	11
2	John Mahaffy (C)	1943-44	28	9	20	29	0
16, 26	Troy Mallette (LW)	1989-90—1990-91	150	25	26	51	557
26	Dave Maloney (D)	1974-75—1984-85	605	70	225	295	1113
12	Don Maloney (LW)	1978-79—1988-89	653	195	307	502	739
5	Felix Mancuso (RW)	1942-43	21	6	8	14	13
16	Jack Mann (C)	1943-44—1944-45	9	3	4	7	0
19	Ray Manson (LW)	1948-49	1	0	1	1	0
14	Henry Maracle (F)	1930-31	11	1	3	4	4
39	Todd Marchant (C)	1993-94	1	0	0	0	0
42	Dave Marcinyshyn	1992-93	2	0	0	0	2
29	Ray Markham (C)	1979-80	14	1	1	2	21
25	Mario Marios (D)	1977-78—1980-81	166	15	52	67	356
6	Gilles Marotte (D)	1973-74—1975-76	180	10	66	76	131
4	Bert Marshall (D)	1972-73	8	0	0	0	14
22	Don Marshall (LW)	1963-64—1969-70	479	129	141	270	40
17	Clare Martin (D)	1951-52	15	0	1	1	8
16	Charles Mason (RW)	1934-35—1935-36	74	6	14	20	44
32	Stephane Matteau (LW)	1993-94	12	4	3	7	2
26	Brad Maxwell (D)	1986-87	9	0	4	4	6
34	Jim Mayer (RW)	1979-80	4	0	0	0	0
12	Sam McAdam (LW)	1930-31	4	0	0	0	0
20	Dunc McCallum (D)	1965-66	2	0	0	0	2
28	Dan McCarthy (C)	1980-81	5	4	0	4	4
9, 39	Rob McClanahan (LW)	1981-82—1983-84	141	33	43	76	77
21	Bill McCreary (LW)	1953-54—1954-55	10	0	2	2	2
19	Bill McDonagh (LW)	1949-50	4	0	0	0	2
14	Bob McDonald (RW)	1943-44	1	0	0	0	0
6	Bucko McDonald (D)	1943-44—1944-45	81	7	15	22	14
11	John McDonald (RW)	1943-44	43	10	9	19	6
22, 28	Mike McDougal (RW)	1978-79; 1980-81	3	0	0	0	0
6, 27	Mike McEwen (D)	1976-77—1979-80; 1985-86	242	42	92	134	141
18	Sandy McGregor (RW)	1963-64	2	0	0	0	2
14	John McIntyre (C)	1992-93	11	1	0	1	4
25	Tony McKegney (RW)	1986-87	64	29	17	46	56
17	Don McKenney (C)	1962-63—1963-64	76	17	33	50	10
14	John McKenzie (RW)	1965-66	35	6	5	11	36
14, 19	Jack MacLeod (RW)	1945-50—1952-53; 1954-55	106	14	23	37	10
18, 12							
4, 6	Mike McMahon (D)	1963-64—1965-66; 1971-72	61	0	13	13	50
21, 37	George McPhee (LW)	1982-83—1986-87	109	21	24	45	247
16	Brian McReynolds (C)	1990-91	1	0	0	0	0
12	Dick Meissner (RW)	1963-64—1964-65	36	3	5	8	0
30	Larry Melnyk (D)	1985-86—1987-88	133	4	21	25	281
28	Joby Messier (D)	1992-93—1993-94	15	0	2	2	6
11	Mark Messier (C)	1991-92—1993-94	230	86	196	282	224
18, 12, 9	Larry Mickey (RW)	1965-66—1967-68	19	0	2	2	2
11	Nick Mickoski (LW)	1947-48—1954-55	362	88	93	181	129
9	Rick Middleton (RW)	1974-75—1975-76	124	46	44	90	33
12	Jim Mikol (D)	1964-65	30	1	3	4	6

RANGERS ALL-TIME REGISTER

Number	Name & Position	Yrs. Played	GP	G	A	PTS	PIM
4	Hib Milks (LW)	1931-32	45	0	4	4	12
32, 23	Corey Millen (C)	1989-90—1991-92	19	4	5	9	12
40, 10	Kelly Miller (RW)	1984-85—1986-87	117	19	36	55	76
32, 26	Kevin Miller (RW)	1988-89—1990-91	103	20	37	57	67
24	Warren Miller (RW)	1979-80	55	7	6	13	17
21	Bill Moe (D)	1944-45—1948-49	261	11	42	53	163
5	Lloyd Mohns (D)	1943-44	1	0	0	0	0
24	Randy Moller (D)	1989-90—1991-92	164	7	38	49	378
16	Larry Molyneaux (D)	1937-38—1938-39	45	0	1	1	20
15	Hartland Monahan (RW)	1974-75	6	0	1	1	4
40	Jayson More (D)	1988-89	1	0	0	0	0
11	Howie Morenz (C)	1935-36	19	2	5	7	6
8	Elwin Morris (D)	1948-49	18	0	1	1	8
2	Jim Morrison (D)	1960-61	19	1	6	7	6
21	Mark Morrison (C)	1981-82; 1983-84	10	1	1	2	0
19	Brian Mullen (LW)	1987-88—1990-91	307	100	148	248	188
14	Don Murdoch (RW)	1976-77—1979-80	221	97	93	190	110
9	Murray Murdoch (LW)	1926-27—1936-37	508	84	108	192	197
14	Mike Murphy (RW)	1972-73—1973-74	31	6	5	11	5
15, 10	Ron Murphy (LW)	1952-53—1956-57	207	41	60	101	141
18	Vic Myles (D)	1942-43	45	6	9	15	57

N

Number	Name & Position	Yrs. Played	GP	G	A	PTS	PIM
34	Vaclav Nedomansky (RW)	1982-83	35	12	8	20	0
15	Jim Neilson (D)	1962-63—1973-74	810	60	238	298	766
13	Sergei Nemchinov (C)	1991-92—1993-94	230	75	86	161	85
47	Steve Nemeth (C)	1987-88	12	2	0	2	2
21	Lance Nethery (C)	1980-81—1981-82	38	11	12	23	12
8	Bob Nevin (RW)	1963-64—1970-71	505	168	174	342	105
24	Dan Newman (LW)	1976-77—1977-78	100	14	21	35	59
9	Bernie Nicholls (C)	1989-90—1991-92	104	37	73	110	116
25	Graeme Nicolson (D)	1982-83	10	0	0	0	9
30	Chris Nilan (RW)	1987-88—1989-90	85	11	14	25	332
19, 11	Ulf Nilsson (C)	1978-79—1982-83	170	57	112	169	85
16	Brian Noonan (RW)	1993-94	12	4	2	6	12
14	Mattias Norstrom (D)	1993-94	9	0	2	2	6

O

Number	Name & Position	Yrs. Played	GP	G	A	PTS	PIM
14	Warren Oatman (F)	1928-29	27	1	1	2	10
5	Buddy OiConnor (C)	1947-48	238	62	102	164	12
25	John Ogrodnick (LW)	1987-88—1991-92	338	126	128	254	106
12	Eddie Olczyk (LW)	1992-93—1993-94	83	16	21	37	54
19	Mark Osborne (LW)	1983-84—1986-87	216	60	71	131	302

P

Number	Name & Position	Yrs. Played	GP	G	A	PTS	PIM
11	Wilf Paiement (RW)	1985-86	8	1	6	7	13
14	Aldo Palazzari (RW)	1943-44	12	2	0	2	0
2	Brad Park (D)	1968-69—1975-76	465	95	283	378	738
27	Joe Paterson (LW)	1987-88—1988-89	41	1	4	5	149
6	Larry Patey (C)	1983-84—1984-85	16	1	3	4	16
3	James Patrick (D)	1983-84—1993-94	671	104	363	467	541
9, 18	Lynn Patrick (LW)	1934-35—1942-43; 1945-46	455	145	190	335	270
2, 15	Muzz Patrick (D)	1937-38—1940-41; 1945-46	166	5	26	31	133
11	Stephen Patrick (RW)	1984-85—1985-86	71	15	21	36	100
16, 40	Mark Pavelich (C)	1981-82—1985-86	341	133	185	318	326
18	Jim Pavese (D)	1987-88	14	0	1	1	48
12, 16	Mel Pearson (LW)	1959-60; 1961-62 1962-63—1964-65	36	2	5	7	25
3	Fern Perreault (LW)	1947-48; 1949-50	3	0	0	0	0
4	Frank Peters (D)	1930-31	44	0	0	0	59
21	Gary Peters (C)	1965-66	63	7	3	10	42
24, 17	Michel Petit (D)	1987-88—1988-89	133	17	49	66	377
11	Gordon Pettinger (C)	1932-33	35	1	2	3	18
32	Dave Pichette (D)	1987-88	6	1	3	4	4
2, 16	Alf Pike (C)	1939-40—1942-43; 1945-46—1946-47	234	42	77	119	145
2, 25	Bob Plager (D)	1964-65—1966-67	29	0	5	5	40

RANGERS ALL-TIME REGISTER

Number	Name & Position	Yrs. Played	GP	G	A	PTS	PIM
24	Pierre Plante (RW)	1978-79	70	6	25	31	37
8	Walt Poddubny (C)	1986-87—1987-88	152	78	97	175	125
29, 41	Rudy Poeschek (RW)	1987-88—1989-90	68	0	2	2	256
14	Bud Poile (RW)	1949-50	28	3	6	9	8
19	Johnny Polich (RW)	1939-40—1940-41	3	0	1	1	0
20	Greg Polis (LW)	1974-75—1978-79	275	65	76	141	196
19	Larry Popein (C)	1954-55—1960-61	402	75	127	202	150
11, 2	Babe Pratt (D)	1935-36—1942-43	307	27	97	124	299
17	Dean Prentice (LW)	1952-53—1962-63	666	186	236	422	263
15	Noel Price (D)	1959-60—1960-61	7	0	0	0	4
47	Pat Price (D)	1986-87	13	0	2	2	49
17	Jean Pusie (D)	1933-34	19	0	2	2	17

Q

12	Leo Quenneville (F)	1929-30	25	0	3	3	10

R

Number	Name & Position	Yrs. Played	GP	G	A	PTS	PIM
7, 9	Don Raleigh (C)	1943-44; 1947-48—1955-56	535	101	219	320	96
19, 14	Jean Ratelle (C)	1960-61—1975-76	862	336	481	817	192
5	Mel Read (F)	1946-47	6	0	0	0	8
11	William Regan (D)	1929-30—1930-31	52	2	1	3	53
11	Oliver Reinikka (F)	1926-27	16	0	0	0	0
5	Leo Reise, Jr. (D)	1952-53—1953-54	131	7	20	27	124
2	Leo Reise, Sr. (D)	1929-30	14	0	1	1	8
10	Steven Rice (RW)	1990-91	11	1	1	2	4
18	Dave Richardson (LW)	1963-64—1964-65	41	3	2	5	25
41	Steve Richmond (D)	1983-84—1985-86	77	2	12	14	263
18	Mike Ridley (C)	1985-86—1986-87	118	38	63	101	89
4	Vic Ripley (LW)	1933-34—1934-35	39	5	14	19	12
19	Alex Ritson (LW)	1944-45	1	0	0	0	0
21	Wayne Rivers (RW)	1968-69	4	0	0	0	0
5	Doug Robinson (LW)	1964-65—1966-67	73	16	26	42	10
25, 24	Mike Robitaille (D)	1969-70—1970-71	15	1	1	2	15
16	Leon Rochefort (RW)	1960-61; 1962-63	24	5	4	9	6
5	Normand Rochefort (D)	1988-89—1991-92	112	7	15	22	108
12	Edmond Rodden (F)	1930-31	24	0	3	3	8
17, 27	Mike Rogers (C)	1981-82—1985-86	316	117	191	308	142
5	Dale Rolfe (D)	1970-71—1974-75	244	13	66	79	190
19	Len Ronson (LW)	1960-61	13	2	1	3	10
9	Paul Ronty (C)	1951-52—1954-55	260	45	114	159	62
2, 15	Jim Ross (D)	1951-52—1952-53	62	2	11	13	29
22	Bobby Rousseau (RW)	1971-72—1974-75	236	41	116	157	30
15	Ronnie Rowe (LW)	1947-48	5	1	0	1	0
44	Lindy Ruff (D)	1988-89—1990-91	83	3	12	15	135
29	Reijo Ruotsalainen (D)	1981-82—1985-86	389	99	217	316	154
19	Duane Rupp (D)	1962-63	2	0	0	0	0
16	Church Russell (LW)	1945-46—1947-48	90	20	16	36	12

S

Number	Name & Position	Yrs. Played	GP	G	A	PTS	PIM
21	Simo Saarinen (D)	1984-85	8	0	0	0	8
4, 3 2, 5	Larry Sacharuk (D)	1972-73—1973-74; 1975-76—1976-77	75	9	11	20	18
26, 8	Kjell Samuelsson (D)	1985-86—1986-87	39	2	6	8	60
16, 4	Derek Sanderson (C)	1974-75—1975-76	83	25	25	50	110
5	Chuck Sands (F)	1943-44	9	0	2	2	0
28	Tomas Sandstrom (RW)	1984-85—1989-90	407	173	207	380	563
6	Glen Sather (LW)	1970-71—1973-74	188	18	24	42	193
17	Chuck Scherza (C)	1943-44—1944-45	27	5	5	10	29
18	Ken Schinkel (RW)	1959-60—1963-64; 1966-67	265	34	55	89	77
11	Lawrence Scott (F)	1927-28	23	0	1	1	6
21, 2	Earl Seibert (D)	1931-32—1935-36	202	27	41	68	338
16	Rod Seiling (D)	1963-64—1974-75	644	50	198	248	425
16	George Senick (LW)	1952-53	13	2	3	5	8
6, 5	Eddie Shack (RW)	1958-59—1960-61	141	16	26	42	236
18	Joe Shack (LW)	1942-43; 1944-45	70	9	27	36	20
27, 21	David Shaw (D)	1987-88—1991-92	240	17	57	74	314
6	Bobby Sheehan** (C)	1978-79	15	4	3	7	2

RANGERS ALL-TIME REGISTER

Number	Name & Position	Yrs. Played	GP	G	A	PTS	PIM
23	Ray Sheppard (RW)	1990-91	59	24	23	47	21
	Johnny Sherf** (LW)	1937-38	1	0	0	0	0
3	Fred Shero (D)	1947-48—1949-50	145	6	14	20	137
4	Alex Shibicky (LW)	1935-36—1941-42; 1945-46	322	110	91	201	161
4	Alex "Babe" Siebert (LW)	1932-33—1933-34	55	9	11	20	56
16	Dave Silk (RW)	1979-80—1982-83	141	30	33	63	112
41	Mike Siltala (RW)	1986-87—1987-88	4	0	0	0	0
21	Reg Sinclair (RW)	1950-51—1951-52	139	38	31	69	103
20, 11	Ed Slowinski (RW)	1947-48—1952-53	291	58	74	132	63
14, 20, 10	Clint Smith (C)	1936-37—1942-43	281	80	115	195	12
15	Dallas Smith (D)	1977-78	29	1	4	5	23
21	Don Smith (RW)	1949-50	10	1	1	2	0
19	Floyd Smith (RW)	1960-61	29	5	9	14	0
17	Stan Smith (C)	1939-40—1940-41	9	2	1	3	0
12	Art Somers (C)	1931-32—1934-35	145	19	37	56	82
16	Glen Sonmor (LW)	1953-54—1954-55	28	2	0	2	21
15, 16, 21	Irv Spencer (D)	1959-60—1961-62	131	4	20	24	81
19	Red Staley (C)	1948-49	1	0	1	1	0
8	Allan Stanley (D)	1948-49—1954-55	307	23	56	79	272
4	Wally Stanowski (D)	1948-49—1950-51	146	3	14	17	54
4	Harold Starr (D)	1934-35—1935-36	45	0	0	0	38
21	Bud Stefanski (C)	1977-78	1	0	0	0	0
21	Pete Stemkowski (C)	1970-71—1976-77	496	113	204	317	379
5	Ulf Sterner (LW)	1964-65	4	0	0	0	0
16	Gaye Stewart (LW)	1951-52—1952-53	87	16	27	43	30
12	Ron Stewart (RW)	1967-68—1972-73	306	44	37	81	74
13	Jack Stoddard (RW)	1951-52—1952-53	80	16	15	31	31
21	Blaine Stoughton (RW)	1983-84	14	5	2	7	4
21	Neil Strain (LW)	1952-53	52	11	13	24	12
15, 10	Art Stratton (C)	1959-60	18	2	5	7	2
10	Art Strobel (LW)	1943-44	7	0	0	0	0
9	Doug Sulliman (RW)	1979-80—1980-81	63	8	8	16	34
7	Red Sullivan (C)	1956-57—1960-61	322	59	150	209	300
25	Peter Sundstrom (RW)	1983-84—1985-86	206	48	62	110	70
5	Bill Sweeney (C)	1959-60	4	1	0	1	0

T

Number	Name & Position	Yrs. Played	GP	G	A	PTS	PIM
19	Dean Talafous (RW)	1978-79—1981-82	202	42	60	102	91
26, 35	Ron Talakoski (RW)	1986-87—1987-88	9	0	1	1	33
17	Spence Tatchell (D)	1942-43	1	0	0	0	0
15	Bill Taylor (C)	1947-48	2	0	0	0	0
19	G. Bill Taylor (C)	1964-65	2	0	0	0	0
12	Ralph Taylor (D)	1929-30	24	2	0	2	28
18, 5	Ted Taylor (LW)	1964-65—1965-66	8	0	1	1	6
8, 10	Paul Thompson (LW)	1926-27—1930-31	216	35	33	68	144
14	Fred Thurier (C)	1944-45	50	16	19	35	14
10	Esa Tikkanen (LW)	1992-93—1993-94	98	24	37	61	132
6	Mark Tinordi (D)	1987-88	24	1	2	3	50
18, 17	Walt Tkaczuk (C)	1967-68—1980-81	945	227	451	678	556
12	Zellio Toppazzini (RW)	1950-51—1951-52	71	15	14	29	31
14	Wes Trainor (RW)	1948-49	17	1	2	3	6
14	Guy Trottier (RW)	1968-69	2	0	0	0	0
4	Rene Trudell (RW)	1945-46—1947-48	129	24	28	52	72
8	Darren Turcotte (C)	1988-89—1993-94	325	122	133	255	183
6	Dean Turner (D)	1978-79	1	0	0	0	0
17	Norm Tustin (LW)	1941-42	18	2	4	6	0

V

Number	Name & Position	Yrs. Played	GP	G	A	PTS	PIM
5, 2	Carol Vadnais (D)	1975-76—1981-82	485	56	190	246	690
11	Sparky Vail (LW)	1928-29—1929-30	50	4	1	5	18
40	Dennis Vial (D)	1990-91	21	0	0	0	61
8	Steve Vickers (LW)	1972-73—1981-82	698	246	340	586	330
11	Carl Voss (C)	1932-33	9	2	1	3	4

W

Number	Name & Position	Yrs. Played	GP	G	A	PTS	PIM
15	Frank Waite (F)	1930-31	17	1	3	4	4
14, 36	Gord Walker (LW)	1986-87—1987-88	19	2	4	6	19
25	Peter Wallin (RW)	1980-81—1981-82	52	3	14	17	14

RANGERS ALL-TIME REGISTER

Number	Name & Position	Yrs. Played	GP	G	Statistics A	PTS	PIM
	Eddie Wares (RW)	1936-37	2	2	0	2	0
8	Grant Warwick (RW)	1941-42—1947-48	293	117	116	233	179
14	Billy Warwick (LW)	1942-43—1943-44	14	3	3	6	16
7, 15	Phil Watson (RW)	1935-36—1942-43; 1944-45—1947-48	546	127	233	360	471
21	John Webster (LW)	1949-50	14	0	0	0	4
39	Doug Weight (C)	1991-92—1992-93	118	23	47	70	78
24	Jay Wells (D)	1991-92—1993-94	143	3	16	19	241
12	Len Wharton (D)	1944-45	1	0	0	0	0
41	Simon Wheeldon (C)	1987-88—1988-89	11	0	2	2	6
17, 39	Rob Whistle (D)	1985-86	32	4	2	6	10
19	Sherman White (C)	1946-47; 1949-50	4	0	2	2	0
14	Doug Wickenheiser (C)	1988-89	1	1	0	1	0
20	Juha Widing (C)	1969-70	44	7	7	14	10
6, 24	Jim Wiemer (D)	1984-85—1985-86	29	7	3	10	32
17	Tom Williams (LW)	1971-72—1973-74	25	1	3	4	6
14	Bert WIlson (LW)	1973-74—1974-75	66	6	2	8	68
17	Carey Wilson (C)	1988-89—1989-90	82	30	51	81	102
16	Johnny Wilson (LW)	1960-61—1961-62	96	25	15	40	38
4	Bob Wood (D)	1950-51	1	0	0	0	0
14	Bill Wylie (C)	1950-51	1	0	0	0	0

Y

Number	Name & Position	Yrs. Played	GP	G	A	PTS	PIM
19, 39	Tom Younghans (RW)	1981-82	47	3	5	8	17

Z

Number	Name & Position	Yrs. Played	GP	G	A	PTS	PIM
31	Rob Zamuner (C)	1991-92	9	1	2	3	2
24	Joe Zanussi (D)	1974-75	8	0	2	2	4
21	Sergei Zubov (D)	1992-93—1993-94	127	20	100	120	43

RANGERS ALL-TIME REGISTER

Goaltenders

Number	Name	Yrs. Played	W-L-T	GP	MINS	GA	AVG	SO
1	Andy Aitkenhead	1932-33—1934-35	47-43-16	106	6570	257	2.42	11
1	Lorne Anderson	1951-52	1-2-0	3	180	18	6.00	0
31	Hardy Astrom	1977-78	2-2-0	4	240	14	3.50	0
35	Steve Baker	1979-80—1982-83	20-20-11	57	3081	190	3.70	3
1	Gordie Bell**	1955-56	**1-1-0	2	120	9	4.50	0
1	Bill Beveridge	1942-43	4-10-3	17	1020	89	5.24	1
1	Lionel Bouvrette	1942-43	0-1-0	1	60	6	6.00	0
1	Johnny Bower	1953-54—1954-55; 1956-57	31-35-11	77	4620	202	2.62	5
1	Steve Buzinski	1942-43	2-6-1	9	560	55	5.89	0
1	Lorne Chabot	1926-27—1927-28	41-25-14	80	5037	135	1.61	21
30, 00, 35	John Davidson	1975-76—1982-83	93-90-25	222	12,449	742	3.58	7
1	Bob DeCourcy	1947-48	0-1-0	1	29	6	12.41	0
1	Dave Dryden	1961-62	0-1-0	1	40	3	4.50	0
1, 16	Emile Francis	1948-49—1951-52	7-9-5	22	1280	68	3.19	0
1	Jimmy Franks	1942-43	5-14-4	23	1380	103	4.48	0
33	Bob Froese	1986-87—1989-90	36-43-8	98	5350	324	3.63	1
1	Bruce Gamble	1958-59	0-2-0	2	120	6	3.00	0
1	Bert Gardiner	1935-36; 1938-39	1-0-0	1	60	1	1.00	0
1, 30	Ed Giacomin	1965-66—1975-76	266-169-90	539	31,646	1441	2.73	49
33	Gilles Gratton	1976-77	11-18-7	41	2034	143	4.22	0
1	Glen Hanlon	1982-83—1985-86	56-56-13	138	7690	473	3.69	0
30	Glenn Healy	1993-94	10-12-2	29	1368	69	3.03	2
1,20	Jim Henry	1941-43—1945-46; 1947-48	47-44-17	109	6583	346	3.15	4
31	Corey Hirsch	1992-93	1-2-1	4	224	14	3.75	0
1	Percy Jackson	1934-35	0-1-0	1	60	8	8.00	0
1	Dave Kerr	1934-35—1940-41	157-110-57	324	20,230	698	2.07	40
44	Terry Kleisinger	1985-86	0-2-0	4	191	14	4.40	0
1	Julian Klymkiew	1958-59	0-0-0	1	19	2	6.32	0
1	Harry Lumley	1943-44	0-0-0	1	20	0	0.00	0
30	Cesare Maniago	1965-66—1966-67	9-19-4	34	1832	108	3.54	2
1	Ken McAuley	1943-44—1944-45	16-65-15	96	5740	537	5.61	1
1	Jack McCartan	1959-60—1960-61	3-7-2	12	680	43	3.79	1
31	Peter McDuffe	1972-73—1973-74	4-2-1	7	400	19	2.85	0
1	Joe Miller**	1927-28	**2-1-0	3	180	3	1.00	1
41	Ed Mio	1981-82—1982-83	29-24-11	66	3865	225	3.49	2
1	Dan Olesevich	1961-62	0-0-1	1	40	2	3.00	0
23,1	Marcel Paille	1957-58—1962-63; 1964-65	33-52-21	107	6342	362	3.42	2
16	Lester Patrick**	1927-28	**1-0-0	1	46	1	1.30	0
	Marcel Pelletier	1962-63	0-1-1	2	40	4	6.00	0
1	Jacques Plante	1963-64—1964-65	32-52-13	98	5838	329	3.38	5
1	Chuck Rayner	1945-46—1952-53	123-181-73	377	22,488	1122	2.99	24
35	Mike Richter	1989-90—1993-94	111-26-13	215	12,029	613	3.06	9
35	Curt Ridley	1974-75	1-1-0	2	81	7	5.19	0
1	John Ross Roach	1928-29—1931-32	80-63-37	180	11,310	407	2.16	30
1	Al Rollins	1959-60	1-3-4	8	480	31	3.88	0
30	Terry Sawchuk	1969-70	3-1-2	8	412	20	2.91	1
1	Joe Schaefer	1959-60—1960-61	0-1-0	2	86	8	5.58	0
31, 35	Ron Scott	1983-84—1987-88	3-7-4	16	796	51	3.84	0
30	Don Simmons	1965-66; 1967-68—1968-69	7-9-4	21	997	58	3.49	0
1, 31, 1, 33	Doug Soetaert	1975-76—1980-81; 1986-87	35-40-15	103	5226	372	4.27	1
1	Doug Stevenson	1944-45	0-4-0	4	240	20	5.00	0
25	Dave Tataryn	1976-77	1-1-0	2	80	10	7.50	0
1	Wayne Thomas	1977-78—1980-81	34-43-11	94	5288	320	3.63	5
34	John Vanbiesbrouck	1981-82; 1983-84—1992-93	200-177-47	449	25,380	1458	3.45	16
30, 1	Gilles Villemure	1963-64—1967-69; 1970-71—1975-76	96-54-21	184	10,472	457	2.62	13
31	Steve Weeks	1980-81—1983-84	42-33-14	94	5313	339	3.83	1
1, 31	Dunc Wilson	1974-75—1975-76	6-11-3	23	1260	89	4.24	0
1	Hal Winkler	1926-27	3-4-1	8	514	16	1.87	2
1	Lorne Worsley	1952-53—1962-63	204-271-101	583	34,675	1789	3.10	24

**Denotes Playoff Statistics